World Philosophies

An Historical Introduction

David E. Cooper

Copyright © David E. Cooper, 1996

The right of David E. Cooper to be identified as author of this work has been
asserted in accordance with the Copyright, Designs and Patents Act 1988.

First published 1996

Reprinted 1996

Blackwell Publishers Ltd
108 Cowley Road
Oxford OX4 1JF, UK

Blackwell Publishers Inc.
238 Main Street
Cambridge, Massachusetts 02142, USA

British Library Cataloguing in Publication Data
A CIP catalogue record for this book is available from the British Library

Library of Congress Cataloging in Publication Data
Cooper, David Edward.
World philosophies: an historical introduction / David E. Cooper
p. cm.
Includes bibliographical references and index.
ISBN 0-631-18866-5 - ISBN 0-631-18867-3 (pbk)
1. Philosophy - Introductions. 2. Philosophy - History. I. Title.
BD21.C656   1996
109 - dc20
95-5864
CIP

Typeset in 11 on 13 pt Bembo
by Best-set Typesetter Ltd, Hong Kong
Printed in Great Britain by T. J. Press Ltd, Padstow, Cornwall

This book is printed on acid-free paper

• CONTENTS •

· ACKNOWLEDGEMENTS ·

Nobody should be rash enough to embark on writing a history of world philosophies – ones from the earliest times to the present, from Kyoto to Boston, from Copenhagen to Benin – without relying on more than a little help from critically-minded friends. I should like to thank Peter Harvey, Keith Pratt, Joy Palmer, Paul MacDonald, 'Paddy' Fitzpatrick and Kalyan Sen Gupta for reading and commenting on individual chapters. I am also grateful to a number of anonymous readers recruited by the publisher for their comments on particular chapters. My greatest debt, however, is to Robert L. Arrington and Anthony O'Hear, both of whom, like the character in a long-running antacid commercial, devoured 'the whole damn thing'. In return, their comments, detailed and meticulous, have provided me with much food for thought, converted into revisions which have made the final product a good deal better than the original one.

I am grateful, as well, to the University of Durham for granting me two periods of research leave during the writing of the book, without which it would doubtless not have been finished before the history of philosophy pressed on and some new philosophical movement emerged that I would then have had to include in a final chapter.

Last but not least, I express my thanks to my long-standing publisher, Blackwell's: especially to Stephan Chambers who persuaded me to undertake this book, to Steve Smith who persuaded me to finish it, and to the production team who have seen it to the bookshelves.

1
• INTRODUCTION •

• 'World Philosophies' •

The title of this book is ambiguous. 'World philosophies' might refer to philosophies from around the world, or it might mean something like 'world-views', theories on the grand scale *about* 'The World'. My title is intended to bear both senses, so it is a pun.

It is not necessary to be a devotee of 'political correctness' to regret that the great preponderance of histories of philosophy, many passing themselves off as 'general', deal only with Western thought. A few Arabs are sometimes included but, so to speak, as honorary Westerners, deemed worthy of inclusion for their commentaries on Aristotle and hence their influence on mediaeval Christian thought. Exclusion of the Indian, Chinese and Japanese contributions to philosophy was forgivable, perhaps, at the beginning of the nineteenth century, when the German philosopher Hegel passed his scathing verdicts on those traditions: for precious few of their works had been translated. It was less excusable a century later, after the explosion in oriental scholarship, when Edmund Husserl expressed doubt as to the very existence of non-Western philosophy. Today, after a further century of scholarship and translation, such an exclusion ought to seem absurd. If to many people it does not, this must be mainly due to the feeling – encouraged, admittedly, by some enthusiasts for 'the wisdom of the East' – that these traditions are too indelibly 'religious', 'irrational' and 'mystical' to warrant a place on today's hard-nosed, 'analytical' curriculum. This book will have failed in one of its aims if that feeling persists with the reader to the end.

A better reason, arguably, for keeping non-Western philosophies out of the curricular sun would be that life is short, especially the life of the undergraduate. No student – indeed, no teacher – has time to savour the riches of all philosophical traditions: better then, some would say, to restrict attention to the tradition of the culture in which the students have grown up. But, in the first place, many of the ideas of, say, ancient India and Kamakura Japan are no more and no less 'relevant' to the contemporary culture of young Britons or Americans than those of ancient Greece and mediaeval France. Second, in philosophy as in gastronomy, the sensible response to an overstocked larder is surely to choose the best items, not those which happen to lie on one side or the other of an imaginary line. I am unimpressed, incidentally, by the consideration that few teachers or students are likely to be masters of Sanskrit, Mandarin and other mediums of non-Western philosophy. Most are not masters, either, of the languages in which Plato, Aquinas and Kant wrote, but that is no reason for students to be kept away from these thinkers.

The present book, then, attempts to redress an imbalance: the 'world philosophies' it presents are indeed from 'around the world', sizeable chunks of it, at any rate: India, China, Japan, the Near and Middle East, and Africa, as well as Europe and North America. Doubtless, there are other parts of the world which have made their contribution to philosophy, but which I do not discuss. Total comprehensiveness, however, cannot be my aim in a book which would otherwise, as Vikram Seth charmingly puts it at the beginning of his massive novel, 'strain your purse and sprain your wrists'.[1]

Indeed, it is not only geographical comprehensiveness that the book lacks: for its subject is not philosophy at large, but philosoph*ies*. 'Philosophy', as the name of a very general intellectual activity, does not have a plural, no more than does 'music'; and philosophies no more exhaust the field of philosophy than music consists entirely in the outpouring of musicals. Philosophies, like musicals, are particular products of the more general activity. The singular of 'philosophies' is 'a philosophy'; and by 'a philosophy', I mean – as 'the man in the street' tends to mean – an account on the grand scale of the nature of reality, the place of human beings within it, and the implications of all this for how people should comport themselves in the world and towards one another. Taoism, Thomism, Cartesianism, and Existentialism – to mention but a few – are philosophies in this sense, and it is on such '-isms' that the book focuses. There are, on the surface at least, some exceptions to be found in the book, like Logical Positivism, whose champions would certainly reject that theirs were philosophies in the sense just characterized. But these are best seen as self-conscious reactions against grand accounts like those mentioned, and in that respect parasitic upon them. Anyway, it is unclear that, despite the intentions of their authors, these reactive exceptions avoid offering accounts of the very kind they condemn.

It is partly out of consideration for readers' purses and wrists that my focus is philosophies, not philosophy at large. This focus enables me to ignore a great range of philosophizing, especially in the areas of logic and the theory of knowledge, except of course where considerations from these areas have had a marked input into systematic philosophies. It thereby enables me, too, to be brief with many thinkers who, in more general histories of philosophy, receive the more expansive coverage they doubtless deserve. Socrates and Gottlob Frege, for example, were great philosophers, but neither was the creator of *a* philosophy in the sense characterized: hence their modest treatment in this book. (Incidentally, the book is not, in the main, done 'by blokes', as Australian students are wont to put it, but by movements or '-isms'. Only three thinkers, Plato, Aristotle and Kant – each too big, as it were, to squeeze in others next to him – have whole sections of chapters devoted to them.)

It is not just considerations of length, however, which explain my restricted focus, for it serves, too, to redress another imbalance. 'Grand theory' has, for much of the twentieth century, been suspect. Many philosophers have disowned the ambitions of their predecessors to construct comprehensive philosophical systems. This has been reflected in several recent histories of the subject which, consistent with this suspicion, tend to concentrate on the 'methods' employed by past philosophers, or on their solutions over the ages to particular knotty problems. Such histories have their value, but we need to be reminded that many of the great philosophers *were* ambitious, and that the yardstick by which they would have wanted to be judged is the overall adequacy of their synoptic vision of things. In my view, they were right to want to be so judged, for it is the construction and criticism of the great '-isms' which are the life-blood of the subject, giving vitality to the philosophical enterprise as a whole. It is in relation to these that the methods of argument employed, or the problems tackled, by philosophers assume their importance and fascination. Without the system-builders to scoff or carp at, moreover, it is difficult to see how those who engage in this would ever have been in a job.

The French philosopher Henri Bergson may have exaggerated in judging that 'the whole of philosophy is not worth one hour of trouble' if it has 'really nothing to say' on 'the three Ws' – 'Where do we come from? What are we doing here? Whither are we going?'[2] But students set to read many of today's technical journal articles, whose bearing on such questions is at the very least tangential, may justifiably wonder if they are being taught the subject which they thought they had signed up for. And they might surely conclude that they are not when they hear that philosophy is 'really' the semantics of natural language or the piecemeal clarification of puzzling terms. Such news might, of course, come as good news to some students. The present book is one for the rest, and for anyone, indeed, to whom the name 'philosophy' conjures up, in the first instance, the rather amazing story of human beings' efforts to articulate reasoned visions of their world and their place within, or perhaps without, it.

•   'An Historical Introduction'   •

As told here, that story – to move on to my subtitle – is certainly a history in the banal sense of being presented in broadly chronological terms. Since separate chapters are devoted to non-Western philosophies, chronology has to be suspended, of course, when I switch, for example, from nineteenth-century European thought to contemporaneous developments further east or south. Because of such switches, moreover, it sometimes happens that thinkers from one part of the world are discussed before earlier ones from another part – Śaṅkara before Augustine, for instance, or Mao Tse-Tung before Bergson. So the book is, if you will, not a single history, but a set of histories. Even within chapters, moreover, I have not been obsessive about dates. Where thematic considerations make it appropriate, a given philosopher is sometimes discussed before his predecessors from the same period covered by the chapter.

Is the book a history in some more heavyweight sense than that of being broadly chronological in structure? Certainly I do not 'have' a history of philosophy in the manner that Hegel, Marx and Heidegger 'had' histories of the subject. Few are likely to ask, 'Do you find Cooper's history more plausible than Marx's?', but if perchance they do, they shouldn't. For that question would imply that I am promulgating an historical thesis, a large claim – itself philosophical – about the course and destiny of philosophy. I might like to have a thesis, on the same grand scale, to rival such claims as that philosophies are always ideological products of the dominant economic class, or manifestations of Absolute Spirit's progress through time, or ways in which Being has revealed itself over the millennia. But I do not.

On the other hand, this book does have a *Leitmotiv*, a recurrent theme that can be heard in every chapter and which does something, I hope, to gather disparate movements together and to attune readers to certain patterns or rhythms among those movements. Goethe once remarked, 'I hate everything that merely instructs me without augmenting . . . my activity.'[3] Something of that spirit, I suggest, informs nearly all the great philosophies. The motive behind these sytems was rarely, if ever, mere curiosity about the world, their aim almost never 'knowledge for its own sake'. A philosophy, I indicated, involves an account of the place of human beings in the world and of the implications of this for how they should comport themselves. A philosophy, then, is 'practical', though not in the narrow sense of being what is these days called 'applied philosophy' – designed, that is, to provide solutions to particular practical, moral problems, like those of euthanasia or the proper treatment of animals. It is rather that philosophies have typically been constructed by authors with at least one eye out for 'the human condition' and how to 'cope' with it, with an ambition to better our lives by substituting an appropriate stance towards the world for the distorted ones that men and women, in these authors' view, generally adopt.

The book's *Leitmotiv* is a little more specific, however, than simply the 'practical' orientation of the systems it examines. Hegel and, following him, Marx saw philosophy as the endeavour to overcome what they called the problem of 'alienation' or 'estrangement'. By these terms, they meant the sense which many human beings – all of them, perhaps, at times – have of being 'strangers', of not being 'at home', in the world. Reading philosophers from all times and climes, I am struck by the accuracy of this perception of the central inspiration behind philosophical speculation, by the constant recurrence – from the earliest Indian thinkers recorded to twentieth-century existentialists – of the theme of alienation. We can ask of our primitive ancestors, 'Staring at the sun, the sky, were they aware of their own being, and if so, what did they think?', but without much hope of an answer.[4] We might, though, with rather more confidence, guess that when people did become 'aware of their own being', they became conscious, at the same time, of its strangeness, of respects in which, for all their affinity with the animal and wider natural world, they were also set apart from it. For with self-awareness, there would also have come the emergent appreciation of being a creature that can reason and deliberate, make free choices, enjoy beauty and feel resentment, care about the past and the long-term future, string meaningful noises together, depict the world of nature in coloured powders or movements of the limbs, and perhaps receive intimations of a purpose lying beyond this world: an appreciation, in short, of the many ways in which a human being belongs, or seems to belong, to a unique order of life.

With that appreciation, one might further guess, there ensued an experience compounded of exhilaration and unease, of hubris in the uniqueness of one's species and envy of other, less distinguished creatures whose very lack of the capacities just mentioned made for a more settled existence, 'sunk in nature' as Hegel put it. However things struck our early ancestors, there is an intellectual tension latent in these conflicting emotions which was to become, and remain, the spur to philosophical thought: the tension of which Wordsworth writes poignantly, when he says that 'the groundwork of all true philosophy' is 'the difference between . . . that intuition . . . of ourselves, as one with the whole . . . and that [of] ourselves as separated beings, [which] places nature in antithesis' to us.[5] At any rate, many of the philosophies we shall encounter over the following chapters can fruitfully be regarded as attempts to resolve this difference or tension by offering accounts of human beings which do justice to the uniqueness of the species, yet without, so to speak, rendering its members freaks, outsiders or strangers in the world.

The goal of resolving this tension or difference has, it seems to me, given certain rhythms to the history of philosophy. One observes, for example, a constant oscillation between those philosophers who would resolve it by trying to show that we are, as it were, more 'world-like' than at first we seem, and those who argue that the world is more 'human-like' than it may at first appear. The former may insist that we are, after all, only complicated physical mechanisms, deny that we are really possessed of free will, or demonstrate in other ways that we are not so very different from everything else. The latter may argue that nature is, after all, 'spiritual' or purposive, or claim in other ways that everything else is not so very different from ourselves. What hardly any philosopher of the first rank has done is to ignore, or remain sanguine about, the tension. Those, like Kant, who confessed to their failure to resolve it, did so with palpable disappointment, even despair. After all, if the German poet Hölderlin was right and it is both 'divine and good' to be 'at one' with the world, then the failure to resolve the tension is not simply an intellectual débâcle, but a human tragedy.

Recent histories of philosophies do not emphasize the *Leitmotiv* I have described. Indeed, their authors often ignore the concern of, say, Plato, Descartes and Wittgenstein to address 'the problem of alienation', focusing instead on their treatment of today's more 'professional' philosophical problems. Some readers may sympathize with the approach of these authors, finding that 'the problem of alienation' is neither as historically salient nor as philosophically central as I do. But these readers will not, I hope, find this book a waste of their time. The 'professional' problems are not ignored, and my *Leitmotiv*, like that of many musical compositions, is kept fairly discreet. Even those who don't like its sound might perhaps agree that it serves to lend a certain cohesion to what would otherwise threaten to be a cacophony of disparate subjects and developments.

Finally, a few comments on the last word in my subtitle. One respect, certainly, in which the book is an introduction is that it concentrates on presenting and explaining, not on criticizing, the philosophers and philosophies considered. Doubtless the very selection of the material, as well as the space devoted to this or that position, reflects critical stances on my part. But except where it has been irresistible, I have resisted the temptation to pass lightning critical comments. Charity, justice or both surely require that one desists from passing hostile verdicts that one is without the space properly to secure. It is a quite different matter, of course, to cite, as I often do, well-known criticisms of a position, ones that themselves belong to the history of our subject.

These days there are too many publishers – my own, it goes without saying, not included – who promote as 'introductions' books which would tax even an advanced postgraduate student. This does not mean that an introduction must be readily absorbable by readers completely virgin in the field. I occasionally daydream of browsers, with no background at all in philosophy, who would see this book on the shelves, like the look of it, take it away and read it with some profit. But the book is designed, primarily, for people who are studying philosophy and allied subjects, with the help of teachers, and so for use on courses. It is, after all, an introductory account of the history of philosophy – or rather, philosoph*ies* – not an introduction to philosophy itself. Since, more accurately, it is a set of histories, rather than a single history, different readers may take different 'routes' through it. Students mainly interested in Indian philosophy and religion, for instance, could pass from chapter 2 to section 1 of chapter 6, and then to section 1 of chapter 9.

Still, I am not too ready to abandon the dream of the receptive 'general reader'. He or she will not, without instruction, find some of the discussions easy, though I have avoided technicalities wherever possible: for I have preferred to engage in relatively detailed examination of a limited number of thinkers and '-isms' than to provide lightning, encyclopaedic coverage of them all. But then the very difficulties such readers encounter may themselves act as a spur to further study of philosophy. Of course, the greater spur should be the story itself of millennia of thinkers, some of them men of genius, who have endeavoured, on behalf of all of us, to articulate our place in the scheme of things and to offer guidance, and sometimes hope, in coping with our condition. I should be pleased if students taking 'Comparative Religion I', 'Modern Philosophy II', or 'Contemporary European Thought' find the relevant chapters of the book help them through their travails. I would be still more gratified if both they and readers with no such urgent objectives come away from the book as a whole with a sense that the tale, if not the telling of it, is one of depth and grandeur.

• Notes •

1 Vikram Seth, *A Suitable Boy*.
2 Quoted in Leszek Kolakowski, *Bergson*, p. 37.
3 Quoted in Friedrich Nietzsche, *Untimely Meditations*, p. 59.
4 Peter Matthiessen, *The Tree Where Man Was Born*, p. 82.
5 Quoted in Charles Taylor, *Sources of the Self*, p. 574.

Part I

• Ancient Philosophies •

· Introduction to Part I ·

It is intriguing to reflect that, despite uncertain dating, the earliest figures discussed in this book – Confucius, the Buddha, the sages who composed some of the most important *Upaniṣads*, and Thales – might all have been alive at the same time. What makes it intriguing, of course, is that these thinkers belonged to three very different civilizations – Chinese, Indian and Greek – between which, as far as is known, there was virtually no intercourse. That philosophical enquiry should have blossomed simultaneously and, it seems, independently in these three cultures is remarkable. Is it any more than that – a mystery to which there must, nevertheless, be a key? It has been suggested, certainly, that there must have been contacts between these cultures, but the evidence is unforthcoming. Still less plausibly, it has been speculated that there is a natural, maturational stage in the development of *homo sapiens* at which philosophizing – rather like the hair on the faces of boys at puberty – suddenly sprouts: a stage unsurprisingly reached at roughly the same time by peoples in different parts of the globe.

These unlikely explanations are responses, however, to the misconceived assumption that philosophy 'began' during the seventh or sixth century BCE. For one thing, granted that philosophizing had certainly arrived by this time, we just do not know enough about the thinking of still earlier civilizations to tell whether it had already arrived with them. For another thing, and more importantly, there is no sharp line to be drawn between thinking which does and thinking which does not deserve to be labelled 'philosophy': between, for example, a 'mere' myth about the origins of the universe and an account of the same which appeals to evidence and reason. The oldest texts I discuss are some Indian ones dating from around 700 BCE, which is why, incidentally, the opening chapter is on India. Other authors might prefer to begin with even older texts from India or China, or perhaps with Homer. Yet others would prefer to wait a few hundred years, starting their story with the later pre-Socratic writers, say, or the sophisticated commentaries on the *Upaniṣads*. Such differences reflect competing judgements on the criteria for counting as philosophy rather than disagreements over the historical facts. Intriguing as it is, then, that a number of great minds should have flourished at the same time in such diverse contexts, it overdramatizes this confluence – and invites unlikely speculations – to hail it as 'the beginning of philosophy'.

'Ancient philosophies' is not an entirely happy title for this part of the book. One reason is that, to many ears, its immediate connotation is systems of Greek thought exclusively. (For this reason, 'classical' would have been even worse than 'ancient'.) Another is that the periods covered in the three chapters of Part I are not the same, with the one on India taking us well into the period corresponding to the Middle Ages in the West. Indeed, some scholars of Indian philosophy themselves refer to the later figures I discuss in chapter 2 as 'mediaeval'. The justification for taking the discussion of 'ancient' Indian thought to such a late date is its continuity. In the West, the arrival of Christianity marked an important caesura in philosophical development, while in China, around the same time, development seems rather suddenly to have atrophied, only being resumed many centuries later. In India, on the other hand, there were no such episodes to warrant breaking off our story so early.

Although the primary texts available to us from the 'ancient' period are, of course, far fewer than those from later periods, I have had to be selective. Some thinkers or schools, to be sure, are self-selecting – Plato and Aristotle, Vedānta and Buddhism, Confucianism and Taoism. Some, like the Chinese 'legalists', I have excluded or only touched upon because their main contributions were not systematic 'world philosophies' in the sense sketched in chapter 1; others, like the Greek 'Eleatics', because their contributions were so similar to ones discussed in connection with other thinkers or schools.

A note, finally, on the romanization of Indian and Chinese names and words. In the case of the former, I have gone less for consistency than familiarity, using those spellings which, to judge from a survey of books on Indian philosophy (by Indians, at least), are most common. (Readers who like to speak the words they read might want to know that 's' when marked with diacritics, as in 'Śaṅkara' and '*mokṣa*', is pronounced 'sh'.) In the case of Chinese, I use the older Wade–Giles system of spelling, not the newer *pinyin* one, so that we stay, for example, with 'Mao Tse-Tung' rather than move to 'Mao Zedong'. This is not because the latter system, in one authority's judgement, 'gives even less idea how the words are actually pronounced' – though for all I know, that's true. The reason is, rather, that most of the source-books and commentaries students are likely to encounter are sufficiently old still to be employing Wade–Giles.

2
· INDIA ·

· 1 The 'Schools' and Their Framework ·

In this chapter, I consider the emergence of various 'schools' (*darśanas*) of
Indian thought from an early, oral tradition of speculation, and their development of systematic philosophies during the first few centuries CE. As noted in
the introduction to this part of the book, Indian philosophy has enjoyed
considerable continuity. One reason for this is an early and persistent penchant
for taking certain texts as authoritative – the *Upaniṣads*, in the case of the Hindu
schools, the sayings of the Buddha in the case of Buddhism, and so on. This has
both encouraged and been reinforced by the dominant 'housestyle' of the
philosophical literature – commentaries on the revered texts, commentaries on
these commentaries, and so on. These factors help explain why, even in the
twentieth century, prominent thinkers share a framework of assumptions whose
sources can be traced back to at least 500 BCE.

Since, on the usual counting, there are some eight *darśanas*, each with its
various sub-schools, continuity is clearly not the same as conformity. Indeed, a
main impression yielded by the literature is one of a furnace of heated debate.
Almost every possible position on almost every central issue seems to have been
occupied by some Indian philosopher. For example, there is no serious account
of perception familiar to Western readers – 'naïve realism', 'idealism',
'phenomenalism', and so on – which was not developed in one or another
Indian system. One would, perhaps, have to be something of an Indian
chauvinist to agree that all 'other teachings . . . are but the sauces and the spices'
to garnish the 'spiritual food' from the 'storehouse' of Indian philosophy.[1] But
it is hard to gainsay the judgement that 'India should not, indeed cannot, be left
out of any general study of the history of logic and philosophy'.[2]

This reference to logic is significant. For a second immediate impression is
one of acute argument and close attention to the credentials of good argumentation. (Though this does not prevent even the greatest thinker suddenly

foreclosing a debate by blunt appeal to an authoritative source, or buttressing an otherwise impressive chain of reasoning by invoking the experiences someone has had in hell.)

Philosophy, Religion and Mysticism

The systematic and argumentative character of Indian philosophy comes as a surprise to readers whose image of the Indian mind has been formed by verdicts, like Hegel's, on its 'dreamlike' nature, or by footage of the Beatles and 'flower people' sitting, eyes glazed, at the feet of an hirsute 'guru' of the 1960s. The image dies hard, of course: and in the kind of bookshop where PHILOSOPHY rubs shoulders with OCCULTISM and NEW AGE, one will find plenty of books by authors with an interest in keeping it alive. It is the image of Indian philosophy as so much ineffable and mystical spirituality or religion. The image is not, of course, *entirely* inaccurate but we are rightly encouraged, in the main, to 'find it spurious and mythical'.[3] A distinguished contemporary Indian philosopher is surely correct to insist that his ancestors' theories of reality were 'no more [and] no less secular than the Western'.[4]

Let us take the three elastic ingredients of this image in turn – religion, spirituality and mysticism. If by 'a religion' is understood an organized institution – replete with a founder, a holy order, temples, ceremonies, and so on – it is obviously a confusion to identify a religion with a philosophical system, even that system (if there is one) to which devotees of the religion generally subscribe. Matters are less clear-cut if we understand by 'a religion' a dogma or doctrine whose central assertion is that there exists a supreme creator, an object of total devotion, with which we should aspire to union. Here, too, it is wise to distinguish between a religion and its philosophical elaboration and apology – not least because each 'world religion' has been elaborated and systematized in a variety of incompatible ways. Aquinas (ch. 5, sect. 4) and Kierkegaard (ch. 8, sect. 3) were both Christians, but distant cousins philosophically. In the case of India, there is a more obvious reason against confusing philosophy with religion in this second sense. None of the systems discussed in this chapter in fact subscribe to the central assertion of a supreme God's existence. Some of them are flatly atheistic (including Jainism, despite its associated religious institutions); and in the rest, God is at most an especially 'pure soul', a fully enlightened human being, or a manifestation of an impersonal cosmic principle.

Whether the main Indian philosophies are religious in a further sense of being imbued with an essentially 'spiritual outlook' depends on how that expression is taken. If a 'spiritual philosophy' is one which holds that only mind or spirit genuinely exists – so that the material world is some kind of illusion or 'mental construct' – then only a few Indian systems qualify. But, in a less demanding sense, we might call a philosophy 'spiritual' if it denies that our everyday, earthly existence and experience are the only ones available to us, and urges us to seek for a plane of existence and experience where we are 'liberated' or 'emancipated' from the physical and psychological constraints of ordinary life. In this sense, all the main Indian schools are 'spiritual' – 'religious', if you will – in outlook.

Must a 'spiritual philosophy', so understood, be a *mystical* one? If a mystic is one who enjoys direct experience – though not through ordinary perception or introspection – of an order of being that cannot be adequately articulated in any language or conceptual scheme, then mysticism is indeed granted a place by the schools. It is 'not by speech, not by mind, not by sight', according to the *Kaṭha Upaniṣad*, that this order of being can be 'apprehended', yet it is nevertheless there to be 'discerned' by 'one liberated from the mouth of death' in a state of advanced meditation (360, 353).[5] Claims of this kind are found in all the philosophical systems. But three important points should be noted before concluding, without further ado, that these systems are therefore mystical.

First, the possibility of mystical experience is always *argued* for: so that it is on rational grounds, not through 'intuition', that the feasibility of mystical knowledge is established. Second, it is generally accepted that rational, philosophical understanding is a prerequisite for the mystic's direct acquaintance with reality. Without it, the meditator is unwarranted in construing his experiences as valid apprehensions of truth. Finally, despite the ineffability of what the mystic apprehends, a good deal can be said in advance concerning what this is *not*. Many passages in the *Upaniṣads* are devoted to showing that *Brahman* ('absolute reality') is not mind, space, a god, or whatever. Such demonstrations do not rely on mystical experiences, but on arguments. What these three points add up to is that, if we must dub the Indian philosophies 'mystical', this cannot excuse us from getting to grips with them as the complex rational systems which their respective champions took them to be. It is now time to obtain an overview of these systems and of the assumptions which they shared.

The Indian Schools

The standard convention is to divide the main Indian philosophies into six 'orthodox' schools and two 'unorthodox' ones, Buddhism and Jainism. It is a further convention to divide the six 'orthodox' schools into three pairs, as follows: Sāṃkhya and Yoga; Vaiśeṣika and Nyāya; and Vedānta and Mīmāṃsā. The rationale for this is the alleged affinity between the members of each pair, though one sometimes hears the further claim that the second member of a pair is primarily concerned with the practical application of the teachings of the first member. (This claim, as we shall see, is certainly false in at least the case of Sāṃkhya-Yoga.) There is a Joker missing from this pack, the 'materialist' school named after its founder, Cārvāka, which flourished around 600 BCE. Our knowledge of Cārvāka's teachings comes almost entirely from his Buddhist, and other, opponents. Apparently Cārvāka taught that there exists nothing but matter and that the goal of life should be a thoroughly hedonistic one, 'good digestion and no conscience'.[6] It is an interesting comment on the temper of Indian philosophy that the materialist school failed to survive. Still, its legacy, however ghostly, can be discerned in the writings of the longer-lived schools, all of which treat seriously the materialist threat.

What makes the 'orthodox' schools orthodox is their supposed acceptance, as authoritative, of the Hindu scriptures known as the Veda (a Sanskrit word originally meaning 'knowledge'). This is the vast corpus of works − religious verses (*mantras*), treatises on sacrifice, instructions for meditation, and philosophical speculations (*Upaniṣads*) − composed and assembled during the millennium after the Aryan invasion of India around 1500 BCE. For the history of philosophy, as distinct from that of religion, however, this distinction between 'orthodox' and 'unorthodox' is an uninteresting one. 'The notion of "Vedic" authority', writes one recent commentator, 'is a myth'.[7] With the exception of the *Upaniṣads*, the Veda was rarely the subject for commentary and, great though they may be, the *Upaniṣads* were less an iron constraint on the 'orthodox' schools than a spur to speculative interpretation − unsurprisingly, given their vagueness and ambiguities. 'Although the different schools ... moved within the space opened up by the [sacred] texts', one authority explains, they 'realized quite different interpretive possibilities'.[8] The texts which more effectively constrained the teachings of the schools were just as much outside the Veda as the sermons of the Buddha were − for example, the *Bhagavad-Gītā* in the case of the Vedānta school. More crucially, the distance between some 'orthodox' and 'unorthodox' thinkers is often less than that between different 'orthodox' writers. The rejection, by Buddhism and Jainism, of Vedic authority owed less to philosophical objections than to distaste for the sacrificial practices and social institutions (notably, the caste system) given blessing in the Vedic texts.

Some authors go further in dismantling the conventional divisions. There is, writes one, a 'myth of the schools'. In particular, 'Vedānta', 'the most haloed term of Indian philosophical thought connotes nothing. It is ... mere verbiage'. The most we are entitled to speak of are 'styles', not 'schools', of philosophy.[9] This is exaggerated: Indian philosophers seem to have viewed themselves as belonging to schools and were, to a degree, organized as such. Still, one has to concede that thinkers from one school sometimes share more with those from a second than with their fellows. But we need not agonize over this issue. In subsequent sections of this chapter I describe a number of

Indian philosophies, and whether we assign them to schools, sub-schools, super-schools, styles, or whatever, is of little moment. My use of the conventional labels for these philosophies is strictly for convenience.

If it is an exaggeration to call the emergence of the *Upaniṣads* 'the most remarkable event in the history of philosophic thought',[10] it is a pardonable one. Despite their obscurity on many issues, these works provided the framework for the schools, 'unorthodox' ones included. This framework was shaped, not only by a certain tone and theme, but by specific concepts and assumptions which are embryonically developed within those texts. The tone that pervades the *Upaniṣads* and the writings of the schools is one of intense seriousness. By this, I mean the sense that a proper understanding of the cosmos and of ourselves is not the goal of idle curiosity, or of a search for knowledge for its own sake. Rather, it is upon such understanding that, quite literally, our salvation – our emancipation from the grimness of our everyday condition – turns. Our lives – our actions, attitudes, emotions – are distorted ones, precisely because they are fuelled by an almost universal misunderstanding of our place in the scheme of things.

The *Leitmotiv* of the *Upaniṣads*, variously developed and modulated in the schools, is that this misunderstanding, with its consequent evils, resides in a failure to appreciate that both the cosmos and ourselves are, in essence, very different from how they ordinarily appear. In particular, there is the failure to recognize that, at the essential level, there is a fundamental affinity – identity, even – between ourselves and the rest of reality. In the *Upaniṣads*, this affinity is expressed in the famous equation of *Brahman* and *ātman*, of 'absolute reality' and the 'soul'. As Śvetaketu's father explains to him in the *Chāndogya Upaniṣad*, 'That which is the finest essence – this whole world has that as its soul. That is Reality. That is *ātman*. That art thou ["*Tat tvam asi*"], Śvetaketu' (247). The schools will variously interpret this statement, and some – notably Buddhism – cannot accept its manner of expressing the fundamental affinity between the world and ourselves. But the sense of some such affinity persists throughout the Indian tradition, and the failure properly to grasp it continues to be regarded as the culprit which is, at root, responsible for the grimness of the human condition. (This needs considerable qualification in the case of Sāṃkhya and Yoga thought. See sect. 2.) When the modern Bengali poet Tagore refers to the sense that 'I was no stranger in this world, that the inscrutable without name and form had taken me in its arms',[11] he echoes a sentiment expressed more than two and a half thousand years before in the *Chāndogya Upaniṣad*: 'I shall remain here [i.e. in my everyday existence] only so long as I shall not be released (from the bonds of ignorance). Then I shall arrive home' (249). False beliefs and conceptions have made us feel insecure strangers and aliens in the world, so that, as a recent writer puts it, 'man's naive at-oneness with the living universe, his essential innocence or sense of fellow feeling, is lost'.[12] This lost innocence may be irretrievable, but a reflective sense of 'at-oneness' can be achieved through philosophical thought. Or such is the conviction of Indian philosophy.

Rebirth, Action and Law

The common framework within which the schools operated has more structure to it, however, than that provided by the tone and theme just sketched. For it contains a number of more specific doctrines, also presaged in the *Upaniṣads*. Nomenclature varies in some cases, but I will refer to them as the doctrines of *saṃsāra*, *karma*, *dharma*, *mokṣa*, *duḥkha*, and *avidyā*. Although these doctrines are variously interpreted by the schools, they have a common, minimal content. '*Saṃsāra*' is often used to refer, simply, to the mundane world of ordinary experience, the world of 'becoming' – but always on the background assumption that this is a world in which all living creatures undergo a cycle of rebirth or transmigration from one body to another. The belief that each creature has lived countless previous lives and, until 'liberated', will continue to live further ones, seems to have become engrained by at least 500 BCE. Since it is not found in the earlier parts of the Veda, a reasonable guess is that this belief was inherited from the pre-Aryan culture that flourished before 1500 BCE, but which continued to exert an influence – in art, religion and mythology – long after that.

A crucial question which arises concerns what it is, exactly, that transmigrates. If by 'a creature' is meant a being with a given body, then obviously it cannot be *that* which proceeds to occupy other bodies. 'Self' and 'soul' are often offered by way of answers: but not only would these answers be rejected by Buddhists, they are anyway too bland, since most of the schools distinguish different kinds of self or soul, not all of which could be candidates for rebirth. For the present, I will postpone the question and borrow the label used in the *Maitrī Upaniṣad* for the transmigrating entity – 'the elemental soul' (*bhūtātman*). Three more tractable questions about *saṃsāra* are the following. First, why is it supposed that there is this cycle of rebirth? (The appeal, familiar among 'reincarnationists' in the West, to apparent memories of experiences that could only have been had in previous lives is rarely made – though the Buddha, during the first watch of his night of enlightenment, is alleged to have vividly recalled his previous incarnations.) Second, what allows us to say that the 'elemental soul' presently harnessed to creature X is the one which, in an earlier incarnation, was attached to creature Y? (Once again, the criterion of memory is rarely invoked.) Finally, what explains why an 'elemental soul' comes to occupy the particular bodies that it does? Or is it just luck, good or ill?

Answers to these questions are furnished by the second doctrine of *karma* ('action'). 'According as one acts', explains the *Brihad-Āranyaka Upaniṣad*, 'so does he become . . . One becomes virtuous by virtuous action, bad by bad action' (140). This sounds fairly innocent, but a peculiar twist soon turns this thought into a moral-cum-psychological equivalent to the law of the conservation of energy. Becoming such-and-such through one's actions – enjoying or suffering their 'fruits' – is not something which only occurs by and large; rather, it is something which *necessarily* ensues. Now since not all one's actions can 'bear fruit' within a given lifetime – some of them, after all, are performed only shortly before death – then a future lifetime is guaranteed in which the fruit is borne. What makes the 'elemental soul' currently occupying body X the one which previously occupied body Y is precisely the load of karmic effects which it carries as a result of actions performed during the occupancy of Y. (Jains treat this as more than metaphor, regarding *karma* as a kind of stuff which sticks to the 'soul'.) Moreover, the reason it now occupies X in particular, and is furnished with an appropriate character and set of dispositions, is that these are properly suited, properly 'deserved', in the light of its previous actions. As the *Maitrī Upaniṣad* has it, 'there is indeed . . . "the elemental soul" – he who, being overcome by the bright or the dark fruits of action, enters a good or evil womb, so that his course is downward or upward' (140).

Perhaps surprisingly, almost no arguments are offered in support of the doctrine of *karma*. But Indian philosophy would not regard this as a criticism, replying that, in Western thought too, few arguments are found to support the universal assumption that all events are subject to causal laws. And to the objection that the actual mechanics of *karma* are a mystery, the response will be that no one understands either how, in the final analysis, one event can cause or produce another.

Although the doctrine of *karma* is rarely argued for, it is embedded in the third, and wider, doctrine of *dharma*. This word has several senses. Buddhists, for example, use it to refer both to the corpus of the Buddha's teachings and to the ultimate elements out of which grosser things are constructed. More pertinently, it can mean something like 'duty' or 'moral obligation' – a sense discussed in section 5. It will emerge, there, that a person's *dharma* is generally reckoned to obtain in virtue of his 'station in life', his place in the social order and, ultimately thereby, in 'the order of things'. It is this sense, that of 'the order of things', which is relevant in our present context. The doctrine of *dharma* teaches that everything, in the mundane world at least, occupies an explicable place in an intelligible whole. 'Everything', here, means everything: there are no 'cosmic accidents', God does not play dice. And where ordinary causal explanations are insufficient – as they are in the case of human character, feelings, and actions – the slack is taken up by *karma*. *Dharma* cannot allow, for example, that being born with a surly, jealous disposition is mere 'bad luck' –

so there must be an explanation, the person's rotten behaviour in a previous incarnation. In many of its uses, '*dharma*' might be translated by that equally protean word 'law', and readers might compare the doctrine with the Christian concept of Natural Law (see ch. 5, sect. 4), which also straddles the moral and material orders.

Liberation, Ignorance and Suffering

Many Westerners cite the doctrines so far described, especially that of *karma*, to buttress their popular image of the 'fatalistic' Indian mind. But this is quite wrong, as consideration of the next doctrine demonstrates. According to this doctrine, it is possible to attain 'liberation' ('*mokṣa*') from *saṃsāra*, the cycle of rebirth, and thereby enter into a timeless, unchanging state (such as the famous *nirvāṇa* of the Buddhists). While, in the more theistic of the *Upaniṣads* and Vedāntic writings, liberation is held to depend, in part, on something like the grace of God, the general tendency is to insist that it must primarily depend upon one's own efforts. If it did not, the countless exhortations, by the Buddha and others, to strive for liberation would be pointless.

Karmic 'fruits', it should be emphasized, are not the results of the physical deeds one performs, but of the intentions or motives behind them. Killing a man will bear very different 'fruits' according to whether it is done out of jealousy, say, or out of military duty. So *karma* is not some underlying physical mechanism which grinds on irrespective of the decisions and intentions of the agent. Admittedly, these will be the decisions and intentions of someone whose character and dispositions are already formed through previous conduct, but nothing determines that they must now make those choices to which they are at most *inclined*. Looked at in one way, the doctrine of *karma* is as far removed from 'fatalism' as any could be: for it summons us to a sense of personal responsibility of enormous rigour. There can, after all, be 'no excuses' for the way we are – for our jealousy, our meanness, or whatever – if these are the result, in the final analysis, of our own freely decided actions. There is no moral 'bad luck' to comfort us for our shortcomings.

Earlier, I noted that 'emancipation' from our everyday condition is the final ambition of philosophy. This emancipation, we now see, is *mokṣa* – liberation from *saṃsāra*. Predictably, the various schools offer conflicting answers to such questions as 'How is liberation attained?' and 'What is the state of the liberated person?' It is difficult, then, to say much of a general kind about *mokṣa*. But the following, at least, is common ground: the paramount prerequisite for liberation is right knowledge or understanding of the self and its relation to the cosmos. This is the doctrine of *avidyā* ('ignorance', 'nescience'). This is not the kind of 'ignorance' we are now in about the weather in New York next

Christmas, but a set of stubborn, natural, yet false beliefs about the self and reality (such as that the self is necessarily connected up with a body). It is these beliefs that must be discredited, through philosophical argument and meditation, if liberation is to be won. What are immediately responsible, of course, for one's remaining in the cycle of rebirth are desires and motives for action, since it is these which produce karmic 'fruits'. But the idea is that, with 'enlightenment', such desires and motives, feeding off a false conception of self, will evaporate, to be replaced by disinterest in action. With 'cessation from every illusion', says the *Śvetāśvatara Upaniṣad*, 'there is a falling off of all fetters [i.e. desires] . . . [and so] cessation of birth and death' (396).

But why this talk of 'fetters', and why the loaded terminology of 'liberation' or 'emancipation' to describe the end of the cycle of rebirth? After all, some people might welcome the prospect of further lives. And even if we grant that this is due to 'ignorance', why shouldn't 'ignorance' here, as elsewhere, be bliss? The answer to these questions is provided by the final shared doctrine of *duḥkha*. It concerns the predominantly unsatisfactory character of mundane life, which makes this something from which it is imperative to seek release.

'*Duḥkha*' is usually translated as 'suffering', but this is misleading. Indian philosophers, it is true, like to dwell on the unpleasant side of life − pain, disease, dying − and to dispel the attractions of pleasure. Pleasures are ephemeral, they leave us with 'hangovers', we become addicted to them, yet bored as soon as they have been enjoyed. But even mundane lives which, by any normal criteria, would be regarded as genuinely contented, are condemned as *duḥkha* − and surely not even the darkest spectacles can totally blot out the existence of such lives. Nor is the verdict on life as suffering warranted by the insistence, among the Nyāya school especially, that even the most respectable mundane contentments fall badly short of the pure bliss experienced by the enlightened visionary. Love-making and playing the piano hardly deserve to be called 'suffering' simply because they fail to match up to something 'higher'. Anyway, not all the schools depict the liberated state in terms of bliss and happiness.

The fact is that *duḥkha* should not be construed as a psychological condition, such as suffering, at all. A better construal is:

> *Duḥkha* . . . is neither physical suffering nor mental frustration, nor . . . the obsession . . . with the uncontrollable transience of our pleasures. It is a profound awareness − a realization that our existence is necessarily conditioned; *saṃsāra* is a prison-house. Cessation of *duḥkha* implies [an] unconditioned state of freedom.[13]

This requires a qualification. In mundane life, we are in a condition of *duḥkha* even if we are *not* aware of being 'conditioned' or 'imprisoned'. There is a crucial distinction, here, between genuine and merely apparent cessation of *duḥkha*. People are very efficient at blinding themselves to their everyday condition. By 'grasping at' or 'attachment to' things or other people, and by identifying themselves with their bodies or characters, they can suppress the sense of being strangers in a world that stands over against them and 'conditions' them. Their ignorance may be bliss, but it is also culpable self-deceit, a kind of bad faith. Genuine cessation of *duḥkha* – that is, *mokṣa* – secures the sense of being 'unconditioned', not through a disingenuous immersion in mundane life, but through the recognition that this is not, *au fond*, one's true life at all. It is never the 'true self' that is imprisoned, but only the *ersatz* one with which, in our 'ignorance', we confuse it.

These, then, are the interrelated doctrines which constitute the common framework of the Indian philosophical systems. We can now see more clearly what these systems try to achieve, and how. The goal is to provide a comprehensive account of ourselves and the wider reality to which we belong that will not only dispel the 'ignorance' (*avidyā*) inherent in our everyday beliefs, but exhibit the fundamental unsatisfactoriness (*duḥkha*) of an existence founded on those beliefs. This comprehensive account must be so communicated and meditated upon that people will no longer have an interest in performing the actions which, through the strict operation of the moral law (*dharma*), bear the karmic 'fruits' which bind us to the cycle of rebirth (*saṃsāra*). With this achieved, philosophy will have completed its task of enabling human beings to attain liberation (*mokṣa*) from mundane existence, its ills and illusions.

A worry experienced by many Western and contemporary Indian readers is how much of this impressively coherent edifice can remain if one is unable to swallow the doctrines of rebirth and karmic desert. None of the other doctrines could, of course, survive in just the forms described above. *Mokṣa*, for instance, cannot be liberation from the cycle of rebirth if there is no such cycle. However, suitably modulated, much in these doctrines remains for serious consideration. All of them, after all, lend expression – sometimes exaggerated, perhaps, sometimes poetic, but never absurd – to the themes that are the very lifeblood of philosophy.

I shall focus, in the following sections, on the philosophies of Sāṃkhya-Yoga, Advaita Vedānta, and some schools of Buddhism. Some law of irony dictates that it is the ones I do not discuss in which some readers have most interest. But decisions have to be made, and there is some consensus that the systems mentioned are the most influential ones. (The nineteenth-century revival of Indian philosophy, for example, was essentially a revival of Vedānta (see ch. 9, sect. 1).)

Certainly they are the ones likely to be of most interest to the more general reader. There has, to be sure, been considerable interest recently among professional philosophers in the Nyāya school, primarily on account of its sophisticated discussions of perception.[14] But not only are these extremely technical and often tangential to the main concerns of this book, they also surround issues given their due in later chapters. I shall, of course, mention Nyāya and other schools at appropriate points, where their views conveniently contrast with those of the schools on which I focus.

• 2 Sāṃkhya and Yoga •

Among the 'orthodox' schools, Sāṃkhya – with its close stable-mate, Yoga – is second in influence only to the Vedānta schools. It is often said that it is the oldest of the philosophical systems. Certainly some of the *Upaniṣads* express Sāṃkhyan thoughts, but since these were composed fairly late on, that is hardly decisive. The central doctrine of the earlier *Upaniṣads* – the identity of *ātman* ('self') with *Brahman* ('absolute reality') – is at odds with the dualistic opposition, in Sāṃkhya and Yoga, between 'soul' (*puruṣa*) and 'nature' (*prakṛti*). Despite that, these systems share what I have called the tone and theme of the *Upaniṣads* – the serious conception of philosophy as essential to emancipation or liberation, and the notion of an affinity between self and the world which it is the task of philosophy to illuminate. Moreover, the six doctrines (of *karma*, *mokṣa*, etc.) which figure in the *Upaniṣads* are, suitably interpreted, embraced by these two systems.

Most probably, the main elements of Sāṃkhyan thought are of very ancient pedigree, gradually receiving sophisticated articulation over the centuries. The main text, Īśvarakṛṣṇa's *Sāṃkhya-kārikā*, is now usually dated around 200 CE, though its author claims to be recording the ideas of one Kapila, a figure lost in the mists of time. The main Yoga text, Patañjali's *Yoga-sūtra*, is probably later still, though this time the author claims a more elevated early source – the god Īśvara. (Of course, the *practice* of *yoga*, a physical and meditational discipline, is of great antiquity, being inherited by the Aryan invaders from the earlier Indus Valley civilization.)

Etymologically '*sāṃkhya*' means 'discrimination' or 'discernment', and the school which borrows this name indeed focuses upon one particular and paramount discrimination. *Yoga* means something like 'join' or 'yoke', and is an apposite name for the discipline advocated by the Yoga school. I shall not distinguish between the systems of the two schools until later since, on most large matters, they are in full agreement. Hence I shall be helping myself to texts from both schools and, unless otherwise indicated, I intend my account of Sāṃkhya to cover Yoga as well.

Sāṃkhya

If Sāṃkhya were the oldest system, that would not be surprising, for one may view it as elaborating what must surely have been primordial responses to the burgeoning reflection by human beings upon themselves, the world about them, and the relation between the two. I have three such responses in mind. First, the sense – so pervasive in ancient thought – that the world, for all its apparent variety, is a single coherent whole. Second, the sense that human beings are a unique kind of creature, set off against and separated from the natural order. And third, the sense – by way of an antidote to the previous one – that human beings are central in the scheme of things, that everything else is 'for their sake', so that, after all, there is some vital and meaningful link between themselves and 'the ponderous enormity of things', as Tagore put it.

In Sāṃkhya, these rough-hewn responses are articulated by its three central propositions. First: with one notable exception, everything in the cosmos is an ingredient in a single material substance, *prakṛti*. Second: the notable exception is an infinite number of distinct 'souls', or *puruṣas* – 'pure' consciousnesses, devoid of any material features. Third: *prakṛti* exists 'for the sake of' the *puruṣas*, for it has evolved so that the latter may eventually exist in a condition of liberation, achieved by full appreciation of the absolute distinctness of a *puruṣa* from material nature. Let us begin with the notion of *prakṛti*. According to some Indian schools, notably Nyāya and Vaiśeṣika, the natural world is composed out of an infinite number of elementary atoms. Sāṃkhya does not deny that there are elements which compose larger bodies, but holds that everything, including these elements, evolve from a single, dynamic substance. But why is this held, given that everyday perception suggests a vast plurality of distinct, independent objects in the world about us? Well, certainly we do not *perceive prakṛti*. (For Sāṃkhya, in fact, we never perceive natural objects directly, only pictures or representations of them constructed by the 'mind-organ' (*manas*).) And while, in advanced states of meditation, a person may have direct intuition of the 'oneness' of nature, this is not the basis for postulating the existence of *prakṛti*. Rather, we know of it through rational inference based on a proper understanding of *causality*.

The crucial premise of the argument is that effects are somehow contained in their causes. If they were not, the idea goes, then anything might cause anything, so that there would be no order in the universe – which there plainly is. Granted this premise, we can then trace every conditioned, caused state of affairs back to a source which contains it, so that nothing genuinely novel or independent of that source can ever arise. Such is the point of Īśvarakṛṣṇa's claim that *prakṛti* must be the one 'general cause of this many-sided universe' on account of 'the difference and non-difference of cause and effect' (15–16).[15]

(The smoke can be differentiated from the fire, but is only a manifestation of a potentiality within the fire.)

Although there is only the one substance, *prakṛti*, this is not a *simple* substance, for it is an amalgam of three 'threads', called *guṇas*. Strictly, '*prakṛti*' is the name of that initial state of the cosmos when the *guṇas* are in perfect equilibrium – a state which then evolves into the world as we know it after that equilibrium, for reasons which are unclear, gets disturbed. A good deal of the energy of Sāṃkhyan writers is spent detailing the course of this evolution. Roughly, the story is one of the increasing complexity and differentiation of matter. In the early chapters of the story, there is, so to speak, just one plot: matter as a whole evolves through various stages. But, at a certain point, there is a bifurcation. Matter with a preponderance of one of the *guṇas* develops into the elements composing the external world and then into the familiar material objects – tables, trees, and so on – around us. Matter of a more refined kind, meanwhile, develops into the perceptual senses (sight, hearing, etc.), the 'conative' senses (desire, will, etc.), and the 'mind-organ', whose primary function is to order the data received through the senses.

It is essential to note that the Sāṃkhyan doctrine is *not* a dualism of mind versus matter. Perceiving, desiring, remembering are mental episodes or processes, but for Sāṃkhya, they are also material ones – distinguished from other material processes only by their refinement. (Compare the view of contemporary materialists that mental states are certain highly complex brain-states (see ch. 10, sect. 4).) Thus, when Sāṃkhyans call one stage in the evolution of *prakṛti* '*buddhi*' ('intelligence'), they do not mean that matter is really 'spiritual' in nature, but that matter must evolve to a point where its most refined activities can also be described in psychological terms.

Sāṃkhyan dualism is one between matter (including mind) and *puruṣa*. So let us turn to this notion. Whereas *prakṛti* is a single, though complex substance, dynamic and evolving, there is a plurality of distinct *puruṣas*, each of which is absolutely simple and passive, a pure consciousness. In the words of the *Sāṃkhya-kārikā*, a *puruṣa* is 'a witness, isolated, neutral, cognizing, and inactive' (18). What it directly 'cognizes' or 'witnesses' is not the external world, but mental states and processes, including the 'pictures' of the world synthesized by the 'mind-organ' from incoming perceptual data. A perception, for example, is analysed into three components: the external object, its mental representation, and the consciousness or 'witnessing' of this representation. It is difficult, but crucial, to distinguish between the last two elements, and to recognize that the former belongs in the realm of *prakṛti* as much as the external object represented does. Unlike the mind, Patañjali explains, *puruṣa* is 'unchanging, unmoving', and since '*buddhi* [intelligence] is made up of the *guṇas* . . . [it] is opposed to That [i.e. *puruṣa*]'.[16] Lower animals can perceive and desire, and so be said to have minds. After all, they respond to stimuli received through sense-organs, and behave in goal-directed ways. But they are not conscious: so the consciousness possessed by higher animals and human beings is not a property of mind, but of an entity outside of nature, namely *puruṣa*.

Since the only *objects* of consciousness are mental states and processes, *puruṣa* cannot itself be an object of its own consciousness – no more than a source of light, to use a favourite analogy, can shine upon itself. We can, then, only know of *puruṣa*'s existence by rational inference. At least three arguments for its existence are presented, as in the following passage of Īśvarakṛṣṇa's:

> Since the aggregate of things is for the sake of another; . . . since there is super-intendence; and since there is activity for sake of isolation, the soul exists. (21)

The second clause recalls a point from the previous paragraph. Because mental processes *per se* are never conscious, they require 'superintendence' or 'witnessing' by some entity outside of nature to become objects for consciousness. For a desire, say, to be what we misleadingly describe as a conscious desire, it must be 'superintended' by something – that is, *puruṣa*.

But the passage quoted suggests two further and very different arguments for *puruṣa*, ones which yield the third central proposition of Sāṃkhya. They are both teleological arguments, to the effect that *puruṣa*'s existence is required in order to lend sense and purpose to what would otherwise be inexplicable. It is required, first, to explain our striving towards 'isolation' – that is, towards 'liberation' or *mokṣa*. If there were nothing but *prakṛti*, no 'souls', there could be nothing to be liberated. In Sāṃkhya, as in other systems, it is not made clear exactly who or what gets liberated. What is clear, however, is that liberation is only achieved when the liberated one makes an absolute discrimination between *prakṛti* and what he, she, or it truly is – a pure consciousness. It is the failure to make this discrimination that explains continuing attachment and 'clinging' to the material world of the senses, pleasure and pain, and hence continuing entrapment in the cycle of rebirth.

The second teleological argument – indicated in the first clause of Īśvarakṛṣṇa's passage – holds that *prakṛti*, the whole natural order and its evolution, must have a point. Since *prakṛti* is the *whole* natural order, this point must lie outside of it and what could this be except *puruṣa* and its liberation? The reasoning behind this premise seems to be that, while the cosmos has no divine designer behind it, everything that we observe is seen to contribute to something larger than, or beyond, itself – like a piece of wood to the finished table. Once all *puruṣas* are liberated, *prakṛti*, having completed its task, will, it seems, evaporate. In Īśvarakṛṣṇa's picturesque analogy, *prakṛti* is compared to a dancer, a striptease one suspects, who 'having exhibited herself on the stage withdraws'. Likewise, '*prakṛti* withdraws from the soul when she has manifested herself to it' in all 'her' distinctness from it (59). An important lesson of this second teleological argument is that, despite the absolute contrast between nature and soul, the former is, so to speak, on the side of the latter. Only stupidity, obstinacy or a clinging to the things of the world prevent that liberation of the soul which nature itself seeks to further. In this respect, at least, Sāṃkhya sees an 'affinity' between the soul and its world. In another picturesque analogy, the two are compared to a blind man and a cripple who co-operate in order to make up for what each of them lacks.

Yoga

Discounting the superannuated speculations on the constitution and evolution of matter, there are still a number of serious problems with the Sāṃkhya system, most of which champions of rival systems were quick to raise. But before glancing at some of these, I need to mention the respects in which the Yoga school departs from the orthodox Sāṃkhyan line. It has been said that the author of the *Yoga-sūtra* 'merely rehandles the Sāṃkhya philosophy . . . adapting it to a rather superficial theism in which he exalts the practical value of meditation'.[17] Patañjali's theism may indeed be 'superficial', but it is misleading to describe him as exalting the merely 'practical' value of meditation. Something of greater philosophical moment than that is at stake.

Against the atheism of Sāṃkhya, Yoga philosophy argues for the existence of a god, Īśvara, on two grounds. First it is held, in a manner prescient of the famous 'ontological' argument of Christian theologians (see ch. 5, sect. 4), that the very notion of a *perfect puruṣa* – that is, of one which has never been tainted by association with the material world – implies the existence of such a being. Second, *yogins* – adepts in the meditational techniques of yoga – testify to enjoying direct experience of this being. But Īśvara plays only a modest role in the system. Unlike the god postulated by the Nyāya and Vaiśeṣika schools, he is not the creator of the world, even if he is able, in some obscure way, to co-ordinate the careers of *prakṛti* and the *puruṣas*. Still less is he an all-embracing principle of reality of the *Brahman* variety, being just one among an infinity of *puruṣas* and set off against nature. Īśvara's main function is to serve as an exemplar of a completely liberated existence – 'to show the supreme essence', as Patañjali puts it, of *puruṣa*-hood – reflection upon whom will be one, but not the only, meditational route towards enlightened understanding.

More interesting is the importance given by Yoga to meditation, whether upon Īśvara or not. Part of the value of meditation is indeed 'practical', in the following sense: someone who rightly discriminates between *puruṣa* and *prakṛti* is nevertheless liable to remain subject to various inherited dispositions (*saṃskāras*) to confuse the two and so return to a state of 'affliction' and 'attachment'. To prevent such recidivism, to 'uproot' these dispositions, prolonged immersion in meditative states, where *puruṣa* is quite unaffected by the machinations of nature, is required. But there is more to the emphasis than this.

It is often said that whereas, for Sāṃkhya, liberation is achieved through philosophical knowledge, this is achieved, for Yoga, through meditation. But it is better to say that there is some discrepancy here over the character of philosophical knowledge. Yoga stresses that the true natures of *puruṣa*, *prakṛti*, and their relationship, cannot be fully articulated in conceptual or linguistic terms. They can, however, be directly intuited by a *yogin* in that advanced state of meditation – the last of eight steps – known as *samādhi*. This state is itself ineffable, and almost the only thing we can be confident of is that it is quite unlike any normal mental state. Indeed, it can hardly be called a mental state since, in *samādhi*, there is complete 'restraint of mental operations' (which is Patañjali's definition of '*yoga*'). In such a state, *puruṣa* 'rests in itself', no longer even tempted to identify itself with the mental processes – themselves belonging in the sphere of *prakṛti* – with which everyday consciousness is 'tainted'. That said, one should not exaggerate the difference between Sāṃkhya and Yoga on the issue of true philosophical knowledge. Those readers who found persuasive the Sāṃkhyan arguments for the separation of *puruṣa* from *prakṛti* will not thereby have achieved instant liberation since, not even for the Sāṃkhyan, is philosophical knowledge equated with mere intellectual assent to a doctrine. It remains, however, that the two schools – like many other pairs of schools in the history of philosophy – put different weights on the benefits of conceptual reflection and of 'mystical' insight respectively.

Some Problems

Other Indian schools were quick to highlight a number of problems in the Sāṃkhya-Yoga doctrines. It is useful to divide these problems into three groups. First, there are those which are endemic to dualist theories in general, including ones familiar in the West, such as that of Descartes (see ch. 7, sect. 3). How, if at all, can the two 'worlds' – material and non-material – interact or connect up? To speak, as Sāṃkhyans do, of mental matter being sufficiently refined or translucent to 'reflect' *puruṣa* is to offer metaphors instead of answers. And how, if the only objects of which a *puruṣa* can be conscious are material, can it have reason to suppose that other *puruṣas* exist as well? Why shouldn't everyone else be *prakṛti* and nothing more?

Second, there are the problems which arise from the *particular* version of dualism espoused by Sāṃkhya-Yoga – above all, the insistence that *puruṣa* is a pure, unchanging consciousness, distinct not only from the external world but from mental processes as well. Can sense be made of such an entity? How does one convince a person that, despite the obvious differences between his feeling the intense pain of toothache and quietly enjoying his favourite CD, his consciousness is the same unchanging one in both cases? Then there is the problem of counting or 'individuating' *puruṣas*. If they are absolutely simple, devoid of all distinguishing features, why should it be supposed that there is a plurality of them? By what criterion can it be known that Jack and Jill do not share the same pure consciousness, or that the consciousness of each of them is not a different one every week?

Finally, there are those problems which result from yoking the dualist doctrine with the six common framework doctrines of Indian thought. Two especially urgent questions concern *puruṣa* and *mokṣa*. We are told that *puruṣa* is, and always has been, entirely distinct from *prakṛti*. But then, as the great Vedāntin philosopher Rāmānuja objected: if the soul is anyway 'eternally free, then there can be no bondage and no release'.[18] The usual answer is that one (who exactly? *Puruṣa*? The 'mind'?) must first experience 'bondage' – or rather, the illusion of 'bondage' – in order then to experience liberation. But why should that be so? The other problem concerns the condition of *puruṣa* after complete liberation and the dissolution of the material world, including the body and 'mental operations'. *Puruṣa* was introduced to us as a consciousness of these operations. But in that case, when these dissolve, what is left for it to be aware of? It appears doomed to become a mere nothing.

It is only fair to add that problems in this final group plague other Indian systems as well. All the orthodox schools find it difficult to explain why the 'true self' – *puruṣa*, *ātman*, or whatever – should labour under the illusion of belonging to the material, empirical world, thereby remaining in 'bondage'. But the schools I now turn to at least strive to escape the difficulties created by the dualism of Sāṃkhya–Yoga. It is not, perhaps, historically accurate to treat the Vedāntic and Buddhist systems as only emerging by way of critical response to this dualism, but it is heuristically convenient so to regard them. In their respective alternatives to Sāṃkhya, we encounter a pattern often repeated in the history of philosophy. If the sense of an ultimate divide between human and all other existence, of the kind articulated by Sāṃkhya, is a 'primordial' response to reflection on the human condition, then attempts to close that divide, of the kinds we shall now encounter, are hardly less perennial.

• 3 Advaita Vedānta •

Modern Indian writers sometimes complain that Westerners tend to identify India's philosophical tradition with just one of its elements, Vedānta. This charge testifies to the fascination exerted by Vedānta, and even those who level it often agree that here, nevertheless, is 'the most perfect expression of Indian thought'.[19] 'Vedānta' means 'end of the Veda', and can refer either to the Upaniṣads (the last portion of the Vedic scriptural corpus) or to the later systematization of their alleged meaning. The second is our present concern. (That Vedānta, in this sense, *is* faithful to the Upaniṣads would be challenged, of course, by the other orthodox schools.) In fact, the main commentaries of the Vedānta philosophers take as their texts, not so much the Upaniṣads, as the Bhagavad-Gītā and, above all, the succinct, indeed gnomic utterances – one of them consists of a single word only – known as the Brahma-sūtras (or Vedānta-sūtras) of Bādarāyana, variously dated between 200 BCE and 200 CE.

Certainly the Vedānta school cannot supply *the* correct interpretation of the Upaniṣads and the other texts in the 'triple basis', for the simple reason that it comprises a number of rival sub-schools. These go by the names of Advaita (non-dualist), Viśiṣtādvaita (qualified non-dualist), and Dvaita (dualist). Here, I focus on Advaita Vedānta, leaving discussion of the others until chapter 6. The leading Advaitin exponent is Śaṅkara, India's most celebrated philosopher if we exclude the Buddha and Gandhi, and it is upon his views that my account is mainly based. (I will not enter the vexed debate over Śaṅkara's originality in relation to various predecessors, notably Gauḍapāda.[20]) Recent scholars put his dates fifty or so years earlier than the traditional 788–820 CE. At least his dates are more certain than the details of his short life, which are shrouded in myth. He can, for example, only have written a fraction of the Herculean opus once ascribed to him. Mythical too, presumably, is the course in the erotic arts he took by occupying the body of a particularly priapic King for a few weeks. Legend also has it that Śaṅkara died of ulcers wished upon him by a rival sage, who then suffered the same fate at the behest of one of Śaṅkara's disciples.

Śaṅkara has been called 'the Eastern Thomas Aquinas', and not simply because of his extraordinary industry and untimely death. Like Aquinas's, Śaṅkara's writings display a sometimes uneasy blend of appeals to scriptural authority and to formal reason. And both of them undertake the task of providing illuminating analogies to facilitate our understanding of what are, finally, inexpressible truths.

The Central Claims

Illuminating analogies are certainly welcome since, taken at face value, the main theses of Advaita Vedānta are bizarre. Like all orthodox systems, it accepts the six doctrines sketched in section 1. We ordinary humans are in bondage to a wretched cycle of rebirth through the karmic deserts of our desires. Liberation from this cycle can only be attained through overcoming ignorance of how we and the world really are. For Śaṅkara, it is a non-dualist reading of the

Upaniṣads which best systematizes these doctrines, blessed as they then are by infallible authority.

The central Advaitin claims – 'simple and devastating'[21] – are:

1 Nothing is truly real except *Brahman*[22] – unitary, seamless, ineffable being.
2 What we ordinarily consider real – physical objects, persons, God, and so on – belong to a world of appearance or illusion (*māyā*).
3 Individual selves are also appearances, mere 'reflections' of a single Self or 'pure consciousness', *ātman*.[23]
4 Since reality is one, *Brahman* and *ātman* must be identical, in which case *Brahman* is pure consciousness.
5 Belief in the existence of the apparent world is due to ignorance (*avidyā*) in the form of 'superimposing' (*adhyāsa*) upon *Brahman/ātman* what does not belong to it.
6 Since we are stuck in the cycle of rebirth through desires which depend on our ignorant belief in the physical world and individual selves, liberation is attained through experiencing the identity of *Brahman* and *ātman*, thereby overcoming 'the delusion that there is a world' (TT 87).[24]

Nothing is real, then, besides a single, indescribable mode of being, pure consciousness, which is to be experienced in a 'self-luminous flash', which is also the attainment of liberation. So stated, Advaita Vedānta is everything Westerners in search of exotic Eastern wisdom could hope for. Whether such a bald statement is adequate, however, is something we need to examine.

The central claims are supposed to elucidate the 'great sentences' (*mahāvākyas*) of the *Upaniṣads*, such as 'Neti, neti' (*Brahman* is 'not this, not this'), and above all 'Tat tvam asi' ('That thou art'). This latter, holds Śaṅkara, is not a figurative way of saying that *Brahman* and *ātman* have some resemblance or affinity. It is a statement of strict identity: '"that" and "thou" refer to one and the same entity' (TT 375). Nor, as for the Mīmāṃsā school, is it a mere peg for reflections leading to right performance of ritual. It is genuinely expressive of a truth. There is a problem here, however, since *Brahman* and *ātman* are not 'things' which can be directly designated by words. 'That thou art', therefore, only 'indicates' a truth which is to be grasped, finally, through a wordless 'direct intuition'. Taken literally, 'that' and 'thou' refer to items in the world of appearance, so that their equation would be false. This obvious falsehood, however, prompts us to give the words a special 'hearing' (*śravaṇa*) which primes us to experience the truth they struggle to express.

Let us accept this as an accurate exercise in scriptural hermeneutics. Still, that hardly helps us understand, with any precision, the 'elucidation' of the 'great sentences', nor the arguments behind the central claims. The best procedure, which Advaitins themselves often adopt, is to compare and contrast these claims with the dualist position of the Sāṃkhya and Yoga schools discussed in section 2.

The Critique of Dualism

Underlying this critique is the powerful conviction that it would be depressing if dualism were true. The attempts of Sāṃkhyans to discover some affinity or co-operation between nature and the soul cannot compensate for the sense of alienation, of being a 'stranger' in the world, which a sharp division between the conscious and natural orders must inspire. Only through recognizing an essential identity of Self and reality can human beings 'attain the state beyond fear or danger' (TT 88). As one commentator puts it, only the doctrine of 'a being of self-awareness which needs nothing else to be there' can bring with it that 'sense of completeness [which] is also *ananda* (delight)'.[25]

Despite the attacks on dualism, Advaitins build upon a number of Sāṃkhya or Yoga assumptions. Like the Sāṃkhyans, they posit the existence of a Self which is pure consciousness, a mere 'witness', and repeat the argument that mental processes are not, *per se*, conscious but need to be 'illuminated' by a consciousness. To this, Śaṅkara adds an argument usually credited to Descartes: 'It is inconsistent to deny [the] Self, for it is that very Self that would do the denying' (B 127). Since the Self is not the empirical mind or ego, Advaitins also accept the Sāṃkhyan conclusion that it is cardinal 'ignorance' to confuse the two. There is agreement, finally, that everything in the world of experience has a single ultimate ground or cause. The Sāṃkhyan argument here – that all effects are somehow 'contained in' their cause – is, according to Śaṅkara, valid as far as it goes. (But it does not go far enough, failing to recognize that the effects of this ultimate cause do not merely lack novelty, but *reality* too.)

These points of agreement soon give way to dissension, however. Dualism, argue the Advaitins, is clearly inconsistent with the monistic thrust of the *Upaniṣads*. Sāṃkhya sins on two counts here. First of all, it holds that there exist *many* souls or pure consciousnesses (*puruṣas*). This, it is argued, is not only scripturally deviant, but unintelligible. Once a person is stripped of everything that belongs in the empirical order – body, perceptual senses, emotions, intellect, and so on – he is thereby deprived of anything that could serve to distinguish him from another person. Just as there is only one Space, despite its many enclosures within pots and jugs, so there is only one Self, despite its local associations with, or reflections in, an apparent plurality of individual souls (*jīvas*) and minds. (Take away the pots and jugs and it would be *obvious* that nothing distinguishes one region of space from another.)

Even if Sāṃkhya were to concede that there can only be one *puruṣa* (like the Advaitin *ātman*), however, it would be guilty on a second count – its central contention that *puruṣa* is entirely distinct from the natural order, *prakṛti*. Once again, it is logic, and not just scripture, which this offends. *Prakṛti*, recall, was alleged to exist and evolve 'for the sake of' *puruṣa*. Śaṅkara comments on this as follows: 'Nature cannot exist to serve the soul since there cannot be any mutual relation between the two and since nature is non-conscious' (TT 221). He is making two points, of which the first is that *prakṛti* would have to be conscious – which everyone agrees it is not – in order to adopt any purpose, including that of evolving for the sake of the soul's liberation. Second, and more crucially, nature and the soul, on the Sāṃkhyan account, belong to such opposite realms that no contact or interaction between them is intelligible. Metaphors like that of the lame man and the blind man co-operating (see p. 28 above) are no use since, here, the two parties belong in the same, natural order (B 154). Nor is it any good appealing, in the manner of Yoga (and, for that matter, of some followers of Descartes), to a God who connects up the activities of nature and the soul. There is indeed a God, Īśvara, but he is not a creator or facilitator, being only a 'personification' of *Brahman*. And even if Īśvara were a separate entity – a special *puruṣa* – his connection with nature and his ability to influence it would be just as puzzling as what he is brought in to explain.

Something, indeed, must be real. If it were not, there would be nothing on which to 'superimpose' our erroneous conceptions. Fortunately we know from scripture, experience of ourselves, and pure reasoning what this is – *ātman*. Hence *Brahman*, the whole of reality, must be equated with *ātman*, and not divided into *ātman* and something else. The relation between this 'something else' and *ātman* would then be incomprehensible. Positing its existence, therefore, could play no role in explaining the one thing we do know, conscious experience. We are forced, then, to deny the reality of a material world (including minds which, recall, are supposed to be composed of a special matter). Liberation indeed requires a Sāṃkhyan discrimination between the Self and everything else. But this is only a first step, to be completed by the further one of appreciating that it is provisional, that really there was nothing to discriminate between. I am indeed nothing material, for there is nothing material for me to be. Only when I see this do I cease feeling a stranger in a world whose nature would be alien to my own, and therein resides the promise of freedom, self-completeness, and 'bliss'.

Māyā

The price for such 'bliss', however, seems to be the total abdication of commonsense. Is it not more sensible to accept that the connection between *ātman* and the empirical world is incomprehensible than to deny all reality to this world? The scriptures do not speak unambiguously for the latter option, and even if they did, we are unlikely to be impressed by the argument that they could not be wrong since they had no human author to whom error could be attributed.[26] Moreover, Advaitins are hardly in a position to deny that something is real simply because it is incomprehensible, since this is just what they allege *Brahman/ātman* finally to be.

There is, of course, one very well-known way of trying to accommodate a denial of material reality to commonsense. This is to insist that material things are 'in the mind' – or, better, that they are somehow 'reducible' to actual or potential perceptions or 'sense-data'. But this brand of Berkeleyan idealism (see ch. 7, sect. 3) is not available to Śaṅkara. For him, perceptions, feelings, and sensations – as distinct from the pure 'witnessing' of them – are no more real than external physical objects. For example, 'suffering does not (really) exist' (TT 385). Moreover, he denies that the world is, as it were, contained in or spun out of the imagination. This world of appearances, *māyā*, is either beginningless or the playful creation (*līlā*) of *Brahman* in its personified form of Īśvara (B 151). (It is worth noting that '*māyā*', usually translated as 'illusion' or 'appearance', originally had the sense of 'magical creation'.) In some sense, it is already there – albeit illusorily – for all of us to encounter.

That Advaita Vedānta is not a kind of idealism in any obvious sense merely compounds the difficulty of deciphering its seemingly mad denial of any reality besides pure consciousness.[27] The offence to commonsense is to some degree alleviated by Śaṅkara's doctrine of 'two levels'. At the 'lower' level, we can rightly distinguish between real and unreal objects (the drinker's bottle and the pink elephants he then 'sees'), between distinct causes and effects, between different persons, and between a true god and heathen imposters. So, at this level, we are not forced to regard everything we ordinarily believe as false. It remains, though, that at the 'higher' level, no objects are real, effects of the one cause (*Brahman*) are merely apparent, no individual selves exist, and even the 'true' god is but an appearance. The comfort this distinction offers to commonsense is surely slight, for we are left wondering why, at *any* level, our ordinary belief in an empirical world should be rejected.

Śaṅkara tries to proffer further help, this time by furnishing some analogies for the relation between *Brahman* and *māyā*. It is like that between the sea and its froth, or Space and the spaces within pots, or the sun and its reflections in pools. But these analogies evoke significantly different conceptions: the second, for example, is suggestive of a pantheistic outlook not indicated by the others. More seriously, while all three doubtless suggest that the ingredients of *māyā* are dependent on *Brahman*, none of them supports the conclusion that these are less than real. There is no sun in the pool, but its reflection is real enough, and swimmers in the Mediterranean sea know all too well that froth can be real. Śaṅkara, then, understates when he remarks 'No analogy is perfect' (B 173).

The suspicion must dawn that the denial of *māyā*'s reality cannot be taken at face value and is due to an eccentric definition of 'real'. This is reinforced by Śankara's claim that the objects of ordinary, 'lower' knowledge are 'unreal' in that they are not 'constant and eternal' (TT 129, B 297). It looks, then, as if 'real' is simply being defined so that anything which changes or is eventually destroyed, like my house or my body, cannot be real. If so, then commonsense is after all secure, for it is not threatened by the fact that very little qualifies as real in this arbitrary sense of 'real'. So is the doctrine of *māyā*, at first hearing so radical, a dull one dressed up in exciting, but misleading terminology? I think not. Śankara's position is not the mad one it may have initially seemed, but nor is it dull. Let us return to the drunkard's pink elephants, which disappear when he awakes. What makes them 'unreal' is not the mere fact that they disappear, but that the experience of them is contradicted by the man's waking experiences. 'Seeing' them does not cohere with more reliable experience. What Śankara means by 'real' and 'true' is that whose presumed existence *cannot* be contradicted by more reliable experience.

Unfortunately for commonsense, even the elephants in the zoo fail to be real on this count. Although they are real relative to the pink ones, they are not finally real. The only difference is this: 'the dream world is sublated each morning when we awake, whereas the waking world remains until ultimate realization of *Brahman*'s identity with the Self (*ātman*)' (B 172). There is, it is alleged, a reliable experience − a 'direct intuition', a 'self-luminous flash' − which contradicts ordinary waking experience. In this visionary experience, whose authority is vouchsafed by scripture, all distinct objects evaporate, as does any separation between them and the pure 'witness' whose experience it is. In these respects, at least, the nearest that we non-visionaries can approach to this condition − and that is not very near − is the state of deep sleep.

As this very partial analogy implies, the special experience which contradicts our ordinary conceptions is indescribable. Śankara offers an interesting reason why this must be so, one that helps us understand his relegation of the empirical world to the status of *māyā*. Any experience which could be articulated would, for that very reason, belong to the merely apparent order. This is because that order is, in a sense, created and sustained by language. 'Gods, men, and the world originate from *śabda*, word . . . Words precede things' (B 139). The thought here, perhaps, is one which not a few philosophers in the twentieth century have proposed, sometimes under such headings as 'linguistic idealism' or 'linguistic relativism'. Being as such is without shape and structure, since these are the contribution of creatures, ourselves, who carve up reality according to the linguistic categories without which thought and action would be impossible. Since the languages we speak are, in the final analysis, conventions − since we do not have to use just the categories we do rather than others − then the world about which we speak is itself a product of convention.

Substitute 'convention' for 'appearance' in Śaṅkara's description of the empirical world as one of mere appearance, and several features of his position fall into place. Only *Brahman* is truly real, in the sense that everything except plain being, as such, issues from the 'superimposition' of the conventional. This superimposition is to be understood as the articulation of reality through the contingent, conventional categories which language supplies. And the visionary experience or direct intuition which contradicts our ordinary experiences is one in which words and concepts seem to lose all necessary connection with reality, and in which there is at least a glimmer of a seamless whole into which the objects of everyday classification are absorbed.

If this is a reasonable interpretation of Advaita Vedānta, its position is neither mad nor dull. But even those sympathetic to its general drift will be critical of some of its components. At least three important issues might be raised. First, a great deal turns, in Śaṅkara's account, on the direct intuition which allegedly reveals the apparent or conventional character of empirical reality. Too much, some will say. For one thing, how should we adjudicate between the intuition Śaṅkara speaks of and other visionary experiences which seem to testify to very different conceptions of reality? Certainly one would welcome arguments of a less precarious kind for Śaṅkara's conventionalist conclusion. Second, does Śaṅkara's conventionalism go far enough? In particular, he holds on to the idea of a permanent Self, in the form of *ātman*, as belonging to – indeed constituting – reality. Is he entitled to? Finally, it will be asked whether the denigration of the empirical world as mere convention is compatible with the stated aim of making us feel 'at home' once more. Can I really stop feeling a 'stranger' by identifying myself with a reality of which there can be no articulate experience, and of which my closest intimations – prior to 'liberation', at least – occur while I am fast asleep?

These are all issues which suggested themselves, several centuries before Śaṅkara, to a succession of remarkable philosophers proclaiming allegiance to the greatest of the unorthodox schools and religions – Buddhism. It is to some of their discussions I now turn.

•   4   Buddhism   •

There are the Vedānta, Sāṃkhya, etc. philosophies, but no 'Hindu philosophy' as such. 'Buddhism', however, refers both to a religion and to a set of philosophies, so that some care must be taken to distinguish between the two. It is a moot point, in fact, whether Buddhism is a religion except in a purely institutional sense (see p. 15 above). There is Buddhist devotion and ritual, but there is no omnipotent, creator God, and the 'gods' which are sometimes spoken of are inferior in status to enlightened men and women, denizens of certain strange worlds which do not usually impinge upon human life. Thus 'there is no place for worship, prayer, nor for many other things which are usually included *by definition* in the category of "religion" '.[28] Buddhist 'faith', for example, is simply the conviction, inspired by the example of the Buddha and later saints, that liberation from the world of suffering is possible.

More than with any other major religion, moreover, there is a wide gap – admittedly with many intermediate positions – between the relatively esoteric doctrines studied by monks or scholars and the 'popular' beliefs which inspire the everyday practice of the larger congregation. This is a distinction sanctioned, to a degree, by the Buddha himself, whose various sermons are tailored for very different audiences. There is, for example, an uneasy relation between the 'esoteric' ideal of 'extinction' (*nirvāṇa*) and the 'popular' concern with acquiring the 'merit' needed for a desirable rebirth. Arguably, the complicated and rather bleak message of Buddhist philosophy would not have generated a 'world religion' if unleavened with a simpler and less demanding one at the popular level.

The Buddha and His Teachings

Unlike Hinduism, Buddhism has an identifiable founder – Siddārtha Gautama, a scion of the noble Śākya clan from the south of present-day Nepal. Traditionally he is believed to have lived between *c.*566 and 486 BCE, but recent scholars tend to date him rather later, say 480–400 BCE. Mollycoddled inside his father's palace until nearly thirty years of age, Gautama was deeply disturbed by his belated witnessing of disease, old age, and death in the surrounding city. Resolving to understand the cause and cure for such human misery, he abandoned his wife and son to become a wandering ascetic. After six years of unsuccessful attempts, including extreme self-mortification, Gautama eventually achieved enlightenment during his famous night of meditation beneath a Pipal tree, thereby attaining the status of a *buddha* ('enlightened one'). Through his personal charisma and brilliant sermons, the Buddha soon attracted a large following, and the remainder of his life was devoted to organizing an order (*saṅgha*) of monks and nuns, converting influential rulers to his doctrines, preaching to all strata of society, and tirelessly elaborating his teachings.

The Buddha's appeal is comparable, in some respects, to Martin Luther's. There is not only the inspired oratory but the insistent call to a sense of individual responsibility for one's own salvation, incompatible with the elevation of a special priestly caste to sovereign authority in such matters. (Many of the Buddha's followers hailed from the noble *kṣatriya* caste, traditional rivals of the priestly *brahmins*.)

The Buddha's teachings on several topics can be identified with certainty, but on others – especially those of philosophical nicety – his position is less clear. Part of the problem is textual, since even the 'authoritative' Pali Canon, which purports to record his sayings, was only written centuries after his death. And later texts, of greater philosophical sophistication, cannot pretend to register the Buddha's actual words. The authors of these texts employed the rather elastic principle that whatever did not actually contradict his known utterances could be taken as his view.

A more interesting problem with identifying the Buddha's own philosophical stance is that he was sometimes impatient with, sometimes benignly critical of, the more speculative reaches of philosophy. For one thing, obsession with speculative questions interfered with the more important and urgent task of achieving emancipation. The sensible man will take a well-tried cure without bothering first to work out the underlying medical principle. But more than that, there is an empiricist streak in the Buddha's sermons, leading him to regard various speculative questions as at best unanswerable, at worst nonsensical. On the so-called Ten Open Questions, such as 'Is the world finite?' or 'Does a *buddha* live again after death?', Gautama refuses to express an opinion: they are not 'profitable . . . not concerned with the Truth' that we could conceivably hope to know (61).[29] The empiricism – and not, as some have thought,[30] the philosophical 'incompetence' – behind this refusal remains, as we will see, an important ingredient in Buddhist thinking.

Of the teachings on matters where the Buddha certainly did have an opinion, the ones which are by far the best known in the West are those of the Four Noble Truths, the Eightfold Path, and *nirvāṇa*. (Everything in Buddhism seems to come with a number – the Four Signs, the Three Marks, the Three Afflictions, etc. – doubtless as a mnemonic in what was, for many centuries, an oral tradition.) The Four Noble Truths, in one of their innumerable statements, are: 'Sorrow (*duḥkha*), the cause of sorrow, the end of sorrow, and the path of eight stages which leads to the end of sorrow'.[31] More fully: (a) life as a whole is *duḥkha*: suffering, sorrow, frustration – to cite just some of the inadequate translations (see p. 22 above); (b) *duḥkha*, and indeed the whole cycle of rebirth, is due to 'craving' – primarily for worldly life and its supposed pleasures, but also for the delights of heaven, and even for *nirvāṇa*; (c) since craving can be overcome, there can be an end to *duḥkha* and the cycle of rebirth; and (d) the strategy for overcoming craving is to follow the Eightfold Path.

The steps on this Path are roughly divisible into the pursuits of the intellectual and moral virtues and those of meditation. Names vary in translation, but here is one representative list: 'right belief [or understanding], right purpose, right speech, right action, right living, right endeavour, right mindfulness, right contemplation' (19). *Nirvāṇa* means extinction, as when a candle's flame is extinguished, and is the condition, therefore, whose possibility is promised by the Third Noble Truth and whose attainment is the goal of the Eightfold Path.

Two points need to be made about these teachings. The first is that they are not, in the bland forms just stated, at all peculiar to Buddhism. Rather they contain, and do not exceed, the six doctrines (of *karma*, *saṃsāra*, *mokṣa*, etc.) which are the common property of all the Indian systems (see sect. 1). Distinctively Buddhist themes only emerge when one probes deeper into the explanation of 'craving', 'right belief', and so on. But second, as soon as one does probe deeper, competing tendencies in Buddhism emerge. Take the concept of *nirvāṇa*. The Buddha himself seems resolutely to have resisted any attempt positively to describe *nirvāṇa*, for although it 'exists', it can only be understood as the negation or cessation of any existence with which we are familiar (47). Later Buddhists veered between construing it as total annihilation, as some kind of joyous 'place' (very much a minority view), and as something which is not separate from or subsequent to everyday existence at all.

'No Self' and 'Dependent Origination'

The truly distinctive theses of Buddhism, whatever their various elaborations, are those of 'No self' (*anātman*) and its close neighbour, 'Dependent origination' (or 'Conditioned arising', *paṭicca-samuppāda* in Pali). Some Western commentators, otherwise sympathetic to Buddhism, have found it hard to take the 'No self' doctrine seriously, treating it as an exotic oriental device for warning us against selfishness.[32] Presumably they had not read David Hume (see ch. 7, sect. 2) who argued for a very similar doctrine. (One can only be amused, too, at the pretensions to revolutionary originality of 'death of the self' fashions in contemporary French intellectual circles (see ch. 10, sect. 5).)

Buddhism without 'No self' – without the claim that 'Everything is Not-self' – is a bit like Christianity without the Trinity, and certainly the Buddha himself takes the doctrine with great seriousness. This is because the 'craving' that keeps us in bondage is rooted in belief in a persisting self. Hence the attempts we have earlier encountered in Sāṃkhya and Vedānta, to distinguish the self from what might be confused with it, do not go far enough. Belief in a persisting self, of however elevated and 'pure' a kind, preserves just that 'craving' and 'attachment' we should seek to overcome. Not only that, but rejection of the reality of this self, in any shape or form, will cut through all those knotty problems faced by rival systems in explaining the connection of the self to the rest of reality. By ridding our conceptual scheme of the self, we are also rid of such mysteries as the 'co-operation' between *puruṣa* and *prakṛti* or the 'reflection' of the one Self (*ātman*) in the empirical world.

The 'No self' doctrine has two stages. First, there is the famous 'chariot' argument. As the monk Nāgasena explains to King Milinda, 'just as it is by . . . the co-existence of its various parts that the word "chariot" is used, just so is it that when the *skandhas* [constituents of a person] are there we talk of a "being"', such as Nāgasena.[33] Examining a chariot, we encounter only a number of connected parts – axle, wheels, and so on – each of which changes and may be replaced over the course of time. Likewise, examination of Nāgasena over the years reveals only a shifting set of physical features, feelings, moods, and so on. In neither case do we observe a permanent, unchanging entity 'supporting' the parts or features. If, by 'self', we simply *mean* this shifting set of connected constituents, then indeed we can speak of a person as a self, an empirical self. But since people are almost irresistibly inclined to suppose that 'self' refers to a permanent, unchanging entity 'uniting' these constituents, it is not overdramatic for Buddhists to state their conclusion by saying that there is no self at all. (Some interesting explanations of this inclination are suggested, including the one resurrected by Nietzsche and Wittgenstein, that the very occurrence of the pronoun 'I' in the language tempts us to think there must be some discrete object to which it refers.)[34]

A second stage is required, however, for the above reasoning only establishes that a persistent self cannot be identified with anything discoverable at the empirical level. That, of course, is a conclusion which would be endorsed by Sāṃkhyans and Vedāntins, who emphasize that *puruṣa* or *ātman* is not to be confused with anything physical or psychological. Their view, that the self is an eternal, unchanging being outside of the natural, empirical order, may well be, as the Buddha charmingly puts it, 'wild, wriggling, scuffling' (22) – but why? Well, Buddhists certainly raise some real difficulties with this view, mainly concerning the relation between this 'pure' self and the natural order. For example, if the self is a pure consciousness quite distinct from the bodily and psychological processes it 'witnesses', why is it that our conscious experience is constrained by our perceptual apparatus? Why, say, should the self's awareness of visual data depend on the use of the eyes, rather than of the nose or nothing at all? The main Buddhist strategy, however, is not to attempt knock-down arguments against the 'pure' self, but to show that it plays absolutely no explanatory role. In the best empiricist spirit, therefore, the idea of such a self will then 'simply wither away'.[35]

An important part of this strategy is to show that, contrary to the usual assumption, the self is not required by the doctrines of *saṃsāra*, *karma* and *mokṣa*. We can explain the notions of rebirth, moral desert, and liberation without appealing to the existence of an abiding self. Rebirth need not be interpreted as the occupation of a new body by such a self. Rather, it is the continuation, in association with a different body, of that shifting set of constituents and dispositions which 'make up' a person. Such continuation *across* lives is no more puzzling, essentially, than continuation *within* one life. We can speak of the middle-aged King Milinda as the same person as the young Prince Milinda despite all the intervening changes in body, character, feelings and thoughts. The same applies with *karma*. If the King can be responsible for, and suffer the consequences of, actions he performed as a Prince, even though he is no longer, as we might say, 'the same man', then his reborn 'continuation' can equally enjoy the 'fruits' of the King's actions. As for *mokṣa*, this is simply the cessation of craving and ignorance, an event which does not require the postulate of an eternal self. To press the question of who or what exists after this cessation is pointless: it is one of those questions which the Buddha rightly dismisses as 'not profitable'.

The next and related part of the 'withering away of the self' strategy is to offer a *complete* account of human life, from birth to death and beyond, which at no point appeals to the existence of a soul or self (except in the innocent 'collection of constituents' sense). And here we reach what I called the second distinctive thesis of Buddhism: Dependent Origination. I shall consider the radical twist given to this thesis by some later Buddhist philosophers in due course; for the moment I am concerned only with its bearing on the 'No self' doctrine.

The thesis states, in the most general terms, that everything – or nearly everything – depends for its existence on something else. 'From the arising of that, this arises . . . from the cessation of that, this ceases.'[36] By 'dependence' is intended, for the most part, not the causal dependence of one thing on another, but either the dependence of a thing on its constituents, or its logical dependence on something further. (In this latter sense, A depends on B if the existence of A cannot even be conceived in the absence of B.) In its application to the 'No self' doctrine, the thesis usually postulates a closed chain, whose twelve links are the various ingredients or stages in human life, none of which could therefore exist without the other links. So, to break into the chain at an arbitrary point, a person's 'cravings' for honour, pleasure or whatever, are a precondition of his 'grasping' after worldly things which, by the operation of *karma*, guarantees his continuing existence and rebirth, and hence a further dose of ageing, suffering and *duḥkha*. At the same time, 'craving' presupposes a capacity for feeling, itself dependent on sensory perception, and thereby on embodied agency. One could only be a genuine agent if one discriminated between different goals of action and was possessed of will and motivation, which in their turn rely on a 'spiritual ignorance' concerning the pointlessness and indifference of worldly goals. The circle is closed when we recognize that this ignorance feeds upon the suffering and confusion for which it is ultimately responsible.

Two features of this story are worth emphasizing. First, to repeat, it is a story in which no role is offered to a soul or 'pure' abiding self – or rather, it has an off-stage part, as a being which, in our ignorance and distorted need for stability and security, we imagine to be real. Second, the story implies a recipe for salvation and liberation: for if, ultimately, everything – motives, agency, craving, rebirth, and so on – presupposes 'spiritual ignorance', then by heeding and absorbing the teachings of the Buddha, the chain is broken and a person is freed from the cycle of rebirth and from 'suffering'.

'Mind Only' and 'The Middle Way'

The doctrine of 'No self', central as it is, does not amount to a total philosophical vision of how things are. As so far stated, for example, it is silent over the status of the external world. But during the millennium after the Buddha's death, Buddhist philosophers did develop such total theories and I want to consider some of these. Any account of this development must mention the gradually emerging 'schism' into the two great traditions of Buddhism, Mahāyāna ('Great Vehicle') and Hīnayāna ('Inferior Vehicle'). The latter term was pejoratively applied by devotees of Mahāyāna to the doctrines of the early Buddhist schools, among which the main survivor was the Theravāda tendency ('Ancient Way of Thought'). The origin of this schism is obscure, but it came to centre on the soteriological issue of whether the proper ambition is to become an *arhat* ('worthy one') bent on his own enlightenment or, as Mahāyāna holds, a *bodhisattva* (one on the path to Buddhahood), whose commitment is to 'lead all beings to absolute *nirvāṇa*'.[37] This dispute, though of considerable interest for ethics, is not in itself germane to our present concerns. What does matter is a divergence between the two traditions over more speculative philosophical issues. Put crudely, most thinkers of the Theravāda persuasion adopted a realist and atomist metaphysics. The external world is real enough, and consists in an infinity of basic, simple elements (*dharmas*) out of which everything else is constructed – just as the empirical self is from its constituents. A fundamental philosophical task on this view is the analysis of grosser items of the world's furniture into their basic constituents. This is undertaken in the vast *Abhidharma* literature that grew up from the third century BCE.

Just as crudely, the Mahāyāna schools are anti-realist, anti-atomist, or both. The two most important of these are the Yogācāra (or Vijñānavāda ('consciousness doctrine')) thinkers wedded to a 'mind only' (*citta-mātra*) view, and the Madhyamaka ('middle way') school – both of which flourished during the first four centuries CE. As the epithet 'mind only' suggests, the Vijñānavādins were idealists. Happy enough with the atomist urge of earlier Buddhism, they deny there is anything – anything, at least, of which we could possibly have knowledge – to be broken down into constituents other than the mind. 'The external world is merely thought seen as a multiplicity [of objects].'[38]

The prime motivation, here, is that parsimonious empiricist streak that we already noted in the Buddha's approach: don't postulate the existence of anything for which there can be no empirical evidence. The great Vijñānavādin, Vasubandhu's, basic premise – familiar to readers of Bishop Berkeley – is that we could never distinguish between the presence of an external object, if such there were, and our own perceptions: hence there can never be experiential evidence that there exists an object distinct from these perceptions. Vasubandhu's robust responses to obvious objections against idealism are often ingenious. How, to take just one of these objections, can objects exert the causal influence on us which they surely do, if they are figments of imagination? By way of reply, Vasubandhu cites the telling, if indelicate, analogy of the woman in an erotic dream who certainly manages to exert her influence on the dreamer, to the point of causing ejaculation.[39] For Vijñānavādins, the merits of the 'mind only' doctrine are not merely intellectual. It is, they argue, our inveterate tendency to suppose that there exist external objects confronting us which is responsible for the correlative sense of ourselves as very special objects – selves or subjects – so confronted. Hence, to free ourselves from the conception of external reality is also to open ourselves to acceptance of 'No self', and so to the prospect of liberation. There is some irony, therefore, in the fact that critics from the second main Mahāyāna school discern, in the 'mind only' doctrine, a danger of reinstating the notion of a substantial self. After all, they point out, Vijñānavādins themselves speak of a 'storehouse consciousness' (ālaya-vijñāna), a warehouse of images mistakenly taken as external objects, which suggests that the mind is a kind of immaterial 'place' in which 'the external world' is somehow contained.

Whatever the justice of that charge, it is to this second school, the Madhyamaka, that I finally turn – with a brevity partly excused by my returning to their views in the section on Zen in chapter 6. The most eminent champions of Madhyamaka are the second-century south Indian monk Nāgārjuna, and his later interpreter, Candrakīrti, though similar views also permeate the Prajñāpāramitā ('perfection of wisdom') sūtras which emerged during the first few centuries CE. In the opinion of many, the writings of Nāgārjuna and Candrakīrti have few rivals in terms of philosophical ingenuity and sophistication, whether in India or elsewhere. Their position is not, however, an easy one to pigeon-hole (though readers of chapter 10, section 5 might notice parallels with some of the views there described). Certainly, Madhyamaka sets itself against the realism and atomism of Theravāda Buddhism, but not for the most obvious reasons. If realism is wrong, it is not because 'external' objects are 'in the mind', like the woman in Vasubandhu's erotic dream. And if atomism is wrong, it is not because there are gross physical objects which resist analysis into ultimately simple constituents.

The place to begin, perhaps, is with those remarks of Nāgārjuna which have invited the charge of 'nihilism' – for instance, 'There absolutely are no things, nowhere and none, that arise' (78).[40] But this charge is too hasty. What Nāgārjuna is denying is the existence of 'things' in the philosophers' sense of 'substances' – things, that is, which enjoy independent 'being-in-themselves', which exist purely 'from their own side', without any necessary reliance on anything else. What we have here is a generalization and radicalization of the 'No self' view of persons. First, it is extended to apply to things as well as persons, for 'what we call "self"', explains Candrakīrti, 'refers to any nature . . . objects could have in which they relied on nothing else. The non-existence of this is what we call "no-self"'.[41] Second, it is radicalized, since *nothing* – not even 'basic atoms' – enjoy independent 'own being' (*svabhāva*).

The point is not that everything is causally connected with something else – for causal connections between things or processes would imply just that degree of distinctness among them which is being denied. The idea, rather – this time, through a radicalization of the 'Dependent Origination' doctrine – is that everything in the phenomenal world is logically, or conceptually, interdependent, so that it does not even make sense to imagine any particular thing existing in isolation. Just as the relatives in a family require one another in order to be the cousins, brothers or whatever which they are, so things or processes in general require one another in order to be what they are. Nāgārjuna offers various arguments for this conclusion, but here is the best known one. Substances or 'things-in-themselves' would have either to be beginningless, which they are obviously not, or to originate. But they cannot originate, 'neither out of themselves, nor out of non-self, nor out of both, nor at random' – which exhausts the possibilities (78). A substance cannot be self-causing, while the idea that something quite distinct is its cause is also wrong, for if A is utterly distinct from B there is no reason why it should have produced B rather than C or D. So, causal connections between substances must be rejected: on the other hand, their behaviour could not be random, since empirical experience is orderly. It follows that there are no such substances.

On reflection, then, the phenomenal world turns out to be an 'emptiness' (*śūnyatā*), containing no things in the heavyweight philosophical sense of independent substances. But it is not therefore a 'nothing'. (Madhyamaka is 'the middle way' between asserting the existence of substances or 'selves' and total nihilism.) The phenomenal items we pick out in ordinary experience – tables, trees, persons – are, so to speak, carved out of a seamless, monistic network, according to our practical interests and the conventions of our linguistic and conceptual schemes. Such items are, then, doubly 'relative'. Any given item depends for its identity upon its place within the total network, its contrasts with other items – rather as, some would argue, a word depends for its identity and meaning on its position within a whole language. In addition, the phenomenal world is relative, in its structure, to human beings, their practices and conceptual schemes.

One implication drawn by Madhyamaka from this account is of special interest. The conventional, phenomenal world is not, properly regarded, a different world from the one of 'emptiness'. The latter, rather, is what we discern when we properly appreciate that the former does *not* consist of independent 'things-in-themselves'. But it was precisely in terms of 'thinglessness' and 'selflessness' that the Buddha defined '*nirvāṇa*'. Hence we reach the conclusion that 'We call this world phenomenal, but *just the same* is called *nirvāṇa*' when viewed, *sub specie aeternitatis*, without the categories of ordinary, conventional experience.[42] So we have the triple equation: *saṃsāra* = *śūnyatā* = *nirvāṇa*. There is just one world or reality, viewed from the increasingly adequate perspectives of ordinary experience, philosophical relativity, and 'selflessness'. In the now familiar spirit of empiricism, Nāgārjuna and Candrakīrti dismiss as senseless any speculations about the nature of *nirvāṇa* as a special 'place' or 'plane' separate from the familiar world as understood by true philosophy.

It is hard to exaggerate the importance of this triple equation for the understanding of liberation and enlightenment. Although I postpone further discussion of this until the section on Zen Buddhism in chapter 6, the general thought should be clear enough. It is aptly put by Nāgārjuna when he writes that, for the person who recognizes the identity of *saṃsāra*, *śūnyatā* and *nirvāṇa*, 'everything stands in its proper place within the harmonious whole'; while, for the person who does not, 'everything is out of joint' (43). Enlightenment, an end to *duḥkha* ('out-of-jointedness' would not be a bad translation), and *nirvāṇa* are not to be attained by distinguishing our selves (or our Self) from an alien or illusory natural order, as Sāṃkhya or Vedānta proposed. For there are no selves or Self in their sense, and no order, real or illusory, which is alien to us. There is but the one world in which, like everything else, we are inextricably interwoven. Liberation is no longer a matter of escaping from that world to another, purer one, but of obtaining a right philosophical perspective upon it – a perspective which will carry in its train, for the person who can truly *live* it, a sense of the insubstantiality of things and selves. And when that sense goes deep with us, 'grasping' after the things of the world, for the supposed sake of our selves, comes to look pathetic and futile.

• 5 Ethics and Indian Philosophy •

I have so far said little about Indian moral philosophy. It was not, after all, in terms of their distinctive ethical doctrines that the schools under discussion in previous sections were distinguished from one another. More important, there was, for reasons we shall come to, a relative dearth of moral theory, in comparison at least with the voluminous debates about reality and knowledge. Indeed, in turning to Indian moral philosophy, we do best to consider initially, not any works of technical philosophy, but two more popular ones. These are in fact the most widely read works of Indian literature, in the West at least: the first (by several lengths) is the *Kāma-Sūtra* ('Pleasure Sutra'), and the second is the *Bhagavad-Gītā* ('Song of the Lord'). The contrast seems vivid: the one a manual on the erotic arts, bedside companion of generations of lovers; the other an elevating discourse on duty and devotion, a constant inspiration for figures, like Gandhi and Albert Schweitzer, not noted for their hedonistic approach to life. Here, perhaps, in microcosm is that 'baffling paradox of a country . . . felt by almost every foreigner to be, at one and the same time, the most spiritual and the most immoral'.[43] One such foreigner was Hegel, who observed that, in India, 'the other side of worship consists in a wild tumult of excess'.[44] Our concern is not with the sociological accuracy of these verdicts, but with whether the seemingly incongruous pursuits of spirituality and 'immoral excess' both get their warrant – as Hegel believed – from mainstream Indian philosophy.

Dharma and *Mokṣa*

The discussion might begin by noting that, on closer inspection, the contrast between the goals of the *Kāma-Sūtra* and the *Bhagavad-Gītā* is not as clear as at first appeared. Although '*Gīta*-freaks', as they were sometimes known during the Indophilia of 1960s America, often like to play it down, the immediate purpose of the Lord Krishna's words is to persuade the reluctant archer, Arjuna, to do his duty as a member of the warrior–noble caste and go into battle, even if this means killing relatives and erstwhile friends. According to the author of the *Kāma-Sūtra*, Vātsyāyana, meanwhile, 'this work is not intended . . . merely as an instrument for satisfying our desires', but to enable men and women properly to perform the marital duties attached to the 'householder' stage of their lives.[45] Both works, then, exhort to the carrying out of the duties conventionally and traditionally belonging to the complex of *āśrama-varṇa-dharma* – the moral law governing people's behaviour according to their 'stage of life' and their caste affiliation. (Were Arjuna a *brahmin* and not a *kṣatriya*, he would have no duty to fight; and were someone a young student or aged 'forest-dweller', not a married 'householder', he would be obliged not to practice the precepts of the *Kāma-Sūtra*, but to be celibate.)

There is a further similarity between the two works. Vātsyāyana says that the person 'acquainted with the true principles of [erotic] science . . . is sure to obtain mastery over his senses'.[46] And these 'principles' indeed encourage a certain cool control, detachment even, on the lover's part, and certainly not any kind of bacchanalian abandon or frenzy. A central message of the *Gītā* likewise is, as we will see, that one's actions should be performed in an 'unattached' style, to such a degree, indeed, that they are hardly one's *own* actions at all. In both books, then, we are not only enjoined to perform our duties of caste or stage of life, but to do whatever we do in a particular, detached manner. Softening the contrast between the 'spirituality' of the one and the 'immorality' of the other serves, of course, to blur the Hegelian vision of an Indian culture in which serious moral reflection can find no space between the excesses of contemplative withdrawal and sensual gratification.

But a related and problematic contrast or tension nevertheless remains. A clue to this is the relative paucity of ethical discussion by the Indian schools. This seems due, in part, to a general agreement over the rules of right or virtuous behaviour. (An exception, of course, was the Materialist school (see p. 17 above) with its ideals of 'eating delicious food, keeping company of young women, using fine clothes, perfumes, etc.'[47]) Even Buddhists, despite their criticisms of various brahminical privileges and practices, broadly endorse the duties attaching to caste, as well as to stages of life. And the same list of more general virtues – truth-telling, compassion, non-violence, temperance, and so on – is subscribed to by writers from all the schools. Some thinkers – notably Jains, who proscribed 'violence' towards insects and microbes – may have pressed these virtues to lengths which others found excessive, but there seem to have been few real moral 'rebels'.

A more interesting reason, however, for the relative dearth of moral philosophizing is the subordinate place apparently assigned to moral behaviour and concerns within a person's life. The proper goal of life is liberation from life, *mokṣa*. The duties and virtues which obtain within this life can hardly be of paramount concern if the true aim is a condition outside of that life. This is especially so when we recall that, according to the doctrine of *karma*, it is good and virtuous actions as much as evil and vicious ones which 'bear fruit' and thereby ensure continued 'bondage' to the cycle of rebirth. As it is said in the *Kauṣītaki Upaniṣad*, the person who 'knows' *Brahman* is 'devoid of good deeds, devoid of evil deeds' (305).

But a real problem now emerges. If the only proper goal is *mokṣa*, why should a person be concerned *at all* with the moral dimension of life, with the performance of *dharma*? Is morality, as some cynics might suggest, simply a set of regulations which it is useful for ordinary folk to obey, thereby providing a stable social background propitious for leisured meditation by the few with a realistic chance of liberation during their present lives? This is not the usual answer given. The more common line is to argue that moral behaviour on a person's part is an important *means to* an end of that liberation. There are two aspects to this answer. First, the *karma* resulting from a virtuous life guarantees a better rebirth – one, that is, in which the person's prospects for *mokṣa* are better than in the former life. (He or she will, perhaps, be reborn as a person with access to the true sacred teachings, and not as an animal or ignorant peasant.) Second, virtuous behaviour is an excellent training for developing those physical and psychological traits – self-discipline, mastery over the senses, absence of self-centredness, and so on – which facilitate acquisition of the philosophical and contemplative understanding on which *mokṣa* depends. Lecherous drunks, for example, are unlikely to enjoy the required peace of mind. Thus Śaṅkara writes that *dharma* is a 'preliminary' or 'auxiliary to the acquisition of knowledge of the Self' (SB 107).

These answers, if well-taken, mean that the sphere of *dharma* is not purely tangential to that of *mokṣa*, for there are reasons why a person bent on the latter should concern himself with the former. Still, the relation of morality to life's true goal remains a merely instrumental and contingent one – a contingency emphasized by Śaṅkara's remark that certain special people may dispense with this instrument and achieve enlightenment despite paying 'no attention to the duties of caste and stages of life' (SB 109). (Patañjali also thinks that some *yogins* can succeed through 'faith' alone, thereby bypassing the preliminary moral discipline of *yoga*.)

This is a position with which many Western philosophers find it difficult to sympathize. Morality, they argue, can neither be merely instrumental in value, nor occupy a position subordinate to other concerns. The moral life is not a means to some further aspiration, but that in and through which a person realizes his highest aspirations as a human being. Nor can it be subordinate, since we identify a person's moral convictions precisely as those which, for him, outweigh or 'trump' all other considerations. It is because Indian philosophy, as they see it, denies the intrinsic and sovereign value of morality that commentators like the sociologist Max Weber have denied that this philosophy operates with a genuine concept of morality at all. But it is not just Western observers who have been unhappy with the status accorded to morality in the traditions of some of the Indian schools, as we shall discover in chapter 9, section 1. Indeed, in the work mentioned at the beginning of this section, the *Bhagavad-Gītā*, we already encounter an early attempt to reconcile the demands of *mokṣa* and *dharma* in a way that does full justice to both.

The Bhagavad-Gītā

This anonymous work, probably written around 200 BCE, is a short interlude in the massive epic, the *Mahābhārata* – condensed on Indian television into ninety-five episodes and by Peter Brook into a single evening's entertainment.

The epic recounts the rivalry and eventual civil war, some centuries earlier, between two branches of a royal clan. Shortly before the start of the decisive battle, the leading hero of one side, Arjuna, is riding in his chariot between the lines of troops. He is assailed with doubts. Will the issue be successful? Even if it is, will it warrant the carnage? How can he kill cousins and former friends? His charioteer, as it happens, is Krishna, incarnation of the god Vishnu, and the *Gītā* records Krishna's attempt to dispel Arjuna's doubts. 'Think . . . of thy duty and do not waver. There is no greater good for a warrior than to fight in a righteous war' (2.31).[48]

Some of Krishna's arguments need not detain us, such as the one that Arjuna will not really be killing anyone, since no one ever really dies; while those concerning the religious, 'consecrative' dimension of doing one's duty are taken up later (ch. 6, sect. 1). We focus, rather, on the central claim that there are '*two* roads of perfection' – the 'path of action' or 'works' (*karma-yoga*), and not simply, as many imagine, the 'path of wisdom' (*jñāna-yoga*) (3.3). The actions of a warrior, properly performed, can therefore lead to liberation from the cycle of rebirth as effectively as meditation can. Or better, perhaps, meditation is itself a kind of action, 'for not even for a moment can a man be without action'. So it cannot be 'by refraining from action [that] a man attain[s] freedom' (3.4–5).

But actions must be performed in a certain way in order for this freedom to be attained. As we might expect from the doctrine that it is not actions as such, but the motives behind them, which bear karmic 'fruit' (see p. 21 above), Arjuna's reasons for fighting must be 'pure, free from the bonds of desire' (3.9). He must not be motivated by a desire for glory, nor even by the more altruistic desire to see his own people prosper. Duty for duty's sake must be his sole consideration. But why doesn't *that* consideration, however elevated it may be as a motive, bear karmic 'fruit'? Krishna's response to this question takes us to the heart of his case.

An action can only 'bear fruit' for a person's future if it really is *his* action: and Krishna's point is that, by right reflection on the nature of agency and action, a person can so sever himself from his actions that they can no longer really be regarded as *his*. There are two parts to this reflection. First, 'all actions take place in time by the interweaving of the forces of Nature', though the deluded person 'thinks that he himself is the actor' (3.27). It is not Arjuna, therefore, but Nature, the beginningless process of cause and effect, which is really responsible for the events which we call 'his' actions. Second, even if at a lax, everyday level it is permissible to describe Arjuna as the responsible agent, we must be clear that this is not the 'real' Arjuna – not, that is, his true self, a *puruṣa*, which is quite distinct from the body and intelligence engaged in the action. (The influence here of Sāṃkhya and Yoga should be evident.) Arjuna – the 'real' one – should think to himself '*I* am not doing any work . . . It is the servants of my soul that are working' (5.8–9). Distinguishing himself from the agent of 'his' actions, Arjuna can no longer suffer or enjoy their 'fruits'. He is liberated.

Such is Krishna's strategy for elevating the performance of *dharma* from its role as a (dispensable) means towards the goal of *mokṣa* into a direct, self-sufficient 'path of perfection'. If it succeeds, the tension between spiritual preoccupations and the practical concerns of ethics is released. But, of course, it raises a host of critical questions. For example, if the crucial thing is *niṣkāma-karma* – total and self-conscious detachment from one's actions – can it matter what those actions are? What if Arjuna were a *mafioso* assailed by doubts as to whether he should perform his duty to 'the family' and gun down some rival drug-traffickers? Would Krishna's arguments still apply, and if not, why not? Nor is the conclusion of the *Gītā* likely to allay the worries of those, like Max Weber, who doubt that the Indian perspective allows for a genuine conception of morality. There are at least two reasons for this. To begin with, it seems essential to anything that we in the West would recognize as a 'moral point of view', not only that human beings are responsible for many of their actions, but that they should *want* to be regarded as responsible. A person's maturity and human dignity, it might be argued, reside in a willingness to assume responsibility for the consequences of his behaviour and for becoming the kind of person he makes himself. From this perspective, it is not only mistaken, but a form of bad faith, for a person to divest himself of responsibility by pretending that his actions are not really his at all. That, perhaps, is why many Western readers are chilled by those paintings, in more gaudily illustrated editions of the *Gītā*, which portray the serene and smiling Arjuna scything his way through the enemy as if through a field of corn.[49]

A second worry for many Western thinkers is that it is unclear that the *Gītā*, or any of the systems considered in this chapter, operate with anything like a Western notion of a moral self, subject, or agent. Crucial, it seems, to our moral discourse is the idea of a person who is certainly *of* this world, an embodied, motivated agent: but who is not, thereby, simply a victim or creature of fate or natural necessity. He can, within limits, transcend the physical and psychological constraints of his situation in the world – not least, through moral will and effort. But what, in Indian thinking, corresponds to a moral subject so conceived? Not, it appears, a person *qua* mind-and-body, for this, according to the *Gītā*, Sāṃkhyans and others, is but a plaything of the forces of nature. Is it, then, the 'true' self – *puruṣa*, *ātman* or whatever – which is the moral subject? But this, we are told, is not of this world at all, but a mere spectator or 'witness', to whom it makes no sense to ascribe a capacity for moral effort or will. It is hard to see where, between an embodied puppet and a dehumanized consciousness, the notion of a moral subject is to be found room. It is difficult to understand, therefore, how a person, through moral action – or indeed anything else – is supposed to realize his or her nature in some kind of harmony with the rest of reality.

At this point, one is bound to feel the attractions of the Buddhist repudiation of the kind of self to which the other schools appeal. And, to be sure, Buddhists have tried to find a place for moral behaviour on foundations very different from those provided in the *Gītā*. I shall consider that attempt in chapter 6, where I also take up the 'devotional' themes of the *Gītā* which I have so far ignored. The views of several more recent Indian thinkers, themselves unhappy with the ethical dimensions of their tradition, will be discussed in chapter 9.

• Notes •

1 B. Baba (trans.), *The Yoga-Sūtra of Patañjali*, Preface.
2 B. K. Matilal, *Logic, Language and Reality*, p. 249.
3 Daya Krishna, *Indian Philosophy*, p. 4.
4 J. N. Mohanty, *Reason and Tradition in Indian Thought*, p. 290.
5 References to the *Upaniṣads* are to page numbers of R. E. Hume (trans. and ed.), *The Thirteen Principal Upanishads*.
6 Quoted in M. Hiriyanna, *Essentials of Indian Philosophy*, p. 58.
7 Krishna, *Indian Philosophy*, p. 9.
8 Mohanty, *Reason and Tradition in Indian Thought*, p. 273.
9 Krishna, *Indian Philosophy*, pp. 12–13, 170.
10 S. Dasgupta, *A History of Indian Philosophy*, vol. I, p. 31.
11 Rabindranath Tagore, *Gitanjali*, p. 87.
12 Sarvepalli Radhakrishnan, *Eastern Religions and Western Thought*, p. 43.
13 B. K. Matilal, *Logic, Language and Reality*, p. 348.
14 See Mohanty, *Reason and Tradition in Indian Thought*, and B. K. Matilal, *Perception*.
15 References to Īśvarakṛṣṇa are to section numbers of S. S. Sastri (trans. and ed.), *The Sāṃkhya-Kārikā of Īśvarakṛṣṇa*. (I sometimes amend the translation.)
16 Baba, *The Yoga-Sūtra of Patañjali*, p. 2.
17 Mircea Eliade, *Yoga*, p. 7.
18 In G. Thibaut (trans.), *The Vedānta-Sūtras*, p. 490.
19 M. Hiriyanna, *Essentials of Indian Philosophy*, p. 151.
20 Dasgupta, for example, thinks Śaṅkara did little more than make some earlier doctrines more explicit. *A History of Indian Philosophy*, vol. I, p. 470.
21 Karl H. Potter (ed.), *Encyclopedia of Indian Philosophies*, vol. III, p. 32.
22 *Brahman* is to be distinguished from Brahmā (the Hindu God), the *Brāhmaṇas* (treatises on ritual), and the *brahman* (or brahmin) caste. Originally referring to prayers or magical verses, the word came to signify the power or force invoked by the verses. In the *Upaniṣads*, the connection with ritual is severed, and '*Brahman*' refers to the supreme principle or ground of the universe.
23 In the *Ṛg-Veda*, *ātman* is the 'vital breath' which leaves a man at death. Only later, in the *Upaniṣads*, does it become the true Self or Soul of man.
24 References to Śaṅkara are to page numbers of *The Thousand Teachings* (TT); *Brahmasūtrabhāṣya* (B), as reduced in Potter, *Encyclopedia of Indian Philosophies*; and *A Samkara Source-Book*, vol. 5 (SB), 1989 (*see under* Alston, A. J.).

25 Pratima Bowes, 'Mysticism in the *Upaniṣads* and in Śaṅkara's Vedānta', in K. Werner (ed.), *The Yogi and the Mystic*, p. 59.

26 On this argument, see B. K. Matilal, *Perception*, p. 32.

27 Not an 'obvious' kind of idealism, but Śaṅkara's position has affinities with those of Hegel and other German Absolute Idealists. See ch. 8, sect. 2.

28 Steven Collins, *Selfless Persons*, p. 6.

29 References to the Buddha are to page numbers of G. Parrinder (ed.), *The Sayings of the Buddha*.

30 Notably De la Vallée Poussin and A. B. Keith. See Theodore Stcherbatsky, *The Conception of Buddhist Nirvana*, pp. 25ff.

31 J. Mascaro (trans.), *The Dhammapada*, p. 63.

32 See Collins, *Selfless Persons*, pp. 7ff.

33 *The Questions of King Milinda*, p. 45. This is one of the clearest authoritative presentations of the Buddha's thought: due largely to King Milinda's (2nd century BCE) constant refrain of 'Give me an illustration!', to which his instructor, the monk Nāgasena, patiently responds. If Milinda, the great Buddhist Emperor Asoka, and the Buddha's own royal protectors are anything to go by, the monarchs of that time in India belonged to a rather different breed from the hunting and horse-racing rulers of recent European experience.

34 See Collins, *Selfless Persons*, pp. 100ff.

35 Peter Harvey, *An Introduction to Buddhism*, p. 52.

36 *Saṃyutta Nikāya*, II, 28. Quoted in Harvey, *An Introduction to Buddhism*, p. 54.

37 *The Diamond Sūtra*, p. 23.

38 *Laṅkāvatāra Sūtra*, 154. Quoted in Harvey, *An Introduction to Buddhism*, p. 109.

39 *Viṃśatikā-Kārikā*, in S. Anacker (trans.), *Seven Works of Vasubandhu*, p. 162. For a detailed discussion of Vasubandhu, see B. K. Matilal, *Perception*, Part III.

40 References to Nāgārjuna are to page numbers of *Madhyamaka-Kārikā*, I, 1, as reprinted in T. Stcherbatsky, *The Conception of Buddhist Nirvana*, p. 78.

41 Quoted in Tsongkapa, *The Principal Teachings of Buddhism*, p. 123.

42 Candrakīrti, *Prasannapadā* (Commentary on Nāgārjuna's *Madhyamaka-Kārikā*), as reprinted in T. Stcherbatsky, *The Conception of Buddhist Nirvana*, p. 206.

43 Daya Krishna, *Indian Philosophy*, p. 7.

44 G. W. F. Hegel, *The Philosophy of History*, p. 157.

45 In R. Burton (trans.), *The Illustrated Kāma-Sūtra, Ananga-Ranga, and Perfumed Garden*, p. 18.

46 Ibid.

47 Quoted in Arthur C. Danto, *Mysticism and Morality*, p. 52.

48 References are to chapter and verse of *The Bhagavad-Gītā*, 1976.

49 The simile is Danto's, *Mysticism and Morality*, p. 99.

3

· CHINA ·

· 1 The Character of Chinese Philosophy ·

This chapter covers the development of the most important schools of Chinese philosophy during its early and most flourishing period from Confucius (*c.*551–479 BCE) to the establishment of Confucianism around 100 BCE, during the Han dynasty, as what we might now call 'an official ideology'. Like most commentators, I speak of 'schools', but the term can be misleading. Among Chinese thinkers, there was neither the institutional grouping, nor the self-consciousness of belonging to a particular tendency of thought, to be found among Indians. Indeed, it was only during Han times that thinkers from earlier centuries were squeezed, sometimes uncomfortably, into such familiar categories as Confucian and Taoist.

In the standard work on Chinese philosophy, these centuries are referred to as 'The Period of the Philosophers', with everything that came later labelled 'The Period of Classical Learning'.[1] This can, unfortunately, suggest that after the early period (until the twentieth century, at least) little happened beyond commentary on the classic texts. Not only, however, were there distinctive Chinese contributions to Buddhist thought, but the Neo-Confucianist philosophies of the Sung and Ming dynasties are of considerable interest in their own right. These developments are discussed in sections 2–3 of chapter 6. The main trends in nineteenth- and twentieth-century Chinese (and Japanese) philosophy are considered in section 2 of chapter 9.

The Chinese tradition, like the Indian, has enjoyed remarkable continuity. Confucius' views recall the speeches of his hero, the twelfth-century BCE Duke of Chou, an early and enlightened proponent of 'the divine right of kings'. (The sovereign has 'a mandate of Heaven', but only so long as he exercises 'virtue' by caring for the people.[2]) With Confucius' disciples there begins the practice of taking certain texts as authoritative and, later, the growth of 'schools' dedicated to preserving and spreading a master's message. In the case of Confucianism, a further factor guaranteed continuity: for after being brutally

suppressed during the Ch'in dynasty (221–207 BCE), Confucian teachings were adopted for the training of the imperial civil service. With various hiccups, Confucianism enjoyed this privileged status until the overthrow of the final, Manchu dynasty in 1911. If there is any truth in the familiar idea that the Chinese mind needs to balance the sobriety of Confucianism with the romanticism of Taoism, then the longevity of the former helped to secure the (admittedly shaky) survival of the latter.

The Chinese and Indian traditions may both have enjoyed great continuity, but there are marked differences in their character. The story is told of Bertrand Russell, on a visit to China, asking a Chinese colleague for his opinion of Western philosophy. The reply came that so much 'brain-bashing' was bad for the liver, and that a sensible man would prefer to sit by a river, listening to birdsongs. Such anecdotes fuel the popular notion that the Chinese mind has no real affinity with philosophy. As evidence for this, some like to cite the fact that, until a nineteenth-century coining, the Chinese language had no equivalent, etymologically speaking, to our word 'philosophy' ('love of wisdom'). This is like arguing that the Germans don't go in for breakfast since their word for that meal is not structured into 'break' and 'fast'. The popular notion goes back at least to Hegel, who thought that, whereas for the Indians everything was 'dreamlike' spirituality, to the Chinese 'everything which belongs to Spirit – morality, . . . inward religion, science and art – is alien'.[3] Certainly, the reader who opens a work attributed to Confucius, Mencius or Lao Tzu at random is less likely to find a metaphysical discourse on reality or the self than an instructive tale about a farmer ruining his crops or some prudent advice to a ruler on the appointment of officials. Certainly, too, there have been recurrent outbreaks of hostility towards philosophy, from the book-burnings of the Ch'in Emperor to the persecutions during Mao's 'cultural revolution'.

But verdicts like Hegel's are exaggerated. The classic texts are not all instructive tales and down-to-earth advice, and for the Emperor or Mao to conduct their persecutions, there had to be some philosophers to persecute. A more temperate verdict than Hegel's is A. C. Graham's. In Chinese philosophy

> . . . interest has always centred in human needs, in the improvement of government, in morals, and in the values of private life. Philosophers have seldom shown much concern for truths which serve no obviously useful purpose.[4]

It is judgements like this which prompt the two epithets most commonly applied to Chinese philosophy, 'humanistic' and 'practical'.

Humanism and Practice

' "Humanism" is the one word that characterizes Chinese philosophy', writes one commentator.[5] But care must be taken with this versatile word. Obviously the classical Chinese philosophers were not humanists in the European Renaissance sense of scholars who were rediscovering and disseminating classical literature. Nor were all of them humanists in the sense of admirers or glorifiers of human nature. The Confucian Hsun Tzu, for example, bluntly declared that 'man's nature is evil'. It is misleading, as well, to state that Chinese humanism resides in its 'frankly proclaim[ing] a man-centred universe'.[6] For it was certainly not the general belief either that the universe exists 'for the sake of' man, or that it is some kind of human conceptual construct.

In a more relaxed sense of the term, however, 'humanism' is not a bad label for the main thrust of Chinese philosophy. To begin with, hardly any major figure believed that there existed a God who created the universe and served as the source of value and purpose in life. (In later, degenerate forms of Confucianism and Taoism, there appeared – alongside other accretions, like alchemy – a host of spirits, demons, and gods, but these were not creators or moral legislators.) Second, it was generally accepted that the goals at which men and women should aim were in and of this, their familiar worldly life. This meant, in part, that such goals were to be achieved during that life and could not, therefore, be the rewards awaiting us in an afterlife, if such there be. More importantly, it meant that people were to realize their proper goals without abdicating from or transcending their natural, empirical existence. Even with Hsun Tzu, there is no hint of the idea, so prominent among many Indian thinkers, that people's true aim must be 'liberation' from the ordinary world and their material selves. Finally, it was the prevalent view that the proper brief of the philosopher was to reflect upon these human goals and establish the right means for their attainment.

This takes us on to the second epithet, the 'practical' character of Chinese philosophy. Once again, some care is needed. 'Practical philosophy' is often used as a semi-technical term for ethics and other areas of philosophy which examine how people ought to act, think or feel. As we have just seen, practical philosophy, in this sense, is indeed the main business in the Chinese tradition. But this hardly serves to distinguish that tradition from the Indian or Greek ones. Śaṅkara and Plato, too, insisted that their real concern was a practical one, to teach men how they ought to be. The difference – both interesting and difficult to explain – is that, for the Chinese, it was much less apparent that the more speculative and metaphysical reaches of thought could have the bearing on human affairs and behaviour which their counterparts in India or Greece supposed. One finds relatively little discussion in the Chinese classics of the reality of the external world, the relation between mind and body, or the identity of the self – all issues which, for Śaṅkara and Plato, must be resolved before a true appreciation of man's proper ambitions is possible.

It would be wrong, though, to exaggerate the practical, anti-speculative predilections of Chinese thought. Such exaggeration is, perhaps, encouraged by an excessive focus on the two best known classics, *The Analects* of Confucius and the *Tao Te Ching* ('The Way and its Power (or Virtue)'). In these two works, especially the first, speculation as to the ultimate nature of reality and man's place within it occupies, admittedly, only a modest space. But even here we should recall, for instance, the resounding opening of the *Tao Te Ching*, with its appeal to an ineffable source of both Heaven and Earth (see sect. 4). In the more expansive writings of Mencius, and above all Chuang Tzu, we encounter considerable speculation over matters whose bearing on questions of moral behaviour is less immediate – innate knowledge, for example, or the relativity of truth. Nor should one ignore a hoary tradition of cosmological speculation, of the kind which informs the famous book on divination, the *I Ching* ('Book of Changes'), and which was to become incorporated in the systems of later Confucian and Taoist authors.

Explaining 'The Chinese Mind'

Let us agree, however, that 'we could demarcate the Chinese mind in terms of its greater *emphasis* upon, and consequent *development* of, the practical as against the theoretical mind'.[7] Why should there be this difference, albeit one of degree, from other great traditions? Appealing to something called 'the Chinese character' is unhelpful: at the very least, we should look for an illuminating diagnosis of that 'character'. Nor does consideration of the historical climate in which the classic texts emerged take us very far. This was during 'The Period of the Warring States', one whose name might indicate a premium on practical deliberation and little enough leisure for detached abstract speculation. But then Europe during the Thirty Years War or the quarter century after the French Revolution was not a haven of peace and stability – yet these were periods during which philosophies on the grandest speculative scale were composed.

Some more interesting suggestions look to the nature of the Chinese language. It has been proposed that the ideographic, pictorial quality of that language's written characters militates against a 'separation of the sensible from the non-sensible' and thereby against the development of 'conceptual abstractions'.[8] The idea seems to be that, as he or she reads, the Chinese necessarily remains in symbolic contact with the visible empirical world that the characters cannot fail but evoke. Alternatively, it has been argued that the language's lack of inflection has saved the Chinese from having to reflect on the abstract categories – thing, quality, the past, and so on – which pair off, to some degree, with the syntactic categories of a language like English (nouns, verbs, tenses, and the like). Because of this, traditional philosophical problems concerning the relationship between linguistic or conceptual structure and the structure of reality have assumed no salience for the Chinese mind: instead, it is able to enjoy the 'illusion of looking through language at reality as though through a perfectly transparent medium'.[9]

It is not easy to assess such proposals, as we know from the continuing debate over the 'Sapir–Whorf hypothesis' of the 'determination' by its grammar of a linguistic community's conceptual capacities. For one thing, there is a chicken-and-egg problem. Maybe the Chinese were disposed to develop and retain pictorial languages because of an antecedent antipathy to abstraction. For another, it is hard to pitch the proposals at the right level. Taken to mean that the Chinese are *debarred* by their language from abstract speculation, they are clearly too strong. Taken to mean that the language exerts *some* pressure against such speculative indulgence, the proposals do not go deep enough to be illuminating.

Suppose we grant, though, that the language plays its role in restricting the opportunity or appetite for the more metaphysical flights of philosophy. This would not be incompatible with searching elsewhere for a key to the practical orientation of Chinese philosophy. This key, I suggest, is that of the theme or *Leitmotiv* sounded in chapter 1, which often recurs in this book. Philosophy, I urged, is predominantly inspired by the sense, among reflective people, of being 'alienated' or 'separated' from the rest of the order of things. Philosophical systems can typically be viewed as attempts to dispel that sense, and I have already charted some of the attempts made in that direction by the philosophers of India.

An implication of this suggestion is that in a culture whose reflective spirits are relatively free from this sense of 'separation', we should not expect the same enthusiasm as elsewhere for the construction of metaphysical systems. The Chinese, perhaps, is just such a culture. It has been persuasively argued, at any rate, that a Chinese sense of human 'harmony with the cosmos' has precluded one important '*motive* for developing theoretical thinking'. More fully:

> [T]he reason why the Chinese mind has not developed strongly in the direction
> of the construction of theoretical . . . structures is that Chinese philosophy has,
> from the beginning, seen man as being at home in nature.[10]

If, as for Mencius, people both are and understand themselves to be 'in the same stream as Heaven above and Earth below' (7(A), 13),[11] the impetus to construct metaphysical structures which establish that this is how matters indeed stand is lacking. In particular, it seems that few Chinese thinkers experienced the pull of the thought that the natural world is a 'foreign "other"' to the self or ego. Hence there were few, if any, analogues in the Chinese tradition to the efforts, in India and Greece, either to provide that thought with a rational foundation or to unmask it as an illusion.

A sense of 'harmony with the cosmos' does not, of course, leave philosophy with nothing to do. For one thing, that sense is a vague and amorphous one, inviting elaboration in various and conflicting ways. For another, there remains the question of how such a sense is to be properly translated into a style of living, so that different 'philosophies . . . evolve which point the way to maintaining, enhancing or, if it is lost, recovering that initial harmony with the world'.[12] Plenty of such philosophies, as we will see, did evolve during the classical era of Chinese thought. Naturally, locating the relative antipathy of Chinese philosophy towards speculation in a settled and comfortable vision of man's place in the order of things only pushes the question of explanation back one step. Why – in contrast, say, with India – should that vision have prevailed? Whether by way of explaining that vision, or simply enriching our depiction of it, we need to relate it to a further striking tendency of Chinese thinking, this time concerning the nature of knowledge.

Knowledge and Harmony

It would be wrong to suppose that the relative dearth of Chinese attempts to articulate systems of theoretical knowledge was due, simply, to lack of interest in such knowledge. For the classic texts are pervaded by a reasoned deprecation of the value of theoretical knowledge, relative to that of other modes of knowledge. At least three themes deserve to be distinguished here. The first might be dubbed that of 'affective knowledge'. The Chinese word usually translated as 'mind' – *hsin* – can also mean 'heart': in fact, though, it fuses both concepts, and might be better translated as 'heart–mind' or 'the thinking heart'. What this indicates is the absence of the dichotomy, familiar in the Western tradition, between the mind as the 'organ' of knowledge and the 'heart' as the centre of mere passion and subjective feeling, between the 'cognitive' and the 'affective'. For Mencius, especially, it is through the 'germs' of feeling and sentiment that we come to know and understand, especially in the moral arena. For example, we come to know our duties through the sense of shame that certain actions inspire. It cannot be through the construction and testing of theories that wisdom is achieved, since 'what [a person] knows without having to reflect on it is what he truly knows' (7, 15).

The second theme is that of the primacy of 'know-how'. It is not especially controversial that knowing how to do something is irreducible to knowing *that* such-and-such is the case – to so-called 'propositional knowledge'. If knowing how to cook a perfect cake were a matter, simply, of knowing that one should do X, Y and Z, we could all become supreme chefs by reading recipe books. What is characteristic of the Chinese sages is not simply a tendency to admire practical know-how over propositional knowledge, but the insistence that knowledge of the most important matters is, properly analysed, of the former, not the latter, kind. For Confucius, for example, moral knowledge is knowledge of 'the Mean', of acting in a way that is neither excessive nor deficient. Now this knowledge is manifested not in the 'inflexible' citation of principles, but in 'flexible' and intuitive responses to situations, of a kind which cannot be captured in formulas. And for Chuang Tzu, the most important knowledge of all – that of 'the Way' – resides, not in an acknowledgement of a set of true propositions but, primarily, in an easy, unforced behaviour that 'goes with the grain' of the Way.

A third theme, that of the ineffability of knowledge, is seen as a corollary of the second. Whether or not Shaw was right to hold that it is those who can't do something who teach it, it is certainly true that many people who can do it can't teach or explain it. Many a great chef or batsman would agree with Chuang Tzu's wheelwright that theirs is 'a knack which cannot be explained'. Combined with the claim that the most important knowledge we seek is a kind of practical know-how, it follows that such knowledge may not, even in principle, be articulatable in words. 'Those who know the nature of things do not try to explain it in words; and those who try, show thereby, that they do not know.'[13] So another reason for deprecating the value of theory construction – or simply never making a place for it – is that, where knowledge matters most, it is an illusion, a hubristic intellectualism, to suppose that any adequate theories could be constructed at all. This is not, incidentally, the ineffabilism with which we became familiar from our discussion of the Indian schools. What is indescribable is not the knowledge furnished by a vision too profound and too remote from ordinary experience for language to reach down to it. It is, rather, the kind of knowledge implicit in an effortless practical mastery that would only be obstructed, or even lost, by the adept's fruitless attempt to regiment it into a systematic theory.

Here we discern a connection with that sense of harmony with the world which in itself, as we saw, renders one motive for theoretical speculation inoperative. None the worse for being a cliché of romanticism, it has often been observed that to take the theoretical stance is already to put oneself at a distance from the world of one's enquiries. Physicist or metaphysician, the theorist must disengage from everyday involvement, take stock, analyse, regiment, and impose coherent structure. The ideal perspective of the scientist or philosopher, it sometimes sounds, is 'a view from nowhere', pared of all the 'prejudices' which suffuse our natural engagement with the world and one another. Conversely, knowledge in the mode of practical know-how is necessarily engaged. The best chef is the one immersed in his cooking, not the one who continually takes stock and consults Elizabeth David. If the Chinese philosophers are right and the knowledge which really counts is in just this mode, then such knowledge belongs only to the person who is integrated with the world which is his theatre of action. The sense of 'harmony with the cosmos' and the deprecation of theoretical knowledge, then, are not two distinct ingredients of the Chinese attitude. For the reverse side of that deprecation is the elevation of another mode of knowledge which *is* a style of harmonious engagement with the world.[14]

It is, then, the concept of harmony which sets the parameters for Chinese philosophy – and not only for philosophy. Here, for example, is an eloquent summary of the Chinese endeavour in the arts:

> [A]esthetic undertaking . . . is a natural and organic activity for humankind, a part of self-realization and self-refinement, practices that resonate with things in nature, proper adaptations to the physical and social landscape; in short, an orientation . . . that brings both the creator and audience close to the Way.[15]

Harmony, of course, is a highly ramified concept, and Chinese philosophers duly examine it in its many ramifications: harmony within, and between, the self, the family, and 'the Great Society'; harmony between heaven, earth, and man; harmony as a cosmological principle, a balance between the 'negative' and 'positive' forces of *yin* and *yang*; harmony as a set of 'correspondences' between the 'five elements' of nature and their human analogues; harmony as adaptation to the direction of the Way.

The various loosely-knit Chinese schools may be approached as competing, sometimes overlapping attempts to elucidate the idea of harmony and to instruct human beings on the proper path towards the attainment of harmony. Fortunately for the reader keen to survey these schools, the traditional count of 'the hundred schools' of the classical era had been reduced, by the Han period, to some half dozen – the result, in some cases, of the disappearance of these text-based communities of scholars, and in others, of the imposition of broader categories of classification. Of these broader groupings, it is upon Confucianism and Taoism that I focus, pausing by way of an important *entr'acte* to consider a school – that of Mohism – which, though short-lived, appeared to formulate a moral philosophy which has turned out to be a hardy perennial in Western soil.

• 2 Confucianism •

If the criterion is a headcount over the centuries, the influence of Confucius' teachings may have been greater than those of any other individual – of any, at least, whose message was not a religious one of salvation and immortality. For two millennia, the education and administration of the world's most populous country was shaped by these teachings, distorted though they may often have been. The course of Confucianism has some parallels with that of Buddhism. In both cases, a relatively simple and popular message is proclaimed by a founding figure and disseminated by devoted disciples. Within two hundred years, that message is elaborated and set against a more theoretical background. Later, the message goes through more baroque variations in the hands of writers keen to integrate it with other influential intellectual currents. So, in this discussion, we need to separate Confucius' own teachings from their interpretation and elaboration by Mencius and Hsun Tzu, and from the later efforts at synthesis by Confucians of the Han dynasty.

The Teachings of Confucius

Confucius – the name is a latinization of 'K'ung Fu Tzu' ('Master K'ung') – was born around 551 BCE, in the state of Lu, the son of an impoverished, but aristocratic family. Largely self-taught, he went on to occupy various administrative positions in his native state, though almost certainly not the elevated ones formerly imagined. According to one story, he finally resigned from public office when the ruler, who had taken to dancing girls, proved unworthy to follow the precepts which Confucius had tried to instil in him. For many years, he wandered from state to state, unsuccessfully offering his advice and services to their rulers. Such rejections, sometimes violent, cut deep with Confucius who had a high estimation of his political prowess. 'If anyone were to employ me, in a year's time I would have brought things to a satisfactory state' (XIII, 10).[16] During the last few years of his life, he lived in relative seclusion with the students and disciples he had accumulated, dying around 479 BCE.

Like Socrates, Confucius never wrote any work, *The Analects* being put together from his sayings by students. Contrary to earlier legend, it is now clear that he did not write substantial sections of such famous works as the *I Ching*. *The Analects* is a short book, consisting of advice to rulers, moral tales, rather dull observations on Confucius' person (he did not talk while eating, liked his drink, but could hold it, and so on), and shining through all this, some nuggets of moral philosophy. On other issues of philosophical interest, such as the afterlife, he maintained a sceptical silence.

Unlike Socrates – or Jesus and the Buddha – Confucius has not retained his awesome reputation. Once proclaimed by European enthusiasts as 'the patron saint of the Enlightenment', his star was soon to fade, with Hegel, for one, judging that he never rose above mediocrity. More recent judges sometimes sympathize with readers who find his teachings 'commonplace and unexciting'.[17] Why this fall from favour? Doubtless, generations of 'Confucius, he say . . .' jokes, and the popping out of his more banal proverbs from the inside of Chinese crackers, have not contributed to an august image. And people of leftist inclinations have presumably been swayed by the mangling he received at the hands of Mao Tse-Tung and his ideological henchmen. More serious, however, are the several elements in the currently received, popular impression of Confucius which are unappealing to contemporary taste.

First, there is the impression of Confucius as a diehard conservative, with a nostalgia for the twelfth-century BCE Chou rulers that rivals, in eccentricity, Evelyn Waugh's yearnings for thirteenth-century Christendom. Related to this is Confucius' alleged insistence on the rigid performance of age-old rites and customs: in particular, those associated with 'filial piety', thereby betraying a bizarre predilection for a 'virtue' which inspired later Confucians to cut lumps off their arms, cook them, and feed them to ailing parents. Finally, his supposed ideal of devotion to public service is not just dull and uninspiring but to the modern mind – with its jaundiced perception of politicians and civil servants – not even a worthy one. How much more appealing the romantic individualism which the Taoist masters are thought to have preached!

It will help us appreciate Confucius' real position to correct these misconceptions (though one should add that there are respectable commentators who would deny that they are misconceptions). He was, of course, a conservative. 'I am for the Chou' (III, 14), he proclaimed, meaning the glory days of that dynasty many centuries earlier: and he could get splenetic about the corruption of some ancient dance-form. It was not, however, nostalgia alone which explains Confucius' admiration for an earlier order. He believed, first, that in his own day 'those in authority have lost the Way and the common people have, for long, been rootless' (XIX, 19). And he also thought that these earlier times had been propitious ones for the emergence of a certain kind of individual – the *chun tzu* – who represents humanity at its best. This word originally meant 'princeling' and is often translated as 'gentleman', which has a number of misleading connotations. Better, arguably, would be 'superior person'.

Nor does nostalgia or blind conservatism fully explain Confucius' insistence on the performance of traditional *li* (often translated as 'rites', but applying more widely to a whole body of social duties and customs). No doubt the performance of *li*, without any motive of 'profit', makes for social harmony and stability, but Confucius' main argument is rather different. 'Unless a man has the spirit of the rites . . . he will wear himself out . . . become unruly, intolerant' (VIII, 2). The *li*, that is, provide the disciplined channels through which the *chun tzu* is able to put his morality into practice (XV, 18). Without them, the best of wills can find no tried and tested outlets for behaviour. Mencius was later to compare the rites to exit gates, without which there would be no point to being 'on the Way' of righteousness. There would be nowhere to go. (5(B), 7).

Confucius' argument applies to the rites of 'filial piety' as much as to any other, but two further considerations emerge in support of this virtue. It is when 'mourning for one's parents' that 'a man realize[s] himself to the full' (XIX, 17): for here is a supreme example of behaviour from which there can accrue no personal profit. Not only that, but it *sets* an example which will inspire in others a disinterested urge to lead the moral life. A main point in the Confucian classic, *The Great Learning*, is that the moral example set within the family soon spreads throughout 'The Great Society'.[18] These considerations also apply to the duty to serve in public life. The *chun tzu* 'takes office in order to do his duty' even when he knows that no benefit may accrue (XVIII, 7), and in such disinterested action he behaves in accordance with the 'basic stuff' of his humanity. The public official, morever, is well-placed to teach by example. The 'gentleman' administrator's virtue 'is like the wind; the virtue of the small man is like grass. Let the wind blow over the grass and it is sure to bend' (XII, 19).

What these responses to the received, unflattering image of Confucius indicate is that his primary concern is less to provide a 'rationalization . . . [of] originally existing institutions',[19] than to secure the (re)emergence of a certain kind of human being – the *chun tzu*. But what, in more detail, is such a person like? We know, of course, that he is a moral being, one who guides his behaviour by Confucius' version of the 'Golden Rule': 'Do not impose on others what you yourself do not desire' (XII, 2). To obtain a fuller picture, though, we need to examine a central term in *The Analects*, '*jen*' – for it is in his pursuit or exercise of *jen* that the 'superior person' is distinguished.

Raymond Dawson lists fourteen attempted translations of this word, including such horrors as 'man-to-manness' and the neologistic 'hominity' alongside the more likely 'virtue', 'humanity', and – most popular of all – 'benevolence'.[20] But, disputed as the concept is, these translations are inadequate on one or both of two counts. Either they are too narrow or they fail to bring out what seems to me the essentially *inner* nature of *jen*. Thus, a person of *jen* will mourn his parents, but this is hardly something we would include under 'benevolence'. And Confucius makes it clear that a benevolent man who 'gave extensively . . . and brought help to the multitude' may nevertheless not have *jen*. We cannot straightforwardly read possession of *jen* off from behaviour, since it is an inner quality, only indirectly manifested in actions. It is 'found within himself' (XV, 21), a 'native substance' or 'basic stuff' (*chih*) (XV, 18). *Jen* underlies a whole range of virtues – simplicity, magnanimity, modesty, and so on – and cannot, therefore, be equated with them.

As a fifteenth attempt, I would propose 'inner moral force'. The force metaphor at any rate gels with the image of *jen* as something which, like the wind, both exerts a pressure among men and, lest it 'wear itself out' and become 'unruly', must be constrained and channelled (through the discipline of the rites). Confucius' reasons for cultivating the *chun tzu* with his 'inner moral force' mainly appeal to harmony, in several of its ramifications. At the most cosmic level, a life that manifests *jen* accords with the Way of Heaven, for 'Heaven is author of the virtue that is in me' (VII, 23). (It is unclear just how Confucius understands Heaven – whether as God or simply as an overarching principle of order and purpose.) At the social level, the *chun tzu*, provided he heeds custom and tradition, helps to promote harmony in the family, the wider community, and the State. The effective bonds keeping men and women together in peace and co-operation are those which come from 'inside' them – love, a sense of duty, piety – not simply the external sanctions of rewards and punishments.

Confucius' most interesting observations, however, concern *jen* and harmony at the level of the individual. The *chun tzu* is a balanced person, someone at one with himself, who will not be toppled from his course either by the urges of passion or by the blandishments and threats of other people. Thus he is 'easy of mind, while the small man is always full of anxiety' (VII, 37), and able to 'overcome' himself (XII, 1) – not in the almost literal sense intended by many Indian thinkers, but in that of integrating his various facets into an harmonious whole. In a nice image, Confucius speaks of *jen* as a beautiful 'neighbourhood' in which the 'superior man' 'feels at home' (IV, 1–2). To extend the metaphor in my proposed translation, it is as if *jen* were a gravitational force, giving weight and stability to a person's life. It is because the *chun tzu* is in harmony with himself, moreover, that in his behaviour and feelings he follows the Mean. He never goes 'over the top', but not because he does or feels too little. One aspect of the Mean is especially important. A life is not properly human if it is lived mechanically or solely for profit: but blind moral enthusiasm, an undirected overflow of good will and love for mankind, also have their dangers. These must be checked by and channelled through *li*, the customs and social duties that go with one's station in life. This is why only 'a well-balanced admixture' of *jen* and 'acquired refinement' produces the *chun tzu* (VI, 18).

Confucius, if my interpretation is right, is not a reactionary worshipper of tradition and customary duty for their own sake, but the preacher of a moral vision of some force and depth – a vision of the moral person whose humanity is fully realized. It is a vision, moreover, from which many of us might learn today. The insistence on a 'well-balanced admixture' of an inner moral source and a respect for the well-tried rules of right conduct might serve to correct the respective exaggerations of those who see morality merely as a device for regulating self-interested behaviour and those who locate it in the 'authenticity' of private conviction.

Human Nature

On two matters, observed a disciple, 'one cannot get to hear [Confucius'] views', human nature and the Way of Heaven (V, 13). Given that the *jen* of the 'superior person' is supposed to accord with both of these, the Master's silence here is disappointing. Let us start with human nature. There are at least three issues which the Confucian needs to address. First he must establish that human nature does not preclude the emergence of the *chun tzu*, that people *can* act out of elevated motives, and not simply enlightened self-interest. Second, if the 'superior' life is to be an ideal for all human beings – as Confucius claims – then it must be shown that the potential *chun tzu*'s 'basic stuff' is not the privileged endowment of exceptional beings, but belongs to human nature itself. Otherwise, the ordinary person has no more prospect of developing *jen* than of acquiring the physique of Hercules or Marilyn Monroe. Finally, it needs to be shown not merely that we have a capacity to lead the 'superior' life, but that we are predisposed to do so. Otherwise it will be no more reasonable to speak of that life being in accordance with human nature than a life spent in a perpetual haze of opium – for this, too, is a life we are *capable* of.

It was to precisely these issues which Confucius' most famous successor, Mencius – a latinization of 'Meng Tzu' ('Master Meng') – turned his attention, goaded by Confucius' critics. By Mencius' time (*c.*372–289 BCE) there had developed theories of human nature which, if true, rendered the Confucian ideal nugatory. To begin with, there was the idea that 'appetite for food and sex is nature' (6(A), 4), that – more generally – our 'internal' nature is primarily to pursue self-gratification. Mencius' response is to cite examples of human psychology – a person's compassionate urge to save a child from drowning, a ruler's revulsion at the sight of an animal on its way to sacrifice – which establish that even the hardened egoist is spontaneously moved, on occasions, by a moral sympathy from which there is nothing personally to profit. Such sympathy, therefore, belongs to human nature. At any rate, someone totally devoid of the 'four germs' of compassion, sense of shame, courtesy, and the ability to discriminate between right and wrong, 'is not human'. 'Man has these four germs just as he has four limbs' (2(A), 6). 'Reason and rightness', he adds, are 'common to all hearts', as is evidenced by the pleasure or delight experienced by whoever pursues them (6(A), 7).

Mencius is not denying that we are also born with tendencies to rather less savoury behaviour and feelings. The point, rather, is to insist, first, that the moral urge is also innate, and does not require explanation, therefore, in terms of enlightened self-interest or social conditioning: and second, that moral sympathy will, under 'neutral' conditions, outweigh the less savoury motives. Our limbs, by way of analogy, do not merely give us a capacity to move, but predispose us to – for something has to go wrong if we are not to walk, clutch or stretch. Likewise, for Mencius, morality is natural in that the 'four germs' predispose us to virtue. Like seeds of barley or trees, external obstruction or interference is required if they are not to grow. In yet another analogy, man's tendency to moral behaviour is compared to water's flowing downwards. 'A great man is one who retains the heart of a new-born babe' (4(B), 12): *jen* does not have to be 'welded' on to him 'from the outside', since virtue is a natural inclination of his 'original heart'. To be sure, there can be plenty of obstructions – corruption by others, bad education, struggle for scarce goods – which pervert men's behaviour: but none of these gainsay the existence of that 'original heart'.

There is something else Mencius means when he speaks of 'reason and rightness' as natural. When we ask 'What is the nature of man?', we may be asking, like Aristotle, 'What differentiates man from all other animals?' The difference, says Mencius, is 'slight' but crucial, and the 'superior person' is determined to maintain it, thereby distinguishing himself from the brutes and realizing what is proper – unique – to his nature as a human being (4(B), 19). This is, of course, his capacity for reason and morality.

This point needs bearing in mind when we assess the position of another eminent Confucian, Hsun Tzu (*c*.298–238 BCE), which at first glance looks diametrically opposed to Mencius'. According to William James, the former is as 'tough-minded' as the latter is 'tender-minded' in his estimation of human nature.[21] Certainly, Hsun Tzu roundly declares that 'man's nature is evil', with goodness being the product of artifice, education, threat of punishment, and so on.[22] In calling our nature evil he means that we are born with appetites and a 'fondness for profit' which, left unchecked, lead human beings into 'wrangling and strife . . . violence and crime'. Against Mencius, he argues that if human nature were good, various phenomena are hard to explain – the speed with which many people's behaviour becomes evil, for instance, or the patent need in society for law and moral education. Worse still, it is evident that people *learn* to act morally and need *effort* to improve themselves. This makes it quite wrong to describe goodness as natural, since 'nature' here simply *means* 'that part of man which cannot be learned or acquired by effort'. If a warped piece of wood must be straightened through force, it is absurd to describe it as straight by nature.

There is surely some shadow-boxing between the two Confucians here. Mencius is only too aware of how fragile and easily obstructed are the 'germs' of morality, so that grim descriptions of actual human behaviour, of the kind Hsun Tzu provides, come as no surprise or refutation. Nor does he deny that we are also born with less worthy predispositions. Second, the two men mean different things by 'nature'. For Mencius, goodness is natural in that, first, it distinguishes us from the brutes and, second, it is something people will exhibit in their lives provided that circumstances are not too adverse. This is perfectly compatible with holding that moral learning and effort play their role – which is what is *excluded* by Hsun Tzu's definition of 'natural'. Finally, even for Hsun Tzu, 'the essential faculties needed to understand . . . ethical principles and the potential ability to put them into practice' are part of a person's 'make-up'. Certainly his is not the view of philosophical egoism that, in a sense, people never act ethically, but always out of self-interest, however enlightened. Hsun Tzu's man is not the Hobbesian individual whose overriding consideration is always self-protection. Even if the wood starts off warped, it really does become straight. One might say that it has it in its nature to be straight.

If I am wrong here, and Hsun Tzu is as 'tough-minded' as Hobbes (see ch. 7, sect. 3) and considers morality as nothing but a necessary artifice for securing social co-operation, then he is less of a Confucian than usually imagined. At any rate, he is not faithful to the Confucian ideal as I interpreted it – for that is the ideal of a 'superior person' who does not merely accommodate himself to society's norms, but in doing so is true to his essential nature and thereby 'at one' with himself. Of Confucius' two great followers, it is therefore Mencius who has the better claim to that title.

'The Way of Heaven'

Such was the standing of Mencius and Hsun Tzu that it became important for Confucians of the following centuries to show that their positions were indeed reconcilable. For example, Tung Chung-Shu (second century BCE) – author of the wonderfully named *Luxuriant Dew from the Spring and Autumn Annals* and an adviser to the Han Emperor – argued that, while there is a Mencian 'congenital goodness', the extra goodness of the 'superior person' is entirely acquired. And while Mencius was right to regard *jen* as an ingredient in our inborn nature, his rival was correct to regard 'inordinate desire' as another. More interestingly, he holds that, with these two ingredients, 'the self works in the same way as Heaven'.[23] Man is the cosmos in miniature.

Confucius had stated that the virtuous man lives in the Way of Heaven, but as we learned from his student, one could not get to hear any further views from him on this matter. Mencius was slightly more voluble, borrowing from the favoured cosmology of his time to establish that the *chun tzu* is indeed 'in the same stream as Heaven above and Earth below' (7(A), 13). It was believed, apparently, that Heaven and Earth were composed of the same substance, *ch'i*, but in its refined and gross forms respectively. According to Mencius, the 'superior person', not leadenly rooted in the world of material desire, cultivates 'a flood-like *ch'i*' within himself, which is sufficiently refined to 'fill the space between Heaven and Earth'. In this manner, man bridges the gap between the two, making of the cosmos a balanced whole. His is a *ch'i* which 'unites rightness and the Way' (2(A), 2).

It is this brand of imaginative speculation about man's relation to the cosmos which the Han Confucians, eclectically borrowing from older traditions, made their main pursuit. A peculiar aspect of this was the use made of the doctrine of the 'Five Elements'. Heaven, it was held, employs the elements of wood, fire, soil, metal and water, among which certain relations hold: wood fuels fire, for example, while soil begets metal. Rather in the manner elaborated by mediaeval alchemists, there exist systematic 'correspondences' between these elements and human life. For instance, fathers stand to sons in the 'begetting' relation of soil to metal, so that a perverse or improper paternal relationship would be 'unnatural' in the strong sense of defying a law of nature. Tung Chung-Shu draws political wisdom from the system of 'correspondences'. Thus, since 'wood is the agent of the Minister of Agriculture' and metal that of the Minister of the Interior, then it is the duty of the latter to punish the former if he behaves corruptly, because metal is the appropriate instrument for cutting down wood.[24]

Of more abiding interest than quaint excursions into Cabinet responsibilities was the use made of that venerable pair of concepts, *yin* and *yang*. It is precisely because 'Heaven has the *yin* and the *yang*', while human nature is composed of 'congenital goodness' (a *yang* feature) and 'natural emotions' (a *yin* feature) that, for Tung Chung-Shu, 'the self works in the same way as Heaven' and the Ways of Heaven and man are 'one'.[25] Popular expositions of these terms in the West tend to stress only the opposition of *yin* (dark, feminine, soft, hidden, etc.) and *yang* (bright, masculine, firm, open, etc.). But, as the famous symbol for this pair – a circle divided by an 'S'-shaped line into a black and a white half, with each half containing a smaller circle of the opposite colour – is intended to indicate, it is the mutual dependence and penetration of the two which is crucial. Men and women have need of one another, and there cannot be shadow and brightness except in relation to each other. The imagery of *yin* and *yang*, then, evokes 'a unity of polarities engaged in creative interaction and an infinite process of transformation', one which is, moreover, 'regarded as intrinsically valuable and self-fulfilling'.[26]

There are at least three ways in which the doctrine of *yin* and *yang* is supposed to integrate human existence with reality as a whole. Since the various facets of human psychology belong to one or other of the two principles – the mind can be in motion or at rest, for example – then a person is subject to the same interplay of forces as everything else in nature. But because of this, secondly, an imbalance of the two forces within a given person will reverberate throughout the world. It was believed, for example, that the imbalanced behaviour of a ruler could produce floods and other natural disasters. Finally, and most importantly, the relation between *yin* and *yang* elements in a person can and should emulate the one deemed to obtain in Heaven. Though Heaven, like everything else, contains *yin* elements, it is essentially *yang* in nature, and must therefore act so as to block the infection of this nature by *yin* – as a mat serves to block dirt, in Tung Chung-Shu's analogy. Likewise, the 'superior person' blocks the infection of *jen* (*yang*) by 'inordinate desire' (*yin*). He is someone who knows 'how to avoid injuring desire and yet to have a rest from emotion, and thus fit in with Heaven . . . prohibiting what Heaven prohibits'.[27] Thereby is attained that Confucian harmony with the Way of Heaven at which the Master only hinted. It is a harmony, as we might expect from section 1, which is achieved, not through intellectual understanding, but through a practical mastery of one's life and emotions. And it is the kind of harmony on which later Confucians, like Chu Hsi in the twelfth century CE, continued to reflect, as we shall discover in chapter 6.

• 3 Mohism •

A main target of Confucian apologists during the two centuries before its violent eclipse under the Ch'in dynasty (221–207 BCE) was the Mohist school, named after its founder, Mo Tzu (*c*.479–438 BCE), Master Mo (latinized as Micius). The course of Mo Tzu's reputation is something of a mirror image of Confucius'. Having briefly competed with Confucius in influence, political and intellectual, his name all but disappears from Chinese scholarship for two thousand years. But as Confucius' star fell during the nineteenth and twentieth centuries, Mo Tzu's rose, to the point of being described by one influential modern figure as 'perhaps the greatest mind China has produced'.[28] In China itself, his rugged championing of the common people and his plea for austerity today for the sake of welfare tomorrow have improved his current stock – despite his religious strain and enthusiasm for population growth. And in the wider world, he might be seen as an early advocate of that uneasy combination which constitutes the modern 'liberal consensus' – egalitarianism, utilitarianism, respect for all humanity, and material progress.

Mo Tzu is one of the more intriguing personalities in the history of philosophy. Various meanings of the word '*mo*' ('black', 'branding') have encouraged speculation that he may have been an Indian or a former criminal.

Certainly he seems to have been of very humble origin and, by way of career, a military engineer and leader of a kind of private army dedicated to protecting smaller states against outside aggression. This band of 'knights-errant' – similar, one imagines, to the military-cum-religious Orders of mediaeval Europe – was one of rigid discipline, committed to 'enjoy equally and suffer equally', and owing total obedience to its leader. It is related that, facing defeat by the Ch'in army, 181 Mohists followed their then leader in committing suicide.

It is not only his veering between the lives of scholar-monk and man of action which makes Mo Tzu intriguing: there are also some unusual, perhaps paradoxical, pairings among his opinions and attitudes. A champion of the common man, he advocates complete submission to authority – 'What the superior considers right, all shall consider right' (35);[29] a military leader, he is against militarism; a preacher of 'universal love', he displays an almost obsessive hatred of Confucians – they 'stuff away food like hamsters, stare like he-goats, and walk around like castrated pigs' (127); a no-nonsense welfarist of the 'gas and water' school, he calls on the spirits and God to punish evil; a proponent of equal concern for all people, he insists on the special duties of group loyalty. Some of these paradoxes will perhaps dissolve, or at any rate become easier to understand, as we examine Mo Tzu's position.

Against Confucianism

Mo Tzu clearly regards combatting the baleful influence on his times of Confucianism as his most urgent task. Not only does its remote and elitist message offer no remedy for the ills of this, the period of the Warring States, but the effete amusements and adherence to expensive rituals condoned by Confucians exacerbate those ills. So what are Mo Tzu's objections to the tenets, real or imagined, of Confucianism? We might begin with his arguments against its alleged fatalism, the first of which is a pragmatic one. A proper test of a theory is 'whether, when [it] is put into practice . . . it brings benefit to the state and the people' (118). By this test, fatalism must be rejected, for teaching it would 'overthrow righteousness in the world' – through, for example, encouraging people to think that, with the future fixed in advance, there is no point to effort or endeavour. A second argument is that fatalism would render pointless or perverse any punishment from Heaven for our deeds – a notion which, if accepted, would further weaken our motivation to act rightly. Arguably, Mo Tzu misses his target with these arguments, for it is not clear that Confucius was a fatalist: for while we are indeed under 'the Decree of Heaven', this is something we are only too able to violate.

Mo Tzu's second objection to the Confucians is to their deprecation of the importance of Heaven and the spirits. Mohism, it has been said, is the only

Chinese philosophy that 'requires the existence of God and spirits to ensure the world's moral order'.[30] The Confucian Heaven, recall, is not akin to God: it is nothing to worship or sacrifice to, for example. And Confucius was sceptical towards the existence of spirits. The Mohist Heaven, however, does seem to be describable as God, for it has a will, it loves, it punishes (by delegation to the spirits), and it responds to sacrifice and petition. Mo Tzu's argument for such a Heaven is by what might be called 'moral induction'. Just as what is right for a subordinate to do is decided for him by a superior, all the way up to the level of the ruler, the Son of Heaven, so what is right for this Son to do must be decided for him by a yet higher authority – Heaven or God itself. Ultimately, therefore, 'I measure [benevolence and righteousness] by the clearest standard in the world (i.e. the will of Heaven)' (83). (Despite the terminology, there is no reason to think that Mo Tzu regards this divine will as something outside or transcending the natural order: it seems, rather, to be a will immanent in that order.)

Once it is recognized that there is, and must be, this 'clearest standard', if morality is to have a firm basis, then all human practices and conventions can be measured against it. It may be an ancient tradition among the inhabitants of K'ai-shu to eat the first-born child, but that cannot justify the practice. More generally, it is wrong to 'confuse . . . what is customary with what is right' (75). And here we reach a third objection for, as Mo Tzu sees it, Confucians are guilty of an unthinking respect for custom in the form of *li*, the rites. Indeed, their insistence that the 'superior person' is one who emulates ancient practices is incoherent, for someone must have initiated those practices: since, by the Confucian definition, *he* cannot have been a 'superior person', why then should his practices be emulated?

It is not clear that the careful Confucian is open to these criticisms. For Confucius himself, as for Mencius, the *chun tzu* is not defined by his adherence to custom: rather, *li* provide the disciplined channels through which people are able to direct their moral energies. The Mohist may seem to be on more secure ground when he complains of the excessive expenditure of time and resources on the rites, notably those of mourning – a lavishness, he believes, which goes against the desire of Heaven. (The wood for coffins can be really quite thin, says Mo Tzu.) But whether this expenditure really is excessive depends, in part, on whether the Confucian is right in holding that we have special obligations to certain people, notably our parents, which override a concern for the well-being of people in general.

It is at this stage that Mo Tzu's best-known and most important objection to Confucian ethics emerges. In his terminology, theirs is an ethic of 'partial love' (*pieh ai*), for it demands that compassion and other moral sentiments be particularly directed towards some people, such as one's own family, and not others. What Mo Tzu – and Heaven – demand, however, is 'universal (or undifferentiated) love' (*chien ai*). 'Universality is the source of all the great benefits in the world and partiality is the source of all the great harm . . . [Hence] partiality is wrong and universality is right' (40–1). Mo Tzu backs this up with another pragmatic argument, this time against *broadcasting* the doctrine of 'partial love'. Either your audience will accept it or they will not: if they do, they will act partially towards you, while if they don't, they will hate you for your pernicious message. Either way you lose out.[31]

For three reasons, the distance between Mohist and Confucian may be less than Mo Tzu imagines. First, Mo Tzu sometimes speaks as if the alternative to 'universal love' is total indifference, even hatred, towards most people. But the Confucian can reply that special obligations towards the objects of 'partial love' are perfectly compatible with a general respect for human beings which enjoins us, for example, not to meddle in their lives. Second, Mo Tzu fails to refute the Confucian conviction, described earlier, that 'filial piety' and other instances of 'partial love' set inspiring examples of selfless duty which will promote a more generalized moral concern in and for the wider community. Finally, his examples of 'universality' turn out not to illustrate 'impartial' duty or love at all. In one of them, he urges us to help a friend in need – clothe him and feed him in the way we would our own father. But despite the claim that these would be the 'actions of the universal-minded man' (42), it is surely essential to the force of the example that the person in need is a *friend*. It is far from obvious that I have a duty – one which it would be anyway impossible to discharge – to clothe and feed everyone who is in need. What this, and other of Mo Tzu's examples, suggest is not that we should be entirely 'impartial' in our compassion, but simply that our obligations are rather wider than some people have supposed.

So far, though, we have not uncovered the wholly alternative conception of morality which Mo Tzu seemingly develops, and on the basis of which more telling objections to Confucianism might be raised.

Utilitarianism

Any book on Chinese philosophy will tell its readers that Mo Tzu was an early, perhaps the earliest, proponent of a utilitarian moral philosophy. He indeed proclaims that the business of the moral person is 'to promote what is beneficial to the world and to eliminate what is harmful' (40). And his pragmatic refutation of fatalism, his economic objections to the rites, and his defence of 'universal love' as 'the source of all great benefits', seem to confirm the usual judgement. Still, it is possible to query the aptness of that admittedly elastic label, 'utilitarian' – though this is something I defer for the time being, as I do the question of how Mo Tzu's alleged utilitarianism sets him apart from the Confucians. The immediate task is to determine what kind of utilitarianism, if any, Mohism embraces.

In its most pristine form, utilitarianism is the doctrine that the sole criterion of the rightness of an act is its contribution to overall utility. But here agreement among its advocates ends. Jeremy Bentham defined the maximum utility at which acts should aim as 'the greatest happiness of the greatest number', with happiness understood in terms of pleasure and the absence of pain. Other utilitarians, however, diverge from this in one or both of two directions. First, they might characterize utility in a different way – arguing, perhaps, that happiness and pleasure are too 'intangible' to be measured or to serve as the concrete goals of policy. Instead, they may argue, utility should be defined in terms of certain 'goods', like material comfort, which we should aim to secure. Second, some utilitarians think it unrealistic to aim at utility for 'the greatest number'. For Bentham, taken at his word, the interests of *all* people, and indeed of all animals, present and future, are germane to determining the rightness of an action. For some of his critics, though, it can only be the interests of a limited range of people (and animals) – those of one's own nation, say, or those presently alive – which it can be realistic and relevant to consider.

Mo Tzu's position seems to diverge from Bentham's in both of these ways. He understands the benefits or utility at which policy should aim not in psychological terms, like happiness, but in economic and political ones. Population increase, wealth and order are the three great benefits. And what the ordinary person 'worries about' is not obtaining pleasure, but food, clothing and rest – which are what we should secure for him (111). Mo Tzu would surely have been impatient with Benthamite attempts to weigh all pleasures and pains against one another in a 'felicific calculus'. In his diatribe against musical entertainments, the point is less that the pleasures derived are outweighed by their cost than that such pleasures, being those of the effete and idle, are of no weight whatsoever. The benevolent man will not even 'consider' these 'delights' (110). Second, despite his rhetoric of '*universal* love', it is clear that Mo Tzu's benevolent person does not measure his actions by their effects on *everyone*. The good ruler, for example, has the interests, not of all people, but of all *his* people at heart. It is worth adding, though, that Mo Tzu insists on our obligations to future generations, including one to be fertile and increase the population. Long periods of chaste mourning are condemned on this count.

Mohist utilitarianism, if the label is appropriate, is then a welfare utilitarianism, the exercise of which, at any rate for purposes of practical policy, aims at benefitting particular communities. This is a position, it would seem, sufficient to set the Mohist at odds with the Confucian. For one thing, the insistence that we should endeavour in all our acts to produce benefits sounds incompatible with the Confucian precept of duty for its own sake. For Mo Tzu, the Confucian *chun tzu* who takes public office knowing that he will achieve nothing is not only irrational, but evil. The idea of doing things for their own sake, he suggests, is barely intelligible: what would it mean to build a house for its own sake instead of for shelter and comfort? For another thing, the Mohist seems to reverse the Confucian relation between virtue and righteousness. For Confucius and Mencius, the right actions to perform are those to which the person of virtue, of *jen*, is disposed. Mourning a parent is right because that is a natural manifestation of *jen*. For the Mohist, however, the virtuous or benevolent person is identified as such through his performance of actions which are right according to the criterion of benefit. Thus, whereas Confucians had condemned the shooting of enemy soldiers in flight as incompatible with the nature of 'the superior man', Mo Tzu defends such behaviour on the ground that 'the world will be . . . rid of harm' (129).

But the sharpness of these disagreements is blurred when we reflect on two features of Mo Tzu's position – ones which might also give pause before labelling him a utilitarian. The first belongs to his theology. There is no reason, of course, why a utilitarian cannot be a religious believer (think of all those reformist Victorian worthies). But Mo Tzu sounds to set up the authority of God, the Will of Heaven, as the very criterion of right and wrong. Recall his remark that the will of Heaven is 'the clearest standard in the world'. My action is right in the final analysis, it seems, not *because* it produces benefits to the world, but because it is demanded of me by Heaven. As it happens, 'Heaven desires life . . . wealth . . . [and] order'(79), but the possibility remains that Heaven might have desired something else, in which case my duties would not have been of a utilitarian kind. The second feature is Mo Tzu's hostility towards many of the deepest and most important human emotions. 'Joy and anger, pleasure and sorrow, love and hate, are to be got rid of',[32] and such emotions are referred to as 'depravities'. He would, no doubt, argue that these emotions are obstacles to impartial execution of practical policies for improving the general welfare. But it is hard to avoid the impression – confirmed, perhaps, by Mo Tzu's own lifestyle – that he is here presenting a vision of the ideal man, of the kind of person we should strive to become, irrespective of utilitarian considerations. The truly human being is the dispassionate, austere, self-disciplined one – the hardy peasant, or a member of Mo Tzu's own corps of 'knights-errant'.

These features do not, of course, cancel the undeniably utilitarian elements in Mo Tzu's account; no more than they erase his real differences with Confucianism over the practical requirements of morality. But they do, perhaps, indicate that Mohism is less distant from the mainstream of classical

Chinese philosophy than admirers and critics have supposed. As with Confucianism and Taoism, the Mohist vision is of an ideal or superior person, identified less by his performance of certain actions than by his character or inner moral resources. More explicitly even than these rivals, Mohism understands the superior person to be one whose life is led in harmony with the Way of Heaven. Such harmony is nothing so baroque in flavour as the balancing of *yin* and *yang*, in emulation of their balance in Heaven, which was recommended by the Han Confucians. It is, arguably, the idea familiar in the Christian pantheist tradition of adjusting one's own will and desires to those of a higher moral Person immanent in the natural order.

• 4 Taoism •

The Mohist call, we have seen, was for a life of intense moral seriousness – something lacking, as Mo Tzu saw it, in the Confucian acquiescence in the performance of conventional rites. It was from a very different angle that Confucianism was criticized by representatives of a tendency whose influence has not merely persisted but, in recent years, found a whole new audience in the West – Taoism. Some of this new audience, doubtless, are attracted not to the philosophical Taoism discussed here, but to its later occultist forms; while, for others, the appeal lies in what sound like early manifestos of ecology, feminism and, *a fortiori*, 'eco-feminism'. More generally, Taoism enjoys a romantic image that Confucianism certainly lacks, one strengthened by the legends of Taoist sages spurning the administrative positions which Confucians so assiduously sought. Whereas Confucianism attracts 'those who wear official buttons and those who kowtow to them', wrote Lin Yutang, it repels others by being 'too decorous, too reasonable, too correct'. The person with 'a hidden desire to go about with dishevelled hair . . . and bare feet goes to Taoism'.[33] In the popular imagination, the conflict between the two philosophies encapsulates the eternal tensions between town and country, discipline and freedom, reason and romance, prose and poetry.

There are reasons to hesitate, however, before accepting this black-and-white picture. For one thing, Confucius himself does not always figure badly in Taoist texts. While he is sometimes the butt of criticism and ridicule, he more often appears as a Taoist *manqué* – a wise man not quite able to grasp the deepest truths. In one passage of Chuang Tzu's, he even converts someone to the principles of Taoism (5d).[34] Second, it appears that many Chinese people throughout the ages have managed to accommodate the precepts of both philosophies within their lives – applying them, perhaps, to different areas of these lives, rather as people today may adopt different kinds of standards when at work and when back-packing through the mountains. Third, Taoism is a diffuse tendency, without a founder, like Confucius or Mo Tzu, whose teachings set broad limits to membership of the schools which took his name. Even when we exclude later 'magical' Taoism, with its demons, quest for immortality, and experiments in alchemy, there remain significant differences between the main Taoist thinkers. Chuang Tzu, for example, is less sympathetic than Lao Tzu to Confucian concerns.

Importantly, moreover, two broad aims of Taoist thought are identical with those of Confucianism, and indeed of nearly every Chinese school. These are to delineate the nature of the 'superior person' and to demonstrate that what makes this person superior is the harmony between his nature and the Way. Although it is the concept of the Way (*tao*) which gives Taoism its name, this concept, we have seen, is common currency among the Chinese schools. For both Confucius and Mo Tzu, the 'superior person' is in accord with 'the Way of Heaven'. That said, there are a number of respects in which the Way figures more centrally in Taoist writings. To begin with, the Taoist Way is not simply the manner or direction in which heaven, earth or nature operates: it is the source or origin of everything. Second, there is much more discussion in Taoist writings, especially the *Chuang Tzu*, of the Way and its relationship to the empirical world than in the works of other schools. In particular, a serious effort is made to *deduce* the proper course of human conduct from the supposed tendencies of the Way. There is no longer the impression, as there was with the other schools, that a writer is simply investing 'the Way of Heaven' with just those features he needs it to have in the light of an ethical position to which he is already committed. (Mo Tzu, for instance, offered no argument for thinking that Heaven esteems what Mo Tzu esteems – welfare, life, order.)

I postpone the attempt to explain what, for the Taoists, the Way *is*, beginning with the more tractable question of the kind of human life that would accord with the Way. The discussion will focus on the two great Taoist figures, Lao Tzu and Chuang Tzu – or rather, on the two works traditionally attributed to them, the *Tao Te Ching* and the *Chuang Tzu*. It is unclear that there ever was an historical person, Lao Tzu, living in the sixth century BCE and answering to the descriptions provided in an unreliable history book written five centuries later and in various legends (the calibre of which can be judged by the claim, in one of them, that he spent eighty-two years in the womb). What is clearer is that the *Tao Te Ching* was probably a fourth-century compilation of teachings by various sages or 'old masters' (which is what *lao tzu* means). In that event, it can hardly be much earlier than the collection of teachings attributed, more reliably, to Chuang Tzu (*c.*369–286 BCE). He seems to have been a real historical figure, probably an official in the Lacquer Garden of Meng, and the author of at least the first seven (or 'inner') chapters of the work bearing his name.

Nature and *wu wei*

'All artificiality is false', says Chuang Tzu (4a), and the person whose life is dominated by artifice cannot be a 'true man': he is alienated from himself.[35] 'Artifice', here, refers to social conventions, rules of etiquette and art, private property, and much else that characterizes a civilized culture. Morality, too, comes under this hammer. 'Exterminate benevolence, discard rectitude', demands Lao Tzu (19).[36] But such remarks can mislead, for the Taoists were certainly not moral nihilists in the sense of denying that one life can be better than any other. The lesser point of such remarks is to complain that, even in a community which requires a code of moral rules, the kind urged by Confucians, such as the performance of innumerable rites, was excessive and oppressive. The more important point is that the very existence of a code, of duties and obligations, is a sign that things have gone wrong, that the Way is in disuse. '[W]hen the Way was lost there was . . . benevolence; when benevolence was lost there was rectitude; when rectitude was lost there were the rites' (Lao Tzu, 38). It is, then, the 'artificial' character of a civilized society, the maintenance of which requires a moral code, which is the real Taoist target.

Such a critique implies, of course, a conception of a 'natural' form of life, in accordance with the Way, from which 'artificial' existence is a fall. This is often interpreted as a call for 'primitivism', for returning to a 'state of nature' presumed to have existed before civilized society. There are passages which seem to support this. 'The adoption of conventional ways,' says Chuang Tzu, 'has been the ruin . . . of primordial nature . . . the ruin of the world' (16b). We are enjoined to emulate the behaviour of animals or natural phenomena, to admire the gardener who refuses to employ machines, to make ourselves like Lao Tzu's simple 'uncarved block' before its sculpturing into the artificial forms of society.

Despite such 'green' passages, however, it is not the 'primitive' which Taoists have primarily in mind by the 'natural'. For one thing, they think it possible, if difficult, for a person to live 'naturally' and authentically *within* an advanced culture: this is possible even for the ruler of an empire, to whom much of Lao Tzu's advice is directed. Some of the Taoist heroes, moreover, who do live 'in the Way', are hardly of the 'primitive', Tarzanesque variety, but skilled craftsmen (wheelwrights, bell-makers) or contemplatives immersed in a world of abstractions. (This is not to deny that, in the Taoist tradition, there is also admiration for the wild 'man of the mountains' or the poetic wanderer, subjects of countless paintings and novels.) Most significant of all, however, is that the natural phenomena we are enjoined to emulate are very carefully chosen – the grazing cow rather than the hunting tiger, the gently rolling stream rather than the exploding volcano. This is because only the former adequately symbolize or illustrate the tendency of the Way. The 'natural' life admired by the Taoist is natural because it accords with the Way, not because it is the one led in a 'state of nature', even if this latter can provide useful metaphors for the 'natural' life.

But why should grazing cattle or water, not tigers or volcanos, serve as the metaphors for the 'natural' life? It is because they illustrate the central Taoist ideal of *wu wei* (non-action). 'Make of non-action your glory [and] ambition', exhorts Chuang Tzu (7f). Non-action is not, of course, to be taken literally here: we are not being exhorted to spend our whole lives asleep or in trance. *Wu wei*, rather, is the manner and spirit in which we act. The manner of our actions should – to cite just a few of the favoured epithets – be submissive, weak, feminine, yielding. The person of *wu wei* does 'not contend', 'lets things be', 'goes with the grain of things', and his spirit is one of 'indifference', 'apathy', 'affable impassivity'.[37] A favourite illustration is that of the swimmer who goes, unresisting, with the current.

Wu wei is not only the ideal of human behaviour but, one might say, the way of the Way. If the pliable swimmer is a symbol of human *wu wei*, the water in which he swims is a symbol of the Way itself. 'Because water excels in benefiting [things] without contending with them . . . it comes close to the Way' (Lao Tzu, 8). Like water, the Way influences without 'dominating': it is the source and sustainer of life, but does not interfere with it. Joseph Needham is correct to say that *wu wei* is 'refraining from activity contrary to nature',[38] provided that 'nature' here is understood as the nature of the Way. To live in the manner and spirit of *wu wei* is to live naturally because it accords with the Way. 'To let oneself be is to follow the Way' (Chuang Tzu, 22e).

This accord with the Way, it might seem, is sufficient reason for living 'naturally', but Lao Tzu and Chuang Tzu are keen, in their different ways, to elaborate the case for *wu wei*. The former's emphasis is upon the pragmatic advantages to a person of being submissive and non-contentious. In particular, the person who 'goes against the way will come to an early end' (55); by not contending 'you will meet with no danger. You can then endure' (44). So marked is this emphasis that some have regarded Lao Tzu as a cynic, the purveyor of an 'old-roguish wisdom . . . [a] brilliantly wicked philosophy of self-protection', designed to enable a person to survive, and indeed to come out on top, during violent and destitute times.[39] Certainly there are passages where he might be read as telling us only to *pretend* to be submissive and yielding in order, really, to dominate, and where the 'feminine' he praises appears to be the seductress who uses her 'weakness' to entrap a man. 'If you would take from a thing, you must first give to it . . . The submissive and weak will overcome the hard and the strong' (36).

But the accusations of cynicism and 'old-roguish wickedness' are exaggerated. For Lao Tzu, just as it is a fact about the natural world that water eventually wears away the rock, so it is a fact of social life that submissiveness and pliability eventually overcome the dominant and the rigid – and it would be silly for people not to recognize this and to benefit from doing so. There is no reason to suppose that he is advocating only the simulation of *wu wei*. That, in grim and violent times, there are self-protective advantages in being submissive and non-contentious is perfectly compatible with insisting that this is how we should also be in smoother times when there is less of a strategic premium on such behaviour.

Chuang Tzu, though less concerned with survival in a dangerous environment, also draws attention to the advantages of *wu wei*. It promises 'supreme contentment' (18a), 'a resurgence of vitality' (19a); above all, perhaps, 'non-action does not wear one out' (7f) – rather as the knife of the butcher who follows the natural contours of the carcass never wears out. But the emphasis in Chuang Tzu is on some deeper ethical dimensions of *wu wei* – on the 'perfect freedom' and return to one's 'true being' that it offers. This suggests that he has a deeper conception of *wu wei* than has so far emerged. Exploring this will help us understand his conception of the Way itself. Let us proceed by examining Chuang Tzu's alleged 'relativism'.

Relativism, freedom and the 'true man'

An interesting difference between the two Taoist Masters concerns the status of opposites or contraries. Lao Tzu follows a familiar Chinese line, epitomized by the *yin/yang* relation, that the structure of reality is fundamentally polar, harmony residing in the balance of opposites. Prudent people, we saw, will be acutely conscious of opposites like strength and weakness. According to Chuang Tzu, however, 'heaven and earth are one, the *yin* and the *yang* are one, and likewise the opposed aspects of all contraries' (17a). Since, in reality, 'there is no contrast . . . there is no distinction' either (2a). This peculiar claim is soon qualified, though. It is only 'in the absolute sense' that there is neither great nor small, good nor evil: such 'things are relative' (17a).

Some of Chuang Tzu's arguments for this conclusion are hardly persuasive. A person's opinions about things change, so how do we know that the sixtieth is any more true than the other fifty-nine? To which a reasonable answer is that, even if we don't, that hardly shows that no opinion *is* correct. Again, he points out how quickly opposites, 'fleeting modalities', can pass into each other, pleasure into pain, action into laziness, for example. But, if anything, this observation implies the very distinctions Chuang Tzu seems to deny – as does the claim that what is great or good in one set of circumstances may be petty or evil in another. Nor is the conclusion that 'there is no absolute morality, but only an opportunist expedience' (17a) secured by the banal thought that the rightness of an action depends in certain ways on circumstances. (You don't hand over the knife you promised someone if he intends stabbing his mother.) The rules of any sensible morality will, of course, be sensitive to the conditions under which they are to be applied.

At certain points, however, a more persuasive position – what might nowadays be called 'linguistic relativism' – is urged. 'There is, in reality, neither truth nor error . . . nor other distinctions . . . There are only diverse aspects, which depend on the point of view' (2c). The reason for this, it emerges, is that all judgements and distinctions are functions of the language we speak. That distinctions are language-relative would not matter, of course, if language were a true representation of reality. But it is not, being 'no better than a clacking of hens' (2c). More soberly put, the things we ordinarily distinguish are 'designated by words, to which nothing corresponds in reality' (2e). It seems that for Chuang Tzu, here illustrating once more the 'practical' tendency of Chinese thought, a language is simply a convenient device, the test of whose adequacy is communicative success, not its accurately picturing reality – something which, given our immersion in language, we can never know that it does.

If one recent commentator is right in holding that this view of language, as 'not . . . representing reality, not stating truths, but guiding actions and co-ordinating social interaction',[40] was commonplace in Chinese thinking, that would explain why Chuang Tzu does not bother to provide arguments for it. His interest is in the implications of this view for human freedom and authenticity. The link is provided by the notion of *wu wei* which, for Chuang Tzu, is not merely a matter of a relaxed, 'laid back' approach to life. The person who follows *wu wei*, we saw, does not impose or contend. The deep meaning of *wu wei*, in Chuang Tzu's hands, is the refusal to impose, either upon reality or on other people, a particular language-relative perspective. Apparently competing discourses and perspectives should be treated with detachment, amusement even. The story is told of some monkeys angry at the offer of three taro roots in the morning and four in the evening, but happy with four roots in the morning and three in the evening (2c). There is no real difference in what they get, so they are silly to make an issue of it. The point of the tale, perhaps, is that there is no real difference either, in practical terms, between apparently competing discourses and perspectives: it is just that people suppose there are and try to enforce one at the expense of others. This is what the precepts of *wu wei* enjoin us to avoid. Except for everyday, pragmatic purposes, we should 'neglect' the distinctions which our particular language honours, not 'let them penetrate the palace of the mind' (5c). In a 'multicultural' spirit, we should respect the traditional concepts and wisdom of the villages, but it would be wrong for the villagers to think their 'maxims are the expression of the Way', since these do not 'extend to the affairs of other earthly beings', with different, but equally valid, ways of 'co-ordinating social interaction' (23j).

In taking this *laissez-faire* attitude towards 'competing' discourses and perspectives, the sage is emulating the Way itself. For the Way, too, allows for a variety of perspectives, but without dictating any one of these. It 'influences everything' by making it possible for us to speak and think in co-operation, 'whilst remaining indifferent' to the particular schemes of speech and thought which are developed (22b). The sage, by refusing to adhere to or impose a particular 'science, tradition, precedent . . . imitates the indifferent opportunism of heaven'. And this is why, Chuang Tzu adds, the sage 'has nothing to suffer, from heaven, beings, men' (15b). This gives a clue to the relation between *wu wei*, as just interpreted, and human freedom.

Chuang Tzu's concept of freedom is not at all that of a Promethean imposition of the will, upon the world or people, familiar in modern Western thought. Rather, it is to be understood in the Stoic manner as 'non-dependence'. The sage is 'perfectly free' because he 'no longer depend[s] on anything' (1c). This is because he is not committed to any particular perspective on things, recognizing the sheer contingency of the things which are picked out for appreciation or condemnation in any particular linguistic culture. 'Do not be enslaved to the world' (28j), by the obsessive pursuit of honours, for example: for, from other viable perspectives, these 'honours' would be objects of disdain or ridicule. Because he is indifferent and 'lets the cosmic wheel turn', 'the superior man is touched by nothing' (1d) – and therein resides his freedom.

Therein, too, resides 'truth to oneself' since, paradoxically put, the sage will be indifferent and without any special commitment to himself. Personal life and advantage do not matter to the person who adheres to *wu wei*, for among the conventional distinctions which he does not take seriously is that between distinct persons. 'There are no such things as distinct beings . . . there does not exist, in reality, this something closer which one calls mine, and this something further away which one calls yours' (2b). One of the things, then, which 'makes a true man' is the refusal to 'artificially distinguish individual human cases', his own included (6b). We are entering Indian territory here, though at what crossing is unclear, since Chuang Tzu's remarks are sketchy. Maybe his thought is the Sāṃkhyan one that it is the empirical ego which is an artificially distinguished 'part of the great mass', an ego not to be confused with an individual transcendental self (see p. 26). Or maybe it is more akin to Śaṅkara's (see p. 33): there is not even this latter individual self, since there is only the one Self of absolute reality. Either way, however, it is clear that the 'true man' regards as merely conventional the distinction between persons or individuals as ordinarily conceived. The question then turns to how this insight is properly reflected in the life of the 'true man'.

In two different, and at first glance antithetical, ways, it seems. On the one hand, there is the way of the contemplative sage, abstracted from the empirical world and fully occupied with discernment of the Way itself. On the other hand, there is the way of the skilled craftsman, effortlessly immersed in the exercise of his trade. But, for Chuang Tzu, there is no antithesis here, only different routes to acquaintance with the Way. The crucial element, in both cases, is the setting aside of the conventional distinctions of everyday life – in particular, that between oneself and other people and things. The sage achieves this through an 'ecstatic contemplation' in which he brings 'all the parts together into one' (17a). The craftsman, like the sculptor of a wooden belfry, does so through 'the fusion of [his] nature into one with that of the trees', during which process he loses all concern for himself and 'even the notion of [his own] body' (19j). Whether through a 'vision' that rises above the world of artificial distinctions or a practical immersion that, so to speak, takes him beneath it, the 'true man' is no longer dependent on convention.

The large question, however, seems to remain: what *is* the Way with which the sage and the craftsman, by their different routes, have become acquainted?

The Way

On several points concerning the Way, the Taoist Masters are in agreement. The Way, although it somehow 'influences' the world, is not simply 'the way of the world', a tendency or direction which things have. For it is also a source, 'the beginning of heaven and earth . . . the mother of the myriad creatures' (Lao Tzu, 1). But it is not at all a creator God, being entirely 'without substance'. The Way 'from which beings emanate,' says Chuang Tzu, 'cannot properly be called the author of these beings' (25j). Finally, according to the famous opening of the *Tao Te Ching*, 'The Way that can be spoken of is not the constant Way': a view echoed in Chuang Tzu's rhetorical question 'What is the good of looking for impossible terms to express an ineffable being?' (2e).

But there are differences too: for example, over the reason for the Way's ineffability. Lao Tzu's argument is unclear, but on one interpretation seems to be that, since the world contains (or could contain), for each property X, things which are X and things which are non-X, the Way itself can be neither of these. For if it were X, say, that would exclude its being the source of what is non-X; this is impossible since it is the source of everything. So we are unable to describe it as having any particular property.[41] In Chuang Tzu's case, the ineffability of the Way is a consequence of his 'relativism'. All the properties and distinctions we ascribe to the world are imposed upon it through linguistic convention. None of these, therefore, are available for describing the Way: for if the Way has any features at all, these would 'really' belong to it, and not by artifice or convention.

For whatever exact reason, the Way is ineffable; this, together with its lack of 'substance', suggests that our question 'What *is* the Way with which the sage and craftsman are acquainted?' may be an unhappy one. The point is not that we will not get the kind of answer we were hoping for, a nice meaty description of the Way – though indeed we shall not. Rather, the question primes us to think of the Way as some kind of thing or being, distinguished from others only by its peculiarly immense, recessive or intangible nature. But this is precisely the attitude from which the Masters try to wean us: hence their fondness for expressions – non-being, void, empty, between being and nothing – designed to discourage the conception of the Way as any kind of entity, however special.

Indeed, the thought may occur that our question was the wrong way round. Perhaps the wisdom of the sage and craftsman is not to be explained in terms of their acquaintance with the Way: rather, the Way is to be understood in terms of their wisdom. Perhaps 'acquaintance with the Way' simply *is* the abstracted state of the sage or the immersed activity of the craftsman. Both of them, recall, have set aside everyday distinctions, either by rising above them or by 'fusing' with things. Maybe this obliviousness towards artifice and convention is all there is to 'following the Way'. There is nothing – no thing – to know over and above this obliviousness. The exhortation to follow the Way then *reduces to* the demand that we should live unencumbered by the contingent linguistic and conceptual schemes through which we conduct our everyday social business.

But while this thought might represent what the Taoist *ought* to be saying, it does not accord with all that he actually says. In particular, it does not account for his insistence that the Way is a source or origin, one which somehow confers on things their 'destiny'. Can explanation of the Way go further, or must we take it or leave it as the 'mystery' which Taoists often call it? One thing we might try is asking why Taoists are *Tao*-ists; why, that is, they prefer to characterize the ineffable source as 'the Way' rather than as 'the One', 'the Absolute', 'Pure Being', or whatever. A twentieth-century admirer of Taoism, Martin Heidegger, wrote '*tao* could be the way that gives all ways'.[42] The force of characterizing the source as 'the Way' is to emphasize that this source is what makes possible – 'gives' – the various ways, the various perspectives or linguistic schemes, which are the currencies for talking about the world. Thereby, the Way also 'gives' or allows the emergence of the objects conventionally spoken of through these schemes since, according to Chuang

Tzu, these objects are artifices of language. The source itself cannot, of course, be described, since any terms used would have to be culled from *within* a given linguistic perspective which has no privileged access to the grounds of its own possibility.

Or rather, the Way cannot be spoken of in any conventional language, any mere pragmatic device for 'social co-ordination'. In an intriguing passage, Chuang Tzu holds out a further possibility:

> I have spoken without art, naturally, according to the impulse of my inner sense . . . preliminary to all discourses, there pre-exists an innate harmony in all beings, their nature. From the fact of this pre-existing harmony, my speech, if it is natural, will make others vibrate, with few or no words. (27a)

This is hardly transparent, but three points seem to be indicated. First, there may be a form of speech which is a 'natural' response to the world. Second, such a form will communicate to other people not through informative propositions, but by 'vibrating' for them; by their spontaneously recognizing the 'natural' response as 'fitting', as Chuang Tzu then puts it. Finally, this 'natural' speech need not be verbal, for it can be one 'spoken without words'.

These points, taken with the preceding discussion, suggest the following interpretation of at least Chuang Tzu's brand of Taoism. The various perspectives or ways whereby we talk about things, and therefore the things so talked about, presuppose a source or ground – the Way. Unfortunately, people fail to recognize that these ways are pragmatic devices, taking them to be representations of reality itself. The possibility is not excluded, however, of a less impositional way of speech, a natural response to things – no longer, of course, the language-relative things of everyday discourses, but things in the 'essence' or 'destiny' imparted to them by the Way. Someone who speaks thus, whether through words or deeds, 'lets things be' what they essentially are. This is not a matter, simply, of setting aside the preconceptions embedded in the linguistic perspective of one's community. It requires, too, a quiet and patient readiness to 'fit' one's words and deeds to the world, to 'vibrate' with the 'pre-existing harmony'. Here we reach the deepest meaning of *wu wei*. There are, then, two broad possibilities for 'following the Way'. First, the way of the sage, the contemplative whose natural responses are simple words, spoken 'without art', and 'perceived spontaneously' to be 'fitting'. Second, the way of the craftsman – or perhaps the swimmer – whose speech 'without words' is an acting upon things which, once again, does not impose or contend, but is an easy response to his materials or environment that anyone with 'a natural sense of right and wrong' can at once see to be 'fitting'.[43]

On this interpretation, Chuang Tzu's conception, whatever the final verdict on its coherence, is surely one of depth and beauty. It is a kind of conception with which we are not yet finished, for readers of Heidegger will recognize its close affinity with his later writings, which are briefly discussed in section 5 of chapter 10.

• Notes •

1 Fung Yu-Lan, *A History of Chinese Philosophy*, 2 vols.
2 See Franz Michael, *China Through the Ages*, ch. 4.
3 G. W. F. Hegel, *The Philosophy of History*, p. 138.
4 A. C. Graham, 'The place of reason in the Chinese philosophical tradition', p. 54.
5 Laurence C. Wu, *Fundamentals of Chinese Philosophy*, p. 6.
6 Lin Yutang, *My Country and its People*, p. 96.
7 Robert E. Allinson, 'An overview of the Chinese mind', p. 10.
8 Chung-Ying Cheng, 'Chinese metaphysics as non-metaphysics: Confucianist and Daoist insights into the nature of reality', p. 167.
9 A. C. Graham, 'The place of reason in the Chinese philosophical tradition', p. 55.
10 R. E. Allinson, 'An overview of the Chinese mind', p. 14.
11 References to Mencius are to book and chapter numbers of *Mencius*.
12 Allinson, 'An overview of the Chinese mind', p. 13.
13 Chuang Tzu, in L. Wieger (trans.), *Wisdom of the Daoist Masters*, p. 178.
14 The primacy of 'know-how' for Chinese philosophers is emphasized by Arthur C. Danto, *Mysticism and Morality*, ch. 6. The *locus classicus* for the distinction between 'knowing how' and 'knowing that' is Gilbert Ryle, *The Concept of Mind*.
15 Kenneth DeWoskin, 'Chinese and Japanese aesthetics', p. 73.
16 References to Confucius are to Book and Chapter of *The Analects*.
17 Laurence C. Wu, *Fundamentals of Chinese Philosophy*, p. 23.
18 In E. R. Hughes (ed.), *Chinese Philosophy in Classical Times*, p. 89.
19 Fung Yu-lan, *A History of Chinese Philosophy*, vol. 1, p. 63.
20 Raymond Dawson, *Confucius*, pp. 37–8.
21 Quoted by D. C. Lau (trans.), *Mencius*, Introduction, p. 1.
22 *Hsun Tzu*, in B. Watson (trans.), *Basic Writings of Mo Tzu, Hsun Tzu, and Han Fei Tzu*, section 23, p. 157. Further quotations are all from this Section.
23 In E. R. Hughes (ed.), *Chinese Philosophy in Classical Times*, p. 301.
24 In W. Baskin (ed.), *Classics in Chinese Philosophy*, pp. 273–4.
25 In E. R. Hughes (ed.), p. 304 and p. 306.
26 Cheng, 'Chinese metaphysics as non-metaphysics', p. 191.
27 Tung Chung-Shu, in E. R. Hughes (ed.), p. 301.
28 Hu Shih, quoted in St E. Nauman, *Dictionary of Asian Philosophies*, p. 279.
29 References to Mo Tzu are to page numbers of B. Watson (ed.), *Basic Writings of Mo Tzu, Hsun Tzu, and Han Fei Tzu*.
30 Lawrence C. Wu, *Fundamentals of Chinese Philosophy*, p. 89.
31 Ibid., pp. 100–1.
32 Quoted in ibid., p. 99.
33 Lin Yutang, *My Country and Its People*, pp. 109–10.
34 References to Chuang Tzu are to Chapter and Section of the *Chuang Tzu* in *Wisdom of the Daoist Masters*. The translator prefers 'the Principle' to 'the Way' as a translation of *tao*: in my quotations, I stick to 'the Way'.

35   See A. C. Graham's discussion of 'self-alienation', *Chuang-tzu: The Inner Chapters*.

36   References are to Chapters of the *Tao Te Ching*.

37   The notion of *wu wei* has *some* resemblance to that of *niṣkarma-karma* ('actionless/non-fruitive action') discussed in ch. 2 sect. 5. But the kinds of 'detachment' enjoined are different, and the former primarily concerns the manner of action, the latter its motive. Certainly the *wu wei*-ish agent need not be performing an action 'for its own sake'.

38   Joseph Needham, *Science and Civilization in China*, vol. II, p. 68.

39   Lin Yutang, p. 112.

40   Chad Hansen, 'Language in the Heart-Mind', p. 85. My discussion of Chuang Tzu is much endebted to Hansen's suggestions, which are more fully expressed in his book, *A Daoist Theory of Chinese Thought*.

41   Such, at any rate, is D. C. Lau's interpretation in the Introduction to his translation of the *Tao Te Ching*, pp. 19ff.

42   M. Heidegger, *On The Way To Language*, p. 92.

43   For a fuller exposition, see my 'Is Daoism green?'

4
· GREECE ·

· 1 Legacies ·

Philosophers, like other people, both inherit legacies and bequeath them. In the case of those early and fructifying thinkers, the Greeks, it is of course the bequest to posterity which commands most attention.

The Greek Bequest

'The legacy of Greece to Western philosophy is Western philosophy.'[1] As an opener, it would be hard to beat this remark of Bernard Williams, just as it would be difficult to improve on his succinct elaboration of it. It is not simply that in philosophy, as in the sciences and arts, Western civilization built on Greek initiatives. For it was the Greeks who performed the division of philosophy into its sub-disciplines, like ethics and metaphysics, which still prevail, and who raised most of the large questions which continue to dominate philosophical discussion. Moreover, in Plato and Aristotle especially, the Greeks graced us with thinkers whose answers to many of those questions remain serious contenders.

It was not the fault of the Greeks, but of events further West, in the Europe of the Dark Ages, that their bequest was to be forgotten after a few centuries, only to be recalled in later mediaeval times. What the mediaevals failed to appreciate in this legacy, the men of the Renaissance and Enlightenment did not, so that by the nineteenth century studies of the Greek classics, including philosophy, were central to liberal education in most European countries. More philistine studies, promoted in the name of 'relevance', have usurped that place, but no one is likely to gainsay the abiding impact of Greek thought on the modern consciousness.

Such indeed has that impact been that in philosophy, as elsewhere, there is the danger of anachronism: of finding in the Greek mind, in accordance with current predilections, what was not there. Even our word 'philosophy' has connotations of an activity – of one relatively disjoint from science, for example – which *philosophía* ('love of wisdom') could not have had for the Greeks. In the following pages we shall have occasion to note the danger of treating Plato and Aristotle as if they were contributing to debates in some modern journal. For example, some of Aristotle's remarks on 'ethics' sound distinctly odd until we remind ourselves that this Greek word meant something different from, and registered different concerns from, our transcription of it.

In some circles, fear of anachronism has prompted a challenge to the whole Renaissance and Enlightenment vision of the Greeks as the bequeathers of 'sweetness and light' to posterity. The fashion, in those circles, is to emphasize the 'strangeness' to us of the Greeks, their darker, irrational and more primordial side. Friedrich Nietzsche was at first scoffed at, but is now frequently admired, for understanding the Greek genius in terms of a perception of 'the primal Oneness amidst the paroxysms of intoxication': a 'tragic', Dionysian perception which only just saved the Greeks from the 'unleashing' of the 'savage beasts of nature' lurking within their souls.[2] We need not go that far: but nor should we exclude in advance an encounter with currents in Greek thought that do not flow with the sweeter streams that preoccupied the attention of earlier generations of graecophiles.

The presence of these darker currents only confirms what is anyway apparent from a brief survey of Greek thought – its great variety. In the case of the Indian tradition, rich as it was, a framework of concepts common to all the schools could be identified. But between the positions of such near contemporaries as Parmenides and Heraclitus, or Democritus and Plato, the philosophical divide is immense. Any attempt to characterize *the* Greek philosophical mind, therefore, would be even blander than the corresponding one I undertook in the case of China. The sheer variety of Greek philosophies means that my coverage must be selective. The great trio of Socrates, Plato and Aristotle are of course included, as are various thinkers of the later Hellenistic period, mainly Stoics and Epicureans. Among the so-called pre-Socratic thinkers – some of whom, confusingly, were younger than Socrates – I focus on the 'naturalists' and the Sophist, Protagoras: partly because of the fire they drew from Plato and Aristotle, partly because of the enduring attraction in the West of the ideas they initiated, and partly because these ideas importantly distinguish Greek thought from anything discussed in the previous chapters on India and China.

Among the notable victims of my selectivity is Pythagoras (sixth century BCE), he of the theorem about right-angled triangles which has been the bane of so many schoolchildren. In his less mathematical moments, this guru-like figure, the founder of a sect, preached in favour of the transmigration of souls between men and animals, and against the eating of beans, perhaps because of their perceived likeness to items of genitalia. There is, of course, more to be said about him than that 'he had some strange ideas about . . . dieting, religion and music', which exhausts one author's account.[3] But the more interesting of his views, including the reincarnationist one and a doctrine of mathematical harmony in the world, were elaborated by Plato and are best discussed when we come to him.

More significant omissions are Parmenides and his pupils Melissus and Zeno, who flourished during the fifth century BCE in the south of Italy, where there was a large Greek population. Parmenides and Melissus taught that reality is a single, changeless and motionless whole, in which nothing ever comes into being or is destroyed: an unpropitious-sounding doctrine which, nevertheless, they defended with some ingenuity against the commonsense which they despised.[4] I do not discuss the doctrine, partly because a strikingly similar one (based on not dissimilar arguments) was considered in section 3 of chapter 2, and partly because it is not one to have passed, with rare exceptions, into mainstream Western philosophy. A work more concerned with logic than the present one, however, would discuss the famous paradoxes of motion which Zeno devised in order, according to Plato, to defend Parmenides against the commonsense view of a plural world of changing, moving objects. The best-known is designed to demonstrate, in Aristotle's words, that 'the quickest runner can never overtake the slowest, since the pursuer must first reach the point whence the pursued started, so that the slower must always hold a lead'.[5] When Achilles starts, the tortoise is, say, twenty metres ahead at point A. Clearly he must get to A in order to catch the tortoise, which by then has reached point B, from which it has moved on by the time Achilles gets to B – and so on *ad infinitum*, according to Zeno. *Every* point Achilles must pass in order to overtake the tortoise is one the latter has already crawled beyond. (Zeno, one should add, despite being Parmenides' 'favourite', also devised arguments against his teacher's account of reality.)

The Greek Muse

Some of the views mentioned above – metempsychosis (or transmigration of souls), and the static, monistic vision of reality – were almost certainly imports from further east, and there has always been speculation over the Greek debt to the civilizations of Asia Minor, India and North Africa. Today, if some disturbing reports are true, subscription to the 'Black Athena' thesis, that the debt to that last region was almost total, is a pre-condition of appointment to certain 'politically correct' Departments of Classics in the USA. A respectable motive behind less extravagant speculations, however, is the desire to answer a genuinely puzzling question. How was it that around the middle of the first millennium BCE there should have been such a sudden flourishing of philosophy, literature, architecture and much else among a scattered people, for the most part warlike and rude, unblessed by wealth and the stability of ancient empire? The thought that much must have been borrowed from elsewhere becomes a tempting one, especially when one reflects that some of the factors adduced to explain 'the glory that was Greece' cut both ways. Granted, for example, that the Greek religion did not have a priestly caste to constrain and discourage innovative thought, it was also a peculiarly chaotic polytheism with little of the intellectual substance that Indian thinkers found in the sacred works of their tradition. Granted, too, that the *póleis* ('city-states') were robust communities, often encouraging initiative, they were also frequently at war with one another and hardly provided, it would seem, ideal conditions for leisured contemplation.

One advantage Greek thinkers certainly possessed was an efficient and economical written language in which to record and disseminate their views. But, just as it was implausible to blame a pictorial language for the relative absence of abstract thought among the Chinese, so one suspects an argument from hindsight behind the great historian Jacob Burckhardt's claim that Greek was 'brilliantly capable of detaching itself from the world of particulars' and hence 'intimately suited to philosophical discourse'.[6] The Greek language arguably played an important, indirect role, however, in facilitating intellectual debate: for it was in terms of their possession of a common tongue that this people of mixed tribal stock primarily identified itself *as* a people. Despite its dispersion about the Aegean and the Mediterranean, therefore, this people formed a large constituency for the dissemination of ideas. It is worth noting that many important philosophers, such as Heraclitus and Parmenides, came from regions far from the country we today call 'Greece'.

The sense of identity generated by a common language was reflected in frequent Pan-Hellenic gatherings, such as the Olympic Games. An interesting feature of these gatherings, not only the Games, was their competitive nature. Dramatists and poets, as well as athletes, would pit their skills against one another. This agonistic penchant, one might speculate, was itself conducive to a lively philosophical arena in which the weapons were ideas rather than javelins. Certainly, many of the philosophical writings – especially those in dialogue form – manifested the cut-and-thrust critical enthusiasm which professional philosophers, these days at any rate, regard as essential to progress in their discipline. Maybe, too, the competitive spirit was indicative of an individualism among the Greeks which was lacking among other civilizations of the time. The oracle at Delphi famously commanded 'Know thyself!', and Heraclitus explained his philosophical endeavours as 'searching for myself'. The sentiment implied by such remarks – the urge towards self-sufficient individual understanding – is not one found among the Greeks' neighbours, nor even among the sages of India or China. Arguably it is one that must be present for distinctive philosophies to abound.

In the final analysis, however, there is not much we can now do to explain the flowering of the Greek genius in philosophy and other fields. We might indeed follow the advice of the Roman poet Horace, in his *Ars Poetica*, to 'turn over the pages of the Greeks by night and by day', and perhaps we cannot improve on the reason he gives: 'The Muse gave the Greeks genius.' We do not know what, if not 'the Muse', inspired 14,000 Greeks at a time to attend whole days of dramas, by Sophocles or Aeschylus, which today play to a handful of devotees. Nor do we know what, besides 'the Muse', sustained four centuries of intensive philosophizing.

I have, of course, moved from the matter of the Greeks' legacy to Western philosophy to that of the legacy, or lack of it, which they inherited. Inadequate as reflections on language or forms of political organization may be in explaining the origins of Greek philosophy, there is however one inheritance, so far unmentioned, which certainly guided the direction taken by its earliest practitioners.

The Homeric Legacy

Whether or not we follow Aristotle in bestowing the label 'the first philosophers' on certain thinkers of the early sixth century BCE, it is clear that these men did not spring out of an intellectual vacuum. For they were the recipients of earlier ideas about the world, the gods and men which, for all their lack of system, were suggestive of a philosophical vision. What these men, like all educated Greeks of their time, inherited above all, however, was the Homeric legacy. The great eighth-century BCE poet did not, presumably, invent the philosophical themes which run through his works, the *Iliad* and the *Odyssey*, but it is there that they received their earliest remaining articulation and, through the recitation of these works, formed the background against which later speculation would proceed.

Homer's two epics are, of course, good ripping yarns about the stirring events of some four centuries earlier, the fall of Troy to the Achaean Greeks and the perilous journey home to Ithaca of one of those warriors. But, throughout, the poet is not content simply to tell a coherent narrative in which, at a commonsense level, this or that event is placed in an intelligible context. For he is concerned, too, to reflect upon the significance of the events and to offer underlying explanations for them. It would be too strong, perhaps, to speak here of a 'framework' of explanation, since Homer does not attempt to impose unity and coherence among the motley kinds of explanations he proposes at different points. Still, for all the variety and tensions among the accounts he offers, one can discern certain general convictions as to why things happen as they do which constitute an intellectual legacy.

At first glance, it is indeed the variety and tensions which are striking. Why do things turn out for people as they do? According to the chief of the gods, Zeus, it is because of their 'own wickedness'; it is 'a lamentable thing . . . that men should blame the gods . . . as the source of their troubles' (*Odyssey* 1).[7] But elsewhere it is precisely these gods who are held responsible, as the dying Patroclus points out to his victor, the Trojan hero Hector: 'Boast while you may. The victory is . . . a gift from Zeus and Apollo. *They* conquered me' (*Iliad* 16). In other places it is not the gods at large but Zeus in particular whose will is in control of the *dénouements* of human affairs. And sometimes, it is not the gods at all, but impersonal destiny or Fate which explains events. Thus the ghost of Patroclus, still unwilling to accept personal responsibility for his defeat by Hector, switches the blame from Zeus and Apollo to 'the dreadful Fate that must have been my lot at birth' (*Iliad* 23). There are passages, finally, where the fortunes of men are put down neither to their own deeds nor to the machinations of the gods or Fate, but to the natural rhythms of the cosmos. As trees lose their leaves but put on fresh ones in spring, 'in the same way one generation flourishes and another nears its end' (*Iliad* 6).

At one level, then, an almost embarrassing variety of explanations is available for a given event. But showing through this variety is a set of convictions about the nature of explanation. The first of these is that the explanations which usually satisfy us for everyday practical purposes are insufficient, since they do not demonstrate the real necessity of what happens. Why did Patroclus die? Well, because he had been stunned and his spear shattered, so that he was easy prey for Hector, who delivered a fatal blow to the belly. But this only invites further questions, such as 'why was Hector in the right place at, from Patroclus' point of view, the wrong time?' It is only when we can understand why each of the ingredients contributing to the death had to be as they were that explanation is truly achieved. Homer's vision of the operation of necessity in the world is one which he bequeathed to his poetic successors, the great fifth-century tragedians. It is the vision of the Chorus in Aeschylus' *Agamemnon*, 'sure that always events and causes hold sequence divinely ordered, and next by last controlled', or of the Chorus in Euripides' *Bacchae*, for whom 'truths more than mortal . . . belong to very nature [and] reign in our world, . . . fixed and strong'.[8]

A second conviction is a corollary of the first. Since ordinary observation of the familiar world about us will not reveal the necessity which governs it, there must be what Euripides calls 'the unseen world'. Whether this is the world of the gods and their plans, of invisible natural forces, or of the darker powers imagined by an earlier religion (and still symbolized by the god of 'frenzy', Dionysus (the Romans' Bacchus)), it is there that the processes unfold which dictate how events in the seen world fall out.

But a further conviction is occasionally expressed by the figures who populate Homer's epics, and more emphatically still by the figures – sometimes the same ones – who appear in the later tragedies. Not only do events in the visible world have to occur as they do because of processes in an unseen world, but these processes themselves take place in obedience to a single overriding principle – that of *justice* (*dikaiosúne*). Human beings and the lesser gods may temporarily upset the scales of justice, but eventually Zeus will intervene precisely because they have 'driven justice out' (*Iliad* 16). Justice, on this view, is not so much an ideal at which to aim, but something to which, despite many hiccups, the world inexorably tends. Justice, Aeschylus explains, guides 'good and evil . . . to their sure end by their appointed ways', and Fate is no blind force, but 'weaves out the world's design' so that each may receive his due portion.[9] Almost all the greatest tragedies were the tales of men or women who must of necessity pay, usually with their lives, for an injustice committed, however innocently. It was not Oedipus' fault that he killed his father and married his mother, but he has to go into exile because, as it is explained to him, 'there is a measure in all things'.[10] The vocabulary in which the necessary operations of the cosmos are most commonly described is borrowed, moreover, from the juridical sphere. Men receive their 'due portions', things go their 'appointed ways', and 'Law eternal wields the rod'.

'The first philosophers', then, stood to inherit a mixed legacy. On the one hand, a motley collection of appeals to the gods, Fate, nature or whatever, by way of explaining the course of events. On the other, a compact set of convictions about the general shape which adequate explanation must take. Such explanations must exhibit the necessity of events in terms of the processes of an 'unseen world' – processes which themselves unfold in accordance with the overriding imperative of justice. Put crudely, these 'first philosophers' attempt to simplify or co-ordinate the Homeric motley within the context provided by those convictions.

• 2 Naturalism and Relativism •

The 'first philosophers' and their successors who will primarily concern us in this section, Aristotle also called 'naturalists' (*phusiológoi*). He contrasts them with 'Hesiod and all the theologians' who 'posit[ed] gods as the principles' explaining the course of events, and to whom, he adds, 'it is not worthy of us to pay serious attention', indulging as they do in 'mythical subtleties'.[11] What distinguishes the naturalists, according to Aristotle, is their belief that 'principles in the form of matter were the only principles of all things'. They believed this, he thinks, on the grounds that only something material could serve as the persisting substance which, while changing its properties, remains as the 'It' which undergoes these changes.[12]

The idea that these early thinkers were obsessed with the so-called 'problem of change' – 'What is it which persists for us to be able to say that *it* changes?' – is probably anachronistic. It is safer to assume that they were interested, simply, in looking for the best candidate to explain the various phenomena we observe around us, and found it in some form or another of material process. This sounds very much like the kind of exercise which we take scientists to be engaged in, and not a few commentators suggest that Aristotle's label of 'naturalists' is more apt than that of 'first philosophers', which anyway invites anachronistic interpretations.

Certainly there are reasons to regard the naturalists as prototypical scientists, with their conviction that phenomena are governed by 'principles in the form of matter'. We find them, for example, trying to explain in material terms happenings – like earthquakes and rainbows – previously credited to the gods. Several of them, too, were what we would now called 'applied scientists'. Thales was an inventor and meteorologist, and Anaximander a cartographer. (Practical in their intellectual interests, they seem to have been less so in the arts of living and dying, if legend is to be believed. We hear that Thales fell into a well while staring at the stars; Heraclitus buried himself in manure to cure his dropsy; and Empedocles spoiled his attempt to persuade posterity that he had been whisked up into heaven by leaving behind a slipper on the edge of the volcano into which he had jumped.) But one should not overdo the scientific credentials of the naturalists. Unlike Hippocrates and his fellow students of medicine, they seem to have made little or no use of experiment and controlled observation in support of their speculations. If F. M. Cornford is right, most of them would have regarded these as redundant, since they regarded themselves as seers, receiving truth through inspired revelation. If so, they are as much the ancestors of the *shamans* of Siberia as of today's hard-headed scientists.[13] But perhaps the most important consideration – to which I shall turn later – is the role played in their explanatory endeavours by something quite alien to contemporary natural science, the operation of justice in the cosmos.

From Water to Fire

The three main early naturalists – Thales, Anaximander, and Heraclitus – were Greeks, but not from Greece, hailing instead from the cities of Ionia in today's tourist-belt Turkey. In the sixth to fifth centuries BCE, Ionia was still a haven of the older Aegean civilization that, in Greece itself, had been overrun by the ruder Dorian invaders at the end of the second millennium BCE. In the cases of the first two thinkers especially, their views must largely be a matter of conjecture, since they are known to us only through a few fragments and reports by later authors, notably Aristotle.

It is Aristotle who refers to Thales (c.625–c.545) as 'the founder' of natural-istic thought, attributing to him the belief that the underlying material principle is water. It is unclear why he held this belief. Perhaps he was impressed by the versatility of water in turning itself into other material forms – steam, ice, and so on – and by the essential role of water in sustaining life. But clearly, it is the question Thales raised – 'What is the original source or substance of things?' – which is important, and not the particular answer essayed. He is important, too, because of the more interesting responses which his unlikely answer elicited from his successors.

The first of these, Anaximander (c.610–c.540), was struck by the problem of how a single element, like water, could generate the others, earth, fire, and air. His solution was that 'the material principle' was not any element, but of 'some other *ápeiron* ['unbounded', 'indefinite' or 'infinite'] nature, from which come into being all the heavens and the worlds in them' (DK 12 A9).[14] It has been speculated that this *ápeiron* was akin to the ineffable, qualityless *Brahman* or *tao* of Asian thought. But this seems unlikely given that the *ápeiron* is said to be spatially extended, and so presumably material in character. It is 'indefinite', not because it has no features at all, but because it is both spatially unlimited and distinct from any element known to us.

But this, as Heraclitus (c.540–c.470) saw, leaves it a puzzle as to how the world was formed out of this indefinite something. More generally, the world cannot have been generated from something different from itself, so 'it always was and is and will be'. It is, in fact, 'an ever-living fire, kindling in measures and being extinguished in measures' (DK 22 B30). This may seem a retrogade step, returning to the implausible Thalean identification of the underlying stuff of reality with a single element. But we need to distinguish between the familiar, literal sense of 'fire', in which fire is just one element among several, and the extended sense in which Heraclitus intends it. Everything is 'fire' only in the sense that, in crucial respects, it is *like* fire: or, better, ordinary fire is an especially vivid instance of the kind of process which everything, properly understood, really is. Indeed, Heraclitean 'fire' sounds like the prototype for what we now call 'energy' and naturally illustrate by examples of processes like combustion.

Heraclitus drew an important conclusion from the 'fiery' nature of every-thing. A fire is a constantly changing process, and if everything is like fire in this respect, then things do not have the stability and permanence we naïvely assume. Hence his famous dictum, 'It is not possible to step into the same river twice' (DK 22 B91). This was later trumped by Cratylus, who said you cannot step into the same river once either, since the river your foot eventually plunges into is different from the one it was when you began to move your foot.

Heraclitus' conclusion marks a significant departure from the views of his predecessors. Thales and Anaximander, while claiming to uncover aspects of reality not available to the ordinary senses, were not concerned to challenge the testimony of the senses. They were adding to, not replacing, our familiar understanding of things. But if Heraclitus is right, not only does 'nature like to hide itself' (DK 22 B123), it is something of a deceiver. For much of the time, nature appears to us to consist of stable objects which retain their identity over time, when in reality everything is undergoing the kind of flux and change which we readily observe in, say, the flickering flame of a candle. This schism between reality and appearance, as we will see, gets widened still further by those later naturalists known as the 'atomists'.

So far, we have looked only at the naturalists' conceptions of the external world. What do they have to say about the soul? In keeping with an older tradition, they regard the soul as that which imparts life and movement to material bodies. It is clear that most of them took this life-imparting power to be material in nature. Thales, indeed, appears to have thought that any object with the power to move, like a magnet, must have a soul – not, presumably, because the magnet is endowed with a conscious spirit, but because its soul *is* its power to move. Heraclitus is more specific: the soul is composed of 'fire' of a special kind, which allows it to run about the body, getting it to move. This provides him with an unusual argument for temperance. As 'fiery', souls should be kept dry. Since 'a dry soul is wisest and best', the drunkard endangers his health and wits by getting his soul 'moist' (DK 22 B117–18).

It is sometimes said that the naturalists should not be described as holding a materialist view of the soul, since the alternative dualist account, and indeed the whole 'mind/body problem', were unknown to them. But this, as Jonathan Barnes points out, is surely 'a miserable bit of argumentation', even if the 'naturalists' were as philosophically virgin as it assumes.[15] One may as well argue that no one should be described as travelling east who cannot articulate the distinction between east and west. The soul's being material means that, for the naturalists, there is an obvious sense in which human beings are very much in and part of the cosmos. They are, so to speak, made of the same stuff. But, as we shall now see, there is a more interesting sense in which these thinkers perceived an affinity between human affairs and cosmic processes.

'The Naturalization of Justice'

Part of the Homeric legacy to the naturalists was the conviction not merely that things are governed by unseen processes, but that these processes themselves obey a certain necessity. The question is therefore raised as to why the various underlying 'principles' proposed by these thinkers operate as they do. Why, for example, does Anaximander's 'unbounded' generate and sustain elements in such a way that no one of these is allowed to eliminate the rest – turning the cosmos into a giant puff of air or an enormous lake? Or why doesn't the Heraclitean 'fire' consume everything, leaving the world a heap of ashes? The short answer is that such disasters would offend the precepts of justice in accordance with which the cosmos functions. Justice requires a balance and equality among competing claimants for power, so that 'tyranny' exercised by one element over the rest is no more compatible with justice than the political tyranny practised by an autocrat.

The most famous testament to this conviction is Anaximander's assertion that the 'coming-to-be' and destruction of things happen 'according to necessity', for 'they pay penalty and retribution to each other for their injustice according to the assessment of Time' (DK 12 A9). If the world is to remain in a just balance then, for example, the heat and drought of summer must be 'atoned for', and 'punished' by the later cold and rains of winter. The same point is repeated and expanded by Heraclitus. We have already noted his remark – an early intimation, it sounds, of the conservation of energy principle – that the underlying 'fire' kindles and extinguishes in equal measure. This measure or equality is then reflected at the level of the visible world of elements and things. It is a measure, he makes clear, required for the sake of justice, so that the sun, for instance, 'will not overstep its measure; otherwise the Furies, ministers of justice, will find it out' (DK 22 B94). The world, as Heraclitus sees it, is characterized by pairs of 'opposite' features and elements, like hot and cold, between which there is hostility, the one trying to obliterate the other. Justice, as many political philosophers have argued, does not exclude, but rather presupposes, conflicts, since it consists in a fair compromise which prevents the potentially warring parties actually taking up cudgels. Similarly, for Heraclitus, 'one should know that war is common, and justice strife' (DK 22 B80). The just cosmos is the one in which the 'opposites' each receive their due, so that the wholes of which they are parts are not torn asunder by open hostility.

Such claims amount, according to one commentator, to 'the naturalization of justice'. Justice is no longer 'inscrutable' or 'imposed by arbitrary forces', but 'one with "the ineluctable laws of nature herself"'.[16] It is tempting, of course, to the modern mind, to suppose that these claims are purely figurative, mere rhetorical flourish. The juridical terminology is to be taken no more seriously than, say, the mildly erotic vocabulary – 'coupling', 'attraction', and so on – which chemists employ when talking about the behaviour of molecules. Or perhaps the claims should be regarded as symptoms of a still primitive mentality, not yet free from the animism and totemism which reflected earlier man's childish tendency to personify the world.[17] Or maybe we should see the claims as the product of a failure to make distinctions that are obvious to us, but were not to the Greeks, nor indeed to many later peoples: for example, the distinction between 'law' (*nómos*) in its juridical sense of a prescription and 'law' in the sense of a regularity in nature.[18] Without such a distinction, it is fatally easy to import into natural science concepts whose proper abode is jurisprudence.

The first of these suggestions ignores the earnestness with which the naturalists clearly took their talk of naturalized justice. Heraclitus' argument for obeying the laws of one's city was precisely that 'all human laws are nourished by one, the divine [law]' which governs everything (DK 22 B114). That *we* would be speaking figuratively when complaining of the injustice of a peculiarly long and harsh winter, as if it were an unduly severe gaol sentence, does not mean that Anaximander or Heraclitus would have been. Nor is the comparison between the naturalization of justice and primitive animism persuasive. It suggests that the naturalists were populating the natural world with little homunculi or spirits trying to govern the behaviour of trees or clouds according to precepts. But that, of course, was not their proposal. Justice, whether in nature or society, may issue from or embody a divine will, as for Heraclitus, but that is very different from personification of the processes of the natural world.

As to the final suggestion, it is true that many Greek thinkers move smoothly back and forth between 'law' in its prescriptive sense and 'law' in its regularity sense, without apparently noticing the difference. Hesiod, for instance, combines in a single sentence references to the law that animals eat each other and the law that men should treat each other justly. But the question should surely be pressed as to why the Greeks ignored this distinction, if this is what they did. For us, the most obvious motive for drawing the distinction is that the laws of the city can be broken in a way that natural laws cannot. But, for at least two reasons, this consideration would have been less salient for the naturalists. For one thing, the modern idea that seemingly irregular natural events are not really so — that it is we who have failed to uncover the strict regularities which operate — is hardly an obvious one. It is perfectly understandable that peoples of earlier times should have recognized only general trends, not strict regularities, in nature — ones which, therefore, could be 'bucked' by events. At the same time, we saw that it was a firm conviction that human beings cannot, at least in the long term, disobey the laws of their city or of a wider morality with impunity. Oedipus can rule in Thebes for many years, but eventually he must go into exile, blind, because 'there is a measure in all things'. Given these considerations, the gulfs between the laws of the city and natural laws — and, relatedly, between the spheres of justice and of merely material processes — would not have had the importance for the naturalists that they have for us.

Whatever the motives or the muddles behind the naturalization of justice, it clearly helped to secure, in the minds of the naturalists, that integration of human beings with their world which has been the ambition of many other philosophers to secure. Men are not simply in and part of nature because they are made of the same general stuff. In addition, the very laws which govern their behaviour, which make it right or wrong, are but instances of a wider law, a universal *lógos*, to which everything is subject. Human lives take on significance by partaking in the process of a cosmos which itself gains value and meaning through the perception of it as a just city writ large.

Satisfying as such a vision might have been, justice was soon to be 'denaturalized', and returned with a vengeance to the sphere of human affairs, by the fifth-century successors of the naturalists. Let us turn to that reversal.

Atomism and Relativism

The reversal was the repudiation of appeals to an objective order of justice in attempts to explain the operation of the natural and social worlds. As the Homeric age receded, the idea that material processes, like the coming and going of the seasons, were under the sway of a principle of justice, was striking many minds as an anachronistic pendant of an earlier, 'mythical' stage of consciousness. Increased contact with other societies in the known world served, moreover, to cast doubt on the presence among all peoples of any single concept of justice.

In two related ways the explanatory role of justice was challenged. First, those later naturalists we know as the 'atomists' offered a picture of the natural world as a vast conglomeration of interacting atoms, within which no room needed to, nor could, be found for the operations of justice. Second, historians and philosophers – particularly among those itinerant teachers of prudential wisdom, the Sophists – were arguing that judgements about justice were relative to individuals or societies. Clearly, these two tendencies supported one another. If justice, as a cosmic process, is redundant in explaining the order of the natural world, is it really required either for explaining the conduct of human affairs? And if justice is anyway, so to speak, in the eye of the beholder, it can play no role in the objective explanation of the natural world.

Moderns with a tendency to scoff at the cosmological efforts of the early naturalists usually stop smiling when they reach Leucippus (5th C. BCE) and Democritus (c. 460–c. 370) the leading atomists. For it is hard to deny the affinity between their account of reality and the classical physics of Newton. The following passage of Aristotle's might almost describe the views of an orthodox eighteenth-century CE scientist:

Democritus holds that the nature of what is eternal consists of little substances, unlimited in quantity . . . and space, unlimited in magnitude . . . the substances are so small that they escape our perception . . . from these, as from elements, he generates and combines the visible and perceptible masses. (DK 68 A37)

These tiny substances were taken to be indestructible and solid, coming in various shapes which enable them to lock onto one another so as to form grosser bodies. Most important, and the reason for calling them 'atoms', is that they are indivisible, and therefore the ultimate building-blocks of reality. Democritus, it seems, argued for this last feature on several grounds. The atoms are too small to cut with even the thinnest blade; they contain no 'voids' or interstices that could be penetrated; and anyway 'we cannot cut without limit', so there must be *something* which cannot be further divided (DK 67 A13).

It is not difficult to see why the atomists should have thought that, on their theory, 'nothing happens at random, but everything for a reason and by necessity' (DK 67 B2), and that any appeal to a process of justice would be redundant. The 'stuffs' spoken of earlier – water, the 'unbounded', 'fire' – were too gross and undifferentiated to provide much hope of explaining, naturalistically, either their internal workings or the ways they produce the things and events of the familiar, visible world. But if the underlying 'stuff' is a conglomeration of minute parts, some promise is held out of discerning law-like regularities in the ways they combine and generate macroscopic bodies. The problem which might remain as to why these regularities should be as they are was not one, apparently, which taxed the atomists.

One problem *did* tax Democritus, however. If reality consists of un-perceivable atoms, what is the status of our ordinary judgements about the external world – its colours and smells, for instance? His answer is brutal: all such judgements are false, and represent only a 'bastard' claim to knowledge (DK 68 B11). The reasoning appears to be this: perceptual judgements vary according to conditions and to the people making them. No reason can be given for preferring one such judgement to other conflicting ones. If we do prefer some to others – insisting, say, that the table is really brown, but only looks yellow – this is a matter of convention. 'By convention sweet, . . . by convention colour: but in reality atoms and void' (DK 68 B9). Perceptual judgements purport to describe the world as it is, but the real world has few, if any, of those features, like colour, which are perceived. This was a view partially revived in the seventeenth century, as we shall see in chapter 7, by philosophers impressed by Galileo's mechanics.

With greater frankness and perspicuity, perhaps, than these later thinkers, Democritus recognizes that a dilemma arises from this relegation of perceptual claims to 'bastard' knowledge. The senses, it seems, are our *entrée* into understanding the nature of reality. So, if their testimony is never true, what evidence can they ever provide us with that any account of the world – the atomist one included – is right? If atomism is true, so that perceptual judgements are all false, then there can be no reason to believe it is true. Or, as Democritus more robustly puts it, speaking in the person of the senses: 'Wretched mind! Do you take your evidence from us and then overthrow us? Our overthrow is your downfall' (DK 68 B125). He can see no escape from this dilemma, concluding that a man must admit 'that he is separated from reality' (DK 68 B6).

In later antiquity, Democritus was known as 'the laughing philosopher' – not because his surviving words are especially rib-tickling, but because of a cheerfully ironic and jaundiced view of the human condition. It is not surprising, perhaps, that there is nothing in our lives 'to be taken seriously', given that we are merely 'a movement of atoms and infinity'.[19] Consistent with this view, the nearest he comes to offering moral advice are downbeat precepts for achieving contentment and 'good spirits'. One policy recommended is *Schadenfreude*: we should 'look at the lives of those in trouble, bearing in mind how mightily they are suffering' (DK 68 B191).

Advice on how to prosper in an essentially meaningless world was also the speciality of many Sophists, including one whose views have a particular affinity with Democritus' – Protagoras (*c*.485–415). (According to the painting by Salvator Rosa in the St Petersburg Hermitage, Democritus admired Protagoras for, among other things, his skill at tying together fire-wood.) Whether or not he agreed with Democritus, in the latter's sceptical mood, that there is a real world, but one entirely beyond our ken, he certainly agreed that our ordinary empirical (and evaluative) judgements do not state truths about such a world. Instead of concluding, however, that all such judgements are false, he argues that they are all *true*. At any rate, this is what he argues according to Socrates, who construes his famous remark, 'Of all things a measure is man', as meaning that 'individual things are for me such as they appear to me, and for you in turn such as they appear to you'.[20]

The reasoning is Democritean. Perceptual judgements vary according to conditions and perceivers, and there can be no objective criterion, but at best a convention, for regarding only some as correct. But Protagoras, instead of treating such judgements as failed attempts to state what reality is like, treats them as true reports of how things strike the speaker. He is not, therefore, denying the laws of logic in holding that both 'This is sweet' and 'This is not sweet' are true. Rather, the former is elliptical for something like 'I find it sweet', and so does not conflict with one's friend's reply 'This is not sweet' (i.e. 'Well, *I* don't find it sweet'). In short, Protagoras is a relativist. Judgements are true relative to experiences of speakers about which they cannot be wrong.

Protagoras carries his relativism into the area of moral judgements, in particular ones about justice. 'In affairs of state, . . . the just and the unjust . . . are in truth to each state such as it thinks they are . . . and in these matters no citizen and no state is wiser than another.'[21] If Socrates' interpretation here is right, then Protagoras sometimes makes judgements true relative, not to individuals, but to states or societies, thereby embracing what we now call 'cultural' or 'social' relativism. This is an awkward position, for suppose that what seems just to me is different from what seems just to my fellow citizens. If a *man* is the measure, I can't be wrong; if society is the measure, then I can. Be that as it may, the idea that principles of justice are not woven into the fabric of the world, nor innately planted in the human soul, but artifacts which vary from society to society, was becoming common currency by the end of the fifth century – and not only among philosophers. In the same way that 'Democritus eliminates Aeschylean cosmic justice', so the historian Thucydides 'excludes it from history'.[22] The behaviour of states during the Peloponnesian war demonstrated that states will only follow what pass as the rules of justice when it is beneficial for them to do so. All too frequently it is not, and when it is not, it is neither wrong nor irrational to override these rules.

By the latter part of the fifth century, in short, justice had been thoroughly 'denaturalized'. According to atomist cosmology, material nature is nothing but a movement of atoms in space, and devoid therefore of value and purpose. And for Sophists like Protagoras, grasp of moral principles is no part of human nature, since these principles are the products of local convention. There were, however, dissenting voices, none louder than that of Socrates – though it was left to his greatest pupil, Plato, to reconstruct, in the grand style, a conception of reality apparently discredited by the alliance of atomism with relativism.

• 3   Plato •

By the time of Plato's youth, the following set of views would have been familiar and, one suspects, fashionable in Athenian intellectual circles. The real world, to the extent that we can know it at all, is a material mechanism, composed of 'atoms' and devoid of value and purpose. Among its occupants are human beings, distinguished only by the special matter – 'spherical atoms', perhaps – of which their souls are made. Judgements about the familiar world presented to us by the senses are either all false or all true, depending on whether they are treated as misguided attempts to say how things really are or as incorrigible expressions of subjective experiences. Since reality is itself devoid of value, judgements about justice, right, beauty and the like, can only register approval or disapproval, an estimate of what a person or society finds useful or beneficial in the prevailing circumstances.

For convenience, I shall call this the 'scientistic' position, not least because it is so similar to that adopted by many thinkers in recent times who congratulate themselves on a robust scientific perspective. Plato's critique of this target, then, is not of merely antiquarian interest. But on what grounds did he reject it? To answer that, we should first glance at the inspiration he received from his mentor, Socrates.

Socrates and Knowledge

Socrates (469–399) never wrote anything, and nearly everything we know about him must be gleaned from the dialogues of Plato, in the great majority of which he appears as the main speaker. This has created a hoary problem. When is Socrates expressing his own views, and when is he a mere vehicle for Plato's? I shall follow the modern wisdom that, in the early dialogues, it is the historical Socrates whose views are presented, while in the middle and later dialogues – with the introduction of the theory of Forms – 'Socrates' is a mouthpiece for Plato himself.

Socrates is one of history's most intriguing and controversial figures – for some, the rational person's substitute for Christ; for others, like Nietzsche, a 'typical criminal', a decadent 'buffoon who got himself taken seriously'.[23] His impact on his Athenian contemporaries was similarly dramatic and various. For some, like Plato and the brilliant demagogue and general, Alcibiades, an object of veneration and love; for others, notably those who condemned him to death in 399 BCE for corrupting youth and impiety towards the city's gods, a dangerous nihilist, despite his years of courageous military service. His feats-at-arms are not the only indication that this short, unprepossessing plebeian was something of an iron-man. He could stay up all night, drinking his friends under the table, and then go off, fresh as a daisy, for a hard day's work. More significantly, in relation to his moral views, he had an unusual degree of control over his appetites and emotions – managing, for example, to sleep chastely next to the beautiful, promiscuous Alcibiades, to whom he was strongly attracted.[24]

It is ironic, yet understandable, that Socrates should have been charged with the corruption of young minds. Ironic, because his purpose was to defend the possibility of moral knowledge against sceptics and relativists; understandable, because most of his opponents in the early dialogues are not these Sophists, but rather brash young men with a misplaced confidence in their understanding of various traditional virtues. Euthyphro and Laches, for example, are quickly brought to see that they do not know what piety and courage are. Moreover, instead of supplying them with answers, Socrates leaves things in suspense – hence his reputation as a 'sting-ray' who leaves his victims numb (*Meno* 80).[25] Indeed, he was keen to disown any knowledge of these matters himself, interpreting the Delphic oracle's judgement that he was the wisest of men to mean that he, unlike others, did not claim to know what he did not know (*Apology* 21). Unsurprisingly, then, and despite his criticisms of the Sophists, Socrates won the reputation of numbering among them.

The knowledge of the virtues which Socrates disowned was of rather a special kind. For one of his crucial assumptions is that not only he, but people in general, have a type of knowledge, however implicit and inchoate, of justice, piety, or whatever. They must do, otherwise there could be no explanation of their coming to realize that their clumsy attempts to characterize these notions were *mistaken*. How can a person recognize that it is wrong, say, to define piety as obedience to the will of the gods, unless he has some grasp of what piety is? What people, including Socrates himself, usually lack is a cogent definition of 'piety', 'justice', and the like – one which will reveal why the various things naturally recognized to be pious (or just) are so, and why they are virtues, always to be admired. Put differently, they lack an explicit grasp of a standard to which the many things called 'pious' or 'just' may be referred. This cannot be acquired by simply enumerating actual instances of some virtue, nor by generalizing from some empirical feature that such instances may display. Just actions, on occasions, may take the form of keeping promises, but justice cannot be defined as promise-keeping, since one can imagine cases where keeping a promise would be quite wrong.

More generally, the standards by which we judge things in the empirical world to have a certain feature cannot be derived from observation of that world. Take equality (of length, weight, etc.), for example. We speak of two sticks or two stones as equal, but 'these equal things are not the same as absolute equality' (*Phaedo* 74). It is only by reference to this absolute standard, never strictly instantiated in the observable world, that things can be judged more-or-less equal. The same applies when we judge faces to be beautiful or actions just. Nothing in this messy, unstable, confused world is absolutely beautiful or just: yet it is only in relation to an absolute standard that we can recognize that something is not beautiful or just, or that it approximates to one of these desiderata.

For Socrates, the ambition to attain explicit knowledge of these standards is no mere academic pastime. While a rough and ready ability to form 'true opinions' about virtues may suffice for much of the time, we often confront 'hard cases' where something more exact is required. Thus, it is a serious and difficult matter for Euthyphro, in the Dialogue that goes by his name, to decide whether piety allows him to prosecute his own father for manslaughter. More generally, Socrates believes that since the virtues must be beneficial to those who practise them – and since no one willingly does what he knows will harm him – there is clearly a premium on acquiring the appropriate knowledge or wisdom. The claim that 'virtue must be a sort of wisdom' is a depressing one if we believe that few people are disposed towards wisdom. But Socrates was, in this respect, an optimist, believing – as Plutarch was to put it – that 'no man is so surrounded and lapped about by fortune with the so-called good things of life that he is completely out of reach of philosophy', the route to wisdom.[26]

But nor did he underestimate the difficulties in the way of attaining wisdom. For one thing, those 'so-called good things of life', like sex, are only too likely to intrude into the impartial pursuit of knowledge. Moreover, such knowledge cannot consist in piecemeal understanding of the virtues, since each of these is a virtue only in so far as it is integral to the good life. 'Virtue is one', so that justice, piety and the rest 'are parts of it' (*Protagoras* 329). Wisdom, then, involves the considerable capacity to appreciate 'the unity of the virtues', an holistic vision of their respective places in the moral life. Socrates, we saw, said that he had not himself acquired the kind of knowledge of which he speaks, and tells us little about what it might consist in and about how we might achieve it. It is to these large lacunas that his most famous pupil was to address himself.

Plato and his Influence

Plato (427–347) came from the opposite end of the social spectrum to Socrates, and numbered among his aristocratic relatives some of 'The Thirty Tyrants' who briefly ruled Athens after the defeat by Sparta. Such connections may have put Plato in bad odour when democracy was re-established, but the main reason for his leaving Athens was probably the execution of Socrates on the order of the new democrats. During his years away, Plato made the first of three eventual visits to Sicily in the roles of royal tutor and political adviser. Legend has it that, on this first trip, he was enslaved by the king and ransomed with money later used by Plato to set up his famous Academy in Athens, where most of his subsequent teaching was conducted. Like Socrates, Plato was a man of strong passions, yet great self-control. He appears to have fallen in love with Dion, the man responsible for his visits to Sicily, and Dion's death affected Plato – and perhaps his philosophy, too – as strongly as that of Socrates many years earlier.[27]

Few would deny that Plato is the most influential figure in Western philosophy, even if they would want to moderate A. N. Whitehead's old saw that all subsequent philosophy has been footnotes to Plato.[28] It is not simply that he raised most of the issues about knowledge, reality, truth, good, beauty or government, which have become the staple of philosophical discussion. Nor that his are the first surviving writings in which such issues are given extended, and always interesting, treatment. In addition, he is the paradigmatic representative of a perennial, 'other worldly' tendency which has never ceased to attract or repel, the emotions as much as the intellect. In our own century, when that tendency, in its various manifestations, has for the most part repelled, Plato is the man you love to hate. For philosophers as various as Heidegger, Dewey, Wittgenstein and Derrida, a central target has been 'Platonism'.

That label suggests, of course, that Plato himself advanced a single, cohesive 'big' theory, something which many commentators would question. Indeed, much of the fascination exerted by Plato owes to the tensions and shifts in his views. (Compare the strikingly different political proposals urged in the *Republic* and the later *Laws*.) It is not quite that Plato is all things to all men, but as one commentator observes, it is as if there are two different philosophers, Pato and Lato – the one a virtual mystic, urging us to dwell on and in a spiritual, eternal world divorced from the grubby material one; the other, a hard-headed analyst, urging on us rational solutions to puzzles about meaning, mathematics and moral terms. The former 'would have been at home in a Zen Buddhist monastery'; the latter perhaps in Harvard or Oxford.[29] In what follows, therefore, it is important to bear in mind that I shall only be highlighting certain features of Plato's thought, and that both the selection of these features and my treatment of them are very different from those enjoined by other commentators.[30]

The Forms

Socrates, we saw, argued that we have some kind of knowledge, not derived from ordinary observation, of what justice, beauty, equality, etc. are; otherwise we could not recognize mistaken definitions of such notions. But of the nature of this knowledge already possessed and its objects, he says little. Plato's bold proposal is to take this terminology of knowledge *already* possessed and of *objects* of such knowledge quite literally.

> [B]efore we began to . . . use our . . . senses we must somewhere have acquired the knowledge that there is such a thing as absolute equality; otherwise we could never have realized . . . that all equal objects of sense . . . are only imperfect copies. (*Phaedo* 74)

When recognizing instances, or mistaken definitions, of justice, equality or whatever, we are therefore *recollecting*, however dimly, a previous acquaintance with certain 'things' or 'objects', of which these instances are 'copies'. Plato supports this proposal by stressing how teaching often gives the impression of merely drawing out from a pupil something he must already grasp – as with the slave boy in the *Meno*, who does not need to be told a geometrical theorem, merely 'reminded' of it by prompts.

Plato calls these recollected objects, these exemplars of which observable things are 'copies', the 'Forms' or 'Ideas' (*eíde*, sing. *eîdos*). He leaves us in no doubt that the Forms have their own 'grade of reality', and are not therefore mere psychological constructs or 'convenient fictions' (like 'perfect competition' in economic theory). 'Absolute beauty and goodness', for example, 'exist in the fullest possible sense' (*Phaedo* 77). Since our acquaintance with them precedes 'the use of our senses', the Forms cannot themselves be objects of an empirical or physical kind. In various places, Plato offers us imaginative 'myths' recounting how, in our pre-bodily existence, we have been escorted through the world of the Forms, 'a reality without colour or shape, intangible but utterly real' (*Phaedrus* 247).

With the existence of the Forms postulated, Plato provides them with further explanatory roles and ourselves, therefore, with further reasons for accepting their reality. How, for instance, do we explain something becoming more beautiful? It cannot be sufficient to point to various physical changes, for this would not explain why the changes are in the direction, specifically, of beauty. There is, in the final analysis, only 'one thing that makes the object beautiful', namely 'the association with it of absolute beauty' (*Phaedo* 100). There is one argument for the Forms often attributed to Plato which, however, he almost certainly does not deploy. The Forms, it gets said, are required by Plato to provide words with their meanings. 'Hair', for example, cannot mean this or that hair in particular: so it must stand for that which all hairs have in common – the Form of hair. But this cannot be Plato's view, for despite later reservations, he does not think that there is a Form associated with each general term. There is a Form of X only where, roughly speaking, Xs are the sort of things for which there is a standard, an ideal to which to approximate. Hair and mud, to use his own examples, do not have Forms. Some muds may be especially good for making mud-pies, but there is no standard for judging mud *per se*.[31] There is a Form of beauty, but this is not what beautiful things have in common, rather an exemplar which things somehow copy or 'participate' in.

Not only do the Forms exist 'in the fullest possible sense' but, says Plato, they have a greater degree of reality than things in the empirical world. Among the reasons for this, apparently, is their being both eternal and unchanging – though why these features should confer greater reality is hardly clear. (The thought seems sometimes to lurk that things are counted as real relative to our pursuits, and that it is the eternal and unchanging which engages the concerns of those with the highest pursuits.) Easier to grasp, perhaps, is his insistence that the reality of the Forms is *primary*, since everything else depends upon their existence. Empirical objects are what they are because they participate in the Forms (*Phaedo* 161), whereas the latter have no such dependence on anything outside of themselves. In the *Timaeus*, Plato explains the dependence as follows: in the beginning, there is a kind of formless tohu-bohu, called the 'receptacle', which then 'receives . . . the resemblances of all eternal beings [i.e. the Forms]' through the agency of a divine 'Craftsman' (*demiurgós*). The world as we experience it is then the result of an intelligent agent creating it in the likeness of ideal patterns – existing independently of him – which he apprehends.

These remarks show that Plato does not, as is sometimes charged, regard the empirical world as mere illusion. I may, of course, be *under* an illusion concerning it, failing to recognize that it is but a copy of the Forms, just as I may mistake a waxwork Jack the Ripper for Jack himself. Plato speaks of ordinary things 'hovering' between being and non-being (*Republic* 479). Relative to his reflection in a pool, Narcissus is real, but not relative to the Form of beauty – of which he is a copy in the way the reflection was of him. This 'hovering' status of ordinary things is one reason why they cannot be objects of true knowledge (*epistéme*), but only of 'opinions'. But there are other reasons for this, of a Heraclitean hue. These things are constantly changing or in flux, so it is impossible to fix their natures in definitive formulas of the type 'This is . . .'. Not only are the features of 'this' unstable, but 'this' will itself be 'in the process of change while [one] is making the assertion' (*Timaeus* 50). Such things, moreover, display opposite features – large relative to one standard, small relative to another, for example. So it is only of the Form of largeness that it can be said, without qualification and with certainty, that it is large (*Republic* 479).

Knowledge also involves a kind of understanding which creatures whose experience is confined to the empirical world – like those trapped in the famous Cave, whose contents are at best dim copies of the Forms (*Republic* 514ff) – cannot possess. (In the Cave allegory, prisoners are confined to watching the shadows cast by puppet-like figures. The analogy is with those of us confined to the sphere of mere 'opinions'.) For a person who truly knows can explain what he knows (*Phaedo* 76) – which is beyond the capacity of someone who merely has a true opinion about something since, ignorant of the Forms, he is unable to grasp why the thing is as it is. He must know the relevant Form because a crucial aspect to understanding what something is consists in knowing 'how it was best for that thing to be' (*Phaedo* 97). We do not understand what it is to be a man, say, unless we appreciate the standard for being a perfect man – and this is to have knowledge of a Form.

Indeed, we do not have complete knowledge of the Forms themselves unless we grasp how each of them contributes to, or is an ingredient in, a perfect whole. (This is Plato's twist to Socrates' doctrine of 'the unity of the virtues'.)

Hence, the epitome of knowledge is a grasp of that Form of Forms, the Form of the good – that 'source not only of the intelligibility of the objects of knowledge, but also of their being and reality' (*Republic* 509). With a 'vision' of this Form, the philosopher's ascent from the Cave – from the shadows on the wall to the things that cast them, from these to the Forms of which they in turn are copies, and from these Forms to the good of the whole in which they figure – is complete.

We are now in a position to appreciate several of Plato's replies to the 'scientistic' account sketched earlier. The only ingredient in that account with which Plato has any sympathy is the idea that judgements about the sensible world have a truth which is at best relative to perceivers. Sense experience cannot furnish objective knowledge of reality, but for Plato this is not, of course, because that reality is a conglomeration of atoms beyond the reach of perception. That conglomeration would at best furnish the matter, the 'receptacle', for the 'Craftsman's' modelling of the world on the Forms – and it is these which constitute the highest 'grade of reality'. Nor, finally, is the world devoid of purpose and value. It is, in fact, 'the fairest of creations', being a copy of those ideal exemplars, the Forms (*Timaeus* 29). Everything in creation, moreover, and indeed the Forms themselves, are finally intelligible only by reference to that supreme Form of the good which, like the sun, illuminates them.

The Soul

Since some of us, the true philosophers, can attain full knowledge of the Forms which the rest of us only dimly 'recollect', the question arises as to how such an attainment is possible. This question divides into three. What kind of beings are we that make this attainment possible? What kind of acquaintance and relation must we have with the Forms? What is required in practical terms – educational ones, say – for attaining such knowledge? The short answer to the first question is that we must be creatures who possess immaterial souls. Since the Forms are immaterial and we are acquainted with them prior to being equipped with the bodily senses, then we too must be, or contain, something immaterial. 'The theory that our soul exists even before it enters the body surely stands or falls with the soul's possession of the ultimate standard of reality' (*Phaedo* 92). This bare claim is embellished, in ways not required by the argument, with doctrines inherited from Pythagoras, and probably imported from further east. The soul not merely predates its association with a body, but survives bodily death and is reborn in another body, human or animal, depending on its performance in the previous incarnation.

Plato, then, is a dualist, but of what kind, exactly, is unclear, since he offers different accounts of the relation between soul and body. Sometimes he speaks of the two as entirely different in kind, but elsewhere allows that the soul can be 'permeated by the corporeal', 'ingrained' with it through 'constant association', or 'fastened' to it as with a rivet (*Phaedo* 81ff). In some of the dialogues, moreover, the soul is not a simple, seamless unity, but consists of different 'parts', some of which, if not exactly physical in nature, are at any rate especially 'weighed down' by the body. Thus the soul is compared to 'a winged charioteer and his team acting together' – the charioteer being the rational part of the soul which prevents the 'horses' of 'appetite' and 'spirit' (*thumós*) from dragging it down from the world of the Forms to that of the body and the senses (*Phaedrus* 246ff). (*Thumós* is barely translatable. A man of 'spirit' displays pugnaciousness, indignation, and courage in defence of his honour – qualities admirable enough in a Homeric hero, and antipathetic to sensuality, but not always conducive to the life of reason.) In a similar tripartite division of the soul in the *Republic*, the 'just' person is defined as the one whose reason keeps the other elements of the soul in their proper place, so that there is no 'civil war' among them (441ff).

As these metaphors suggest, the parts of the soul form a hierarchy, and it is with the higher, rational part that a person is properly identified. On Plato's telling, at least, it is because his rational part will survive that, in the hours before drinking the hemlock, Socrates knows that *he* will survive his body, that 'sepulchre', 'prison' and 'contamination'. Plato obviously had a sense, as vivid as a Calvinist's, of the soul beleaguered by the body and its insistent demands – a sense at some odds, perhaps, with the ephemeral, twilight reality accorded to physical things elsewhere in Plato's discussion.[32]

Why, puritanism apart, should we identify ourselves so resolutely, however, with the soul, or rather just one part of it, given that a 'living being' is a 'combination of soul and body' (*Phaedrus* 246)? A sensible person will recognize that whatever he or she wants out of life – happiness, pleasure – requires self-discipline and self-control. For unless order is imposed upon the pleasures, they are liable to cancel one another out. The delights of getting drunk and of mathematics, for example, do not mix well. So what a person really wants is not to be 'mastered by pleasure' – for that is to 'act beneath oneself' – but, instead, to 'be his own master' (*Protagoras* 357f). But, as that terminology implies, it is with the self that does the mastering that a person identifies himself – and not with the desires he controls, or gets controlled by. He is the rational self that he 'acts beneath' when impulse and appetite take over.

There is, though, a deeper reason why a person's true being is the rational part of the soul, one that raises the question of the soul's relation to the Forms. It is, of course, the rational soul – and not the two 'horses' liable to drag it down – that can truly understand the Forms. It can do this precisely because it is 'akin to reality . . . and unites with it' (*Republic* 490). The rational soul is of a 'similar, kindred nature' to the Forms, so that it can become 'assimilated' with them. Like them, it is eternal, immaterial, invisible and good. Now since the Forms have a higher 'grade of reality' than the empirical world, it follows that the part of the soul which is most akin to them, and least embroiled in the physical world through appetite, is its most real part – the true 'I'. How the final meeting between the soul and the Forms takes place, Plato does not explain, except in allegorical terms. But it is in this idea of 'kinship', of an affinity of substance, that we find Plato's alternative to the naturalists' accommodation of man to his world. For them, human beings are integral parts of the world because they too are composed of matter. For Plato, human beings – their rational souls, that is – are also integrated into reality through the 'kindred nature' they share with the Forms.

If Plato tells us little about 'the final meeting', he has a lot to say about our preparation for it – about the political and educational system which prepares the philosopher for full knowledge. These are the great themes of his most famous work, the *Republic*.

Politics, Education and Love

After his diatribes against the 'contaminating' influence of worldly indulgences, and his insistence that the proper goal is knowledge of a realm distinct from the everyday world, one might expect Plato to teach that the way of the philosopher is one of solitary, yogic detachment. After all, does not 'the philosopher's occupation consist precisely in the freeing . . . of soul from body'? (*Phaedo* 67). Yet, austere and elevated though it may be, the philosopher's way is not one of disengagement from the world. His engagement in it is threefold: political, educational and erotic.

Despite its title, the *Republic* is not directly a work on politics, but an examination of 'the just soul'. The State is discussed, in the first instance, only to provide a useful analogy, for if we can 'find justice on a larger scale in the larger entity', that should help us identify justice in the soul (368). The just State, it emerges, is one in which each class in the community – philosopher-kings or guardians, auxiliaries (soldiers, roughly), and workers – 'does its own thing', practising its specific virtue (wisdom, courage, and discipline or temperance, respectively). This is because justice is a matter of 'keeping what is properly one's own and doing one's own job' (433). The soul has three parts – reason, 'spirit' and appetite – corresponding to the classes in the State, and the specific virtue of each part is the same as that of the corresponding class. The just soul is one in which each part performs its proper function. Thus, the 'charioteer' of reason must rule over 'spirit' and appetite as do the philosopher-kings over the other classes.

Political considerations soon come to occupy Plato for different reasons. The ideal State is not simply a metaphor for the just soul, but a precondition for the philosopher's 'occupation'. No individual, not even the budding philosopher, is 'self-sufficient' (369). Unfortunately, 'there's no existing form of society good enough for the philosophic nature, with the result that it gets warped' (497). Institution of the just State, therefore, is as much for the philosopher's sake as for that of the whole community. The 'philosophic nature' cannot flourish, for example, where there is social instability and competition for wealth and women. The republic will be organized, therefore, to prevent such disruptions. For instance, the guardians are not allowed to own wealth.

But philosophers are not to be contemplative idlers, kept at the public purse, for they have an obligation to *rule*. Plato is well aware that people whose sights are set on the 'higher grade of reality' may find the messy business of government an unwelcome distraction. The allegory of the Cave is as much concerned with the problem of getting the enlightened philosopher to go back down into the Cave – to instruct others – as with his earlier ascent out from it. It is the philosopher's duty to return partly because he owes his privileged education to the State. More important, perhaps, someone who knows the Forms, and above all the Form of the good, will 'love' them. But to love them entails the desire that the everyday world should approximate to them as far as possible. Thus, the philosopher who knows what justice is will feel bound to contribute towards the institution of justice on earth. This he can do only by playing his part in the government of the just State.

There is another reason why 'the philosophic nature' cannot flourish in isolation from social institutions. It needs to be *educated*. (Plato is perhaps insufficiently perturbed by the chicken-and-egg problem of what comes first – the republic, which educates its rulers, or the rulers, who are required for the republic to function.) Even if the final stage of wisdom is a 'mystic vision' of the Form of the good, this presupposes a long (thirty-five years!) preparation. A platonic education, as one might guess, is not a matter of stuffing heads with factual knowledge. Indeed, 'we must reject the conception of education professed by those who say that they can put into the mind knowledge that was not there before'. Just as eyes which are used to the dark must be 'turned from darkness to light', so 'the mind . . . must be turned away from the world of change until its eye can bear to look straight at . . . the brightest of all realities . . . the good' (518). This is to be achieved in two main stages: first, through a kind of 'character training' whereby the novitiate is taught the mental and physical self-discipline which arm him against the siren-calls of the senses and of fashionable opinion. Second, through gradually inducting him into the more abstract intellectual disciplines – mathematics and philosophy –

which acquaint him with a realm of objects increasingly remote from the mere 'reflections' of reality encountered in the 'darker' world of change.

There is little in the puritanical and rigorously intellectual education recommended in the *Republic* which prepares the reader of Plato for a third dimension of the philosopher's engagement with the world and his fellows. This is the erotic dimension. In an amazing speech from the *Symposium*, Socrates endorses the claim of a mysterious priestess, Diotima, that 'supreme knowledge' is the natural goal of a process which begins with a man's 'feeling of love for boys' (211). In the *Phaedrus*, this same knowledge originates with the 'heaven-sent madness' experienced by a man for the boy he loves. For Socrates, Plato and many other Greeks, incidentally, it is only young men who are the proper objects of a mature man's love (*éros*).[33]

Do these claims recant the position in the *Republic*? Or is Plato arguing that there are two quite different routes, the intellectual and the erotic, each of them self-sufficient, towards knowledge of the Form of the good? Both suggestions suffer, arguably, from exaggerating the differences between the *Republic* and the other dialogues just mentioned. This is not to deny that, in the latter, Plato seems to be attributing a role, both in education and in the good life, to certain emotions missing or more muted in the former. (It has been speculated that the change was due to Plato's own experience of falling in love with Dion of Sicily.)[34] Still, there are important points of continuity.

It should be emphasized, first, that despite a little 'touching in the gymnasium', the erotic love spoken of by Plato is chaste – so his point is certainly not the *Kama-Sūtra* one (see pp. 47 f.) that sexual virtuosity is a means to higher things. The crucial consideration relates to the doctrine of 'recollection'. We come to know the Forms by recollecting our acquaintance with them in a prenatal existence. This requires 'aids to recollection', which in the more 'intellectual' passages of the *Meno* or the *Republic* are things like diagrams, reminding us of, say, perfect equality. In the *Phaedrus* the primary symbol of, or spur to the recollection of, the Form of beauty is the beauty of a young man. Thus the 'mad' lover is 'reminded by the sight of beauty on earth of the true beauty' (249). For Plato, it seems, it matters little whether the supreme Form is described as the Form of the good or as that of beauty. (Indeed, *kalón* can mean either 'beautiful' or 'good'.) The good or beauty is that harmonious whole within which other Forms have their place and value, and which is reflected in the visible world that 'copies' it. The philosophic lover will recognize that what he really appreciates in the boy is a harmony or symmetry shared by many other things, and not only physical ones. It is akin, for example, to the harmony which constitutes justice, whether in the State or the soul. Having thus ascended 'from one instance of physical beauty to . . . all, then from physical beauty to moral beauty', it remains to pass 'from moral beauty to the beauty of knowledge, until . . . one arrives at the supreme knowledge [of] absolute beauty' (*Symposium* 211). The boy in the gymnasium was, after all, but a preview and a reminder of a good and beautiful harmony, the love of which is the source of all our other aspirations.

While our ultimate ambition must be emancipation from the visible world, this is not, then, a place in which we are 'strangers', and from which we must stand entirely aloof. This is not because, as for the naturalists, we are of the same stuff as it. Rather it is because this visible world is a reflection of the real world with which our souls enjoy a kinship, and because the way to emancipation takes us through an engagement with our fellow beings – as participants in a political system, in an educational enterprise, and in adventures of the heart.

• 4 Aristotle •

If Plato is the West's most footnotable philosopher, Aristotle (384–322) is its most notable thinker, for his compass far exceeded the sphere of philosophy. It reduces his achievement to describe him as mastering the disciplines of logic, biology, zoology, physics, rhetoric, poetics and political science, since it was he who invented them. It is inconceivable that anyone should emulate that achievement, for however radically someone might revise the boundaries of the disciplines, these would still be revisions within Aristotle's framework. The more scientific of his enquiries have, of course, been superseded, but one should recall that the logic and biology of the man who, for the mediaevals, was not only 'The Philosopher' but 'The Scientist', stood virtually unchallenged until the modern era. His contributions in these areas will not be our concern. Those which will be – in metaphysics, philosophical psychology, ethics and theology – are as alive for us as they were for Aristotle's contemporaries.

Early bibliophiliac misadventures ensured that only about a fifth of Aristotle's output has survived, mainly in the form of lecture notes from his later years, when teaching at the Lyceum, which he founded in Athens.[35] Although he had been a pupil at Plato's Academy, Aristotle came from that growing power in Greece, Macedon, where his father was a royal physician. In what must have been fascinating sessions, Aristotle tutored Alexander the Great, who repaid his teacher by instructing the subjects of his empire to furnish the philosopher with data germane to his zoological researches. Little is known about Aristotle the man, beyond the thinness of his legs and the fastidiousness of his dress. But he is reputed to have been witty and dignified, with not a little hauteur, 'admirable rather than amiable' and not perhaps unlike the men held up for our esteem in his ethical writings.[36]

Readers coming from Plato to Aristotle experience a change of climate. The style is more technical and dry, unleavened by allegories, myths and social chit-chat. They find, too, an unplatonic appeal not only to the 'authority' of sense-experience (*Metaphysics* 981),[37] but to the value of everyday opinions. Everything seems more 'down to earth', 'solider' as W. B. Yeats put it – an impression famously captured by Raphael in *The School of Athens*, where Plato points towards the heavens, Aristotle towards the ground. Scholarship has emulated art, for recent opinion has had it that Aristotle's was a gradual 'movement from otherworldliness towards . . . a conviction that the "form" and meaning of the world is . . . embedded in its "matter" '.[38] But this image is questionable, perhaps underplaying Aristotelian themes uncongenial to modern philosophical sympathies. For example, most recent discussion of Aristotle on 'the good life' has focused on the social virtues, at the expense of what is, for him, 'the highest form of activity' – divinely inspired contemplation. The Aristotle of the next few pages has a somewhat more platonic hue than Raphael and recent scholars give him.[39]

Only somewhat, however, for Aristotle is certainly critical of Plato. We might see him as endeavouring to forge accounts of reality, the soul and the good life, which steer between the opposing excesses of Platonism and the 'scientistic' naturalism discussed earlier. 'All men by nature desire to know' (*Met.* 980) and understanding is man's true goal. Moreover, the world – natural and moral – lends itself to such understanding. The possibility exists, then, of our making sense of an intelligible order. Plato's error was to have placed this order outside of natural reality, so that emancipation from the physical, a separation of soul from body, is required in order to grasp it. The error of 'scientism', though, is the worse one of depicting the world, ourselves in-cluded, as so much senseless matter. Since there could then be no objective purposes discoverable in nature or man, the good life could not be one of enquiry and discovery. Naturalism and Platonism, in their different ways, preclude the possibility, then, of a person attaining, in this world, the goal towards which his natural 'desire to know' propels him. That would be a cruel irony which Aristotle is unwilling to accept.

Explanation, Form and *Télos*

Aristotle's view of the world emerges in his answers to two large questions, an explanatory and an ontological one. The first looks for the explanation of those regular changes which occur 'always or for the most part', like a plant's growth or the building of a house. The second asks which are the most basic entities, the 'primary substances', on which everything else depends. The two questions are closely related. On the one hand, explanations of changes eventually refer us to the 'causes of that which is *qua* thing-that-is [i.e. primary substance]' (*Met.* 1002). On the other, we only 'have knowledge of a thing when we have found its primary causes' (*Physics* 184). Indeed, as we will see, Aristotle's answers to the two questions are the same. To know what there fundamentally *is*, is also to know what explains why things happen as they do.

'Change' is used widely by Aristotle, to include something coming into being and passing away and also, as a special case, a thing's persisting for a time in an unaltered state. He defines change as 'the actualization of what is potentially' (*Physics* 201). Unpacked, this is much more than the truism that something must be able to become what it becomes. But even left packed, it provides his answer to those who wanted to challenge commonsense beliefs about change. To Parmenides, who denied that change ever occurs; to Heraclitus, for whom change is so constant that nothing lasts long enough for us to say of it that *it* changes (see pp. 96f.); and to the atomists, for whom nothing new ever comes into being, since all change is mere rearrangement of 'atoms'. To deflect these challenges, Aristotle must show that, during change, a dog, say, remains in a sense the same, and in a sense not. If there is no sense in which it is the same, then it cannot be *that* dog which changes; while if it is the same in every sense, the dog has not *changed*. The solution is that the dog becomes *actually* what it had only *potentially* been. Even the bronze turned into a statue *was* a statue before the sculptor got to it – but only, of course, potentially.

To unpack Aristotle's definition of 'change', we need to look at his doctrine of 'the four causes':

> According to one way of speaking, that out of which . . . a thing comes to be is called a cause; for example, the bronze . . . of a statue . . . According to another, the form . . . is a cause . . . – thus the cause of an octave is the ratio of two to one . . . Again, there is the primary source of the change . . .: for example . . . the father is a cause of the child . . . And again, a thing may be a cause as the end. That is what something is for, as health might be what a walk is for. (*Physics* 194)

This foursome was later dubbed the 'material', 'formal', 'efficient', and 'final' causes. Generations of critics have accused Aristotle of using 'cause' in an illegitimately wide way, for surely bronze, ratio or health do not *cause* statues to be sculpted, octaves to be sounded or walks to be walked. The criticism is absurd, for Aristotle was Greek not English, and wrote not of 'cause' but of *aitía*. It is not he who is guilty of misusing 'cause', but his critics of poorly translating *aitía*. For Aristotle a 'cause' is what is cited in answer to questions beginning 'On account of what . . . ?' He is clearly right that people offer answers of all four kinds. Why, or on account of what, was Pavarotti's last note a top C? 'Because when air is set vibrating by the singer's . . .'; 'Because it was in a certain ratio to middle C, and you know what middle C is, don't you?'; 'Because that is what he was trying to produce, and he had the breath, and . . .'; 'Because it made a fitting climax to the recital'. Each answer, in an appropriate context, is in place.

Reference to a doctrine of 'four causes' is misleading for another reason. For Aristotle, the 'material' cause is, in the final analysis, not explanatory at all, while the other three 'coincide'. 'What a thing is [its form], and what it is for, are one and the same, and that from which the change originates is the same in form as these' (*Physics* 198). Material causes drop out of the final picture because matter as such, though it must be 'recognized by abstract thought',[40] is nothing intelligible to us. A dog's life is explained by its nature, and its 'form has a much better claim than the matter to be called nature' (*Physics* 193). Admittedly, to have its carnivorous nature, the dog must have material parts like teeth. But it is the form or function of these parts – their grinding of food, say – not the stuff they are made of, which explains the dog's behaviour. Doubtless, the dog, its teeth and everything else are finally composed of some formless 'prime' matter which somehow 'supports' form and function. But this 'somehow' and the 'prime' matter itself are beyond our understanding, and cannot therefore be invoked in explanations. Here, incidentally, is Aristotle's answer to those who hold that reality is nothing but matter. Not only is there something non-material – form – but formless matter is explanatorily useless.

The 'coinciding' of the remaining 'causes' goes in two stages. First, Aristotle argues that a thing's 'form . . . is an end, . . . the cause as that for which' (*Physics* 199). Then he argues that its 'primary source', the 'efficient cause', is also this form-*cum*-end. Both stages draw on his distinction between actuality and potentiality, and are best understood, initially, in connection with artifacts. The form or essence of a house – the 'what-it-is-to-be-a-house' – is to be a home and shelter, which is, of course, what a house is *for*, its end or function. The changes it undergoes during the building, when only potentially a house, have to be understood by reference to what it will actually become. But what of the man who builds it? Does not he figure in the explanation? Indeed he does, but only as a *builder* – as someone, that is, who has the form of houses in his mind. So it is still the end for which the house exists, present as potential in the builder's mind, which explains how it was built. From the drawing-board to the day of moving-in, there is a single process – from a form which is only potential to one fully actualized in a functioning building.

Aristotle generalizes this account, for like artifacts 'nature is for something' too (*Physics* 198). Ducks develop webbed feet in order to swim, for swimming belongs to a duck's end or *télos*. In general, plants and animals develop from seeds, barring accidents, so as to manifest, in maturity, their essential natures or forms. To know what duckhood is, is to know what normal ducks grow into.

In their case, too, what they are potentially coincides with what they will actually become. And just as the builder had the form of the house in his mind, so the parental seed contains the form which will later be fully manifest – so that, once again, the 'primary source' is form-*cum*-end.

There are, of course, crucial differences between artifacts and nature. Unlike the pile of bricks which grows into a house for the sake of those who will live in it, ducklings do not grow into ducks for the sake of anything beyond themselves. Whereas building requires conscious planning, no one designs ducks or controls their development, since they contain their principle of change 'within themselves'. Aristotle's teleological, or goal-directed, vision of nature, then, is not that of later theologians, who thought of nature as designed by God, to serve His purposes or those of his favourite – Man. Aristotle's ducks are not like Chrysippus' fleas, put on earth to wake us from our idle slumbers.

So Aristotle's account is not subject to the criticisms perennially levelled against 'designer' teleology. On the other hand, his teleogical framework is deadly serious, and not a mere *façon de parler*, replaceable by a purely mechanical account of natural life in terms, say, of natural selection. He was well-acquainted with the 'Darwinians' of his own day, and dismissed them. It cannot, he believes, be 'automatic' or the 'outcome of luck or coincidence' that species are as they are (*Physics* 198–9).

Form and Substance

Aristotle's second main question concerned the fundamental furniture of the world – the 'primary substances'. 'Substance' is, in fact, a tendentious translation of the term *ousía* ('being'), for it suggests, contrary to Aristotle's intentions, some kind of stuff. We are first introduced to the term through a grammatical criterion. 'That which is called a substance . . . primarily . . . is that which is [not] said of a subject' (*Categories* 2). Thus, in 'X is red', red cannot be a substance since it is being said, or predicated, of X. But it is soon made clear that this grammatical distinction is related to one in the hierarchy of beings, for what is predicated of X *depends* on X. 'If the primary substances did not exist it would be impossible for any of the other things to exist' (*Cat.* 2). My complexion, smile and charm, for example, cannot exist independently of my face, which in turn depends upon me. Quite generally, 'all other things are said to be' only in virtue of their connection with substances. Hence, in the final analysis, 'what being is, is just the question, what is substance?' (*Met.* 1028). What *is* it, then? First, as we have seen, substances must be 'independent' in the sense that they, unlike my smile, do not presuppose the existence of anything else. Second, they must be 'definite' – that is, capable of being defined and fully understood. For substances are 'primary' not only in the order of being, but of knowledge. Nothing would be knowable unless substances were, and it is Aristotle's conviction that some things *are* knowable.

Aristotle's early answer to the question 'what things are substances?' was particular objects, such as this individual man or horse (*Cat.* 2). But in the later, labyrinthine discussion of the *Metaphysics*, a different answer is generally preferred. 'Each primary and self-subsistent thing is one and the same as its essence . . . By form I mean the essence of each thing and its primary substance' (1032). So it is no longer I and my horse which are substances, but the human and equine forms or essences. (For Aristotle, there is a single form for each species.) Why this departure from the original and, it would seem, 'robustly commonsensical' answer?[41] Because a horse, say, is a 'whole' or 'composite' of matter and form, and hence dependent upon these for its existence. The individual horse, therefore, does not enjoy the required 'independence' which substances must have. Not only that, but it is insufficiently definite and knowable, since an individual horse has countless features unknown to us. Moreover it is 'composed' of matter, which is, as such, beyond our ken. So the horse fails to meet either of Aristotle's criteria for substance.

Forms or essences, it is alleged, meet both. But this raises some awkward questions. For one thing, we seem able to describe something in terms of its form or essence, as in 'Man is a rational animal' – in which case what becomes of Aristotle's insistence that substance cannot be predicated of anything? Aristotle's answer to this question is opaque,[42] as indeed it is to the more crucial one of whether substances *qua* forms can any longer be regarded as 'independent' and basic. A form was explained to us as an end towards which concrete things, like animals or houses, approach – as a potential which becomes manifest in such things. So does not a form depend upon the things in which, so to speak, it is embedded? Aristotle himself, after all, objected to Plato's Forms on the grounds of their being 'something apart from the individuals' and 'useless', therefore, in explaining the 'comings-to-be' of things (*Met.* 1033). This was not his only objection, for he accuses Plato's doctrine of generating an infinite regress. If the Form of man is both what all men have in common and an exemplar – an 'ideal man', as it were – there would have to be another Form, a 'third man', constituting the common essence of ordinary men and that exemplar – and so on *ad infinitum* (see *Met.* 1038–9).

Despite these objections to Plato, Aristotle does think there are some forms which are changeless, eternal and 'without matter' (*Met.* 1071). Moreover, these are 'prior' and the study of them is 'primary philosophy', understood as the examination of substance. The implication is that materially embedded forms are 'honorary' substances, counted as such only through their analogy or relation to 'prior', matter-free, substance (*Met.* 1026). Aristotle's other name for 'primary philosophy' is 'theology'. But to pursue the clue that this offers, we should first consider his account of another very special substance – the human soul.

The Soul

A living creature, we have seen, has both a body and a form – an end towards which its natural development tends. Does it also have a soul? Aristotle's answer is 'No' – not because it has no soul, but because its soul *is* this form. For him, as for Greeks generally, the soul is what gives life to a body. Since it is form or end which gives life, 'the soul must, then, be substance *qua* form of a natural body which has life potentially' (*On the Soul* 412). Soul stands to body in somewhat the way sight stands to the eye. For seeing is what makes an eye an eye, explaining what it is for and why it operates as it does. Among the disanalogies, however, is this: in advanced creatures, at least, the soul is complex, a 'principle of [various] powers . . . the faculties of nutrition, percep-tion, thought, and . . . movement' (*Soul* 413). At one end of the scale, a plant's soul is simply the faculty to utilize nutriment; at the other end, the human soul is a set of faculties which include all those enjoyed by lower creatures *plus* the capacity for intellectual thought.

This account seems to provide Aristotle with a satisfying way of steering between the materialism of Democritus and the dualism of Plato. These are wrong answers to a question which should never have been posed, for 'we should not ask whether the soul and body are one' or two any more than we should ask this of sight and the eye (*Soul* 412). The soul is form or end, and not therefore an object which is either material ('round atoms') or immaterial. Soul, it seems, is neither distinct from body nor part of it: rather, it is a set of capacities which are realized through physical activity.

So satisfying has this account appeared to some recent philosophers that they regard it as the prototype of such twentieth-century philosophies of mind as behaviourism and functionalism, both of which emphasize the necessity of physical criteria for mental concepts (see ch. 10, sect. 4). Unfortunately for such attempts to conscript Aristotle into modern philosophy of mind, an obstacle emerges at just the point, ironically, where he begins to speak about *mind* (or intellect (*noûs*)). For 'it is reasonable', he writes, that this 'should not be mixed with body', and 'it seems to be a different kind of soul [that] can exist separately' (*Soul* 428 and 413).

His initial argument, here, refers back to his account of sense-perception, where he explained that 'the sense is that which can receive perceptible forms without their matter, as wax receives the imprint of the ring without the iron or gold' (*Soul* 424). The soul somehow receives the shape, say, of something looked at without, as in the case of nutrition, absorbing the thing's matter. Now the very structure of the eye which equips it to receive the forms of shape and colour precludes it from receiving others, such as tastes and smells. If the mind or intellect, therefore, were like perception and exercised through some physical organ, we should expect the range of forms about which it can think to be similarly limited. But it is not, for *any* form can be an object of thought. Mind, it seems, is not constrained by body in the manner of the senses.

Perhaps this argument can be dismissed as a symptom of Aristotle's primitive physiology. Had he lived today, perhaps he would have recognized in the brain an 'organ' with a versatility far beyond that of the eye or nose. But Aristotle goes on to say two things which would be harder to accommodate within a physicalistic picture of mind. First, he speaks of the mind *becoming* the objects of which it has knowledge. 'Actual knowledge is identical with its object' (*Soul* 431). This means that the mind becomes one with forms. These are the so-called 'intelligible' forms. Whereas it is perception which discerns the perceptible forms of flesh, such as temperature, it is mind which discerns 'what it is to be flesh', the intelligible form or essence (*Soul* 429). Prior to knowing forms, mind is a mere 'nothing', a bare capacity. What Aristotle means here is hardly clear,[43] but it is difficult to avoid the conclusion that the mind is indeed 'unmixed with body'. For since the intelligible forms are non-material, and since the knowing mind becomes identical with these, it too must surely be non-material.

Worse is to come, for the assimilation of Aristotle's account to modern ones, when he introduces us to 'another' intellect – so-called 'active' mind – beyond that so far discussed. For this intellect is 'distinct . . . and unmixed . . . In separation it is . . . immortal and eternal' (*Soul* 430). The idea seems to be that just as the body requires the soul to become 'animated' – or as colours require light in order to become 'actual' – so the 'passive' mind requires the aid of 'active' mind in order for its capacity for knowledge to be exercised. Something is required for what is, after all, a mere 'nothing', a bare capacity, to be galvanized into intellectual activity. In *On the Soul*, the remarks on 'active' mind are terse and opaque, but they are similar to ones made in another work on the being which Aristotle calls 'God'. Before we turn to those, it will help to consider the implications he draws for the good life from his view of the human soul.

The Virtues

The *Nicomachean Ethics*, many hold, is the greatest work ever written on practical philosophy. If interest in Aristotle's views lagged during those recent years when moral philosophers confined themselves to 'clarifying the logic of moral language', they are now as intensely debated as ever. Aristotle especially appeals to those who argue that the proper moral ambition is neither, at one extreme, to cultivate a pure 'inner' self nor, at another, to promote the universal good of man, but to live responsibly among one's fellows in whose practices and traditions one shares.[44] Whether it is right to enlist Aristotle on the side of this cause is another matter.

The central topic of the work is *eudaimonía*, usually though, as we shall see, misleadingly translated as 'happiness'. For it is this which provides the answer to the question 'what is the highest of all practical goods?' (1095). *Eudaimonía* is the supreme good since it is the one thing we 'want for its own sake', and which explains our seeking of other goods, like health and money. That *eudaimonía* is not happiness – though it typically brings happiness in its train – is clear from Aristotle's denial that children and animals can enjoy it (1009). It consists, rather, in 'living well or doing well', in certain deliberative activities (*práxeis*), and not in any psychological state which results from these (1095ff). A child or its dog cannot be *eudaímon* since it cannot engage in these mature, intelligent activities. The idea that the good life is one of deliberative activities done with the aim of performing them well or excellently, is not a vacuous one. It serves to exclude certain rival conceptions. The good life cannot, for example, consist simply in 'hanging loose' or in the passive contentment of lotus-eaters. Still, the questions of what the relevant activities are and their criterion of excellence are obviously invited.

Just as we can only know whether an eye is 'doing well' if we know its function, seeing, so we can only identify a human being's appropriate activities by 'grasping the function (*érgon*) of man' (1097). This 'function' is not some end-state which people consciously or otherwise aim at: rather, it is man's form or essence, the 'what-it-is-to-be-a-man'. Now we already know what this is from Aristotle's account of the soul. What distinguishes humans from other creatures is mind or intellect and the associated capacity to reason. So 'the function of man is an activity of the soul in accordance with . . . a rational principle' (1098). This quickly yields Aristotle's considered definition of *eudaimonía*: 'an activity of the soul in accordance with perfect virtue' (1102) – for 'virtue' (*areté*) is precisely the excellence belonging to rational activities well conducted.

The virtues are divided into two classes – the 'intellectual' ones, discussed only late in the book, and the 'ethical' ones. A list of these 'ethical' virtues (*ethikaí areteí*) strikes most readers as a peculiarly mixed bag – the platonic trio of courage, temperance and justice, but also friendship, proper ambition, righteous indignation, wit, and several more. But this is because readers, misled by the usual translation into 'moral virtues', are expecting a list of what we now think of under that label – roughly speaking, dispositions to discharge our obligations to others, by keeping promises and the like. But the Greek expression means 'excellences of character', which are, for Aristotle, dispositions towards just those activities whereby man fulfils his function as a rational being. One may still wonder why some of the items on his list are there. Some, perhaps, reflect the times in and for which Aristotle was writing. Thus the virtue of *megalopsuchía* ('great-souledness'), exhibited by the man whose 'gait is measured, . . . voice deep, . . . and speech unhurried' (1125), sounds like a requirement for an Athenian gentleman – even if, as one Scotsman puts it, such a man is also 'very nearly an English gentleman'.[45] Other items, more interestingly, reflect Aristotle's robust sense that leading the good life requires favourable circumstances. There are 'fine deeds' which can only be done, for example, 'by the help of friends' (1099) – hence the value of a capacity for friendship. More generally, 'man is a political animal' (*Politics* 1253) – one whose nature can only flourish as a member of a society, a *pólis* – who must, therefore, possess the accomplishments which make him an acceptable citizen.

For Aristotle himself, each virtue on the list deserves its place as a disposition to *rational* activities (and feelings). This is because a virtue is a 'purposive disposition, lying in a mean (*méson*) . . . determined by a rational principle . . . a mean between two kinds of vice, one of excess and the other of deficiency' (1107). Courage, for instance, is a virtue since it 'hits the mean' between rashness and cowardice (or, as Aristotle should have said, excessive caution).[46] 'Hit the mean!', it should be stressed, does not counsel moderation and compromise. In some circumstances, a person should be *very* courageous or indignant. Rather, it enjoins us to act and feel in ways that are appropriate in the circumstances. A virtuous person should be willing to risk something, but not his life, for a good, yet minor, cause. To risk nothing or everything is out of proportion, and hence irrational.

It is understandable why Aristotle should be attractive, so far, to those who view the good life as the exercise of the practical virtues through rational participation in the social activities which bind a person to his fellows. But just as Aristotle's account of the soul turned out to be less 'modern' than at first sight, so there emerges an obstacle, in the final chapter of the *Nicomachean Ethics*, to invoking him in support of the above view of the good life. For we suddenly read that 'contemplation is . . . the highest form of activity', so that 'contemplative activity (*theoría*)' is 'perfect *eudaimonía*' (1177). More surprising still, perhaps, Aristotle makes next to no effort to relate this supreme, intellectual virtue to the 'ethical' ones. Certainly his view is not the yogic one that living ethically is simply useful training for the contemplative life. Nor that there are two kinds of human being, suited to one or other variety of virtue. Some conclude that he does not make the effort since any attempt to marry the two kinds of virtue must be 'broken-backed'.[47] If devotion to contemplation really is the ideal, then there is simply no place for a distracting concern for the 'ethical'. For the contemplative, the demands of friendship, magnanimity, justice and the like merely intrude. If this is the right conclusion, the problem it identifies is not, of course, one for Aristotle alone. For it is one faced by anyone who promotes an ideal of life that is seemingly remote from ethical concerns, but who also insists on the importance of ethical behaviour.

Whether or not the conclusion is right, we have yet to understand why Aristotle regards contemplation as 'the highest form of activity'. His answer is contained in the claims that contemplation is 'insight into things . . . divine' by that which is 'more divine than any other part of us' (1177).

God

The notion of God or the divine has now surfaced at the end of all three preceding discussions – of substance, the soul, and the virtues. The absolutely 'prior' and independent substance is a topic for 'theology'; the 'active' mind in the human soul is at least akin to God as described in the *Metaphysics* – immortal, eternal thought; and the 'highest' virtue is contemplation on the divine through the exercise of the most divine part of the soul. The divine is clearly playing a fundamental role in Aristotle's scheme, something one might hardly guess from commentators keen to promote his thinking as thoroughly 'solid'.[48] Before asking whether Aristotle has a coherent theology, we need to know what convinces him that there is a God.

His argument goes in two stages. First he establishes the existence of a 'prime' or 'unmoved mover', and then argues that it merits the title of God. Movement, Aristotle insists, is necessarily eternal, for without it there would be no time – an absurd supposition, since 'there could not be a before and an after if time did not exist' (*Met.* 1071). Now since all ordinary substances are liable to destruction, there necessarily exists an eternal substance which guarantees the continuation of movement. As the source of all movement, this 'mover' cannot itself be moved. Moreover, since all material things are liable to destruction, and can be moved, this eternal 'mover' must be 'without matter'.

This raises the problem of how the 'mover' moves. It cannot do so by causally interacting with the 'starry heavens', whose movements are responsible in turn for those which occur on earth, for then it would itself be 'affected' – a possibility Aristotle rejects. The solution is that the 'mover' 'produces motion by being loved', by being 'the object of desire and . . . thought' for the heavenly bodies which, being themselves intelligent, strive to emulate this 'mover' (*Met.* 1072). Now a substance which is the proper object of love and desire by intelligent beings must not only be good, but intelligent. It must think. What is eternal, 'prior', good, and 'the actuality of thought' surely deserves to be called God. 'Our forefathers' may have indulged in incredible myths, but they were right to suppose that 'the divine encloses the whole of nature' (*Met.* 1074).

With God firmly in place, is it possible to offer an overall and coherent Aristotelian conception of reality and man's place within it? Much falls into focus if the admittedly disputed step, popular among many mediaeval thinkers, is taken of identifying God with the 'active' mind of the soul.[49] It allows us, first, to take as seriously as Aristotle surely intended his reference to 'the divine element' within man which engages in contemplation. Since this element is also 'the true self', the person who eschews the life of contemplation has 'chose[n] to live someone else's life instead of his own' (*Nic. Eth.* 1177). It allows us, next, to exploit the analogy Aristotle draws between 'active' mind's 'actualization' of the objects of thought (the intelligible forms) and light's 'actualization' of colours. Just as we would never see colours without light, so we would never grasp the forms which are embedded in the physical things which they 'animate' unless these forms were actually illuminated, actually present, in the thought of God – a thought in which, with one part of the soul, we can participate. Forms, so to speak, have a double status – as embedded in the things whose development they explain, and as intelligible objects present to thought. (Perhaps there is an analogy with numbers. There is a number of books in front of me, ten say, and the number ten reflected on by the pure mathematician.) Finally, it might help us grasp why only God is totally 'independent' and self-sufficient, the only substance, strictly speaking. Taken one way, the forms depend on the material things in which they are embedded. Taken another way, as intelligible objects present to thought, they do not. Since God's mind, or 'active' mind, just *is* the forms made actually intelligible, it can depend on nothing outside of itself.

Whether or not this account is coherent, it is one which brings Aristotle closer to Plato than many would like. 'In the end,' writes David Hamlyn, 'Aristotle's conception of the relation of the world to God is not dissimilar to Plato's conception of the relation of the world to the Forms.'[50] Differences, of course, remain. 'Active' mind is but one 'part of the soul', and there is not the tendency in Aristotle to denigrate the other parts. These other parts place man firmly in the natural world, and human beings, unlike God, must investigate that world in order to grasp the forms which are the principles or 'causes' of material things. Aristotle, it seems, wants to make man doubly 'at home' in the universe – as an earthly being whose nature is continuous with that of lower creatures, and as a participant in 'active' mind, the mind of God. As we saw when discussing the tension between the 'ethical' and 'intellectual' virtues – between 'doing well' in life and contemplative transcendence of life – Aristotle does not succeed in his ambition. That is no reason not to admire it, or to discourage others from pursuing it.

• 5 Epicureanism, Scepticism and Stoicism •

Aristotle's death followed by one year that of his former pupil, Alexander the Great, in 323 BCE. That date marks the beginning of the period of Graeco-Roman civilization, up to the defeat of Mark Antony at Actium by the future emperor Augustus, known by historians as the Hellenistic era. Athens had long ceased to be the major Mediterranean power, and was indeed conquered by the Romans in 146 BCE. But, as Horace noted, 'Greece took its brutish captor captive', and Athens was to remain, well into the imperial period, the inspirational centre of philosophy.

Such are the massive shadows cast by Plato and Aristotle that it comes as a surprise to learn that during the Hellenistic era and beyond, the most robust contenders in philosophical debate were not the followers of these two giants, but the disciples of schools originating in the late fourth century BCE. These included the Cynics or 'dog sect', so-called not only because of their begging, but because of their founder, Diogenes', disarmingly public emulation of the natural, 'shameless' habits of that animal. More important was a loosely-knit school of philosophers who did not propose any particular metaphysical view, but challenged the credentials of anyone else who did – the Sceptics. But the schools which had the greatest impact upon intellectual and practical life during these centuries were the Epicurean and the Stoic, respectively named after the Greek philosopher Epicurus and the portico (*stoá*) where Zeno of Citium taught in Athens.

Until a decade or so ago, scholarly interest in these two schools was in the doldrums, the prevailing sense being that they represented a dull coda to the achievements of Plato and Aristotle. A further reason, no doubt, was the paucity of surviving texts from the earlier and most lively years of these schools' development. Most of what we know about the earlier figures comes from the writings, largely Latin, of several centuries later. In many of those writings, moreover – especially those of the Stoics Seneca and Marcus Aurelius – the emphasis is almost entirely on these philosophies as recipes for life. Scholarly times have changed, however, and there is now a heightened appreciation of the systematic interweaving of metaphysics and 'philosophies of life' to be found in the thinkers of these schools.[51] The predominantly empiricist and materialist approach of these thinkers, one might add, makes them in some respects more attractive, by currently prevailing yardsticks, than their more illustrious predecessors.

Epicureanism

The word 'epicure' conjures an image of an effete gourmet sat before a dish of truffles and a bottle of Tokay. Even in Seneca's time (c.4 BCE–65 CE), an Epicurean had the reputation of being 'an advocate of soft living'.[52] But the image is certainly false of Epicurus himself, who was 'content with just water and simple bread', and whose idea of extravagance was 'a little pot of cheese' (3),[53] and also of his most illustrious followers, like the Roman poet Lucretius. Epicurus (341–271) founded his famous 'Garden' in Athens as a place where men and women might live together in great simplicity, if not austerity. He was a man able to inspire love and devotion from his friends, and messianic zeal even in people who lived long after him. For Lucretius (c.95–55), he had a 'claim to be called a god', a man whose 'unerring lips gave utterance to the whole of truth' (NU 172, 217).[54]

The 'soft living' image owes, presumably, to Epicurus' claim that 'pleasure is the starting-point and goal of living blessedly' (24). But as we might predict from his diet, the pleasure in question is not of the sybaritic variety. 'It is not drinking bouts and continuous partying and enjoying boys and women . . . which produce the pleasant life' (25). In fact, 'pleasure' seems an inapt term for our principal 'goal of living', which is elsewhere defined as 'health of the body and the freedom of the soul from disturbance (ataraxía)'. Pleasure is only the 'starting-point' of our actions in the negative sense that 'we do everything for the sake of being neither in pain nor in terror' (24). At any rate, this is the aim of those desires which are both 'natural and necessary'. Unnecessary ones, for rich food, sex and the like, whose satisfaction does not serve to liberate us from pain or terror, are not 'a bad thing in themselves', but they tend to 'bring troubles many times greater than the pleasures' they seek, and should therefore be avoided or kept within severe limits (26ff).

So far, Epicureanism may seem to consist in no more than some edifying, if over-familiar, injunctions for a life of sober contentment. But Epicurus and Lucretius are keen to ground these injunctions in a complete theory of nature. There are two reasons for this. First, it is important to show that human beings, generally speaking, do not simply happen to desire 'a body free from pain [and] a mind released from worry and fear', but that nature itself is 'clamouring' for these (NU 60). Man's problem is not that he has a wrong final goal, for investigation of nature will show that his only possible goal is freedom from pain and worry. His problem, rather, is having false beliefs about how such a goal is attained, ones which he *can* do something about. This leads to the second reason for constructing a correct theory of nature. Only such a theory can serve to dispel the main causes of our worry and terror. In Lucretius' refrain, 'this dread and darkness of mind cannot be dispelled by the sun-

beams . . . but only by an understanding of the outward form and inner workings of nature' (NU 218).

The main causes of our unhappy condition, Epicurus claims, are 'superstitions', like 'the eternal expectation and suspicion that something dreadful
[might happen] such as the myths tell about' (14). Instead of sensibly regarding
earthquakes and floods, or the setbacks that sometimes confront us in life, as
natural phenomena occurring in accordance with universal laws, people imagine that they are due to the caprices of the gods who must therefore be
appeased. Worse still is people's fear of death – or rather, of the afterlife. Not
only is that fear 'the most frightening of bad things' (23), but our obsession
with what will happen to us after our earthly life prevents our appreciation of
life as it actually is. The antidote to our fears, then, is a naturalistic account of
a universe in which the gods have no interest or role, and in which human
beings, like other creatures, have no life beyond their earthly one. Someone
who accepts such an account will recognize that 'death . . . is nothing to us;
since when we exist, death is not yet present, and when death is present, then
we do not exist' (23). (Critics will argue that this is hardly enough to dispel a
horror of death. If I suffer a stroke that renders me a contented imbecile, the
fact that I will not then be in a position to regret my condition is no reason for
me, now, not to dread such an eventuality.)

The theory of nature proposed by the Epicureans is a modified version
of one already familiar to us – Democritean atomism (see pp. 100ff.). The
universe consists of atomic bodies and empty space, for 'beyond these two
things . . . nothing can be conceived' (5). The human soul, since it can act
upon and be acted upon by matter, must itself be material in nature. And this
nature is such that the soul cannot but desire pleasure, albeit of the 'negative'
kind mentioned above. Even the gods, whose existence is known to us
through, *inter alia*, our experience of them in dreams, are material. Being
perfectly blissful and self-sufficient, however, they can have no interest in
meddling in earthly affairs. The world is anyway much too imperfect a place to
suggest that the gods have a hand in directing its course. The main modification to the older atomism is the infelicitous notion of 'swerving atoms'. Atoms
do not always follow a straight path, but occasionally swerve aside. The
importance of this, for Lucretius at least, resides in its explanation of free will.
'[T]hat the mind has no internal necessity to . . . compel it to suffer in helpless
passivity . . . is due to the slight swerve of the atoms at no determinate time or
place' (NU 68). Few of us, I suspect, would feel cheered by this promise of a
freedom from compulsion which resides, simply, in random deviations from
the laws of nature.

It is ironic that Epicurus should have based his account of the virtues on a
cosmology which earlier writers had condemned – or praised – for its relativistic or nihilistic implications for morality. Be that as it may, he is convinced

that the virtues are 'natural adjuncts of the pleasant life' – for there is nothing else we can possibly aim at – and that, in fact, 'the pleasant life is inseparable' from practising the virtues (25). Courage, temperance, justice and so on, can all be shown to be necessary for a life free from pain and anxiety. One thing which distinguishes Epicurus from the hedonistic Sophists who populate Plato's dialogues, and which makes him the more attractive figure, is his refusal to allow 'free riding' violations of morality when this is apparently in the interest of an agent. This is not because obedience to a moral norm can have any value additional to that of pleasure, but because any violation is bound to bring with it the kind of anxiety and fear which is the negation of pleasure. 'It is hard to commit injustice and escape detection, but to be confident of escaping detection is impossible' (29). But cannot a person *know*, under some circumstances, that he will escape detection? Epicurus' reply is disappointing: 'the plain statement [of the answer] is not easy' (50).

As for Thomas Hobbes (see ch. 7, sect. 3), 'justice [is] not a thing in its own right' for Epicurus, but arises from 'a pact about neither harming one another nor being harmed' (28). But there is a nice difference between the two philosophers. For while both agree that this 'pact' is to deliver men from fear, the terror of an untimely death which is the prime motive behind Hobbes' contract is one which Epicurus regards as irrational. This difference from Hobbes helps to explain the Epicurean belief that of all the things that contribute most to a good life, 'by far the greatest is the possession of friendship' (28). The worries and fears which most beset us are not of the kind, like a concern for one's property or physical safety, which can be allayed by a well-policed State. What we require, rather, is the company of like-minded, Epicurean friends who will constantly reinforce our occasionally wobbling convictions that we are not the playthings of the gods and that there is 'nothing terrible which is eternal'. In such company, a man will himself 'live as a god among men' (25). For such a man, confident in the scheme of things and self-sufficient, nothing is 'alien to himself' (29).

Skirmishes with the Sceptics

The Epicurean account of nature will only make people 'free from disturbance', of course, if they are able to believe it. Unfortunately, this account inherits from Democritus the problem with atomism which he himself pointed out (see pp. 101f.). Unless the senses can be trusted, there will be no reason to accept atomism (or anything else): but if atomism is true, the senses are a hopeless guide to reality, which has few if any of those features, like colour, which are presented to the senses. Matters were made more urgent by the emergence around 300 BCE of various sceptical philosophers, beginning with

Pyrrho (*c.*365–270), who argued vigorously against any claims to knowledge which go beyond a statement of how things *appear* to be. Adding insult to injury, the Pyrrhonians also hijacked the Epicurean ideal of *ataraxía*, arguing that it is only through 'suspension of judgement' that 'freedom from anxiety follows' (182).[55] The search for knowledge is bound to be ridden with *Angst*, since we find ourselves hopelessly confused by contradictory accounts of things between which we cannot rationally choose. With reality unknowable, the only proper way to accommodate to it is to suspend all beliefs.

According to legend, Pyrrho himself followed a policy of 'relying on the senses for nothing', having to be rescued by friends from falling off precipices or being crushed by wagons. Since he lived to a respectable age, and cannot always have been surrounded by minders, it is more likely that he 'only theorized about the suspension of judgement [and] did not actually act improvidently' (173). Such 'improvident' behaviour would anyway be inconsistent with the Pyrrhonian advice to 'follow appearances' and customary practice while, of course, refusing to claim any validity on behalf of them.

Pyrrhonian arguments, as codified by the first-century BCE philosopher Aenesidemus, are designed to show that we can 'determine nothing'. Nothing, for example, is just or unjust, 'nothing exists in truth . . . [and] each thing is no more this than that' (173). The strategy is to show – often with the help of fanciful illustrations (animals which live in fire, people who can only get warm in the shade) – that how things appear to be varies so much that there can be no sensible method for deciding which appearances accurately represent reality. Stripped of the unconvincing illustrations, the point comes to this: there is no independent way of telling that a perception, say, or a moral conviction represents how things truly are. Nothing rules out the possibility that the person who has it does so for reasons, like the force of social convention, which vitiate its claim to truth. If so, it is not simply that experience does not 'warrant indubitable . . . beliefs about the external world'.[56] Rather, we should suspend all beliefs, of whatever degree, once we admit that there is no procedure for ruling out their production by factors which exclude, or at least do not require, their truth.

Epicureans make various *ripostes* to all of this. Some challenge the coherence of the sceptic's position. 'If you quarrel with all sense-perceptions,' says Epicurus, 'you will have nothing to refer to in judging [those] which you claim are false' (27). But this is beside the point, since the Pyrrhonist rejects the belief that a perception is false as much as the belief that it is true. Again, it is charged that the life of a radical sceptic would be an impossible one of 'total lethargy'. Yet, as we saw, Pyrrho does not advocate suspended animation, but going along with how things appear to us and with convention. A better criticism would have been that there can be no difference between its appearing to Pyrrho that 'each thing is no more this than that' and his believing this to be true – in which case the sceptic is not, as he pretends, without belief. One might think, too, that there is something peculiarly 'inhuman' in the Pyrrhonist stance: for he must treat how things strike him with the same cool detachment with which he might regard the experiences of a perfect stranger.[57]

Another Epicurean strategy is to defend the credentials of sense-perception. There is, it is argued, nothing in his atomist theory of nature which contradicts how things appear to us, for we can explain colours and the like in terms of the impact of 'atoms' on us. Lucretius, indeed, argues that some familiar experiences actually support the atomist account, if only by way of analogy. Just as an army which seems static when viewed from a distance is really a maelstrom of troop and horse manoeuvres, so an apparently immobile object is really a hive of atomic activity (NU 69f). Sceptics are unlikely to be impressed by these replies, however. How can we have good reason to believe that such analogies hold, and why should the mere consistency of a theory with appearances be a warrant for its truth? After all the whole point is that any appearance is compatible with many different beliefs about the external world and cannot, therefore, be used to support any one of these in particular.

It was not the Epicureans alone who faced challenges from scepticism, for so did their Stoic rivals. But, here, the main attacks came from a different school of sceptics – those, like Arcesilaus (316–242) and Carneades (214–c.129), who dominated the New Academy in defiance, one suspects, of Plato's hopes for the future of the institution which he had founded. In a book more concerned with 'the problem of knowledge', the views of these figures would merit closer attention than I give them. Actually, it is not easy to ascertain their views since they had a penchant for arguing both sides of a case. Thus Cicero records his anger at hearing Carneades defending and attacking the merits of justice on successive days in Rome. One thing, at least, is certain – their rejection of the Stoic doctrine of *katálepsis* (apprehension), according to which some experiences or 'presentations' are so clear and compelling that their correspondence to reality cannot be doubted. The Stoic sage, indeed, is defined as one who limits his beliefs to those founded upon such presentations. The Academic sceptics' retort was simple: there can be no such self-authenticating presentations, so that if the sage restricts his beliefs to these, then he must be without any beliefs at all. The argument was that no presentation, even if true, is 'such that there could not be a false one just like it' (167). An hallucination may be as clear and compelling for a perceiver as any veridical experience. Hence the experiential character of a presentation cannot serve as a criterion to determine if it corresponds to reality.

What made the Academics less radical than the Pyrrhonians was their willingness to regard some beliefs as more reasonable and plausible than others. Carneades' importance for more recent epistemology resides less in his sceptical utterances than in his careful consideration of the criteria for reasonable belief.

(Presumably by way of a compliment, Carneades has been described as 'closer to the spirit of modern British philosophy than perhaps any other ancient thinker'.)[58] In particular, he stresses the way in which presentations 'depend upon one another like links in a chain' (168). The more strongly and coherently my perception is linked with further ones, whether mine or of other people, the more reasonable is it to regard that perception as veridical. Whether even the most 'plausible, uncontroverted, and thoroughly tested presentation' amounts, strictly speaking, to *knowledge* might not seem a very substantial issue. If it is not, there is no great reason why Stoics should not replace their criterion of *katálepsis* by one of 'reasonableness'. There would, to be sure, remain other Academic objections – for example, to the Stoic idea of divine providence, which, for Carneades, is not even a plausible one. But to understand these, we must turn to the Stoics' account of the cosmos.

The Stoics' World

I shall refer, for the most part, rather vaguely to 'the Stoics' since our sources (like Cicero) for the views of the main Greek Stoics – Zeno (344–262), Cleanthes (331–232) and Chrysippus (*c.*280–207) – do not always distinguish their individual contributions. The stoic way of life must have been a healthy one, to judge from these men's longevity – further promoted in the case of two of them, perhaps, by their earlier careers as boxer and marathon runner, respectively. Zeno and Cleanthes, it seems, died the deaths often recommended by Stoics, choosing to depart this world when they sensed their span was over. Less edifying was Chrysippus' end for, according to the version one reads, he succumbed either to an overdose of wine or to uncontrollable laughter at one of his own jokes (about wine, as it happened).

Although Stoics and Epicureans are usually contrasted like chalk and cheese, there are striking affinities between them. Both offer materialistic accounts of the world and man, based as they see it on the authority of sense-perception. Both insist that the virtuous life is possible only for someone who appreciates the truth of such an account. And, in substance, the virtuous Stoic life is similar to the virtuous Epicurean one. The standard virtues of courage, temperance and justice figure in both, and Stoic and Epicurean alike emphasize tranquillity, self-sufficiency and resignation to one's own death. (The good man, it was held, would not suffer even on the rack – which invited Jowett's comment that he would have to be a very good man on a very bad rack.) The modern connotations of 'stoical' are much less misleading, therefore, than those of 'epicurean'. But there are, of course, vital differences. Pleasure, which for the Epicurean is the goal of life, is for the Stoic a matter of 'indifference'. Moreover, the rational practice of virtue, which for Stoics *is* the good life, serves for their rivals simply as an instrumental means to that life. Anyway, whatever the similarities between the respective good lives, they are grounded by the two schools in very different theories of nature.

The Stoic theory is more complex and ambitious. Complex, because it is a cocktail of novel ingredients added to some staples of earlier Greek thought – Homeric Fate, the materialism of the naturalists, Heraclitean 'fire', the Socratic equation of virtue with knowledge, the Platonic devaluation of the body, an Aristotelian sense of purpose in nature, and more. Shaken together the result is an ambitious attempt to establish that human beings are 'at home' in the universe, not simply through being of the same stuff as everything else, but through embodying the fundamental principle and purpose of the cosmos. The philosophical task to which the Stoic Emperor, Marcus Aurelius (121–180), dedicated himself between battles against the barbarians was 'to consider well the nature of the universe and my own nature, together with the relation betwixt them'. Such reflection will establish 'what kind of part [I am] of what kind of whole; and that no mortal can hinder me from acting and speaking conformably to the being of which I am a part'.[59] The scale and ambition of the task ensured that it would, in different ways, inspire many later thinkers – Augustine, Spinoza and Kant among them.

The Stoic cosmos is an integrated whole composed of a 'passive' substrate, or mere 'matter', and an 'active' material principle, called *pneûma* ('breath'), described as a 'craftsmanlike fire'. This 'fire' or energy 'holds things together' and, by permeating everything, is responsible for the behaviour of mere 'matter'. *Pneûma* is further credited with purpose, intelligence and reason. Indeed, it may be described as 'an animal, immortal, rational, perfect . . . providentially [looking after] the cosmos' (99). Since that is not a bad description of God, *pneûma* may be identified with God – and also with Fate, 'the rational principle according to which the cosmos is managed' (100). The whole of nature is, in a sense, rational, since everything occurs according to the dispensations of an intelligent God, pantheistically conceived. This does not mean that individual stones, flowers or animals are rational. Rational nature is the privilege of the cosmos as an organic whole and of its most special denizens, human beings, who thereby reflect and participate in the governing principle of the universe.

To raise the most obvious query, why did the Stoics regard the cosmic *pneûma* as 'alive' and rational? Two of the arguments credited to Zeno look unpromising. 'That which is rational is better than that which is not rational; but nothing is better than the cosmos; therefore, the cosmos is rational': and, 'nothing which lacks life and reason can produce from itself something [i.e. man] which is alive and rational' (105). The problem with the first argument is this: granted that it is better for a being *capable* of rationality to be rational rather than irrational, what reason is there to suppose that nature-as-a-whole has such a capacity? The Stoics' answer is an early instance of 'the argument from design'. Consider 'the regularity of the motions . . . of the heaven, and the . . . orderly beauty of the sun, moon and . . . stars; just looking at them indicates . . . that these things are not the result of chance', but require 'someone who is in charge and runs things', in just the way that an efficient gymnasium does (104). Intelligent purpose in the world is something we 'grasp' or 'apprehend' through simple observation. This argument is boosted by reflecting on the ways nature providentially caters for the needs of its creatures – though some of us might be less impressed than Cicero by nature's ingenuity in providing pigs with the right number of teats for their litters (115).

The second argument – that human reason cannot have sprung from a non-rational cause – looks open to such obvious retorts as this: I, together with my brain and rational faculties, 'came from' a zygote, hardly a paragon of reason. But, here, we need to take seriously the Stoic conviction that the cosmos is an organic whole within which each thing is only intelligible, finally, through its relation to everything else. Consider a 'whole', like a football team, as opposed to a mere 'aggregate', like the sum total of redheads. It seems reasonable to say of the team, first, that it must share various crucial features with its members (skill, determination, etc.); and, second, that the members can only have these features because of their membership of a team. A striker can only display skill and determination at football as a member of a football team. Analogously, if the cosmos is a whole in which rational beings are integral parts, then not only will the whole share their qualities of reason but, more crucially, these beings can display rationality only through their membership of the whole. Without a conception of cosmic purposes, there could be no grounds for regarding the purposes which individual men and women pursue as either rational or irrational.

If 'the argument from design' sounds prescient of much Christian theology, so is the Stoics' response to the vexed problem – part of 'the problem of evil' – of explaining away the apparent 'imperfections' of the world. Epicurus, recall, had cited earthquakes, famines and the like as evidence against the existence of a perfect intelligence at work in the world. The Stoics' response again relies on their holism. We cannot pick and choose what we would like to occur, for everything that occurs is, if we could but see it, a necessary part of a whole which we recognize to be good overall. Even the most 'terrible disaster,' said Chrysippus, 'is not without its usefulness to the whole. For without it there could be no good.'[60] Or, as Marcus Aurelius – taking what can only be called a stoical attiude – wrote, 'to be vexed at anything that happens is a separation of ourselves from nature'.[61] I should not be vexed at getting mugged, for that would imply that nature could be as it is without such integral components as my getting mugged.

There is another part to 'the problem of evil'. How, if everything happens in accordance with Fate, can we ever blame, or praise, human beings for their actions? Can we, indeed, speak of *them* acting at all? But such questions refer us to the Stoics' treatment of ethics.

Stoic Ethics

Chrysippus is said to have 'sweated' over the problem of reconciling fatalism with individual responsibility – and to some avail. First, he makes a shrewd reply to the so-called 'lazy argument', according to which there is no point in my going to the doctor, since it is already fixed whether or not I shall get over my illness. This is fallacious since 'calling the doctor is fated just as much as recovering' (130). It was 'co-fated' that I should call the doctor and recover, so that the former was a necessary means to the latter. Chrysippus was also one of the first to argue that there is no incompatibility between holding me responsible for some outcome and the conviction that this outcome was the result of a deterministic causal process. Just as the intrinsic features of a cylinder are required to explain why it rolled when pushed, so typically the intrinsic features of a person, as well as external causes, explain his behaviour. If so, it is proper to hold him responsible for this behaviour. That the person is as he is as a result of Fate is neither here nor there, for it is still *he* – and not external factors alone – who is responsible for the behaviour. Hobbes and Hume are among the later 'compatibilists' who endorsed this reasoning.

Granted that it is appropriate to praise and blame people, which actions properly invite these judgements? What, in other words, constitute the right and the good for the Stoic? The good life is that which benefits a person, and the one thing that does this is living virtuously. Since nature-as-a-whole is a perfect, divine intelligence, the virtuous life must be one which accords with this nature. And since what distinguishes human beings, and makes them share in divine nature, is reason, then the natural life for man is that of reason. The overriding aim is always to act in the manner which is rationally 'appropriate'. Thus we arrive at the following Stoic equations: ' "to live according to virtue" is equivalent to . . . "liv[ing] consistently with nature" . . . which is right reason . . . being the same as Zeus' (136).

This sounds like a more theologically charged version of Aristotle, for whom *eudaimonía* ('flourishing') resides in discharging the distinctive human 'function', reason, through exercising the virtues, for these 'hit the mean' (i.e. are 'appropriate', and neither 'excessive' nor 'deficient'). Two related differences from Aristotle, however, soon emerge. First, among the constituents of *eudaimonía*, for Aristotle, were such desiderata as good health, sufficient wealth and a respected station in life, and some of his virtues – such as 'righteous indignation' and 'magnanimity' – presuppose these advantages. For the Stoics, on the other hand, health, etc. are 'indifferent': they are 'neither good nor bad' and 'neither benefit nor harm' (139). Second, *eudaimonía* depends in part on the success of a person's aims, so that someone who ends up sick and penniless in prison cannot be *eudaímon*. The Stoics, however, argue that the worth of actions is not to be judged 'by their ultimate completion' (152), and someone who ends up like the prisoner need have forfeited no 'benefit'.

These claims attracted much criticism. Is not an ideal of 'indifference' to nearly everything we desire either absurd or impossibly demanding? Certainly, what some Stoics urge sounds 'too good to be true' – Seneca recommending friendships simply in order for us to have people to help, or Marcus Aurelius welcoming an act of treason so that he may have someone to forgive.[62] Properly understood, however, the Stoics' position is not bizarre and has striking affinities with a more recent, and very much alive, tradition of moral thought.

How can we explain the advocacy of 'indifference' to health, beauty, status and so on? If, when ill, I refuse to become 'vexed', because I recognize the necessary place of my illness in the scheme of things, then nor – while well – will I put the same premium on remaining well that someone who *does* get 'vexed' by illness will. In other words, the value a person puts on health is partly a function of how distressed he allows himself to become by its absence. The Stoics urge us to minimize such distress. But, as this suggests, even the Stoic accords some value to health, and insists that it is 'preferable' to illness. 'Of indifferents, some are preferred . . . the preferred are those which have considerable value' (156). It now sounds as if there is a merely verbal difference between the Stoics and the rest of us – with them calling 'preferable' and 'valuable' what we call 'beneficial' and 'good' as well. That would be to ignore, however, the Stoics' reasons for their reluctance to apply these latter terms. These include the following: 'preferable' things, like strength, can be misused, as in the case of a muscular mugger; moreover, there are circumstances in which they would not be preferable. (The example is given of health being undesirable in a society whose warped rulers enslaved and executed the healthy.) As we might put it, health and strength are not 'good in themselves', but only *prima facie* good, relative to circumstances and the use which is made of them. But why, then, do not the Stoics themselves put it like that? Why their keenness to restrict 'good' to actions which do *not* aim at 'indifferents', however 'preferable'?

Answering these questions gets us to the crux of their position. Let us recall their second difference from Aristotle – the irrelevance of 'ultimate completion' to the worth of our aims. This is explained by the Stoics' attempt to identify a good which attaches solely to the person (and his or her aims), and cannot therefore be affected by the vicissitudes of Fate, by luck or unluck. Health depends upon too many factors outside people's control for this to reflect upon *their* worth. The worth in question sounds remarkably like that which Kant and others have called *moral* worth. Hence we might construe the Stoics' narrow use of 'good' as belonging to their attempt to identify a specifically moral sense of the term – a sense which, arguably, earlier Greek philosophers like Aristotle were not concerned to isolate.[63]

Why, though, should I not prove myself worthy by aiming to become healthy? Well, suppose things go wrong and through no fault of my own I contract tuberculosis. In that case, I have, quite simply, failed in my aim. But the kind of good which the Stoics are after – moral good – must not be liable to failure. Moral worth attaches to aims which, so to speak, guarantee their own success, since it cannot be erased by contingencies that do not reflect the worth of the person. What kind of aims, then, might fill the bill? Consider the difference between wanting to be healthy and wanting to be rational in matters of health. If I get tuberculosis, I failed to satisfy the first of these wants: but, provided I took rational steps to avoid illness, I still satisfied the second. *My* worth is to be judged by what is entirely in my power: that is, the exercise of my reason, independent of the fortuitous *dénouements* of that exercise.

Reason, as Chrysippus insisted, needs its 'raw materials', however. 'Be rational!' is a useless exhortation unless we already have some goals which reason is enlisted to enable us to achieve. These 'raw materials' are provided by our natural preferences for health, friendship, beauty, moderate pleasures, and so on. (The Stoics were no puritans. We can drink, though not get drunk, and take lovers, though only if they are friends as well.) But something morally momentous occurs when, as we mature, we recognize that these natural preferences are, except in special circumstances, rational – and rational precisely because they are furnished by an intelligent nature-as-a-whole. For we are then enabled to pursue such goals, no longer simply out of desire, but because we appreciate the rationality of pursuing them. It is when we recognize that they are 'in agreement with nature . . . [that] for the first time we begin to . . . understand something which can truly be called good' (149). When 'agreement with nature' – with the intelligent ordering of the universe – becomes the motive for our 'appropriate' behaviour, we have attained the age of moral reason. Only then can our behaviour have that special worth to which the Stoics restrict the word 'good'.

Whether or not there is such a special worth – whether or not a distinctive moral good should be abstracted from a wider conception of the good – is a question that currently taxes many moral philosophers. The persuasive thought that there is owes much to the Stoics, whose contribution therefore was not a redundant coda to the themes of a more golden age of Greek philosophy.

• Notes •

1 Bernard Williams, 'Philosophy', p. 202.
2 *The Birth of Tragedy*, sects 1 and 2, in Nietzsche's *Basic Writings*.
3 Roy Burrell, *The Greeks*, p. 61.
4 Though see Jonathan Barnes, *The Presocratic Philosophers*, pp. 205ff, who challenges the usual monistic reading of Parmenides.
5 *Physics* 239b14. On references to Aristotle, see note 31.
6 Jacob Burckhardt, *History of Greek Culture*, pp. 277–8.
7 References to Homer are to Book numbers of *The Iliad*, and *The Odyssey*, in E. V. Rieu's translations.
8 Aeschylus, *The Oresteian Trilogy*, p. 78; Euripides, *The Bacchae and Other Plays*, p. 223.
9 Aeschylus, *The Oresteian Trilogy*, pp. 69, 159.
10 Sophocles, *The Theban Plays*, p. 67.
11 *Metaphysics* B 1000a. Elsewhere in the same work, a softer verdict on the 'mythologists' is passed.
12 Ibid., A 983b.
13 F. M. Cornford, *Principium Sapientiae*. But for criticism of Cornford, see Gregory Vlastos' review of this book in D. Furley and R. Allen, *Studies in Presocratic Philosophy*, vol. I.
14 The 'DK' references are to the fragments etc. as numbered by Diels and Kranz. All the fragments I quote can be found, with the same numbers, in such standard works as Barnes, *The Presocratic Philosophers* and G. S. Kirk et al., *The Presocratic Philosophers*.
15 Barnes, *The Presocratic Philosophers*, p. 475.
16 Gregory Vlastos, 'Equality and justice in early Greek cosmologies', p. 84. Note Vlastos' mention of the great Athenian legislator, Solon's, appeal to the justice of the cosmos.
17 For this view, see F. M. Cornford, *From Religion to Philosophy*.
18 For this view, see Barnes, *The Presocratic Philosophers*, pp. 128ff.
19 Quoted in Terence Irwin, *Classical Thought*, p. 51.
20 Plato, *Theaetetus*, 152. On references to Plato, see note 25.
21 Ibid., 172.
22 Irwin, *Classical Thought*, p. 57.
23 *Twilight of the Idols*, in Friedrich Nietzsche, *The Portable Nietzsche*, pp. 475ff. Elsewhere, Nietzsche expresses a much more favourable opinion.
24 For Socrates the man, see Plato's *Apology* and *Symposium* (Alcibiades' speech).
25 References to Plato are to dialogue and page number, following the standard pagination found in the margins of any good translation, such as the *Collected Dialogues*.
26 Plutarch, *The Rise and Fall of Athens: Nine Greek Lives*, p. 248.
27 For Plato's own account of the Sicilian connection see his *Seventh Letter*, a work whose attribution to Plato has, however, been challenged by some scholars.
28 For many centuries, right up to the Renaissance, Plato's influence was *via* the writings of the Neo-Platonists (see ch. 5, sect. 2), most of his own having been lost from view during this period.
29 R. M. Hare, *Plato*, p. 26.
30 An indispensable study is I. M. Crombie, *An Examination of Plato's Doctrines*.
31 On this topic, see J. C. B. Gosling, *Plato*, chs 9–11.
32 See Williams, 'Philosophy', p. 227.
33 See Kenneth J. Dover, *Greek Popular Morality*.
34 Martha Nussbaum, *The Fragility of Goodness*, pp. 228ff. This book is excellent on the role of the emotions and the erotic in Plato.

35 See Luciano Canfora, *The Vanished Library*.

36 Jonathan Barnes, *Aristotle*, p. 1.

37 References to Aristotle are to page numbers of his works, according to the standard pagination found in the margins of good translations, such as *Works of Aristotle*. Many of the passages I cite can be found in J. L. Ackrill (ed.), *A New Aristotle Reader*.

38 W. D. Ross, *Aristotle*, p. 19. The main inspiration for the 'recent opinion' was Werner Jaeger, *Aristotle*.

39 My account is much indebted to Jonathan Lear, *Aristotle*. Other writers, I should stress, e.g. Barnes, *Aristotle*, offer very different interpretations.

40 Ross, *Aristotle*, p. 69. See Aristotle, *On Generation and Corruption*, 329.

41 Barnes, *Aristotle*, p. 46.

42 See Lear, *Aristotle*, pp. 289ff, and Michael Frede, who also argues that Aristotle's basic substances are forms, some of which are immaterial, *Essays in Ancient Philosophy*, pp. 77ff.

43 Those seeking a modern echo might find it in the idea of phenomenologists, like Jean-Paul Sartre, that consciousness is a 'nothing' in itself, because completely 'absorbed' into its objects (see ch. 10, sect. 2).

44 See, especially, Alasdair MacIntyre, *After Virtue*.

45 Alasdair MacIntyre, *A Short History of Ethics*, p. 79.

46 For discussion of this and other Aristotelian triads of mean, excess and deficiency, see J. O. Urmson, 'Aristotle's doctrine of the mean'.

47 J. L. Ackrill, 'Aristotle on *eudaimonía*', p. 33.

48 For example, Irwin, *Classical Thought*, in an otherwise illuminating account, nowhere mentions the place of God in Aristotle's thought.

49 Ross, *Aristotle*, criticizes J. Zabarella for taking this step, p. 183. See also Lear, *Aristotle*, who argues in favour of it.

50 D. W. Hamlyn, *A History of Western Philosophy*, p. 70.

51 The revived interest in Hellenistic philosophy owes much to A. A. Long, *Hellenistic Philosophy*, to which my account, like that of most other recent commentators, is indebted.

52 Seneca, *Letters from a Stoic*, p. 78.

53 References in the text, except to Lucretius (see note 54), are to page numbers of B. Inwood and L. Gerson, *Hellenistic Philosophy: Introductory Readings*. The passages cited can also be found in A. A. Long and D. Sedley, *The Hellenistic Philosophers*, vol. I.

54 References to Lucretius are to page numbers of *On the Nature of the Universe* (NU). This is an amazing, and very long, poem whose plea for the tranquil life contrasts pathetically with the obvious turmoil and anguish in the soul of its author.

55 Sources for the views of the sceptics are relatively late – Cicero (1st century BCE), Sextus Empiricus (fl. 200 CE), and Diogenes Laertius (3rd century CE), especially.

56 Long, *Hellenistic Philosophy*, p. 82.

57 Both these points are made by M. F. Burnyeat in his excellent 'Can the sceptic live his scepticism?'

58 Long, *Hellenistic Philosophy*, p. 106.

59 Aurelius Marcus, *The Meditations*, n.d., p. 26.

60 Quoted from Plutarch in Long, *Hellenistic Philosophy*, p. 169.

61 Ibid., p. 30.

62 Seneca, *Letters from a Stoic*, pp. 49f; Marcus Aunelius, *The Meditations*, p. 12.

63 For an illuminating discussion of these issues, see Bernard Williams, *Moral Luck*, ch. 2.

Part II

• Middle Period and 'Modern' Philosophies •

• Introduction to Part II •

There is no single, handy label for the long period of Western philosophies, let alone for that of ones further east, which the second part of this book covers. I have opted for two terms of art, 'middle period' and 'modern'. 'Middle period' has the advantage over 'mediaeval' of being less irredeemably suggestive of an era of European history. I use the term 'modern' in the sense it acquired among eighteenth-century writers, to refer to the period down to their own century following the demise of mediaeval scholastic philosophy with the onset of what we now call the Renaissance. (The first part of this period is sometimes referred to as 'early modern'.) I shall use 'recent philosophies' to refer to the post-Enlightenment philosophies discussed in Part III.

The 'Western chapters', 5 and 7, in Part II take us from the fusion of late Greek philosophy, Neo-Platonism, with Christianity to the eighteenth-century debate between the figures of 'radical' Enlightenment and their early romantic critics. 'Western', here, needs to be taken broadly, since some of the most significant developments during the middle period took place in the Islamic world, where Arab-language writers – Muslims and Jews – were themselves debating the fusion of Greek philosophy with their own religions. Indeed, it was these writers who, during Europe's 'dark ages', preserved the Aristotelian tradition that was to have such an impact in the glory days of later mediaeval Europe. Such was the break with earlier philosophy marked by the emergence of Christianity and Islam that our starting point in Part II is not arbitrary. Nor, in my judgement, is our closing point. For all the originality of Descartes and other early seventeenth-century thinkers, it is with the revolutionary approach of Immanuel Kant at the very end of the eighteenth century that philosophy was given the new stamp which has most marked subsequent developments down to the present. Hence, our story in Part II ends on the eve of Kant's great contribution.

Chapter 6, on developments in Asian philosophy, covers a shorter period than the two Western ones. In the case of India, this is partly because the discussion in chapter 2 took us into centuries well past *annus domini*, and partly because there seems to have been little development of great philosophical note beyond the one I shall be discussing, Theistic Vedānta, until the nineteenth century (a matter for Part III). In China, the atrophy of philosophy after the ancient period covered in chapter 3 means that the story is not resumed until the Neo-Confucian renaissance between, roughly, the eleventh and fifteenth centuries, after which there was again relative stagnation until the late nineteenth century. An exception to the preceding atrophy and subsequent stagnation was the development of Ch'an Buddhism; but as its better known Japanese name, Zen Buddhism, suggests, it was to be in Japan more than in China that this philosophy received its most sophisticated articulation. Theistic Vedānta, Neo-Confucianism, and Zen Buddhism – the three topics for chapter 6 – may seem a mixed bag. Yet, as we shall see, they are united by a certain reformist zeal as attempts to retrieve pristine messages from ancient traditions that had been corrupted.

5
• MEDIAEVAL PHILOSOPHIES •

• 1 Religion and Philosophy •

As noted in the preamble to Part II, 'mediaeval' is an elastic term. According to the book one picks up, the Middle Ages began with the collapse of the Western Roman Empire in the fifth century CE, the coronation of Charlemagne as Holy Roman Emperor in 800, or the emergence from the Dark Ages around 1100. This chronological uncertainty reflects substantial, not merely terminological, differences among historians: differences, for example, as to whether the Dark Ages were so dark that the brighter period which followed deserves a new appellation. Historians of philosophy inherit the uncertainties of the general historian, and add a few of their own. Was mediaeval scholasticism really dead by, say, 1500? Should not even Descartes, in the seventeenth century, be read as scholastic in his main concerns, as some recent scholars urge?

Was Mediaeval Thought Distinctive?

I shall not agonize over whether there is some distinctive feature of mediaeval thought which provides a criterion for dating the period. I will suggest that there is a distinctive flavour to the philosophies considered in this chapter, so that the division between it and chapter 7, where the Western story is resumed, is not one of mere chronology and convenience. But, should my suggestion be wrong, these latter considerations would suffice to warrant such a division.

My account will begin with a school of thought earlier than the first philosopher who could respectably be regarded as mediaeval, St Augustine. The great Bishop of Hippo figures twice in histories of philosophy: in the coda to books on classical thought and in the overture to ones on mediaeval thought. The so-called Neo-Platonism of Plotinus and his followers is clearly to be regarded as a late movement in Greek philosophy, but it is with this that my account begins because of its immense influence upon Augustine and later mediaeval thought. With a few exceptions, like Erigena in the ninth century, it was to be a long time before Christian philosophy produced figures approaching Augustine in stature. The same is not true of Islamic and Jewish thought, which was already flourishing in the tenth and eleventh centuries. One would hardly guess this from books which treat Muslim and Jewish philosophers as mere conduits of the Aristotelianism which eventually came to dominate scholastic thought, and there is little excuse for Bertrand Russell's remarks that 'Arabic philosophy is not important as original thought', and that 'the Spanish Jews produced one philosopher of importance'.[1] Hence I devote a section to these philosophies in their own right. Returning to the Christian world, few would deny that St Thomas Aquinas in the thirteenth century represents the pinnacle of the mediaeval achievement. His work is the subject of a further section. The final figures I discuss are Aquinas' great scholastic critics, Duns Scotus and William of Ockham, and their contemporaries among thirteenth and fourteenth-century speculative mystics, like Meister Eckhart.

That we should begin with a Bishop and close with monks and friars is an indication of the salient feature of the period: the intimate relation between philosophy and religion. There was not a single notable philosopher, from Augustine to Eckhart, who was not among the faithful of one or other of the three great monotheist, semitic religions. History, as Gilson points out, might so easily have gone differently.[2] All three religions might have remained, as Judaism largely did for more than a millennium, just that – 'mere' religions, simple creeds elaborated in codes of morality and worship. Many, including some of the early Church Fathers and their ideological soulmates in the Islamic world, wished that things had remained so. That they did not was due to a mixture of luck (the survival, despite plenty of book-burning, of Greek philosophical texts); the intellectual honesty of men like Augustine, Saadia and Avicenna, which compelled them to seek an accommodation between their faiths and the undeniable achievements of Greek thought; and a relative tolerance by all but the most conservative religious authorities towards speculations that could, and sometimes did, challenge tenets of the creeds which they defended.

In recent years there has been a revival of interest in mediaeval philosophy, though most university courses still leap-frog over it from the Greeks to Descartes. Given the obvious stature of some mediaeval thinkers, it is less this revival which needs explaining than the doldrums which for so long preceded it. The turgidity of much of the prose, the lack of translations from Latin or Arabic, and the depressing length of many mediaeval writings (sixty volumes in the case of one of Aquinas' works) doubtless played their part. Moreover, mediaeval culture has struck many people as hopelessly remote from their concerns and sensibilities in a way that Greek culture has not. For Matthew Arnold's Oxford, their 'lost causes, and forsaken beliefs, and unpopular names, and impossible loyalties' may have been the 'enchantments of the Middle Age[s]';[3] but for most people, these features confirmed their irrelevance. Cowled monks, troubadors in tights, knights in ponderous suits of armour can seem as alien from modern life as primitive tribesmen do. Mediaeval philosophy in particular surely suffered from its most salient character: the association with religion. Modern philosophers either hostile or indifferent towards religion were not drawn to study Aquinas, who by the end of the nineteenth century had become the 'official' philosopher of Roman Catholicism. Indeed, there was the widespread feeling, expressed by Hegel, that there was no such thing as mediaeval philosophy, only mediaeval theology. Let us ask if there is any justification for that feeling.

Philosophy and Theology

Contemporary enthusiasts rightly plead that some mediaeval debates can be appreciated in relative isolation from the religious context in which they arose: the argument about universals, for example (see pp. 175ff.). But such pleading in effect concedes that the main body of mediaeval thought was theological in shape. Mediaeval writers themselves often distinguished theology from philosophy. Those who disliked the intrusion of Greek ideas into religion often used the term 'philosophy' pejoratively to refer to doctrines inspired by those ideas. One of the best-known Muslim works was titled *Incoherence of the Philosophers*, these being the admirers of Aristotle. The same people were intended by a thirteenth-century rabbi when he proclaimed that 'you ought to know that these philosophers whose wisdom you are praising end where we begin'.[4]

A less loaded distinction, still popular today, was made by Aquinas. Theologians accept as premises, on the basis of faith or revelation, those propositions which philosophy subjects to critical examination: God's existence, say, or His omnipotence. But this has peculiar consequences as a way of sorting philosophers from theologians. For one thing, it will be impossible to allocate thinkers like Aquinas himself to one rather than the other category, since they thought it proper to accept such premises on faith, but also to provide rational proofs for them. It would mean, too, that we should have to reclassify a seemingly philosophical work on religion if it turned out that the author accepted God's existence through faith alone. Again, it would be difficult to classify those thinkers who, although they eschew rational proofs of religious premises, nevertheless offer general justifications for taking testimony and revelation as reliable sources of truth.

In short, the ways in which mediaeval writers themselves tried to distinguish theology from philosophy are not much help in adjudicating the later feeling that mediaeval thought was, in essence, the former. Let us return, then, to our occasionally erratic but always interesting guide, Hegel, and to his reasons for regarding mediaeval thought as theology. For Hegel, 'religion and philosophy have a common subject-matter – God inasmuch as He is absolute'. Nevertheless, theology and philosophy differ in their 'form' of understanding God, and in Hegel's view, the mediaevals never ascended to the higher, philosophical form.[5] While philosophy understands God or the Absolute through 'pure thought', theology tends to do so in 'imaginative' terms which are insufficiently free from those of mythology. Myths represent the gods as supernatural beings, embodied in human or animal forms, and separate from other beings in the natural world, including actual people. Theology, of course, has risen above this primitive conception, but it continues to regard 'the Holy' as a being 'having the characteristic of *externality*'.[6] God is thought of as the external cause of the world; as the legislator, from above, of human morality; and, in the form of the Holy Spirit, as an outside source from which people are illuminated. God is thereby rendered so remote from the world and ourselves that he becomes unknowable, hidden behind a veil: a predicament for which we compensate by trying to draw close to Him through worship and cult. There follows a perpetual 'see-saw' between the mind's conception of God as remote and inscrutable and the heart's efforts to gain 'a sense of His presence' by, for example, the taking of the Host.[7]

Hegel's portrait of mediaeval thought, however, betrays considerable ignorance. There were thinkers, especially those most influenced by Neo-Platonism, who cannot be accused of treating 'the Holy' as 'external'. The portrait anyway relies on building into the term 'philosophy' Hegel's own, hardly indisputable, philosophical position: in particular, his claim that God or the Absolute is not something independent of the natural order and of human consciousness (see ch. 8, sect. 2). Nevertheless, his assessment of mediaeval thought offers a useful perspective from which to regard it, as we shall see in a moment. Philosophers later than Hegel of course have their own suggestions for how theology and philosophy might be distinguished in those areas where their interests draw close. (No one, I take it, denies that there are philosophical issues obviously independent from theology, nor that there are branches of theology – 'dogmatic' and 'pastoral' theology, for instance – remote from philosophical concerns.) But these suggestions do not convince. For example, it is hard to see how the popular suggestion that philosophy is a 'second-order' discipline, examining the concepts which other disciplines deploy, can gain a purchase. God is not an entity whose nature can be studied by empirical means, so one wonders where the difference could be between a theologian's examination of the nature of God and a philosopher's examination of the concept of

God. There is, in my view, little point in pressing the question whether issues like the compatibility of divine omnipotence with human freedom, or the limits on our capacity to describe God, belong to theology rather than philosophy, or vice versa. We might speak of their belonging to philosophical theology, or theological philosophy.

Let me close by pursuing my remark that Hegel's discussion, while failing to secure a verdict on mediaeval thought as 'mere' theology, provides a useful perspective on the age. This is best done by glancing at his account of the characteristic mood of the age, which he called 'the unhappy consciousness'. By this, he meant the attitude of 'the alienated soul', one which views itself as a 'dual-natured, merely contradictory being'.[8] This is the view of someone who sees himself as an embodied, natural creature, but one whose true essence is that part of himself which most resembles a transcendent being, God or 'the Unchangeable'. The 'unhappy consciousness' tries, impossibly, to resolve this duality by suppressing the inessential side. It 'renounces and surrenders its embodied form' in order to 'gain a sense of its unity with the Unchangeable'.[9] For example, it treats the body and 'animal functions' as 'the enemy', to be combatted by the devices of asceticism. Such is bound to be the result when people identify what is most central to them with something beyond or outside their natural, empirical existence.

This is a perceptive résumé of how many mediaeval thinkers encouraged men and women to regard themselves. We will encounter those, for example, who urge that the real self is a pure 'active intellect', like God Himself, but encumbered in our case by the body during our sojourn in this world. We will, to be sure, also encounter those who resist this picture of the self and who argue that the body is an essential part of the human person and a prerequisite for arriving at knowledge of God. Still, it is reasonable to regard these latter philosophers as reacting against the views which would induce an 'unhappy consciousness'. In that case, it is the mood which Hegel describes that sets the agenda for debate, even if plenty of the parties to the debate rejected the terms of the agenda. In short, we can usefully distinguish philosophers of the Middle Ages according to their stance on those doctrines which, if true, would mean that we are indeed depressingly 'dual-natured' creatures, who must either surrender to or struggle against the unhappiness which our condition implies.

• 2 Neo-Platonism and Early Christianity •

Were he granted his time over again, George Steiner remarked, he would devote it to studying the emergence of Christian thought in the confused intellectual climate of the Graeco-Roman world during the first few centuries following the crucifixion. The story is at once complex, fascinating, and in parts untold. Certainly that climate was a confused one with, on the religious front, sundry Jewish and Christian sects, pagan cults, gnostics and hermetists vying for allegiance and, in the world of philosophy, Platonists, Aristotelians, Epicureans and Stoics at once disputing and stealing one another's clothes.

Among early Christians, there was also a dispute: whether to gain respectability for the new religion by grafting its doctrines onto an established system of Greek philosophy, or to isolate and protect the faith against high-faluting metaphysical abstractions. In the latter camp belonged Tertullian (c.160–c.225), who wrote 'What indeed has Athens to do with Jerusalem? . . . Away with all attempts to produce a Stoic, Platonic, and dialectical Christianity.'[10] (His even better known line, 'I believe because it is absurd', further confirms his animosity towards rational philosophers – who would, one suspects, be among those whose sufferings in Hell, in Tertullian's view, provide entertainment for the saved.) This dispute as to whether Greek philosophy *ought* to shape Christian doctrine gradually modulated into a more scholarly and still live debate over the extent to which it had *in fact* done so. At one extreme is the 'view [that] the whole body of Christian dogmas appears as a construction of Greek inspiration erected upon the . . . Gospel'; at the other, the 'view [that] not a single Greek philosophical notion . . . has ever become a constitutive element of Christian faith'.[11]

No one denies, of course, the presence in the New Testament of philosophical terminology. 'Our eyes are fixed,' writes St Paul in Platonic vein, 'not on the things that are seen, but on the things that are unseen: for what is seen passes away; what is unseen is eternal' (2 Cor. 4). The best-known example is St John's apparent invocation of the *logos* at the beginning of his Gospel, the Word which 'when all things began, . . . already was', which 'dwelt with God' and was 'what God was'. But perhaps this was simply the rhetoric of the age, no more indicative of a systematic attempt to exploit Greek metaphysics than a modern writer's casual references to libidos and death-wishes of a commitment to Freudian psychology. After all, no one denies, either, that there were Christian doctrines which provided extremely infertile soil for Greek ideas. These include the doctrine of the creation of the universe *ex nihilo* (and not, as with Plato's 'Craftsman', from pre-existent Forms), and that of the incarnation of God in Jesus, a belief which St Paul said must be 'folly to the Greeks'. A modern theologian agrees with him: it is 'inconceivable for Greek thought . . . that *logos* should become flesh'.[12] But perhaps 'inconceivable' is too strong here and a version of Platonism might be developed that would not be totally unaccommodating of such a doctrine. (After all, the Jewish Platonist Philo of Alexandria (c.20 BCE–c.50 CE) had argued for something like the incarnation of *logos* in the person of Moses.)

I lack the space and scholarship to pass judgement on the general influence of Greek philosophy on Christian thought. I shall, though, discuss one very important chapter in the story by considering the views of the last great philosopher from the Greek world, Plotinus, and the first great Christian philosopher, Augustine – a chapter already written in part by the latter when acknowledging his debt to Neo-Platonism.

Plotinus' Neo-Platonism

In one of biography's great opening lines, Porphyry wrote of his teacher, 'Plotinus . . . seemed ashamed of being in the body.'[13] So 'deeply rooted was this feeling' that he would not speak of his parentage and childhood. It seems, though, that Plotinus (205–70) was born in (hellenized) Egypt, where he studied philosophy in Alexandria. After an unsuccessful attempt to visit India, he arrived in Rome to teach philosophy at the age of forty. A late starter, he only began to write ten years after this. His writings were organized by Porphyry, with a peculiar zeal for symmetry, into groups of nine essays – hence their title, *The Enneads* ('The Nines'). Plotinus was a man of charisma, who gathered about him a circle of disciples devoted to contemplation and austerity. His one venture into the political field was the unlikely attempt to found a city of philosophers, Platonopolis. The Emperor was keen on the project but, perhaps for reasons of 'cost effectiveness', the idea was soon scotched by bureaucrats. Plotinus died a painful death, probably of leprosy, with the grace and fortitude to be expected of a man who scorned bodily life.

It would be unfair to regard Plotinus simply as a coda to Plato or an overture to Augustine. Indeed, his stock is currently rising, with one recent author declaring him 'greatest of the Greek philosophers'.[14] Few would concur in this judgement, but Plotinus is certainly one of the most systematic Greek philosophers and epitomizes one tendency – the transcendental and mystical one – in Plato's own thought. His ambition is to construct a system to accommodate, in terms as nearly literal as possible, Plato's poetic sagas – in the *Phaedrus* and the *Symposium* especially – of the soul's ascent from the earthly to union with the Good.

His shame at being 'in the body' is an expression of Plotinus' belief that 'by a fall, a descent into the body, into matter', the soul has 'trafficked away for an alien nature its own essential [nature]' (I.6.5).[15] The aim of philosophy is to enable the soul, 'detached' from matter, to 'mount' above its ordinary condition and aspire 'not to something alien, but to its very self', as if returning to its 'native land' after years of wandering (VI.9.11, V.9.1). (This 'return' by the soul, Plotinus thinks, is the true message of Homer's *Odyssey*.) The soul's task is not easy, for it has a tendency to self-assertiveness, manifested in its attachment to a particular body which serves to emphasize its distinctness from other embodied souls. Worse still, the prospect of 'detaching' itself from the 'solid ground' offered by the corporeal world and turning to the seemingly 'shapeless' realm of the immaterial, produces in the soul the 'sheer dread of . . . nothingness' (VI.9.3).

The picture, so far familiar, is that of the soul as an immaterial entity, alienated from its essentially intellectual nature through over-identification with an ephemeral bodily world. But from now on, Plotinus' account begins to diverge from Plato's. As the soul 'mounts' towards contemplation of the eternal Platonic Forms (see pp. 107ff.), it loses the individuality provided by attachment to a particular body. It is now 'intellection', the activity of mind, though not of your mind or mine in particular. Following the so-called Middle Platonists, Plotinus argues that the Forms are inseparable from their 'intellection', for they must exist in some medium, as it were, which can only be the 'intellecting' mind. This does not mean that Forms are created by mind: rather that, in this immaterial realm, 'the knowledge of the thing is the thing', 'intellection and being are identical' (V.9.5). Neither Forms nor intellect are conceivable except in their mutual reliance. To this union or fusion, Plotinus gives the name *noûs*.

Noûs, however, is not our 'native land', and 'we must make haste yet higher', towards that which 'produced that realm' – towards what Plotinus calls the One or the Good (VI.7.16). 'Gathered' in the One, the soul finally enjoys 'liberation from the alien that besets' it at any less exalted level (VI.9.11). Strictly, the One cannot be said to *be*, for it is responsible for all being. A being has 'shape', it is a 'this or that', whereas the One is 'without shape', 'neither a this nor a that'. Indescribable and unconceptualizable, the One can only be reached in a mystic vision whereby we are 'made over into unity' with it – a vision, Porphyry tells us, that Plotinus experienced on four occasions (three more than Porphyry himself). Given these resonances with Indian thought, one might almost believe that Plotinus' Indian expedition *had* reached its destination.

The Plotinian universe, then, is hierarchical, descending from the One through *noûs* ('intellection' plus the Forms) to soul – the three so-called 'hypostases'. Soul itself is hierarchically ordered. In its higher activities, such as mathematical contemplation, it merges into intellect. At a lower level, it manifests itself in the everyday reasoning and perception of intelligent creatures, and at a lower level still, operates as the unconscious, 'vegetal' principle animating nature. At these lower levels, soul confronts matter, which, like Aristotle's 'prime' matter, is not any particular kind of stuff, but a formless, unknowable X on which all form and order is imposed. More apt is Plotinus' metaphor of concentric circles – with the spheres of *noûs* and soul 'radiating' out from the central sphere of the One. This metaphor reminds us that everything, matter apart, has a single centre – the 'native land', to which to return.

Why does Plotinus think that the universe must have the structure just sketched? One argument, a 'downwards' or 'centrifugal' one, begins by assuming the One and attempts to show how from this there must 'emanate' the world as we experience it. The argument is inductive in character. The things we encounter in the world of a (relatively) perfect kind 'generate' and 'impart something of themselves' to whatever they produce. Fire imparts warmth, for example. 'How then', Plotinus asks, 'could the most perfect [the One] grudge or be powerless to give of itself?' (V.4.1). It could not, and so 'in its exuberance has produced the new', in the shape of *noûs*, which inherits some of the One's perfection. *Noûs* then 'repeats the act of the One in pouring forth a vast power', namely soul, which in its own exuberant turn 'overflows', via the 'vegetal' principle, into nature. This emphasis on 'the dynamic, vital character of spiritual being' or 'the great dance of the universe', as one authority puts it,[16] has more in common with the speculations of the European romantics and 'vitalists', like Bergson and Teilhard de Chardin, than with Plato's conception of the Forms.

Plotinus' other, 'upwards' or 'centripetal', argument begins with the world as experienced and attempts to show how this must have 'emanated' from the One. The key role is played by the notion of unity. 'It is', we are told, 'in virtue of unity that beings are beings' (VI.9.1). Remove the unity which soul, as an organizing principle in the world, lends to an army or a house, and it ceases to be an army or house. But soul, and indeed an individual soul such as mine, is itself a 'manifold', composed of 'diverse powers', like reason and desire, and so must be 'held together' by something more unitary. This can only be, in the first instance, a Form. I am a (relatively) unitary being only because my 'diverse powers' are aspects of a single Form which I manifest. But the realm of Forms, *noûs*, cannot constitute the final unity. This is partly because the Forms themselves are an 'agglomeration', so something beyond them is needed to confer unity on the 'cosmos' they inhabit. But it is also because the two dimensions of *noûs*, 'intellection' and the Forms 'intellected', though in truth inseparable, necessarily appear distinct to the 'intellecting' mind. 'Considered as at once thinker and object of its thought, [*noûs*] is dual, . . . not the unity' (VI.9.2). The point is the difficult yet interesting one that when we contemplate the realm of Forms, we are bound, by the very subject–object structure of thought, to 'see it from without', as if one thing were seeing another (VI.7.15). That, of course, is an illusion since, as we learnt, 'intellection and being are identical'. But it is an illusion we cannot escape from when engaged in thought. Hence, duality will only be overcome when we 'mount' above any process of an intellectual kind and enter into mystic union with the One through a vision where all sense of a distinction between a subject and an object evaporates. Only in the One, then, do we encounter that absolute unity which, since all beings depend upon unity, must be the ultimate source from which all else 'emanates'.

Beauty and Evil

A variation on this 'upwards' argument from unity occurs in the best-known section of *The Enneads*, on beauty. Everyone has some capacity, thinks Plotinus, for recognizing beauty. But beauty is not simply an object of recognition: it is also 'desired of every soul', and to sense beauty is to be inspired with 'longing and love' (I.6.4). Plotinus, here drawing on Diotima's speech in the *Symposium* (see p. 114), argues that such desire or love must be construed as directed towards beauty itself, which for him is identical with the One or the Good. Some kind of aquaintance with the One, therefore, however dim, is implicit in our everyday experience of beauty.

Plotinus begins by rejecting the familiar view that the beauty we experience around us is due to symmetry. This view cannot apply to a beautiful colour or to sunlight, for these do not have parts which are symmetrically or otherwise related. Moreover, we discern beauty in 'noble conduct, or excellent laws', on which the notion of symmetry has no purchase. The beauty of physical objects, conduct, laws or whatever must, Plotinus concludes, be due to the unity they exhibit. 'On what has . . . been compacted to unity, beauty enthrones itself' (I.6.2). Whatever unity something beautiful enjoys is due to its 'communion in ideal Form'. The beauty of a house, for example, owes to 'the inner idea [being] stamped upon the mass of exterior matter, the indivisible exhibited in diversity'. With some artificiality, Plotinus even tries to account for the beauty of a colour as 'the outcome of a unification'. A patch of colour is a unit 'conquered' out of 'the darkness of matter' by the 'pouring-in' of the Form of light (I.6.3).

Since each Form is unitary, it is beautiful, but it is not in the realm of Forms that we encounter beauty itself. Precisely because a Form *has* beauty, there must be a further source for the beauty it possesses. Hence, contemplation of the Forms only sets up a further 'longing' for that which confers unity and beauty upon them. This further source can only be 'the nature of the Good radiating beauty before it' (I.6.9). In mystical fusion with the One, therefore, we experience that beauty which, all along, was the true object of our desire for, and delight in, the beauties which our senses and intellects discern.

The equation, within the One, of the Good and beauty implies that, for Plotinus, there is an intimate relation between the aesthetic and the moral.

'The ugly is also the primal evil; therefore its contrary is at once good and beautiful' (I.6.6). Ugliness, we know, is due to a departure from unity, to formlessness. This is equivalent to descending into mere matter. A man, for example, becomes ugly when 'immersed in filth or daubed with mud'. Evil is due to exactly the same process. The virtues all involve 'purifying' the soul from its contamination by matter, so that it becomes 'all idea and reason'. Courage, for instance, is 'being fearless of the death which is but the parting of the soul from the body' (I.6.6).

This account of evil prepares the way for Plotinus' solution to a problem that threatens to be a serious one for his account. The Good, in Plato, is not generative, not 'dynamic and vital', and so cannot be blamed for the existence of evil in the universe. But the Good or the One, for Plotinus, is the source of the world. How, then, can it truly be the Good given the presence of so much evil in the world? Plotinus' solution – ingenious and influential – is that all evil is due to that which is evil in itself, matter, but that matter, strictly speaking, does not exist at all. Matter is 'absolute lack', so that 'being is attributed to it by an accident of words: the truth would be that it has non-being' (I.8.5). Whereas the One was 'above' being, matter is 'below' it: for, lacking all form, there can be no sense to the question of *what* being, what 'this or that', matter is. The One is thereby cleared of responsibility for evil in the order of being by the device of putting evil outside of that order. In the language of later theologians, evil is not a positive ingredient in God's universe, but a 'privation'.

Plotinus' practical philosophy is concocted from familiar Greek themes, with a twist added to accommodate them to his doctrine of the One. The Plotinian catalogue of virtues is standard (temperance, prudence, courage, magnanimity, etc.), as are the asceticism he preached and the stoic resignation recommended in the face of hard knocks. ('What more is called for than a laugh?', when beaten up and robbed by 'a gang of lads' (III.2.8).) Like Plato, he distinguishes between the 'civic virtues' and the 'loftier' ones, like wisdom, though unlike Plato he seems to have thought, despite the attempt to found Platonopolis, that political activities were too vulgar to engage a true philosopher. In the case of both kinds of virtue, the purpose is to 'liken' oneself to what is higher, through 'purifying' the soul of its contamination by matter – through ascetic control of the passions, for example. The 'restraint' demanded by civic virtue may suffice for 'the human life of the good man', but falls short of that 'final disengagement' required if the soul is to 'take up instead another life, that of the Gods'. For this, it is necessary to 'fix our gaze above . . . and attain likeness to the supreme exemplar', the One (I.2.7). The true aim of the virtuous life is to prepare the soul for that mystical union in the One where, finally, 'we put otherness away' and return to the source of our being.

Augustine, Neo-Platonism and *Genesis*

Although Porphyry, if not Plotinus, regarded Christian beliefs as 'superstition', the word 'god' occurs frequently in Neo-Platonist writings. Sometimes it occurs in the plural, referring either to the Greek deities or to especially elevated souls. But Plotinus also speaks of God, and here the reference is less clear. The most obvious candidate would be that supreme source, the One, yet Plotinus tells us that we would be thinking 'too meanly' of the One were we to describe it as God. So perhaps the reference is to *noûs*, or to a combination of *noûs* and soul in its higher activities.

Be that as it may, it is clear, on the one hand, that there is no element in Plotinus' metaphysics with which the Christian God could be identified but, on the other, that his system holds considerable promise for any Christian anxious to convert his 'superstition' into a coherent philosophical theology. None of Plotinus' 'hypostases' could be the Christian God for the following reason: He could not be *less* than the One, for then He would not be supreme, but nor can He *be* the One, since this is lacking in will and those personal, moral attributes which, if only by analogy, Christians ascribe to God. In some respects, however, the One does fit the bill. Like God, the One is a supreme and immaterial source of the world, yet in no way 'diminished' through what it generates, nor in any way responsible for the evil to be found in the world. Like God again, the One is our 'native land', the true object of our yearnings, in some kind of union with which we discover our true selves. Moreover, since the One does not forsake its unity through generating *noûs* and soul, these are, in some sense, three-in-one – thus offering a possible model for that most delicate of Christian doctrines, the Trinity.

Few were more anxious than one young teacher of rhetoric in Milan in 384 CE to discover the philosophical resources which would enable him both to demolish the superstition, Manicheanism, to which, despite misgivings, he was still attached, and to embrace in intellectual honesty the orthodox Christianity which attracted him. (The Manichees believed that reality was a battleground between the equally powerful and material forces of good and evil.) St Augustine (354–430) had turned to Manicheanism partly as an antidote to what, by his own rigorous standards, he regarded as his dissoluteness. His profession had taken him from his native North Africa to Italy, and it was here that his reading of the Neo-Platonists provided the sought-after resources. Converted to orthodox Christianity in 386, his plan to live in contemplative retreat was spoiled when he was forcibly drafted as Bishop of Hippo (today's Annaba in Algeria). During the remainder of a long life lived in tumultuous times (Rome had fallen to the Goths in 410), Augustine managed to combine writing, pastoral duties and indefatigable campaigns against heretics, notably the Donatists and

Pelagians. He died, in suitably apocalyptic circumstances, on the eve of the Vandals' sacking of Hippo.

As we know from his *Confessions* – one of the earliest and finest autobiographies – the young Augustine felt something even more intense than Plotinus' 'shame' at being in the body. Unlike Plotinus, he was a man of strong sensual passion, 'floundering in the broiling sea of my fornication' (2.2).[17] Hence his 'inner self was a house divided against itself' with 'the impulses of nature and . . . of spirit . . . at war with one another' (8.8 and 8.5). Occasionally, Augustine could smile at this inner strife, as in his prayer, 'Give me chastity and continence – but not yet' (8.7). Unlike Plotinus, too, he felt unable to resolve this conflict by identifying his true self with 'the impulses of spirit'. This was partly because of a belief that the nature of the self is opaque, since it all too easily 'confounds itself' with what it is not, but mainly because of the dogged suspicion that, perhaps, this 'war' is inevitable, a reflection of the real structure of reality. Perhaps reality truly is an irresolvable conflict between material forces, the higher ones and those of evil. This Manichean tenet, however depressing, at least provided an explanation of the presence of evil and lust in the world. (Augustine was not tempted by such embellishments to this tenet as the belief that eclipses occur in order to veil cosmic battles between the forces of good and evil.)

It was this suspicion which an acquaintance with Neo-Platonism helped Augustine dispel. First, 'by reading . . . the Platonists I had been prompted to look for truth as something incorporeal' (7.20), for they offered an account of a world generated from an immaterial source, so that it was no longer necessary to think of God as an immense 'sea' in which the world, like a giant sponge, is soaked. Second, they convinced Augustine that 'whatever is, is good; and evil . . . is not a substance', as the Manichees held, but a 'privation' of being (7.12). Nothing that comes from God can be bad, for evil is a falling-away from His creation. Naturally, Augustine specifies a number of respects in which Neo-Platonism is, from the Christian perspective, deficient. 'Their pages have not the mien of the true love of God': nor will one 'read in them that the Word was made flesh and came to dwell among us' (7.21 and 7.9). Clearly, important differences must be resolved before Augustine can bring off the 'momentous' feat of 'bringing together' the Plotinian One and the God of 'love, power, justice, and forgiveness'.[18]

The difference on which Augustine focuses in the *Confessions* concerns the Creation. Neo-Platonism is incompatible with creation *ex nihilo* on two counts: first, the One is not responsible for matter, and second, *noús* and soul, though 'emanating' from the One, do not come later than the One and are therefore co-eternal with it. The world is not created, therefore, but has always existed. It is not, however, this conflict with Genesis so much as an apparent inconsistency within that Book which taxes Augustine. God, it would seem, created heaven and earth twice – once before the first 'day', then all over again on subsequent 'days'. Augustine's solution, borrowing as much as he can from Plotinus, is ingenious. The heaven and earth created on the second and third 'days' are to be understood in the familiar way, but in the words 'In the Beginning God made heaven and earth', the terms are to be taken allegorically. 'Earth' refers to 'formless matter', the shapeless 'vehicle for all the composite forms . . . in the world'; while 'Heaven' is 'some kind of intellectual creature', namely the Forms and the 'intellect' in which the Forms are known (12.6ff). This 'Heaven', in fact, is Plotinus' *noûs*, with the difference that it is created and so is 'in no way co-eternal' with God, even though – in a manner barely explained – it 'partakes in [God's] eternity' (12.9). Creation from the first 'day' on then proceeds through God's filling or shaping the formless 'vehicle' through the 'intellectual creature'. (An account of the Creation which relies even more heavily on Neo-Platonic thought was later offered by the Irishman John Scotus Erigena (*c.*810–77). Opponents understandably accused him of an heretical pantheism, incompatible with the doctrine of creation *ex nihilo*.)[19]

Augustine recognized that problems remain: notably, 'What was God doing before He made heaven and earth?' If something prevented His creating earlier than He did, or caused Him to create when He did, then there must, absurdly, have been something besides God prior to all creation. Augustine's rather brutal solution is that time itself only begins with things which are susceptible to change: hence there was no time prior to the Creation during which God was either doing or not doing anything (12.11ff). (I defer further discussion of this problem, which also exercised Islamic thinkers, to sect. 3.)

Another problem concerns the warrant for Augustine's interpretation which dissolved the paradox of 'the double creation' in the opening verses of Genesis. Here he treads a delicate and influential line between fundamentalism and revisionism. On the one hand, faith requires us to take these verses as true, since they are the word of God transmitted through Moses. Even if we cannot know their proper interpretation – and Augustine is tentative about his own – we must believe them. Indeed, unless we first believe them, there is scant hope of ever understanding them. On the other hand, most people are 'still like children', which requires Scripture to address them in a simple manner capable of sustaining them in their faith (12.28). They would hardly have been sustained in this had Genesis indulged in sophisticated platonic talk of *noûs* and the Forms. This consideration provides the interpreter with a presumptive warrant to treat problematical passages as allegorical or metaphorical.

Augustine's attitude towards interpretation of Scripture illustrates his wider stance towards faith and reason. While, as his personal history shows, it is important to try rationally to justify the testimony of faith, it is faith finally which takes precedence. The point is not that where reason definitively contradicts faith, reason must be abjured. Rather we can never have total confidence in our estimation of what is and is not rational. Even where reason seems to support faith – as when it is properly argued, along Plotinian lines, that our sense of beauty and truth is only explicable in terms of a divine source – the arguments display only a 'tenuous form of knowledge', which should never substitute for faith and revelation.[20] Thus while Augustine does offer arguments for God's existence, he does not see these as the 'proofs' which it was soon to become a major theological industry to construct.

Free Will

One of the things Augustine liked in Neo-Platonism was the treatment of evil as 'privation'. If 'for a thing to be bad is for it to fall away from being',[21] then evil is not some Manichean force, but 'non-being'. This hardly suffices, however, to scotch 'the problem of evil' which Christians face. Plotinus' 'non-being' is *matter*, which does not emanate from the One. God, on the other hand, does create matter, so if evil consists in a tendency towards matter, God is not thereby exonerated. Augustine then uses the evergreen ploy of arguing that the evils we observe in the world are required, in ways opaque to us, for the good of the whole. History is compared to a poem whose beauty needs to be 'set off' with ugly antitheses in order to stand out.[22] But this ploy is of no help with a further problem, stemming from the Christian belief that God justly punishes sinners. Granting that sins are blemishes which nevertheless contribute to the good of creation as a whole does nothing to explain the justice of punishing their perpetrators. If anything, it compounds the problem, for the sinners are then doing a useful job – like the 'stooge' in a music-hall juggling act, whose bungling sets off the skill of his partner.

At this point Augustine invokes the notion which occupied more of his, and many later theologians', attention than any other – free will. God is responsible, not for sins, but for our free will which, when misused, results in sin. Since it is we, not He, who are thus responsible, there is no injustice in His punishing sins. That free will is 'a good thing', Augustine takes to be evident: only a 'madman' could 'doubt that that is far superior without which there can be no right living', even if that thing, free will, also makes wrong living possible.[23] Augustine confesses that he does not know why God did not make us like angels, invariably yet freely choosing the path of virtue. But He did create us as we are, potential warts and all, and it would be heresy to suggest that He made a mistake in doing so. Here, once again, faith must not be shaken by absence of understanding.

This strategy for salvaging God's justice will only succeed if freedom of the human will is compatible with God's sovereignty. One argument for supposing it is *not* is stated by Augustine as follows: 'if . . . God foreknows that a man will sin, he must necessarily sin. But if there is necessity there is no voluntary choice.' He clearly rejects this argument. I do not compel you to order a whisky simply by knowing in advance that you are going to. 'Similarly God compels no man to sin, though he sees beforehand those who are going to sin by their own will.'[24] It is less clear *why* he rejects it. Is it because God's foreknowledge necessitates my sin without thereby rendering it non-voluntary? Or is it because not even divine foreknowledge of events renders those events necessary? Augustine's position is probably the latter and more plausible one, which later logicians have expressed in the following way. It is indeed necessary that if God knows that X, then X is the case – otherwise He could not have known it. But that leaves it entirely open whether X is something that *has* to be the case. If 'X' is '2 + 2 = 4', it does; but if 'X' is 'John will order a whisky' then, in the absence of some further argument, it does not.

Augustine, however, recognized in this connection the serious problem, which has continued to dog Christian theology, posed by the doctrine of *grace*. It was Augustine who was largely responsible for the branding as a heretic of his contemporary, Pelagius, who was deemed to have denied this doctrine on the grounds of its incompatibility with free will. Actually it is uncertain what Pelagius *did* deny, but whatever his exact position, Augustine was surely right to insist that on at least some interpretations, the doctrine of grace is compatible with human freedom. If grace is that which enables our acts of will to translate into successful action, that does not diminish our freedom to will. Nor does it if it consists in God's returning a capacity to will to people who have lost it through over-dedicated 'service to sin' and dissipation. The trouble comes when Augustine, citing such Pauline utterances as 'it is God who works in you as to both willing and doing' (Phil. 2: 13), construes grace as a condition, both necessary and sufficient, for anyone's willing or choosing as they do. The point seems to be that, since 'God works in men to will' and since God's intended work 'cannot be resisted by human wills', then everything we will is causally determined by God's own will.[25]

If Pelagius denied grace so understood, was he wrong, let alone guilty of 'unspeakable wickedness', to do so? Can matters really be 'in our own power', if our decisions are determined by God's will? Perhaps they can if, like Augustine at one point, one equates 'having in our own power' with 'being able to do what we will'.[26] For this is tantamount to saying that causal determination of our actions is irrelevant to their freedom. Provided we want to perform an action, and are able to execute what we want to do, then the action is free. That the desire was caused – whether by God or by our genes – is neither here nor there. But, as the many philosophical heirs of Pelagius have asked, does an equation like Augustine's and his 'strong' interpretation of grace really leave us with the freedom we imagined ourselves to possess?

Genuinely to have our lives 'in our own power', they argue, we must have the ability not simply to do what we want, but to determine for ourselves what our wants shall be, in a way incompatible with their being the products of another will – God's. It is unsurprising that at the end of his life, Augustine was to hint that the doctrine of grace may, after all, have proved 'victorious' over his efforts 'to maintain the free decision of the human will'.[27] Unsurprising, too, given the fine distinctions he makes – 'invisible even to a theological microscope', according to Gibbon – that later theologians (Calvinists, Roman Catholics, Jansenists), rivals to the point of killing one another over the issue of grace, could all find something to support their side of the case in Augustine's writings.

Why, one may wonder, was Augustine so attracted to a 'strong' doctrine of grace, given the elasticity, even in St Paul, of biblical references to grace? The reason, I suspect, is his acute experience of that same yearning which attracted him to Neo-Platonism. One theme in the *Confessions*, noted earlier, is the opaqueness of the self. '[T]he powers of my inner self are veiled in darkness which I must deplore' (10.32). But if, as the Psalm has it, 'all human lives are already written in Your record', then at least my inner life has a nature there to be known, if only by God. If, on the other hand, I am possessed of a freedom to stand outside of the determined order of things, then in a sense I am without a nature to be known. The price of such freedom is that its owner is an isolated, arbitrary creature, whose 'inner powers' are without explanation, and in that respect forever 'veiled in darkness'. If this is so, then Augustine's endeavour, at least until his last days, to construe freedom of the will in a manner compatible with a 'strong' doctrine of grace, reflects a desire, shared by Plotinus, to see human beings as integrated into a single, universal order. Recalling Plotinus' yearning for a 'native land', Augustine can sigh, with St Paul, 'for the shelter of that home which heaven will give me' (10.34).

There are many aspects of Augustine's platonized Christianity, including the moral and political themes of *The City of God*, which I have not discussed. Like the ones which I have, these were to be immensely influential in later Christian thought, as we shall see in further sections of this chapter.

• 3   Islamic and Jewish Philosophy •

It can come as a surprise to people familiar only with the recent history of Arab–Jewish relations to learn of the intimacy between Islamic and Jewish philosophy in former times. Ernest Renan perhaps exaggerated in describing Jewish thought as 'nothing but a reflection of Muslim culture',[28] but intellectual developments in these two cultures did indeed largely mirror one another from the tenth to the fourteenth century. To be sure, there were Jewish philosophers before the emergence of Islam, notably the Platonist Philo of Alexandria, but their influence on their co-religionists, always slight, had not endured.

On reflection, the intellectual intertwining of the two religions is not surprising. They shared, after all, the same central doctrines of a single God, responsible for the world's existence and for the eternal fates of the creatures made in His image. In the opening books of the Old Testament, and in its leading figures like Abraham and Moses, moreover, they shared holy texts and prophets. So did the other 'people of the Book', Christians, but the Islamic–Jewish *entente* was further cemented by common hostility to the Christian doctrines of the Trinity and the Incarnation, perceived as corrosive of God's absolute unity. Important, too, were language and geography. The usual medium of Jewish, as of Islamic, philosophy was Arabic, and it was in the lands conquered by the Arabs during the century following Muhammad's death in 632 CE, from Persia in the east to Spain in the west, that Jewish intellectual life, long suppressed in its homeland by Roman persecution, enjoyed a generally tolerant milieu. The Jewish thinker Maimonides (1135–1204) may have fallen foul of the Almohads in Spain, but he could then flourish in Egypt, as philosopher and court physician, at a time when, in Mainz and York, Jews were being burned alive.

Traditionalists and Hellenists

A striking similarity – and very much the theme of this section – *between* the two philosophical cultures was the same deep division *within* them. This is sometimes represented, and was at the time, as a divide between theologians and philosophers (*falāsifa*), but since some of the former were certainly not lacking in philosophical sophistication, let us instead speak of 'traditionalists' *versus* 'hellenists'. For what distinguished the *falāsifa* was the ambition to reconcile religious doctrine, adjusted if need be, with Greek thought of a Neo-Platonist or Aristotelian hue. (Thanks to the attribution of works by Plotinus and Proclus to Aristotle, the hues were often mixed.) It was against this attempt that traditionalists rebelled: neither the Torah nor the Koran were compatible as they stood with Greek metaphysics, and to adjust their doctrines was heresy.

In Islam and Judaism alike, the debate had a certain rhythm. By the beginning of the tenth century there was an established school of 'rational theologians', the Mu'tazalites, keen to justify doctrine by argument: to demonstrate, for example, that God's will was not capricious, but conformed to universal principles of justice. In the writings of Fārābī and Saadia, Muslim and

Jew respectively, this spirit of rational theology had blossomed, by the end of the century, into full-blown attempts to set their religions within a Neo-Platonist framework – one which was soon to yield to the more Aristotelian construction of Avicenna (Ibn Sīnā, in Arabic). These hellenizing efforts soon produced a reaction from such writers as Ghazāli in Baghdad and Judah Halevi in Spain, repelled by what the latter called the unholy marriage 'between the God of Aristotle and the God of Abraham'.[29] A more rigorous Aristotelianism, however, reasserted itself in the works of the twelfth-century Spanish contemporaries Maimonides and the Muslim Averroes (Ibn Rushd, in Arabic). On their fellow-believers, though, these philosophers were to have little impact, victory having already gone to traditionalists such as Ghazāli who, as one commentator puts it, 'effectively sealed the fate of Greek thought in Islam'.[30] The consolation prize for the Aristotelians was their immense influence upon Aquinas and other Christian thinkers. The 'curious consequence' of the great debate between traditionalist theologians and hellenizing philosophers was, therefore, that 'the great Christian theologians were to become the pupils of the Mohammedan [and Jewish] philosophers much more than of the Mohammedan [and Jewish] theologians'.[31]

Traditionalists and hellenists were not, it should be added, the only players on the field. Sometimes aloof from the great debate, sometimes joining it, were those, like the Sūfis, representing a different tendency of thought – mysticism. They will concern us in section 5 of this chapter.

I shall shortly turn to some of the philosophical issues which divided traditionalists from hellenists. These were, of course, taken seriously, but it is easy to feel that they reflected an underlying difference resistant to resolution by philosophical argument. The difference was between competing conceptions of how human beings are to be integrated in the wider order of things. Broadly, the hellenists aspired to portray human beings as integral elements within a rational totality. God, though responsible for the existence of the universe, cannot then be the mysterious, intervening power, the arbiter of good and evil, or the dispenser of grace, of popular religious faith. This portrait, the traditionalists complained, is without room for a God who can make 'a real difference' to the way things go, one able to invite the love and dependence which rescue people from a sense of isolation and abandonment. God as a 'prime mover' of a universe which then runs under its own steam, or a 'pure intellect' trafficking only in abstractions, or a being Himself subject to an impersonal moral law, is not the majestic, miracle-making Person to whom 'the peoples of the Book' turned for succour and a sense of their place in a purposive order. But the God of popular tradition, retorted the hellenists – beyond rational comprehension, issuing moral law by *diktat* – can only deepen the intelligent, educated person's isolation: for, if that is how God is, there is no intelligible order for anyone to grasp or within which to locate themselves. Here, then, is the visceral difference, over the kind of God that human beings truly need, which surfaces in the philosophical disputes.

Infidelity and Hermeneutics

To speak of *disputes*, however, is in a sense to describe matters from the traditionalist perspective, for it was the hellenists' claim, typically, that philosophical reason does not really conflict with the testimony of religion. Cynics treated this claim as disingenuous, a protective device in what were dangerous times, despite the relative tolerance, by usual standards of zealotry, that Islam displayed. The politically influential Ghazāli, after all, thought that the *falāsifa* should be 'branded with infidelity' and perhaps 'punished with death' (249).[32] Averroes and Maimonides doubtless laid themselves open to the charge of disingenuousness through their declared policy of disguising their real meaning from all but the most perceptive readers. Still, there is no overwhelming reason to suspect their convictions that philosophy was, as Averroes put it, 'the friend and milk-sister' of religion (DT 306),[33] and that it was the likes of Ghazāli who weakened the faith by publishing popular tracts in which atheistic ideas, though rebutted, were given an airing.

The attempt to establish the compatibility of hellenism with tradition was made urgent by Ghazāli's famous onslaught, in his *Incoherence of the Philosophers*, upon the first wave of hellenists such as Avicenna. Regarded by some as the most influential Muslim thinker since Muhammad himself, Ghazāli (1058–1111) was a Persian-born theologian who taught in Baghdad, where he wrote his main critical works, until 1095. A spiritual crisis, perhaps compounded by political difficulties, prompted him to leave Baghdad and to turn from teaching to meditation. As we shall see in section 5, he was to gain a new influence among the Sūfi mystics.

Ghazāli aims, in his great book, to refute no less than twenty *falāsifa* doctrines, of which three are held to be infidel. These are 'belief in the eternity of the world' (11), the 'assertion that divine knowledge does not encompass individual objects', and 'denial of the resurrection of bodies' (249). To these one might add the belief, attacked elsewhere, that moral law is not dependent on divine commandment. The point of the seemingly recondite matter of God's knowledge of individual objects is this: as Ghazāli saw it, the hellenists' God was a 'pure intelligence' which could have no acquaintance with material beings. This, he objects, is incompatible both with the Koran ('there does not escape Him the weight of an atom') and with divine justice, which requires God to know the individuals he rewards or punishes. These objections illustrate Ghazāli's general strategy: hellenist beliefs are neither rational nor compatible with scriptural authority and revelation, which alone are 'fit to produce certainty' (163). (The Jewish 'traditionalist', Halevi, agreed and indeed saw a chance, here, to secure the superiority of Judaism, on the ground that Yahweh revealed *His* message to some 600,000 people on Mount Sinai. That number of people could not be wrong.)

The greatest of the Muslim Aristotelians, Averroes (1126–98) – another amazingly industrious philosopher, lawyer and physician like Avicenna before him and Maimonides shortly after – struck back at Ghazāli in a number of works, including *The Incoherence of The Incoherence*. In his concise 'Decisive Treatise', he begins by elevating 'demonstration' over alternative ways – like rhetoric – of securing belief. This is in preparation for the following hermeneutical maxim or principle of interpretation: 'whenever the conclusion of a demonstration is in conflict with the apparent meaning of Scripture, that apparent meaning admits of allegorical interpretation' (DT 292). The maxim is subject to two constraints: it does not operate when there is universal consensus that a text must be taken literally, and allegorical interpretation must accord with the 'rules' of Arabic (no 'loose gun' exegetical pyrotechnics, in other words). (No more than Augustine (see pp. 158f.) does Averroes intend this as a criticism of Scripture.) On the contrary, 'God has been gracious to those . . . who have no access to demonstration' by providing them with images and metaphors which inspire in them the same basic beliefs that the 'elite' arrive at through reason (298). Averroes rejects the question of which general conception of God mankind needs, on the ground that different classes of people – the 'elite' and the 'masses' – need different conceptions. Or better, the 'masses' need a certain *picture*, with which the 'elite' are able to dispense.

The charge against Ghazāli is not that he rejects the need for allegorical interpretation, for like anyone else he is willing to apply this to the flowerier passages of the Koran ('His throne was on the water', and the like). Rather, Ghazāli unduly restricts the scope for such interpretations, and fails to appreciate that, when conducted in accordance with the proper rules, they in no way conflict with the message of the texts. How could they, given that they are uncovering the true hidden meaning of the texts?

Averroes' hermeneutics sound plausible as a strategy for reducing apparent conflicts between reason and revelation. Peculiarly, however, the strategy is hardly used when he turns to the particular issues on which Ghazāli had based his charge of infidelity against the hellenists. Only in the case of the resurrection of the body is his point that an allegorical interpretation is at least permissible, so that any scholar who offers it may be 'excused' if the interpretation is mistaken (299). Concerning the issue of whether the universe is eternal or had an origin, his points are quite different. First he argues that the 'apparent meaning' of Scripture is *not* unequivocally that the universe originated, in which case Aristotelian 'eternalists' are no more engaged in allegorical interpretation than are Ghazāli and the traditionalists. Second, he argues that the dispute over origin *versus* eternity is a largely verbal one, so that the protagonists are therefore 'not so very far apart from each other that some of them should be called irreligious' (296). As for the charge that hellenists deny divine knowledge of individuals, Averroes simply rejects it. Granted that God's knowledge of individuals is very different from mine, Ghazāli was nevertheless 'mistaken . . . in ascribing to [hellenists] the assertion that God . . . does not know particulars at all' (295). On this issue, then, Averroes claims to take Scripture as literally as Ghazāli, so that the need for allegorical interpretation does not arise.

Related remarks could be made about Maimonides' position. In his *Guide of the Perplexed*, he addresses those who feel pulled in different directions by religious commandment and metaphysical reason, and like Averroes he makes a good deal of the distinction between the apparent meaning of Scripture and its 'spiritual' meaning. But it is not obvious how much use he makes of this when tackling issues like that of the eternity of the universe. Indeed, the one clear feature of the *Guide* is its ambiguity on such issues. Not only does the work contain many inconsistencies, but Maimonides cheerfully announces that he will proceed on the basis of contradictory premises. The discerning reader, therefore, will be unsure how to take Maimonides' verdict in favour of a universe created in time, defended partly on the grounds that belief in its eternity 'gives the lie to every miracle, and reduces to inanity all the hopes and threats that the Law has held out'.[34] Is he simply disguising his sympathy, expressed in other places, for the Aristotelian doctrine of eternity?[35] Or is the point that such matters are beyond our ken, with prudence favouring belief in the doctrine which follows tradition? Or is he offering a pragmatic criterion of truth, so that belief in creation in time is true precisely in virtue of yielding a better pay-off? Whatever Maimonides' actual position on this question, hermeneutic considerations of literal *versus* figurative meanings are not involved.

The upshot of these remarks is that the issues which, for Ghazāli, divide traditionalists from hellenists are not dissolved by hermeneutic strategies. Indeed, the hellenists do not really try to dissolve them in this way, despite their initial methodological pronouncements. Let us see, then, how some of these were actually tackled, beginning with the topics – necessity, causality, time and eternity – which clustered around the doctrine of creation *ex nihilo*.

Time and Necessity

All parties to the dispute could agree with Augustine that the creation stories in Genesis, or the Koran, were not to be taken in all literalness. But it was another, and more dangerous, thing to hold that the doctrine of creation *per se* was allegorical. Hellenists were therefore anxious to square this doctrine with their own accounts. The debate followed the usual rhythm: the initial hellenist proposals, a traditionalist critique of these, and a later hellenist response to this critique.

We can begin with the position of Avicenna (980–1037), a Persian who, Russell remarked, 'spent his life in . . . the places that one used to think only exist in poetry'.[36] Indeed, he seems to have lived a life of adventure, women and wine, closer in style to the *Arabian Nights* or the *Rubáiyát* than to the kind his prodigious output would suggest. For Avicenna, there must be a necessary being: otherwise, there would be no final explanation of why anything exists at all. This being is God, 'the cause of all causes or the principle of all principles'.[37] There then follows a baroque account, with both Aristotelian and Neo-Platonist antecedents, of the 'emanation' from God of various 'intelligences', ranging from the one which moves the outermost heavens to that which imprints form on the matter of the sublunary world. This process is one of strict necessity, since although nothing but God is necessary 'by itself', everything which exists is necessitated by God. In what sense, then, does God create *ex nihilo*? Only, it seems, by excluding, through being incompatible with, nothingness. God 'bars not-being', and in that respect 'confers being . . . upon entit[ies]'.[38]

It is easy to predict what Ghazāli would find repellent in this account. If the universe 'emanates' from God, Plotinus-style, through divine 'self-reflection', then it is eternal and so not, in any usual sense, created. Anyway, creation surely suggests more to believers than God's merely keeping 'not-being' at bay, as it were. Equally corrosive of belief is Avicenna's insistence that everything occurs as a matter of strict and eternal necessity. For that seems not only to exclude the possibility of God's intervening in the natural order, through miracles, but to give Him no positive role in keeping that order running. Defenders of Avicenna will reply that any more traditional notion of creation is incoherent and that an intervening God who plays a positive role in running things is incompatible with acceptance of a necessary causal *order* in the world.

Ghazāli's way with the first reply is Augustine's. 'Time did have a beginning; and it was created. And before time, there was no time whatsoever' (36). Hence it is illegitimate to raise such puzzles as 'What was God doing *before* the Creation?' Ironically, Ghazāli is here relying on Aristotle's thesis of the relativity of time to change and motion. There can only be periods of time and a temporal order among events given some regular motion of things which provides a means of measurement. But he inverts Aristotle's conclusion that, since time is infinite, motion must be eternal. Motion had a beginning, Ghazāli insists, so therefore did time. If motion has been going on for infinity, we should have to accept – absurdly, in Ghazāli's view – that infinity can be multiplied since, for example, the sun revolves around the earth twelve times as often as Jupiter (20). We may still speak of God existing *before* the world, but such terminology must be emptied of the temporal connotation with which habit or 'imagination' usually invests it.

Ghazāli's way with the problem about the relation between God and the necessary causal order of the universe is simply to deny that this order *is* necessary. '[T]he connection between . . . cause and . . . effect is not necessary. Take any two things . . . The existence of one is not necessitated by the existence of the other' (185). When two kinds of thing – burning cotton and fire, say – are regularly associated, a connection between them is 'indelibly impressed upon our minds' (189). But 'it is clear that existence *with* a thing does not prove being *by* it' (186), as is soon discovered by a man, his blindness suddenly cured, who at first believes that colours are brought into existence by the opening of his eyes. So far, this sounds like David Hume's thesis (see ch. 7, sect. 2): X and Y are deemed causally connected when their conjunction is so constant that an occurrence of X induces us to believe that Y must happen. But Ghazāli is, rather, anticipating the so-called 'occasionalist' doctrine much favoured in the seventeenth century. 'X causes Y' means that God, 'either directly or through the intermediacy of angels', brings about Y on the occasion of X's occurring. Ultimately, therefore, God is the sole causal agent, and since He acts voluntarily, there is nothing in the order of things to prevent Him from turning a rod into a serpent or rendering a piece of cotton fireproof. The order of things is simply the set of 'norms' which, by and large, God maintains in operation.

Averroes responded in detail to these claims, inspired by the Aristotelian conviction that, if they were right, reality would not be the intelligible structure that our natural search for knowledge presupposes. The denial of a necessary causal order 'implies that nothing in this world can really be known' (TT 319).[39] A causal connection between two things cannot, but for the will of God, be accidental, since a thing is known as the thing it is in virtue of its causal connections with other things. Ghazāli is therefore in the paradoxical position of claiming knowledge about things which, having been stripped of causal connections with one another, can no longer be items of knowledge. Ghazāli's denial of a necessary causal order is paradoxical in a further respect, for a world lacking such order would not manifest that perfect workmanship, spoken of by the Koran, which is a main reason for belief in a wise Creator.

This belief, thinks Averroes, is also threatened by the traditionalist claim that God existed, in splendid isolation, 'before' the creation of time and motion. For since nothing could have prevented Him creating the universe earlier, His doing so when He did looks to be capricious. This is not Averroes' sole objection to supposing that the universe has existed only for a finite time. For anything to come into existence, it must already have been possible for it to do so. But 'that possibility needs something for its substratum . . . which receives that which is possible' (TT 59). If something must already exist in order for anything else to come into being, then clearly existence stretches back to infinity.

This prepares the way for an account of creation which leans on Aristotle, as one might expect from Averroes' opinion that Aristotle was 'given to us by divine providence, so that we might know all that can be known'.[40] God is the 'prime mover'. Himself unmovable, He must be an immaterial being, and since His essence is to impart movement, there must always have been something there for Him to move. He does not create the universe from literally nothing, therefore: rather He produces it by moving and changing matter and 'compounding' it with form (M 109).

But does this kind of 'production' really deserve, as Averroes supposes, to be described as 'creation'? He favourably contrasts the Aristotelian approach, in this respect, with the 'emanation' view of the Neo-Platonists, on which 'becoming is merely the emergence of things' from something they are already 'in' (M 108). That view allows for insufficient action, as it were, by God for Him to be spoken of as creating the world. But so, for most Muslim theologians, does Averroes' account. A God who merely organizes the universe out of raw materials is not a genuine creator. Admittedly Averroes asserts that 'what is potential is equal to nothingness',[41] on the ground that what has yet to be 'compounded' by God with form does not deserve to be called a 'something'. This struck the theologians, however, as a lame attempt to preserve the terminology of the doctrine of creation *ex nihilo*, but without the substance. Maimonides, it is worth noting, was less confident than Averroes about the prospects of reconciling that doctrine with the Aristotelian account to which he, too, was attracted. That is perhaps why, as we saw, he seems finally to plump, if only on pragmatic grounds, for the view that the universe was created in time.

Resurrection, the Soul and Perfection

One of the reasons why hellenists deserved 'branding with infidelity', according to Ghazāli, was their 'denial of the resurrection of bodies'. While it is hardly for philosophy to pronounce on whether God in fact resurrects the bodies of the dead, it is in its province to address a number of related issues – the relation between soul and body, the criteria for personal identity and survival, and conceptions of a perfect existence. The connection between the debate about resurrection and these issues is forged by the expectation that someone who claims, as hellenists usually did, that there is an afterlife but no bodily resurrection, will also argue that soul, personhood and heavenly perfection are independent of bodily existence.

The debate displayed the familiar dialectic: a traditionalist critique of some earlier hellenist accounts, followed by a later hellenist response to this critique. Avicenna, who epitomizes the earlier approach, begins in Aristotelian vein. 'The soul comes into existence whenever a body does so fit to be used by it' as its 'instrument'.[42] However, the soul is not simply the form of the body, the animator and organizer of its activities. Rather, these are functions of what is a separable, immaterial substance. This is true, at any rate, of the higher or rational soul, which must be as immaterial as the forms with which it is acquainted. Avicenna uses an argument – 'the flying man' – which anticipates Descartes' case for the separateness of soul and body and the identification of the self with the former alone (see ch. 7, sect. 3). Imagine a person suspended in the air, denied all awareness of his body and the external world. He will, nevertheless, be aware of himself as existing. Since the object of this awareness is not, *ex hypothesi*, anything physical, it can only be his self as an immaterial entity. Since he conceives himself separately from his body, he *is* separate from it. Moreover, it is this immaterial 'entity which remains one and the same [and which] is truly you', whatever subsequent functions it performs in organizing bodily activity.[43]

There is no reason, therefore, to suppose that a person ceases with the death of his body. He has simply discarded an 'instrument'. Unlike some modern theologians, however, who condescendingly smile at the conception of an afterlife which requires bodily survival, Avicenna is acutely aware of the difficulty of identifying individual souls in the absence of the bodies which ordinarily furnish the criterion for individuation. This is why, for him, there can be no individual souls prior to their association with bodies, nor souls which are always disembodied. '[A]fter their separation from their bodies the souls remain individual', but only because they have acquired 'different dispositions due to their bodies'.[44] It is only through his or her embodied life that a person retains individuality in the afterlife. Since some disembodied souls go to heaven, it follows that the highest form of life for the soul requires no engagement with the physical. 'The perfection proper to the soul is to become identified with the intelligible world' of immaterial forms.[45] Hence it is the duty of a person while still on earth to disengage himself as far as possible from physical concerns, in order to approximate to this state of perfection. As for Aristotle, it is the contemplative life which is our true goal.

Ghazāli's objections to Avicenna are primarily scriptural. The Koran is explicit about the physical pleasures and pains of the afterlife, and there is no scope for treating the relevant passages allegorically. At 'the hour of doom', some will enjoy the water of cool, running streams, while others will have their skins melted by scalding water (Koran, ch. 109). These contrasting fates both require the genuine resurrection of the body. Two of Ghazāli's points about Avicenna's position, however, have a more philosophical inspiration. Without denying that spiritual pleasures are superior to physical ones, he suggests that 'the combination of the two will be conducive to greater perfection' (235). The implication is that an Aristotelian emphasis upon the supremacy of a contemplative life is one-sided. This accords, perhaps, with the place of sensual pleasure as an ingredient in a full human life that Islam, more than most religions, has usually recognized. He is also less confident than Avicenna that we can make sense of an individual soul's existing apart from its body. Avicenna, after all, admits that each body is peculiarly 'fit' for a given soul. Why then should this 'mutual fitness' not be so thorough that it 'makes the immortality of the soul dependent upon the continuance of the body'? (225). That a soul can temporarily exist without a body, while awaiting the latter's resurrection at 'the hour of doom', is a mystery which we must accept on faith.

The later hellenists, Averroes and Maimonides, are sympathetic to their predecessor Avicenna on several counts. The soul is necessarily distinct from the body; the afterlife has no physical dimension to it; and the practical lesson for men is to concentrate upon contemplative activity. Scriptural stories about resurrection are bracing allegories for the benefit of the 'masses'. (Maimonides notes that such stories are anyway rare in the Jewish sacred literature.) The central argument also follows Avicenna. The rational soul 'is not mixed with matter in any way at all' because of its union with the immaterial 'intelligibles', abstract forms or essences (DA 315). But on one crucial count, they reject Avicenna's position, sharing and then radicalizing Ghazāli's worries about the preservation of the soul's individuality in the absence of a body. They argue that with the loss of the body – or even before, in special cases – the soul loses all individuality. We can only speak of souls in the plural because of the distribution of 'intellect' among different bodies. 'A perfect man', as Maimonides puts it, becomes increasingly identified with a purely intellectual 'object of apprehension', so that at death, or even before, 'the soul is separated from the body . . . After reaching this condition of enduring permanence, that intellect remains in one and the same state.'[46] But that state is indistinguishable from the state of any other 'perfect man' who has become identified with the 'object of apprehension'. Intellects, at first distinguishable through the 'impediments' which are their bodies, merge into Intellect. It follows, therefore, that the afterlife is entirely impersonal. 'If . . . the soul does not die when the body dies . . . it must, when it has left the bodies, form a numerical unity', as Averroes puts it (TT 15).

While Ghazāli may have sympathized with the premise, this conclusion of the impersonality of the afterlife would, of course, have horrified him, for more than any other hellenist doctrine this one threatens the fabric of traditional belief. Not only does the denial of personal immortality neutralize religion's main sanction of eternal reward or punishment, but it threatens any vision of an enduring personal relationship with God, and hence removes the greatest succour that religion has to offer to the faithful. It was this doctrine of Averroes and Maimonides which was the main reason why they fell foul of theological authority during their lifetime, and why during subsequent centuries their writings hardly influenced the intellectual development of their cultures.

'Development', perhaps, is not the right word to use in connection with, at any rate, Muslim thought, for after the twelfth century intellectual life atrophied. This is not the judgement only of Western commentators mainly concerned with the Muslim thinkers who had most impact upon Christian thought. A Pakistani scholar refers to the sack of Baghdad by the Mongols in 1258 as having 'ushered in an era of intellectual lethargy, mental stupor and strict conservatism . . . the first to suffer was philosophy itself'.[47] (The revival of Islamic thought in the nineteenth and twentieth centuries is discussed in chapter 9, section 3.) Political and military events doubtless played their part, but this era of conservative dogmatism also confirmed a prediction made by Ghazāli in his *Deliverance from Error* that the *falāsifa*, by challenging some central tenets of faith, would bring philosophy as such into disrepute. Perhaps it confirmed, as well, the wisdom of his remark that once people see themselves *as* traditionalists, they no longer *are* traditionalists. It is one thing to work from within a tradition, like Ghazāli himself, arguing against what are regarded as misguided criticisms. It is another to defend tradition simply because it is tradition. Ghazāli's successors, it can seem, no longer stood within a tradition, but stood outside of it in the manner of guards posted around a temple or mosque.

• 4 Thomism and its Critics •

In March 1277, the Bishop of Paris issued a *Condemnation of 219 Propositions*. Some, like the proposition that a man could be 'adequately generated from putrefaction', sound merely quaint, but they also included the claims that the world has existed from eternity and that intellect is singular (with the corollary that the afterlife is impersonal). When the condemnation of these is taken together with diatribes against the sovereignty of philosophy and 'the sayings of the accursed pagans', the Bishop's target becomes clear.[48] It was 'Latin Averroism', represented by figures such as Siger of Brabant, which was enjoying a vogue in the cathedral schools and the universities, recently developed out of the master–student guilds of the preceding century. Since Averroes was deemed to be the most authoritative commentator on Aristotle – whose works had become available in Latin by the thirteenth century in translations from Arabic and then from the original Greek – an attack on Averroism was also one on Aristotelian influences in theology. The reaction, indeed, had set in earlier than 1277, with St Bonaventure, for example, defending the Augustinian tradition against the intrusions of Aristotelianism.

The question arises as to why, despite the mood manifested in the *Condemnation*, Aristotelianism did not suffer the same eclipse in the Christian world as in the Islamic. The former, to be sure, did not experience a trauma equivalent to the sack of Baghdad, inspiring a return to 'the old ways'. Nor did it boast a traditionalist figure with Ghazāli's combination of acumen, rhetoric and popular appeal. But a main explanation, surely, lies in the achievement of a man who had died shortly before the *Condemnation*. Here was someone who, despite the inclusion of some of his own views among the condemned propositions, had produced a magisterial synthesis of Aristotelian and Christian thought which few reflective Christians could regard as subversive of faith in the manner of Averroism. I refer to St Thomas Aquinas. That Aquinas could be 'condemned' (until 1323), as well as subjected to acute criticism by such thinkers as Duns Scotus and William of Ockham during the century following his death, indicates that he was not, in this period, the paramount authority that he was later to become for the Catholic church. It was many centuries before Popes Leo XIII and Pius X would promote Thomism as the 'official' philosophy of their church, and Catholics open his works 'expect[ing] to find the answer . . . to almost any question in philosophy or theology'.[49] Nevertheless, he soon acquired sufficient stature to be canonized in 1323, notwithstanding a modest record of miracles (the most impressive of which, apparently, was the transmutation of some sardines into the herrings which he preferred).

Thomas Aquinas (1225–74) was the son of a noble Italian family, who were upset by his decision to join the newly founded mendicant Order of Dominican Friars instead of the more well-heeled Benedictines. After a year's imprisonment by his brothers, Thomas became a student of Albert the Great, from whom he inherited an admiration for Aristotle. From 1252 to 1273 he taught and wrote in Paris and at the papal court in Italy, after which he gave up writing as a result of what has been variously interpreted as a stroke, a nervous breakdown and a mystical vision, declaring that 'all . . . I have written seems like a straw to me'. To his readers, it has seemed more like several haystacks, for Aquinas – dubbed 'the dumb ox' on account of his massive size, his reticence and his prodigious work-load – wrote more than any other philosopher in history. The *Summa Theologiae*, one among many huge works, comes to several million words alone. Such feats of production were aided by his ability to dictate different chapters to three or four secretaries at a time, and abetted by a concentration that enabled him to forget, for example, that he was at a banquet next to the King of France. Aquinas died in 1274 as a result of hitting his head against a tree on the way to the Council of Lyons.

Faith, Knowledge and Universals

'The divine rights of grace,' Aquinas wrote, 'do not abolish the human rights of natural reason' (ST 2–2.10.10).[50] His achievement, in the eyes of many Christians, was to produce a system ('Thomism') that maintained a fine balance between faith and reason, emotion and intellect. Greater concessions to the 'rights of grace' would deprive the system of its claim to be a rational theology. Greater concessions to the 'rights of natural reason' would make redundant the faith and feelings which have traditionally bound men and women to the Christian religion. When Aquinas writes that some theological truths 'surpass the ingenuity of the human reason, for instance the Trinity', while 'others can be attained by the human reason, for instance the existence and unity of God' (CG 1.3), he is battling on two fronts. He is opposing the Averroist tendency to reject, or treat as merely figurative, those articles of faith which conflict with the Aristotelian scheme of things. On the other front, he is rejecting the assumption, found in St Bonaventure, that an 'accursed pagan', unenlightened by Christian revelation, is bound to produce a false philosophy. Although it is an exaggeration to describe Thomism as 'Aristotelianism baptized', it is Aquinas' conviction that the Aristotelian scheme, shorn of certain mistakes, provides an impressive account of reality to which Christian belief must accommodate.

Philosophers, as Aquinas sees it, can err in one of two directions, modesty or pretension. They err in the first direction if, like William of Ockham a century later, they suppose that matters divorced from direct human experience, such as the unity of God, are incapable of rational demonstration. They err in the second direction when, as with Averroes' proof for the world's eternity, they pretend to offer demonstrations that are not grounded at all in human experience. They can also err in this direction by pretending that the knowledge which it is most important to seek is of an intellectual kind. Rather, such knowledge is an 'acquaintance' with 'divine things', and is a function less of right understanding than of appropriate affection – 'for things understood are in the mind in the mind's own fashion, whereas desire goes out to things as they are in themselves; love would transform us into the very condition of their being' (DN 2.4).

A suitable tag for the mood of Aquinas' thought is 'moderate empiricism'. Empiricism is evident in remarks like this: 'in its present condition the mind cannot understand anything except by reference to images [*phantasmata*]' which are 'caused by the senses' (ST 1.84.7 and 6). We are not blessed with innate knowledge, prior to all sense-experience. The empiricism is only moderate, however, and this for two rather different reasons. First, images are necessary for knowledge but not sufficient, since it also requires the participation of 'active intellect'. This intellect is capable of utilizing the images that furnish the raw materials for understanding to arrive at knowledge which surpasses the information directly provided by the senses. Hence, 'intellectual cognition extends further than sensitive cognition' (ST 1.84.6). Second, it is only in its *present* condition that the mind is restricted to knowledge 'by reference to images'. Outside of its embodied condition, in the afterlife, the soul can enjoy that direct acquaintance with things – 'divine things', at least – which is the knowledge to which man aspires. It is only then, indeed, that the soul appreciates things as they are in themselves, for in its present condition things are inevitably shaped, for intellectual consumption, according to 'the mind's own fashion'.

Aquinas' account of knowledge and the world is sufficiently important in its own right, and in its bearing upon his theology, to be looked at in more detail. It begins in Aristotelian vein. With the exception of immaterial beings like angels, all substances are composed of matter and form. As for Aristotle, matter is not a determinate stuff, but that which underlies change of form, enabling us to say, for example, that something changed from being grass to being pulp in the cow's stomach. Matter, in the 'determinate dimensions' (DV 10.5) of its spatio-temporal distribution, also enables us to individuate different members of the same species.

Aquinas also follows Aristotle some of the way in his account of substantial form, 'that in virtue of which a thing is what it is' – a man, say. For both of them reject the Platonic view that such forms exist independently of the particular things which embody them. If they were independent, we would not require sense-experience to know them, which would make it inexplicable why God had furnished us with bodies in the first place, given that attainment of knowledge is our proper function (ST 1.84.7). But whereas Aristotle thought that a form is common to the individuals which possess it, Aquinas holds that each substantial form is unique to its possessor. 'There is nothing common in Socrates; everything in him is individuated' (EE 3). Socrates and Plato are both human, but Socrates' humanity is the-humanity-of-Socrates, while Plato's is the-humanity-of-Plato. There is not, in the objective order, a single form, humanity, which the two share.

This creates a problem, however, concerning the acquisition of knowledge. To know or understand something is to grasp it in 'its character of universality' (ST 1.85.2). Put in modern dress, knowing what something is involves bringing it under a concept which, like that of humanity, any number of other things can also be brought under. Now, how is this move to universality made given that 'nature itself . . . exists only in singular things'? Sense-experience admittedly provides us with 'likenesses' of particular things. (Whether these 'likenesses' are physical impressions or psychological ones is a vexed question.)[51] But awareness of such images, of which even simple animals are capable, falls far short of knowing that the thing impinging on our senses is, say, a tree. Aquinas' solution is that 'we should assign some power on the part of the intellect which can make things actually intelligible by the abstraction of the species from material conditions: this is why we postulate the active intellect' (ST 1.79.3). In other words, from the particular data provided by the senses, the intellect abstracts a general concept applicable to all those individuals which resemble one another sufficiently to produce similar images in us. The abstracted species or form, the universal, does not exist in nature. Universality belongs to concepts which, as the products of the 'active intellect', only 'exist in the mind'.

The issue of universals is one on which mediaeval thinkers, from Boethius in the sixth century to Ockham in the fourteenth, lavished considerable attention, with positions ranging from a Platonic 'exaggerated realism' to a 'nominalism', according to which only signs or words are general. Why should philosophers whose main concern was with matters theological have been vexed by the issue? The answer is that both the real and the merely nominal existence of universals raise difficulties concerning God's presumed purpose or capacities. Realists argued, for example, that unless universals actually exist, then our concepts distort reality, discovering generality where there is none. This possibility is incompatible with God's equipping minds adequately to understand His creation. Nominalists, on the other hand, could argue that real universals would limit God's freedom to produce whatever world he willed, reducing His status to that of a chef whose creations are limited by the ingredients already in the kitchen.

This refusal to limit God's will certainly inspired the robust attack on universals by the Franciscan friar William of Ockham (1280–1349) – an attack which, exacerbated by his criticisms of the Pope's wealth, placed him in some danger. Possibly the Black Death saved him from a worse fate. Ockham is adamant that there exists 'no thing really distinct from singular things', hence nothing 'universal or common to them'. If there did, these universals would surely be essential to the existence of things, which would not in that case have been 'created afresh', *ex nihilo*, by God. Ockham also employs less theologically tinged arguments. For example, it is clear that 'every singular thing can be annihilated without the annihilation . . . of another singular thing on which it in no way depends'. How could that be if different things shared a common, essential ingredient? For in that event, destruction of one thing would also destroy the very ingredient on which other things also depend.[52]

More interesting is Ockham's modern-sounding diagnosis of the mistaken belief in universals. Signs have either 'primary intention', standing for things, or 'secondary intention', standing for other signs. Now consider a sentence like 'Species are various.' In structure, this looks like 'Socrates is white', so that we are tempted to suppose that just as 'Socrates' refers to something in reality, so must 'species'. In fact, though, 'species' is a term with 'secondary intention'. 'Species are various' is a misleading way of talking about signs, specifically about the variety of signs like 'man', 'dog', etc. Once this is grasped, we need not imagine that entities like species exist over and above individual things. (He also argued, less promisingly, that 'white', in 'Socrates is white', stands for Socrates and other white individuals.)[53] More generally, Ockham shared the view of the Parisian nominalists that one should 'not multiply the things . . . signified by terms in accordance with the multiplication of the terms' themselves.[54] Some such principle – an instance of Ockham's famous 'razor' ('plurality should not be posited without necessity') – was the defining credo of nominalism. Ockham was not, one might add, a nominalist in the more recent sense of someone who holds that only *words* are general. Most words, he thinks, express 'natural signs', which are mental, not linguistic, items.

Ockham's account is often contrasted with Aquinas', but on the central question of whether universals belong to the objective order of nature they are at one in their negative answer. There are, though, at least two significant differences. The first concerns the manner in which, having learned to apply a sign to certain individuals, we go on to apply it to further cases. For Aquinas, we do this through exercising the concept we have abstracted from the original examples, comparing the new instances with this concept. But Ockham, slashing away with his razor, thinks that 'it is not necessary to posit anything else in the intellect outside of *habit*'.[55] Meeting Fido for the first time, I do not go through any process in order to call him a dog: I simply continue the habit set up by my earlier encounters with Rover and Bonzo. The second difference is that, for Aquinas, our concepts resemble the 'divine ideas' in accordance with which God has created things. Just as we see things in the rays of the sun, so we 'know things in the eternal exemplars from which they derive' (ST 1.84.5). This is why, despite the absence of universals in nature, our concepts are adequate to reality. For Ockham, as we saw, it is incompatible with God's absolute freedom that He should have to create in accordance with anything.

God

The most celebrated section of the *Summa Theologiae* (1.2.3) offers 'five ways' to establish the existence of God, proofs which Aquinas did not invent but stated with special lucidity. One might wonder why, in an age when God's existence was generally taken for granted, Aquinas should devote any more effort to establishing this than a modern geographer would to proving the existence of America. Partly, perhaps, to demonstrate the power of philosophical reason against its detractors but, more importantly, because 'the denial of God's existence can . . . be entertained by the mind', a sane mind at that. Admittedly, the proposition 'God exists' is 'of itself self-evident', in that someone who knows the essence of God must also know that He exists. Unfortunately 'we do not know what the essence of God is', and the relatively little we can know about Him is not blindingly obvious. Hence God's existence is 'not self-evident *to us*' (ST 1.2.1). There is, then, scope for rational demonstration of His existence.

Proofs which presuppose a grasp of God's essence will not, of course, be allowed. This is why Aquinas does not help himself to St Anselm's famous 'ontological' proof, which has invited, over the centuries, discussions so over-subtle that one sympathizes with Umberto Eco's reference to a 'duel of morons'.[56] Anselm (1033–1109), an unwilling archbishop of Canterbury, held that by 'God' is meant 'something-than-which-nothing-greater-can-be-thought', and that since this is an intelligible concept, even 'the Fool' who denies God must admit that this 'something' at least 'exists in the mind'. He then argues that this 'something' cannot exist *only* in the mind, for it would not then be the greatest thing that can be thought. This is because what exists in reality is greater than its *doppelganger* in the mind. So it follows from the definition of 'God' that God really exists.[57]

It is misleading to say that Aquinas simply rejects this argument, for he too thinks that God's essence involves, or indeed *is*, His existence. His complaint, rather, is that Anselm relies on premises, like his definition of 'God', which are not so evident that the sceptic must concede them (ST 1.2.1). Convincing proofs must instead be *a posteriori*, arguing 'from those of [God's] effects which are known to us' in the world of experience (ST 1.2.2). Such proofs display Aquinas' 'moderate empiricism', for although they yield a conclusion which transcends experience, experience is their starting-point.

Although the 'five ways' have a common destination – God's existence – each of them also has its own goal: to establish the existence of God under some particular aspect. They do not simply provide, by overkill, five ways of establishing one and the same item of information but, taken together, reveal different roles which God plays in the scheme of things. Thus the first way argues, in Aristotelian style, for God as the 'first mover', the prerequisite of motion and change. The second argues for God as the 'first among efficient causes'. The point here is not that it is 'unthinkable' for a causal series, such as procreation, to stretch back to infinity. Rather, causal processes are hierarchically ordered or 'subordinated', as when the movements of the stone depend on those of the crowbar, which depend on those of the hand, and so on. Unless there is a base to this hierarchy then, like a house without foundations, it would collapse. At any rate, there would be no explanation of its remaining upright. The Thomist God, therefore, does not simply set everything in motion, but constantly sustains the structure of the universe.

The third way argues that there must be a 'being whose existence is necessary'. Contingent beings are ones which, at some time, did not exist, so that if everything were contingent, there would have been a time when nothing whatsoever existed, making it impossible to understand how there is now something, rather than nothing. This is Aquinas' elaboration of the familiar idea that not everything can be contingent for then, absurdly, everything would depend on something further for its existence. The fourth way has a Platonic ring. Some things are truer, better and nobler than others, and this is because they more or less closely 'approach something which is the maximum'. This 'maximum' is God, the possessor of all perfections. The last way, arguing for God as the 'final cause', is really two-in-one. Not only does the universe display remarkable harmony, but even the unconscious things within it tend towards definite ends. God is required both as the organizer of this harmony and as the being who directs things towards their goals.

Commentators often suggest that the 'five ways' collapse into one, and it is true that, in a suitably generous sense of 'cause', they all conspire to establish God as the cause of the effects we observe in the world – of motion, say, or degrees of perfection. But to concertina them in this manner surely misses Aquinas' point, which is, as remarked, not simply to prove that God exists, but to articulate the variety of essential roles which He plays.

The Franciscan pair, Scotus and Ockham, were unhappy with the 'five ways', but for opposing reasons. For Duns Scotus (1265–1308), such arguments from our experience of the world lend an unwelcome contingency to their conclusion, God's existence. His own complicated arguments make his title of *Doctor Subtilis* easy to appreciate. ('Dunce', which Scotus bequeathed to our language, was first applied to his followers, not on account of their stupidity, but of their resistance to new theological fashions.) His main argument is that, since God's existence is thinkable, then it is possible, and that since there was nothing outside of God to prevent this possibility being realized, God must therefore exist. God is a being such that 'it can exist from itself; and so does exist from itself'.[58] For the more empirically-minded Ockham, the problem with Aquinas' arguments is not that they prove too little, but too much. Even if experience makes it probable that there is a 'first cause', we are not entitled to conclude that this is a unitary being, nor that it is the same as the one which is the source of perfections.

With God's existence established, Aquinas turns to the question of our knowledge of His nature. Part of the answer is provided by his doctrine of 'analogical predication', a further testament to his 'moderate empiricism'. According to this, terms gleaned from ordinary experience can be applied to God, but only 'inadequately'. We can, of course, describe God in negative terms: He is not snub-nosed, nor a cabbage. 'The controversy hinges on affirmative . . . terms, such as good and wise' (ST 1.13.2). 'God is wise', argues Aquinas, cannot be equivalent to 'God is not stupid', nor to 'God is the cause of wisdom in man'. He is, after all, the cause of hair in man, but we do not describe Him as hairy. So the statement should be taken at face value. The question arises, though, whether 'wise' applied both to God and to Socrates has one sense or two quite different ones. Neither, says Aquinas. It cannot be univocal, since clearly God's wisdom is importantly unlike a man's. In the case of the latter, for instance, 'wisdom' signifies one 'perfection as distinct from another', like goodness, whereas in the case of God, wisdom and goodness are, in an obscure manner, not distinct. But nor is a term like 'wise' equivocal: if it were, 'nothing could be known . . . about God from [His] creatures' when the term is applied to Him.

The proper view is that such 'terms are used according to analogy', rather as 'healthy' is when applied both to a person's urine and to the exercise he takes (ST 1.13.5). Analogy, Aquinas remarks, differs from metaphor. The metaphorical description of God as a father employs a term 'primarily used of creatures'. Terms like 'wise', however, are 'primarily used of God . . . for these perfections derive from Him'. This is so even though we first learn the use of these terms through their 'secondary' application to His creatures (ST 1.13.6). Scotus, it is worth recording, was sceptical towards the 'analogy' doctrine. Either the wisdoms of God and man have something in common or they do not. If they do, the common element determines a univocal sense of 'wise', applicable to God and man alike. If they do not, 'wise' really is an equivocal term.

I now turn to an element in Aquinas' discussion of God's nature, variously regarded as a revolutionary contribution to metaphysics (albeit anticipated by Anselm) and as a jumble of 'sophistry and illusion'.[59] I refer to the 'sublime truth' that 'the essence of God is His existence' (CG 1.22). With God's creatures, we can distinguish the issues of what they are and whether they are, but this is not so with God Himself. But what can the equation of God's existence and essence mean? It sounds unpromising to suppose we can answer the question 'What is God?' by retorting 'He exists', even if God set a precedent for this reply by telling Moses 'I am who I am'. Part of Aquinas' point is the negative one of stressing how limited our understanding of God's nature is, and how different His essence must be from that of anything else. When talking of a thing's essence, we typically contrast this with accidental features, or with those which distinguish the thing from other members of the same species. Since nothing about God is accidental, nor is he a member of a species, talk of His essence cannot have these purposes. Again, we can distinguish what essential quality something has from the particular degree to which it actually possesses it. But this would be idle in the case of God, since He has, or is, all His qualities to a maximum degree (EE 7.6).[60]

Aquinas also seems to intend something positive by his equation. First, he argues that the essence of a substance is typically identified in terms of its 'likeness' to the 'characteristic effects' it brings about. Hence, heat is the essence of fire. Now what is the 'characteristic effect' which God has upon His creatures? Their very existence, of course, which he confers and sustains. 'It follows, therefore', by parity of reasoning with the case of fire, that '[existence] itself is the substance or nature of God' (P 7.2). Second, things exist in different degrees, according to their realization of their potential. In God, however, everything is realized, and so He is 'pure act without alloy of potentiality' (CT 13.11). Put together, the force of these two points, and hence of Aquinas' equation, is that God is the supremely self-realized source and sustainer of the universe.

This is not obviously 'sophistry and illusion', yet there are passages in Aquinas which are hard to render in literal terms, for they speak of existence as if it were a force or quality exuded by God. 'Existence is . . . deepest in all reality since it is the heart of all perfection. Hence, God is in all things, and intimately' (ST 1.8.1). Perhaps such passages can be illuminated by turning to Aquinas' account of how those special creatures, human beings, are to live if they are fully to experience and reciprocate the 'intimacy' which their God proffers.

Beatitude, Virtue and Natural Law

Some half-million words of the *Summa Theologiae* are devoted to ethics and, in many eyes, contain Aquinas' most abiding contribution. Informed modern discussions of contraception, just wars and natural rights are rarely complete without references, approving or damning, to the Thomist position. Even the 'liberation theologians' of Latin America seek support from Aquinas' writings. Blandly stated, Aquinas' ambition is to harmonize the naturalistic approach of Aristotelian ethics with the precepts of Christian morality. As the famous remark 'Grace does not destroy nature, but completes it' (ST 1.1.8) indicates, the aim is not simply to show that our God–given moral purpose is compatible with naturalism. It is, in addition, to show that the basic premises of Aristotle's ethics, supplemented by rational theology and revelation, actually entail a Christian system of morality. This is not to deny that such a system will entail injunctions that conflict with the specific content of Aristotle's recipes for the good life. Aquinas' ethics testifies, once more, to his moderate empiricism. Practical philosophy must begin with observation of man's nature, even though reflection on that nature soon shows that the human good is not to be achieved except in relation to a being, God, who transcends ordinary experience.

So familiar to Christians has Aquinas' project become that we need reminding of the originality it had for his contemporaries. He was writing in a climate dominated by the beliefs, inherited from Augustine and Anselm, that human beings are too corrupt to discern the contours of true morality through their own intelligence, and that anyway moral precepts are God's commands, unavailable except by chance to those who have not heard His voice. Admittedly, the Latin Averroists had attempted to establish moral principles on a purely rational basis, without appeal to God's purpose, but their perceived failure, as attested to by the 1277 *Condemnation*, had cast suspicion even on less radical attempts.

For Aquinas, as for Aristotle, the good is what human beings naturally aim at, 'the end . . . of natural appetite' (CG 3.3). This final end is *beatitude* because, like Aristotle's *eudaimonía* ('well-being', crudely), it 'so satisfies the entire appetite that nought outside is left to be desired' (ST 1–2,1,5). Since, as Aristotle also argued, human nature is distinguished by a propensity for reason and knowledge, it follows that 'the end of the intellect is the end of all human actions' (CG 3.25). The search for beatitude is, therefore, a search for knowledge, even though it also has implications for practical activities. Aristotle was also right to identify some of the virtues with dispositions which are rationally required if human beings are to progress towards their natural end; and right, too, to locate the rationality of these dispositions in their 'hitting the mean' between excess and deficiency (see p. 124).

Aquinas, as a good Christian, must at some point part company with Aristotle. The point occurs when he writes, 'some partial happiness can be achieved in this life, but true perfect happiness cannot' (ST 1–2,5,3): the latter is postponed until the afterlife. The reason is not that Thomist man is slower than Aristotelian man, who *can* achieve *eudaimonía* in this life. It is, rather, that the kind of knowledge in which beatitude consists is of a different kind from that attained by Aristotle's contemplative philosopher. 'Final happiness does not consist in merely rational knowledge' (CG 3.38), but in a 'vision of the divine essence' (ST 1–2,3,8), only available to a disembodied soul in the presence of God. But why should this vision, beatific as it may be, count as the final end towards which man naturally tends? Why is it the good? The answer is that the predominant human desire is to understand. 'There is an inborn desire of knowing cause when effect is seen – this is the spring of wonder.' This desire can only be satisfied by full knowledge of God. Indeed, 'if the mind of rational creatures could never see the first cause of things this natural desire would be pointless' (ST 1,12,1). True contentment, then, where 'nought outside is left to be desired', is the beatitude which resides in knowledge by acquaintance with

God – the only kind that can put to rest our fundamental urge to seek for the explanation of things.

Even in this life, we know enough, through revelation and the story of Christ, to recognize that Aristotle's list of virtues is incomplete. Three additions need to be made, starting with the self-denying virtues like celibacy. Despite some predictable diatribes against fornication and masturbation, Aquinas does not endorse the Augustinian view of the body as a repulsive appendage to which, for our sins, we are chained. The soul, though it finally parts from the body, is originally 'the form of the body' and relies on it for the acquisition of knowledge. Virginity is 'holy', not because sex is obscene, but because it enables a person to 'be more free for the contemplation of the divine' (ST 1–2,152,2). Next, there are the 'heroic' or 'divine' virtues, manifested in 'super-human' acts of courage, for example. These only seem to conflict with the policy of aiming at 'the mean' in one's actions. What would be silly, indeed 'vicious', for an ordinary person – taking on a giant, armed only with a sling, say – is admirable for someone 'divinely moved', and trusting in divine help (ST 1–2,68,1). Finally, there are the 'theological' virtues of faith, hope and, above all, charity, the love of God 'with thy whole soul' and of 'thy neighbour as thyself'. The crucial point about these and the other additional virtues is that they could not be recognized as such by reason alone. Faith, in fact, is required not only for their recognition, but for their exercise, for what they enjoin goes against what would otherwise be natural human behaviour.

When our moral behaviour accords with nature and unaided reason, we are, says Aquinas, acting in accordance with the 'natural law', defined as 'participation in the eternal law by rational creatures' (ST 1–2,91,2). Morality, like everything natural, is under the 'rational governance' of God, and so has 'the quality of law' – a law being an 'ordination of reason for the common good' (ST 1–2,91,1). This proposal has loomed large in political philosophy, implying as it does that the commands of a tyrant who offends against natural morality do not have the status of law. The papal party, in the endless mediaeval disputes over the respective powers of emperor and pope, were quick to seize upon it by way of criticizing imperial insubordination to the Holy See. The imperial party preferred the 'Render unto Caesar' connotations of Augustine's image of the 'two cities', the divine and the secular.

I shall focus, however, on a long-running issue concerning God and morality which the idea of natural law brings into sharp relief. Its pedigree goes back to Plato's *Euthyphro*, where the problem raised was whether the gods love piety because it is good, or piety is good because the gods love it. When the expression 'natural law' became current, among the Stoics and the early Church Fathers, the issue became this: is natural law a set of rational principles which God endorses, or simply the commands of God, unconstrained by any pre-existing criteria? Most early Christian thinkers opted for the latter, 'voluntarist' position, arguing that any other would be incompatible with divine omnipotence. Aquinas' view is that while natural law *is* an 'ordinance' of God, that is not all it is. The principles of natural morality are binding on rational people even if, in the absence of God's governance, they would not have the status of laws. It is customary to contrast Aquinas' position with those of his Franciscan critics, though in the case of Duns Scotus – never the clearest of writers – the contrast is fuzzy. A remark like 'the divine will is the cause of good, and so by the fact that He wills something it is good' sounds like pure 'voluntarism'.[61] But what he means, it emerges, is simply that, without divine ordinance, rational moral prescriptions would not enjoy the status of absolute obligations. Ockham, who insists on the unfettered character of God's will, really does seem to be an uncompromising 'voluntarist'. 'By the very fact that God wills something, it is right for it to be done.' Hence, if He ordered us to fornicate, steal, or even hate Him, these would be meritorious acts.[62]

It is this possibility of God's having ordained a quite different natural law from the one which actually obtains that Aquinas contests. To begin with, it is impossible that natural law could be much different, given human nature as God created it. (It is no limit on God's omnipotence that He cannot do the impossible.) Given our rational capacities and purpose, only certain behaviour could be virtuous – that which manifests rational strategies for the achievement of our purpose. But could not God have furnished us with a totally different nature, requiring us to fornicate, steal, and so on? No, for then human beings would not have 'participated in' God's *own* nature: they would not have been in His image. God made Himself flesh in the form of a man, not a cow or dog, and it was 'most fitting' that He did so (CG 4,54). If by 'man' we mean that being created in order to enjoy a vision of God, then man's nature must be more or less as it is – and so, therefore, must the moral code under which he lives.

For many Protestants, Aquinas is a 'dry stick', a main culprit in the attempt to make a science of religion, a body of doctrine to be established by reason to the detriment of that lived, personal relation to God which is the heart of religion. The reputation is undeserved, notwithstanding the dryness of much of the prose. Granted, the existence of God and the broad contours of how human beings should live are, for Aquinas, matters of rational demonstration. But the Thomist God is far from being the distant God of reason, the 'prime mover', of Aristotle and Averroes. God is 'intimate to' everything in the world, which is suffused with His existence and constantly sustained by Him. This is why people can be 'at home' in this world. A human being is not a soul held in a bodily prison whose bars prevent access to God, but an embodied being equipped to understand, and appreciate the presence of, God if he or she engages in this world with intelligence and piety. By trusting in God, inspired by His presence, a person can obey the call to an 'heroic' life which mere reason could never require. Reason, indeed, can never furnish full understanding of God's essence, for He retains an inscrutable 'otherness', despite all that we 'receive' from Him and all the analogies for His nature that we can glean from the world of experience. He has, however, vouchsafed to us a final vision of His essence, the goal of our inchoate yearnings, and the attainment of a contentment which leaves 'nought outside to be desired'. It is here, finally, that we experience that full intimacy with reality, the earthly glimmerings of which give point to our lives.

• 5 Mediaeval Mysticism •

Of the thousand pages on mediaeval thought in Copleston's *A History of Philosophy*, less than fifty are devoted to mysticism. Why do I dedicate a much higher percentage of my more slender discussion to this area? Some readers, familiar perhaps with Schopenhauer's contrast between philosophy and mysticism, may wonder why I dedicate any at all. Philosophy and mysticism, on his view, are mutually exclusive paths to knowledge. But we must not draw the wrong conclusion from this. It is true, of course, that the knowledge alleged by the mystic is not arrived at by philosophical reasoning. But then, nor is that of the historian or the physicist, from which it hardly follows that there cannot be philosophies of history and of science. We need to distinguish between the training, methods and experiences of the practising mystic, and philosophical discussion and interpretation of these – between, as it is sometimes put, practical and speculative mysticism. Some of the figures discussed in this chapter were adepts, others not. Adepts or not, what gives them a place in it is their philosophically informed sympathy with the possibility and importance of mystical experiences.

There are two reasons why these figures get more attention than, until recently, was their wont. First, the claims of mystics to achieve some kind of union with true reality mean that discussion of mysticism is very much in accord with the guiding theme of this book: philosophy as the enterprise of mitigating the sense of alienation that seems to go with the reflective human condition. Second, in the past few years, interest in mysticism, both scholarly and 'practical', has mushroomed. Mysticism, it seems, appeals to today's ecumenical spirit, promising a basis for the 'transcendent unity of religions', a way of getting beneath the various 'forms' of religions to their 'essence', as one modern Sūfi puts it.[63] In an age of disillusion with authority and institutions, there is also something attractive about the supposedly individual and private way of the mystic. Finally, the very 'mysteriousness' of the mystic's claims seems to cushion them against the attacks from science and modern canons of reason to which the claims of rational theology are supposed to have fallen.

Reasons not dissimilar to these also made mysticism attractive to mediaeval men and women. For example, many Sūfis – at least until they fell foul of Islamic orthodoxy – liked to stress the affinity between their doctrines and those of Christian anchorites, or even Buddhists. In some Islamic and Christian circles, the mystic 'inebriate' was an admired figure, cocking a snook through his behaviour and beliefs at dogma and authority. And throughout the age, there were those, like St Bernard of Clairvaux (1091–1153) or Ghazāli, who felt that reliance on rational theology played hostage to fortune, since clever men might misuse the apparatus of philosophy to discredit religious belief. A greater emphasis on faith and experience would, moreover, have greater immediacy for ordinary men and women. The famous *Imitation of Christ* (fifteenth century) may have been extreme in its anti-intellectual bias, but many people could sympathize with the sentiment that 'a humble rustic who serves God is certainly better than a proud philosopher who . . . considers the movement of the heavens'.[64]

Philosophia Perennis

It is ironic, given the appeal that mysticism has for many ecumenicists, that scholarly debate in recent years has called into question whether there *is* a single animal, mysticism, identifiable as the 'perennial philosophy' underlying the motley 'forms' of religious belief. It has been persuasively argued, in one 'plea for the recognition of differences', that there is no evidence that 'all mystical experience is the same or similar', on the ground that 'there are *no* pure (i.e. unmediated) experiences'.[65] What the mystic experiences is a function of the training, doctrines, and expectations which provide the cultural context in which he or she is placed. The Jewish mystic's state of *devekuth*, 'adhesion' of one's self to the Divine Self, is barely commensurable with the Buddhist's experience of *nirvāṇa*, in which selfhood is absent. This 'contextualist' approach not only drives a wedge between East and West, but emphasizes the variety of mystical experiences attested to by Jews, Christians and Muslims. However one views this denial of a 'common core' to mystical experience, it is certainly true that there were marked differences in mediaeval speculations on mysticism, within as much as between the three great monotheistic religions. For example, that broad mystical movement in Islam known as Sūfism began life as a creed of ecstatic love for God among extreme ascetics, whose wearing of wool (*sūf*) gave the movement its name. It then progressed through a 'pantheistic' phase, whose best-known figure, Al-Hallāj (*c*.858–922), was crucified for his apparent identification of himself, and presumably everything else, with Allah. A more orthodox and philosophically elaborate apology for Sūfism was provided by the great Ghazāli (see sect. 3), drawn to the movement after his abdication from academia and politics. The broadly Neo-Platonic terms of this apology were to be developed by the most systematic of the Sūfi philosophers, the Spaniard Ibn Arabi (1165–1240) – the choreographer, apparently, of the dervishes' whirling, and the inspiration of the Persian poets Rūmi and Jāmi, whose verses have guaranteed an audience for Sūfism beyond the Islamic world. We will encounter similar variations in the speculative forms taken by Christian mysticism.

There is another difficulty in providing any neat characterization of mediaeval mysticism: its continuity with the views of philosophers who would not usually be classified as mystics. Many mystics, and not merely to avoid Al-Hallāj's fate, were keen to stress such continuity, arguing that their doctrines, properly understood, were perfectly compatible with orthodoxy. Certainly it is not difficult to recall elements in the thought of Augustine or Aquinas on which apologists for Christian mysticism might fasten – the stress on the poverty of our conceptual resources for describing God's nature, say, or on the beatific vision as true knowledge of His essence. In some of its forms, at least, mediaeval mysticism should not be seen as disjointed from mainstream theology, but as a current in which elements often submerged by 'proud philosophers' are brought right to the surface.

What are these elements? The pivotal one, perhaps, is the doctrine of divine ineffability. As to why God cannot be adequately described, explanations differed. For the Pseudo-Dionysius (fl. c.500) – the 'father' of 'negative theology' – it is His sheer mystery, His 'super-essential Darkness', which makes it impossible to affirm anything 'positive' about Him, not even eternity or existence.[66] For Nicolas Cusanus, it is because God is 'the Absolute Maximum', in which all 'contradictories' are contained 'with absolutely no distinction'. Language is adequate only for telling us that something is this rather than that, and so cannot reach a being who is no more one thing than another.[67] From the doctrine of ineffability it is a short step, given the close connection between language and thought, to the conclusion that God is beyond conceptual understanding. God's Darkness, says the Pseudo-Dionysius, reduces us to 'absolute dumbness both of speech and thought'. If words are 'foreign to' God, Jan van Ruysbroeck (1293–1381) wrote, then it is not by 'any learning or subtle consideration' that we shall understand Him.[68]

If language and conceptual thought cannot furnish this understanding, then it can only be through direct, 'unmediated' experiences, certain 'essential states' of rapture, perhaps, that we can know God. (Aquinas defined mysticism as 'knowledge of God through experience'.) Moreover, given the now familiar mediaeval principle that there must be some likeness or identity between knower and known, these privileged experiences will manifest a unity or union of the mystic with God. When, in a 'God-seeing' experience, says Ruysbroeck, a man 'meets God without intermediary', he 'becomes one spirit with Him', without separation. Or, in the more ornate idiom of Sūfi poetry:

> To Thy harem dividuality
> No entrance finds – no words of this or that;
> Do Thou my separate and derived self
> Make one with Thy essential![69]

Such experiences of unity, unfortunately, are not easy to come by, and the would-be 'God-seer' must clear the field of vision of various obstacles or veils. One such veil is constituted by the intellectual apparatus, the battery of philosophical terms and concepts, with which too many theologians aspire to understand God. Hence, in the words of Cusanus, we must cultivate a 'learned ignorance', a cognitive innocence receptive to simple, direct experience. Another obstacle is the bodily desires which tie us down to the mundane world. It is, as we saw when discussing Aquinas, easy to exaggerate mediaeval hostility towards the body, but in the Sūfi ascetics and a Christian mystic like St Bernard we encounter again the Augustinian horror of the carnal. For St Bernard, the soul is 'a captive in exile, imprisoned in this body, . . . sunk in its mire', wandering in a 'Land of Unlikeness' which it must first leave if it is to rejoin its real likeness, God (133).[70]

The elements I have mentioned were, I believe, common to nearly all varieties of mediaeval speculative mysticism. But this does not mean there was doctrinal unanimity among them: on the contrary, there were great disagreements over the understanding and elaboration of some of these elements – most of all, over the sense in which, through mystical experience, some kind of unity with God is realized. We can broadly distinguish two influential models of this unity, which I shall call the 'erotic' and the 'absorptive'.

Unity and Love

According to the *Zohar* ('splendour'), the central text of the Jewish mystical tradition known as the *kabbalah*, a person who worships God out of 'love . . . lifts everything to the stage where all must be one'.[71] Countless similar utterances by Muslim and Christian mystics could be cited. The idea that God is a proper recipient, and a giver, of love is hardly confined, of course, to mystical thought. The 'charity' of which the Gospels speak is love of God before it is love of one's neighbour. But the general tendency, in all three religions, had been to emphasize fear, reverence and awe as the primary attitudes towards God. This was a tendency expressly combatted by, among many others, St Bernard. Not only does love 'outweigh' these other attitudes, he writes, but God Himself 'loves rather to be loved' than feared or admired (137). Fear, after all, can be a mark of servility. Moreover, it was not the virtue of love or charity which was emphasized by the mystics, but love as a particular kind of revelatory experience.

It is 'God the Bridegroom' who, says St Bernard, 'would be loved'. Nuptial metaphors like this, or that of a 'spiritual marriage', might suggest that the preferred model for the union of a person with God is that of the love between man and wife. But many other metaphors make it clear, if not quite explicit, that it is not the enduring, dispositional love between a couple which provides the leading analogy, but the particular act of love which consummates a marriage – sexual intercourse, or better, its climax. For St Bernard, the mystic union is not a 'contract', but an 'embrace', a 'kiss'. The 'making one' with God of which Jāmi wrote in the verse quoted earlier takes place 'on that divan which leaves no room for twain'. Another Sūfi poet records the 'passionate yearning', the 'searing ecstasy', by which he is swept away as 'my Lover', God, comes near.[72] The erotic imagery of a writer rather later than our present period, St Teresa of Avila (1515–82), has of course been much discussed, even if it is less explicit than might be predicted from Bernini's Sculpture 'The Ecstasy of St Teresa', which luridly adorns modern covers of her writings.

It is perhaps unnecessary to warn against a certain misunderstanding of the erotic analogy. The authors of such classic erotica as *The Perfumed Garden* or *The Fountains of Pleasure* apparently saw themselves as doing Allah's work in practising or preaching the arts of love, but not even they would have endorsed the view, championed in the Tantric school of Yoga, that sexual union is both a means to and a symbolic enactment of spiritual union. All the mystics who are our current concern condemned 'concupiscence' and saw sexual pursuits as, if not revolting, then certainly a distraction from the proper preoccupations of men and women. We are, then, dealing with sexual intercourse simply as a metaphor, partial but illuminating, for the experience of union with God, and not with its role – which would have been denied – as a training method for such union.

Why should it have been deemed an illuminating metaphor? Sexual climax is doubtless characterized by that mixture of intensity, intoxication, indescribability and sudden release from yearning which mystical experiences are often reported as having. But it is in the elaboration of the union which sexual intercourse involves that the force of the metaphor resides. To begin with, there are the closeness and harmony which, ideally, obtain and are experienced as obtaining between the two partners in such a union. Each wants what the other wants, so that their wills are in accord. This accord is central, for example, to St Bernard's understanding of the mystic union. 'At the ideal limit,

inaccessible in this life but prefigured in ectasy, there would be perfect communion between God's will and ours' (118). Beyond mere harmony, there is
also reciprocity in the ideal act of love. Each partner's pleasure depends upon
the other's pleasure, so that, in more than the clichéd sense, they need one
another. That man needs God's love is, of course, a familiar theme, but it is also
a recurrent theme among mystics that this need is reciprocal. God 'loves only
that He may be loved', says St Bernard: indeed, man and the world only exist
because of God's need for His love to find both expression and reciprocation
(138). A similar thought is important in Ibn Arabi's theology: the 'perfect man'
is 'the epiphany of God's desire to be known; for only [he] . . . loves God and
is loved by God. For [him] alone the world was made'.[73]

A further aspect of sexual union, prominent in romantic literature, is that of
the partners 'losing themselves' in one another or in the act itself. So immersed
are they that no room is left for self-conscious observation. This, too, provides
an analogue for a central feature of the experiences attested to by mystics – for
what the Sūfis called 'dying to self' (fanā). As Al-Junaid put it:

> Lo! I have severed every thought from me,
> And died to selfhood, that I might be Thine.[74]

Some scholars of mysticism, indeed, have treated as a defining feature of
mystical experience that it lacks the 'subject–object' structure of more mundane
experiences.[75] Still, no one thinks that during sexual climax there is literally
only one person, that one or other partner really is no longer a self. Hence the
erotic model is attractive, finally, to those mystics who, for all their talk of
union with God, resist the pantheistic urge to suppose that mystical experience
reveals a strict identity of man's soul with God. It may well be, remarks St
Bernard, that the soul 'seems to be wholly lost' in God, like a drop of water
mingled in wine. But as this defender of orthodoxy – abbot of a great
monastery, scourge of 'dangerous' philosophers like Peter Abelard, and
preacher of the second crusade against the infidel – quickly adds, this does not
mean that the soul and God become one substance.

Absorption

The water in wine image is also used, but with a significant twist, by Meister
Eckhart (1260–1327), a Dominican friar who taught in Paris, and arguably the
most influential of the mediaeval Christian writers on mysticism. He argues that
the union between soul and God is 'more intimate than when a drop of water
is poured into a vat of wine; that would be wine and water, but the other is
transformed into the same so that no creature can detect a difference' (102).[76]

The metaphor of 'dying to self' is similarly radicalized. 'As the soul dies in herself God comes to be her whole life . . . for God and the soul to be one, the soul has to lose her own life and nature' (142). This seems to express something more than an absence of self-consciousness analogous to the lover's experience at the height of passion. Indeed, says Eckhart, we should 'extol detachment above any love', where by 'detachment' is meant such a total abdication from one's natural, 'creaturely' state as to permit 'God and me becoming one' (145). What mystical experience reveals, it seems, is not a closeness of creature and God on the model of two lovers, but that 'all creatures are a pure nothing. I do not say that they are little or something; they are a pure nothing.'[77]

Similar claims are made by Eckhart's many followers, such as John Tauler and Ruysbroeck, as well as by several Sūfis. 'I am He whom I love and He whom I love is I', proclaimed Al-Hallāj: a doctrine of identity with God which inspired him to conclude that 'I am the One Real!' Al-Bistami, who shared this view, could then announce 'Glory be to me! How great is my glory!'[78] As their refusal to recant the pantheism implied by such remarks, and their subsequent executions, show, these two Sūfis intended to be taken quite literally. Eckhart, on the other hand, regarded his position as compatible with Catholic orthodoxy and struggled, unsuccessfully, against the official condemnation of some of his propositions. The attitude of the authorities is understandable, for the passages I quoted suggest a model of mystic union very different from that of two distinguishable persons united in love. They indicate, instead, a conception of the soul absorbed without remainder, a 'pure nothing', into the one, true, divine being: a conception more reminiscent of the metaphysics of Śaṅkara (see pp. 32ff.), with whom Eckhart has often been compared, than of orthodox monotheism.[79]

How, one wonders, could Eckhart and others who employed the rhetoric of absorption pretend to orthodoxy? One way, to be sure, was by a degree of backtracking, treating the rhetoric as excusable hyperbole for something less radical. Thus we find Eckhart explaining his reference to the 'pure nothingness' of God's creatures as meaning that they are so dependent upon God that they *would* be 'reduced to nothing' if He 'turned away' from them. Again, Ghazāli sympathizes with the 'pantheistic' proclamations of the 'inebriate' Sūfis, whilst insisting that all they really experienced was 'unification', not 'identity', with Allah. Their utterances are excused by their having become so 'dumbfounded' by their experiences that 'no capacity remained within them save to recall Allah', so that it was *as if* 'there remained nothing . . . save Allah'.[80] Such disclaimers do not imply a return to the erotic model: there is a difference, presumably, between stressing a creature's insignificance and absolute dependence and emphasizing his role in a reciprocal relationship of love.

Backtracking was not, however, the only way of trying to reconcile absorptive rhetoric with orthodox faith. Two, more theoretical, manoeuvres were also employed, both displaying a Neo-Platonist pedigree. The first is to draw a distinction between, in Eckhart's terminology, God and the Godhead. These are, he insists, 'as different as earth is from heaven'. 'Everything in the Godhead is one, and of that there is nothing to be said. God works, the Godhead does not work . . . in it there is no activity.' The distinction, it seems, is between the God of the Bible, God the Father, active in history, who becomes flesh in the person of Christ, and the ineffable 'wellspring' or 'ground' of everything, including God, which 'passes away' into this Godhead. Strictly, then, it is not God, a distinct person from myself, with whom I am identified: so orthodoxy is preserved. Rather, it is into 'the wellspring of the Godhead' which I, like the God I pray to, return to without trace when 'I go back into the ground, into the depths' of my being (134–5). A similar distinction, it seems, is made in the *kabbalah*, between the God of Israel and *En Sof* ('the unlimited'). 'All things are in Him and He is in all things', according to the *Zohar*, whereas it would be heresy to confuse oneself with the God who appeared to Moses.[81]

There is a second manoeuvre discernible in the *Zohar*. At the point where 'Kabbalism comes nearest to Neo-Platonic thought,' explains one commentator, 'the consensus of Kabbalistic opinion regards the mystical way to God as a reversal of the procession by which we have emanated from God'.[82] Crucial, here, is a distinction, somewhat parallel to that between the 'active God' and the Godhead, between the mundane, 'created' soul which has emanated from the source of all beings and the soul, as yet 'uncreated', existing within that source. Mystical experience is then a foretaste, as it were, of the soul's return to this original source. Such is certainly the view of some of Eckhart's followers. For Tauler, the soul strives to return 'to that centre . . . where it used to be in its uncreated state'.[83] For Ruysbroeck, souls have 'come forth in eternity, before they were created in time'. God has willed that 'we shall go forth from ourselves' into the created world, but also that 'we shall reunite ourselves in a supernatural way with [His] Image' in which we have our eternal life.[84] The appearance of orthodoxy is thereby saved, since there is a clear distinction between God and the creaturely soul. But since this soul is an emanation into the created world of a soul which exists within the divine mind, mystical union is after all a return to an original state of identity with, or immersion in, God.

On either of the two models of mystical experience, the 'erotic' and the 'absorptive', which I have sketched, speculative mysticism of the Middle Ages registers with a particular salience the ambition to overcome a sense of isolation or homelessness by urging that there is, after all, an intimate union between the human soul and the ground of all existence. This union is no mere postulate for the thinkers I have discussed, but one of which we can have a vivid taste, or at least foretaste, in certain privileged experiences. There is, of course, a price to be paid for ensuring the intimacy of the individual person with the reality which is his source. It is the price which Hegel, as we saw at the beginning of this chapter, called 'the unhappy consciousness'. For the more that the mystic stresses his identity with God, the more alien the mundane, physical world in which he is temporarily stuck becomes. The more one is seen to be 'like' God, the more must the ordinary world appear, in St Bernard's words, as a 'Land of Unlikeness'. Here, for example, is Eckhart's recipe for arriving at that state of detachment or 'death' in which, alone, one can truly 'see God': '. . . you are aware of nothing within you . . . having escaped from earthly species and forgotten your honourable estate and all temporal happenings, you have entered oblivion . . . of [everything] save the sheer ascendency of your soul' (142). There is no echo here of the theme which, for example, informs Zen thought (see pp. 222ff.), that union with reality is realized precisely through a human being's quiet engagement in and with the everyday world. Indeed, one wonders what is left of a *human* being in Eckhart's man of detachment, a stranger to his fellows and to the events of his daily life. In chapter 7 we shall see how, as the Middle Ages drew to a close, attempts were made to integrate human existence into the scheme of things which did not require sacrificing the conditions that make such an existence distinctively human. Arguably, it is the making of these attempts which mark the passing of the Middle Ages and the birth – or, as it is said, a rebirth, a renaissance – of another age.

• Notes •

1 Bertrand Russell, *History of Western Philosophy*, p. 420.
2 Etienne Gilson, *History of Christian Philosophy in the Middle Ages*, p. 544.
3 Matthew Arnold, *Essays in Literary Criticism*, Preface.
4 Moses of Burgos, quoted in Gershom G. Scholem, 'General characteristics of Jewish mysticism', p. 156.
5 G. W. F. Hegel, *Introduction to the Lectures on the History of Philosophy*, p. 124.
6 G. W. F. Hegel, *The Philosophy of History*, p. 377.
7 Hegel, *Introduction to the Lectures on the History of Philosophy*, p. 134.
8 G. W. F. Hegel, *Phenomenology of Spirit*, p. 126.
9 Ibid., p. 134.
10 Quoted in T. Irwin, *Classical Thought*, p. 203.
11 Gilson, *History of Christian Philosophy in the Middle Ages*, p. 5.
12 J. D. G. Dunn, *Christology in the Making*, p. 243.
13 'On the life of Plotinus', in Plotinus, *The Enneads*, p. cii.
14 Stephen R. L. Clark, *God's World and the Great Awakening*, p. 205.
15 References to Plotinus are to Book, Tractate and Chapter of Plotinus, *The Enneads*. With minor amendments, I use the MacKenna translation, though I am told this is less reliable at certain points than the one by A. H. Armstrong, a usefully potted version of which is found in his *Plotinus*.

16 Armstrong, *Plotinus*, pp. 34, 39.

17 Augustine, *Confessions*. References are to book and chapter.

18 Henry Chadwick, *Augustine*, p. 29.

19 *On the Division of Nature*, quoted and discussed by F. Copleston, *A History of Philosophy*, vol. 2, pp. 122ff.

20 Augustine, *On Free Will*, in A. Hyman and J. Walsh (eds), *Philosophy in the Middle Ages*, p. 49.

21 Quoted in Christopher Kirwan, *Augustine*, p. 62, which contains an excellent discussion of Augustine on evil and free will.

22 Augustine, *The City of God*, XI. 18.

23 Augustine, *On Free Will*, p. 54.

24 Ibid., p. 61.

25 Quoted in Kirwan, *Augustine*, p. 127.

26 Augustine, *On Free Will*, p. 59.

27 Quoted in Kirwan, *Augustine*, p. 128.

28 Quoted in Majid Fakhry, *A History of Islamic Philosophy*, p. 306.

29 Quoted in Isidore Epstein, *Judaism*, p. 205.

30 Ahmed S. Akbar, *Postmodernism and Islam*, p. 85.

31 Gilson, *History of Christian Philosophy in the Middle Ages*, p. 183.

32 Abu Hamid Al-Ghazāli, *Tahafut Al-Falāsifah* (Incoherence of the Philosophers). References in the text are to page numbers of this work.

33 References to Averroes are to page numbers of 'The Decisive Treatise . . .' (DT); *Tahafut al-tahafut* (TT); 'Long Commentary on De Anima' (DA); and C. Genequand (trans.), *Ibn Rushd's* Metaphysics (M).

34 Moses Maimonides, *Guide of the Perplexed*, book II, ch. 25.

35 As suggested by Leo Strauss, whose views are carefully discussed by Oliver Leaman, *An Introduction to Medieval Islamic Philosophy*: a book to which I am much endebted in this section.

36 Russell, *History of Western Philosophy*, p. 417.

37 Quoted in Fakhry, *A History of Islamic Philosophy*, p. 167.

38 Ibid., p. 170.

39 On Ghazāli and Averroes on causality, see L. E. Goodman, 'Did al-Ghazāli deny causality?'

40 Quoted in Gilson, *History of Christian Philosophy in the Middle Ages*, p. 220.

41 Quoted in Dominique Urvoy, *Ibn Rushd*, p. 84.

42 *The Deliverance*, in Hyman and Walsh (eds), *Philosophy in the Middle Ages*, p. 257.

43 Quoted in Fakhry, *A History of Islamic Philosophy*, p. 182.

44 *The Deliverance*, in Hyman and Walsh (eds), *Philosophy in the Middle Ages*, p. 258.

45 Quoted in Fakhry, *A History of Islamic Philosophy*, pp. 165–6.

46 Maimonides, *Guide of the Perplexed*, book III, ch. 51.

47 C. A. Qadir, *Philosophy and Science in the Islamic World*, pp. 123–4.

48 *Condemnation of 219 Propositions*, in Hyman and Walsh (eds), *Philosophy in the Middle Ages*, pp. 542ff.

49 David Knowles, 'The historical context of the philosophical work of St. Thomas Aquinas', p. 13. I am using 'Thomism' to refer to the views of Aquinas himself, not to the long Catholic tradition inspired by them.

50 References to Aquinas are to Parts, Books, Sections etc. of his works. Those cited are *Summa Theologiae* (ST), *Summa contra Gentiles* (CG), *De Veritate* (DV), *De Potentia Dei* (P), *De Ente et Essentia* (EE), *Compendium Theologiae* (CT), and *De Divinis Nominibus* (DN). Most of the passages quoted may be found either in Aquinas, *Selected Texts*, ed. by T. Gilbey, or Aquinas, *On Politics and Ethics*, ed. by P. E. Sigmund. Leisured readers will doubtless want

to consult the sixty-volume Blackfriars translation of the *Summa Theologiae*, 1963–75.

51 See John Haldane, 'Aquinas on sense-perception', for a useful discussion of this question.

52 *Commentary on the Sentences*, in Hyman and Walsh (eds), *Philosophy in the Middle Ages*, p. 619.

53 *Summa Totius Logicae*, in Hyman and Walsh (eds), *Philosophy in the Middle Ages*, p. 615. This 'two-name theory' of Ockham's is castigated, as 'one of the worst disasters in the history of logic', by Peter Geach, 'Nominalism'.

54 Quoted in Hyman and Walsh (eds), *Philosophy in the Middle Ages*, p. 605.

55 *Commentary on the Sentences*, in ibid., p. 630.

56 Umberto Eco, *Foucault's Pendulum*, p. 65.

57 *Proslogion*, in Hyman and Walsh (eds), *Philosophy in the Middle Ages*, p. 150.

58 *The Oxford Commentary*, in ibid., p. 560.

59 For the first judgement, see Gilson, *History of Christian Philosophy in the Middle Ages*, p. 365; for the second, see Anthony Kenny, *Aquinas*, p. 60.

60 On this point, see Peter Geach, 'Aquinas'.

61 Quoted in Copleston, *A History of Philosophy*, vol. 2, p. 547. For a useful discussion of the various mediaeval positions on this issue, see John Haldane, 'Medieval and renaissance ethics'.

62 Quoted in ibid., vol. 3, p. 104.

63 Seyyed Hossein Nasr, *Sūfi Essays*, p. 38.

64 Thomas à Kempis, *Of the Imitation of Christ*, n.d., p. 5.

65 Steven T. Katz, 'Language, epistemology, and mysticism', pp. 25, 65, 26.

66 *Mystical Theology*, chs 2–5, in N. Smart (ed.), *Historical Selections in the Philosophy of Religion*, pp. 52ff. The Pseudo-Dionysius was so-called, not because he was some kind of theological imposter, but because he was confused, for many centuries, with a much earlier figure, Dionysius the disciple of St Paul.

67 Nicolas Cusanus, *Of Learned Ignorance*, p. 53.

68 *The Adornment of the Spiritual Marriage*, in F. C. Happold (ed.), *Mysticism*, p. 290.

69 Jāmi, *Salaman and Absal*, in *Four Sūfi Classics*, p. 17.

70 References to St Bernard are to page numbers of Etienne Gilson, *The Mystical Theology of Saint Bernard*.

71 Quoted in Epstein, *Judaism*, p. 242.

72 Al-Nuri, quoted in A. J. Arberry, *Sūfism*, p. 62.

73 Arberry, *Sūfism*, p. 101.

74 Quoted in Arberry, *Sūfism* p. 63.

75 See, for example, Sallie B. King, 'Two epistemological models for the interpretation of mysticism', p. 275.

76 References to Eckhart are to page numbers of U. Fleming (ed.), *Meister Eckhart*.

77 Quoted in Copleston, *A History of Western Philosophy* vol. 3, p. 189.

78 Quoted in Abu Hamid Al-Ghazāli, *Mishkat*, p. 122.

79 See especially, Rudolf Otto, *Mysticism East and West*.

80 Ghazāli, *Mishkat*, pp. 122–3.

81 Quoted in Epstein, *Judaism*, p. 235.

82 Gershom G. Scholem, 'General characteristics of Jewish mysticism', p. 154.

83 Quoted in Gilson, *History of Christian Philosophy in the Middle Ages*, p. 443.

84 In Happold (ed.), *Mysticism*, p. 292.

6
• DEVELOPMENTS IN ASIAN PHILOSOPHY •

• 1 Theistic Vedānta •

The developments discussed in this chapter took place mainly in the period from the eleventh to the sixteenth century CE, though with various overtures and codas and at somewhat different times in the three civilizations considered – India, China and Japan. Rough contemporaneity is not the only feature the developments shared. As we shall see, each of them was at once reformist and reactionary, purporting to recover a purer, original message from the accretions and distortions inflicted, since 'the golden days', on an ancient philosophy. These ancient philosophies are among those discussed in chapters 2 and 3. I begin with the recovery by Indian philosophers of, as they saw it, the theistic message of Vedāntic thought. (On 'Vedānta', see p. 30.)

The world of the Vedas, the early scriptural corpus of Hinduism, is populated by a host of deities, proper objects of sacrifice and prayer. In the so-called 'creation hymns' of the *Ṛg-Veda*, moreover, there is speculation on the existence of a supreme God, an 'overseer in highest heaven', 'the Lord of immortality'.[1] Yet we saw in chapter 2, perhaps to the surprise of some readers, that none of the 'orthodox' schools of Indian philosophy there discussed offers a central place in the scheme of things to God or the gods. In the Yoga system, Īśvara was simply an especially exemplary *puruṣa* or soul; while in Śaṅkara's Advaita Vedānta, he belonged to the illusory world of *māyā* and was at best a symbol of ineffable and impersonal *Brahman*. As for the Sāṃkhya and Mīmāṃsā schools, these were flatly atheistic.

Unsurprisingly, a gulf was to grow between the doctrines of these schools and popular religious belief. In particular, the abstractions of Advaita thought, which by the eleventh century had become the dominant 'orthodox' philosophy, might satisfy the transcendental yearnings of intellectuals, but did not address – even in the case of those who found it intelligible – the emotional needs of ordinary men and women. As Rudolf Otto observed, Śaṅkara's conception of reality as featureless *Brahman* can easily induce a feeling of 'icy-coldness'.[2] To be sure, Śaṅkara saw himself as dissolving the barrier between human beings, in their mundane existence, and the spiritual order, and hence as providing succour to those, like the poetess Mahādevī, gripped by the worry that 'This world/ And that other/ [I] cannot manage them both'. But it was a strange dissolution that required the denial of the reality of individuals and of everyday existence. And the kind of succour sought by Mahādevī was not the promise of a 'Oneness' in which she, like everyone and everything else, would be absorbed without trace, but of a spiritual reality from which people could at once be distinguished, as beings in their own right, yet with which they could somehow 'identify'. By allocating human beings to the world of *māyā*, and by making of spiritual reality something impersonal and featureless, Śaṅkara apparently excludes both distinction and identification.

Bhakti

Put differently, Śaṅkara seemingly shuts out the possibility for a meaningful and satisfying attitude of devotion (*bhakti*) – for whatever the proper stance towards the *Brahman* of Advaita, it is surely not that. But it was just this devotional urge which was manifested in the *bhakti* sects that had mushroomed by the eleventh century, most notably those devoted to Śiva and Vishnu, elevated by their respective followers from the relatively modest gods of an earlier literature into Supreme Beings. The flavour of this devotionalism, often erotic in its language and imagery, can be gauged from the poems of Mahādevī, who writes, for example: 'I grieve for you [Śiva] . . . I'm mad for you. I lie lost, sick for you, night and day'. Later, another poetess, Mīrā Bāī, writes: 'O Friend [Vishnu, this time], I am mad with love . . . Mīrā's pain will vanish only when the Beloved (God) Himself becomes the physician'.[3] The erotic tone – evident, too, in the stories of the *gopīs* (milkmaids) who uncontrollably lust after Krishna (an *avatar*, or embodiment, of Vishnu) – is significant, for the goal of devotion was regarded as a real union with God. But it can also be misleading, for at least in the hands of the theistic philosophers who will shortly concern us, the devotion recommended is not an overheated, bare-breasted emotion but, in the words of one of them, Rāmānuja, 'a steady remembrance', or 'keeping-in-mind', of God (16).[4]

It was one thing, however, for the sects to replace the 'icy-cold' metaphysics of Advaita by a devotional theology, quite another to demonstrate any warrant for this substitution in the scriptures. To be sure, everyone conceded that there are passages in the *Upaniṣads* which seem to affirm a theistic conception and to advocate worship of a Creator-God. For example, the *Śvetāśvatara* urges us to 'Worship . . . the adorable God who dwells in your own thoughts . . . the God who is the cause of all.'⁵ Equally undeniable were the devotional sections of the *Bhagavad-Gītā*. In discussing this famous work (see pp. 49ff.), I considered its argument that a person could aspire towards *mokṣa* or liberation through performing actions – the trick being to perform them 'for their own sake', and without the motives responsible for the accumulation of karmic effects and, thereby, for a further rebirth. But in the latter half of the book, Krishna makes clear to Arjuna that he is indeed the *avatar* of the Supreme God and drops his guise as a charioteer, revealing Himself in His full divine glory – a God of love, moreover, expecting love in return from his creatures, who are 'even dearer to me [when they] have faith and love' (12.20).

Krishna makes clear too that a, indeed *the*, proper path to liberation is precisely such faith and love. It is sometimes said that the *Gītā* adds this as an extra path to those of wisdom and (disinterested) work or action. But it would be more accurate to say that the ways of knowledge and action are here given their deeper interpretation. 'Only by love can men . . . know me' (11.54), and 'a man attains perfection when his work is worship of God' (18.46). The knowledge that brings liberation is not intellectual understanding, but a mode of acquaintance with *Brahman*, inseparable from an experience of it as an object of love. And non-egoistic action, properly perceived, is action performed in a spirit of dedication to God.

But appeal to these texts is not decisive. They were, after all, well known to Śaṅkara, who tried to explain them – or explain them away – in a manner consonant with his non-theistic metaphysics. (The strategy, similar to that of some modern Christian theologians, was to treat the theistic passages 'symbolically'. In both cases, the reception among the devout has been unenthusiastic.) Moreover, there remain the monistic-sounding 'Everything is One' dicta of the principal *Upaniṣads* (and of some chapters in the *Gītā*), on which Advaita metaphysics is primarily based. Even if a plausible alternative interpretation of these passages is provided, there remains the task – if we want to progress beyond theology to philosophy – of showing that the Advaitin position is incoherent, that a theistic metaphysics is rationally supportable.

The best known figures to whom these jobs of scriptural reinterpretation and philosophical criticism fell were the South Indian sages, Rāmānuja (1017–1137) and Madhva (1197–1276). (If the usual dates of these and other significant Vedāntins of the period, like Veṅkaṭa (1268–1369), are even approximately correct, theistic Vedānta can be recommended for longevity.) Both alternated between itinerant debating – invariably defeating their Advaitin adversaries, according to the legends – and setting up sects and temples dedicated to Vishnu. Their influence on later Hindu devotionalism, right down to the twentieth century, has been immense (see ch. 9, sect. 1). There are, we shall see, important differences between Rāmānuja and Madhva, indicated by the respective names of their philosophies, Viśiṣṭādvaita ('the non-duality of qualified being(s)') and Dvaita ('dualism'). Given the differences between them, and between them and Śaṅkara, one might ask why all three are grouped as Vedāntins. Perhaps, as we saw suggested earlier (see p. 17), there is no good reason. It is insufficient, certainly, that all three insist on the authority of the *Upaniṣads*, for so did the other 'orthodox' schools. Maybe they share little beyond taking the concept of *Brahman* as central, and the gnomic aphorisms of Bādarāyaṇa's *Brahma-* (or *Vedānta*) *Sūtras* as the primary text for commentary.

The Rejection of Advaita

The common aim of theistic Vedāntins was to discredit the Advaita doctrine of an absolute reality, *Brahman*, which is totally without quality and difference, and of which material things and selves are but the illusory appearances. This doctrine, they held, is unfaithful to scripture, logically incoherent and incompatible with religious devotion. It is this last charge that explains the peculiar animus against Śaṅkara and his followers which pervades the theistic literature. The Advaita doctrine, says Rāmānuja, is the work of 'men . . . destitute of [the] qualities which cause individuals to be chosen by the Supreme Person', purveyors of 'hollow and vicious arguments' (39). Madhva sees no distinction between the doctrine and atheistic Buddhism, and his disciples regarded him as sent by God to destroy the claims of Śaṅkara, whom they declared to be the son of a demon.

To understand their interpretation of the scriptures, we need to grasp certain epistemological and linguistic assumptions which Rāmānuja and Madhva deployed against the Advaita interpretation. First, they assumed the priority of perceptual knowledge. As good Vedāntins, they do not deny that scripture, where its meaning is plain, trumps all other claims, including those founded on perception. But a crucial constraint on interpreting a scriptural passage is consistency with our general perceptual experience. Since this experience is, undeniably, of distinct objects and selves, the presumption is already against an interpretation of the texts which treats such experience as illusory. Indeed, such an interpretation is doubly perverse. In order to trust that we have read or heard the words of a text correctly, all of us − Advaitins included − have to rely on sense-perception. Worse still, since these texts belong in the empirical world, the Advaitin must concede that the support he adduces for his doctrine is drawn from what is, according to that doctrine, a realm of illusion. As Rāmānuja puts it, 'if perception . . . is based on the imagination of plurality, scripture is also in no better case − for it is based on the very same view' (73).

Two of the important assumptions about language on which the theistic critique draws both concern structure. For a language to communicate about reality, there must be some correspondence between the two. Now since language is structured – into words, parts of speech, and so on – it follows that reality must also be structured. But this creates a problem for the Advaitin, for suppose, as he does, that there is an unstructured, undifferentiated realm of reality. In that case, nothing can be intelligibly said about it. But does not Śaṅkara concede that *Brahman* is ineffable? He does, but as his voluminous output proves, he does not take the concession seriously. Śaṅkara, to be consistent, should have kept his mouth shut, like the Zen Masters who refused to enter into discussions about reality. Anyway, if there is nothing intelligible to say about *Brahman*, surely the scriptures on which Śaṅkara relies are so much hot air.

The second point concerns the structure of propositions. Consider a sentence of the form 'A is F, G, and H'. According to Rāmānuja, this illustrates 'co-ordinative' or 'correlative predication', where there is 'an application to one object of more than one word having different grounds for their occurrence'.[6] The point is that different predicates are applicable to a subject only in virtue of genuinely different elements within the structure of that subject. Consider, then, the famous Upaniṣadic statement, '*Brahman* is reality, knowledge, infinite'. Śaṅkara had construed this in a negative manner, as denying that *Brahman* is illusory, spatially bounded, and so on. But, if the statement is to be taken literally, this is wrong, and we should read it as attributing different positive aspects to *Brahman* in virtue of its distinguishable elements.

This raises the question, though, of why we should take the scriptures literally. Here we encounter a further assumption about language, to the effect that words are to be taken literally unless there is good reason not to. There is nothing arbitrary about this principle since, without it, nothing would constrain our interpretation, and communication would soon break down. In the special case of scriptures, it would do no honour to the God who is their source to suppose that the words are figurative except when they are quite obviously so. (The Vedāntins did not entertain Pascal's rather Machiavellian God who speaks in 'ciphers', which He knows that 'concupiscent' people will misread.)[7] Since this exception clause does not apply to a statement such as '*Brahman* is reality, knowledge, infinite', and since there is a plausible literal reading of it as an instance of 'correlative predication', the Advaitin's construal has no warrant. (The most important Upaniṣadic claim on which these considerations are brought to bear is the famous 'That thou art', with its apparent equation of the self and *Brahman*. Since there here emerges a significant difference between Rāmānuja and Madhva, I postpone discussion until later.)

These epistemological and linguistic considerations constitute a strong presumption against the Advaita interpretation of scripture. But can the theists provide arguments of a more direct kind against Śaṅkara's spiritual monism? Clearly, they believe so. Rāmānuja's follower, Veṅkaṭa, assembled some one hundred arguments against Śaṅkara, of which, sadly, only sixty-six survive. One set of arguments is directed against Śaṅkara's denial of a plurality of selves in favour of a single seamless consciousness, *Brahman* itself. What needs to be shown is not only that consciousness requires a subject or self as its source, but that there are many such subjects. Rāmānuja's argument is that 'the permanency of the conscious subject is proved' by the fact each person has direct, intuitive knowledge of himself as a persisting subject of temporary conscious states. This may sound more like blunt assertion than argument, but the point is that the burden of argument rests upon the person who would deny the testimony of such a vivid and self-authenticating intuition.

The Advaitins do, in fact, offer one such argument against plurality, whether of selves or material objects. To say there is a plurality of things means that each is different from the next. But what can be meant by saying that difference exists? Only, surely, that there is more than one thing, a plurality. But then we are moving around in a circle and have made no sense of either plurality or difference. Madhva has a neat response to this argument, one to warm the hearts of today's 'deconstructivists'. To recognize a difference between A and B, we do not *first* have to identify them as discrete objects; nor, to identify them as such, do we *first* have to recognize their differences. Rather, to perceive something as A (or B) simply *is* to grasp its differences from other things – rather as, according to some recent views, to identify a word as 'dog' just is to grasp its contrasts and similarities with other words in the language. 'To perceive objects is to perceive their uniqueness, and it is this uniqueness which constitutes difference.'[8] So the chicken-and-egg argument against plurality fails: the chicken and the egg arrive together.

The target which the theists find most inviting is the Advaita account – or lack of one – of the relation between *Brahman* and *māyā*, the illusory world of appearance. Madhva, for example, argues that either these two are identical or they are different. Either way, the Advaitin is in trouble. If *māyā* is different from *Brahman*, then reality is not after all undifferentiated and 'One'. But if they are identical, then *Brahman* inherits the defects of the empirical world – ignorance, evil, and so on – contrary to its depiction as a reality without blemish. The Advaitin might reply that the objection is too crude. *Māyā* is not real, like *Brahman*, but nor is it unreal, like things in a dream. It has a special status not captured by the terms 'real' and 'unreal'. Madhva, a keen enforcer of the Law of the Excluded Middle, will have none of this. Something is real or it is unreal: it cannot hover somewhere between the two. As for the suggestion that *māyā* is 'superimposed' on *Brahman* by ourselves, this raises more problems than it solves. How can we superimpose perceptual properties on what is supposed to be beyond perception? And who are the 'we' responsible for the superimposition, given that we are supposed to be part of what gets superimposed?

God, Selves and the World

Suppose the effectiveness of the above critique of Advaita is granted. With what do the theistic Vedāntins replace it? On several matters, there is agreement between the Viśiṣṭādvaita system of Rāmānuja and the Dvaita system of Madhva. Both postulate, on scriptural authority, the existence of a Creator-God, Vishnu, now identified with *Brahman*. Both insist that there really exist a plurality of persons and a material world. (A person is a conjunction of an eternal self with a series of material bodies that constitutes its various incarnations. In standard Indian fashion, this self is a mere 'witness' or 'pure consciousness', with feelings, intelligence, and the like, understood as the subtle operations of matter or *prakṛti*.) Both agree that liberation from the cycle of rebirth depends upon the grace of God, dispensed to those with an appropriately devotional knowledge of God. And both accept a double sense – causal and moral – in which the operation of *karma* depends on God. An action of mine will only produce 'fruit' with the 'permission' of God; and that only some actions, such as the performance of duty, are associated with 'good fruit', is due, not to an impersonal moral order, but to the will of God. As Madhva puts it, '*Karma* does not guide the Supreme Being . . . it is the Supreme Being that guides action' (567).[9]

But this common platform disguises the different ways in which Rāmānuja and Madhva conceive of the relation between God, his creation, and our selves. At issue is how seriously to take those famous lines of the scriptures, such as 'That thou art', which on the surface proclaim an identity between *Brahman*, selves, and the world – lines which no Vedāntin can simply ignore. Defying chronology, let us begin with Madhva's position, which is more straightforward and so strikingly similar to Christian views as to inspire speculation about the influence on Madhva of the missionaries he may have met. For Madhva, God really is a quite distinct being from everything else. The scriptural passages in which He is said to be *prakṛti* can only mean that matter is the medium through which His will is exercised, and that nothing happens in the material world without His agreement. '*Prakṛti* is *Brahman* . . . for the reason that He moulds forms out of . . . the material cause, in which He (also) . . . makes everything.' Nor, he argues, is there 'any conflict' between such texts as 'That thou art' or 'I am *Brahman*' and 'the understanding of the separateness (from the self) of the Lord' (558). The lesser point of such texts is to stress the dependence of the self upon God, but their primary aim is to draw attention to the *similarity* between the two. 'Since the essence of the self consists only of wisdom, bliss and other qualities similar (in some degree) to those of *Brahman*, there proceeds the statement that the self is one with (like) *Brahman*.' It is clear, for Madhva, that only if 'the Supreme Lord is absolutely separate from . . . selves' is He 'exalted far above selves', in a manner that renders Him a fit object of worship and devotion (565).

Here is one of the points with which Rāmānuja takes issue. Devotional love is directed, not towards a supreme power that is 'absolutely separate' from ourselves, but towards a being with whom we can experience intimacy. What is sought after by those, like Mahādevī, who 'cannot manage . . . this world and that other', is not an awesome God who belongs entirely to 'that other' world, but a God who allows us to experience, in Tagore's wonderful line, 'the bliss of the touch of the play of the one in the many'.[10] Anyway, Madhva's construal of 'That thou art', as an elliptical statement of similarity, is hardly compatible with the principle, mentioned earlier, of treating such texts as literally as possible, nor with the unmistakable spirit of 'unity' with *Brahman* that pervades the *Upaniṣads*.

The task, as Rāmānuja conceives it, is to steer between the arid Advaita doctrine of a featureless reality devoid of all differentiation and a dualism which hives us and our world off from God. Put differently, the task is to do equal justice to *Brahman*'s transcendence and immanence. He takes his lead from two Upaniṣadic texts – '[*Brahman*] thought, may I be many, may I bring forth', and the reference to *Brahman* as that 'of whom all beings are the body'. *Brahman*, he argues, may be thought of in three different ways: in its 'pure' state as knowledge or 'omniscience'; as that which 'brings forth' the plurality of selves and material things; and as 'effect', that of which these selves and things are 'aspects'. To use Aristotelian terminology, *Brahman* is at once the 'efficient' cause of the world and its 'material' cause, the 'substrate' of which all beings are aspects. Thus, in 'That thou art', 'that' refers to 'pure' *Brahman* and 'thou' to the individual self, its point being to indicate that there is 'one thing subsisting in a twofold form' – *Brahman* as 'pure' and as 'effect' (130). More generally, the Upaniṣadic statements which assert identity with *Brahman* are to be taken as proclaiming that everything has *Brahman* as its 'self' or substrate.

Meat is put on these bare claims when Rāmānuja develops the idea of the world as the 'body' of *Brahman*. '[T]he entire aggregate of things, intelligent and non-intelligent, has its Self in *Brahman* in so far as it constitutes *Brahman*'s body' (134). This is not mere analogy: things are the body of *Brahman* in just the sense that the body at this desk is *my* body. Of course, a rather special sense of 'body' is involved here since, in *Brahman*'s case, his body includes human selves. 'Body' is defined as 'any substance which a sentient soul is capable of completely controlling and supporting for its own purposes, and which stands to the soul in an entirely subordinate relation' (424). These relations of control, support and subordination obtain, it is held, as much between *Brahman* and individual selves and things as between myself and my body.

Not much needs to be said about 'control' here: *Brahman* controls the world with the same efficacy as I normally do my physical movements. But 'support' and 'subordination' need closer examination. *Brahman* not only supports things and selves in that, without him, they would not exist – no more than my body would, for long, were I dead. More crucially, they cannot be conceived as existing without him, for they are 'modes' of *Brahman* and, as such, cannot be 'rendered intelligible apart from [him]'. The same is true of my body in relation to myself: for once we distinguish between the body as a mere lump of meat and the body, in its 'primary' sense, as a locus of action, an instrument of will, it is clear that this latter could not intelligibly exist without the person whose body it is. A related point is made by the claim that the body – *Brahman*'s or mine – is 'subordinate' to or an 'accessory' of its possessor. 'The accessory is that whose nature it is to be given over to the tendency to render due glory to another; that other is the principal.'[11] Just as the significance for me of my body is to enable me to achieve goals and realize my aspirations, so the *raison d'être* of the world is to make manifest, and thereby 'render glory' to, the goodness of *Brahman*.

It needs stressing that the I-and-my-body relation does not serve simply as a model for that between *Brahman* and the world. By emphasizing how my body is controlled, supported, and subordinated by me, Rāmānuja is insisting on the autonomy and dignity of the indivual human self. This is significant in the context of a theological position which might be read as reducing people to mere 'aspects' of a divine substance. It is important to Rāmānuja that we do not view the relation between *Brahman* and ourselves from just one of two legitimate perspectives. Looked at 'from above', starting from 'pure' *Brahman*, we see the world, ourselves included, as emanations or 'modes' of a single substance. Looked at 'from below', starting from our position as active agents in the world, *Brahman* can appear as a remote cause. Failure to shift from the first perspective encourages the Advaita sense of the world as mere appearance; while a preoccupation, like Madhva's, with the second nurtures a sense of 'absolute difference' between *Brahman* and ourselves, which 'implies the abandonment' of Vedānta (135). We need to combine the two perspectives into a vision of 'identity-in-difference', of a world whose denizens enjoy an autonomy compatible with a devotional recognition that their existence and significance are due to a being that thought, 'May I be many!'

In all of this, surely, there is a brave effort to reconcile the polarities, perennial in the theological imagination, of transcendence and immanence. Whether or not the ingenious analogy – as we, at any rate, are likely to perceive it – between the body of a person and the body of *Brahman* renders the effort successful is, of course, less clear. More generally, it remains an open question whether the theistic Vedāntins – on textual, theological or philosophical grounds – have discredited their Advaita rivals. Certainly they do not sufficiently address the possibility, so important to Śaṅkara (see p. 36), of a mystical vision that 'contradicts' the testimony of everyday, pluralistic experience in rather the manner that, on our awakening, the sight of the sun shining through the window dispels the illusions of that night's dreams. And while it cannot be denied that many Indian men and women – Mahādevī and Tagore, for example – find it impossible to reconcile the absolute monism of Advaita with devotion to the divine, nor can it be denied that many others have experienced no such tension. We might close with the words, written at the beginning of the twentieth century, by one of the most reflective Indian philosophers of modern times:

> The Advaitin would whole-heartedly join in the traditional worship and would be false to himself if he professed contempt for it, though he would recognize that the contemplation of [its] abstract significance is itself part of the worship and at a certain stage may be the whole spiritual activity . . . [For] although *bhakti* implies individuality, it represents the individual's joy in surrendering his individuality.[12]

• 2 Neo-Confucianism •

In Fung Yu-Lan's massive history of Chinese philosophy, six of the seven chapters covering the period from the founding of the Sung dynasty in 960 CE to the collapse of the dynastic system in 1912 are devoted to Neo-Confucian thinkers – an indication of the success of these philosophers in their struggle to 'repossess the Way'. The expression is an apt one since, for all their originality, Neo-Confucians perceived themselves as regaining something which had been lost since that first flowering of Confucian thought described in chapter 3. Central to the spirit of that early thinking had been the ideal of the 'superior person' (*chun tzu*). It was in order to cultivate such persons that scholarly learning and performance of 'ritual' (*li*) had originally been advocated. By the Sung era, however, many Confucians were conceding to their critics that learning and *li* were no longer respected 'for the sake of one's self' – of one's betterment as a person – but as a means, simply, to advancement in official life.[13]

'Repossession' referred, however, not only to the retrieval of the original moral spirit of Confucianism, for what also needed to be regained was the philosophical initiative which, it seemed, had long been lost to its rivals, Taoism and Buddhism (the latter having extended its influence into China since around 300 CE). Few readers of chapters 2 and 3 would deny that Taoism (in Chuang Tzu's version at least) and Mahāyāna Buddhism offered philosophies of greater depth and scope than anything to be found in the relatively sketchy remarks of Confucius or Mencius. So the challenge was on to forge a systematic philosophy that could compete with Taoism and Buddhism, and at the same time serve as the foundation for the traditional ideals of Confucianism.

The challenge, moreover, was an urgent one, for Confucians perceived their two rivals as moral and political dangers. To begin with, both of them relegated the importance of social duty and 'propriety', such as those required by 'filial piety'. Whether inspired by the romantic anarchism of some Taoists or by a Buddhistic sense of the mundane world as 'illusory', this relegation was 'a crime of the greatest magnitude'.[14] Moreover, despite their rhetoric of 'truth to oneself' and 'selflessness', Taoists and Buddhists could both be accused of insincerity and selfishness. Insincerity because, for all their claims to have 'renounced' the world, these people 'still drink when they are thirsty and still . . . set their feet on earth'.[15] Selfishness because they had replaced moral obligations to others with an obsession with either physical longevity or personal emancipation from 'the world of suffering'.

Despite these criticisms of the alleged amoralism of Taoism and Buddhism, the Neo-Confucians were able to appreciate the value of other ingredients in their rivals' teachings and keen to integrate these with their own. There is truth, therefore, in the familiar idea of Neo-Confucianism as a synthesis of several philosophical tendencies. This will become clearer as we elaborate its main objectives and the central claims subscribed to, with important variations, by its leading representatives.

Old and New in Neo-Confucianism

Neo-Confucians earn the name through their reaffirmation of the social morality prescribed by Confucius. The 'superior person' lives in accordance with *jen* ('inner moral force'), whose primary manifestation is the readiness to discharge the duties of one's stations in life – as father, say, or imperial official. Reaffirmed, too, is the double sense in which *jen* was reckoned to be 'natural'. Not only does the 'superior' life harmonize with 'the Way of Heaven' but, as Mencius urged, it grows from man's innate endowment, his 'natural goodness' (see ch. 3, sect. 2). Particular importance was also attached to the traditional emphasis upon learning. 'The way to learn has been lost to us', complained Ch'eng I,[16] partly because people, misinterpreting Mencius, had come to the lazy conclusion that sagehood could be attained by relying entirely on their innate knowledge; and partly because people had fallen for the quack promises of instant enlightenment made by Buddhists and Taoists. Seriousness in the search for virtue and knowledge, Chu Hsi reminded his contemporaries, 'does not mean to sit still like a blockhead . . . with the mind thinking of nothing' (607).[17]

In one of the ironic turns which enliven the history of our subject, the distinctive, 'neo', element in Neo-Confucianism is borrowed from the repertoire of its rivals. This is the theme of 'holism', of a unity or 'oneness' of everything that goes beyond the mere 'harmony' spoken of by Confucius and Mencius. As the Ming dynasty philosopher Wang Yang-Ming was to put it, the 'great man . . . regards Heaven and Earth and the myriad things as one body . . . the world as one family and the country as one person. As to those who distinguish between the self and others, they are small men' (661).[18] Such remarks might have been lifted from the pages of Chuang Tzu or a Mahāyāna *sūtra*. The ingenuity and novelty of Neo-Confucianism reside in its attempts to demonstrate that holism, far from warranting an anarchistic or transcendental disdain for the affairs of society, entails commitment to, precisely, the precepts of Confucian ethics. The reflective response to the unity of self and cosmos is neither an undirected 'universal compassion', nor a separation of the 'true self' from the everyday, socially engaged persona. Indeed, it is those reactions which should be seen as forms of attachment to the self. What holism requires is the authentic selflessness of the person committed to an unstinting discharge of his or her duties as parent, friend, ruler, official, or whatever. At the ethical level, holism entails what Theodore de Bary calls 'Confucian personalism', 'the concept of the person as most truly itself when most fully in communion with other selves' through a network of moral obligations.[19]

I spoke of Neo-Confucian attempts to ground Confucian ethics in a doctrine of holism, for we need to distinguish between the two broad streams of Neo-Confucian thought respectively inspired, in a happy example of fraternal rivalry, by the eleventh-century brothers Ch'eng I and Ch'eng Hao. The first is variously refered to as 'orthodox', 'rationalist', 'the school of principle (*Li-hsueh*)', and 'the Ch'eng-Chu school' (after the first brother and his twelfth-century admirer, Chu Hsi). The second is alternatively called 'unorthodox', 'idealist', 'the school of heart–mind (*Hsin-hsueh*)', and 'the Lu-Wang school' (after Chu Hsi's sparring partner, Lu Hsiang-Shan, and the aforementioned Wang Yang-Ming). The sloganizing way to distinguish the two schools is to say that the 'orthodox' advocates 'the investigation of things', while the 'unorthodox' emphasizes 'the investigation of mind'. But that is too bland to be of any help at this stage. To appreciate what is at issue, we need to consider the views of two leading protagonists, the 'orthodox' Chu Hsi and the 'unorthodox' Wang Yang-Ming. This will also be the best way to fill out our sketch, so far rough, of Neo-Confucian thought.

Principle and 'The Investigation of Things'

After the classical sages, the philosopher to exert most influence in China was Chu Hsi (1137–1200), an influence by no means confined to the ivory tower and one extending, as we shall see in section 2 of chapter 9, down to the twentieth century. As writer, educational reformer, and editor of the

Confucian corpus, he shaped the training and *esprit de corps* of the Chinese civil service. During an energetic life, Chu Hsi oscillated between periods in high office and disgrace, the latter on account of the forthright manner in which he practised his preaching that officials were duty-bound to point out to superiors, the Emperor included, the errors of their ways. Chu, it seems, was a born philosopher, harassing his father, at the age of four, with questions about the afterlife. Whether, as an adult, he added anything substantially new to the ideas of earlier Neo-Confucians, like Ch'eng I, is a matter of some contention. It is not disputed that he provided the most systematic account of 'orthodox' thinking.

Chu's starting point is 'the problem of evil', which had plagued Confucianism since its early days. He agreed with Mencius that, by nature, man is naturally good, but admitted that Mencius himself had no real answer to critics, like Hsun Tzu, who marshalled evidence for a less favourable verdict on human nature. According to Chu, both Mencius and his critics failed to make a crucial distinction between man's 'original' and 'physical' natures. The claim that our nature is good is ambiguous, and true only of the former nature. 'We fall into evil only when our actions are not in accordance with our original nature' (617).

Man's 'original' nature, like that of everything else, is constituted by *Li*, variously translated by 'principle', 'form' and 'pattern' (and not to be confused with *li* = 'ritual'; hence my use of a capital 'L'). This notion is to be understood by way of contrast with that of *ch'i* – 'ether', 'material fluid' or, as I prefer, 'material force'. A person's or a thing's 'original' nature – or simply its nature, left unqualified – is its *Li*. 'Man's nature is nothing but principle'. On the other hand, 'physical nature refers to principle and material force combined' (613–14). The idea seems to be that *Li* makes something the kind of thing it is – a man, a dog, a tile: it constitutes the 'essence' of its kind. To be a dog, say, a creature must be a physical substance, composed out of *ch'i*, which 'fits' the principle or pattern that determines the category of dogs. Not only that, but a thing's *Li* serves as a paradigm or exemplar to which it must approximate in order to be good of its kind. The more a dog deviates from its principle – by losing its teeth, say, so that it is no longer carniverous – the less it lives up to the canine ideal.

It is hard to make the intended idea here more precise, since Chu's words permit various interpretations. The idiom of a 'pattern' which determines a thing's kind and serves as an exemplar may suggest an affinity with Plato's theory of Forms (see ch. 4, sect. 3), and this is reinforced by two further claims. First, Chu tells us that *Li* 'exists before physical form . . . principle is prior' (634), seemingly hinting thereby at a distinct 'world' of abstract entities. Second, he postulates a single overarching principle, 'the Great Ultimate' (*t'ai-*

chi), which is at once the unity of 'all principles put together' and 'the principle of the highest good' (640–1). The echo here is of Plato's 'Form of the Good'. Against this, Chu insists that *Li* is only 'prior' to physical objects in the sense that nothing could be the object it is unless it fitted a certain pattern. In practice, 'principle is not a separate entity . . . without material force, principle would have nothing to adhere to' (634). This sounds more like Aristotle: principles exist only in and through the things which fit them.

But perhaps any assimilation of *Li* to Greek Forms is mistaken; as Joseph Needham argues, '*Li* was not in any strict sense metaphysical . . . but rather the invisible organizing fields or forces existing at all levels within the natural world.'[20] The *Li* of a dog is then that natural – perhaps genetic, as we would now say – endowment which underlies the features and behaviour of normal dogs. Fido's 'physical' nature is a combination of this endowment, shared with other dogs, and of the *ch'i* responsible for his particular features – his aggression, say, or curly tail. That principle of principles, 'the Great Ultimate', might then be construed as the most general structural patterns and forces underlying the physical processes of the world, most notably the universal operation of '*yin* and *yang* succeeding each other in an unceasing cycle' (641).

It is not crucial to decide between these interpretations in order to appreciate Chu's solution to 'the problem of evil'. The charm of the *Li* versus *ch'i* distinction is virtually to immunize the belief in natural goodness against empirical refutation, for any failure to exhibit *jen* can be put down to a bad dose of *ch'i*. *Ch'i* apparently varies from being 'turbid' to 'clear', and only in the latter case does it permit a person's natural virtue to come through. Our most general moral duty is to 'clarify' our *ch'i*, by reducing the selfish desires which obstruct the natural dispositions towards benevolence and righteousness.

But if the doctrine of *Li* immunizes the belief in natural goodness against empirical refutation, it also seems to debar it from empirical support. Why, given that lots of people behave pretty badly most of the time, should one make any assumption of their natural goodness? It is at this point that Chu appeals to the central Neo-Confucian tenet of holism. All *Li*, as we know, are connected up to one another in 'the Great Ultimate': hence, 'every person has in him the Great Ultimate' (640). Put differently, the Way, which is 'inherent in nature', is 'inherent in the self': 'one's nature is the framework of the Way' (617). Consequently, a person is only authentically himself when his actions and feelings reflect the unity with everything – other people included – in which he truly stands. Such actions and feelings are, conveniently, the very ones enjoined by the Confucian virtues. *Jen*, in particular, is marked by an impartiality and sympathy which directly testify to a sense of 'the unity of all things and the self' (595). Our nature is that whereby we are intimately related to the cosmos: hence, to act and feel in consort with that nature is to develop the virtues, for these are the antidote to a selfishness which would otherwise turn us into so many isolated atoms.

Chu Hsi must answer two questions before his position can lay claim to Confucian orthodoxy, however. Why, in order to live well, should a premium be put on learning, on 'the investigation of things' (*ko-wu*)? And why, if *jen* and the virtues have universal scope, should emphasis be placed on such restricted duties as those of a son to his father? By 'the investigation of things', Chu means the examination of their *Li*, their essential natures. In much the same rationalist spirit we associate with Spinoza, he believes that it is only through rigorous examination of essences – and not, say, through a Buddhistic 'emptying of the mind' – that we can come to grasp the ordered unity of the cosmos. 'The mind that leaves something outside is not capable of uniting itself with the mind of Heaven' (629), of achieving a final 'harmony [with] and penetration [into]' reality. But there is a more direct reason for 'investigating things'. If, especially in human affairs, 'we know why things are as they are, we will not be perplexed . . . our action will not be wrong' (611). Bad, selfish behaviour is often explicable by sheer error, by the mistaken belief that to prosper a person must 'look out for Number One'. Proper examination of human relations shows, however, that it is by acting on one's 'original' impulses, like sympathy, that a person achieves peace and happiness.[21]

It is in these terms that Chu answers the second question, concerning the Confucian's stress on restricted duties, like those of filial piety and loyalty to a ruler. Although everyone is connected to everyone else in a grand 'family', some connections are patently closer than others. 'Investigation' of human beings incontrovertibly reveals that a person feels greater emotional commitment to some people – family, friends – than to others. A morality which ignores this and exhorts us to total impartiality – like Buddhism, in Chu's estimate – sets a standard which cannot be met. Or rather, if it is to be met, this can only be through the gradual and gentle extension of human sympathy from its basis in family relations and friendship. Set the bar too high and no one will even try to jump it: set it at a level that people can comfortably clear then, with practice and dedication, they will eventually reach a level that, had it been set at the beginning, would have frightened them off.

'The Investigation of Heart–Mind'

As is the fate of many influential philosophers, Chu Hsi's views had, within two hundred years of his death, ossified into dogma, remote in spirit from anything he had advocated. The main critic of this tendency, and the leading 'unorthodox' or 'idealist' Neo-Confucian, was Wang Yang-Ming (1472–1529) – or, to give him his proper name, Wang Shou-Jen. Like Chu, Wang alternated between high office and periods of disgrace due to his bluntly expressed criticisms. Like Mo Tzu, much earlier, he combined philosophy with military expertise, specializing in the suppression of uprisings against the Ming dynasty. He was less able, it seems, to combine philosophy with conjugal matters, spending his wedding night in discussion with a Taoist priest over immortality.

Had Wang confined his attack to the degeneration of 'the investigation of things' into idle curiosity and the accumulation of data, he would not have been an especially controversial figure. But, despite an admiration for his great predecessor, he also holds Chu Hsi's own views responsible for this tendency. Had Chu not told us to study and 'pay attention to everything'? – an instruction which, taken seriously, would mean close study of, say, the *Li* of bamboos. Wang, in fact, had tried just this, but only to 'become sick' (689): for not only did the essence of bamboos have no bearing on the important issues of moral life, but it was absurd to expect the 'tremendous energy' demanded for investigating the *Li* of everything.

He has a deeper criticism of Chu, however. Like all Neo-Confucians, Wang teaches a doctrine of holism. 'I . . . form one body with Heaven, Earth, and the myriad things' (661). Now Chu had argued that the way to appreciate this unity was through the objective investigation of the *Li* of things. But this, in Wang's view, will actually obstruct such an appreciation. When people 'search for the highest good in individual things . . . the mind becomes fragmentary, isolated, broken into pieces' (662). The complaint is the recurrent one that the 'objective stance' – viewing the world as so many objects for detached examination – distances a person from that world, thereby destroying the prospects for a sense of integration with everything. Seeking 'the principle of things outside the mind' means that the mind is 'closed to', or closed off from, the world (681).

But if there *is* an objective world of *Li*, is it not disingenuous simply to ignore it? Wang's retort is that there is no such objective world: hence his constant reiteration of 'mind is principle' or, more fully, 'mind is the nature of man and things, and nature is principle' (674) – a set of equations specifically denied by Chu Hsi. This may indeed sound like idealism, but Wang's position is as ambiguous as Chu's. Certainly there are passages where he seems to be expounding a doctrine of *esse est percipi* ('To be is to be perceived'), as when he remarks that 'flowers are not external to the mind' (685). But a less drastic construal is more likely. Flowers are 'not external', not because they are 'in' the mind, but because they are things we encounter in experience and not the invisible, unknowable substances that 'lie behind' what we perceive. What makes something a flower, its *Li*, is not therefore some objective essence, but its location in a network of human experience and behaviour. In the absence of this network, there is no reason to count something as a flower rather than as anything else, which is why, without the 'knowledge inherent in man, there cannot be plants and trees, tiles and stones' (685). This dependence of things on human experience is encapsulated in Wang's very definition of 'a thing' as 'that to which the will is directed' (675). A thing is not 'in' the mind, as if inside some ethereal medium, for mind 'has no substance of its own' (685). Rather, it depends on mind only in the sense that, in the absence of human purposes and concerns, it would lose its identity as the thing it is – a tile, say.

One can now see why, for Wang, the 'investigation of things' that really matters is at the same time an 'investigation of the heart–mind (hsin)'. A thing is something 'for us'; to understand it is not to grasp some metaphysical form or invisible physical force, if such there be, which it possesses, but to appreciate how it figures as an object of human perception, feeling and purpose. The principle or Li of filial piety, for example, is not a rule etched into the objective, mind-independent order of the cosmos, awaiting our discovery, but the expression of a human disposition. It is, simply, the 'will directed towards serving one's parents' (673).

By denying a distinction between Li and mind – and thereby between our 'original' and 'physical' natures – Wang is unable to offer Chu Hsi's answers to the pressing questions of how evil is possible and how right behaviour is to be determined. (For Chu, it was explained, evil actions do not reflect on the goodness of our 'original' nature; it is by appeal to the Li, which defines this nature, that right and wrong are determined.) Wang's strategy is to reject these questions as traditionally posed. If the problem of evil is why people behave badly despite their natural knowledge of what is good, then it is a pseudo-problem. That a person acts badly is sure evidence that he does *not* really know what is good. 'Those who are supposed to know but do not act simply do not know' (669). Wang proposes the identity of knowledge and virtue – as one might predict from his 'behaviourist' denial that the mind is a substance, a theatre of 'inner' operations divorced from dispositions to act. He does, in fact, concede *a* sense in which human nature is good, but not one which makes the emergence of bad behaviour problematic. Our 'innate goodness' is simply the state of 'equilibrium before the feelings are aroused'; when that happens people 'cannot help being darkened . . . by material desires' (683). Neither in the state of equilibrium nor in their 'darkened' condition have people yet risen to knowledge of the good – so there is no puzzle as to why they do not act on such knowledge.

But if we cannot appeal to innately known Li, how can we objectively determine what is good? Wang again rejects the assumption on which the question rests – that we can stand outside of all our feelings and dispositions and subject them to objective moral scrutiny. In twentieth-century parlance, Wang is a 'non-cognitivist' in ethics. Good and evil 'are not present in things at all'

(678): such terms register our favourable and unfavourable attitudes towards things. 'When you want . . . flowers, you will consider . . . weeds evil. But when you want . . . weeds, you will consider them good. Such good and evil are all products of the mind's likes and dislikes' (677).

None of this, however, excludes criticism of selfish desires and actions, for these are at odds with 'the principle of nature', which is one of the unity of things and people in 'one body'. It is the person who cultivates sympathy and generosity, the promptings of *jen*, whose life not only expresses the unity of things but enjoys the 'tranquility' of the equilibrium state prior to the arousal of selfish feelings. To someone who retorts 'So what! Unity and tranquility are nothing to me', Wang's reply, one suspects, must be silence. Not the silence of the moral nihilist, for whom all discussion of right and wrong is hot air; but the silence of someone who recognizes that moral discussion must start somewhere, and that this place has not been reached by the interlocutor for whom love, sympathy, tranquility, and a sense of living in accord with the way of things, matter not at all.

Two Schools?

Are there, then, two schools of Neo-Confucianism, 'orthodox' and 'unorthodox', represented by Chu Hsi and Wang Yang-Ming? A lot turns, of course, on uncertain interpretations of these philosophers. If Chu's 'principles' are akin to the Forms of either Plato or Aristotle, and if Wang really is an idealist of the *esse est percipi* ilk, then the metaphysical divide is a large one. But there seemed no great reason to understand their positions in these ways. Chu's principles are, more probably, in and of the natural physical world, one whose existence Wang does not want to deny.

But an important difference remains, of philosophical temperament, perhaps, more than of specific doctrine. An alternative label for the 'orthodox' school is 'rationalist': and this usefully indicates a kinship between Chu's approach and the conviction of European rationalists, like Descartes, that our everyday conceptions may not be in order as they stand. These conceptions are to be validated, or invalidated, on the basis of a rational foundation attainable through the detached, objective enquiries of specialists. So, for Chu, that conception of a unitary world which is required to secure the precepts of Confucian ethics, is to be confirmed through investigation of the *Li*.

Wang, on the other hand, is friendlier towards 'the plain man'. Specialist, detached enquiry may turn up information for the curious, but it cannot overturn – and is not required to justify – our everyday conception of the world as it is 'for us', in relation to perception and purpose. The unity of the cosmos is secured by the simple thought that every thing is what it is because of the place it occupies in a single, broad field of practical vision – ours. As for the justification of Confucian morality, again the plain man is right to rely on 'gut' feelings of sympathy, decency, and so on. That these feelings can be given no objective warrant from the detached standpoint of 'the investigator of things' is neither here nor there. Morality operates from within the perspective of men and women as they actually are. Whether Chu and Wang are right to suppose that 'the investigation of things' and 'the investigation of heart–mind', respectively, will yield the particular virtues of Confucian morality, is of course a further question.

• 3 Zen Buddhism •

Buddhism has had a bad press in this chapter. Among Śaṅkara's theistic critics, the charge against him of 'closet Buddhism' was a serious one, while for Neo-Confucians, the pretensions of Buddhists to 'detachment' from the everyday world were both egoistic and disingenuous. But Buddhism had also become a target of internal criticism, none more robust than that of the Zen schools. Here, as one historian puts it, if with some exaggeration, was a genuine 'reformation or revolution in Buddhism'.[22]

For the followers of Zen, other Buddhists had lost the original message of Gautama, the Buddha, at any rate that 'unspoken' one epitomized in his 'Flower Sermon' when he enlightened his most perceptive disciple by simply holding up a lotus flower. It was this 'special transmission outside the scriptures' that needed to be recaptured. To the extent that any 'scriptures' had communicated the true message, these were the classic Mahāyāna texts, such as the *Diamond* and *Laṅkāvatāra Sūtras*. But even the best interpreters of these texts, the Mādhyamikas (see pp. 44ff.), had been tempted into false directions. Against their better judgement, some of them had veered towards 'transcendentalism', a false contrast between the 'empty' phenomenal world and an eternal *nirvāṇa* – towards, in effect, a 'closet Vedāntism'. As for the 'Pure Land' school, which had been gathering in popularity since the fourth century CE, its identification of *nirvāṇa* with a heaven populated by a pantheon of divine Buddhas, commanding worship and dispensing grace, represented a theism antithetical to Gautama's intentions.

It is not only as a 'reformist' movement that Zen qualifies for attention. There are, today, American sons and daughters of the 'flower power' generation of the 1960s who, with or without filial gratitude, bear the Christian name 'Zen': a testament to the fascination this form of Buddhism exerted in the West during the twentieth century. Some of the reasons for this would, no doubt, be approved by the old Zen Masters themselves: the urge to live simply and spontaneously within an increasingly complex and artificial society, for example, or the sense that a spiritual existence can dispense with the baggage of scriptural scholarship, idolatry and mythology. But other reasons would not be approved by them, being based on popular misunderstandings of Zen. Many Westerners, for instance, construe Zen references to 'sudden' enlightenment as promising a 'quick fix', a safe alternative to LSD in the quest for spiritual experience. Others are attracted by some methods of Zen practice, especially the use of *koans* – riddles, bizarre anecdotes, paradoxes – which are reckoned to confirm that Zen preaches a mysterious irrationalism welcome in an age dominated by science.

This charge – or boast – of irrationalism has, unfortunately, been encouraged by the man most responsible for acquainting the West with Zen, D. T. Suzuki. 'Zen is the most irrational, inconceivable thing in the world', he writes, 'not subject to logical analysis or intellectual treatment'[23] – which raises the question of what Suzuki himself was doing in his many works on Zen. He is surely failing to draw two distinctions. The first is that between Zen philosophy and Zen enlightenment. The latter, to be sure, requires an 'intuition' or mode of experience that cannot be provided by a philosophical articulation of reality. But a claim of this kind, of course, is common currency among Indian philosophies and many others, such as Plotinus'. Second, Suzuki is eliding Zen philosophy and Zen practice. The shouts, slaps and *koan* absurdities, which are supposed to induce enlightenment, might well be described as 'irrational' methods. But that does not exclude the possibility of an articulate philosophy in terms of which the use of such devices is warranted. Just such an articulation is what we find in the writings of many Zen Masters. It matters little whether we say that Zen is a philosophy that justifies certain practices or, with Masao Abe, that 'Zen is not a philosophy' but a practice which 'embraces a profound philosophy'.[24] (Compare a similar option in the case of Marxism.) Either way we can discern in Zen writings a reasoned account of reality and human existence.

'*Zen*' is the Japanese rendition of the Chinese '*ch'an*', in turn derived from the Sanskrit word '*dhyāna*', meaning 'meditation'. (An etymology which, we shall see, can mislead.) Legend has it that Zen was 'brought to' China in 520 CE by an Indian, Bodhidharma, who set the blunt tone of the school by telling the Emperor that the latter's many good deeds had 'no merit' and that 'nothing is sacred'. But it is more accurate to think of Zen as gradually evolving through a fusion of Mahāyānist and Taoist doctrines. The first extended work of an undoubtedly Zen character was *The Platform Sūtra* of Hui-Neng (638–713), supposedly an illiterate seller of firewood who, while employed in the thresh-ing-room of a monastery, so impressed its Head that he was elevated to the position of Sixth Patriarch (Bodhidharma having been the First). Although Zen, or Ch'an, Buddhism was to enjoy great success during the T'ang dynasty, despite its internal schisms and occasional persecution, it was to be in Japan that its influence would be most abiding. There, certainly, it was also to receive its most acute philosophical articulation, in the writings of Dōgen (1200–53). Dōgen is usually credited with founding one of the two main Zen sects, Sōtō, offspring of the schism in China. But it is not until the eighteenth century that the divisions between this and the rival Rinzai sect become sharply delineated, largely through Hakuin's (1685–1768) institutionalizing of the use of *koans*, which has since become the Rinzai hallmark.

The distinctive contributions of Zen are to be found both in fundamental Buddhist doctrine and in the implications drawn from this for practice. But it is worth stressing that the Zen Masters did not see themselves as promulgating new doctrines, but rather as retrieving an original teaching that had been encrusted with false interpretations. When they proclaim that 'there is not much in Buddhism after all',[25] the point is that what is needed is not so much a new theory, but the dismantling of theories which have come to disguise an essentially simple message.

'We *are* the Buddha–Mind'

According to the *Laṅkāvatāra Sūtra*, 'all beings are already in . . . *nirvāṇa*', and since being in *nirvāṇa* is to be enlightened, this means that, in the words of Hui-Neng, 'enlightenment and intuitive wisdom [*prajñā*] are from the outset possessed by men of the world'.[26] And since to be enlightened is to have Buddha-mind, it means we already possess Buddha-mind here in the world. For Dōgen, it is better to say that we *are* Buddha-mind, lest the idiom of 'possession' suggests that we are selves which merely happen to have a certain feature. Whatever the exact formulation, here is a fundamental tenet of Zen. But can it really be the intention to deny the 'noble truth' that, ordinarily, we live in a state of 'suffering' (*duḥkha*) due to 'ignorance'?

At a minimum, the point of the above pronouncements is to deny that enlightenment owes to anything like the 'grace' entertained by 'Pure Land' Buddhists. We possess Buddha-mind in at least the sense that the potential for enlightenment is wholly within our own nature. But denied, too, is another 'Pure Land' heresy: that Buddhahood is the prerogative of beings in a heavenly afterlife. As Hui-Neng stated on his deathbed, 'apart from sentient beings there is no Buddha-mind'.[27] More generally, it is denied that enlightenment is a condition 'outside' or 'above' the phenomenal world: so it should not, for example, be assimilated, in the manner of some Mahāyānists, to the state of *Brahman*. The Buddha himself, it is held, taught a doctrine of *nirvāṇa* which accommodates beings as they are and not 'the attainment of heaven'.

Such denials, however, hardly warrant the dramatic claim that we are *already* enlightened. That I have the potential to be a novelist does not mean that I am one. Nor does the fact that only sentient beings can be enlightened entail that this is what they all are. How, moreover, is Zen to explain the usual view that the Buddha *attained* enlightenment one night beneath the Bodhi tree? By saying, perhaps, that until that night his enlightenment was only 'dormant'. But then one suspects that this is only a peculiar and misleading way of expressing the usual view that, before that night, he was not enlightened at all, but the victim of ignorance.

Doubtless, the Zen claim is unnecessarily paradoxical, but there is a serious and subtle point to it which distinguishes it from the standard view. I am pretty ignorant of chemistry: that is, I lack various items of knowledge, let alone a grasp of chemical theory. I am unable to provide answers or solutions to perfectly good questions, like 'What is wood composed of?' Now, is the alleged ignorance under which we labour prior to enlightenment – to appreciating, above all, that there is 'No self' (see pp. 40ff.) – at all parallel? The Zen reply is that it is not, so that describing our condition as one of ignorance, to be made good by new knowledge, is badly misleading. What we need is not to pick up some new information, but as the *Laṅkāvatāra* puts it, 'a turning round of consciousness'. The Buddhist slogan of 'No self' is to be understood not as a solution to a well-formed question about the nature of the self, but as a way of rejecting such questions. It is not a solution, but a dissolution. This is why Zen Masters like to describe our normal condition, a symptom of which is the pressing of such a question, as a disease. 'I merely cure disease,' says Lin-Chi, 'and set people free.'[28]

Zen diagnoses the disease which makes us press on with bad questions about the self as due to our capacity for self-reflection, for making judgements of the kind 'I can see that I am a rotter'. Such judgements seduce us into making a double error: setting up a 'me' – the rotter – as the object of self-reflection, and imagining an 'I', a pure 'witness', as its inner subject. In truth, of course, there is neither this object nor this subject, only that loose bundle or series of perceptions and thoughts which we call 'a person'. The pressing of questions about the self's nature is, therefore, both fruitless and frustrating. We should be dispensing, not answers, but a 'medicine for the mental paralysis which comes from excessive self-consciousness'.[29]

There is a further reason why 'ignorance' is an unhappy word for our normal condition, for this is, to a degree, our own creation. The grammar of self-reflective judgements engenders the idea of a self or subject not only as a pure 'witness', but as the controlling centre of will, the hidden director of our thoughts and actions, the referent of the 'I' in judgements of the form 'I did X' or 'I decided on Y'. This latter idea, once it has taken root, feeds on itself. Seeing myself as the pilot of my ship, I live accordingly: setting and doggedly pursuing goals and projects, trying to control my future and that of the people and things about me. The effect is to reinforce the sense of myself as a discrete self which persists unchanged over time – the self which sets goals and later achieves them. My misunderstanding of myself, then, is due not only to the confusions inspired by self-reflection, but to the perverse attempt to live in a manner which embodies those confusions.

It is in this context that Zen Masters describe the 'cure' for our condition as a 'letting go'. Dōgen, for example, exhorts us to 'just let body and mind drop off': to recognize, that is, that decisions and intentions are, in the final analysis, events which 'just happen', and not the dictates of a controlling subject (149).[30] We would not need to 'let go' if we had not been bamboozled through an excess of self-consciousness and had retained what Zen sometimes calls our 'straightforward' mind. This is the mind of the simple person, immersed in everyday affairs, with neither the time nor the inclination to pursue fruitless questions about the self. 'Whatever runs counter to the mind and will of ordinary people hinders . . . the law of Buddha', writes one sage, in a demotic mood inspired, one suspects, by Taoist idealizations of the simple life of cognitive innocence.[31] The idea that our normal, confused situation is a fall from one of original innocence lends further point, of course, to describing us as enlightened 'from the outset'.

Is there no difference, then, between the innocent condition of the 'straightforward' mind and that of the sage? The Zen priest Takuan offered a useful analogy when he compared the movement from innocence through 'sickness' to sagehood with going up a musical scale. One reaches the note with which one began, but in a higher register. Likewise the 'highest stage' of wisdom is a return to a 'first stage . . . [when] intellectual calculations are lost sight of and . . . no-thought-ness prevails'.[32] The difference between the two stages is like that between the good health of a person cured of an illness and that of one who was never ill. It is because the 'highest stage' marks a return that Zen Masters speak of it as a 'homecoming', a return to oneself after a period of seeming division, of subject set against object. This recovery of oneself is not, of course, a rediscovery of *a* self. In the beautiful simile of the travel writer and student of Zen, Peter Matthiessen, 'to glimpse one's own true nature is a kind of homegoing . . . that needs no home, like that waterfall on the upper Suli Gad that turns to mist before touching the earth and rises once again into the sky'.[33]

'Mountains are once more mountains'

The second distinctive contribution of Zen at the level of doctrine concerns the nature of the external world and our relation to it. Not that this is an entirely separate matter from the nature of the self, since Zen shares the standard Buddhist view that our conception of things is shaped by that of selves. With the recognition of 'No self' there comes the recognition that trees and stones are not individual substances underlying phenomenal properties. The 'self' of his chariot 'dissolves' alongside that of the King himself (see p. 41). For much of the time, indeed, it seems that Zen accepts the radical views of the Mādhyamikas, like Nāgārjuna, with their triple equation of *nirvāṇa*, *śūnyatā* (emptiness) and *saṃsāra* (the empirical world). Since nothing in the empirical world can, on analysis, be conceived to exist independently of its relations to everything else, this world is 'empty' of substances. But *nirvāṇa*, properly understood, is precisely the condition of 'no substance'. So *nirvāṇa* is not a different world from *saṃsāra*, but the same one perspicuously viewed without the false categories of substance and self, and without, therefore, the preconceptions that incline us to 'grasp after' worldly things. Zen seems to agree, too, that the articulation of the world into classes of things is the product of human convention. Thus Hui-Neng says that 'all things were originally given rise to by man', echoing perhaps the *Diamond Sūtra*'s remark that ' "seizing upon a material object" is a convention of language'.[34]

But there is a twist to the story, for alongside the insistence that the world is a seamless network of relations within which individual things can only be picked out through convention, there are many passages in Zen writings which also insist on the independence and 'in-itselfness' of a material thing. Dōgen, for instance, tells us to 'see things properly . . . accept them the way they are', and to 'accept things as they come – i.e. independent' (11). Unless we do so, we devalue the empirical world, treating it as a mere 'nothing' or reducing it to the status of the Hindu's *māyā*. And this would bring with it not so much a welcome refusal to 'grasp after' things as an uncaring indifference to our world and its inhabitants.

But how can we reconcile passages like Dōgen's with the doctrine of *saṃsāra* as 'empty'. Crucial here is a famous statement by Ch'ing-Yuan (Jap.: Seigen): 'Before a man studies Zen, to him mountains are mountains . . . ; after he gets an insight into . . . Zen, mountains to him are not mountains . . . ; but . . . when he really attains to the abode of rest, mountains are once more mountains.'[35] At the first, naïve stage, we take a mountain to be an independent item in reality. At the second stage – when, say, we have read our Nāgārjuna – we recognize that mountains are 'empty' and without, it seems, any reality of their own. But at a third stage of true Zen enlightenment, we transcend this second stage and return to something like our first perception.

How are we to interpret this third stage? The usual suggestion commentators make is as follows. At the second stage, it has been recognized that the terms in which we talk and think about the world are irretrievably anthropocentric and conventional and serve as a veil, distorting our perception of things. We think of a mountain itself as big and beautiful when, in truth, these adjectives merely express human measurements. We must strive, then, to cultivate a mode of direct experience – wordless and non-conceptual – in which mountains, or whatever, are perceived for what *they* are, 'in themselves'. But this suggestion is not coherent. If it is anthropocentric and language-relative to speak of something as a mountain, why is it not equally so to perceive or experience it as a mountain? Creatures from a very different background – Martians, say – might not find it at all natural to see what is before them as mountains. Maybe they would find it natural to perceive what we would call three adjoining mountains as a single item of experience, a 'trimount' perhaps. Yet the Zen Masters, like Ch'ing-Yuan, are insistent that, at the third stage, it is mountains, trees and the like which we experience 'for what they are'.

Any interpretation of this third stage must, moreover, take note that nothing is what it is except in relation to everything else. But how can this be done while proclaiming, with Dōgen, that each thing is 'independent'? We get a clue, perhaps, from the school of painting associated with Japanese Zen, the *sumi-e*. At first sight, the bent tree depicted on an almost blank scroll seems to have been abstracted from any context. But, on a closer view, the empty background (the mist in the valley) and a few further strokes (the hint of a mountain crag, of a crow) serve to emphasize the life and environment of the tree in a way that a more crowded canvas, by Constable perhaps, could not. Its precarious roots in the crag, its being blasted by the wind, its being perched on by the crow, serve to bring out the uniqueness of just that tree, precisely by depicting its relations to these items in its environment. Still in the realm of forestry, Dōgen writes that the 'entire universe manifests itself in . . . a tall bamboo' (89). (Dōgen, apparently, had more luck with bamboos than Wang Yang-Ming who, recall, was made sick by staring at a bamboo in the hope of discovering its 'principle'.) The bamboo, as it were, 'gathers' its environment around it, and through doing so takes on its special identity.

The Mādhyamikas were not wrong to insist that an object is nothing outside of its relations to everything else. But this can suggest that the object is merely dissolved and has no reality of its own. Such is the viewpoint of the person at Ch'ing-Yuan's second stage. At the higher, third stage it is finally appreciated that the mountain or tree has its reality precisely through being the particular locus or node of relations that it is. Far from dissolving into a network of relations, its place in this network guarantees its identity and independence – that is, its difference from everything else. As Abe puts it, 'in the Zen awakening . . . mountains are really mountains . . . in themselves . . . and yet there is no hindrance between [things] – everything is . . . interfusing'.[36] There is, of course, no question of escaping from the background of human practice and language against which things stand out for us as discrete items of experience, of ascending to an objective 'view from nowhere'. But that is perfectly compatible with focusing on the particular place that any given object occupies in our scheme of things, and nothing else, at any rate, could count as seeing it for what it really is.

Meditation, Everyday Life and Morality

The distinctive philosophical contributions of Zen are, if I am right, the idea that enlightenment is not the overcoming of ignorance or misperception, but the dissolution of wrong-headed questions which seduce us into a fruitless search for the self, and the claim that things in the world retain their concrete individuality, not as logically independent substances, but as unique nodes in a holistic network of relations. It remains to bring out the characteristic implications for practice which Zen draws from these ideas. Here we may divide practice, for convenience, into the three areas of meditational techniques, everyday behaviour (from drinking tea to shooting arrows), and moral action.

'Zen', derived as it is from a word meaning 'meditation', is something of a misnomer, for what is advocated is very far from the navel-gazing, the recitation of *mantras* and names of Buddhas, or the inducement of trance-like visions popularly associated with Eastern meditation. Hakuin calls meditators of this ilk 'dead silkworms in their cuccoons', and suggests that reciting 'the grain-grinding song' is as effective as reciting the name of a Buddha.[37] On one point, there is general agreement among the Zen Masters: in Dōgen's words, Zen meditation is 'not the means to enlightenment, but . . . itself . . . natural enlightenment' (38), the operation of 'Buddha nature'. In part, this reflects the Buddha's own strictures against trying to achieve enlightenment while having one's mind fixed on enlightenment as a goal. But it also registers the Zen conviction that enlightenment is not entry into some further, transcendental state, but the conduct of thought without self-reflection and 'intellectual calculations'. To the extent that this is the condition of a person during *zazen* ('sitting meditation'), he or she already manifests enlightenment.

This calls into question the popular view of Zen as preaching a doctrine of 'sudden enlightenment'. Certainly the Masters sometimes speak of sudden, intense moments of insight into 'No self', the 'oneness' of everything and 'Buddha nature', but these staccato experiences are no more to be equated with enlightenment than occasional pangs of ecstacy are with sexual enjoyment. In its more careful statements, Zen endorses Hui-Neng's opinion that 'there is no sudden or gradual', though since 'some are keen and others dull', there is 'slowness and speed' in 'awakening'.[38] The 'knowledge' of the enlightened person is not the accumulation of information, nor the grasping of some theory – and not, therefore, the kind of thing which a person acquires rapidly or gradually. A person may take a day or a decade to appreciate that the questions he has been asking are senseless, but the appreciation itself – accompanied or not by a gasp of relief – is neither quick nor slow.

If meditation is not a means to an end, the question arises why there are Zen *techniques* at all – notably, the use of *koans*. It is worth recalling that the systematic use of *koans* is restricted to one school, the Rinzai, and that this was a late development. And it is worth noting that rival schools are critical of this use precisely because it smacks of a means–end strategy. (They also complain that a student may confuse his relief at 'solving' a brain-teasing *koan* with genuine enlightenment.) So it would not be entirely unreasonable to regard *koan* practice as a corruption, motivated by the need to impose discipline on the burgeoning numbers of young boys sent to Zen monasteries for their education. It is difficult to make a judgement here, partly because Rinzai Masters are secretive as to the 'point' of *koans*, partly because the *koans* are a very motley collection indeed. But there are at least two kinds of *koan* whose 'point' is not incompatible with the general thrust of Zen. First, there are the iconoclastic anecdotes – a monk spitting on a statue of the Buddha, say, or tearing up a revered scripture – whose purpose, presumably, is to ween a student off any theistic conception of Buddhism to which he may have become attached. Second, there are those 'funny' questions – Hakuin's 'What is the sound of one hand clapping?', most famously – which are supposed to illustrate the possibility of raising questions which, at first glance, seem well-formed, but on further reflection are based on a false presupposition. This will be good training for 'seeing through' such apparently sensible questions as 'What is the "I" which is aware of myself?'

An important and, for many people, attractive aspect of Zen is the conviction – inspired, surely, by Taoism – that several dimensions of enlightened meditation are transferable to extra-monastic practical life. Hakuin, who stresses Zen 'activity in the midst of the phenomenal world', thinks enlightened practice may actually be easier for the warrior than for the monk, presumably because he is less prone to periods of idle self-reflection.[39] Thus, the mind's freely 'flowing from one object to another' without becoming 'stopped' or fixated, which is the mark of authentic *zazen* meditation, is clearly a desideratum, too, in an activity like swordfighting.[40] Still, care must be taken over what is being recommended here. The swordsman who stops and stares at the point of his opponent's sword will not last long, but it is not obvious that we would entrust ourselves to a Zen brain-surgeon whose mind flowed too freely from the scalpel to the limpid eyes of the nurse. However, it is not this kind of spontaneity and lack of concentration which is advocated.

Three things we surely would expect of our brain-surgeon are, first, that he should respect his instruments and not impose some alien use upon them; second, that he should be ready to respond to contingencies instead of following an inflexible plan; and third, that he should not be preoccupied with himself. These, and not an undisciplined spontaneity, are the virtues of the freely flowing mind, be it engaged in *zazen*, serving tea or shooting arrows. The tea-master, in handling his implements, honours the materials of which they are composed – clay, iron, wood – for their unique properties (for the unique manners, that is, in which they 'gather' the world about them). The swordsman, recognizing that in the final analysis things 'just happen', does not dictate, insensitive to the unexpected, a rigid pattern on the course of the contest. And only the bad archer will focus on himself and his ambitions. Indeed, the enlightened archer will recognize that there is no self which stands behind the shooting; that it is closer to the truth to say, not 'I shot the arrow', but 'It shot'. For him, 'bow, arrow, goal and ego, all melt into one another', as a twentieth-century German student of Zen archery experienced it.[41]

That an enlightened existence can be led 'in the midst of the phenomenal world' and 'worldly affairs' means that, for Zen, there is not the tension between the pursuit of enlightenment and a commitment to social morality which some Buddhists, as well as critics of Buddhism (such as the Neo-Confucians), have alleged. 'Social obligations', Dōgen insisted, are no 'hindrance' to enlightenment, since this is not confined to the solitary meditator. But the question remains why anyone should be especially bothered about discharging such obligations. If Zen can be practised with the sword and bow, why not become a free-booting *samurai*, of the type familiar from the films of Kurosawa, lending one's services to the highest bidder with scant attention to any 'social obligations'?

It is not enough, here, to recall the Buddha's imperative of 'universal compassion'. For one thing, plenty of Buddhists who agree that we should *feel* such compassion have nevertheless advocated the solitary or monastic pursuit of one's own enlightenment away from 'worldly affairs'. For another, it has never been clear to some critics why, if release from *saṃsāra* is the urgent matter, a person should be distracted by concern for others. To these critics, the call to compassion appears to be merely tacked-on. There is, to be sure, the argument that someone who sincerely wills his own freedom is committed to willing that of others too. Equally, though, there are many who remain unconvinced by this. Why should it be irrational to be concerned solely for my own freedom or liberation through enlightenment?

The Zen – and, more generally, the Mahāyāna – reply to this is that such solipsistic concern would *not* be irrational on the usual view of ourselves as distinct, substantial selves. But that view is mistaken; we are not so many discrete egos. As Dōgen puts it, 'myself-is-yourself, yourself-is-myself and the entire universe form one unity' (105). More soberly expressed, the universe is a seamless network of phenomena which, with considerable arbitrariness and convention, we have sorted into those loosely connected bundles we then misleadingly call 'selves' and 'substances'. Just as we can imagine a people who carve up the external world differently from ourselves, so we can imagine a people who count persons differently – perhaps regarding two identical twins as a single bifurcated person, or a man whose life changes radically as two persons in succession. Once this is appreciated, it then becomes irrational to limit concern to one's own enlightenment. One can no longer say, '*This* bundle of experiences, and its future, is my sole concern because it is *mine*'. For there is no 'I' underlying or standing behind the bundle as its owner. Once the truth of 'No self' is recognized, the force of that distinction between myself and others, which prompts the query as to why I should extend compassion to these others and bother myself with 'social obligations' to them, is attenuated. If a false self-consciousness stands in the way of properly 'interfusing' with the things in the world about us, how much more does it impede a sense of interpersonal community?[42]

• Notes •

1 Quoted in R. Zaehner, *Hinduism*, pp. 42–3.
2 Rudolf Otto, *Mysticism East and West*, pp. 151–2.
3 Quoted in Deidre Green, 'Living between the worlds: *bhakti* poetry and the Carmelite mystics', pp. 131ff. As the sub-title suggests, Green compares the words of the two Indian poetesses with the sexually charged writings of St Teresa of Avila.
4 References to Rāmānuja are to page numbers of *The Vedānta-Sūtra*, (trans.) G. Thibaut, p. 16.
5 In R. E. Hume (trans. and ed.), *The Thirteen Principal Upanishads*, p. 409.
6 Quoted in Julius Lipner, *The Face of Truth*, p. 29. I am much indebted to this lucid account of Rāmānuja's thought.
7 Blaise Pascal, *Pensées*, pp. 205f.
8 Quoted in Surendranath Dasgupta, *A History of Indian Philosophy*, vol. IV, p. 79. The argument which Madhva is criticizing was rehearsed by Nāgārjuna (see p. 45) and, two thousand years on, by F. H. Bradley (see p. 356).
9 References to Madhva are to page numbers of Sarvepalli Radhakrishnan and Charles Moore (eds), *A Source Book in Indian Philosophy*.
10 Rabindranath Tagore, *Gitanjali*, p. 59.
11 Quoted in Julius Lipner, *The Face of Truth*, p. 131.
12 Krishnachandra Bhattacharyya, *Studies in Philosophy*, vol. 1, pp. 123–4.
13 See Wm. Theodore de Bary, *The Liberal Tradition in China*.
14 Chu Hsi, in Wing-Tsit Chan (ed.), *A Source Book in Chinese Philosophy*, p. 604.
15 Ch'eng I, in ibid., p. 564.
16 Ibid., p. 550.
17 References to Chu Hsi are to page numbers of Chan (ed.).
18 References to Wang Yang-Ming are to page numbers of ibid.
19 De Bary, *The Liberal Tradition in China*, p. 27.
20 Joseph Needham, *Science and Civilization in China*, vol. 2, p. 475.
21 See A. C. Graham, 'What was new in the Ch'eng-Chu theory of human nature?', in Wing-Tsit Chan (ed.), *Chu Hsi and Neo-Confucianism*.

22 Hu Shih, quoted in Chan (ed.), *A Source Book in Chinese Philosophy*, p. 425.

23 D. T. Suzuki, *Zen Buddhism*, p. 13.

24 Masao Abe, *Zen and Western Thought*, p. 4.

25 Lin-Chi [Jap.: Rinzai], in Chan (ed.), *A Source Book in Chinese Philosophy*, p. 449, n. 95.

26 *The Diamond Sūtra with Supplemental Texts*, p. 67; P. B. Yampolsky (trans.), *The Platform Scripture of the Sixth Patriarch*, p. 135.

27 Yampolsky, *The Platform Scripture of the Sixth Patriarch*, p. 180.

28 In Chan (ed.), *A Source Book in Chinese Philosophy*, p. 447. Zen talk of 'dissolving' questions and 'curing' us from pursuing them has suggested to some authors a parallel with the views of Ludwig Wittgenstein. See, for example, John V. Canfield, 'Wittgenstein and Zen'.

29 Alan W. Watts, *The Way of Zen*, p. 162.

30 References to Dōgen are to page numbers of *Shōbōgenzō*.

31 Ikkyū, quoted in Watts, *The Way of Zen*, p. 203.

32 Quoted in D. T. Suzuki, *Zen and Japanese Culture*, p. 100.

33 Peter Matthiessen, *The Snow Leopard*, pp. 232–3.

34 Yampolsky, *The Platform Scripture*, p. 151; *The Diamond Sūtra*, p. 27.

35 Quoted in *Zen Buddhism*, p. 14.

36 Abe, *Zen and Western Philosophy*, p. 18.

37 In P. B. Yampolsky, *The Zen Master Hakuin*, pp. 54, 133.

38 Yampolsky, *The Platform Scripture*, pp. 54, 133.

39 In Yampolsky, *The Zen Master Hakuin*, pp. 35, 69.

40 Takuan, quoted in Suzuki, *Zen and Japanese Culture*, p. 95.

41 Eugen Herrigel, *Zen in the Art of Archery*, pp. 73, 86.

42 The argument just rehearsed is to be found in many works of Tibetan Buddhism as well, for example Tsongkapa, *The Principal Teachings of Buddhism*. For an interesting recent application to ethics of the relative arbitrariness of criteria for the identity of the self, see Derek Parfit, *Reasons and Persons*, esp. ch. 15 and appendix J.

7

FROM RENAISSANCE TO ENLIGHTENMENT •

• 1 Humanism and the Rise of Science •

The period of European philosophy covered in this chapter is the four hundred years, roughly, from the early Renaissance around 1400 to the romantic reaction against the Enlightenment around 1800. The starting date is relatively arbitrary, since the chronology of the Renaissance is hardly more exact than that of the Middle Ages. Certainly some 'proto-Renaissance' figures, like the poet Petrarch (1304–74), will earn a mention. One thing not in dispute is that at least the second half of our period is one of the richest in the history of the subject. Descartes, Spinoza, Hume, Rousseau and Kant – to mention only a few – are the staple of philosophy courses in the West and appear on anyone's list of The Great Philosophers. (The main discussion of Kant, however, is postponed until chapter 8, reflecting his unique influence on the century which followed his death in 1804.) Their period is sometimes dubbed 'modern', and the previous two centuries 'early modern'. But this labelling perhaps reflects both an exaggerated estimate of the novelty of Descartes, 'the father of modern philosophy', and a jaundiced view of Renaissance philosophy. Maybe the verdict that philosophy, unlike the arts, was 'at a low ebb' during the Renaissance betrays a predilection for achievements in logic and metaphysics over those in moral and political thought, the primary concern of Renaissance thinkers.[1]

The plot of the chapter is as follows. During the great motley that was Renaissance thought, when scholasticism, rediscovered Greek systems, occultism, kabbalism, and much else were either clashing or being blended in bizarre syncretic brews, two broad intellectual movements stand out – humanism and the rise of the natural sciences, the topics for section 1. In some respects, these two movements complemented one another, notably in a displacement of theology from its central place in understanding the world, men and their morals. Both movements, for example, proclaimed kinds of heroes – man-as-artist, or man-as-technologist – unrecognized by the mediaevals. But in other respects, there was tension between the two movements. Humanists, as the first great historian of the Renaissance explains, tended to emphasize the uniqueness and 'subjective side' of the individual, together with a daunting 'sense of moral responsibility'.[2] This emphasis could easily compete with that of the new scientists on the me-chanistic character of the universe, one in which human beings themselves might appear to be mere machines. Again, the stress of many humanists on the frailty of human understanding, its subjective and relativistic character, could conflict with any confidence that scientists, provided they follow the right methods, can arrive at a complete and objective account of the world.

Such conflicts had, by the seventeenth century, crystallized into two large sets of issues. The first of these concerned the epistemic situation of human beings. What can we know with certainty? If there is much that we cannot, how should we live our lives in the light of uncertainty? The second concerned man's metaphysical status. What kind of being is he? Is he 'the image of God', albeit in a post-mediaeval sense, or a 'speck of dust' in a mechanistic universe?[3] If the latter is true, what could the proper life for a human being be? The debates on such issues, beginning with that of the sceptical challenge, will occupy sections 2–4. By the middle of the eighteenth century, stances on these questions had polarized. Crudely put, the keenest champions of Enlightenment, 'the Age of Reason', developed the early scientists' confidence that human beings are elements in an ordered universe which is fully transparent to the well-educated understanding, one which will generate rational and universal principles of moral behaviour. Against them stood the descendants of humanism, the romantics, who shared neither the faith in the epistemic prospects of science and reason, nor the picture of human beings as elements like any other in a law-governed universe, nor the optimism in a universal morality transcending differences between tribes or nations. The rivalry between Enlightenment *philosophes* and their romantic critics is the topic of section 5.

I do not, as most treatments of this period do, devote separate sections to 'the rationalists' and 'the empiricists'. These names are sometimes used merely for abbreviated reference to, respectively, Descartes, Spinoza and Leibniz, and Locke, Berkeley and Hume. But on some matters which will concern us, such as the nature of reality and the self, the differences within these foreign and home teams are at least as great as those between them. More properly, 'rationalism' and 'empiricism' indicate broad attitudes towards philosophical method and the acquisition of knowledge. These topics are not ignored, but nor do they loom so large as to warrant the customary rationalist *versus* empiricist division of the material.

Renaissance Humanism

The Renaissance, for Walter Pater, was a 'movement, in which the love of the things of the intellect and the imagination for their own sake' inspired the search for 'means of intellectual or imaginative enjoyment', thus 'directing [people] not only to the discovery of old and forgotten sources of this enjoyment, but to the divination of fresh sources thereof'.[4] Among these 'old and forgotten sources' were classical texts unavailable to the mediaevals. In its original sense, 'humanism' refers to a 'concern with the study and imitation of classical antiquity', manifested in the pursuit of the 'humanities' or *studia humanitatis* – which included poetics, rhetoric and history – in contrast with such mediaeval preoccupations as geometry, logic and theology.[5] The term then came to indicate, more loosely, a broad concern with the human situation and the improvement of Pater's 'intellectual or imaginative enjoyment', to the exclusion of those drier reaches of scientific and philosophical enquiry which Petrarch denounced as 'futile curiosity'.

Philosophy was not the central concern of most humanists, their main attention being directed towards literature and the arts or to such 'relevant' pursuits as education, statecraft and rhetoric. Hardly any major humanist figures were professional university philosophers, most of whom continued working within the scholastic framework. The greatest figure of the northern Renaissance, the Dutch scholar Erasmus (1466–1536), for instance, devoted most of his energy to educational reform and the simplification of Christian teachings. But humanist philosophizing there was. Its most obvious features were a reborn interest in long-forgotten classical schools of thought, including Stoicism and Epicureanism; its anti-scholastic animus; and a shift of attention away from logic and metaphysics to ethics and political theory. These features were connected. Whether through the scouring of obscure libraries or the influx of scholars during the fifteenth century from Byzantium (threatened and finally taken by the Turks), a huge number of texts – by Plato, Lucretius and Sextus Empiricus, for example – were rediscovered. An immediate effect was to present impressive rivals to the Aristotelianism which had taken such a grip on mediaeval philosophy. This helped to cement disillusion with scholasticism, which many saw as a game in which grown men could amuse themselves by discussing whether God might have manifested Himself in the form of a gourd instead of that of Jesus. Petrarch had already denounced the Aristotelianism imported from Arab scholars as the product of a 'rabid dog'. For Martin Luther, Aristotle was a 'buffoon', while Erasmus complained that you could 'extricate yourself faster from a labyrinth than from the tortuous obscurities' of the mediaeval schools.[6] Erasmus also complained of the bankruptcy of mediaeval moral thought in particular – of writers who could seriously maintain it was worse to tell a lie than to let the whole world perish. In the rediscovered texts of antiquity, where the nature of the good life was the main focus, there lay the promise of vigorous and saner contributions to ethical and political reflection.

The sheer variety of revived classical influences, compounded with those of Catholic and Reformist Christianity, as well as ones of a more exotic hue, such as kabbalism and Zoroastrianism, produces an impression of humanist philosophizing as febrile and chaotic. It would indeed be hopeless to distil it down into a number of doctrines unanimously subscribed to by humanist thinkers. Certain themes, nevertheless, stand out. First and foremost was the broad theme of individualism and 'the dignity of man'. Pico was hardly exaggerating the sentiment of his contemporaries in referring to man as 'a great miracle and a being worthy of all admiration' (4–5).[7] This theme devolves into several subsidiary ones, for example that of the individual's responsibility for shaping his life as a whole. Humanists were generally hostile to Lutheran or Calvinist doctrines of predestination and grace. More amorphous, but equally acute, was the sense that the individual human being, in his or her uniqueness, equipped with a particular repertoire of feelings, tastes and aspirations, is *interesting*. This was reflected, at the literary level, in the emergence or re-emergence of such genres as letters, confessions, memoirs (notably Benvenuto Cellini's and François Villon's), and biographies.

The best-known work in this last category, Vasari's *Lives* (of the artists), doubly illustrates a further aspect of the 'dignity' theme. It introduces a new kind of hero, the man of *virtu*, which is not the type of Christian virtue extolled by Aquinas, but that which earns glory and renown, above all through creative endeavour. It is Michelangelo – painter, sculptor, poet – whom everyone should 'admire and follow . . . as their perfect exemplar in life, work, and behaviour'.[8] Second, many of the works discussed in the book are themselves depictions of *virtu*: Michelangelo's own brooding sculpture of Lorenzo de Medici, for example, or Titian's portrait of the imperious Doge Andrea Gritti. The faces of men and women even in religious paintings look out with an independence and pride absent from mediaeval icons.

What was not missing from the mediaeval understanding, of course, was the idea that man is unique: he is, after all, the pinnacle, perhaps even the purpose, of God's creation. But – and this is the second theme – most humanists rejected the mediaeval attempt to characterize what is special about human beings in terms of their relationship to God. As Erwin Panofsky remarked, humanism had as much to do with distinguishing the human from the divine as with elevating the human over everything else in nature.[9] Renaissance atheists and those, such as Machiavelli and Pomponazzi, who treated the rise of world religions as natural, historically explicable phenomena, could not, of course, define the distinctively human in theological terms – but nor did several

Christian thinkers. Contrast Aquinas' notion of human happiness as acquaintance with God with Erasmus' more earthly conception of happiness as 'being
willing to be what you are', a willingness that should encourage us to 'clap
[our] hands, live well, and drink'.[10] Or contrast Vasari's 'perfect exemplar' of
the species with 'the perfect man', encountered in chapter 5, who exists,
originally, as an idea in the divine mind. Contrast, finally, the typical humanist
ideal of 'the whole man', a unity of spirit, character and body, with the
standard mediaeval strategy for preserving man's special kinship to God –
namely, the elevation of some part of the human being, his 'active intellect'
perhaps, to the status of his 'essence'. In the climate which fostered that
strategy, the admiring studies of human anatomy undertaken by Leonardo da
Vinci or Vesalius would have been unimaginable.

Leonardo, in particular, was keen to draw in the warts and all, and this
symbolizes a third theme: the humanists' interest in the 'all-too-human'.
The 'folly' in praise of which Erasmus wrote was, in part, a cheerfully
ironic acceptance of people's inability to achieve the certain knowledge,
above all concerning God, which scholastic theologians as well as Luther
professed. Such scepticism was reinforced through renewed acquaintance
with the Greek sceptics, as well as by travellers' tales of exotic beliefs and
moral practices among distant peoples. Nor was it man's epistemic frailty alone
which attracted the humanists' attention. Unlike the mediaeval contemplative,
the new hero, the man of *virtu*, was not one to opt out of everyday affairs.
His capacity to exercise *virtu*, therefore, is threatened by the operations of
fortune and fate, as well as by the foibles of lesser men in less than perfect
societies. The virtuous individual must, in consequence, recognize the limitations which life in the real world imposes, and devise a practical philosophy
suited to that world rather than to the sanitized environment enjoyed by
monkish drop-outs.

These three themes – dignity, independence from the divine, and human
frailty – are broad ones on which different humanists played many variations.
It will be instructive to glance at those played by two very different, but equally
representative, figures of the Renaissance – Pico and Machiavelli.

The Dignity of Man and *Realpolitik*

Giovanni Pico Della Mirandola (1463–94), to give him his full operatic-
sounding name, was a young man – brilliant, brash and beautiful – difficult for
his fellows not to admire and resent in equal measure. At the age of twenty-
three, he arrived in Rome – 'like some knight-errant of philosophy', says Pater
– to announce no less than 900 theses designed 'to resolve any question
proposed . . . in natural philosophy or theology' (50). When thirteen of these

theses were condemned, Pico defended them, upon which the Pope condemned the remaining 887. As a fanfare to the 900 theses, Pico wrote his most famous work, now known as the *Oration on the Dignity of Man*, an amazingly syncretic essay in which Pico draws upon the Orphic mysteries, hermetic, kabbalistic and magical sources, as well as upon more orthodox authorities, such as Plato and Augustine. Its first aim is to defend the remark that man is a 'being worthy of all admiration'. In a crucial passage, God says to Adam: 'The nature of other creatures is defined and restricted . . .; you, by contrast, . . . may, by your own free will, . . . trace for yourself the lineaments of your own nature . . . We have made you a creature neither of heaven nor of earth . . . in order that you may, as the free and proud shaper of your own being, fashion yourself in the form you may prefer' (7).

This 'existentialist' passage is as bold a statement of the theme of human dignity as one could hope for. A human being is 'worthy of all admiration', not because of his intrinsic nature, but because he is a free, creative being with the capacity to make of himself what he will – whether to 'descend to the lower, brutish forms of life' or to rise to 'the superior orders' (8). This Promethean ideal explains Pico's enthusiasm for magic and hostility towards astrology. Through 'good' magic, a person makes himself 'lord and master' over the powers that threaten his autonomy (56), which is incompatible with the belief that our lives are governed by the stars.

The *Oration* also sounds the second humanist theme: man's dignity is not due to sharing in divine nature. Human beings are *sui generis*, akin to neither animals, angels, nor God. It is true that they should try to approximate to God's nature through contemplation, but anyone who succeeds in this ceases to be human, and is instead 'some higher divinity, clothed with human flesh' (11). *Human* dignity does not depend on success in this enterprise, but on the capacity freely to undertake it, to *make oneself* like God. Nor is Pico prepared to condemn the less contemplative aspects of human life. What is required is a compromise, 'an inviolable compact of peace between the flesh and the spirit' (20). Indeed, for all the Promethean tone of the essay, Pico is well aware of the human frailties which may impede the capacity to make the best of ourselves. 'It is not granted to us', for example, 'flesh as we are' to attain knowledge of the highest things 'by our own efforts' (15). This is why we must scour diverse ancient texts in an effort to divine the common truths which underly their variety. 'The confrontation of many schools . . . might illuminate our minds more clearly, like the sun rising from the sea' (47). Pythagoras, Hermes Trismegistus, the *Torah*, Plato and Aristotle, Pico believed, all turn out to be saying the same thing – a belief he devoted the remainder of his short life to confirming.

All three of the humanist themes identified earlier are, then, to be found in Pico's *Oration*. So they are, in another key, in the writings of a fellow

Florentine, born only a few years later, Niccolo Machiavelli (1469–1527). We turn, here, from one of the most mellifluous names in the history of philosophy to perhaps its most sinister, one which has been transformed into an epithet for the cynical pursuit of *Realpolitik*. Even the motive behind the most famous work by this career diplomat, *The Prince*, was unedifying: for here was a man of known republican sympathies trying to ingratiate himself with the recently restored ruling family of Florence, the Medicis, by dedicating to their leader a recipe for power and glory.

Those who regard Machiavelli as a mere cynic can cite plenty of remarks in support of this judgement. 'A wise lord . . . ought [not] to keep faith when such observance may be turned against him', for example, or 'it is necessary . . . to be a great pretender and dissembler' (98).[11] The hero, more-over, whom he 'offer[s] . . . for imitation to all those . . . raised to government' (41) is none other than Cesare Borgia, a man who could appoint a henchman to do his bloody work and then execute the fellow in order to divert criticism from himself. But the charge of sheer cynicism is too hasty. There is no reason, first, to doubt the sincerity of Machiavelli's insistence that, in bellicose times, the people are better off in a society ruled by a resolute prince, cruel and devious though he may need to be. Their society will be more secure and prosperous. Nor was he obviously lying when insisting that it is only because most men, being bad, 'will not keep faith with you, [that] you too are not bound to observe it with them' (98). Most importantly, though, the qualities Machiavelli urges upon his prince are ones which, in his view, really are morally admirable. They belong to *virtu*, and the prince's behaviour only 'looks like vice' (85) when we piously disregard its real-life context. This may be better or worse than cynicism, but it is at any rate different.

There is not, for Machiavelli, unlike Aristotle and Aquinas, anything natu-rally virtuous in living as a social being. Society, like its morality, is an artificial product for satisfying individuals' selfish desires with minimal strife. Since the sole 'end which every man has before him [is] glory and riches' (140–1), the man of *virtu* cannot be distinguished by the goals he pursues, but only by the effectiveness with which he pursues them. Behaviour varies in effective-ness according to the times, with those for which Machiavelli wrote putting a premium on qualities like guile and hardness. But, whatever the times, *virtu* always requires, above all, a sense of realism. This is not simply the recognition that how things actually are is very different from how they might ideally be, but a sense of history, of where one's society and oneself are placed in the cyclical rhythms of the world (which Machiavelli put down to astral influ-ences). He is a poor specimen whose 'behaviour is out of harmony with his time and the type of its affairs'.[12] Machiavellian man is less Promethean than Pico's, since he is subject to limiting factors − fate or *fortuna*, and his innate temperament – about which he can do nothing. What he can do is fully to recognize these limitations and then act resolutely and boldly in the light of this knowledge. After all, 'fortune is a woman' (143), and like most women, she favours the brave.

All three humanist themes recur, then, in Machiavelli's philosophy: individualism, for not only are human beings 'atoms' which come together with preformed desires, but these desires are themselves ones for purely individual satisfaction; the complete absence of any reference to God in the characterization of human nature and *virtu*; and human frailty, seen as man's subjection to cosmic forces. In Machiavelli's treatment, the themes have a harsher tone than in Pico's, and both sets of variations will be heard, over and over again, during the following centuries.

The Rise of Science

In 1543, the year of his death, the Polish clergyman Nicolaus Copernicus published his hypothesis of a rotating earth that revolves around the sun. During the following century, up to the publication of Descartes' *Meditations* in 1641, Gilbert presented his theory of magnetism, Galileo established the laws of falling bodies and inertia, Kepler showed that planetary orbits were elliptical, and Harvey demonstrated that blood circulated the body. Boyle and Newton were yet to come, but the list of those mentioned warrants the description of the latter part of the 'early modern' period as one which witnessed the rise of science. The warrant is strengthened by striking technological successes in, for example, printing, optics, navigational equipment and military hardware. The names of the early scientists figure in a history of philosophy, less because of their proneness to philosophical speculation than because of the impact of their work, in both its methods and its results, upon the great philosophers of the seventeenth century, such as Descartes, Hobbes and Locke.

Indeed, the 'early modern' period produced, at its tail-end, the first outstanding philosopher to regard scientific enquiry, suitably obedient to his own prescriptions, as the best prospect for securing both knowledge and 'the commodity of human life'. This was no less a grandee than the Lord Chancellor of England, Francis Bacon (1561–1626). No one warms to this rather cold and corrupt toady as a man; not so as a thinker. For Pope, he was 'the wisest, brightest, meanest of mankind'; or, as someone in a recent novel puts it, 'Bacon's a pig, but he has talent.'[13] Though strangely ignorant of some of its main triumphs, like Galileo's, and lacking in appreciation of the importance of mathematics, Bacon was sensitive to the scientific momentum of his age. He was not a practising scientist himself, one of his few experiments being his last, for he died of a chill caught while stuffing a chicken with snow to test its preservative qualities.

One thing we at once learn from Bacon's writings is that science of an 'orthodox' kind (by present standards) was not the only form which enquiries into nature took during this period. Beyond his diatribes against the Aristotelian influence, there are those directed against 'superstitious' and 'fantastic learning'. Here the targets included the Italian 'philosophers of nature' and the enthusiasts of magic and alchemy. The former, who had included Pico and his teacher Marsilio Ficino, looked less to observation and experiment than to Neo-Platonism and Pythagorean number mysticism in support of their theories of nature. So, too, did the magi of the time, like Paracelsus (whose real name was the wonderful Theophrastus Bombastus von Hohenheim), who were more respected by many of their contemporaries than, say, Copernicus was. Theoretical backing for magic came, primarily, from the doctrines of 'sympathies' and 'signs'. If everything emanates from the One, there must exist concordances between even the most diverse phenomena – stars and human faces, for example. Such 'sympathies' manifest themselves through resemblances between things, which therefore serve as 'signs' of one another, readable by the skilled peruser of 'the Book of Nature'. 'Is it not true,' asks one magus, 'that all herbs, plants, trees and other things . . . are so many magic books and signs?'[14] The adept who discerns the 'sympathy' between, say, the brain and a walnut, is then in the position to effect changes in the one – curing headaches, for instance – by operating on the other.

Beliefs of this kind come together with other exotic ones in the writings of one of philosophy's authentic wildmen, Giordano Bruno (1548–1600). The contrast with Copernicus is striking. The Pole was right, Bruno said, to hold that the earth moves, but not to do so on grounds of mathematical simplicity and elegance. Rather, there are infinite universes, each a unitary, animated whole in which everything moves. Nor is it through empirical and mathematical methods that we will efficiently grasp and deal with nature. Rather, we should consult the lore of the ancient Egyptian hermetists who 'with magic and divine rites . . . ascended to . . . the divinity by that same scale of nature by which the divinity descends to the smallest things by the communication of itself'.[15] Bruno was optimistic to think he could persuade the ecclesiastical authorities that these beliefs were compatible with Catholic orthodoxy. In 1600 he was burned alive in Rome, becoming in later centuries both a symbol of martyrdom to the cause of science and, among romantics, an early hero in the fight against a merely scientific understanding of the world.

One may wonder why Bacon, who after all asked whether we 'ought rather to laugh . . . or to weep' over the claims of magic, devoted so much energy to refuting it (83).[16] Part of the answer is that magic, albeit with 'scanty success', was a rival to 'orthodox' science in what was, Bacon held, the proper, practical aim of science, to 'command nature in action' and thereby to contribute to 'human utility and power' (19 and 16). Magic, alchemy and the like had failed in this task, not least because of secrecy among the adepts. Command over nature can only be secured by a *public* science, a view Bacon elaborated in his description of a utopian scientific community, 'the House of Solomon', in his *New Atlantis*.[17]

There was a further motive for discrediting the magi and the 'philosophers of nature': they operated with a model of knowledge that could only impede progress in understanding the natural world and its processes. On this model, as Michel Foucault puts it, to know things is 'to gather together the whole dense layer of signs with which . . . they may have been covered; . . . to rediscover . . . the forms from which they derive their value as heraldic signs'.[18] This is to treat nature as a hermetic language, a repository of hidden meanings to be recovered by the gifted reader of its 'book'. For Bacon and his fellows, this 'enchanted' vision of nature must be set aside if nature is to be investigated for what it is, and its processes and structures to be examined piecemeal and in their own right. The only meanings are those located in that inadequate instrument, human language, which 'wonderfully obstructs the understanding' (49). Our proper business is to reform the meanings presently expressed by our words, not to compound the problem by supposing that nature itself is a giant array of meanings that we must master.

Science and Religion

Another thing we learn from Bacon, if taken at his admittedly questionable word, is that the rise of science did not bring an immediate divorce of science from religion after centuries of unequal partnership. Most of the early scientists, like Boyle and Newton after them, were devout and construed the wondrous mechanisms of nature as redounding to the further credit of the divine designer. Bacon claimed that scientific enquiry would confirm God's existence and 'advance our reason to the divine truth'.[19] Moreover, it is through the knowledge and power that such enquiry promises that 'man is a god to man' (118). This thought, that man approximates to God precisely through scientific and mathematical knowledge, is more explicit in Galileo. 'With regard to those few [truths] which the human intellect does understand, I believe that its knowledge equals the divine in objective certainty, for here it succeeds in understanding necessity.'[20]

It was not uncommon, either, for the early scientists to employ their discoveries in aid of biblical interpretation. Galileo argued, for example, that Joshua's command to the sun to stand still was much easier to effect on Copernican than on Ptolemaic geocentric premises. The aid could be mutual, with scientists still citing theological support for their hypotheses. Even Descartes was to adduce God's immutability as evidence for inertia: if God simply preserves what He has created, then the quantity of motion in the universe must be constant.

Nevertheless, as one historian puts it, even if 'conventional references to . . . a separation' or 'divorce' of science from religion are 'defective', there was during this period an increasing 'differentiation' of their spheres.[21] *Pace* the example of Descartes, there was greater reluctance to find scientific wisdom in the Bible, which, as Galileo nicely remarked, teaches how to go to heaven, not how the heavens go. There was even greater reluctance to reject plausible hypotheses because of a conflict, real or apparent, with scriptural authority. In the fourteenth century, Nicole Oresme used the very reasonableness of the hypothesis that the earth rotated as an *objection* to unaided reason. If it can come up with something so flatly opposed to Scripture as that, what possible trust can we have in it? Galileo and his contemporaries could no longer argue in that manner. The mood, by now, was Bacon's, critical of attempts 'to found a system of natural philosophy on the first chapter of Genesis [and] other sacred writings', and entreating us to 'give to faith that only which is faith's' (62).

An especially important element in the differentiation of science and religion was the virtual abandonment of appeals to 'final causes' – those Aristotelian ends or purposes in things which had for centuries been supposed to have been set for them by God. For Bacon, the search for final causes had 'intercepted the . . . diligent enquiry of all real and physical causes . . . to the great arrest . . . of further discovery'.[22] Some may not have thought that this made God otiose in the explanation of things, but others did. Sir Thomas Browne, in *Religio Medici*, insisted that on the discoverability of final causes 'hangs the providence of God'.[23]

Browne, perhaps, was prescient in suspecting that the conception of a purely mechanical universe would transmute into one of a universe so autonomous and explanatorily self-sufficient that there could no longer be any reason to invoke God at all. It required less prescience to predict that the idea, mentioned above, of man-as-scientist approximating to God, might give way to a notion of human dignity and pride that required no reference to God. Something similar, after all, was to be found among the humanists discussed earlier. Bacon cited with approval the saying, 'the glory of God is to conceal a thing; the glory of the king to search it out' (118). Someone was eventually bound to ask whether the glory of the king's search really required the thing to have been concealed by *God*.

The rise of science was, of course, to have other influences on subsequent philosophy than those of a theological sort. For two of these, Bacon can once again take fair credit. The first is a self-conscious concern with the methods for establishing knowledge. The contemporary 'state of knowledge', thought Bacon, was 'not prosperous' (7). Various 'idols . . . beset men's minds' (47), from personal prejudices to insensitivity to counter-evidence and over-confidence in the clarity of supposedly *a priori* principles or 'first notions'. Bacon was optimistic about establishing 'certain conclusions' in science, but for this to occur 'the entire work of the understanding [must] be commenced afresh, and the mind . . . guided at every step; and the business be done as if by machinery' (34). The most important part of this 'machinery' was a complicated procedure of induction, based upon carefully organized data or 'natural histories', for identifying the 'forms' or 'essences' of 'natures', such as heat and colour.

The notion of forms or essences indicates a second influential move made by Bacon and some of the early scientists: a sharp distinction between the scientific and manifest images of the world, between, that is, an account of the invisible, underlying structures of nature and the plain man's view of it. Bacon's forms are not Platonic or Aristotelian ones, contrasted with matter, but the inner and material 'latent processes' or structures of things. The form of heat, for instance, is a 'motion . . . acting upon the smaller particles of bodies' (162). This form is not simply some interesting feature of heat; rather, 'the form of a thing *is* the very thing itself', in which case a 'thing in reference to man' – the 'apparent' thing – is quite different from the the thing in itself (142). It is a small step from Bacon's view to Galileo's claim that properties like colour and odour are merely subjective, with the only objective ones being those, like motion and shape, which lend themselves to mathematical treatment. Here is the origin of the great seventeenth-century debate over 'primary' *versus* 'secondary' qualities between those who could and those who could not stomach the apparently depressing thought that the world is, in large part, a very different place from how it appears to be.

• 2 Scepticism •

First-year philosophy students often gain the impression that the main obsession of philosophers has been with the question of whether anything can be known. During the many centuries which divided the chroniclers of Greek scepticism from the Renaissance, when their chronicles were rediscovered, doubts about the general attainability of knowledge were, however, scarcely raised, important as debates about the knowability of some particular matters, like God's existence, of course were. The sixteenth-century revival of scepticism, however, was to have an immense impact on modern philosophy, to the extent, it has been claimed, that '*modern* philosophy from Descartes to Kant can be seen as [so many] attempts to answer the challenge of modern scepticism, or to live with it'.[24]

Another impression students often gain is that scepticism is, at worst, a futile intellectual game and, at best, their lecturers' ploy for getting them to analyse terms like 'know', 'believe' and 'justification'. It is important, therefore, to realize that, for the thinkers discussed in this section, whether to answer or to live with the sceptical challenge was an urgent and momentous issue. Upon its resolution depended the proper estimate of the human condition and the right conduct of life. To be sure, there were those, like Hume, who thought that scepticism was idle in that it could not be lived: but this, they argued, itself had deep implications for our condition and conduct.

There are several reasons why, during this period, discussion of scepticism was more than a mere intellectual exercise. To begin with, the fledgling sciences had yet to prove themselves, so that if Bacon's optimism about their prospects was to be taken seriously, scepticism about establishing the laws of nature would have to be refuted. Admittedly, there were some, like Gassendi and Mersenne, who argued that it hardly mattered if these laws described reality as such, since they could still serve as reliable guides to experience. But for most writers, this either conceded too much to the sceptics or, with its talk of 'reliability', begged the question against a really radical sceptic. Second, the period was, by and large, a deeply religious one in which, nevertheless, orthodox beliefs were under attack from various directions – atheism, Protestantism and deism (which denied the existence of divinely revealed knowledge). The pressure was on, then, to defend the claims of traditional faith. In the process some strange alliances were formed: some of the traditionalists, as we shall see, enlisted scepticism on *their* side.

A third factor resulted from the Renaissance endeavour to delineate the essential aspects of the human individual. Two themes which emerged from this, we saw, were the seemingly contrasting ones of human dignity and frailty. People are frail in many ways, no doubt, but the dimension that came to be stressed most – by Montaigne and Pascal, for instance – was the fragility of human understanding. To accentuate the positive side of man, his dignity, therefore seemed to require either a less sceptical view of our intellectual capacities or, as with Pascal, the deduction of human greatness from these 'wretched' capacities. Finally, we should recall that the brand of Greek scepticism most enjoying a revival was Pyrrhonism, which was as much a recipe for the happy life as a pronouncement on the limits of knowledge (see pp. 130ff.). By witholding belief and simply going along with prevailing opinion, a person avoids the distress which is all too liable to accompany committed allegiance and a febrile pursuit of certainty. To debate scepticism again, after a pause of one and a half millennia, was therefore to revive, in however different an historical climate, an ancient examination of the good life.

Fideism

Nowadays, a main first connotation of the term 'sceptic' is someone agnostic or hostile towards the claims of religion. It then seems odd that during and after the Counter-Reformation, many Catholics supported allegiance to their faith by appealing to scepticism. They belong among those usefully labelled 'sceptical fideists'.[25] It becomes less odd when two factors are borne in mind. First, the scepticism appealed to was a critique, primarily, of reason and sense-experience as sources of knowledge, and hence of a kind compatible with allowing certainty through other sources, including faith and authority. Second, most of the *arguing* was being done by critics of Catholicism: hence, to discredit rational argument – as well as Protestant appeals to 'an inner light' or 'voice of conscience' – served to leave the older faith intact. As Gentian Hervert put it, if nothing can be known, then Calvinism cannot be known.[26]

This raises the question why one should stick with Catholicism, rather than suspend all belief on religious matters. To this question, two different responses were to emerge. One, very much in the Pyrrhonian spirit, was that a relaxed, unfanatical conformity with the prevailing, traditional faith was the best guarantee of that peace of mind, or 'apathy', which had been the ambition of the Greek sceptics. The other was that scepticism clears the way for a committed 'leap of faith', and in such a manner that the 'leap' should be in the direction of Christianity and the Church which has for so long protected it. Let us examine the scepticism which elicited these responses by considering the views of Montaigne and Pascal, men whose literary brilliance has been an obstacle to appreciation of their philosophical importance.

A minor aristocrat, Michel de Montaigne (1533–92) engaged in law and local politics until, in 1571, withdrawing to his *domaine* to reflect and write, briefly re-emerging into public life as Mayor of Bordeaux during the 1580s. His famous *Essays* might better be called '"assays" of Montaigne's character undertaken by himself . . . of his ideas and of those of the authors he read . . . judged against his own'.[27] In their determination to 'only look for knowledge of myself', the *Essays* are at once a climax to Renaissance dissections of the individual and an anticipation of the 'solipsistic turn' taken by Descartes. Born nearly a century later, Blaise Pascal (1623–62) was a child prodigy, working out many of Euclid's principles for himself at the age of twelve. Conveniently for his father, a tax-man, Pascal then invented a calculating machine, a prelude to later important work in geometry and mechanics, including a proof that vacuums can exist and the invention of the world's first bus line. He came, however, to take a dismissive view of his contributions to science, especially after an intense religious experience in 1654, recorded in a 'Memorial' which he thereafter kept sewn inside his clothes. It was during these last years that, despite terrible illness, he wrote down most of the *pensées* (thoughts) which constitute his most important work.

Although they were to argue for religious faith on different grounds, the two Frenchmen were largely at one in their assessments of the human condition and in their sceptical sympathies. To begin with, both accentuate the Renaissance theme of human frailty. 'Man is only a reed', wrote Pascal, 'the weakest in nature' (200), and the human condition, in isolation from God, is like that of condemned prisoners who await their end with 'grief and despair' (434).[28] Stripped of knowledge of God, according to Montaigne, man is a 'pitiful, wretched creature' (13),[29] barely superior to the beasts above which he wrongly exalts himself. The primary reason for this unenviable position is man's inability to attain the knowledge and certainty for which he yearns. He is, says Pascal, 'equally incapable of knowing and of not desiring to know' (75). This incapacity is total, for the scepticism of both writers is thoroughgoing in its scope and degree. 'There is no single proposition' – in ethics, science, philosophy, or whatever – 'which is not subject to . . . controversy', claims Montaigne (141). Pascal agrees, for 'nothing shows [man] the truth, everything deceives him' (45). There is, one should add, an apparent equivocation in Pascal, for he sometimes writes as if total scepticism were impossible for creatures with our nature. There are intuitive certainties of the 'heart', such as the axioms of geometry, which no argument could reduce. His considered position, however, seems to be that even these certainties are legitimate only if, through faith, we assume that it is God who is 'moving [our] heart' (110).

There is considerable overlap, too, in the ways the two authors support their sceptical conclusions. Thus, with all the relish of a twentieth-century 'cultural relativist', they chronicle the wild variations, in time and place, of opinions on just about everything. Custom and fashion dictate a person's beliefs far more effectively than reason and observation. 'Another region, other witnesses [would] stamp a contrary belief on us' (8), wrote Montaigne, a view echoed by Pascal's remark that it is a 'funny sort' of belief which is 'true on this side of the Pyrenees, false on the other' (60). One type of variation, that of sense-experience, is especially important, since such experience is often held to provide the foundations for knowledge about the world. The variable deliverances of the senses are enough to convince Montaigne that 'the senses do not embrace an outside object but only their own impressions of it'. If so, we are in the predicament of someone with a portrait of a man he does not know, unable to ascertain the resemblance between the copy and the original (185–6). Reason, some say, can serve to establish that our impressions properly represent the world, but there are at least three problems with this suggestion. First, as Pascal points out, reason only comes into operation on the basis of those intuitions of the 'heart' which are also being called into question. Second, he adds, reason cannot be used to buttress the testimony of the senses, since they are 'at war'. 'Reason and senses . . . are engaged in mutual deception' (45). What we 'see', for example, can be distorted by what we think we ought to be seeing. Finally, a question Montaigne presses, what is the status of reason itself? People differ widely on what they regard as rational principles, and to settle the differences we must either invoke the very principles that are in dispute, thereby begging the question, or cite further ones which would in turn require justification. 'No reason can be established except by another reason. We retreat into infinity' (185).

Unsurprisingly, neither Frenchman has any time for the alleged proofs of God's existence and goodness offered by natural theology. Such speculations can, for Montaigne, at best serve as a 'finger-post . . . an elementary guide . . . on the road leading to knowledge' of God (11). Pascal at first seems to differ, insisting that the world is full of signs indicating God's presence. He soon makes clear, however, that these can only be read by people already committed in their faith. As for 'metaphysical proofs for the existence of God', these can have 'little impact', and then only briefly, since 'an hour later [people] would be afraid they had made a mistake' (190). Even if these 'proofs' were more impressive, they would at most establish the remote 'God of philosophers and scholars', not the 'God of Abraham, Isaac and Jacob'. Otherwise put, the 'proofs' could only secure deism, which, with its rejection of revelation and miracles, is 'almost equally abhorrent to Christianity' as atheism is (449).

Despite their low opinion of reason, and of natural theology in particular, Montaigne and Pascal both offer arguments for joining them in their faith. Montaigne's approach is inspired by Erasmus who, in his duel with Luther, had written that he would 'readily take refuge in the opinion of the sceptics wherever this is allowed by . . . the Holy Scriptures and the decrees of the Church, to which I . . . willingly submit'.[30] Montaigne's argument for such submission is a Pyrrhonian one in terms of contentment and peace of mind. When reason strays from 'the beaten track traced for us by the Church, she . . . becomes inextricably lost; she whirls aimlessly about' (91). In order to save myself from 'endlessly rolling' – to be 'led back home' – I must accept the Church's 'choice and remain where God put me' (149): I must 'keep to the beaten track' (137). No other 'choice' could have a *more* rational backing and would involve us in a fruitless, anxious quest for beliefs and rules of conduct which is unnecessary if we gently submit to a seasoned tradition which supplies them for us ready-made.

There is none of this 'half-hearted conformism' in Pascal,[31] who was highly critical of much Catholic orthodoxy and sympathetic to the Jansenists (named after a Bishop whose almost Calvinist doctrine of grace invited condemnation by the Pope and persecution by Louis XIV). Presumably, Pascal recognized that Montaigne's argument would, not so many miles to the east, justify submission to Islam rather than to the Holy Church. Endorsing a blank-cheque for submission to whatever the prevailing tradition might be was anyway impossible for a man who, on that night in 1654, had experienced 'the God of Abraham, Isaac and Jacob' and recognized that 'total submission to Jesus Christ' was the only proper surrender (913). That said, Pascal's famous 'wager argument' for cultivating religious belief is one in favour of *any* faith which promises eternal happiness. We are, he says, compelled to wager on whether God exists or not, since reason cannot decide the issue. Nevertheless there is a rational way to wager, given that unbelief *may* entail the forfeiture of everlasting happiness. 'Let us weigh up the gain and loss involved in calling heads that God exists . . . if you win you win everything, if you lose you lose nothing. Do not hesitate then; wager that he does exist.' If the recommended wager turns out to be mistaken, you will still 'gain even in this life', for you will live in confident expectation of a happy afterlife, avoiding 'noxious pleasures' and passions (418). Indeed, the argument is mainly directed towards those who are prone to such pleasures and passions. No one can simply switch on religious belief, but people can 'diminish the passions' which are an obstacle to such belief.

Elsewhere, Pascal exhorts us to specifically Christian belief. Like Montaigne, he emphasizes man's 'wretchedness', but unlike him he manages to discern a certain 'greatness' in this condition. In part, this is because 'there is greatness in knowing one is wretched' (114), something denied to the animals that Montaigne so much admired. More important, though, man's sense of wretchedness is a sign that 'he must have fallen from some better state' (117). Our yearning for this 'better state', moreover, is a sign that redemption is possible. These two 'blazing' truths – our fall into corruption and the promise of redemption – can only be fully appreciated through love of and submission to the person of Christ, the redeemer incarnate (449). It is in Christ that the 'hidden God' (*Deus absconditus*) reveals Himself to those who 'seek Him with all their heart' (427). Because He is, specifically, the God of Abraham, and only reveals Himself to those committed to finding Him, the signs of His existence will mean nothing to the detached, rational enquirer. The latter will at most conclude that there is a God who at 'a flick of the fingers . . . set the world in motion; after that he [has] no more use for God'.[32] This view Pascal attributes to Descartes, whom he 'cannot forgive' for it. Let us, then, turn to Descartes, whose judgement on scepticism and its relation to religious belief is sharply at odds with those of Montaigne and Pascal alike.

Cartesian Doubt

René Descartes (1596–1650), 'universally acknowledged as the father of modern Western philosophy',[33] was educated at the Jesuit College of La Flèche, an experience which encouraged him to abandon 'literary studies' and 'seek no knowledge other than . . . in myself or . . . the great book of the world' (24).[34] The plan to construct a system of thought 'upon a foundation which is all my own' (27) was crystallized by an intense, prophetic experience which Descartes had, when soldiering, in the famous 'stove-heated room' one night in 1619. Never especially industrious, Descartes did not publish this system until 1637 in his *Discourse on the Method*, a preface to various works on geometry and science. Most of his subsequent writings, including the *Meditations on First Philosophy*, defended and elaborated this system. By the 1640s, Descartes – now living almost reclusively in Holland, whose tranquillity and, more strangely, climate appealed to him – was one of the most celebrated thinkers in Europe and, not least through his correspondence with other leading thinkers, one of its most influential. He remained immune to the enticements of fame until 1649 when, unfortunately, he accepted an invitation to Stockholm from Queen Christina. There, the rigours of composing librettos for ballets and giving freezing, pre-dawn tutorials to the Queen induced a fatal pneumonia in a man given, from his student days, to spending much of his time wrapped up in bed.

As the early abandonment of book-learning suggests, Descartes was impressed, like Montaigne, by the unfortunate influence of scholarly fashion and hallowed names, like Aristotle's. Unlike Montaigne's, however, the sceptical position which Descartes rehearses and then tries to refute relies hardly at all upon such vagaries of fashion. It is altogether too radical and general – calling into question, for example, the very existence of an external world – to gain any support from the foibles and diversity of human beliefs. This raises the question why Descartes took scepticism so seriously, especially when it challenges even those beliefs which 'no sane man has ever seriously doubted' (75). Surely we should submit to those beliefs that we can anyway hardly help having.

For two reasons, one methodological, the other more practical, this is not Descartes' attitude. If the aim is to build a system on 'a foundation which is all my own', then I must first 'cast aside the loose earth and sand so as to come upon rock or clay' (34): the best strategy, here, is to follow the sceptic as far as possible until we reach those beliefs, if any, which are so firm that doubt is impossible. Only by building upon such a foundation, by small and certain steps, can I have confidence in the resulting edifice. Second, there are many beliefs that people should try to secure but which are not of a kind they cannot, strictly speaking, help having. These included the beliefs about nature which scientists like Galileo were broadcasting. Not only did these offer a promising account of the natural world, in Descartes' view, but – here echoing Bacon – they offered the prospect of our becoming 'the lords and masters of nature' (47). Science in Descartes' day, we should recall, was not the established enterprise it is today, but a fledgling only too liable to be shot down by its opponents.[35] Unless scepticism about the prospects for truly representing nature could be scotched, why should we be so keen to protect this fledgling? More important still were beliefs in the existence of God and the immortality of the soul. These are beliefs which, sadly, a person can live without: nevertheless, it is in 'the contemplation of the divine majesty' that there reside 'supreme happiness in the next life' and 'the greatest joy of which we are capable in this life' (98). Any scepticism which calls God and immortality into question must, therefore, be refuted.

Descartes makes his job of refutation tough by a persuasive presentation of the sceptic's position, with which he provisionally sympathizes in his resolve to 'reject as if absolutely false everything in which I could imagine the least doubt' (36). The first stage of doubt is familiar enough. Using examples like the jaundiced man's perception of something white as yellow, which show that 'from time to time . . . the senses deceive', Descartes concludes that 'it is prudent never to trust' the senses completely (76). But what of so vivid an experience as my 'sitting by the fire, wearing a winter dressing-gown'? The answer leads to a second stage of doubt. Granted, it is hard to think of the senses deceiving me here, but I have surely had equally vivid experiences in dreams, when lying undressed in bed. Since there are 'never any sure signs' of waking *versus* dream experiences, I can never be certain that any of them correspond to how things actually are in the world. Still, even for me to dream, there must surely exist 'corporeal nature in general, and its extension' (78), shape, size and so on to furnish the materials of which my dreams are composed? The reply introduces the third and most radical stage of doubt. We can intelligibly imagine that God – or, if that is too impious, a 'malicious demon of the utmost power and cunning' – 'has employed all his energies in order to deceive me' (79). Not only may he have furnished my mind with ideas – of the sky, the earth, flesh and blood – to which there corresponds nothing in external reality, but he may have made me 'go wrong every time I add two and three or count the sides of a square' (78). If such a possibility is imaginable and we are without the means to refute it, then in accordance with his 'resolve', Descartes must 'reject as if absolutely false' all his previous beliefs about the world, including its geometry and mathematics.

The sceptic now encounters his nemesis, however, in the so-called *cogito*. As Descartes puts it in his *Principles*, 'We cannot suppose . . . that we, who are having such [doubts], are nothing. For it is a contradiction to suppose that what thinks does not, at the very time when it is thinking, exist. Accordingly, this piece of knowledge – *I am thinking, therefore I exist* [*cogito ergo sum*] – is the first and most certain of all to occur to anyone who philosophizes in an orderly way' (161–2). I can imagine the demon deceiving me about almost everything: but by the very act of imagining this, I am guaranteed that there is something he cannot deceive me about – my own existence.

Descartes now recaptures the ground earlier yielded to the sceptic. He does so by adopting as 'a general rule that the things we conceive very clearly and very distinctly are all true' (36), for it was these features of *cogito ergo sum* which assured him of its truth. This rule is first deployed to establish that God exists. It is 'very evident by . . . natural light' that we *im*perfect beings could not even have the idea of God unless it was 'placed in us by something which truly possesses the sum of all perfections', namely God Himself. Without this implant, an idea of perfection would have been produced from imperfect resources, which contradicts the principle that 'what is more perfect cannot be produced by . . . what is less perfect' (166). The next clear and distinct proposition on which we can rely is that God is no deceiver and so would not produce in us tendencies to believe what is false. We can then trust those beliefs which do not result from our misusing our wills so as to affirm things for which we have no clear evidence. In this way, the truths of mathematics can be reinstated, as too can those beliefs about the external world and its properties as 'comprised within the subject-matter of pure mathematics', such as extension and motion. After all, we have a powerful tendency to believe that many of our ideas are produced in us by external things, so that 'I do not see how God could be understood to be anything but a deceiver if the ideas were transmitted from a source other than corporeal things' (116). On one important matter, though, the sceptic was right: 'secondary' properties, like colour and smell, do not belong to external things in a form that corresponds to our experiences. Rather, they are effects in us of the 'primary' qualities, such as motion.

Descartes' rebuttal of scepticism has attracted less attention and admiration than his sympathetic rehearsal of it. Certainly the latter is more impressive than the former, and of greater lasting influence. It is not simply that some of the arguments in the rebuttal are feeble, like the one about our incapacity to think of perfection without God's having planted the idea in us. In addition, many have claimed, Descartes' whole strategy is circular. As contemporaries were quick to point out, he seems to hold that 'you . . . cannot know anything clearly and distinctly until you have achieved clear and certain knowledge of the existence of God': the trouble being that the proof of God's existence itself relies on prior knowledge of some clear and distinct truths, notably *cogito ergo sum* (139). Without the proof already in place, how can we have confidence in the premises?

To this objection Descartes replies that there are some ideas so clear and distinct that when we attend to them it is impossible to doubt their truth. Here, our certainty does not presuppose God's existence and trustworthiness. What *is* possible, however, is general doubt as to the reliability of one's rational faculties. The atheist can only reassure himself by the arduous task of going through his ideas, attending to each, and examining it for its indubitability.

People armed with the proof of God's existence, on the other hand, need only remind themselves of that proof to be reassured that 'the intellectual faculty which He gave them cannot but tend towards the truth' (142), and hence that any clear and distinct idea will be true. They need not continually be putting those ideas on parade – something which would be incompatible with scientific progress – in order to restore confidence.[36] A more telling criticism of Descartes is his failure to specify any reliable marks of clarity and distinctness, a failure made worse by some of the dubious candidates for this status which he offers. These include the principle that what is more perfect cannot be produced by the less perfect; the conviction, essential to his account of error, that our judgements are 'not determined by any external force'; and even the maxim that God is no deceiver. (Why, if God sometimes works in mysterious ways, as Descartes concedes He does, should not deceit be an ingredient in His overall, beneficent plan?)

Descartes' evident reliance on some well-worn scholastic principles, and the thoroughly traditional nature of some of his ambitions – to establish the existence of God and immortality, or to show that in our absolute freedom of will, at least, we are made in the 'image and likeness' of God – raise the question of his title to being 'the father of modern philosophy'. This issue is better addressed after examining Descartes' views on the relation between mind and body in section 3, as are some connected problems concerning that little phrase, target of countless commentaries, parodies and even cartoons, *cogito ergo sum*.

Few philosophers supposed that Descartes had adequately answered the sceptic, and a rich variety of alternative responses soon came on offer. One of these, which basically concedes the sceptic's case, we have already discussed: the fideist line as continued by Pascal, and later by Pierre Bayle in his influential *Dictionnaire historique et critique* of 1697, albeit in a slippery form which invited charges of atheism. Among those keener to refute scepticism, a familiar strategy was to try to reduce the gap between thought and reality which the sceptic exploits when asking how we can know that the two correspond. This strategy can be found both among those rationalists who followed Descartes in trying to secure knowledge by the 'natural light' of reason, and among those of a more empiricist bent who looked for certainty in the testimony of sense-experience. The details of their efforts follow in later sections, but one illustration of this anti-sceptical strategy is worth giving in the present context.

For Bishop Berkeley, a great merit of his famous doctrine that *esse est percipi* (to be is to be perceived) – that there are *no* objects external to the mind – is that it refutes scepticism. As the full title of one of his works explains, 'the design . . . is plainly to demonstrate the . . . perfection of human knowledge . . . in opposition to sceptics and atheists'. The doctrine achieves this

because all 'scepticism follows, from our supposing a difference between *things* and *ideas* . . . So long as we attribute a real existence to unthinking things, distinct from their being perceived, it is not only impossible for us to know . . . the nature of any [such thing], but even that it exists.'[37] Only if we regard 'sensible things', like trees and tables, as so many 'ideas which exist only in the mind', can we be sure both that they exist and that they are as they appear to be to ordinary perception. Considered as a strategy for refuting scepticism, however, this seems like throwing out the baby with the bath-water. Indeed, when Pierre Bayle denied the existence of 'external objects' for reasons which overlap with Berkeley's, both Bayle and his readers took the denial as a *confirmation* of scepticism. Many of Berkeley's readers, too, concluded that 'all his arguments, though otherwise intended, are, in reality, merely sceptical'.[38] The words are those of Hume, whose own response to scepticism we now turn to consider.

Hume's Naturalism

David Hume (1711–76) trained as a lawyer in his native Edinburgh, but rejected this career so as to indulge his 'ruling passion' for literature and philosophy. Financial exigency, however, forced him to lead a peripatetic life, in England, Italy and France, where his work ranged from tutoring to diplomacy. His attempts to get a Chair in philosophy failed, partly because of obstruction by the pious Scottish clergy, who accused him of atheism, partly because his earlier writings anyway drew little attention, his *magnum opus*, *A Treatise of Human Nature*, falling 'dead-born from the Press', as he put it. In fact, he was always to be honoured abroad more than at home, becoming during his Paris days something of a darling of the *encyclopédistes*. In the twentieth century, British philosophers have made up for their earlier neglect of Hume, with A. J. Ayer, for example, describing him as 'the greatest of all British philosophers'.[39] With a few exceptions who proved the rule, like the vituperative Dr Johnson and the paranoid Rousseau, Hume seems to have been liked by everybody. This confirms his own description of his mature self as 'a man of mild disposition . . . open, social, and cheerful humour . . . little susceptible of enmity' (D 239).[40]

One of the charges brought by those obstructive clergymen was that of 'universal scepticism', and ever since 'the first thing anyone hears of Hume is that he was a sceptic'.[41] The issue, however, is complicated, for while Hume described himself as a sceptic, his comments on Pyrrhonian or 'excessive' sceptics, 'a fantastical sect' (T 183), are hostile. That hostility, though, is tempered by conceding that 'a small tincture of Pyrrhonism' is an antidote to dogmatism and engenders a properly 'mitigated' scepticism (E 111). The 'mitigated' sceptic urges both 'a degree of doubt, and caution . . . which ought ever to accompany a just reasoner' and 'the limitation of our enquiries to such subjects as are best adapted to the narrow capacity of human understanding' (E 111–12).

Mitigated this might be, but it is still radical since it emerges that the only subjects adapted to our 'narrow capacity' are mathematics and 'experimental reasoning concerning matter of fact and existence'. All else is 'sophistry and illusion', to be 'committed to the flames' (E 114). Most of metaphysics and theology go up in the conflagration, since we cannot have knowledge about most topics in these areas. 'The essence of the mind [is] equally unknown to us with that of external bodies' (T 267); and we are as 'ignorant of the ultimate principle which binds [things] together' as of that which 'unites our successive perceptions' into selves (T 636), and of the 'inconceivable' properties of the Deity (D 190).[42]

Hume's scepticism goes further than this, moreover. For while he does not reject beliefs in external bodies, selves and causal powers, he does deny that we can have any good reasons, whether deductive or evidential, for these beliefs. Since there is no contradiction in imagining them to be false, the existence of the things they are beliefs in cannot be deduced by pure reasoning. Nor does the direct 'evidence of our memory and senses' establish their existence. 'The mind has never anything present to it but [its] own perceptions' and so cannot 'reach any experience of their connection with [external] objects' (E 105). Nor does it 'reach any experience' of the self, since all that introspection reveals is successive perceptions, feelings etc., and not that which 'binds them together'. As for causal powers, while 'the senses inform us of the colour, weight, and consistency of bread', they do not reveal any powers 'which fit it for the nourishment of a human body' (E 21).

If beliefs in external bodies etc. are to be justified, then, it must be through rational inferences from the meagre data supplied by the senses. Now the only reasoning capable of taking us 'beyond the evidence of our memory and the senses' has its 'foundation in the relation of cause and effect' (E 16). This means, for Hume, that such reasoning involves inferring B from A on the basis of the 'constant conjunction' between A and B observed in the past. This form of inference, however, relies on the principle that the future will resemble the past. This principle, unfortunately, is not *a priori* true, and any arguments in its support culled from experience will be circular, for they are bound to be 'founded on the supposition of this resemblance' (E 24). We cannot even argue that it is *probable* that the future will resemble the past, since all judgements as to something's probability presuppose that the past is a pretty reliable guide to the future. The moment we suspect it might not be, we can no longer judge, for instance, that the bread will even probably nourish us.

Even if inferences based on past experience had a rational foundation, this would not secure beliefs in external bodies, selves and causal powers. Only mental 'impressions' are perceivable, hence external bodies etc. are not, and cannot therefore have been observed in 'constant conjunction' with anything that *is* observable, from which their existence might be inferred. For example, to infer that 'the perceptions of the senses [are] produced by external objects', I must constantly have witnessed this production in the past – but that, of course, I cannot have done, since all I can witness is the passing parade of 'impressions'. 'Here,' then, 'experience is, and must be entirely silent' (E 105).

Although such beliefs cannot be justified, they can be *explained* by an ultimate 'principle of human nature': the association of ideas engendered by 'custom or habit'. For example, because of the conjunction of heat and flame in our experience 'we are determined by custom alone to expect the one from the appearance of the other' (E 28). The necessity with which such expectations occur is then illicitly transferred to nature itself. Again, we are accustomed to observing an object in a single, flowing sequence of perceptions. This sets up a tendency to suppose that something identical persists even during an interrupted sequence of distinct, but resembling perceptions. Their occurrence in a 'chain . . . make[s] the whole seem like the continuance of one object' (T 261). Here is the source of our belief, not only in external bodies, but in an unchanging self which binds together a set of distinct experiences.

What more is needed, one might ask, to warrant the clergymen's verdict of 'universal scepticism'? Not only can we know next to nothing of the essence of matter, self and causal powers, but the very belief in such things is the result of 'custom' and 'fancy' alone. Yet, says Hume, it is precisely through 'custom' and 'fancy' that we 'save ourselves from . . . total scepticism' (T 268). His point is not that of the 'common-sense school' of his Scottish contemporaries, to the effect that custom is itself evidence for a belief, which ought to outweigh sceptical arguments even when their flaws cannot be detected. Hume never indicates that the arguments are flawed; nor does he treat custom, in the relevant sense, as *evidence* for a belief. His point, in part, is the pragmatic one that total scepticism would make it impossible to act. 'The great subverter of Pyrrhonism . . . is action . . . and the occupations of everyday life' (E 109). But there is more to it than that. By focusing on action, the pragmatist underplays the role of our natural beliefs in our *thinking*. These 'must be taken for granted in all our reasonings' (T 187), and judgement is as much 'determined by our nature as are our breathing and feeling'. Here, Hume's 'naturalism' differs from 'fideism': there is no question of *trying*, in the face of scepticism, to cultivate beliefs which we anyway accept by 'absolute and unconditional necessity' (T 183).

The pragmatic response, moreover, does not explain why we shouldn't indulge in sceptical thoughts when at leisure from 'the occupations of everyday life'. But for Hume, famously, 'reason is and ought to be the slave of the passions' (T 415) – not simply because action can only be motivated by 'passions', but because our natural 'sentiments' should not be subjected to the corrosive test of reason. There is nothing rational, for example, about the natural sympathy we have for people and animals, and which, for Hume, is the basis for moral judgement. But to point out that such sentiments are not rational should not do anything to make them evaporate. The same goes for our basic, natural beliefs.

What makes scepticism frightening is the move from the correct observation that the framework of our natural beliefs and sentiments is without rational foundation to the conclusion that all our thinking and behaviour are irrational. But this move is mistaken. Applauding a judgement or action for its rationality, and criticizing it for its irrationality, are practices that go on *within* that framework, which is not itself to be appraised in those terms. Appreciation of this does not refute the sceptic's arguments – nothing can – but it 'breaks the[ir] force' (T 187). By recalling the fundamental role played by our nature, the sceptic's nihilistic onslaught on our beliefs is reduced to the unsurprising reflection that our reasonings, good or bad, presuppose a framework too all-encompassing to itself be the subject of such evaluations.[43]

A coda is needed, however. Hume describes how metaphysical speculation seems 'cold, and strain'd, and ridiculous' after a good dinner and game of backgammon (T 269). Taken out of context, this apparently confirms the impression of Hume, suggested by the autobiography written just before his death, as a hale fellow well-met, for whom philosophical questioning was a pastime, for which a sensible man should substitute a board-game. We know, however, that the young author of the *Treatise* suffered anxiety, and this is attested to in the section from which the backgammon passage is taken. What the dinner and the game 'cure' are 'philosophical melancholy', 'despair', and 'forlorn solitude' – hardly words to describe a frivolous pastime. Indeed, Hume explains, there are many people, like himself, in whom an irresistible urge for philosophical speculation 'springs up naturally' (T 271). If so, human nature cannot be the stout bulwark against scepticism that, elsewhere, Hume suggests. For, despite the 'despair' and 'solitude' it entails, pressing scepticism to its limits is itself an ingredient in the nature of some people – those, presumably, of whom it is true that ''tis almost impossible for the mind of man to rest' (T 271).

Such people – to recall the Renaissance theme which gave such edge to discussions of scepticism – cannot, moreover, escape from being *weak*. Hume curses himself for his weakness in succumbing to fruitless philosophical enquiries, but insists too on the weakness of our natural, everyday understanding. Whatever we do, then, we display our weakness, whether by easy acquiescence in our feeble capacities or by indulgence in pointless attempts to overcome our limitations. In the end, therefore, Hume leaves the proper conduct of our intellectual lives in a quandary. On the one hand, he can hardly want us all to emulate those 'many honest Gentlemen' in England (not, it seems, Scotland) who are totally immersed in domestic affairs and amusement, and 'do well to keep themselves in their present situation', steering clear of philosophy. On the other hand, 'the gross earthy mixture' in this gentlemanly character is one that philosophers 'stand in need of' (T 272). Or, as Hume puts the dilemma a few pages earlier, 'fain would I run into the crowd for shelter and warmth; but cannot prevail with myself to mix with such deformity' (T 264).

• 3 Dualism, Materialism and Idealism •

In this and section 4, we encounter some of the grand metaphysical systems which proliferated during the seventeenth and eighteenth centuries.[44] Most of these aspired to be comprehensive, to provide integrated accounts of almost any philosophical topic one cares to mention, from space and time to God and the will. The central aspiration, however, was to explain the relationship between mind and matter, or more broadly, the location of human being within the larger universe. This was unsurprising given the Renaissance legacy of tension between the humanist emphasis on the uniqueness of man and the growing scientific vision of the world as simply a physical mechanism. How, the question loomed, could man's unique dignity be secured if he is a 'speck of dust' in a material universe?

One answer to that question which has immediate appeal is to distinguish between two orders of being or substance, the mental and the physical. As 'thinking things', the main proponent of this dualist answer, Descartes, said, human beings do not belong in the physical order and, not being 'determined by any external force', live in the 'image of God'. We begin with Descartes' dualism, not only because it was the first, chronologically, of the systems elaborated, but because the others defined themselves in contrast to it. It was the perceived failure of dualism which made the construction of rival systems imperative. The failure did not consist simply in the allegedly insoluble conundrums to which dualism gave rise – notably, the problem of 'interaction' between mind and matter. For many thinkers, additionally, dualism was deeply unsatisfying emotionally, managing less to locate human beings *within* than to displace them *from* the rest of reality. Thus, to anticipate, Berkeley found it 'repugnant' that there should exist anything other than mind: something as 'stupid' as matter would be incommensurable with and alien to mind, including that of God, who did not need to create matter in order to furnish us with 'signs' for the proper direction of our lives.[45]

There were two broad types of critical response to dualism. Those of the first type accepted the question as posed by the dualist – 'Do both kinds of substance, one straightforwardly material, the other straightforwardly mental, exist?' – but came up with a negative answer. Thus a materialist, like Hobbes, insists that only matter exists, while an idealist, like Berkeley, insists that only mind does. These responses to dualism will occupy us in the present section. In section 4, however, we turn to systems whose champions rejected the question as posed. So, in Spinoza's monism, to anticipate once more, the mental and the physical are *attributes* of a single substance which, in itself, is neither of these.

Cartesian Dualism

For Descartes, the sceptical buck stopped with the certainty of his own existence. I cannot doubt anything unless I exist to do the doubting. Some critics held that he went too far here: doubting may entail 'There exists thought', but not that there is an 'I' doing the thinking. Part of Descartes' answer is that it is 'very well known by the natural light . . . that wherever we find some atttributes or qualities, there is necessarily some thing or substance . . . for them to belong to' (163). Ownerless thoughts are a nonsense. But part of the answer, too, is to concede that, at this stage in the argument, little enough is being said about the nature of this owner, the 'I'. This much, however, can be said about it: it is a 'thinking thing' (*res cogitans*). For it is only in and through thinking that the doubter assures himself of his own existence. (Thinking is construed broadly by Descartes to cover, *inter alia*, understanding, doubting, willing, and perceiving.)

In the *Discourse*, however, Descartes assumes he has shown more than this, namely that he is 'a substance whose whole essence or nature is solely to think' and does not 'depend on any material thing', including his body, from which he is 'entirely distinct' so that he 'would not fail to be . . . even if th[is] body did not exist' (36). The reasoning seems to be that since he has a clear and distinct idea of himself as a thinking thing, but can doubt that he has a body, then his body cannot be essential to, let alone identical with, him. (Avicenna had argued similarly through his 'flying man' example see p. 170.) Critics were quick to detect the fallacy. 'How,' asked Arnauld, 'does it follow from the fact that he is aware of nothing else [than thought] belonging to his essence, that nothing else does in fact belong to it?' (143). After all, someone can know that a figure is a triangle but be unaware that it has a property which is, nevertheless, essential to it. Descartes is more circumspect in the *Meditations*, now insisting that it is only after the proof of God that he can establish the distinctness of mind and body. 'That I can clearly and distinctly understand one thing apart from another is enough to make me certain that the two things are distinct, since they are capable of being separated, at least by God' (115). But this hardly helps: understanding mind 'apart from' body is not the same as understanding that they are 'capable of being separated'. Even if God *could have* separated them, it does not follow that He *did*.

Descartes produces a further argument to 'show . . . that the mind is completely distinct from the body': to wit, that matter, whose essence is extension in space, is 'always divisible', whereas 'the mind is utterly indivisible', since 'I am unable to distinguish any parts within myself' (120). This is not an argument likely to appeal in an age of neuropsychological sophistication, accustomed to speaking of the mind as a set of interlocking sub-systems 'realized' in different parts of the brain. Scientific sophisticates will not be convinced, either, by a third argument at which Descartes hints when he remarks, 'when I considered corporeal nature on its own I discovered no thought in it' (149). Possibly he is right: perhaps matter does not have features that explain how it could be the vehicle of thought. The trouble is that Descartes' own conception of matter is so barren. A material thing is simply extension 'in length, breadth and depth', divisible into parts with 'sizes, shapes, positions, and local motions' (105). If this is all matter is then, as one commentator remarks, 'the possibility that it could have complex properties like *consciousness* seems to be ruled out from the start. Indeed, it becomes hard to see how . . . [it] can *do* anything at all (except lie around, and perhaps be shoved about . . .)'.[46]

If Descartes' arguments are uncompelling, his conclusion also generates an obvious puzzle. Experience suggests, and Descartes himself insists, that a scalded hand 'produces in us the feelings of heat or pain' (118), and that my desire to move my hand produces movement in it. How is such 'production' possible, given that hands belong to a quite distinct order of being from pains and desires? Descartes thinks he knows *where* interactions between the mental and physical occur: in the pineal gland of the brain, 'the principal seat of the soul' (230). It is here that the soul both 'moves' and is 'moved by' the 'animal spirits' or nerves which radiate through the body and carry messages between the hand, say, and the mind. In his correspondence with another regal admirer, Princess Elizabeth of Bohemia, Descartes concedes, however, that this interaction is a mystery.[47] Indeed it is, especially given Descartes' own principle, used in his proof of God's existence, that cause and effect must be similar, since the former somehow contains within it the features of the latter. For Descartes' so-called 'parallelist' followers, interaction is too much of a mystery to swallow. In their account, hands and minds no more influence one another than do two clocks which chime in harmony. Just as the latter phenomenon is due to the clocks having been designed by a clock-maker to unwind in tandem, so the regular concurrence of, for example, scalded hands and pains, is due to God's having designed mental and physical processes to chime with one another.

Although Descartes prefers to stay with the commonsense conviction of causal connections between mind and matter, he too assigns an important role to God. That there are such connections is due not only to God's having initiated them, but to His continuously maintaining them. The spirit of his position is not radically different from the so-called 'occasionalism' of those followers, like Malebranche, who were unable to accept its letter. Malebranche held that, strictly speaking, the scalded hand is not the cause of the pain, but an 'occasion' for God miraculously to intervene by Himself causing the pain. (Ghazāli, recall, held a similar view – see p. 168.) But his argument for this rests on Descartes' denial that the 'connection of two things as remote and incompatible as mind and matter could be caused and maintained in any way other than by the continuous and all powerful will of the author of nature'.[48]

Ultimately, then, the harmony we observe between the mental and the physical is explicable only by reference to God's will. Nor is His will at all capricious here. 'That any given movement . . . in the brain . . . produces just one sensation' is a feature of 'the best system that could be devised' to guarantee 'the preservation of the healthy man' (121). A few unfortunate exceptions apart – like dropsy, which causes the patient to crave the water that will harm him – the mind–body connections which obtain are set up for our good through divine beneficence.

This claim of Descartes' is significant, since it mitigates a depressing implication of his philosophy. Let us recall the question of Descartes' 'modernity' which I earlier postponed, pausing only to remark on some respects in which he was not 'modern'. Despite those respects, there was something genuinely new, at least in the Western tradition, in Descartes' position. It can be summarized by saying that he involves us in an 'egocentric predicament' from which philosophers, ever since, have been trying to extricate us. One aspect of this predicament is epistemological. If 'I can have no knowledge of what is outside me except by means of the ideas I have within me',[49] the problem looms of how I can escape from this internal confinement so as to acquire knowledge of what is 'outside' me. Few critics, we saw, thought that Descartes himself succeeded in regaining the ground earlier conceded to the sceptic.

There is, however, another dimension – at once ontological and emotional – to the 'egocentric predicament'. When Plato and later thinkers who followed him proclaimed the immateriality of the soul, the aim was to demonstrate the soul's intimacy with what is ultimately real – the immaterial Forms or Ideas in which everything else participates. But when Descartes makes a similar proclamation, the effect is to create an 'ontological cleft' between ourselves and the rest of the universe. Whereas Platonic Ideas belong to a reality with which the soul somehow succeeds in identifying itself, Descartes' ideas occur only within the confines of our minds. Those which are not innate in us are the products, simply, of extended stuff. Whereas, then, 'the Platonic soul realizes its eternal nature by becoming absorbed in the supersensible, the Cartesian discovers and affirms his immaterial nature' by severing himself from outside reality.[50]

It is this severance, with its implication of our alienation from nature, that Descartes' claim about the divinely arranged connection between mind and body purports to mitigate. As thinking things, we may indeed be disjoint from nature; nevertheless, the contingent, causal connections between ourselves and the physical world are not merely instituted by God, but take the forms they do precisely because they are the 'best system' for the preservation and well-being of us, God's creatures. In a sense, therefore, the physical world exists as it does for our sake. We cannot close the 'ontological cleft' between ourselves and everything else in the Platonic manner. Still, Descartes is trying to secure the maximum intimacy between the self and the world which is possible once the latter is seen as the pared-down, 'disenchanted' mechanism of the scientists. As we shall now see, his effort was, for some, insufficient.

Hobbes' Materialism

In a Europe more devout than today's, materialism, with its odour of atheism and moral nihilism, was more often darkly implied than boldly stated. The outstanding exception was Thomas Hobbes (1588–1679), best known for his tough political philosophy. Disenchanted by university life, this son of a west of England vicar earned a living mainly by private tutoring to grandees, which afforded him the opportunity of foreign travel, especially to France, where he became part of the Mersenne and Gassendi circle, and contributed some of the 'Objections' to Descartes' *Meditations*. Hobbes was a late starter, older than Descartes, and his main works were not published until after the Frenchman's death, including the *Leviathan*, itself almost a youthful work compared with *Concerning Body* and his translations of Homer, written at the ages of 67 and 86 respectively. Worried by Parliamentarian resentment at his royalist views, Hobbes was 'the first of all that fled', in 1640, to Paris, so as to miss the brewing Civil War. The Puritans allowed his return in 1652, and Hobbes found favour under both them and Charles II, a former tutee. Given his doctrine of absolute obedience to *de facto* authority, Hobbes did not need to be a Vicar of Bray in order to survive so many changes of political and religious climate.

In a replay of Bacon's words, Hobbes declares that the aim of philosophy – which, as for his contemporaries, includes the sciences – aims at 'the commodity of human life'. It is 'the cause of all the . . . benefits' of civilization. This is because its 'knowledge is power', due to being, above all, the study of causes and effects, of 'the generation of bodies'. Philosophy enables us to control or manipulate the behaviour of things and people through knowledge of causes. Political philosophy, for example, primarily examines the causes of war, especially civil war, so as to furnish the knowledge which will 'unite and keep men in peace' (DC I.1.6–8).[51]

Political philosophy is one branch of 'civil' philosophy, the other being ethics, which enquires into men's 'dispositions and manners'. Like the other great division of the subject, 'natural' philosophy, it examines 'bodies', but in the sense of those 'artificial' bodies we call commonwealths or states. The connection between the two divisions is due to more than this play on the word 'body', for in Hobbes' system civil philosophy is founded on natural philosophy. Human behaviour, including political behaviour, is ultimately determined by the motions of physical bodies. Hobbes' ambition, in effect, is to extend the scope of Galileo's mechanics to the arena of psychology and morality.

Philosophy's failure to progress, outside of geometry and physics, has been due to entrenched beliefs in 'bodies incorporeal', such as Platonic Forms and immaterial souls. As, indeed, have the larger ills of society, since it is these beliefs that a 'confederacy of deceivers' – above all, the Papacy – has exploited to 'fright [men] from obeying the laws of their country' (L 442). Hobbes' rejection of immaterial entities invited the charge of atheism: but his view, familiar among Christians before Augustine, was that God is a 'corporeal spirit'.[52] He expends considerable scholarship showing that 'spirit', in biblical texts, refers not to anything immaterial but, say, to especially 'fluid' bodies. Admittedly, theology is banished from philosophy, but this is because philosophy is the rational examination of things through their causes, and God, being 'eternal, ingenerable, incomprehensible' (DC I.1.8), is neither caused nor accessible to reason.

It is hard to improve on Hobbes' own robust statement of his materialism: 'The world . . . the whole mass of all things that are, is corporeal, that is to say, body . . . also every part of body, is likewise body . . . and that which is not body, is no part of the universe: and . . . [hence] *nothing* . . . and . . . *nowhere*' (L 440). Among the things which are 'nothing', therefore, are the universals or forms which, for other philosophers, determine that something is a man, tree, or whatever. There is 'nothing in the world universal but names; for the things named are every one of them individual and singular' (L 19). What makes certain bodies men is not their sharing a universal form, but simply their having the same name applied to them. Hobbes is therefore a nominalist in a stricter sense than Ockham, for whom it was 'natural signs', mental rather than linguistic items, which had general application (see p. 177).

The main victim of Hobbes' materialism is immaterial soul or mind. There is no Cartesian immaterial substance, for '*substance incorporeal* are words, which when they are joined together, destroy one another' (L 256). Hobbes is therefore obliged to provide a physicalist account of mental events and processes. 'Sense' or perception, for example, is 'some internal motion [or 'phantasm'] in the sentient, generated by some internal motion of . . . the object, and propagated . . . to the innermost part of the organ', which is the brain or heart (DC IV.25.2). The story is like Descartes', with the difference that the end-product is not an event in a soul, but an 'internal motion' of the body. As for Descartes, colour and other 'secondary' qualities are 'not inherent in the object, but an effect thereof upon us, caused by . . . motion in the object' (HN 2.9). Hobbes proceeds to offer appropriately materialistic accounts of other psychological phenomena, like imagination. (A nice explanation of erotic dreams is supplied: because the sight of a beautiful woman causes the genitals to become hot, when these heat up spontaneously, during sleep, they 'causeth desire and the image of unresisting beauty' – DC IV.25.9.)

Of particular interest, given the moral and political philosophy to come, is Hobbes' account of 'animal' or voluntary motion. All such motion is 'endeavour', which takes the form of 'appetite' or 'aversion'. Voluntary behaviour, therefore, is a purely mechanical movement towards what yields pleasure or 'delight', or away from what gives displeasure (L 31ff). Pleasure, of course, is a physical phenomenon, 'nothing really but motion about the heart' (HN 7.1). Unlike that of animals, our behaviour is sometimes the outcome of deliberation. But this, for Hobbes, simply means that our desires are often balanced against one another, and that reflection is then required to determine which, if any, is the most powerful. The will is simply 'the last appetite, or aversion', the one that wins out and so brings about the action. It is absurd, consequently, to suppose there are acts of free will in the sense of acts that are not the necessary outcome of mechanical processes. We can only speak of a man acting freely if all we mean is that he is 'not hindered to do what he has a will to'. 'Freedom signifieth . . . the absence of . . . external impediments' to our desires (L 136–7).

Hobbes develops his materialist account of mind with more enthusiasm than care. We are told, for example, that sense perception involves *judgement* of what object is causing the 'phantasms', through 'comparing and distinguishing' them (DC IV.25.5). But it is not explained how these operations are to be treated as 'internal motions'. This kind of objection was raised by Cartesians, but a more interesting question is whether, in crucial respects, Hobbes' position is so very different from Descartes'. Does it any way help us out of the 'egocentric predicament'? It is hard to see how since, for Hobbes as for Descartes, the immediate data of perception are purely 'internal' to the perceiver. Indeed, Hobbes has his own version of Cartesian doubt, 'feigning the world to be annihilated', so that all that 'would remain to [a] man . . . are . . . phantasms, happening internally to him' (DC II.7.1). How Hobbes would justify the inference from the 'phantasms' to the existence of an outside material world is unclear.

Nor is it clear that Hobbes helps to alleviate the more emotional symptoms of the 'egocentric predicament'. Admittedly, we are not special 'thinking things' disjoint in kind from the rest of reality. But in his, as in Descartes', account, the relation between a person and outside reality is purely contingent and causal. In no way does my existence *essentially* depend upon that of anything else: the little bodily mechanism that is me might exist in splendid isolation. Consider, too, that the wider mechanical universe into which Hobbes tries to integrate us, a colourless, soundless swirl of tiny bodies, is one stripped of nearly all the qualities we normally take it to have. Finally, the price paid for integrating human beings into this universe is a heavy one: passive victims of the motions of appetite and aversion, we are without freedom of the will in the sense which, for many people, makes it essential to human dignity.

Hobbes' moral psychology also seems to confirm the fear that materialism creates a further, 'egoistic' predicament, entailing moral nihilism. Certainly he was a 'psychological egoist', for 'of the voluntary acts of every man, the object is some *good to himself*' (L 86). Hobbes, though, would deny that this is incompatible with morality. His aim, indeed, is to derive principles of justice, obligation and legitimate authority from a social contract or covenant that people *would* enter into and carry out in practice *if* they recognized certain 'theorems' or 'laws of nature'. The 'science' of these laws is held to be 'the true and only moral philosophy' (L 104).

Hobbes' much-emulated strategy was to imagine a 'state of nature' from which political and moral authority were absent, and to show how these would emerge as people clambered out of this state. No such state may have existed, but actual societies can approximate to it when, as in Hobbes' times, authority evaporates and civil war looms. People have good reason to rise out of Hobbes' bleakly portrayed state of nature. It is, potentially at least, a condition of 'war of every man, against every man', in which there is 'continual fear, and danger of violent death' and 'the life of man [is] solitary, poor, nasty, brutish, and short' (L 82). The situation is an amoral one, since although people have 'rights of nature', these 'rights' are nothing but the absence of obligation, the liberties a person has to 'use his own power' for self-preservation (L 84). Things are grim not simply because people are selfish, nor because they are behaving irrationally. On the contrary, it is perfectly sensible to behave aggressively – to get one's boot in first – in conditions where there is no 'common power' to enforce peace and co-operation.

Nevertheless, things being so grim, it is also rational to accept the first and fundamental 'law of nature', that everyone should seek peace 'as far as he has hope of obtaining it' (L 85). The rest of Hobbes' account follows quickly. To obtain peace, a rational person will recognize that he must 'lay down [a] right to all things; and be contented with so much liberty . . . as he would allow other men' (L 85). Hence he will covenant to renounce his power and promise to keep faith. But since 'covenants, without the sword, are but words', this social contract can only be made effective by submitting to a 'coercive power, to compel men equally to the performance of their covenants, by the terror of some punishment' (L 109 and 94). This 'coercive power' is Hobbes' sovereign, whom it is always rational to obey, except when one's life is endangered, out of fear. Under the right political conditions, therefore, fear guarantees just that peace and co-operation which, in the state of nature, it made impossible. With the sovereign and his laws instituted, so is morality. Acts can now be just or unjust, since 'injustice is no other than the not performance of covenant' (L 94). Behaviour can now be criticized as ungrateful or arrogant, not of course because it is selfish, but because it threatens the peace which obtains through the sovereign's enforcement of the covenant.

That Hobbes grants absolute power to the sovereign is due less to the logic of social contract theory than to his jaundiced view of human behaviour under less absolutist regimes. Later social contract theorists, with a sunnier view, were not similarly absolutist. In John Locke's account, for example, people's natural rights in the state of nature are genuine entitlements – to honestly gained private property, for example – which the government of the society set up by the social contract is obliged to protect. If it fails in this task, its overthrow constitutes a just revolution.[53] The main problem with Hobbes' derivation of moral and political principles from his social contract stems not from his absolutism, nor from his egoistic account of human nature, but from his strict determinism. For Hobbes, people do not keep the law because they have promised to, but because it is psychologically impossible for them not to, given their overriding fear of the sovereign's punishment. If they disobey the sovereign, this is not, as it can be for Locke, because they recognize that he has overstepped his authority, but because they cannot, psychologically, do otherwise when they see their lives endangered. For many later philosophers, Hobbes' materialist, determinist psychology is incompatible with a notion of authentically *moral* motivation.

Berkeley's Idealism

Just as we let Hobbes announce materialism in his own words, so we can leave Berkeley to broadcast his contrary, idealist manifesto: 'all the choir of heaven and furniture of the earth, in a word all those bodies which compose the mighty frame of the world, have not any subsistence without a mind, . . . their being is to be perceived or known . . . there is not any other substance than *spirit*' (P 6–7).[54] Berkeley, in fact, reads like Hobbes inverted. Whereas Hobbes imputes the ills of mankind to a belief in 'bodies incorporeal', Berkeley claims that it is upon materialism that the 'monstrous systems' of atheism and scepticism have a 'visible and necessary . . . dependence' (P 92). (Among materialists Berkeley includes not only those, like Hobbes, who think that *only* matter exists, but anyone who thinks that it exists *at all*.) The agenda of Berkeley's system, indeed, is to establish the eternity of the soul and the existence of a God in whom 'we live, and move, and have our being'. He was, we should recall, an Anglican bishop who was disturbed at the remoteness of the 'God of the philosophers' from the intimate God of simpler belief.

Born in Ireland, George Berkeley (1685–1753) was a precocious Fellow of Trinity College, Dublin, where his main philosophical works were written before the age of thirty. In the 1720s he spent an unhappy spell in London where, despite moving in elevated literary circles, his denial of the material world provoked jocularity. (Dr Johnson warned a Berkeleyan disciple not to leave a party lest, when the others ceased having him in mind, he would himself cease to exist.) Money left to him by 'Vanessa', Swift's mistress, encouraged his project of a church mission in Bermuda, though in the event he decided instead to live in Newport, Rhode Island. In 1734 he accepted the bishopric of Cloyne in Ireland, a position he dutifully filled until the year before his death. During his final ten years his only writings were discourses surrounding the virtues of tar-water as a universal panacea. A generous and humble man, he had, according to Pope – rarely lavish in his eulogies – 'ev'ry virtue under heav'n'.

As a teenager, Berkeley was already convinced that the notion of matter was incoherent, superfluous, at odds with common sense, and dangerous. His starting point – the *idée fixe* of his age, inherited from Descartes, Locke and others – was that the only direct objects of perception are contents of the mind, 'ideas', whose 'existence . . . consists in being perceived' (P 2). From this, it can be shown 'in a line or two' that trees, chairs, and so on cannot exist without the mind, and so cannot be material objects as normally understood. The first lightning argument is this: try to imagine trees existing unperceived. If you win, you lose; for in imagining them 'you yourself perceive or think of them all the while', so that they are not after all unperceived (P 23). The second is that trees, etc., are 'sensible things' – 'things we perceive by sense' – and must, therefore, be 'collections of ideas', since *ex hypothesi* we perceive nothing but ideas. In that event, a tree's existence must consist in its being perceived (P 1, 4). Its *esse* is *percipi*.

The first argument clearly confuses imagining, in the sense of conceiving of, with perceiving. The second begs the question against most philosophers and scientists of the time, for whom another virtual *idée fixe* was that a tree is *not* a 'sensible thing', a collection of ideas, but that which *causes* ideas and is 'represented' by them because of their resemblance to the tree. Berkeley's response to this view is that ideas cannot resemble anything that is not perceivable: 'an idea can be like nothing but an idea' (P 52). As it stands, this too begs a question against his opponents, who would concede his point in the case of the 'secondary' properties, like colour and taste, but reject it in the case of the 'primary' ones, like extension and motion.

The best-known statement of this position is John Locke's (1632–1704) who, here as elsewhere, was not so much advancing a novel thesis as lending clarity and coherence to views already formulated by others. (Hence his rather spasmodic appearance in this chapter.)[55] In this instance, Locke is endorsing the position of Boyle and Newton. As he puts it: 'the *ideas* of *primary qualities* of bodies are *resemblances* of them . . . but the *ideas produced* in us by . . . *secondary qualities have no resemblance* of them at all . . . They are . . . only a power to produce . . . sensations in us; and what is sweet, blue, or warm in *idea* is but the certain bulk, figure, and motion of the insensible parts in the bodies themselves' (II.8.15).[56] Locke here presupposes the 'corpuscularian' theory that, in Robert Boyle's (1627–91) words, 'the world is made up of an innumerable multitude of singly insensible corpuscles endowed with their own sizes, shapes and motions'.[57] These corpuscles affect the nerves, brain and mind so as to produce ideas, only some of which resemble the features of the corpuscles themselves.

Berkeley's response to this is to borrow the arguments which Locke *et al.* employ to show that nothing in bodies resembles our 'secondary' ideas, and then apply these arguments to the 'primary' qualities as well. For example, Locke had argued that 'primary' qualities are 'utterly inseparable from the body' (II.8.9), since one cannot conceive of, say, an unextended body. To which Berkeley retorts that the same is true of colour: one cannot imagine extension without colour (D 144). Again, Locke had argued for the mind-dependence of colour and taste on the ground that ideas of these vary with the situation of the perceiver, without there being any variation in the object itself. The same, replies Berkeley, goes for the 'primary' qualities – solidity, for instance, since 'what seems hard to one animal, may appear soft to another' (D 141). The conclusion is that 'the very same arguments which . . . [were] conclusive against the secondary qualities', as intrinsic features of external bodies, are also 'of force against the primary too' (D 145). If so, materialists must concede that matter has *none* of the properties normally ascribed to it, in which case they are postulating something of which we have no understanding at all and which certainly would not deserve to be called 'matter', which means 'extended, solid, figured, movable substance' (D 178).

Berkeley's opponents are not without their replies to this obliteration of the differences between 'primary' and 'secondary' qualities, and anyway he does not tackle their more impressive arguments. (Locke had pointed out that one can change an object's colour and taste by operating on its 'primary' qualities, as when one pounds an almond, but not vice-versa – II.8.20.) More persuasive, in fact, than his attempt to show that the notion of matter is unintelligible are

Berkeley's dogged efforts to show that it neither plays a useful explanatory role, nor conforms to common sense.

Locke himself had conceded that the connection between bodies and ideas was a mystery. There can be no explanation of why certain physical motions produce ideas of blue rather than red, other than that God decided to 'annex such *ideas* to such motions' (II.8.13). Malebranche, we noted earlier, went further. Such motions do not, strictly speaking, produce the ideas; rather, they serve as 'occasions' for God to produce the ideas in us. Berkeley, seizing on these admissions of God into the picture, asks why we require anything other than God, such as matter, in order to account for our ideas. Why, 'since God might have done everything as well without them', does one postulate the existence of material bodies (P 57)? To reply that He needs them as 'instruments' for producing ideas is to demean Him, for instruments are only required by creatures unable to effect things by pure acts of will. God could surely cause me to have an idea of blue simply by willing that I should. Matter, then, is incompatible with the belief that God acts in the most economical way possible.

Given the ribbing and charges of insanity which Berkeley's immaterialism invited, it may seem odd that a main merit of the doctrine, in his view, was its chiming with common sense. 'I side in all things with the mob,' he wrote, 'eternally banishing metaphysics . . . and recalling men to common sense' (PC 408 and 751). He was not, he insisted, denying the existence of trees and other 'sensible things'. On the contrary, by equating them with collections of ideas, he was guaranteeing their existence. In two further ways, moreover, this equation agrees with common sense, unlike the 'corpuscularian' doctrine. It entails first that trees, etc., really are perceived by us, and second that we can *know* about their features. As noted earlier, scepticism, in Berkeley's view, exploits the gap which materialists open up between our ideas and the unperceivable bodies alleged to cause them.

Really to be 'siding with the mob', Berkeley needs to show that he can, within his own terms of reference, account for the commonsense distinction between veridical and illusory perceptions, and for the value of scientific enquiry. He does both by appealing to the connections and coherence among ideas. A veridical perception is one that coherently connects up with other ideas in a way that illusions and dream experiences do not. The scientist who examines things under a microscope is simply, but usefully, establishing connections and order among ideas in a systematic manner, and 'the more a man knows of the connexion of ideas, the more he is said to know of the nature of things' (D 190).

Berkeley's toughest task, however, is to accommodate the commonsense belief that trees etc. still exist when no one is actually perceiving them. If Dr Johnson's joke, about something ceasing to exist if nobody thinks about it, is apposite, then clearly Berkeley is not 'with the mob'. Especially in his early notebooks, Berkeley toyed with a 'phenomenalist' analysis of unperceived objects: to refer to such objects is to refer to the perceptions we *would* have if we were appropriately situated. Even in the *Principles*, he writes 'if I were out of my study I should say [the table] existed, meaning thereby that if I was in my study I might perceive it' (P 3). But his usual view is surely the one immortalized in Ronald Knox's two limericks. In the first, the puzzle is posed how 'this tree / Continues to be / When there's no one about in the Quad'. The second indicates Berkeley's solution: 'Dear Sir: Your astonishment's odd; / I am always about in the Quad. / And that's why the tree / Will continue to be, / Since observed by *Yours faithfully*, GOD'. Clearly, says Berkeley, objects do not depend on *my* mind, since they exist 'after my supposed annihilation', and 'during the intervals between the times of my perceiving them'. The same is true, of course, 'with regard to all other finite created spirits'. It follows, therefore, that 'there is an *omnipresent eternal Mind*, which knows and comprehends all things and exhibits them to our view' (D 180–1). In short, 'sensible things' are never literally unperceived; they are always ideas in God's mind, if no one else's.[58]

Berkeley's unusual defence of belief in the existence of things unperceived by us has conveniently provided a proof for God's existence. Since many of my ideas clearly have a source outside of me, and since this source cannot be matter, 'they must exist in some other mind, whose will it is they should be exhibited to me' (D 169). This talk of God prompts Hylas, the 'stooge' in the *Three Dialogues*, to ask how we have an idea of such a being, or indeed of any spiritual substance. Philonous replies that we do not, since spirit cannot be imagined. We do, however, have a 'notion' of spirit, for 'I know what I mean by the terms *I* and *myself*' through immediate, intuitive acquaintance with myself as an 'indivisible unextended thing, which thinks, acts, and perceives' (D 181). By analogy with my own case, I have some understanding of other spirits, including God. I cannot, Berkeley explains, regard myself – as, perhaps, Hume did – simply as a 'system of floating ideas, without any substance to support them' (D 184), since ideas are 'inert', whereas I am an active creature of will or volition. It is because I am directly acquainted with volition that I have no trouble conceiving of God creating ideas in me through His volitions.

God as the furnisher of my ideas and perceptions provides Berkeley with his solution to the epistemological side of the 'egocentric predicament'. I need not worry that my ideas are all that there is, since they do have an 'outside' source. Nor need I worry that they fail to correspond with some external, material reality, since there isn't one. Equally significant is his response to the 'emotional' threat posed by the 'egocentric predicament', the sense of estrangement from the rest of reality. It is crucial to appreciate that Berkeley takes himself to have established the existence of a God, unlike that of his opponents, whose 'presence' is always with us and in whom, almost literally, we have our being. The whole 'mighty frame of the world' is, in effect, God's epiphany, for it consists in nothing but those ideas of His which He has willed us to share. 'We need only open our eyes to see the sovereign Lord of all things', unobtruded by matter (P 148). A new and vivid sense is thereby given to the ancient notion of the world as God's *logos*, upheld 'by the Word of His Power' (P 147). The world is not, as it was for the mediaevals, the *book* of God, since written words have only an indirect connection with their creator. Rather, it is the *speech* of God, so many immediate expressions of, and testaments to, His presence with us.

• 4 Monism and Monadology •

The systems discussed in the previous section shared a common assumption: the basic ingredients of reality, substances, would have to be either mental or physical. The issue is then whether both these kinds exist, as Descartes held, or only one kind, as Hobbes and Berkeley did. In the present section, we turn to two famous systems, those of Spinoza and Leibniz, which reject that assumption. Given how natural that assumption is, it is not surprising that philosophies which challenge it should be more elaborate and open to interpretation than those which accept it. Spinoza, for example, has been treated as everything from an atheistic materialist to a 'God-intoxicated' mystic. One thing, at least, Spinoza and Leibniz did share with the philosophers discussed in section 3: the primary ambition of solving the 'mind–body problem' or, more widely, locating the place of human beings within reality.

Spinoza and Leibniz are a fascinating couple to compare. Beginning from a number of shared attitudes and premises, they reach radically different metaphysical positions, only for those positions, in turn, broadly to converge in their implications for the nature of human existence and the good life. The comparison is made the more interesting by the very different lives and characters of the two men.

Benedict de Spinoza (1632–77) came from a Spanish Jewish family which had settled in the Netherlands. His rejection of orthodox Judaism, symbolized by a change of name from 'Baruch' to 'Benedict', led to his expulsion from the Synagogue with the hope that 'the wrath and fury of the Lord will be kindled against this man'. He also became unpopular in the political arena, where his liberal sympathies drew him to the circle of the Stadtholder, Jan de Witt, who was blamed for the Dutch defeat by the French and murdered by the mob. With both the Lord and the mob after him, Spinoza chose to live an unobtrusive life as a lens-grinder and did not permit publication of his main work, the *Ethics*, which he knew would attract charges of atheism, until after his death. Spinoza, the man, has many admirers, who describe him, for example, as 'lovable' and 'saintly'. These are strange epithets, perhaps, for someone whose callousness towards all species bar one, humankind, is unsurpassed by any other philosopher. We may, he says, use animals 'at our pleasure, and treat them as is most convenient for us' (IVp37).[59] Despite a retiring life-style and relative paucity of publications, Spinoza's ideas were well-known in *avant-garde* circles and he attracted many distinguished visitors, including a young German diplomat, Leibniz.

Gottfried Wilhelm Leibniz (1646–1716) was an altogether more cosmopolitan and extrovert figure than Spinoza. Born in Leipzig, he had a long career spent in the service of various courts, including those of the future George I of England and the Austrian Empress. He served these in a bewildering variety of capacities – diplomat, librarian, alchemist, inventor, engineer, historian – thereby inviting Bertrand Russell's reproach of 'undue preference to princes and lamentable waste of time in the endeavour to please them'.[60] Philosophy occupied only a fraction of Leibniz's energies, even of those devoted to more theoretical pursuits than draining the Harz mountains and, like Pascal, designing a computer and an express coach. Among his intellectual passions was mathematics, in which area he discovered the Infinitesimal Calculus independently of Newton's slightly earlier discovery. Leibniz's frenetic activities somehow left him leisure to exchange learned letters with some 1,000 correspondents, but not, unfortunately, to write an extended philosophical treatise that would expand upon the *vignettes* in which his system was expounded. Despite this, he was a famous figure at his death and much discussed during the eighteenth century (unlike Spinoza), most notably in Voltaire's *Candide*, where his doctrine of 'the best of all possible worlds', mouthed by Dr Pangloss, is lampooned.

Rationalism

Spinoza and Leibniz, to begin our comparison, were the arch-exponents of 'rationalism', in at least three respects. First, they inherit Descartes' low estimate of knowledge gained through sense-experience. This, says Spinoza, is only 'opinion' or 'confused and mutilated knowledge', in contrast with the kind obtained by mathematicians through reason or clear and distinct intuition (Ip29 and 40). Leibniz draws a similar contrast between the 'confused' belief of an 'artisan' who 'knows by experience' some geometrical truth, and the geometer's knowledge of the reasons for, and necessity of, this truth (BW 170).[61]

More interestingly, both philosophers – this time parting company with Descartes – are so-called 'causal rationalists'.[62] Not only is there nothing inexplicable, a matter of 'brute fact', but it can in principle be demonstrated why everything has to be as it is. This is obviously the view of Spinoza, who claims to have shown 'more clearly than the noon light that there is absolutely nothing . . . contingent' (Ip33). The position of Leibniz, who took himself to be rejecting this 'brutal' determinism of Spinoza, is more complex. Leibniz does distinguish between necessary and contingent truths – between truths of reason and ones of mere fact – and also holds that things are as they are through the 'free decrees' of God. But it emerges, first, that the contingency of a factual truth like 'Caesar crossed the Rubicon' is due only to our lack of knowledge. To an infinite mind which had full understanding of the concept of Caesar, it would be evident that this concept includes the property of crossing the Rubicon, and hence that it would be self-contradictory to deny that Caesar made the crossing. For God's mind, therefore, this truth, like every other, is necessary. It emerges, second, that while God was not constrained by logic to create the world as He did, He is constrained by His own perfection to create according to 'the principle of the best'. Since everything has to be the way it is in order to belong to 'the best of all possible worlds', there is a 'moral absurdity' in supposing anything might have been different. In the end, therefore, there is little to choose between Spinoza's 'brutal' determinism and Leibniz's position that 'everything in the world takes place in accordance with the laws of the eternal truths . . . [with] formal necessities' (PW 140).

Both philosophers, finally, are what might be called 'prescriptive rationalists'. The proper life for human beings is that of reason, and in two respects. Not only should our passions and impulses be firmly under the control of reason but, as Leibniz put it, the rational knowledge of 'necessary eternal truths' is 'able to make us more perfect. This knowledge alone is good in itself; all the rest is mercenary' (BW 170). The two respects are related, since it is through such knowledge that we become immune to the power of the passions. But why should this knowledge and immunity be so crucial to our 'perfection'? Because, to begin with, they ensure our approximation to the mind of God. In understanding 'the sciences in accordance with which God has regulated things', writes Leibniz, the mind 'imitates in its own sphere' what God has performed and is 'an image of the Deity' (PW 202). Spinoza goes even further. If the mind of God is the set of necessarily true ideas in accordance with which nature operates, then to the extent that the human mind is able to grasp these, it is 'part of the infinite intellect of God' (IIp11). For both men, moreover, God is without passion or impulse, so that in this respect, too, the immunity to such forces which reason provides makes us more like God.

Next, it is only through the exercise of reason that we can hope for perfect happiness. In part, this is because the mind naturally strives for understanding and takes pleasure in achieving it. The rational grasp of necessary truths is, says Spinoza, 'affected with the greatest joy' (Vp27). Morever, the appreciation that the order of things is a necessary one not only enables us to 'bear calmly those things which happen . . . contrary to . . . our advantage', but saves us from despair when our best efforts go awry (IV App. 32). Someone with insight into this necessary order will also be saved from the frustrating pursuit of the impossible and, in Stoic fashion, will concentrate on those activities, intellectual ones, least likely to be frustrated by factors outside his control. For Leibniz, at least, a further felicitous bonus of reason lies in its recognition that God's world is one which 'it is impossible to make . . . better than it is . . . for ourselves, in particular' (PW 194). However bad things may seem, they could only have been worse still.

Finally, it is only through the exercise of reason that our freedom is realized. Since everything takes place by necessity, human freedom cannot consist in heroic opposition to the inevitable order of things. Still, we can distinguish between those actions that are determined through our own internal natures and those that are determined by, or rely on the co-operation of, what is external to us. Only the former are free for, as Spinoza puts it, 'that thing is called free which exists from the necessity of its nature alone, and is determined to act by itself alone' (Idef. 7). Strictly, only God can be fully free in this sense, but we can approximate to this condition. To do so, we must, for both philosophers, be 'active': not in the sense of becoming 'men of action', but in that of reducing our reliance on what is outside of us. Indeed, it is not in action, as usually understood, but in intellectual activities such as mathematics that this reliance is minimized. For in such activities, we have 'adequate' ideas of what we are doing, and so can direct the steps we take according to rational principles, a grasp of which belongs to our innate endowment. In Spinoza's case, at least, this intimate connection between reason and freedom provides the basis for a liberal political philosophy. 'The true aim of government is liberty', not so that men may do as they like, but in order that 'everyone's judgement is free and untrammelled' (TTP sect. 20 and Preface). As one commentator puts it, for Spinoza 'man needs political freedom in order to realize that other freedom which constitutes his happiness' – freedom, that is, as self-determination by reason.[63] Only in a liberal society where, for example, no religious creed is imposed, do people experience conditions favourable to rational autonomy.

Naturalism and Substance

Besides their 'rationalism', Spinoza and Leibniz share a commitment to a kind of naturalism. We are, says Spinoza, 'part of the whole of nature, whose order we follow' (IV App. 32). But their point is the more specific one expressed in Leibniz's 'law of continuity'. This requires that 'all the orders of natural beings form but a single chain' in which it is impossible 'to determine precisely the point at which one . . . ends and the next begins'. We must reject the illusion of 'perfect and absolute separation' of beings: 'men are linked with the animals, these with the plants and these with the fossils, which in turn merge with those bodies which [we imagine] . . . as absolutely inanimate'.[64] This law of continuity is derived from a 'principle of plenitude' to which both philosophers subscribed. According to this principle, whatever can exist, does exist: or, as Spinoza puts it, 'whatever we conceive to be in God's power, necessarily exists' (Ip35). Since it is clearly in God's power that there should be an indefinitely large number of beings merging with one another on a continuum, we should not, therefore, expect there to be any 'gaps' in the natural order. For Leibniz, indeed, it is God's having filled in such gaps, thereby producing maximum variety in nature, that is one reason for the perfection of our world.

Even before they have told us that everything in nature is, to a degree, mind-like, it is clear from their naturalistic attitude towards man's relation to the rest of nature, that the two philosophers' positions are at odds with Descartes' clean division between two kinds of substance, physical and mental. They have harsh things to say about this aspect of Descartes' philosophy. Spinoza, for instance, regards the doctrine of interaction between these substances as so 'occult' that he 'would hardly have believed . . . [it] had been propounded by so great a man' (V Preface). Descartes' trouble, as they see it, is that he did not follow through with his perfectly correct conception of substance as 'the sort of thing that can exist independently of an other . . . thing'. If he had, he would have seen that there cannot be two kinds of substance interacting with one another. For then these substances would be influencing one another, and so could not be the splendidly independent entities required by the very definition of 'substance'. As Leibniz puts it, 'there is no means by which one simple substance could influence another' (PW 175). Spinoza's and Leibniz's doctrines of substance, antithetical as they are, proceed from their common and dogged adherence to this independence criterion of substancehood.

The startling conclusion that Spinoza draws from this criterion is that there can exist one and only one substance (not just one *kind* of substance), which he dramatically refers to as 'God or Nature'. Since nothing can be outside of this one substance, it is reality-as-a-whole. He reaches this conclusion via two definitions and two propositions. First, he defines 'substance' as 'what is in itself and is conceived through itself' (Idef. 3). This is his way of stating the independence criterion which, he soon makes clear, rules out any causal interaction between substances. Next he defines 'God' as 'a being absolutely infinite, i.e. a substance consisting of an infinity of attributes' (Idef. 6). By attributes, Spinoza means the essential properties in terms of which we conceive a substance. The first of the two crucial propositions is that 'there cannot be two or more substances of the same nature or attribute' (Ip5), for there would then be no way of telling them apart and no reason, therefore, to suppose there is more than one. The second proposition is that God's existence is necessary (Ip11). Here the main argument is that, since God's existence is possible, He could only fail to exist if some other substance prevented His existence. But that is ruled out by the assumption that no substance can influence another, whether by way of giving or of 'taking away' its existence.

Spinoza then moves to his conclusion. 'Except God, no substance can be or be conceived', in which case 'whatever is, is in God, and nothing can be or be conceived without God' (Ip14–15). For suppose there were a second substance. Either it would share God's attributes or it would not. The first of these possibilities is ruled out by the premise that there cannot be two substances sharing the same nature or attribute. The second is excluded by the definition of 'God' as possessing 'an infinity of attributes'. God has, as it were, soaked up all attributes: there are none left over for another substance to possess.

Spinoza's conclusion that everything is 'in' the single substance, God, must not be confused with the tame thesis that everything is created by God, nor with idealist doctrine that everything is a phantasm in the divine intellect. Spinoza pours scorn on those who 'feign' that God is a person whom we could regard as the purposeful creator of a world outside of Himself or as someone who dreams up the world. Spinoza is a pantheist: God neither creates nor dreams the world, since He or It *is* the world. This is why Spinoza is happy to refer to reality-as-a-whole as 'God or Nature'. It may be difficult for us to see Nature, in all its variety, as a single substance. This is why it helps to think of it not only as *Natura naturata*, the outcomes or products of a causal process, but as *Natura naturans*, this very process considered as the active 'expression' of God as cause (Ip29). By reflecting that causal processes are the 'expression' of a single being, it will then become 'evident . . . that the whole *Natura naturata* is only one being' (CW 333). (Some modern 'eco-philosophers' see in such claims a precursor of the 'Gaia hypothesis' of the universe as a single organism.)

Spinoza's monistic doctrine of a single substance on which everything depends encounters its polar opposite in Leibniz's view that there is an infinity of independent substances. For Leibniz, too, ordinary physical objects cannot be substances: because they depend not upon something greater than themselves, but upon something less. A physical object, in fact, is 'merely an aggregate of . . . other things' (PW 175), rather like a flock of sheep. These 'other things', considered as physical parts, are also mere aggregates, for a 'portion of matter' is like a pond, each of whose 'liquid parts is itself a . . . pond' (PW 190). Ultimately these objects and their parts must be resolvable into 'simple' substances, or 'monads', that do not themselves have parts.

Although without parts, a monad must, first of all, have 'qualities'. Indeed, it is not anything over and above its qualities. If it were, there could be a second monad sharing just those qualities: but this would defy Leibniz's 'law of the identity of indiscernibles', according to which if object A (my dog, say) is indistinguishable from object B (my best friend, say), then A and B are one and the same object (my dog *is* my best friend). Second, a monad cannot be a physical, extended thing. If it were, it would be divisible into parts and so a mere aggregate. Monads, then, are 'incorporeal automata' and 'might be called souls' (PW 181–2). They are animate, 'living things', not to be confused with the indivisible atoms of physics, a notion Leibniz rejects. Third, monads can exert no causal influence on each other: otherwise they would not be independent. As Leibniz famously put it in his *Monadology*, 'monads have no windows, by which anything could come in or go out' (PW 179).

Two urgent questions which this denial of causal influence prompts are: 'How, then, do monads manage to change, to take on and lose properties?' and 'How are monads related to one another so as to constitute a single world or "plenum"?' Leibniz sketches answers to both questions when he writes, 'efforts in all substances . . . are, strictly speaking, only in the substance itself; and what follows from them in other substances is only by virtue of a *pre-established harmony*' (PW 129). It must, first, be through its own 'internal principle', not any outside influence, that a monad changes. A monad is 'big with the future', its subsequent career being the unfolding of its intrinsic nature. ('In a manner of speaking,' one commentator puts it, 'monads are gonads'.)[65] In keeping with his description of monads as 'souls', Leibniz calls this internal principle of change 'appetite'. The behaviour of each monad, then, is due to something analogous to a sentient creature's desires.

Second, monads belong to a single world since each of them unfolds in perfect harmony with the rest. Indeed, each of them 'represents the whole universe' (PW 189) since, in principle, one could read off from it what every other monad is like, rather as one might work out from one photo of a cube what other photos, taken from different perspectives, would look like. This convenient harmony is due, as we might expect, to God's having created just those monads, and not others which it was logically open to Him to create, which *do* form an harmonious system. (Created monads, while independent of one another, are not totally independent, since their existence depends on God.) This – the explanation of harmony – gives Leibniz his best-known argument for God's existence.

Mind and Body

The baroque metaphysics of both philosophers, I suggested, were partly motivated by the urge to provide a more satisfactory account of mind–body relations than Descartes'. It seems at first sight, though, that Spinoza's monism commits him to ruling out either mind or body, while Leibniz's symphony of 'soul-like' monads has no room for the physical. But they would regard such suspicions as resting on the naïve assumption that things must be straightforwardly mental or physical.

For Spinoza, mind and body are two attributes under which we humans, at least, are obliged to conceive of the one substance, God or Nature. They are not, then, distinct substances mysteriously interacting or correlated, but distinct ways in which a single reality is thought of. Body is understood in terms of extension, particular physical objects being 'intermittent thickenings'[66] of extended matter capable of more or less discrete motion and states of rest due, Spinoza suggests, to a kind of 'striving' (conatus) to 'persevere in [their] being' (IIIp8). Mind, meanwhile, is understood in terms of the ideas or concepts it forms and operates with.

Spinoza's is not the dull thesis that we find in reality both mental and physical phenomena, but the radical one that whatever is physical is also mental, and vice versa. Any 'mode of extension', such as a physical object, and 'the idea of that mode are one and the same thing, but expressed in two ways' (IIp7). It is not just in the case of human beings that for each bodily state there is a corresponding idea (a puzzling claim, given that we are not conscious of most of our bodily states). We are told, for example, that an extended circle and the idea of it 'are one and the same thing . . . explained through different attributes' (IIp7). Spinoza concedes that he 'cannot explain these matters more clearly', although he does have a discernible argument for his claim. Suppose my leg hurts, in which case I have an idea, however inadequate, of the bodily damage. Now this idea can only be explained by other ideas since 'the modes of each attribute involve the concept of their own attribute, but not of another one' (IIp6). In other words, explanations at the physical and mental levels are entirely disjoint. (Someone who says 'I reached that conclusion because my neurones were firing in a certain way' is guilty of transgressing a conceptual boundary.) It follows that my idea of the damage to my leg cannot be explained in terms of the physical cause of the damage, a thorn, say. The cause of the idea, rather, must be an idea of the thorn, whether or not I and/or the thorn are aware of it. Generalized, the argument guarantees that for each physical description of the links in a causal chain, there will be a corresponding mental one.

Granted that Spinoza's account avoids the problems of interaction and sheer brute correlation between mind and body, can any sense be made of it? Many have been tempted, like Leibniz, to construe him as, at heart, a materialist who, perhaps fearful of 'the wrath of the Lord', retains the jargon of God, mind and ideas. On this view, Spinoza holds the universe to be purely material, with thought being a property of very sophisticated material processes. But this squares neither with his insistence that *everything* has both mental and physical attributes, nor with his refusal to equate these attributes, nor with his conviction that reality is a proper object of love and awe. Perhaps we should take seriously his claim that Nature or body, like mind, '*expresses* God's essence' (IIdef.1). The thought is then the ancient one of the world as the word or *logos* of God, but with the added insight that, to be this, the world must have two aspects, just as the words of a natural language must. Looked at one way, words are physical items, such as spoken sounds; looked at another way, they are the bearers of meanings or ideas. Both aspects are necessary, since sounds without meaning would not be words, and meanings must be expressible in some medium. As God's word, then, reality must be at once a system of ideas or meanings, and a physical system in which these are embodied.[67] Body and mind, then, are the necessary and parallel forms which a God who can express Himself must take. The whole business doubtless remains a mystery, but then Spinoza was, after all, nurtured in the tradition of Maimonides and the *kabbalah* as much as that of Descartes and 'the modern philosophy'.

Despite their contrasting doctrines of substance, Leibniz grants several of Spinoza's claims about the relation between mind and body. There can be no interaction between the two; explanations in mental and in physical terms are never to be mixed; and every physical thing or event is, in some sense, mindlike. Leibniz, though, faces an initial problem which Spinoza did not: that of finding any room at all for the physical in a universe composed of 'incorporeal' monads. Often he speaks quite happily of a physical order and its laws, but he is also able to say that 'extension, mass and motion are no more things than images in mirrors . . . chimeras created by our own minds'.[68] His considered judgement, perhaps, is that while material properties are indeed 'relative to our perceptions', there is no reason to insist that they are 'nothing but appearance . . . deprived of all reality' (PW 22 and 63–4) *provided* we remember that bodies are mere 'aggregates' of the true elements of reality, monads.

Bodies, of course, are not *physically* composed of monads: rather, they are 'constituted' out of the only features monads can have, their 'perceptions'. Roughly, that is, a tree is a function of – and nothing over and above – certain 'perceptions' had by monads. I put 'perceptions' in quotes, since these need not be conscious experiences. Even in the case of the human soul, let alone of 'lower' monads, 'there are at all times an infinite number of perceptions . . . without reflexion' (PW 155). These *petites perceptions* enable Leibniz to make his own sense of the commonsense idea that there are physical events of which no one is consciously aware.

Given that bodies are 'well-founded', in that they are constituted by something genuine, monads, the question then arises of the relation between body and mind. Generally, Leibniz restricts the term 'mind' to those monads which are 'rational souls'. Such a soul is distinguished from other monads, not only through having 'apperceptions' [i.e. conscious perceptions] – a feature it shares with the souls of some animals – but through 'acts of reflection' and 'knowledge of necessary and eternal truths' (PW 183). Like any monad, a mind 'represents' or 'mirrors' the whole universe: but there is one portion of the universe it represents in a peculiarly 'distinct' way. This is the body with which it is 'united'. There is not, of course, any interaction between the mind and its body, since the latter, in the final analysis, is simply an 'aggregate' of monads – and between monads, as we know, any 'influx is inexplicable' (PW 174). This is why we must not try to explain mental occurrences in terms of physical ones, nor vice versa. 'Souls act according to the laws of final causes by appetitions. Bodies act according to the laws of efficient causes by motions' (PW 192). (Though, once again, in the *final* analysis the behaviour of bodies is a function of the 'appetites' of the monads which constitute them.) How, if there is no interaction between a mind and its body, are they so marvellously co-ordinated? The answer predictably appeals to the principle of pre-established harmony. 'This harmony of corporeal and spiritual . . . can arise only from the one common cause, that is, God' (PW 174), who has created the monad which is my mind and the monads which constitute my body to chime with one another in elegant unison.

Their solutions to 'the mind–body problem' indicate how Spinoza and Leibniz 'place' human beings within reality. First, although a person, being a mind united with a body, belongs to both the mental and physical orders, this does not make him a schizoid creature. For Spinoza, those orders are but two aspects of the one substance, God or Nature; while for Leibniz, not only do these orders necessarily combine in perfect harmony, but the physical is, ultimately, a function of soul-like monads. Second, human beings are not sharply cut off from other creatures, as they were for Descartes. Rather there is smooth gradation, according to a 'law of continuity': and this means that the terms in which we speak of human beings are also applicable, albeit in an attenuated form, to other beings. Thus, it is not only the human mind which, for Spinoza, 'strives . . . to persevere in its being', but every thing: indeed, it is this *conatus* that is responsible for a thing's unity and persistence and hence for its very status as a discriminable entity. For Leibniz, even the humblest monad has 'perceptions' and 'appetites'. Such strivings and perceptions may not be, as some of ours are, conscious, but for those willing to speak of unconscious processes, the continuity of lesser beings with ourselves is not thereby threatened.

For neither philosopher, finally, are we removed from nature by possessing a will that is free to defy natural regularities. The denial of free will may seem a high price to pay for guaranteeing our integration with the natural order, but not so high as the one exacted by Hobbes' materialism. On Spinoza's and Leibniz's accounts, we are not mechanical puppets, pushed and pulled by desires and aversions alone. Much of what we do is self-determined, the expression of our inner, rational constitution. Moreover, we achieve an important freedom, an immunity from hopeless passions, simply through recognizing the rational necessities that govern the universe. More than that, such knowledge guarantees that, in Leibniz's words, we become 'images of the divinity itself' (PW 192), or that, as Spinoza might have said, we truly hear the word of God.

The views on substance, mind and body considered in this and the previous sections were not the only ones expressed during the period. One might mention the anti-Cartesian stance taken by the Cambridge Platonists of the seventeenth century. Ralph Cudworth (1617–88), for example, defended a 'scale . . . of entities and perfections in the universe . . . from higher to lower' against Descartes' cleavage between intellects and everything else.[69] His close contemporary Henry More (1614–88), who sometimes sounds like Spinoza, speaks of a nature permeated by soul. Of more lasting influence was the minimalist attitude towards substance taken by some empiricist philosophers. By this, I mean the view that even if substances exist, we have little or no idea of them, so that they cannot significantly contribute to understanding our experience and concepts. A good example is provided by Locke's remarks on personal identity. This 'consists . . . not in the identity of substance but, . . . in the identity of *consciousness* (2.27.19). If I remember standing alone on Waterloo Bridge last Sunday, I *am* the person who was on the bridge. Whether this consciousness is embedded in an immaterial or material substance, whether it hops from one to the other – these are questions we cannot decide, and which we need not decide in order to understand the concept of a person.

Hume concurs in dismissing the relevance of substance to the issue of personal identity, but makes a more general point: 'neither by considering the first origin of ideas, nor by means of a definition are we able to arrive at any satisfactory notion of substance' (T 234). The most familiar definition, 'something which may exist by itself', will not distinguish substances, since anything, in Hume's view, can be conceived to exist alone, there being no necessary connections in nature of which we have an idea. Reference to substances, then, only confuses our attempts to understand the notions of self, physical object, space and time. I postpone discussion of this minimalist attitude until we encounter Kant's response to it in chapter 8. It is now time to descend from these heady matters to the rather more concrete issues which divided the champions of European Enlightenment from their romantic critics.

• 5   Enlightenment and Its Critics •

'Enlightenment' was the name of an ambition, described by Kant as 'man's emergence from his self-incurred immaturity'.[70] Such an ambition was not confined, of course, to the eighteenth century, but 'Enlightenment' has come to refer to a movement of that time whose members – scientists, educationists, as well as philosophers – were, as never before or since, fired by this prospect of people's growing out of a condition of dark ignorance and prejudice through their own resources. The stimulus for this optimism was the success of natural science in the previous century. Applied to the study of human nature, it was proclaimed, the methods of science would not only enable people to understand themselves and the laws of their behaviour, but put them in a position, at long last, to control and improve the human condition. Confidence both in systematic scientific understanding of a common human nature and in the moral fruits of this understanding provided the basis for Enlightenment optimism. If, as the French philosopher and educationist Helvétius (1715–71) insisted, 'morality ought to be treated like all the other sciences, and founded on experiment', then practical philosophy should enjoy the same triumphs as natural philosophy.[71]

Natural and Moral Science

In section 1, I spoke of the tension between the humanist emphasis on the unique dignity of human beings and the incipient scientific picture of them as merely some elements among others in a mechanical universe. A main Enlightenment ambition was to relieve this tension. Does it not, for a start, mark human beings out for special admiration that they alone, utilizing only their own resources – observation, imagination, reason – are capable of constructing an adequate conception of the universe? If in addition they can extend this systematic understanding to themselves and thereby take charge of their destiny, then their position in nature is surely an elevated one.

Natural science had progressed as much through what its practitioners rejected as through the experimental methods which they advocated. Moral scientists should follow suit. Just as Bacon and others had rejected appeals to 'final ends', so teleological conceptions of human nature should be abandoned. The only human goals were those which individuals set themselves, or would do if properly enlightened.[72] Again, since God had been relegated to the status of a designer who does not actively intervene in natural processes, the moral scientist would eschew reference, if not to God Himself, then at any rate to divine providence in human affairs. For Voltaire (1694–1778), the Lisbon earthquake did not show there was no God as first cause of the world, but it did make nonsense of Pangloss' conviction that God is continually watching over our welfare. Next, the practical, like the natural, philosopher must break free from traditional authority and look at human nature afresh. For the editor-in-chief of the French *Encyclopedia* – the great thirty-five volume repository of Enlightenment wisdom – Denis Diderot (1713–84), the true philosopher is one who, 'trampling underfoot prejudice, tradition, . . . authority . . . dares to think for himself, to ascend to the clearest general principles . . . to admit nothing save on the testimony of his own reason and experience'.[74]

Finally, the moral scientist's investigations will, like the natural scientist's, replace armchair speculations on nature by empirical hypotheses and experiment. Although the Enlightenment is often refered to as 'the Age of Reason', most of its enthusiasts were thoroughly empiricist in outlook. Of the great rationalist system-builders, Leibniz was primarily admired for his mathematical work and only managed to inspire a few disciples, like Christian Wolff, among philosophers, while Spinoza had to await resurrection by romantic critics of Enlightenment, such as Goethe. The most admired seventeenth-century philosopher was the one most imbued with the new scientific spirit, John Locke. In the area of epistemology, indeed, a favourite Enlightenment preoccupation was to extend and radicalize Locke's emphasis on the role of sense-experience in human understanding. Typical was Condillac's (1715–80) optimistic attempt to demonstrate how all operations of the understanding could be inferred on the sole basis of a person's possession of the sense of smell. This person must, for example, be able to make judgements, since judgement is 'only the perception of a relation between two ideas', such as two smells.[75] In the areas of ethics and aesthetics, Enlightenment thinkers were especially sceptical of unaided reason's capacity to establish standards of good and beauty. Hume's insistence, noted earlier (see p. 250), that reason is slave to the passions – and hence that it is through sentiment, or some such affective faculty, that good and beauty are discerned – was just one of many similar proclamations.

Histories of the French Revolution invariably describe the famous triplet of ideals, 'Liberty, Equality, Fraternity', as products of Enlightenment. So, in a sense, they were. It is important to recognize, however, that for early Enlightenment thinkers, at least, these were not primarily political notions. Some of them, like Voltaire and Hume, were in fact distinctly patrician in their political outlook. Liberty and individualism were construed, in the first instance, in the intellectual terms attested to in Diderot's sketch of the true philosopher cited above. What mattered was individual freedom as a state of mind that would serve as the antidote to man's 'self-incurred immaturity': for immaturity, as defined by Kant, is 'the inability to use one's own understanding without the guidance of another . . . The motto of Enlightenment is therefore: *Sapere aude*! Have courage to use your *own* understanding!'[76] Equality and Fraternity, likewise, were not originally slogans of demoticism. Voltaire and many others were thoroughly contemptuous towards mass opinion on moral, aesthetic and political matters. It was possible to reconcile this elitism with a notion of equality or fraternity, however, by insisting that all human beings are bound together by a common nature and sentiment, and then attributing the errors of popular opinion to distorting factors that could, in principle, be eradicated through enlightened education. Such was Hume's view about taste. 'Few', he argued, 'are qualified to give judgement on any work of art', but this is because most people 'labour under some defect, or . . . disorder', such as prejudice or lack of relevant experience. The 'principles of taste' are themselves universal, so that when these 'defects' are corrected, everyone will share in 'the joint verdict [which] is the true standard of taste and beauty'.[77]

Radical Enlightenment

There is a useful, if fuzzy, distinction to be drawn between the Enlightenment views which predominated during the first half of the eighteenth century and the harsher, more radical ones which later prevailed and whose epicentre was the Paris *salon* of Baron d'Holbach (1723–89). Hume, for one, whose outlook was formed in the milder atmosphere of the Scottish Enlightenment, found the temperature in this *salon* too extreme.

During the earlier part of the century, a leading doctrine was that of the 'moral sense (or sentiment)' school. According to its leading representative, Francis Hutcheson (1694–1746), an examination of human nature shows that God has 'given us a moral sense to direct our actions'. Unlike the sense of smell, say, this moral sense is affective, a capacity for sentiment or feeling. We are so constituted by nature as to have an affection for those actions which stem from love and benevolence. There is, then, 'in human nature a disinterested ultimate desire of the happiness of others, and . . . our moral sense determines us to approve actions as virtuous which are apprehended to proceed . . . from such a desire'.[78] Hume similarly spoke of a natural 'sympathy' as the basis of morality.

Partly in response to the anthropological data collected by Montesquieu and Diderot, confidence in such universal sentiments as benevolence weakened. If morality is truly to 'possess stability; to be at all times the same, for all individuals of the human race', wrote d'Holbach, its 'solidity' must rest on the one indubitably universal fact about human beings, that they are 'in love with their happiness . . . occupied with their own preservation'. Ethics may then be seen for what it really is, a procedure employed by self-interested individuals 'who live together in society that they may with greater facility ascertain [their] ends'.[79]

This shift from moral sentiment to egoism and hedonism entailed a move to a more robust form of utilitarianism than that proposed by Hutcheson and Hume. For Hutcheson, the moral value of what he, ahead of Bentham, called 'the greatest happiness of the greatest number' is due to its being something aimed at by those people whose motives appeal to our moral sentiments – benevolent people. For Jeremy Bentham (1748–1832), on the other hand, the principle of utility, according to which every action is judged by its tendency to 'augment or diminish happiness', is a direct consequence of nature having 'placed mankind under the governance of two sovereign masters, *pain* and *pleasure*'.[80] If we can desire nothing but pleasure and the absence of pain, it is pointless to erect principles enjoining us to desire something else. The job of the moralist and reformer is then the mechanical one of devising a 'felicific calculus' for maximizing the balance of pleasure over pain. Neither Bentham nor his French predecessors adequately explained how self-interested individuals can be concerned with the happiness of society at large. Rather, it was optimistically assumed that, in the well-organized society, the common good would be achieved through each person pursuing his or her own satisfaction. In such a society, it is as if, to use Adam Smith's famous image, there is a 'hidden hand' at work, serving to harmonize people's interests. One notable victim of this hedonistic utilitarianism was the theory of 'natural rights' which some Enlightenment thinkers, like Diderot, had taken over from Locke. If utility is the sole measure of how people should be treated, then talk of a natural right to property is at best a rhetorical device for drawing attention to the tendency of property-owning to promote utility in society, at worst a bit of 'nonsense on stilts', as Bentham called it.

A further implication of egoistic hedonism was that there could no longer be any principled objection to the pursuit of ordinary – and, indeed, extraordinary – sensual pleasures. At any rate, there could be no reason in advance to heed the exhortations to austerity of churchmen and contemplative philosophers, like Spinoza. 'Nothing is forbidden us by nature,' declaimed the Marquis de Sade, 'nor has she dictated us laws.'[81] If sexual enjoyment, in particular, is harmless fun, there can be no reason to forbid it. Most figures of the radical Enlightenment, admittedly, were not advocates of a strenuous sensual life, but only because they deemed it imprudent. The sole objection d'Holbach can make to 'the voluptuary' is that dissipation has its price, not least the difficulty of combining it with the intellectual pleasures available to those less disposed to libertinism.

The claim that we are motivated only by pleasure and the avoidance of pain reminds one of Hobbes, and it was he, rather than Locke, who was the hero of radical Enlightenment thinkers. For Hobbes, this claim followed from his materialistic, deterministic account of human behaviour, and this was to become the orthodox account within d'Holbach's circle. The titles of La Mettrie's books, *Man the Machine* and *Man the Plant*, speak for themselves, while d'Holbach shows his Hobbesian credentials by holding that the will is simply 'a modification of the brain . . . determined by the qualities, . . . agreeable or painful, . . . that act upon [the] senses'. Because of this, a person 'acts necessarily . . . [as] a result of the impulse . . . from [what] has modified his brain, or disposed his will'.[82]

There was no room in this view of the world, including man, as a physical mechanism, for the operations of an intervening God. Such, to be sure, had been conceded by Voltaire and other deists earlier in the century. In their view, we can know next to nothing about God: He does not act in the world, and reason can place no credence in the descriptions of Him to be found in revealed texts. On the other hand, argued the deists, reason requires that the world must have a first cause, and since the world exhibits enormous ingenuity of design, its maker is a proper object of admiration and worship, if only as the colourless 'Supreme Being' paid homage to by the French revolutionaries. Deism, however, was to give way, in more radical circles, to total agnosticism or atheism. Hume, to his consternation, was told by d'Holbach that of eighteen fellow-diners in his *salon* fifteen were atheists and three had not yet made up their minds.

True to their impatience with abstract speculation, the radicals' objections to religion were practical rather than logical or metaphysical. Better to be rid of all gods, including the deists', than to permit the continuing obfuscation by religious belief of clear-headed morality and politics. For Bentham, it is 'religionists' who have been responsible for that 'principle of asceticism' which has so obstructed acceptance of the principle of utility, with its frank admission of the importance of pleasure. D'Holbach is more vitriolic: 'theology . . . is the true source of all those sorrows which afflict the earth; of all those errors by which man is blinded; . . . of those vices which torment him; of those governments which oppress him'.[83]

One might wonder how the above account of human beings and their place in the world could have inspired in Enlightenment radicals the dithyrambs on the greatness and dignity of man which pepper the pages of their books. The selfish, calculating creature, his behaviour mechanically determined by the 'sovereign masters' of pleasure and pain, depicted on this account does not obviously deserve Condorcet's description of him as a perfect creature, dwelling in Elysium. The Marquis de Condorcet (1743–94) was, perhaps, abnormally optimistic, his best-known work *The Progress of the Human Mind* being penned while on the run from the guillotine. Still, the defence he offers for his high estimate of civilized mankind in his century was not atypical. To begin with, the achievement of Enlightenment thinkers in formulating a rational and systematic account of the human condition, however unromantic, was itself a tribute to man's intellectual endowment. It should be with 'a sort of pride' that we recognize our capacity to arrive at truth without deference to tradition, 'the superstitions of antiquity', and 'the abasement of reason before the transports of supernatural religion'.[84]

Second, it was the conviction of Condorcet and fellow-thinkers that, harsh as the truths they proclaim may be, these alone hold the key to human perfectibility. Hobbes thought it important to broadcast his moral psychology in order to discourage his contemporaries from civil war, with its risk of a return to the state of nature. For Condorcet, the point, more positively, was to encourage human beings to embark on a virtually limitless path of progress. All that has so far prevented their embarkation has been prejudices and super-stitions now blown away. Thus 'the philosopher who laments the errors, the crimes, the injustices which still pollute the earth' can be 'consoled' by this new understanding of 'the human race, emancipated from its shackles [and] the enemies of its progress, advancing with a firm and sure step along the path of truth, virtue and happiness'.[85]

The Early Romantic Critique

Romanticism is associated more with poets, like Wordsworth and Hölderlin, or with literary critics, such as the Schlegel brothers, than with those regarded primarily as philosophers. In this chapter I do not discuss the 'high' romanti-cism of the poets and literary critics: this will receive attention in section 2 of chapter 8. Our present concern is with various figures – Vico, Rousseau, Hamann, Herder – who, whether described as romantics or not, prepared the way for the full-blooded romanticism that was to come through their critiques of Enlightenment ambitions. It is no accident that these critics generally hailed from what Herder called 'simple country seats', like Königsberg and Geneva, rather than the big cities, 'those slagheaps of human vitality' (192).[86] The cosmopolitan intellectual of Paris or Edinburgh had, as they saw it, lost contact with ordinary understanding and foisted on humanity at large attitudes peculiar to himself.

None of these critics was more caustic than J. G. Herder (1744–1803). Educated, like his friend Hamann, in the bleak East Prussian Königsberg of Kant, with whom he enjoyed less easy relations, Herder became a Protestant clergyman, finally settling, after several years of wandering, in the even more remarkable little town of Weimar, whose most famous citizens, Goethe and Schiller, he was to influence. 'Light,' said Herder, challenging the prevailing metaphor of his century, 'does not nourish men.' At best, it nourishes only the head, not the heart (193). Far from Enlightenment being a reason why there is now more virtue in Europe, it is the 'very reason there must be less' (212). Enlightenment, indeed, is the vain 'boast of the European upstart who deems himself superior to the other parts of the world' (315).

Much of this animus against Enlightenment was directed against the doctrine, so apparent in Condorcet, of progress. According to that doctrine, Enlightenment represented the pinnacle of human progress, so that the earlier an age, with the exception of odd blips like the Greeks, the darker it must have been. Primitive man, in particular, was at worst an unthinking beast, at best a pathetic bungler in the art of reason. Among the critics of this doctrine, therefore, we find a re-evaluation, sometimes a celebration, of the primitive. For the Neapolitan philosopher of history, unsung in his own times, Giambattista Vico (1668–1744), condescending judgements on earlier peoples were due to a 'vanity of scholars' which obstructs appreciation of these peoples in their own terms by imposing those of the scholars' own times (160f.).[87] An earlier epoch, remarks Herder, will look much less dark and 'bleak' when considered 'according to its instrinsic nature and aims' (192). Herder was an early sufferer from 'colonial guilt', condemning European attempts to 'subjugate the other continents . . . defraud and plunder them' and then to defend this in terms of intellectual superiority (221). When primitive thought is seen in its own terms, argued Vico, it is not a bungled, childish version of modern reason: rather, it manifests a 'poetic logic' of its own, a complex way of interpreting reality according to metaphors, one 'so sublime that . . . nothing equal, let alone greater, arose' thereafter (214).

Even when there is a common scale on which to compare earlier with modern times, argues Herder, that comparison hardly favours the latter. The 'savage' who loves his family and tribe is 'a truer being than that shadow of a man, the refined citizen of the world: he is 'sounder and stands more firmly on the ground' (309 and 316). This reversal of the usual Enlightenment verdict implies, of course, a less exalted opinion of the qualities on which Enlightenment thinkers congratulated their century, above all its rationality. 'I am unable to comprehend,' says Herder, 'how reason can be presented so universally as the single summit . . . of all human culture' (199). The figure most associated with this devaluation of reason, however, was Rousseau.

Born in Geneva and largely self-educated, Jean-Jacques Rousseau (1712–78) spent a migratory youth, finally arriving in Paris where he tutored and devoted himself to writing. He was a contributor to the *Encyclopedia*, but his *annus mirabilis* came in 1762 when he published two enormously influential works, the didactic novel on education, *Emile*, and *The Social Contract*. Rousseau seems to have taken his own motto, 'To exist is to feel' (E 253),[88] very seriously, for his life was one of largely undisciplined and irresponsible passion. The five children he sired on one of his mistresses were all abandoned to a foundling's home. Never easy company, Rousseau became increasingly victim to a persecution complex. The good-natured Hume, ignoring d'Holbach's warning that he would be warming a viper in his bosom, offered Rousseau – now in trouble with the French authorities – sanctuary in Britain, and was duly rewarded by total ingratitude and animosity.

Contrary to a popular impression, Rousseau's ideal was not 'the noble savage': indeed, he was contemptuous towards those who would 'retire to the woods', since we cannot regain our 'original simplicity' (D 228). The savage may have his noble happiness – 'when he has dined, [he] is at peace with all nature' (D 223) – but this 'happiness would not attain to the highest point, the pride of virtue', since his is an amoral condition (E 256). For Rousseau, the ideal condition, which we can partially recapture, was one between primitiveness and civilization, when human beings were no longer amoral but not yet corrupted. Corruption and civilization arrived together, as the products of private property. 'The first man who [said] . . . "This is mine" . . . was the real founder of civil society', but of crime, war and murder, too (D 192).

The effect of property and civilization is to have made us calculatingly rational in the pursuit of our self-interest, at the expense of natural innocence and sympathy. I am then 'ever at strife, between my natural feelings, which spoke of the common weal, and my reason, which spoke of self' (E 255). The idea that it is through feeling or sentiment that we discern the good was, we saw, a commonplace of early Enlightenment thinkers. But Rousseau goes much further in exalting the authority of feeling over reason. 'Thank heaven we have now got rid of philosophy', exclaims the Savoyard Vicar in *Emile*: 'we may be men without being scholars'. Nor is it only in moral matters that by 'feelings alone . . . we perceive fitness and unfitness' and that 'what I feel to be right is right' (E 249ff). It is feeling which assures me that there is a God; that I have a soul and free will; and that life cannot be a purely material, mechanical phenomenon. If reason denies these deliverances of feeling, it neither can nor should be listened to: for it then denies everything which makes our condition worthwhile.

Rousseau, arguably, exaggerates both the reliability of feelings as a source of knowledge and the extent of Enlightenment reliance on reason. It is worth glancing, therefore, at some other writers' criticisms of the predominantly empiricist epistemology of Enlightenment, foreshadowing as they do such later perspectives as 'relativism', 'conventionalism', and 'constructivism'. That last term certainly seems appropriate for Vico's doctrine that 'the true (*verum*) is what is made (*factum*)'. The idea is that it is only in so far as a person, whether God or man, has constructed something, that he can properly be said to know and understand it. Only God can fully know the natural order, since He made it. Man, however, can have mathematical and geometrical knowledge, since the 'world of shapes and numbers' is one he 'fashions for himself', not one which exists independently of his own constructions (54). Herder, too, was to deny the 'independence' of mathematics, arguing that its truths are the products of conventions we lay down for the use of symbols.

In both Vico and Herder, moreover, there are intimations of the idea, later made famous by Dilthey, that understanding of history and culture is different in kind from that obtained by natural scientists. At any rate, it has been said that, for Vico, understanding of an age requires 'empathy', a vicarious participation in or identification with a mentality different from the historian's own.[89] For Herder, too, ordinary empirical investigation can yield only a 'weak silhouette' of a culture. To obtain real understanding of it, 'you must enter the spirit of a nation' and 'share' its thought (181). Since the historian's 'empathetic' capacity so to 'enter the spirit' of an age is conditioned by the spirit of his own age, an inevitable relativity infects historical understanding.

It is, though, in Hamann's and Herder's remarks on language that readers find the most prescient criticisms of objective knowledge. The standard Enlightenment view of language, found in Condillac, for example, followed Locke's lead in regarding 'the use of words . . . to be sensible marks of ideas' (3.2.1). Language, that is, is simply a vehicle for conveying already formed ideas or thoughts from one mind to another. For the Prussian pair, there are two things badly wrong with this view. First, it makes language inessential to thought, just as any vehicle is to the existence of what it carries. J. G. Hamann (1730–88) – whose esoteric writings, in which 'nothing has a beginning or a middle or an end',[90] earned him the title 'The Magus of the North' – announced against the Lockean view that 'the bone on which I . . . shall gnaw myself to death' is the axiom that 'reason is language'.[91] Herder makes the same point: 'the reasoning power of the mind is inconceivable without the use of language' (137). Words and symbols are not *vehicles* for conveying thought, but the very *medium* in which thought takes place. This would have no dire consequences, perhaps, for the possibility of objective knowledge if languages were all essentially the same. But this Hamann and Herder deny, raising as a further objection to the Lockean view that languages do not so much register or 'mark' our thoughts as shape them. 'We find the history of each race in its speech', writes Hamann, so that, for example, the nature of mathematical thinking in a given culture 'depends on the nature of its speech'.[92] For Herder, 'our mother tongue embodies the first universe we saw' and is 'the essence of [the] tradition' through which the 'thoughts and feelings' of a race or people are perpetuated. Here, perhaps, are the earliest intimations, in the West at least, of that 'linguistic relativism' which was to become an important tendency in twentieth-century philosophy.

Individuals and Communities

If the ways in which a person 'sees' the universe are a function, in part, of the 'mother tongue' and traditions of a whole people, then a threat is posed to another platform of Enlightenment thought, its individualism. In the first instance, I suggested, this individualism was to be understood as a plea for independence from an 'immature' reliance on inherited ways of thinking. Clearly, there are limits to that independence if, as Herder holds, immersion in a tradition is a precondition of thinking at all. Another aspect of individualism is also threatened. Implicit in the Enlightenment assumption of a common human nature is the view that nurture and society can do little or nothing to alter the basic structure of human aspirations and fulfilment. Different societies may channel those aspirations in different ways, but a society is essentially a collection of individuals with pre-formed desires who come together in order more efficiently to satisfy those desires. Such a view of society was common to both social contract theorists and utilitarians.

Herder was not the first to challenge this view, for it was also one of Rousseau's targets. At first blush, Rousseau belongs solidly to the individualist tradition of social contract thought. The great problem of politics is to ensure that a person, despite surrendering 'all his rights . . . to the whole community', nevertheless 'may still obey himself alone, and remain as free as before' (S 12). No society has yet solved this problem: although 'man is born free, . . . everywhere he is in chains' (S 3). The solution is for each of us to contract to put 'his person and all his power under the supreme direction of the General Will, and in our corporate capacity, we receive each member as an indivisible part of the whole' (S 13). In obeying the General Will, I in fact obey myself alone and so remain free. This is so even if I am forced to obey it, for then I am being 'forced to be free'. This is, perhaps, less sinister than it sounds, though it is not easy to determine just what Rousseau means by 'the General Will'. Certainly, it is not to be equated with the unanimous expressed wills – the 'particular' wills – of the citizens, let alone with a majority of such wills. For Rousseau, all of the people *can* be fooled all of the time. The General Will is 'always for our own good, but we do not always see what that is' (S 22). But nor, despite its personification in some passages, is the General Will the will of a mysterious corporate person which exists independently of ordinary, flesh-and-blood men and women.

The General Will expresses, rather, what each of us *would* will if only we were not self-deceived, prejudiced, and corrupted by living in modern, property-based societies. In such societies, I am incapable of recognizing my true good, which is what I really desire: hence my real aims are always frustrated, so that I cannot be said to be free. I only obey myself when I do what I truly desire, even if I must be 'forced' to see what this is. The good society is not a machine for people efficiently to satisfy their selfish, pre-formed desires. Rather, it 'transform[s] each individual ... [from] a complete and solitary whole, into part of a greater whole from which he ... receives his life and being' (S 32). It does so by ensuring that people 'respect the sacred bonds of their ... communities' and 'love their fellow-citizens' (D 229). This is why the Rousseauian society must be a small one, about the size of Corsica, 'in which every member is known by every other', and in which there are no smaller associations, like trade unions, which might divert people's loyalty and love away from the community as a whole. Despite its title, then, the message of *The Social Contract* is not that a society should be a contractual device set up by self-interested parties, to which they then owe allegiance only because it serves their interests. Rather, a society should be a community in which people for the first time since their 'fall' from a nobler, less corrupt form of existence are released from selfishness through identification with their fellows, and so are 'no longer torn in two', but 'at one' with themselves (E 257).

Herder is even more passionate than Rousseau in denouncing the view of society as a mere device for satisfying pre-existent desires, and more insistent still on individuals' dependence on their community for their identity and nature. 'I am nothing ... the whole is everything' (222). It is useless, for example, to look for a common human nature in people's desire for happiness, since what counts as happiness depends on the culture to which one belongs. 'Human nature is not the vessel of an absolute, unchanging ... happiness ... Even the image of happiness changes with each condition and climate' (185). Moreover, there is an important difference between Rousseau's and Herder's 'communitarianism'. Rousseau does nothing to dispel the idea that the society he advocates could be engineered into existence, the creation perhaps of a political genius, the superhuman 'Legislator' of whom he speaks. Nor, it seems, would Rousseau's small-scale societies differ from one another significantly. For Herder, on the other hand, the community is a national culture, defined by its unique history and so quite different from any other. Thus he ridicules those who advocate that we become 'philanthropic citizens of the world' and 'no longer have a fatherland' (209). Rousseau could agree that 'no one of us became man by himself alone': but, for Herder, this is not simply because, to be a true person, one must belong in a community. In addition, the community must have a tradition, for 'the whole structure of a man's humanity is connected by a spiritual genesis ... with his countrymen and forefathers' (312). Even the virtues a person displays will be a function of a particular national culture. A morality for 'all times and places' would be a 'foam which dissolves in the air': a living morality is one which nourishes 'the veins and sinews of one's own people' (203). It was Herder, not Rousseau, who articulated the *Volksgeist* ideology which has inspired both fascism and today's 'multiculturalism'.[93]

These attacks on Enlightenment conceptions of individualism and universal morality, like those on the ideals of 'disengaged' reason and objective knowledge, all manifested a mood of discontent with what the romantics saw as a monochrome and enervating vision of the world and human beings. Goethe, recalling his student days in Strasbourg, tells how d'Holbach's *Système de la nature*, with its mechanistic account of reality, 'appeared to us so grey, . . . so corpse-like . . . that we shuddered before it as before a spectre'.[94] Herder complains that those who dismiss as 'prejudice' all but 'mechanized' rational thought will themselves 'feel like a machine', a 'cog', for they will have sacrificed what 'they have more need of . . . heart, warmth, blood, humanity, life' (200). Worst of all, perhaps, Enlightenment atheism or deism threatens to destroy our appreciation of the world, and of ourselves in particular, as the epiphany of God. The history of human beings, for Herder, is not so much the story of a biological species, but 'God's epic . . . a fable with a thousand variations full of immense meaning' (215). For Hamann, we must regain our sense of reality as divine *logos*, so that we may say 'Speak that I may see Thee!' and recognize that 'this wish was fulfilled in the creation, which is a speaking to the creature through the creature'.[95]

With statements like these, we virtually arrive at the pantheism of 'high' romanticism, and are already able to appreciate how our recurrent *Leitmotiv* of alienation and integration, introduced in chapter 1, was developed in the modern era. For writers like Herder, Hamann and Rousseau, the effect of the rise of the sciences – both natural and practical – had been to generate an Enlightenment conception of human beings as morally and metaphysically isolated atoms, estranged from their fellow men, the cosmos as a whole, and their own selves. In chapter 8, after examining the position of Kant, who posed the issue of estrangement in new and stark terms, we shall see how later romantics continued and intensified the attack on the Enlightenment conception.

• Notes •

1 The verdict is D. W. Hamlyn's, *A History of Western Philosophy*, p. 123.
2 Jacob Burckhardt, *The Civilization of the Renaissance*, p. 129.
3 See Edward Craig, *The Mind of God and the Works of Man*, for an excellent account of the conflict between these two pictures.
4 Walter Pater, *The Renaissance*, p. 1.
5 Paul Oskar Kristeller, 'Humanism', p. 113.
6 Desiderius Erasmus, *Praise of Folly*, in *The Erasmus Reader*, pp. 158–9.
7 Giovanni Pico Della Mirandola, *Oration on the Dignity of Man*. References are to page numbers of this book.
8 Giorgio Vasari, *Artists of the Renaissance*, p. 233.

9 Erwin Panofsky, *Meaning in the Visual Arts*, p. 24.

10 Erasmus, *Praise of Folly*, pp. 157, 168.

11 References to Machiavelli are to *The Prince*.

12 Quoted in A. J. Parel, 'The question of Machiavelli's modernity', p. 269. This article usefully reminds us of the ways in which Machiavelli was certainly not 'modern'.

13 Umberto Eco, *Foucault's Pendulum*, p. 413.

14 Crollius, quoted in Michel Foucault, *The Order of Things*, p. 21.

15 Quoted in Frances A. Yates, 'Bruno, Giordano', p. 407.

16 References to Bacon are to *The New Organon*.

17 Unsurprisingly, Bacon has become something of a villain for modern environmentalists and critics of technology. Theodor Adorno and Max Horkheimer, *Dialectic of Enlightenment*, p. 4, hold him responsible for encouraging 'patriarchal' domination over 'a disenchanted nature'.

18 Foucault, *The Order of Things*, p. 40.

19 Quoted in Anthony Quinton, *Bacon*, p. 42.

20 Galilei Galileo, *Dialogue Concerning the Two Chief World Systems*, p. 103.

21 John Hedley Brooke, *Science and Religion*, p. 81. I am much endebted to this book for my discussion and examples.

22 Quoted in Quinton, *Bacon*, p. 44.

23 Quoted in Brooke, *Science and Religion*, p. 54.

24 Richard H. Popkin, 'Scepticism and modernity', p. 15. This author's *The History of Scepticism from Erasmus to Spinoza*, is the authoritative work on scepticism in the period it covers.

25 See Terence Penelhum, 'Scepticism and fideism'.

26 Quoted in Popkin, *The History of Scepticism from Erasmus to Spinoza*, p. 18.

27 M. A. Screech, *Montaigne and Melancholy*, p. 13.

28 References to Pascal are to the standard (Lafuma) numbers of his *Pensées*.

29 Michel de Montaigne, *An Apology for Raymond Sebond*. References are to page numbers of this, Montaigne's longest essay. Sebond, a fifteenth-century theologian whom Montaigne had translated, disappears after the first few pages and the 'apology' seems to consist in showing that the arguments of Sebond's critics cannot be any better than his own.

30 Quoted in Penelhum, 'Scepticism and Fideism', p. 293.

31 The phrase is Penelhum's, p. 297.

32 'Sayings attributed to Pascal', in Pascal, *Pensées*, p. 355.

33 John Cottingham, 'Introduction' to *Descartes: Selected Philosophical Writings*, p. vii.

34 References in the text are to page numbers of *Descartes: Selected Philosophical Writings*.

35 See Bernard Williams, 'Descartes's use of skepticism', pp. 344f.

36 See Williams, 'Descartes's use of Skepticism', and Anthony Kenny, *Descartes*, pp. 188ff, for defences of Descartes against the charge of circularity.

37 *Three Dialogues Between Hylas and Philonous*, in George Berkeley, *Philosophical Writings*, pp. 115, 83–4.

38 David Hume, *An Enquiry Concerning Human Understanding*, p. 107.

39 A. J. Ayer, *Hume*, p. 185.

40 References to Hume are to *An Enquiry Concerning Human Understanding* (E); *A Treatise of Human Nature* (T); and *Dialogues Concerning Natural Religion* (D).

41 Craig, *The Mind of God and the Works of Man*, p. 81.

42 I see no reason to follow the view of Hume's logical positivist admirers, still apparent in A. J. Ayer's *Hume*, that these professions of ignorance are *ironic*, mimicking the attitude of those naïve enough to think that it could even be *meaningful* to speculate about matters transcending all empirical evidence. For an effective criticism of the logical positivists' claim

to be Hume's heirs, see Craig, *The Mind of God and the Works of Man*, pp. 120ff.

43 On this way of putting Hume's response to the sceptic, see P. F. Strawson, *Scepticism and Naturalism*, pp. 10ff, where useful comparisons and contrasts are drawn between Hume and Wittgenstein.

44 Between them, John Cottingham, *The Rationalists*, and R. S. Woolhouse, *The Empiricists*, provide reliable and readable coverage of the systems I discuss.

45 See *Alciphron*, Dialogue 4, in *The Works of George Berkeley*, 1948–57, vol. 3.

46 Cottingham, *The Rationalists*, p. 123.

47 See Kenny, *Descartes*, pp. 223–4.

48 Nicolas Malebranche, *The Search After Truth*, p. 338.

49 *Descartes: Philosophical Letters*, p. 123.

50 Charles Taylor, *Sources of the Self*, p. 146.

51 References to Hobbes are to *Leviathan* (L); to part, chapter and section of *De Corpore* (Concerning Body) (DC), 1839–45; and to chapter and section of *Human Nature* (HN), 1839–45.

52 Quoted in Frederick Copleston, *A History of Philosophy*, vol. 5, p. 8.

53 See the second of John Locke's, *Two Treatises of Government*.

54 References to Berkeley are to *Three Dialogues Between Hylas and Philonous* (D), to Section numbers of *Principles of Human Knowledge* (P), both in *Berkeley: Philosophical Writings*; and to *Philosophical Commentaries* (PC), as numbered in *The Works of George Berkeley*, vol. I.

55 John Locke (1632–1704) taught at Oxford, where he had the rather ominous title of 'Censor of Moral Philosophy'. Most of his career, however, was spent in public service, at first through the patronage of the first Earl of Shaftesbury, whose son he tutored – rather successfully, since the second Earl was himself to become an important philosopher of the 'moral sense' school. Locke felt in danger during James II's reign, only returning to England after 'the Glorious Revolution' in 1688, the justification of which was an expressed aim of his *Two Treatises of Government*. Locke became Commissioner of Trade in 1696, dying a few years later, as many would like to do, listening to the Psalms.

56 References to Locke are to book, chapter and section of Locke, *An Essay Concerning Human Understanding*.

57 Quoted in J. O. Urmson, *Berkeley*, p. 100.

58 There is, it should be added, much controversy over Berkeley's account of unperceived things. See, for example, the several articles on this in C. B. Martin and D. M. Armstrong (eds), *Locke and Berkeley*, and Urmson, *Berkeley*, who defends the 'phenomenalist' interpretation of Berkeley's analysis.

59 References to Spinoza are to the part and proposition (p) (or definition, axiom etc.) numbers of his *Ethics* (some of the quotes are found in the various corollaries, scholia, etc. following the propositions in this work, which apes the style of works of geometry); also to *Tractatus Theologico-Politicus* (TTP), in *Spinoza: The Political Writings*, and to *The Collected Works of Spinoza*, vol. I (CW).

60 Quoted in Cottingham, *The Rationalists*, p. 26.

61 References to Leibniz are to his *Basic Writings* (BW), and *Philosophical Writings* (PW).

62 For this notion, see Jonathan Bennett's very lively *A Study of Spinoza's Ethics*, pp. 29ff.

63 Roger Scruton, *Spinoza*, p. 101.

64 Quoted by Arthur O. Lovejoy, *The Great Chain of Being*, p. 145.

65 G. MacDonald Ross, *Leibniz*, p. 107.

66 Bennett, *A Study of Spinoza's Ethics*, p. 48.

67 For a related interpretation, see E. M. Curley, *Spinoza's Metaphysics*.

68 Quoted in Ross, *Leibniz*, p. 89.

69 Quoted in Copleston, *A History of Philosophy*, vol. 5, p. 60.

70 'An answer to the question: "What is Enlightenment?"', in Kant, *Political Writings*, p. 54.

71 *On the Mind*, in J. B. Schneewind (ed.), *Moral Philosophy from Montaigne to Kant*, vol. II, p. 416.

72 See Alasdair MacIntyre, *After Virtue*, ch. 5, on the importance of the denial of *telos*.

74 Quoted in Taylor, *Sources of the Self*, p. 323.

75 Quoted in Copleston, *A History of Philosophy*, vol. 6, p. 31.

76 Kant, *Political Writings*, p. 54.

77 'Of the standard of taste', in Hume's *Essays*, pp. 246–7.

78 *An Inquiry into the Original of Our Ideas of Beauty and Virtue*, in Schneewind (ed.), *Moral Philosophy from Montaigne to Kant*, pp. 510ff.

79 *Système de la Nature*, in ibid., p. 439.

80 *An Introduction to the Principles of Morals and Legislation*, in ibid., pp. 462f.

81 Quoted in Taylor, *Sources of the Self*, p. 336.

82 *Système de la Nature*, 1966, p. 228.

83 Ibid., in Schneewind (ed.), p. 444.

84 Antoine-Nicolas de Condorcet, *Sketch for a Historical Picture of the Progress of Human Mind*, p. 136.

85 Ibid., p. 201.

86 References to Herder are to J. G. Herder, *On Social and Political Culture*.

87 References to Vico are to his *Selected Writings*.

88 References to Rousseau are to *Emile* (E); and to *A Discourse on the Origin of Inequality* (D) and *The Social Contract* (S), both in *The Social Contract and Discourses*.

89 See Isaiah Berlin, *Vico and Herder*.

90 Isaiah Berlin, quoted in Michael Rosen, 'The first Romantic?', p. 3.

91 Quoted in Terence J. German, *Hamann on Language and Religion*, p. 7.

92 Ibid., p. 132.

93 See Alain Finkielkraut, *The Undoing of Thought*, on Herder's influence on 'multiculturalism'.

94 Quoted in Copleston, *A History of Philosophy*, vol. 6, p. 50.

95 Quoted in German, *Hamann on Language and Religion*, p. 41.

Part III

· Recent Philosophies ·

Introduction to Part III

Publishers do not like the word 'recent', fearing that it will badly date a book when a subsequent edition still refers to events of years ago, now forgotten, as 'recent'. This book, however, would have to go into many, many reprints before nineteenth- and twentieth-century philosophies, measured on the rather leisurely scale of the history of ideas, cease to be recent. I would have titled Part III 'nineteenth and twentieth-century philosophies' were it not, for reasons already given, for the appearance of Kant at the beginning of chapter 8. 'Modern' was already pre-empted, having been used, as a term of art, to refer to philosophies from the Renaissance to Enlightenment. Anyway, it would be confusing to label those twentieth-century thinkers 'modern' who pride themselves on being 'postmodern'. So, 'recent' it is, bland and vague though the term may be.

In the case of Western thought, the period covered in Part III is from Kant right down to philosophers who not only are still alive but, in some cases, are called 'young' in the kindly parlance of academia. In the East and in the Islamic world, the story starts a little later, with the mid to late nineteenth-century impact of Western thought on their philosophical traditions, an impact which the inheritors of those traditions are still addressing. In Africa, the story starts still later, in the mid-twentieth century, with the contentious attempts to identify a venerable tradition of African philosophizing, to understand traditional belief systems, and to articulate the notion of 'negritude' or 'Africanness'.

Selectivity has been a problem throughout in writing this book. It becomes acute when considering nineteenth and especially twentieth-century philosophies, partly because lack of distance from them makes it difficult to judge what is most significant, what is most likely to last, but mainly because of the sheer volume of material. I can never remember the exact figures, but I seem to have heard, for example, that more philosophy has been written since 1980, measured by tonnage of paper, than was written during the preceding four centuries. The book's focus on philosoph*ies*, large-scale systematic accounts of the world and the place of human beings in it, and the *Leitmotiv* of 'the problem of alienation' announced in chapter 1, provide some criteria for inclusion and exclusion. Despite that, each knowledgeable reader will have his or her complaint that this philosopher, but not that, has been left out, or that this '-ism', but not that, has been included. Such readers are best referred to one of the many good surveys of twentieth-century philosophy (Western, at least), written from an angle, typically, that allows greater coverage than this book does of the developments in logic and philosophy of language which, in the judgement of some, are the outstanding contribution of philosophy in the twentieth century.

8

• KANT AND THE NINETEENTH CENTURY •

• 1 Kant •

Immanuel Kant so set the agenda for nineteenth-century philosophy that few of its important figures could avoid defining their own positions in relation to his. Thirty years after the publication of *Critique of Pure Reason* in 1787, Goethe's friend Mme de Stael wrote of it: 'almost all of which has been accomplished . . . in literature as well as philosophy, has flowed from the impulse given by this performance'.[1] Both the German Absolute Idealists and Schopenhauer and Nietzsche, discussed in sections 2 and 3 respectively, were explicitly responding to the problems Kant bequeathed and trying to improve on his solutions. On other thinkers, notably Kierkegaard (sect. 3), Marx (sect. 4) and the British Idealists (sect. 5), Kant's influence was less direct, being mediated by that of the greatest of the German Idealists, Hegel. For yet other writers – materialists and positivists (sections 4 and 5) – Kant was representative of a position to which they were entirely antipathetic. The 'impulse' given by Kant could still be felt at the end of the nineteenth century, most obviously among the Neo-Kantian school in Germany, but in less predictable quarters, too. The American pragmatist C. S. Peirce, for example, read Kant every day for three years, knowing much of his work by heart. Neo-Kantians and pragmatists are among those discussed in section 5.

Kant's Inheritance

If much flowed from Kant's philosophy, much flowed into it as well, so that to no other philosophy, perhaps, is the image of a watershed more apt. We can begin by sketching how the themes of chapter 7, in reverse order, were taken up by Kant. First, we should note the important, but ambiguous, place he occupied in the debates between Enlightenment thinkers and their critics. I quoted his famous endorsement of Enlightenment as 'man's emergence from his self-incurred immaturity', and in other respects, too, Kant often sounds like a typical *Aufklärer*: in his insistence on a universal morality, for example, or his preference for a republican 'enlightened despotism'. But elsewhere, he writes more in the romantic spirit. As the title of his greatest work suggests, he rejects extravagant claims made on behalf of reason, and references in *Critique of Judgement* to the artistic genius's insights into an ineffable, supersensible reality were to inspire the romantic idea that it is through art, not philosophy or science, that knowledge of the deepest things is attainable. As for the doctrines of radical Enlightenment – materialism, determinism, atheism – these are on Kant's hit-list of '-isms' whose roots must be 'severed'.

His objection to these 'dogmatic' doctrines is that they go beyond anything which experience could possibly establish. The same objection applies to the other '-isms' discussed in chapter 7: to the metaphysics of Leibniz, for instance, Kant's prime example of reason pressed beyond its proper limits. This suggests sympathy with a sceptic like Hume, the man who awoke Kant from his 'dogmatic slumbers'. But it is one of Kant's central claims that restricting knowledge to the testimony of the senses is incoherent. Reason should not be dogmatic, but nor so modest as to confine its scope to the data of the senses.

Kant's attempt to steer between dogmatism and scepticism is not motivated by purely epistemological considerations, but also by the larger issue discussed at the beginning of chapter 7: the tension between the humanists' emphasis on 'the dignity of man' and science's reduction of human beings to 'specks of dust' in a mechanical universe. For Kant, the tension results from his 'ever increasing admiration' for both 'the starry heavens above me and the moral law within me'. When I view myself in relation to the former, this 'annihilates, as it were, my importance as an animal creature . . . a mere speck in the universe'. Reflection on the moral law within me, however, 'infinitely raises my worth as that of an intelligence . . . independent . . . of the whole world of sense . . . not restricted to . . . this life but reach[ing] into the infinite' (P 161–2).[2]

Dogmatism and scepticism cannot do justice to both these perspectives on ourselves. In its materialist forms, dogmatism denies my independence of 'the whole world of sense', and in its idealist forms, my membership of such a world. Scepticism is no better, since it denies my right to confidence in either perspective. The problem, however, to which Kant constantly returns is that even the broadly empiricist position he seems to advocate offers only a one-sided resolution of the issue. Even a liberal empiricism becomes dogmatic when it 'confidently denies whatever lies beyond the sphere' of experience, thus doing 'irreparable injury' to morality, since this requires that we see ourselves as members of a 'supersensible' order (A 471/B 499). Some writers applaud Kant's empiricist account of human understanding and lament, as inconsistent with this, his speculations about God, immortality, and the like.[3] But, for Kant, to remain within the limits of what we understand is to deny the possibility of morality. It is no *more* important to scotch metaphysical excess than to 'check the dangerous pretensions of understanding' to confine within its limits 'the possibility of all things in general' (J Pref. 3). Understanding may answer the first of the three great questions, 'What can I know?', but not 'What ought I to do?' and 'What may I hope?' (A 805/B 833).

The life of Immanuel Kant (1724–1804), remarkable only for its uneventfulness, does not match the drama of his philosophy. Stories are told of *Hausfrauen* in Königsberg – the native town from which he hardly stirred – telling the time by his movements. These may be exaggerated, but his life was certainly one of unbending habit. Up at 5 a.m., work, lectures on just about everything at the undistinguished local university, lunch, a walk, more work. It was eleven years from his appointment to a Chair at the age of forty-six before Kant published *Critique of Pure Reason*, with his other main works appearing in the industrious decade which followed. A diminutive man, Kant was the object of almost universal respect, whom even his erstwhile sparring-partner, Herder, could only recall with 'the deepest gratitude and reverence'.[4] Surprisingly, given his generally humourless and turgid prose, Kant enjoyed the reputation of a witty host and ladies' man until, to his and his friends' chagrin, he lapsed into senility. Hopefully, he had no presentiment of his beloved city's fate, conquered, rebuilt and renamed by Joseph Stalin after his stooge, Kalinin.

Experience and Understanding

Kant's account of understanding emerges from his criticisms of those he calls dogmatists and sceptics. The latter insist that knowledge derives from sense-experience. Since this can only provide particular and contingent items of information, sceptics cannot accept claims about necessary, universal features of reality. The only necessary, *a priori* truths – ones requiring no empirical confirmation – which sceptics allow are uninformative 'analytic' ones, like 'All bachelors are unmarried', where the predicate is already 'contained in' the subject. What sceptics cannot admit are 'synthetic *a priori*' truths: ones, that is, which are necessary, independent of confirmation by experience, yet informative as to the nature of reality. (In a synthetic truth, like 'All bachelors have kidneys', the predicate is not 'contained in' the subject.)

Dogmatists are happy to allow synthetic *a priori* truths, and rightly, since 'it is easy to show that there actually are . . . judgements which are necessary' and 'indispensable' both to common sense and to science (B 5). These include the truths of mathematics, of Newtonian physics, and such principles as that everything has a cause. Dogmatists unfortunately conclude that, since such knowledge is not furnished by the senses, it has no essential relation to experience. Instead, they appeal to special metaphysical insights into reality, or to innate knowledge planted in us by God. On the essential relation between knowledge and experience, the sceptics are nearer the truth. There is no knowledge 'save only in regard to things which may be objects of possible experience' (B 148): for, except through 'sensibility', in 'no other way can an object be given to us' (A 19).

But how, in that case, *can* there be synthetic *a priori* knowledge? To see how, we must embrace an alternative overlooked by dogmatists and sceptics alike: some truths are necessary 'because only as . . . presupposing them is anything possible as *object of experience*' (B 126). If this is so, the sceptics' problem of how *a priori* knowledge could arise from experience disappears: for unless these truths held, there could be no experience. Nor, if synthetic *a priori* truths are preconditions of experience, does one need to make dogmatic appeals to some special faculty which provides insight into them. Reflection on how experience is possible will suffice.

It will suffice, first, to establish that objects of experience must be located in space and time. Space, for example, is not a property we predict that all objects possess on the basis of past experience. If it were, then to imagine a world without objects would be to imagine the absence of space. But we 'can never represent to ourselves the absence of space', only its lack of occupancy (B 39). Space and time are 'forms of all intuition [sensory states, roughly]', 'conditions of sensibility', at least for us humans, without which we cannot envisage perceiving any object. It is therefore *a priori* true that an object is spatio-temporal, since if it were not it could not be an object of possible experience.

Kant's attempt, in his 'transcendental deduction', to show that *a priori* concepts or 'categories', like substance and causality, are also preconditions of experience, is one of the densest parts of a book not celebrated for its limpid prose. Experience, he argues, is not a matter simply of receiving sense-data, but also of a self-conscious creature's employing its understanding to apply concepts to such data. Hence, experience is impossible except under the conditions required for conceptual judgement and self-consciousness. Those conditions are supplied by the 'categories'. More fully: our 'intuitions' or sensory states must, in order to constitute a genuine experience – of a stone, say – be organized so as to be brought under concepts. Experiencing a stone entails making a conceptual judgement: for while 'thoughts without content are empty, intuitions without concepts are blind' (A 51). Further, however, an experience cannot be 'unowned': it must be someone's, that of some 'I'. Hence 'it must be possible for the "I think" to accompany all my representations' (B 131). Otherwise, something could be represented but not *thought* by anyone, which is absurd. Experience, therefore, must obey the conditions necessary for my representations to 'stand together in one self-consciousness', for what Kant inimitably calls the 'transcendental unity of apperception' (B 132).

Now for my perceptions so to 'stand together', they and everything else that 'can come to empirical consciousness must . . . be subject to the categories' (B 164–5). If they were not, sensory states would be insufficiently stable and ordered to be combined, conceptualized, and referred to a single self-conscious creature over the course of time. But, then, these states would not be *experiences* at all. The required stability and order is only possible, the argument continues, if our experience is of substances – enduring 'objects in space outside of me' (B 275) – subject to causal laws. Unless these were what I experienced, I could not be 'conscious of my own existence as determined in time' (B 275). I don't, after all, *perceive* the 'I', my enduring self, but only a passing parade of sensory states. Hence the idea of *my* permanence presupposes that of the objects which I experience outside of, but alongside, me. Descartes had matters back to front: far from first establishing my existence and then inferring that there are external objects, I could not conceive of myself as an enduring subject unless I experienced enduring external objects.

Why, though, must these objects obey strict causal laws? Well, although they endure, objects must visibly change: otherwise I could not experience time, since time *per se* is not perceivable. In that case, I am able to distinguish between perceptions of change, such as water freezing, and a mere succession of sensory states (as when I look at different bits of an unchanging scene one after another). The distinction is that, in the former case, the perceptions *had to* occur in the order they did. Try as I might, I cannot experience the ice before the water: hence my experience of the freezing is of an event which, like all events in the outside world, is 'subject to the concept of the relation of effects and causes' (B 163).

To summarize a dense argument: experiences can only be enjoyed by creatures able to ascribe these to themselves, as more-or-less enduring subjects. They can do so only if their experiences are of more-or-less enduring objects in the external world. But they can distinguish an order of experiences as objective only if it is 'irreversible', and so causally governed. Hence at least two 'categories', those of substance and causality, as well as the two 'forms' of space and time, are *a priori* conditions of experience.

Transcendental Idealism

Kant's argument naturally invites the following query: 'Granted that objects as experienced *by us* must conform to the conditions you mention, need they do so as they are "in themselves"? If not, aren't you a kind of idealist, treating objects as "products" of our sensory and cognitive apparatus?' Kant, by way of reply, is happy to accept that he is an idealist of a kind. 'Knowledge has only to do with appearances, and must leave the thing in itself . . . as not known by us' (B xx). Space and time, he insists, are conditions of our sensibility, not of things in themselves; and the principle of causality, likewise, only governs objects *qua* appearances to us. But this 'transcendental' idealism, Kant stresses, is not to be confused with the 'empirical' kind purveyed, he believes, by Berkeley. This latter brand denies 'the existence of objects in space outside us', construing objects as 'ideas', contents of inner experience. It is, therefore, an absurd view since, as already noted, 'inner experience is possible only on the assumption of outer experience' (B 274–5). Objects are indeed appearances, but not *mere* appearances, like the figures in a dream: they are things-as-they-appear-to-us.

But what of things considered apart from how they appear to us? Kant is adamant that there are such things, that 'the thing in itself [is] indeed real *per se*' (B xx). For a start, it is incoherent to suppose that 'there can be appearances without anything that appears' (B xxvii). Second, since sensibility is a purely receptive faculty, something must act upon it in order to produce perceptions. This something cannot be an object in space and time, for these, recall, are purely 'forms' of perception. Hence, it must be a 'non-sensible cause of [our] representations', a thing in itself (A 494). Finally, I myself am not a denizen of the empirical world of appearances alone, but also a thing in itself belonging to 'a non-sensible intelligible world' (B 431). Were I not, then like all merely empirical objects, I would be subject to causal laws, hence not free. In that case, I could not be a genuine moral agent. The doctrine of things in themselves, then, yields the 'inestimable benefit, that all objections to morality . . . [are] silenced' (B xxxi).

It follows from Kant's account of synthetic *a priori* knowledge, however, that nothing can be known of the nature of things in themselves. The correspondence between knowledge and its objects, after all, is not due to our having made the former conform to the latter: rather, 'objects must conform to our knowledge' through the conditions our minds impose upon anything occurring as an object of experience. It is we, so to speak, who are 'giving the orders' to objects, not vice versa.[5] Things in themselves, however, 'conform to laws of their own', and cannot therefore be given orders and have 'categories' and 'forms' imposed upon them by us. So we can know nothing about them: not through experience, obviously, but nor *a priori*, since the only *a priori* features are those imposed by us. Kant famously compared the move from 'conforming knowledge to objects' to 'conforming objects to knowledge' with the 'Copernican revolution' in astronomy, which showed that our perceptions of the planets are due not to their motion, but to ours (B xvi–ii).

This conclusion is confirmed by the 'antinomies' which arise when we try to obtain knowledge of how things are in themselves. Staple questions of metaphysics, like 'Did time begin?' and 'Did a necessary being cause the world?', are irresolvable, since the contradictory answers they generate transcend any possible resolution through experience. Among those who insist on raising such questions, some (the 'empiricists') insist that things in themselves obey the same conditions as appearances, while others (the 'dogmatists') deny this. But the 'proofs' which each group offers are 'baseless deceptions' (B 535). Kant might now be expected to advise metaphysicians to shut up shop. But, for a start, such advice would be useless. Reason is 'burdened by questions' which it is 'not able to answer': but it is not 'able to ignore' them either (A vii). This is because of an insatiable appetite to discover the grounds for, and unity within, whatever is already known. Reason would only be gorged if, impossibly, it could grasp reality as a harmonious, necessary whole. In the meantime, it must press on, however vainly, with the quest for knowledge of a 'transcendent' soul which unites our experiences, of the cosmos as a systematic whole, and of a God who is the absolute condition of everything.

Kant insists that, though inapplicable to experience, these three 'ideas of reason' – soul, cosmic totality and God – are not 'superfluous and void' (A 329). First, they have an important 'regulative employment', since 'we interrogate nature in accordance with' them (A 645/B 673). Unless scientists proceed *as if* the world were a systematic whole, they will not be inspired to discover ever further connections between apparently disparate phenomena. Their efforts may come to a halt at some point, but they are never justified in conceding that this point has been reached. Second, the 'ideas' are crucial in permitting the 'transition from the concepts of nature to the practical [i.e. moral] concepts' (A 329). If reason were confined to understanding, and hence to employing concepts applicable to experience, there could be no such thing as practical reason. For, in the moral domain, the 'ideas' of the soul's freedom and immortality and of God are essential: and these are notions which, if applicable at all, apply to things in themselves. To be sure, the validity of these 'ideas' can never be a matter of theoretical knowledge: but nor, Kant thinks he has shown, can their *in*validity. No proof of God's existence is valid, but nor is any disproof. To recall an earlier remark, theoretical reason must not lay rash claim to know what is beyond our ken: but nor must the understanding pontificate, from within its limited domain, on 'the possibility of all things in general'. It is, then, for the sake of preserving the possibility of morality and religion that Kant 'found it necessary to deny *knowledge*, in order to make room for *faith*' (B xxx). Let us now follow him in the 'transition' from nature to morality.

The Moral Law

This 'transition' is away from nature, since the natural world, by Kant's earlier arguments, is governed by causal laws, whereas morality presupposes human freedom. The point is not simply that '"ought" implies "can"', though it is indeed through reflecting that there are things one ought to do that a person recognizes that he must have a capacity for free choice – 'a fact which, without the moral law, would have remained unknown to him' (P 30). Freedom from nature, in the sense of natural inclinations and desires, is also required for the 'good will', which is the only thing that 'can be called good without qualification' (F 17). Certain qualities, like courage and cool-headedness may be generally desirable, but unless directed by the good will, even these can be dangerous. Indeed, the very 'coolness of a villain . . . makes him more abominable' (F 18). Anyway, such qualities are mere 'gifts of nature' and so can confer no distinctively 'moral worth' on the actions which display them. Only actions done out of good will – out of a sense of duty and 'respect for the [moral] law' – have moral worth. If, as Kant says, 'I should follow this law even to the thwarting of *all* my inclinations' (F 25), then moral action entails a freedom to transcend my natural, creaturely self.

Moreover, if the moral worth of actions is entirely due to their being done out of 'respect for the law', it is independent of any results they achieve and of any desire to achieve these. Moral acts, therefore, cannot be motivated by natural purposes, like health and happiness, which explain much of our behaviour. Finally, for an action to be moral, the law out of respect for which it is performed must be a self-imposed one. The good will displays 'autonomy' – 'that property of it by which it is a law to itself' (F 70). Obedience to a law simply because it is the Pope's, the Emperor's, or even God's has no moral worth, for it is then inspired by a natural motive, like love or fear. (God, no doubt, does demand obedience to the moral law, but then He can only be recognized as God because He is successfully 'compared with our ideal of moral perfection' (F 36). If so, His word cannot be the *criterion* for moral good.)

In several senses, then, the very possibility of morality requires its insulation against natural processes. This view, reminiscent of the stoics' approach (see pp. 133ff.), puts Kant at odds with mainstream Enlightenment approaches. Utilitarianism, for example, is wrong-headed, not only because it measures the worth of an action by its consequences, but because – especially in the egoistic versions of Helvétius and Bentham – 'the springs it provides for morality . . . undermine it' (F 72). Moral acts cannot be motivated or 'sprung' by amoral self-interest. The 'moral sense (or sentiment)' approach fares scarcely better, since this too defines morality in terms of 'subjective impulses', like sympathy, failing to appreciate that the 'dignity' of duty is all the greater, 'the less the subjective impulses favour it' (F 54). Kant's moral hero is the person who acts out of duty despite a powerful inclination not to. More generally, Kant rejects the Enlightenment strategy of deriving moral principles from human nature. Seeking these principles among 'empirical motives . . . substitutes for morality a bastard' which no one who has 'beheld her in her true form' could confuse with virtue (F 55).

Kant has further objections to any naturalistic approach. One of its effects is to render moral imperatives merely 'hypothetical', enjoining us to perform actions only if, say, they promote happiness. This is to treat moral commands as 'rules of skill' or 'counsels of prudence', of the form 'Do X, if you want Y!', instead of as 'categorical' imperatives whose authority no one can evade by pleading 'Well, I don't happen to want Y'. Second, a morality rooted in human nature restricts the scope of the moral law to human beings. However, 'if a law is to have moral force . . . it . . . is not valid for men alone', but for all rational beings (F 11). The good will, after all, is independent of empirical conditions, including those which serve to distinguish human from other life. It must, then, be the will of a rational being as such, human or otherwise. This has important implications. First, the moral law must be 'formal', in the first instance not telling us *what* we should do, but providing a general recipe for determining the principles or 'maxims' on which we should act. Otherwise it would not be applicable to *all* rational beings, many of whose circumstances may be very different from human ones. Second, the maxims for which the moral law provides a recipe must be ones which all rational beings *can*, in principle, follow. A maxim which only I and my fellows can follow cannot be one binding on all rational creatures.

Kant concludes that the moral law is encapsulated in the following 'categorical imperative': 'Act only on that maxim whereby thou canst at the same time will that it should become a universal law' (F 49). A maxim like 'Keep your promises, except when it's inconvenient!' defies this imperative since it could not be universally acted upon. Promising would soon die out if people broke promises whenever it was convenient. Or take 'Don't bother to help people in need!' This is not something a person could seriously will to serve as a general principle, since he would then 'deprive himself of all hope of the aid he desires' from other people when the chips are down (F 52). (This example shows, importantly, that it is not the categorical imperative by itself which settles the maxims that human beings should adopt. These will depend, as well, on certain facts about human beings, such as that they often desire help from others.)

Kant offers some allegedly equivalent formulations of the categorical imperative, including the command to treat a rational being 'never as a means only', but always 'as an end in itself' (F 58–9). This command is 'equivalent' to the original imperative in that to violate the one is to violate the other. If one of my maxims requires me to treat other people as means, it is not one which people could universally accept – not, certainly, the victims of my treatment. Conversely, a maxim that operated in a rational 'kingdom of ends', whose 'citizens' respected one another's ends, would be universalizable. This is because, these people being rational, their ends cannot contradict one another: they must be harmonious. Still, 'the formula of ends' surely expresses a conviction not apparent in the original categorical imperative: that there is a uniquely 'intrinsic worth' and 'dignity' in a rational will (F 64). Without this conviction, indeed, it is hard to see why we should feel obliged to obey the categorical imperative. In that case, the command to treat others as 'ends in themselves' is less a reformulation than the 'source of [the] categorical imperative' (F 56).

Kant's approach soon attracted a variety of criticisms which time has not staled. The poet Friedrich Schiller complained that the categorical imperative was 'empty': it does not entail the maxims, like 'Always keep promises!', which Kant wants it to, nor exclude silly ones like 'Eat a donut a day!' Kant might have forestalled this charge by paying more attention to human psychology, which, he indeed admits, is relevant when applying the categorical imperative to *human* conduct. Maybe 'Eat a donut a day!' is not one we can imagine a rational human being promulgating. (Things might be different for Martians, so constituted that a donut a day keeps the doctor away.) Other critics found Kant's equation of the good will with a sense of duty impossibly 'cold'. Certainly, his descriptions of human relations – marriage is a contract for the 'reciprocal use of [the] sexual organs'[6] – do not always betray a 'warm' view of life. But Kant is far from denying that we should admire generosity and kindness: it is just that, as 'gifts of nature', they lack that specific worth for which he reserves the term 'moral'. Someone who mistreats dogs does not act immorally, since they are not rational, but he acts 'inhumanly' and his 'heart' can be judged by this behaviour (LE 240–1). Morever, Kant insists, full recognition of other people as ends in themselves involves more than the 'negative' duty not to treat them as means. I must also 'endeavour . . . to forward the ends of others', to make them 'as far as possible . . . *my* ends also' (F 59). Despite the sour remark on marriage, this suggests that people should extend to one another the sympathy and friendship which help them in their efforts to attain their ends.

The problems which preoccupied Kant were rather different from the ones raised by his critics, and concerned the very possibility of moral action. First, since such action may have to be done against all inclination, it must be 'determined' by reason 'directly, not through an intervening feeling of pleasure' (P 24). But to explain how reason alone can prompt action is 'beyond the power of human reason'. In the 'total absence of springs' to action, how can action be sprung (F 95–6)? Second, and relatedly, while moral acts must be free, 'we could not prove [freedom] to be actually a property of ourselves' (F 80). Matters are, in fact, worse still, since according to *Critique of Pure Reason*, everything which happens is causally determined. Kant's solution looks rather desperate: as an empirical self in the physical world, I am subject to causality, but as an 'intelligence', I am free. At any rate, 'there is not the smallest contradiction in saying that a *thing in appearance* . . . is subject to . . . laws, of which the very same *as a thing* . . . *in itself* is independent'. Hence a person must 'think of himself in this twofold way' (F 90). Perhaps there is, strictly, no contradiction here, but as Kant concedes, the free 'I' is no more comprehensible than any other thing in itself: hence, we cannot 'comprehend the necessity of the moral imperative'. That we at least 'comprehend its incomprehensibility' (F 97) is surely small comfort. Far from reconciling the two perspectives upon myself as a 'mere speck in the universe' and as a being of 'infinite worth', Kant seems to make the gap unbridgeable by cutting me into two selves, one which belongs within the universe, another which does not. How can I be put back together again?

Beauty, Purpose and Unity

Kant's aim in his third and final *Critique* is to discover 'a ground of unity' between 'the sensible realm of nature and the supersensible realm of . . . freedom' (J II). It must be possible to 'throw a bridge' between them if the moral law can take practical effect: for that requires that freedom has an 'influence' in nature, that the supersensible can effect the sensible (J IX). We need, he says, to find 'a middle term' between the understanding's application of concepts to nature and reason's deployment of transcendent, supersensible 'ideas' (like those of God and freedom). This middle term is provided by 'reflective judgement', by which Kant understands the judgement through which we 'ascend from the particular in nature to the universal' in the effort to 'establish the unity' and system of empirical laws and phenomena (J IV). The key 'principle' with which reflective judgement operates is that of 'the purposiveness of nature'. For empirical phenomena to be judged reflectively, that is, 'they must be considered in accordance with [the] unity they *would* have *if* an [intelligent being] . . . had furnished them to our cognitive faculties . . . as a system' (J IV). A bridge from nature to freedom is then thrown: purposiveness, so defined, requires us to think of 'the world . . . as a product of an intelligent' free agent, of God in effect (J 75). The precedent is then set for regarding *my* activity, as a 'sensible being' within nature, as at the same time an exercise of freedom. The idea of freedom will then cease to be an awkward postulate, required to ensure morality, but otherwise incongruous with the idea of nature.

Kant's strategy is to reveal familiar aspects of our experiences and practices which at least *intimate* the operation of freedom and the supersensible within nature. One such aspect is the aesthetic. Judgements of beauty are also 'reflective', since they discern pattern and harmony in objects, which are thus experienced *as if* they were designed for our appreciation, as being 'purposive without [actual] purpose' (J 17). Indeed, it is aesthetic experience which 'occasions' the notion of purposiveness in objects, making it available for 'reflection upon nature' (J VIII–IX).

Beauty serves in other ways as a bridge from nature to freedom and morality, so that it 'promotes . . . sensibility . . . to moral feeling' (J IX) and may be regarded as an analogue or 'symbol of morality'. Like a moral judgement, an aesthetic one is universal, for the pleasure I take in a beautiful object is one I expect everyone to share. This is because aesthetic, like moral, satisfaction, is 'entirely disinterested' (J 5), so that the pleasure I take in beauty is independent of *my* particular aims and inclinations. This already implies a 'certain elevation' above the 'mere' pleasures of the senses – gastronomic, erotic, or whatever – and an independence from 'empirical laws'. This connection with freedom is confirmed by realizing that the source of aesthetic pleasure is the opportunity a beautiful object affords for the 'free play of the cognitive faculties' (J 9). The imagination is free to 'gather together' the shapes and colours of a flower into different structures and forms, as is the understanding to bring these forms under any number of 'indeterminate' concepts. The 'excitement' of, and creative 'harmony' between, these faculties explain the pleasure we take in the flower. Such pleasure enables us to pass 'without any violent leap, from the charm of sense to . . . moral interest' since, although prompted by sensible objects, it is nevertheless a '*free* satisfaction' (J 59).

One kind of aesthetic pleasure, with its *frisson* of fear, might seem hard to fit into this account. This is experience of the *sublime*, of 'the boundless ocean in . . . tumult; the lofty waterfall of a mighty river, and such like'. These are too immense and chaotic to be 'gathered' by our faculties into 'purposive' structures. Kant argues, however, that the sublime too testifies to freedom and the supersensible. Sublimity really resides in *us*, who refuse to cower before the wild storm or roaring torrent, so displaying the 'courage to measure ourselves against the apparent almightiness of nature'. We feel a sense of security in recognizing that we are 'above' nature. Hence, the very phenomena which might seem most likely to reduce us to 'specks in the universe' have the opposite effect, inspiring in the soul a sense of the 'sublimity of its destination, in comparison with [mere] nature' (J 28).

Kant now turns to exploring how the notion of 'purposiveness', first occasioned by aesthetic experience, is employed in understanding nature. Without it, indeed, 'the understanding could not *find itself* in nature' (J VIII). One reason for this is that natural processes, organic ones at least, can only be explained teleologically, in terms of purposes to which things are adapted. No 'future Newton' will ever be able to explain 'the production of a blade of grass' in mechanical terms, without recourse to the idea of 'design' (J 75). Second, scientists would not strive to discover unity and system among the laws of nature unless they thought of it *as if* created by an intelligent cause. Provided the principle of 'purposiveness' is regarded as a 'merely regulative' one, guiding scientific investigation, it does not contradict the principle that we should 'explain all . . . occurrences in nature . . . by mechanism, as far as is in our power' (J 78).

So far, this is no advance from the position in the first *Critique* where, recall, freedom and purpose were denied any real role in an empirical world governed by mechanical causality: it was simply that things could be seen *as if* purposely designed. But, first, Kant's greater appreciation of a sense of 'purposiveness' imbuing everyday experience and scientific practice now makes him more insistent on applying 'the concept of design to nature if we wish to understand it' (J 75). Second, and crucially, his attitude to mechanical causation has changed. Though I must look for causal explanations of things, 'I do not thereby say: *They are possible in this way alone*', merely that I must so 'investigate [them] as far as I can' (J 70). In other words, the principle of mechanical causation is no less a 'regulative' principle than that of 'purposiveness'. Both express *perspectives* which, in different contexts of enquiry, we need to adopt.[7] The two principles are no longer invidiously compared, with one providing an *a priori* condition of experience, the other providing a merely *as if* account of experience. In their proper place, each principle must be deployed 'as far as we can': but the places do not collide and neither enjoys special privilege.

Here, at an age when most people are content to prune their roses, is Kant's final effort to accommodate the two images of ourselves as 'specks in the universe' and as beings of 'infinite worth'. There cannot, to be sure, be a *compromise* between the two: it is not that we are very large specks of only nearly infinite worth. That there cannot, however, should no longer be regarded as generating the problem or incomprehensible mystery that it earlier seemed to do. We no longer face the problem of fitting freedom and morality into a mechanical world that excludes them, since mechanism is now seen as just one perspective on reality. Nor, therefore, do we have to allocate the moral self to a different world, with the consequent mystery of how to throw a bridge between the two worlds. It may indeed be uncomfortable to regard ourselves for some purposes (medical ones, say) as mere mechanisms, and for others (political ones, say) as free moral agents. But that is the penalty we pay for enjoying a uniquely complex status in the universe. It is a penalty which, as we shall see in the next section, some of Kant's followers found too severe.

• 2 Absolute Idealism •

It was the poetry of 'high' romanticism, as much as the prose of Kant, which inspired the systems, constructed by German philosophers around the turn of the eighteenth century, to which the title of this section refers. It was not even a German poet, but William Wordsworth, who penned this virtual manifesto for their endeavours:

> The groundwork of all true philosophy is . . . the difference between . . . that intuition of . . . ourselves, as one with the whole . . . and that [of] ourselves as separated beings, [which] places nature in antithesis to the mind, as . . . thing to thought.[8]

These words express the characteristic romantic ambition of unity, as do those of Friedrich Hölderlin, whose fictional hero, Hyperion, announces his desire 'to be one with all that lives, to return in blessed self-forgetfulness into the All of nature' (160).[9]

Romantic Unity

For Hölderlin and other poets, Enlightenment was the culmination of a process of human beings' alienation from their world, God, each other, and themselves. The vehicle of this process was scientific knowledge, which, complains Hyperion, 'has spoilt everything' by encouraging him 'to distinguish myself from what surrounds me' (161). Several doctrines of 'the Age of Reason' contribute to our alienation: the claim that colours and sounds are merely 'subjective' effects in us of material motion, the deists' view of God as a remote designer, and the utilitarian picture of people as selfish pleasure-seekers. Some doctrines, like materialism, admittedly implied, in their way, that we are integrated in the cosmos. But the message that we are made of the same stuff as everything else only integrates us into the world by denying aspects of our existence, such as our freedom, which a truly integrative vision would honour.

It is, however, the whole stance of scientific reason which causes Hyperion to distinguish himself from what surrounds him. For it is a disengaged stance which compels a person to set aside, in favour of cool observation, those emotions which people in earlier times took to reveal their place in nature. The romantic yearning, as Charles Taylor explains, was to retrieve an ancient sense of nature as an 'inner source', a 'life-force' that 'courses through' us. This sense enables us to regard our own lives as an 'expression', richer than any other, of underlying 'Life', and not the mere products of mechanical laws.[10]

Despite their harsh verdict on 'the Age of Reason', the romantics were not pessimists. Hölderlin, for one, anticipates the day when 'mankind and nature will combine in an all embracing deity' (232). The process of alienation may even have been necessary for attaining a mature sense of unity. I can only understand myself as 'one with all that lives' if I have first experienced its 'otherness'. If I am to 'return' to myself, there must have been a 'going forth'. What, though, is to be the vehicle for a return to unity? Not, for most romantics, philosophy, since this has been too much in cahoots with science. Enlightenment philosophers had either denied those aspects of human life which fit the scientific picture badly or, like Kant, had left their relation to the natural world a mystery. The playwright Heinrich von Kleist wrote of the 'shattering' effect of Kant's division between appearances and things in themselves. By placing the real, including our selves, behind a screen of appearances, Kant ensured that we must fail in our 'one great aim' – Truth.[11]

Yet it was Kant, in his *Critique of Judgement*, who gave the romantics a lead. There he had claimed not only that the 'supersensible' realm of freedom and the natural world are somehow brought together in judgements of beauty, but that the artistic genius is able to provide intimations of that realm. The genius is, moreover, himself an embodiment of creative freedom at work in a material medium. These hints were seized upon by the romantics. We cannot, perhaps, *think* our dual status as natural and free beings, but as Friedrich Schiller explained, we can *practise* it by exercising an artistic 'play-drive' (*Spieltrieb*) through which we freely form the material products we then perceive.[12] And while the 'supersensible' may be indescribable, it can be made manifest in art – perhaps through those 'symbols' which, for Goethe, let us 'see the universal in the particular' and so 'acquire' a sense of the transcendent.[13] Or, given 'the impossibility of reaching the Highest by reflection', perhaps it is allegory and myth which are the proper vehicles of a pantheistic feel for the deity's presence in nature.[14]

In short: philosophy, with its dissective analyses, can only aid the divisive procedures of scientific reason. A different medium for returning us to a sense of unity is therefore needed: that of the artist and poet, whose activities and products alike can embody that higher 'life-force' which 'courses through' all existence.

Self and Nature

There were, unsurprisingly, philosophers unwilling to admit the irremediable complicity of their discipline in the divisive programme of science. There can be, in Wordsworth's sense, a 'true philosophy', able to dissolve through argumentation such antitheses as that between thought and thing. Of these philosophers – none of them an easy read, I should warn – it is Friedrich Wilhelm Schelling (1775–1854) who best deserves the title 'the philosopher of romanticism'.[15] As a precocious youth he was, like Hegel, a friend of Hölderlin, and later married the ex-wife of a leading romantic literary guru. What appealed to the romantics in his brand of idealism was the status accorded to nature, art and myth. Nature is not a mechanism, but 'alive', 'slumbering spirit' or 'mind made visible' (I 42).[16] Art, more than reason, 'brings the whole man . . . to . . . knowledge of the Highest', and mythology – a kind of collective art-form – is the proper 'medium for the return of science to poetry' (S 232–3).

Schelling's system, however, is a critical continuation of that of Johann Gottlieb Fichte (1762–1814), for it was he who first converted Kant's philosophy into a doctrine of Absolute Idealism. Blandly put, the doctrine holds that reality as a whole is 'constituted' or 'posited' by an infinite 'Self'. Fichte spent his career elaborating this *Wissenschaftslehre* (science of knowledge) in works such as the ill-named 'Clear as Daylight Report', teutonically subtitled 'An attempt to compel the reader to understand'.

Fichte starts from our 'intuition of the absolute self-activity of the self', of our freely exercised intelligence (44).[17] The problem is to explain why, despite this awareness of freedom, sense-experience is 'accompanied by the feeling of necessity' (6), of our being compelled to perceive things as we do. The solution must depend upon which of two stances we adopt: the 'idealist' one, which holds that things are the 'products of the intelligence', and the 'dogmatic' one which treats them as things in themselves, external to intelligence (9). This choice will, in part, reflect the 'sort of man one is': in the dogmatist's case, for example, the sort who requires the comfort of belief in a fixed, independent reality. Fichte does, however, offer some arguments for the idealist option, the best of which is this: if, as Kant insists, causality is a relation we impose among items of experience, it makes no sense for a dogmatist to speak of things beyond experience causing our perceptions. Dogmatists are unable, then, to 'demonstrate the passage from being to representations' or perceptions (18).

With things in themselves abolished, an object's existence can only be 'derived' from that of the self: reality is 'transfered to it *from the self*' (100). The claim that it is the 'I am' which is the sole original reality prompted the wit Heinrich Heine to wonder how Frau Fichte put up with her husband. (Perhaps she didn't, for Fichte died of a fever which she transmitted to him.) But Fichte does not, of course, have in mind an individual person by 'Self' and 'I'. Rather, they name the 'primordial action of the intellect', originally unconscious, which then divides and finds individual expression in finite selves like you and me. In his later writings, indeed, Fichte prefers 'God' or 'Life' to 'Self' or 'I'. 'Only one thing exists in itself: God . . . pure Life . . . For through His being all being is given, and neither in nor outside of Him can a new being arise.'[18]

Although Fichte cannot imagine 'how people could have failed to understand' his position (24), he concedes the need to explain to them why this 'primordial' Self must posit a 'not-Self' in the form of 'external' reality. It needs to in order to be aware of anything, for 'if I am to [re]present anything at all,

I must oppose it to the [re]presenting self' (105). Consciousness, that is, requires objects, which must therefore be furnished by the Self which, in some sense, they are 'in'. But Fichte's original problem remains: why does the Self feel constrained, 'passive in relation to the not-Self [and] unaware of its own activity' in producing the world? The solution is that the Self is aware of its activity as a 'striving' (Streben), an effort to maintain itself in its pristine, undivided nature. Now, whatever strives requires obstacles to overcome, a field of action in which to test itself, rather as a monk can only *try* to remain chaste when submitted to temptation. Hence, not only does the Self need to posit the not-Self by way of a challenge to itself, it also needs to feel 'restricted, its forces rebuffed . . . in the physical world' (234). Frankenstein's monster, recall, took on a life opposed to that of its creator. Fichte's natural world cannot do quite that, but if it is to serve as a proper field of action for the Self's moral endeavours, it must *appear* to be alien and independent.

It is over this treatment of nature as a kind of assault course for moral commandos that Schelling takes issue with his erstwhile mentor. At this stage in a long career which ended in more or less orthodox Christianity, Schelling still accepted the idealist premise of an 'act' whereby a potentially self-conscious Absolute posits 'not only the [individual] self . . . but everything else' (S 42). As he sees it, Fichte's position, with its unacceptable consequence of an antagonistic relation between man and nature, exaggerates the role of 'subjective consciousness'. It comes dangerously close to that 'relative' or 'empirical' idealism, castigated by Kant, which treats external reality as a mere content of the mind. (Fichte does sometimes speak as if this reality were an illusion: 'all reality is reduced to a beautiful dream'.)[19] Objectivity or nature is not the product of subjectivity or mind as ordinarily understood: both are, rather, equally authentic 'posits' of the Absolute. This is why nature is 'slumbering spirit' or, in its 'active' aspect, *Natura naturans* – Spinoza's term for nature as a dynamic, purposive whole.

Schelling is so anxious to prevent his idealism collapsing into a form of subjectivism that he refers to his system as 'ideal-realism' (S 41) and to the Absolute as 'the Indifference'. The Absolute is not subjectivity rather than objectivity, nor vice versa, but their identity, one which is only apparently sundered into mind and nature. The inspiration, here, is once again Spinoza – enjoying a revival among the romantics – for whom the one true substance is indifferently regarded as mind or nature (see p. 271 above). This identity or 'Indifference', Schelling holds, is an ineffable mystery: hence it is not through philosophical articulation, but through art and the 'collective intuition' of religion and myth, that it can be 'contemplated' (I 55).

This view of the Absolute as an ineffable identity proved unacceptable to Schelling's fellow-student, his senior in years but less of a *Wunderkind*, Hegel. Schelling is the target of Hegel's reference, in his first great work, to the

'monochromatic formalism' of the 'single insight, that in the Absolute everything is the same'. Since nothing can really be distinguished from anything else in Schelling's Absolute, it is 'the night in which all cows are black' (PS 15–16).[20] (A prickly fellow, Schelling took what he regarded as Hegel's mixture of plagiarism and apostasy as bitterly as Fichte had taken his own criticisms of the *Wissenschaftslehre*.) Hegel's contention was that if, as Schelling accepted, the Absolute is potentially self-conscious 'intelligence', then it *must* lend itself to 'articulated cognition' by its most privileged vehicles, rational human beings. Let us examine how one of those vehicles, Hegel himself, provides it.

Hegel's Logic

Georg Wilhelm Friedrich Hegel (1770–1831) was at first regarded as a pedestrian disciple of Schelling. But, in 1807, with the publication of *Phenomenology of Spirit*, he began the construction of a metaphysical system, perhaps the most ambitious and complex in the history of the subject, which has since exerted enormous influence. In social philosophy alone, he has been variously hailed as the inspiration for Marxism, Fascism and participatory democracy. Born in Stuttgart, Hegel taught at a school and various universities before holding a Chair in Berlin from 1816 until his death, like his predecessor Fichte's, from fever. One suspects he died content, for not only had his political philosophy become official Prussian ideology, but his metaphysics implies, as we shall see, that his articulation of it fulfils the whole purpose of history. In person, Hegel might not have struck most people as the realization of history. Though more cosmopolitan than Kant, he seems to have been a dry stick whose dinner conversation was, if Goethe's report is accurate,[21] as tortured as his prose. One wonders how his students, let alone his schoolboys, coped with pronouncements like 'the living being is a syllogism whose very moments are syllogisms', delivered moreover in thick, halting Schwabian tones.

Hegel's ambition was to provide a systematic account of absolute reality as a whole. This requires him to reject Kant's view that reason's attempt to go beyond the understanding and grasp reality as a whole results in irresolvable antinomies. Moral and aesthetic experience may, for Kant, intimate that reality is a purposive whole, but its nature remains 'incomprehensible'. Schelling, we saw, agreed. Hegel, too, agrees that *if* the understanding were the sole means to grasping the whole, this would remain 'something mysterious'. This is because the understanding operates with divisive, 'opposite' concepts like 'finite' and 'infinite', or 'freedom' and 'causality'. Hegel insists, however, that reason can 'transcend the understanding' and 'contain opposites': hence the whole, or the 'mystical', is not 'inaccessible to thinking' (EL 82).

Dialectical thought, as he calls it, leads us not into antinomies, but towards 'the resolution of the contradictions' encountered by the understanding. What Kant and Schelling overlooked is 'the tremendous power of the negative' (PS 32). It is precisely in encountering a contradiction that reason is compelled to 'sublate' (*aufheben*) its previous conception of things and progress to a higher stage, free of *that* contradiction but, very likely, containing another one which in turn prompts a further dialectical resolution – and so on. Hegel soon complicates matters by stating that dialectic is not simply a process of thinking, but is at work in reality itself, in nature and in history. Or rather – to complicate matters further – thought and reality are not finally to be distinguished. 'Being is thought' and 'what is actual is rational' (PS 54, 10). 'The Concept (or . . . subjectivity) and the object are . . . the same' (EL 193), even if – to add a final twist – they must at first be regarded as 'diverse'.

To make some sense of this, let us follow the order of Hegel's three-part *Encyclopaedia*, beginning with his *Logic*, which examines our concepts as a systematic whole, and then proceeding to the implications of this system for the natural and human worlds which he draws in his philosophies of nature and spirit respectively. (Let us postpone, for the moment, his difficult idealist claim that reality is somehow the product of, yet indistinguishable from, what he calls the Idea.) Hegel's manoeuvre in the *Logic* is like the Grand Old Duke of York's. We are marched up through a series of concepts until we reach the highest one, the Idea, and are then marched down again, but this time armed with what we have learned at the top. The upward march is mainly in the waltz rhythm of dialectical reason, which produces a 'synthesis' from the two terms of a contradiction. Less picturesquely: if we start from an uncontentious, but therefore 'empty' conception of reality, we are driven by the contradictions which this and later, fuller conceptions generate, to arrive, finally, at a conception of reality as a unitary, purposive and spiritual whole. This conception is the Idea, which can only be grasped at the end of a process in which the earlier, 'one-sided' conceptions have been incorporated into a consummating whole (PS 20).

Here I can only sketch, with a minimum of 'Hegelspeak', the highlights of this dialectic. The 'emptiest' conception of reality is that of mere *being*: but this is so indeterminate that, as Plotinus saw, we might as well describe reality as a *nothing*. Still, by 'synthesizing' those two conceptions, we arrive at the notion of *becoming*, an oscillation between being and nothing, and thereby at a conception of reality as constituted by 'determinate beings', each distinguished from another as what it is *not*. Unfortunately, the notion of a distinct, determinate being is incoherent: for if it is defined by the 'boundaries' that separate it from other things, we can only think of it in relation to the latter, which in turn can only be thought of in relation to a wider network, and so on. Reality cannot, therefore, be conceived as a *collection* of distinct objects, since the thought of an object soon refers us to the whole to which it belongs (EL 92–3). We might then think of this whole as a system of causal laws, ones of 'reciprocal interaction', which make things what they are. Causal laws, however, unless 'grounded' in something further, are only contingent and cannot explain why things *must* be as they are. Nor, however, can the whole be 'grounded' in something further, since there can be nothing 'external' to it. Hence we must think of the whole as governed by 'internal' or conceptual necessity, not causal. Moreover, as independent of anything 'external', this whole must be regarded as 'free'. 'The truth of necessity is thereby freedom' (EL 158).

Conceptual relations are usually thought of as 'subjective', as features of minds and their operations. But, for Hegel, concepts cannot be mere mental abstractions from reality: they and their connections must be embodied in reality. On the other hand, it is only something mind-*like* which can undergo conceptual processes, for they 'take place under the dominion of . . . purpose' (EL 212). We cannot therefore treat reality as a merely 'mechanical' or 'chemical' process. Instead, we must regard it as a purposive whole, the working out of the goal of a rational 'self'. The so-called external world is therefore only a 'wrapping' under which rational purpose 'lies hidden'. Subjectivity and objectivity – conceptual and actual processes – are now united in the final conception, the Idea, of reality as a purposive self-like whole (EL 212).

Nature and History

Most commentators are more impressed by the use to which Hegel puts this grand final vision than by the tortuous arguments leading up to it. Natural and historical processes are, for Hegel, concrete manifestations of the Idea or Spirit. 'History is the development of Spirit [*Geist*] in time, as Nature is . . . of the Idea in space' (PH 72). If the *Logic* is 'the presentation of God, as He is . . . before the creation of nature and of . . . finite mind[s]',[22] the philosophies of nature and spirit are, so to speak, presentations of God at work.

Given Hegel's vision of the Idea, we should expect natural processes to mimic the conceptual process that culminated in that vision. And so they do, says Hegel. For example, just as the conception of reality as a collection of discrete, finite objects is inadequate, so are the objects themselves. No more than the conception of them are the objects self-sufficient. This is why they are subject to change and destruction: they 'bear the germ of death within themselves' (EL 92). Again, the conceptual superiority of purposive explanations over 'mechanical' and 'chemical' ones is mirrored at the level of nature by the emergence of purposive living organisms from merely chemical processes.

Much more influential is Hegel's account of human history, not least because of its appeal even to those, like Marx, who rejected the underlying metaphysics of Spirit. History is the story of our becoming conscious of what we are, of 'finding ourselves in the world' (EL 194) and recognizing that we are not 'alienated' from the rest of reality, that 'everything in heaven and earth' is permeated by human thought. (In Hegel, one now sees, his and our *Leitmotiv* of alienation and its overcoming positively booms out.) For Hegel, history is the story of something greater as well – Spirit, God, the Idea – of which we rational creatures are the 'vehicles'. But the tale he tells remains gripping without that further claim.

Phenomenology of Spirit begins with man naïvely 'at home' in his world, 'sunk in nature', like an animal. It ends with his reasoned sense of 'self-conscious freedom at peace with itself' (PS 12). In between are the millennia of alienation, during which human beings struggle to appreciate their uniqueness and freedom without feeling 'cut off' by these from the natural world. The struggle is hard, since the more we view ourselves as parts of the natural order, the less easy is it to discern ourselves as truly free. Early on in this struggle, the tactic is to overcome what seems external or alien, but this paradoxically demonstrates dependence on the external: without it, there would be nothing to overcome. Anyway, how could victory over dumb nature furnish a satisfying sense of one's freedom? It could not, which is why the goal of self-conscious freedom 'attains . . . satisfaction only in another self-consciousness' (PS 175). Hence the ensuing attempt to assert one's freedom by enslaving other people. The paradox, now, is that it is the slave, not the master, who more nearly grows 'conscious of what he truly is', an independent being. This is primarily because, through work, he 'forms and shapes' his environment, thereby glimpsing that the world is not 'out and out other', but the product of human purpose (PS 195).

Still, a slave is a slave and not fully independent. Hence different strategies arise: to assert one's freedom by denying or downgrading the external world, so that there is nothing – or nothing that matters – to be 'cut off' from and constrained by. Here we encounter the sceptic, who denies this world altogether, and the Stoic who, indifferent to the world, identifies himself with his inner life. We encounter, too, 'the unhappy consciousness' of mediaeval religion (see p. 149). The physical world is not denied, but despised: hence such practices as asceticism and flagellation, and the yearning for a heaven of spirits no longer confined by bodily shackles. 'The unhappy consciousness' is therefore totally alienated, 'split in two' between the physical and spiritual realms.

This same split is there, but no longer perceived as cause for gloom, in the dualist theories of the 'Age of Reason'. Their strategy is to regard the world as a material mechanism intelligible to us rational creatures because of a divinely pre-established harmony between nature and mind. We are now at the threshold of once again finding ourselves 'at home' in the world, but have not yet crossed it. That we have not is apparent, first, from the Enlightenment view of our relationship to God as one to a remote, external designer; and second, from the Kantian view of human beings as rational selves struggling against their physical and emotional natures. We will temporarily leave Hegel's story at this threshold, since its completion requires an understanding of his moral and political philosophy, of which more later. First, I take up some unfinished business.

Hegel's history, recall, is meant to be the story of Spirit's or the Idea's progress in time. This reflects his idealist insistence that everything is a 'posit' or 'product' of Spirit. 'Spirit is the cause of the world' (EL 8), and this doctrine, Hegel holds, is the philosophical articulation of the 'deep' Christian insight that 'God created the world from nothing' (EL 128). By this doctrine, Hegel does not mean that the world is an illusion or dream. He is no 'subjective' or 'empirical' idealist. Nor does he mean that Spirit or God is a 'soul-thing' which created a world independent of itself. Spirit exists only in and through its 'expression' by nature and human beings.

Among the things Hegel certainly does intend are the following. There are no brute, unconceptualized sensory data, nor unconceptualizable entities like Kant's things in themselves. Second, matter cannot explain the things we experience in the absence of purposive agency, and both nature and human history can only be understood in terms of their goal – self-conscious freedom. In these and other respects, the world is more 'intelligent' and 'mind-like' than usually thought. Critics disagree as to whether Hegel intended more than this. 'Hegel's idealism . . . is ambiguous: [the] claim that . . . the [world-]process as a whole is, or is analogous to, a mind . . . might be interpreted as a thoroughgoing spiritualist doctrine or as a relatively modest doctrine concerning the conceptual structure of the world and humanity's historical development.'[23] On the second, 'modest' interpretation, Hegel's position would be the interesting, yet unstartling one that there can be no experience of the world except through concepts which human beings have historically developed. It is hard to square this, however, with Hegel's references to the world as 'caused' by Spirit and as the 'superficial outer rind' of the Idea (EL 8).

It may help to reflect on the following remark: 'nature is not something other than the Idea . . . , but the Idea . . . in the form of [its] uttering [Entäusserung]' (EL 18). Here we have the thought, similar to Spinoza's (see p. 272), that the Idea stands to the world as language does to its physical expression. Just as a system must, in order to count as a language, find a means of being expressed, so the Idea or Spirit requires 'vehicles' in the form of finite minds like our own. It requires, therefore, the existence of a spatio-temporal world as well: for minds have to be embodied, since their coming to consciousness and self-consciousness is possible only through intercourse with things in nature. Moreover, since nature can be thought by we 'vehicles' of Spirit, it must itself be articulated in accordance with the conceptual system of the Idea, and so is itself an expression of Spirit. Whether, so construed, Hegel's is a 'thoroughgoing spiritualist doctrine' could be debated. But his ambition was surely that of 'establishing anew the Greek *logos*, on the basis of the modern, self-knowing spirit'.[24] For Hegel, as for many earlier writers we have encountered, nature and history are the speech of God.

Ethics, Politics and Absolute Spirit

The Absolute Idealists, we saw, shared the romantics' preoccupation with unity, and this is apparent not only in the metaphysical efforts just described, but in their treatment of culture – of science, art, morality, politics, philosophy and religion. All of these must be closely related, since all are manifestations of the single 'I' or Spirit of which we are the 'vehicles'. Let us, then, turn to their attempts to incorporate these human practices within their general metaphysical vision.

In Kant's ethics, a pivotal role was played by the notion of freedom. Not only is the sense of duty testimony to our freedom of choice, but 'the good will' must be autonomous, legislating for itself principles of conduct. The autonomy and freedom of other people are, moreover, crucial considerations in determining conduct towards them. If anything, freedom is emphasized still more by the Idealists. Freedom is not only *our* most important feature, it is the essential aspect of reality itself, the absolute 'I' or Spirit. Through the realization of our freedom, the Absolute is realized. This is not incompatible with reality's possessing a rational and necessary order, for as Rousseau and Kant saw, true freedom is not that of whim or caprice, but of willing acceptance of what is rationally demanded. 'The highest independence of man,' wrote Hegel, 'is to know himself as totally determined by the absolute Idea' (EL 158). *Un*freedom, after all, is constraint by something 'external': once this 'something' is recognized as rational, the sense of its being a constraint evaporates. Only madmen resent the 'constraints' of the laws of logic.

With such a debt to Kant, it is no surprise that the Idealists promulgated their own versions of the categorical imperative. Schelling, for example, regards the proper demand that we should will only our own self-determination as 'nothing else but the categorical imperative . . . which Kant expresses'.[25] Self-determination, he argues, is the one thing that *all* rational beings can will, regardless of circumstance. Kant's dichotomy between the free, rational self and the empirical self, slave to the mechanisms of desire, is rejected, however. We can, of course, distinguish between actions that issue from reflection and ones inspired by, say, lust. But it is the whole human being, not just half of him or her, who strives for independence and self-determination. Even lust must be viewed in terms of this striving, for, as Fichte puts it, 'my impulse as a being of nature and my tendency as pure spirit [are] . . . one and the same original impulse'.[26] The moral agent is not at war with his 'lower' self, for pleasure and desire, properly channelled, play their role too in the self-determining life.

It is on Kant's isolation of a rational, moral self from the fuller context of life that Hegel focuses his criticism. He sees it as a prime symptom of that dualist thinking which characterized 'the Age of Reason', the point at which we broke off our sketch of his history of consciousness. For Hegel, a principle of duty arrived at from the armchair, by disengaged logic, is bound to be 'utterly indifferent to . . . any content' (PS 644). Kant's categorical imperative is 'empty', since any maxim of conduct can avoid inconsistency if formulated with care. The imperative, therefore, gives *carte blanche* to mere conviction, to doing whatever feels right, and hence to irresolvable moral posturings. Kant's error is to have elevated a morality of individual duty [*Moralität*] over the ethical order [*Sittlichkeit*], the public norms and principles which hold sway in a society. It is only as a participant in the latter, as a citizen, that a person's duties can be determined. The laws and customs of a community provide the content that armchair moral reasoning cannot. The community, though, has to be of the right kind: it has to be an authentic *State*.

Hegel's theory of the State, we saw earlier, helped spawn a wide variety of later ideologies. Dramatic references to the State as 'the perfect embodiment of Spirit' (PH 17) and 'a secular deity' (PR Add. 272) seem to favour a fascist interpretation, but let us look more closely. Like almost everything in Hegel, the State can be viewed from two dialectical perspectives: historically, as the outcome of less adequate forms of political organization, and conceptually, as 'sublating' or synthesizing 'one-sided' conceptions of social life. Reason demands the emergence of the State, and what reason demands, history eventually supplies. Historical precursors of the State include the Greek *pólis* and the Roman Empire. Both were doomed to extinction, but for opposite reasons: the former, because its unity was founded on unreasoned emotion; the latter, because it was held together only as a system of 'abstract right'. The former lacked the rational resources, the latter those of loyalty and patriotism, to contain dissension within tolerable limits and to respond to external threats.

Hegel's notion of the State becomes clearer with his claim that it is 'the unification of the family principle with that of civil society' (PM 535). The 'family' is a community held together by 'love', a 'union of hearts' and, as it were, a 'single person'. What it lacks are rational procedures for protecting individual interests: a lack made good in 'civil society', but at the price of any sense of community. Civil society is, in effect, society as viewed by social contract theorists like Locke: a 'heap of atoms', a collection of individuals rather grudgingly come together in order to pursue their interests more effectively than they could in the state of nature. Civil society is inherently unstable, for it cannot call on a sense of loyalty to keep the lid on the conflicts, like that between rich and poor, which are bound to arise. So, when the lid is off, anything goes: for nothing dictates obedience to the law except self-interest. When this is no longer served by the society, opposition to it takes the form of '*negative* action . . . the *fury* of destruction' (PS 589). The French Revolution and its Terror are the penalties paid by a society that is not a genuine community, and in which freedom is equated with the unobstructed pursuit of individual interests.

The State combines the 'moments' of truth in the 'family' and civil society. It is a community, resting on bonds of love and loyalty, but one in which citizens recognize themselves as autonomous individuals. In so doing, they do not regard government and its laws as 'alien' or as a 'necessary evil': rather, they willingly submit to them as the instruments of a rational system. Hence, 'when the State . . . constitutes a community . . . [and] when the subjective will of man submits to laws – the contradiction between liberty and necessity vanishes' (PH 39). Citizens do not resent the State, since they appreciate that they can only become individuals, only take on human identities, through participating in a community whose laws, traditions and ethos lend shape to their lives. They even see that 'all the worth which the human being possesses, . . . he possesses only through the State' (PH 39).

One might, after a claim like that, expect Hegel to propose an ingeniously novel form of political organization. Disappointingly, the Hegelian State is modelled on the constitutional monarchy of Prussia. There is limited, indirect franchise, with members of one of the Chambers representing the professions. There is rule of law and, by the standards of the time, considerable freedom of expression. What Hegel likes about these arrangements is their tendency to encourage individuals' identification with their State. The king, symbol of State unity, is a person whom the citizens can love; the loyalty they feel towards their professional guild is transferred to the State through the guild's participation in legislation; freedom of expression persuades them that their voices count. Hegel is aware of the difficulty in securing people's emotional identification with their community. Since Rousseau's recipe of a very small state, in which everyone knows each other, is unrealistic, the emergence of something like a 'general will' must be facilitated by constitutional arrangements. One thing is surely clear: despite slogans like 'the State is a secular deity', there is nothing remotely fascistic in the political arrangements he prescribes.[27]

The large claims Hegel makes for the State's role in realizing human freedom might make one think that, for him, political life is the supreme human activity. But this is not so: there are the higher activities of 'Absolute

Spirit' – art, religion, and philosophy. (A main merit of the State is that it provides the stable conditions under which these activities can flourish.) To understand Hegel's point about art, religion and philosophy, we need to recall two aspects of his view of freedom. First, freedom requires awareness of that freedom. 'A man is only free when he knows himself [to be free]' (PH 76). Second, we are aware of ourselves as free only when we cease regarding the world as 'out-and-out other', and instead see it as a mind-like manifestation, like ourselves, of Spirit. The activities of Absolute Spirit are articulations of this freedom, for they try to 'restore [our] unity' with the world after millennia of alienation from it (HP 42). It is through these activities that we become self-consciously free and 'at home' in the world.

Art and religion achieve this only partially, for they reveal the truth about human beings' unity with the cosmos only *symbolically*. (Schelling thought this was the most we could hope for, the Absolute being ineffably mysterious.) For example, the Christian doctrine of creation *ex nihilo* is a symbolic expression of the truth – awaiting rational articulation in Hegel's philosophy – that reality is nothing but Spirit. The happy conclusion of Hegel's philosophy, then, is that this very philosophy is the purpose of reality. Through its expression in Hegel's writings, Spirit becomes once more 'at home with itself', no longer alienated from nature, but this time at the level of articulate, rational self-consciousness (HP 80). This monumental conclusion was, unsurprisingly, soon to be challenged from a variety of quarters.

• 3 Philosophies of the Will •

Readers may turn with relief from the three thinkers just discussed in section 2, with their often impenetrable prose, to the very different trio which will now occupy us. Schopenhauer, Nietzsche and Kierkegaard are among the great stylists, and to this owe much of their belated influence on literature as well as philosophy. It is no accident, perhaps, that none of them were, except briefly, university teachers – a profession, in Nietzsche's view, of 'old maids', 'maggots' and 'chatterers'.

The title of this section is not ideal. For one thing, the notion of the will, of the 'striving' nature of the subject, was an important one for the Absolute Idealists, especially Fichte. Indeed, the idea that reality should be conceived by analogy with the human will has a long pedigree, one we have already encountered in Heraclitus and Leibniz, for example. For another thing, the role that the will plays among our trio is not the same in each case. But with these reservations, the title suitably highlights a crucial aspect of their thinking, and the one upon which their enthusiasts of the following century were to focus.

Schopenhauer and the Will to Live

Arthur Schopenhauer (1788–1860) belonged to a rich family of Danzig merchants, which allowed him, after brief flirtations with the family business and university lecturing, to enjoy the leisured existence of a man of letters. 'Enjoy' may be the wrong word, since even as a boy he tended, said his mother, to 'brood over the misery of things'.[28] He was embittered by the muted reception of *The World as Will and Representation* in 1818, and by his failure to woo students away from Hegel in Berlin; fortune did not smile until 1851, with the success of a collection of essays and aphorisms. By the time of his death, Schopenhauer was something of a cult figure, and his *magnum opus*, now expanded by fifty chapters, was having or was soon to have its impact upon, among others, Wagner, Tolstoy and Nietzsche. Despite his admiration for the gentle ways of the Indian sages, Schopenhauer was an unpleasant man. At least his shoddy treatment of women had the merit of consistency with the vitriolic view taken of their sex in 'On women'. (Deception is to the woman, he claimed, as claws are to the lion – and so on.)[29]

The two main ornaments in Schopenhauer's study – a statue of the Buddha and a bust of Kant – are a good clue to his overall philosophy. Let us begin with the aspects which owe to, but crucially deviate from, Kant. For Schopenhauer, as for his hero, the empirical world is 'my representation', since it is 'conditioned by the subject' who perceives and conceptualizes it (I 3).[30] Space, time and causal relations are not features of reality in itself, but imposed upon it by ourselves. Schopenhauer is, therefore, a transcendental idealist, rejecting both 'empirical idealism' and 'realistic dogmatism' on the ground that these treat something – mind and matter, respectively – as the unperceivable cause of our representations. That must be wrong since, as Kant showed, causality is a relation *among* representations, not between them and something else.

Kant was also right, says Schopenhauer, to insist that there must be a thing in itself, for we cannot escape the conviction that reality is more than our representation of it. Emotionally we cannot escape it, for without this conviction the world 'would pass us by like an empty dream' (I 99): it would be the 'veil of *māyā*', with nothing behind it. Intellectually we cannot escape it, for we are driven to understand the world as a whole in terms of an 'inner force' which holds our representations together coherently. By insisting that the thing in itself is unknowable, however, Kant prematurely gave up on solving 'the riddle of the universe'. He was right to do so if by 'know' one means 'perceive' or 'conceptualize', but he ignored a different, direct mode of knowledge. 'A way *from within* stands open to us to that real inner nature of things to which we cannot penetrate *from without*' (II 195). It is through *self*-knowledge that we can grasp the thing in itself: in particular, knowledge of ourselves as *will*.

Admittedly, we reason and think as well as desire and strive, but these intellectual faculties are subservient to the will. Like Freud, Schopenhauer piles up examples of unconscious desires distorting our rational activities.

The knowledge I have of my will is not of private, inner volitions, but that familiar non-inferential kind of knowledge of my body which enables me to tell, without looking, that I am now raising my foot. I am, therefore, no 'winged cherub without a body': indeed, 'my body and my will are one'. Or better, what I call 'my body' when I am aware of it through perception is the same as what I call 'my will' when I am aware of its activities in the non-inferential manner just illustrated. 'Willing and acting . . . are one' (I 99ff). Not much can be said about this embodied will, partly because it appears to us only under the aspect of time, in passing motives and actions, not as it is independently of categories we impose. Articulate knowledge also requires a distance between the knowing subject and the object known which does not obtain between me and my will. For such reasons, my will is 'not completely knowable . . . [and] does not appear quite naked' (I 197).

Still, Schopenhauer knows enough about it to make the grand claim that the will is not only the 'inner force' of human life, but the 'key to the inner being of every phenomenon in nature' (I 105). As such, and as non-spatial, non-temporal and unperceivable, it deserves the title 'thing in itself'. Schopenhauer's first argument for this conclusion is of the 'what else?' kind. 'What other kind of . . . reality could we attribute to the material world', given that reality cannot be represented and that the only unrepresentable thing we know of is the will? (I 105). The second argument is reminiscent of Schelling. If we look hard at nature – at nest-building, the metamorphosis of stagbeetles, rising sap, and even flowing water – we should conclude that everywhere 'the will is obviously at work . . . but in blind activity'. Everywhere we turn, there is 'impulse, . . . persistence and determination' (I 118).

The charitable thing is to regard such claims, not as the conclusions of seriously proposed arguments, but as the expression of a powerful, and not unfamiliar, vision. In Van Gogh's paintings, for example, 'the world . . . seems charged with a . . . boundless energy, as if permeated by a pulsating life and force . . . like that implicit in Schopenhauer's conception of the will'. It is clearly a vision which can 'to some eyes, in some moods . . . seem both compelling and authentic'.[31]

It will set the scene for the climax of Schopenhauer's philosophy to ask why, congenital rancour apart, he was so hostile to the 'sham philosophy' first concocted by Fichte, then 'applied' by Schelling, and 'ripened into real charlatanism' by Hegel, 'a man with a common mind' (II 12–13, 590). This animosity seems odd, given that he too subscribes to a kind of idealism, a vision of reality as mind-like. Admittedly, Schopenhauer affirms, while the three 'charlatans' deny, the thing in itself, but they are talking of different things.

Schopenhauer's thing in itself is the 'inner principle' manifested in human behaviour and in nature: something the Absolute Idealists did not deny. What they *did* deny was the thing in itself as the unperceivable, external *cause* of appearances: but so, too, did Schopenhauer. The real difference is over the character of that 'inner principle', which, for Schopenhauer, is a good deal less mind-like, less 'ideal', than for his opponents. First, the will is not an 'intelligence' or 'subject' which 'posits' the natural world. Nor is it purposive in the sense of tending towards some final goal, like freedom or self-consciousness. Crucially, its processes are not, like those of Hegel's Spirit, rational. Rather, it is 'blind activity', to which reason is subservient.

It is this power and blindness of the will which, for Schopenhauer, make the world and human life so wretched. We arrive, then, at his famous pessimism, one so cheerless that such dark visions of our condition as those of Heraclitus or Lucretius seem bullish by comparison. Existence is a 'mistake', and ours is the worst of all possible worlds, since anything still worse would disintegrate (II 605, 584). The litany of gloom continues: 'pain, not pleasure, is the positive thing'; 'the happiest moment of the happiest man is . . . falling asleep'; 'life is like a payment [whose] receipt is death'; 'life . . . ought to disgust us' (II ch. 46). The central thought is that, as victims of an insatiable will, our lives are a constant, frustrated search for satisfaction, punctuated by moments of respite which soon turn into boredom, upon which we set off once more on our febrile search.

Even this pessimism has its limits, however. To begin with, we can enjoy longer respite from the will through 'disinterested' aesthetic contemplation. We then manage to disengage from the ordinary world and occupy ourselves with the abstract essences or Platonic Forms of things, which the artist of genius is able to make palpable. Except, that is, the composer, whose music permits direct access to the will's operations, and is therefore an 'unconscious exercise in metaphysics' (I 264). A melody, for example, with its build-up and climax, can mimic human endeavour. (It is not explained how such direct access to the horrors of the will are an improvement on our normal condition.) Still more lasting relief from the will is afforded by the moral virtues. By exercising justice and, even more, the benevolent sympathy which unites one with others, a person resists the egoistic demands of the will. Albeit unconsciously, the virtuous person discerns the deep truth of 'the metaphysical identity of all beings' (II 600–1). Individuals are an illusion or superficial aspect of reality, since the will is common to everyone and everything. In one commentator's graphic metaphor, 'it is as if we are all pimples on the ocean of cosmic pus which constitutes the will'.[32]

Rejection of the reality of individual selves, as well as the emphasis on life as suffering, are Buddhist themes, of course. But the real reason for the statue of the Buddha in Schopenhauer's study is still to emerge. Virtuous behaviour was still a 'symptom' of taking individual wills as real and at best 'a means of advancing self-renunciation'. True salvation requires continuing this renunciation and completely 'denying the will-to-live', a 'euthanasia of the will' (II 606 and 637). This sounds like a recipe for suicide, and some of Schopenhauer's followers, like Eduard von Hartmann (1842–1906), did look forward to mankind's 'cosmic' suicide.[33] But Schopenhauer argues that the suicidal person is motivated by the desire to avoid further pain, and so is still in thrall to the will. Dying as a creature of will, he or she must continue to exist somewhere in 'the ocean of pus'. Only total denial of the will ensures the liberation spoken of by the Buddhists and releases us into the 'nothingness' of *nirvāṇa*.

One wonders how, if will is our 'inner principle', we *can* overcome it, and what, if anything, happens to us if we succeed in doing so. To these questions, Schopenhauer's answers are sketchy. It seems that the will, though it is our essential nature, produces a surplus intellectual energy capable of then turning against it, like an ungrateful child against a parent. We can, then, try to overcome the will, though ultimately this is something that just happens with some people, albeit after suitable preparation through aesthetic contemplation and the exercise of moral virtue. It is most likely to happen during old age when the will has anyway grown tired, or at death's door – a thesis Schopenhauer supports with the testimonies of murderers on the eve of their execution (II 631f.).

As to the fate of one who does renounce the will, little can be said. Whilst still alive, he will indeed differ from most of us. 'Nothing can distress or alarm him' and, like a Buddha, he 'looks back calmly and with a smile on the phantasmagoria of this world which was once able to move and agonize . . . his mind' (I 390). But the final will-less *nirvāṇa* which the person enters cannot be described, for it is a state to which we have access neither through perception nor by knowledge of our bodies. We must, then, be content with the 'darkness and veiled obscurity' of the mystic (II 610–11). From the perspective of human cognition, certainly, *nirvāṇa* can only be called 'nothing'. Yet we have the consolation that this might be 'merely a relative, not an absolute, nothing' (II 612). To us creatures of will, who only understand what we can perceive or conceptualize, this state is indeed a nothing. But 'conversely, to those in whom the will has turned and denied itself, this very world of ours with all its suns and galaxies, is – nothing' (I 412).

Nietzsche and the Will to Power

Nietzsche was a boy of eleven when Kierkegaard died in 1855, but we will reverse the chronological order because of the close connections between Nietzsche's and Schopenhauer's thought. Close, but complex: for the early adulation expressed in *Schopenhauer as Educator* gave way to the judgement that Schopenhauer's was a 'decadent' philosophy (WP 612).[34]

Friedrich Wilhelm Nietzsche (1844–1900) is one of the most striking figures in the history of ideas. His very features – the electric hair, ferocious moustache and blazing eyes, all of them gifts to a portraitist like Eduard Munch – are as etched in the memory as his aphorisms: 'God is dead', 'Some are born posthumously', and so on. Nietzsche's life confirmed his conviction that a philosophy is always a personal reflection of its author. The boyhood in a cloyingly feminine, Lutheran household; the unhappy spell as a Professor in Basel; the overheated friendship with Wagner, whose wife he was in love with, and the painful break with the composer after the first Bayreuth Festival – all find expression in Nietzsche's writings. As do the sick and lonely years wandering around Europe which Nietzsche – hopeless in relations with women and too morbidly sensitive for lasting friendships – spent before his mental collapse in 1889, when trying to protect a donkey from its brutal owner. During his final decade, Nietzsche was a virtual vegetable, incapable of appreciating the fame that his works were beginning to enjoy.

Nietzsche's influence on the literature of the following century – on André Gide, Thomas Mann, Stefan George, and Bernard Shaw, for example – is unparalleled among nineteenth-century philosophers. So too, with the fading of Marx's shadow and the erosion of Nietzsche's reputation as a precursor of Nazism, is his influence on recent philosophy in continental Europe. Even within the cooler Anglo-American tradition, he has been proclaimed 'the greatest moral philosopher of the past century'.[35] His appeal for many recent theologians and feminists is harder to divine, given his scorching remarks on both priests and women.

An unfortunate aspect of his status as 'the first deconstructor of metaphysics' which Nietzsche now enjoys among French 'postmodernists' – whose 'tribute' to his thought is 'to deform it, make it groan'[36] – is that it blinds us to the debt which he owed to earlier thinkers. From Heraclitus, he inherits a vivid sense of the world as an unstable flux; from Hume, or so he thinks, the idea that selves and substances are fictions which do not correspond to anything in the parade of passing phenomena which constitute the empirical world, the only one there is; and from Kant, the conviction that experience and judgement are possible only through our imposition of order on phenomena.

This inheritance is radicalized by superimposing upon Hume's and Kant's claims a Schopenhauerian emphasis on the will and a robust nominalist view of the importance of language. 'Concepts [are] only possible where there are words' (WP 506), for different things fall under a concept only in virtue of the same word being applied to them. Hume did not go far enough in complaining of our tendency to mistake mere similarity for .sameness, since even the similarities we purport to experience are functions of language. 'Dog' does not apply to creatures in themselves similar and forming a natural kind: rather, we make them similar by grouping them under a common label. We have to impose such groupings for communication and action to be possible. For the same reason, we require something like synthetic *a priori* categories. But these are not, as Kant thought, the fixed conditions for any experience to be possible: rather, they are the conditions we stamp upon the flux of sensory data 'for the sake of the preservation of creatures like ourselves' (BGE 11). With different needs, we would have imposed different 'perspectives' on experience – a different mathematics, say.

Nietzsche proceeds from here to some striking claims about truth and knowledge, such as 'truths are illusions of which one has forgotten that this is what they are'.[37] This is his dramatic way of rejecting the view that truth is correspondence between thought or language and reality. Truth cannot be this, since language imposes a structure on what we experience, which, in itself, it is without. Our 'will to power' – our urge to order our lives and the course of our experiences – requires that we 'impose upon becoming the character of being' (WP 617). Knowledge, too, if thought of as a correspondence between belief and reality, is our 'greatest fable'. Even Kant's *a priori* truths are actually 'false judgements', though none the worse for that, since 'belief in their truth' is necessary, at least for creatures like us (BGE 11).

Nietzsche is aware, however, that we require some workable distinction between truth and falsity, knowledge and mere belief. Hence, he offers us a pragmatic notion of truth and knowledge in terms of the 'pay off' which beliefs can have by way of conferring power on us and satisfying our needs. All belief is 'error', but within this error we can distinguish beliefs 'without which a certain kind of . . . being cannot live', and 'one may indeed speak of truth here'. The 'final determinant' of truth, in this sense, is a belief's 'value for life' – 'life', here, understood as will to power and order (WP 584, 493).

Nietzsche devotes less time to defending these claims than to showing why people are reluctant to accept them. Indeed, people's tendency is to go in the opposite direction and postulate a 'true world' populated by such staple ingredients of metaphysics as God, things in themselves, substances and selves. Part of the diagnosis is linguistic. Like Wittgenstein after him, Nietzsche laments our tendencies to suppose, first, that an entity must correspond to each meaningful noun, and second, that the subject–predicate distinction must be paralleled by one between substances and their properties. One reason why 'we are not free of God [is] because we still believe in grammar' (TI 3.5). Particularly tempting is to take 'I' as the name of an enduring entity, a self or soul, which is then illegitimately distinguished from the actions and experiences it does or has. Once we believe in souls, we are ready to accept other substances. Conversely, 'if we give up the soul, . . . the precondition for a "substance" in general is missing' (WP 485).

Grammar, however, could only seduce us if we were willing to be seduced. Nietzsche's explanation of this willingness belongs to moral psychology. Morality is a device used by the 'weak', the 'botched and bungled', to assert their will to power against the 'strong'. It serves not only to constrain the unbooted behaviour of the aggressive, but to nurture self-esteem. This 'herd morality' requires the notion of the self or soul: first, because moral blame and 'resentment' must be directed at something which can be punished for earlier misdeeds; and second, because by distinguishing my self from my actions, I can be consoled that *I*, the 'real' me, am not the weakling those actions suggest. The 'weak', then, 'need the belief in the . . . subject out of an instinct for . . . self-affirmation' (GM I.13).

In fact, it is the 'true world' in general that the 'weak' need to believe in. Unable to take the world as it is – for it is one in which they lose out – they must 'imagin[e] another, *more valuable* one' (WP 579). The denizens of the 'true world', notably God and 'objective' values, are also of strategic value: for if the 'strong' can be persuaded that their behaviour infringes a divinely sanctioned moral law, they are likely to desist from it. Values, including moral ones, are for Nietzsche invented and imposed, not discovered, and different valuations reflect the contrasting needs and routes to power of different kinds of people. The vested interest of the 'weak' is in the moral values, like pity and altruism, for these are 'advantageous to the "suffering"' (WP 266). Despite pronouncements like 'there are no moral facts' (TI 6.1), Nietzsche is not, strictly, a moral relativist. So successful have the 'weak' been in hijacking the meaning of moral terms that it is now true by definition that pity, say, is a moral value (GM I). Someone, like Nietzsche himself, who rejects such values is an 'immoralist' and his own 'table of values' is 'moraline-free', 'beyond good and evil'. Actually, he does not reject moral values *tout court*: they are, after all, suited to the 'herd', but not, as we'll see, to those of a 'higher' breed.

To the extent that he denies 'objective' values, Nietzsche embraces a form of nihilism, 'the radical repudiation of value [and] meaning' beyond those which we confer (WP 1). That the world itself is without value and meaning is the main point of the announcement that 'God is dead'. Nietzsche is keen, however, to dissociate himself from those nihilists who respond to this news in negative, life-denying ways. These include bomb-throwing nihilists 'on the St Petersburg model', who rage against existence, and – more threatening in the long term – purveyors of a 'passive' nihilism, the product of weariness and a symptom of a 'decline and recession of the spirit' (WP 22ff). There is, for example, 'the last man': an easy-going egoist who pursues pleasure, not out of a lust for life, but because he has no real aims, and who tolerates diversity, not out of liberal conviction, but because life is smoother if he brays assent to the ways of his fellow-men (Z Prologue 5). Worst of all are the preachers of a 'new Buddhism', whose 'gloom and unmanly tenderness' make them prefer 'nothingness' to the actual world (BGE 202). Nietzsche's target here, of course, is Schopenhauer. The latter was right to see human existence, and indeed the whole of nature, as the expression of will, but wrong to bemoan it on that count. His 'ideal' of 'extinction' is the opposite to that of 'the most . . . alive, and world-affirming human being . . . who wants to have *what was and is* repeated into all eternity' (BGE 56). Nietzsche believed that the whole course of the world was endlessly repeated, though the real importance for him of 'eternal recurrence' was that a person's attitude towards it – joy or horror – provided the acid-test of an affirmative *versus* a negative view of life.

Nietzsche's notorious Overman (*Übermensch*) is someone who responds to 'the death of God' in a fully 'world-affirming' way. He is 'the sense of the earth' (Z Prologue 3), since it is to his condition that everyone who can aspire should aspire. Contrary to the Nazis' interpretation, Overmen are not to be some ruling elite; on the contrary, they will be pretty solitary beings who disdain politics as 'not worth enough for the most gifted spirit to concern himself with' (D 3.179). It is not politics, but *art*, 'the only counterforce . . . to the denial of life', which is the Overman's medium. (Such, at any rate, is the doctrine of Nietzsche's last writings, as indeed it had been, in a somewhat different form, of his first major work, *The Birth of Tragedy*.) For it is only when a person 'rejoices as an artist' that he fully 'enjoys himself as power' (WP 853). It is not that the Overman is more lavishly endowed with will to power than the rest of us: rather, he faces up to the fact that he is essentially will to power, accepts it, and acts accordingly.

The 'art' which the Overman practises must be taken in a wide sense. For him, the world and he himself are 'works of art': in themselves shapeless, they need to be given form, to be 'created', as much as a symphony or sculpture does (WP 795–6).[38] The Overman 'overcomes' himself, imposing structure and narrative order on the motley of appetites and experiences which we misleadingly dub 'the self'. In its way, morality, too, serves to lend order to people's lives, but moral values inhibit the directions life can take in a manner incompatible with the free creativity of the Overman-artist. They are values for those without the strength to shoulder the responsibility of 'making themselves' and imposing their own 'perspectives' on the world.

Nietzsche's descriptions of the Overman are sketchy: after all, such a person has not yet emerged. Perhaps the fullest indication we get as to the kind of person Nietzsche has in mind is his tribute to Goethe:

> What he wanted was *totality*: he struggled against the separation of reason, the senses, feeling, and will . . . he disciplined himself to wholeness, he *created* himself . . . he said 'Yes' to everything that related to him . . . [and] conceived of a person who would be strong . . . self-controlled, self-reverent, who would dare

allow himself the whole compass . . . of what is natural, who would be strong enough for this freedom. (TI 8.49)

There is an irony, however, in Nietzsche's ideal of the Overman-artist. Not even this figure is able to live with the world just as it is, even if he is able to say 'Yes' to the world in a way that the moralist and the priest, with their self-delusion of a better 'true world', cannot. 'Artists must not see things as they are, but fuller, simpler, stronger' (WP 800). Art may be the supreme manifestation of will to power, an imposition of 'being' upon 'becoming': but by that very token, it also manifests a 'will to falsification'. Indeed, 'we possess art lest we perish of truth' (WP 822). For Nietzsche, then, there can be no life which is fully in harmony with the world, no entirely 'natural' life. Less radically than Schopenhauer, perhaps, Nietzsche nevertheless rejects the romantics' ideal of a life that is at once honest and imbued with a sense of unity with the cosmos. The Overman honestly recognizes that he, like everything else in nature, is a process of will. But in his exercise of that will in the art of living, he is bound, like the sculptor with his initially shapeless materials, to impose forms on the world which, in reality, it is without.

Kierkegaard and the Will to Believe

Nietzsche and Kierkegaard are often paired, with some justice, as the two *enfants terribles* of nineteenth-century philosophy and the twin 'fathers of existentialism'. This is despite the central difference that whereas, for the one, God is 'dead', for the other, the 'God-relationship' is the one thing that should finally matter to us.

One feature they certainly share is the reflection in their works of their lives and personalities. Søren Kierkegaard (1813–55), who rarely left his native Copenhagen, was the son of a rich, pious, manic depressive. The titles of some his books – *The Sickness Unto Death*, *Fear and Trembling*, and so on – do not suggest a sunny disposition on his part either. Indeed, he describes himself as 'melancholy, soul-sick' but, to compensate, of 'immense intelligence' (J 243).[39] After a spell as a young man-about-town, Kierkegaard became engaged and trained for the Church. His sudden renunciation of both marriage and career was something with which, in several of his writings, one can see Kierkegaard trying to come to terms. The most philosophically significant of his works were written during the frenetic years 1843 to 1846. His plan then to retire to the country seems to have been spoiled by the cruel treatment of his views and unprepossessing physique in a Danish periodical. Kierkegaard's revenge, in his later writings, took the form of vitriolic attacks on Copenhagen society and its Lutheran Church.

An odd feature of his best-known works, the 'aesthetic' ones, like *Either/Or*, is their pseudonymous authorship, though without any intention to disguise the real identity of their author. Much ink has been spilled over the import of this 'indirect communication'. Was the point to distance himself from the positions taken in the books? Or to register, as Kierkegaard suggests, his sense that it was divine 'Governance', not a flesh-and-blood man, responsible for the views expounded (CUP 553)? Or could it be that, a century ahead of his time, pseudonymity, along with irony and much else, were among the 'major tools of deconstructive theory' he employed to 'defer' any definite meaning or message being attached to his words?[40] Whatever the answer, it is sometimes risky to ascribe certain views expressed in his writings to Kierkegaard himself, though it would be tedious to obey his instruction never to quote *him*, but only his pseudonyms.

The 'deconstructive' interpretation is not untypical of recent exaggerations of Kierkegaard's freakness as a philosopher. It can be salutary, in understanding him, to stress his continuity with, as well as differences from, earlier thinkers, notably Kant and Hegel. With Kant – though Kierkegaard rarely mentions the great man – there are three important points of contact. First, they are agreed that the data furnished by the senses do not provide a sufficient basis for making judgements about the world. For Kant, the slack is taken up by synthetic *a priori* principles which we contribute. For Kierkegaard, however, our contribution is an exercise of *will*. 'Belief is not a knowledge but . . . an expression of will' and 'doubt can only be terminated . . . by an act of will', a 'will to believe' (PF 82–3). Second, the two men agree that we feel a compulsion to believe some things – notably, that God exists – which not only go beyond the warrant of sensory evidence, but go beyond conceptual understanding. 'We want to discover something that thought cannot think' (PF 37). But whereas for Kant God is a postulate which reason is driven to make in order to explain the world as a totality, for Kierkegaard He is the object of a 'leap of faith'. The Christian God, an eternal being who enters into time in the form of Jesus, is an 'absolute paradox'. It is a 'passion for paradox', not a search for understanding, which inspires that 'leap' (PF 37ff.).

There are strong echoes, finally, of Kant's 'two selves' doctrine. 'Man is a synthesis of the infinite and the finite, of the temporal and the eternal, of freedom and necessity' (SUD 340). For Kant, the 'two selves' are, albeit mysteriously, united: but, in Kierkegaard's view, their unity or synthesis is an *achievement*. It is because few of us succeed in achieving this that 'man is not yet *a self*', but a battleground of warring factions. Here, as with the previous points of contact, what stands out is the role that Kierkegaard, unlike Kant, gives to the will. It is through the will that beliefs about the world, faith in God and the achievement of selfhood are made possible, even if he sometimes suggests that, in the latter two cases, 'grace' may also be required (PF 62).

That the individual faces a 'truly difficult' task in 'holding together' the 'two selves' (CUP 273, 268) implies a criticism of Hegel, a philosopher to whom his relationship is well charted by Kierkegaard himself. If Hegel is right, the embodied person is an 'expression' of infinite Spirit, and once he or she reflects upon this, any sense of being a dual creature will disappear. Kierkegaard complains, however, that Hegel's system cannot accommodate the 'existing individual' at all. An individual's relation to himself is not a 'cognitive' one and 'abstract thought is extraneous to the movement of existence' in which he is embroiled (CUP 278). Each of us is too unique, our situations too concrete, for Hegelian abstractions to provide us with a sense of individuality. It follows that Hegel's system is incapable of guiding me in the 'decisive steps' I must take in life. Indeed, it deters people from facing up to the decisions which shape their lives by treating them as, for example, mere 'accidents' of the State, whose laws and traditions they are to obey. It encourages, instead, a passive identification with the anonymous 'Public'. Hegel, then, is guilty of a 'pantheistic contempt for the individual man' (CUP 317), of submerging him in a totality. The use of 'pantheistic', here, is not mere rhetorical flourish, for another criticism of Hegel is of his treatment of religion as a symbolic expression of the metaphysical truth that absolute Spirit exists only in and through the cosmos which 'expresses' it. This, Kierkegaard argues, is a betrayal of the Christian truth that God is entirely transcendent of the world and ourselves.

Despite these criticisms, the Dane is not without admiration for Hegel. For one thing, he appreciates Hegel's diagnosis of the normal human condition as one of alienation. It is painfully true, as Hegel saw, that someone who sees himself as a distinct, atomic individual may experience a 'terrible . . . cosmic isolation . . . alone with his dreadful responsibility' (FT 107). Hence the attractions of believing oneself to be an integral component in an ethical community and even an 'expression' of the world-spirit. Second, Kierkegaard is impressed by the broad strategy of dialectic, at any rate by the idea that one fully grasps certain matters only by passing through earlier or less adequate stages.

Here we encounter one of the best-known topics of Kierkegaard's thought, the 'stages on life's way'. It has been well-said that he turns Hegel's dialectic not, like Marx, 'upside down', but 'outside in'.[41] For the story he tells is that of a person's inner development from a stage of 'untruth' to one of being 'in the truth'. The 'aesthetic', and first, stage has nothing especially to do with art. 'Aesthetic' figures include Don Juan (the 'sensuous–erotic spirit'), the flippant dilettante who 'plays badminton with life', and the cool seducer who plays with other people's lives. What is common to such figures is that they live 'immediately': they live 'constantly . . . in the moment', 'absorbed in moods', governed by caprice. They are dependent on 'conditions outside [themselves]', on external stimulation, and hence are subject to 'the occasion' (E/O II 234ff). The life of someone at the second, 'ethical' stage, in contrast, is 'mediated' by principles, notably those which apply to his or her station in life, as citizen, mother, or whatever. It is what Hegel called *Sittlichkeit*, social morality, which Kierkegaard generally intends by 'the ethical'. Finally, at the 'religious' stage, it is faith in God which determines one's life – a faith which can conflict with ethical demands. Kierkegaard illustrates this conflict by Abraham's readiness to sacrifice his son at God's bidding. If we admire Abraham for this, it indicates that, for certain people in certain situations, there is a standard higher than the norms of morality. 'Faith's paradox is . . . that the single individual is higher than the universal.' The person of faith's life is not ruled by principles: rather his relationship to principles is determined 'through his relation to the Absolute', to God (FT 97).

It is sometimes suggested that Kierkegaard refuses to plump for one stage of life in preference to the others, and that he is therefore advancing 'the distinctively modern standpoint . . . [that] . . . commitment [is] the expression of criterionless choice . . . for which no rational justification can be given'.[42] It is true, certainly, that he emphasizes the role of the will, as against rational proof, in converting people to the ethical and religious stages. He does, however, offer considerations in favour of living ethically rather than aesthetically, and yet of a willingness as well to 'suspend the ethical' where faith requires it. To begin with, 'everyone who lives aesthetically is in despair', by which Kierkegaard means, not a state of desperate gloom, but a sense that one's life is without point (E/O II 197). But this sense is potentially present even in the ethical life, engaged as it is only with the things of this world. The true 'opposite of being in despair is believing' (SUD 351), for only in the 'God-relationship' is the otherwise senseless, mundane routine transcended. Relatedly, it is only through Christian faith, with the hope of redemption and atonement it offers, that one can cope with the burden of sin that may accompany even the most impeccably ethical life.

Such arguments may sound merely therapeutic: have faith or your life will always be liable to feelings of despair and guilt! But, for Kierkegaard, such feelings intimate what we truly are. In despair, one recognizes that 'a higher form of existence is an imperative' (E/O II 197), and the sense of sin indicates the existence of a God in comparison with whom we are wretched creatures indeed. Through these feelings, moreover, a person recognizes what it is to be a genuine self. The despair which afflicts the aesthetic life is a 'point of departure' for conceding that I have not yet chosen 'this self of mine', that in effect I have not yet chosen to be free, since my life still 'hinges upon a condition outside of itself' (E/O II 218, 240). Guilt, too, is an 'expression of the self-assertion of [my] existence' CCUP 470): an experience of individual responsibility for myself which cannot be unloaded onto society or fate.

Before pursuing this point, we should note a feature of Kierkegaard's thought which, at first blush, seems to contradict the suggestion that the movement through the three stages is a progressive one. I refer to his pronouncement that 'truth is subjectivity'. This Protagorean–sounding slogan seems to preclude Kierkegaard from judging that a certain way of life is better for another person. But despite occasional references to 'a truth which is true *for me*' or to 'inwardness at its maximum proving to be objectivity' (J 178), Kierkegaard does not hold either that the truth of a belief is relative to the believer or that intensity of conviction is a criterion of truth. If it were, no sense could be made of his view that there is more (subjective) truth in a heathen's sincere worship of an (objectively) false God than in a Christian's facile worship of the true God (CUP 179f). Kierkegaard does not deny that there are objective truths: 'if the object to which he is related is the truth, the subject is [in a sense] . . . in the truth' (CUP 178). In many areas of belief, especially religion, we are inevitably confronted, however, with 'objective uncertainties', so that speculation on the objective truth of the beliefs is a waste of time. What we should then do is focus on the 'individual's relationship' to his belief, for this too can be assessed for its truth in a different sense of 'truth' – that, roughly, of sincerity or authenticity.

Far from contradicting the claim that the religious stage is the highest, the slogan 'truth is subjectivity' confirms it, since only the religious person, the Christian in particular, can stand in a fully authentic relationship to his or her belief. First, it is only a passionate faith in God that accommodates what is intimated by the senses of despair, guilt and the infinite, eternal aspect of the self. Such a faith, moreover, is the supreme exercise of that freedom which is inseparable from genuine selfhood. Precisely because the Christian God is an 'absolute paradox', it requires 'tremendous exertion . . . [and] responsibility' genuinely to believe in Him. Finally, the self is only fully individualized through faith, for it is when 'alone before the face of God' that someone 'venture[s] wholly to be oneself, as . . . this definite individual man' (SUD 341). *My* 'God-relationship' is like no one else's, so that it is through commitment to that relationship and 'dying to' the mundane order in which I am relatively anonymous, that my uniqueness is realized.

Since my individuality is secured in the 'God-relationship', this is not a mystic union with God. For Kierkegaard, as for 'negative' theologians, God cannot be understood or described: but unlike most of them, he insists that God is wholly 'other', not the all-embracing One into which, mysteriously, we somehow disappear.[43] In rejecting such a union, Kierkegaard is, like Schopenhauer and Nietzsche – though for very different reasons – abandoning the romantic ambition of unity or integration with the order of reality. I live 'in the truth' not when I recognize myself to be an 'expression' of the Absolute, ultimately indistinguishable (as Hölderlin put it) from what surrounds me, but when I resolve to regard myself as immeasurably distanced from a transcendent 'Power' in which, nonetheless, my existence is 'grounded' (SUD 341).

• 4 Marxism and Social Darwinism •

The philosophers discussed in section 3 had no sympathy for Hegel's vision of history as the rational progress of Absolute Spirit, let alone for his belief that its goal had been reached in the Germany of their century. These antipathies were shared by most of that group of German writers who flourished during the twenty years after Hegel's death in 1831, known as 'Young (or Left) Hegelians'. What united the group was rejection of Hegel's confidence that reason and freedom were already on full display. If, as he put it, 'the rational is the actual', the visible ills of contemporary society surely demonstrated that it was not yet fully 'actual', but still riven with contradictions and doomed to pass. Few of these young men, either, were able to swallow the metaphysics of Absolute Spirit. Spirit there may be, but its properties and operations are simply those of finite human minds.

Towards Marxism

The Young Hegelians did not, however, get their name for nothing. They shared with the master a conception of history as the struggle of human beings to overcome their alienation from nature and one another, and so to enjoy a freedom that would not sever them from the natural order of things. They also shared his confidence in rationality, to the extent of a conviction that this struggle must eventually be victorious, so that people will finally achieve the unity they seek. In these respects, they belonged to the tradition of Hegel in a way that Schopenhauer, Nietzsche and Kierkegaard certainly did not.

The ambivalence of the Young Hegelians towards their mentor was especially apparent in the area of religion. Like Hegel, they regarded religious belief as an essential development in the story of human consciousness, yet one that could not be taken at face value. But whereas Hegel construed Christianity as symbolic of the metaphysical truths he himself articulated, and so as something to cherish, the tendency of his followers was to regard it as a collection of mere myths, expressive of the ills of human life, and hence as something to overcome. For David Strauss, future victim of Nietzsche's polemics and author of the iconoclastic *Life of Jesus* in 1835, Christianity cannot, since it consists of rechauffé Jewish myths, claim superiority over other religions. It was left to Ludwig Feuerbach (1804–72), however, to extend the critique of religion in a manner that was to have an enduring impact upon philosophy and anthropology alike.

Feuerbach's name is best-known from the eleven 'Theses on Feuerbach' in which Marx at once savaged him and betrayed a great debt to him. Today, as Marx's star wanes, Feuerbach's rises. Being a 'precursor' of Marxism is now, in some circles, less of a disadvantage than being its founder. Certainly there is little warrant for Isaiah Berlin's dated characterization of Feuerbach as an 'uninspired mediocrity' who had the luck to ignite Marx's spark.[44] Excluded by his hostility to religion from university teaching, Feuerbach devoted his time to establishing that 'the secret of theology is anthropology'.[45] Human beings, unable to realize an ideal or even satisfactory life under prevailing conditions, project their ideal onto an alien being, God. Religion, therefore, is 'the separation of man from himself', a register of the gulf between how he actually is and how he yearns to be. This gulf is due, in large part, to people's sense of vulnerability in the face of a hostile natural world: a sense that is partially alleviated by construing that world as divinely ordered.

For Feuerbach, religious belief – indeed, belief in general – is not autonomous. 'Thought is a product of being, not being of thought . . . [and] the essence of being is . . . nature.' At times, he sounds like the crudest of eighteenth-century materialists: 'Food becomes blood, blood becomes . . . brain . . . and mind-stuff. . . . Man is what he eats.' But Feuerbach's materialism, though he may have believed that we are nothing but matter, is not a thesis about the stuff of reality. It is, rather, the naturalistic insistence that the development of human consciousness, including religion, can only be explained in terms of the material conditions of life, of human beings' engagement with the natural world of which they are parts. This is why Hegel, for whom natural processes are products of Spirit, must be 'stood on his feet'.

If religious belief is a product of alienation, it also serves to intensify it. By investing in God all that is worthwhile, people come to view themselves as pitiful by contrast, as 'the essence of all nothingness'. Religion must, therefore, be abolished if human beings are to relate to themselves and each other in a proper way. Or rather, 'politics must become our religion': a 'politics' of human relationships in which people's natural urge to live together in freedom and love, standing to one another as 'I' to 'Thou', is released and satisfied.

Absent from Feuerbach's discussion is much by way of economic and social criticism of human conditions. Not so from the writings of Moses Hess (1812–75) who, like several Young Hegelians, was not only a social critic, but a socialist. Hegel was right that the true human ambition is freedom, in the sense of 'the self-awareness of active spirit, the replacement of natural determination by self-determination'.[46] But this cannot be achieved, as Rousseau appreciated, when men are set against the natural environment, each other and their own better selves by a system of private property which fosters exploitation and greed. Nor can people feel 'at home' in a world whose objects are owned and valued only for what they can fetch on the market.

By the early 1840s, then, there were current in Young Hegelian circles both a materialist (or naturalistic) attitude towards the forms of human consciousness and the perception that people's abiding aspirations require the abolition of private property. The scene was set, therefore, for the confluence of these currents. This was to be the project of a young German described by Hess, in 1841, as 'Rousseau, Voltaire, Holbach, Lessing, Heine and Hegel united in one person . . . – Dr. Marx'.[47]

Marx on Alienation

Karl Marx (1818–83), born in the Rhineland to Jewish parents, became Dr Marx in 1841, having switched from the drunken, duelling life of a law student to the serious study of philosophy. Involvement with the most radical Young Hegelians soon forced him into exile, to Paris, then Brussels and finally, in 1848, after the publication of the *Communist Manifesto* and embroilment in the revolutionary events of that year, to London. Unable or unwilling to find regular paid work, Marx devoted the following decades to a massive programme of historical and economic research. His family's straitened circumstances were partly alleviated by his friend and collaborator, Friedrich Engels (1820–95), who ran a textile firm in Manchester, and whose other services to his friend included feigned paternity of Marx's illegitimate son. Marx was not a well-known figure until the gradual success, especially in Russia (despite its shortage of proletarians), of Volume 1 of *Capital* (1867). Engels' boast, in his graveside speech, that Marx was 'the best hated . . . man of his time', yet 'mourned by millions of revolutionary fellow-workers', was hyperbolic.[48] Marx died an unhappy man: ill, burnt-out, bitter at his lack of impact, and broken by the deaths of the two Jennys, wife and daughter.

Engels' boast would have been true only a few decades later. People seeking to show that philosophy can, as Marx put it, not only interpret the world but change it (TF 158),[49] often cite his incomparable influence upon recent history. This is misleading: most of his overtly philosophical writings, during the 1840s, were not published until nearly a century later. It was less Marx the philosopher than Marx the pamphleteer, historian and economist who was to 'shake the world'. Indeed, the Kremlin line on those early writings was that they reflected a youthful romanticism which fortunately disappeared by the time of *Capital*. Other Marxists discern in those writings a profound 'humanism' which can still be observed, by the sensitive reader, in the 'tougher' later works.[50]

In the early works, Marx moves rapidly from criticizing Young Hegelian recipes for religious (especially Jewish) emancipation to a call for communism, the abolition of all private property. The move is made *via* a discussion of 'alienated (or externalized) labour'. Marx shared Hegel's view of philosophy as the endeavour to emancipate people from millennia of alienation. It is because the existence of a proletariat is the most vivid testimony to that condition that 'philosophy can only be realized by the abolition of the proletariat' (HPR 124). This abolition, communism, is also 'the positive abolition of . . . human self-alienation' (EP 149). That is why it should be the goal, and not because, as for 'utopian' socialists, it is required by ideals of equality or universal rights (notions which Marx derided). The point is not, however, that 'private property [is] the cause of externalized labour': on the contrary, it is its 'consequence', in the sense of being a form in which alienation 'presents' or 'expresses' itself (EP 142ff). The roots of both alienation and private property lie deeper.

Religion, too, is an expression of alienation, with its roots in the natural conditions of life. Thus far, Marx agrees with Feuerbach. What the older man failed to recognize, though, was that the 'religious temperament' is a 'social product', the function of 'a particular form of society', not of man's insecurity in the midst of hostile nature (TF 157). 'Religion is the sigh of the oppressed creature . . . the opium of the people', addiction to which blots out awareness of that oppression (HPR 115). It follows that there can be no emancipation from religion through political action alone. Only a revolutionary transformation of underlying social conditions can succeed in this. When it does, there will be no further need for the State, premissed as it is on the conflicts which arise where economic oppression prevails. As Engels was to put it, the State will 'wither away' when there are no longer these conflicts to keep in check.

By 'alienation', Marx did not have in mind that divide between spirit and nature that Hegel had. For Marx, it is a complex phenomenon with several distinguishable aspects. With three of these, we can be brief. 'Under existing conditions', people are alienated from 'the products of [their] labour', from the 'act of production', and from one another. What a man produces does not belong to him and is not, so to speak, an extension of his being; his production of it is something imposed upon him as an 'alien activity'; and he is in hostility with other men, especially 'the master[s] of [his] labour' (EP 137ff). It is worth distinguishing two levels, 'material' and 'conscious', at which these forms of alienation operate. Not only, for example, is labour actually imposed upon the worker, but he experiences it as such: not as something to take pride in, but as an exigency. Not only is he exploited by others, but this colours a whole antagonistic perception of other people.

These themes persist, couched in different terms, in Marx's later works. In *Capital*, the idea that the products of labour become alien to the producer transmutes into that of the 'fetishism of commodities'. According to his 'labour theory of value', the only value of a product is the amount of human effort that went into producing it. Yet under capitalism, products are wrongly assigned a value independent of this input of labour, rather as those other 'productions of the human brain', the gods, get regarded as 'independent beings endowed with life' (C 447).

Granted that people are, in their capacity as workers, alienated in the above respects, why does Marx insist that their lives *qua* human beings are thereby alienated? For an answer, we need to turn to a fourth respect, alienation from one's 'species-being (or -essence)' (*Gattungswesen*). Put crudely, the alienated worker is an estranged human being since it is in work that the essence of humanity is located. To identify the 'species-being' of humans, which each of us should aim to realize in our lives, we must ask what essentially distinguishes human beings from animals. The answer is, the way in which humans *produce*. Animals, such as bees, can produce things, but only 'under the domination of direct physical need'. For people, however, production can and should be a 'free conscious activity', a 'working upon' and creative transformation of 'inorganic nature'. Man, unlike the bee, 'creates according to the laws of beauty', and not simply as a necessary means to subsistence. Or rather, that is how things should be. 'Under existing conditions', work is alienated precisely because it has made of man's 'life activity, his essence, a mere means for his existence' (EP 137ff).

What are these 'existing conditions' responsible for alienation from our essential humanity? It is not, we saw, private property and class divisions, for these 'express' rather than cause 'externalized labour'. The culprit is soon identified. 'How can it be . . . that the forces of their own lives gain control over [people]? The answer, in a word, is – the division of labour.'[51] With the division of labour comes specialization, so that a hunter or a literary critic 'must remain so if he does not want to lose his . . . livelihood'. This intolerably constrains the 'free conscious activity' which manifests our humanity. Hence, in the communist society, with the division of labour abolished, I can hunt, fish, herd sheep and discuss books each day 'without ever becoming hunter, fisherman, shepherd or critic' (GI 177). A further effect of the division of labour is to create the necessity for commerce, which requires that goods take on an 'abstract exchange-value', independent of the value of the labour invested in them. Society is then *en route* to the 'fetishism of commodities'. With considerations like this, we are already engaged with the 'historical materialism' which, by 1846, Marx was articulating.

Historical Materialism

The claim that human beings are essentially distinguished from animals by their capacity for a certain kind of production tells us nothing, as it stands, about the impact of methods of production on people. Marx, therefore, moves far too quickly from the essentialist remark that 'as individuals express their life, so they are' to the conclusion that 'the nature of individuals thus depends on the material conditions determining their production' (GI 164). It was soon to become his ambition, however, to establish that conclusion through the examination of history. Like Feuerbach's materialism, Marx's historical materialism is not a thesis about the stuff of reality. It is, rather, to the effect that the engine which drives human development in all areas of life is 'sensuous practical activity'. Here is the classic statement of the thesis:

> In the social production of their life, men enter into definite relations . . . [of] production [which] correspond to a definite stage of development of their material forces of production. . . . The mode of production of material life determines the social, political and intellectual life process in general. (CPE 159–60)

Marx's scheme is as follows: material forces (the use of resources to produce things) determine the relations of production (property and class relations), which in turn determine the legal and political 'superstructure' of society and its forms of consciousness (religion, philosophy, and so on). The term 'ideology' is sometimes used to refer to this superstructure, but more often only to the forms of consciousness. The point of the term is to stress that these forms are not autonomous, but emerge as functions of economic class interests. Renaissance thought, according to Engels, was merely 'the philosophical expression' of 'the development of the small and middle burghers into a big bourgeoisie' (SW 397).

The dynamics of history are the changes in material forces, owing primarily to technological development, which bring in their wake changes at all the other levels just mentioned. 'The handmill gives you society with the feudal lord, the steam mill society with the industrial capitalist.'[52] Typically, a material change occasions conflict between the dominant economic class and an emerging one better equipped to exploit the new developments. This is why 'the history of all hitherto existing society is the history of class struggles'. In all these struggles, it was the emerging class, the one in tune with the new productive forces, which was victorious. The old property relations became 'fetters' on those forces and 'had to be burst asunder'. It will be no different in the future. Capitalism has unleashed vast productive forces which it cannot effectively develop or control. In wage labour, which becomes increasingly impoverished and resentful, capitalism has produced its own 'grave-diggers. Its fall and the victory of the proletariat are . . . inevitable' (M 203, 209, 217). This victory is the final one, for it marks the abolition of property and hence of class conflict. History as we have known it is over, and a new uncharted history of humanity can begin.

Historical materialism is intended as an empirical theory, to be confirmed or otherwise by historical and sociological evidence. But is it? Critics have argued that Marx's 'technological determinism' is incoherent. It cannot be an *empirical* fact that productive forces determine social relations, which in turn determine a legal/political superstructure, since these three levels cannot be separated. Social relations, notably those of property ownership, are in part *constituted* by legal and political arrangements, and those relations are surely built into the processes of production. It is then a dull truism, not a striking sociological discovery, that where productive forces change, so must the rest.[53] But this criticism is unconvincing. We might, first, distinguish between the relations of *power* that obtain between different classes in society and the legal/political enshrinement of those relations. Second, we can distinguish between the productive forces available and the social relations required to exploit them. That power relations typically generate their own superstructural enshrinement, and that they are generated by the availability of productive forces, would then remain empirical claims.

Marx is not yet in the clear, however. Once he goes beyond manifestos and gets down to detailed explanation, he often concedes that social and political events can effect the development of production, as in the case of the English 'bourgeois revolutions' of 1642 and 1688. If these concessions go too far, what substance is left to his explanatory scheme? No one, after all, denies that there are intimate connections between technology, social relations and politics. If, on the other hand, the concessions are too modest, then not only is Marx denying the obvious reciprocity between these factors, but the resulting 'technological determinism' seems hardly to square with the persistent emphasis on human beings' responsibility for their destiny. Engels might proclaim that men 'make their history themselves', but what does this amount to when, in the same breath, he stresses that 'uncontrolled forces are far more powerful' than those which are planned? (SW 75).

Perhaps, though, Marx's point is this: social and political developments, like those in seventeenth-century England, are not *caused* by technological change, rather they are *functionally* necessary for it to take effect, since otherwise the potential 'fruits' offered by the change would be 'forfeited' ('Letter to Annenkov (1846)', SW 443). If so, we should indeed expect the social and political to impact upon the technological. Nevertheless, it is the latter which finally calls the tune. Given that human beings are rational and wish to improve their material well-being, they will, apart from a few blips, develop those social and political forms that best exploit the current stage of technology. Men do make their own history, then, for their lives are not in the grip of, but rather are rational responses to, the productive forces whose emergence is, in part, the result of the earlier rational strategies of their forebears.[54]

Questions remain, however. Should we really treat as mere blips those long periods of 'stagnation' when people have displayed no obvious urge to change their lives so as efficiently to exploit the productive forces available to them? Perhaps we should if we can put this failure down to recalcitrant factors – lack of education and communication, say – which have impeded the triumph of reason. But can we? Not all of us today would regard as irrational the rejection by traditional societies of the allure of industrial progress. Marxian man may not be the helpless victim of blind forces that he is sometimes portrayed. But if that is because he is a resolute, calculating seeker of increased material well-being, then he is a one-sided figure, less attractive, perhaps, than those depicted by the younger Marx, with their ambition, as yet unrealized, to 'create according to the laws of beauty'.

Social Darwinism

In old age, Karl Kautsky, scourge of 'revisionist' deviation from Marxist orthodoxy, recalled that his 'theory of history was intended to be nothing other than the application of Darwinism to social development'.[55] This intention, though the results may coincide, was the mirror image of Engels' attempt to extrapolate from historical materialism principles governing nature. The 'dialectic' of history – with its 'contradictions' between material forces and social relations, and its revolutionary leaps – finds analogues in the whole of organic life.

It was not Marxism, however, but Social Darwinism which, as the label suggests, swam strongest with the tide of evolutionism in the second half of the nineteenth century. That label, though, was coined as a term of abuse, and remained so during the decades when 'Marxist' was a title of which many intellectuals boasted. Social Darwinism, with its rhetoric of 'the survival of the fittest', was perceived as an apology for unbridled capitalism, colonialism and war. Even if the perception is accurate, these are odd grounds, perhaps, on which to contrast it sharply with Marxism. Marx and Engels were at pains to eschew moral condemnation of capitalism (that was for 'utopian' socialists), and were generally hostile to attempts to reform or soften capitalism, since these might prolong it. Neither of them showed much sympathy for the fate of traditional or primitive societies, for these are anyway 'doomed to extinction' (SW 254). War between the imperalist powers, too, was inevitable, according to many Marxists, and so nothing for a realist to regret.

The contrast with Marxism is further softened by its affinities with the views of the leading Social Darwinist, Herbert Spencer (1820–1903). Like Marx and Engels, he believed that the State would one day wither away – not with the victory of the proletariat, but with the emergence of a rational, liberal society in which, prejudices and delusions abolished, there would be consensus on the aims to be pursued. The overarching aim, moreover, sounds not unlike the one which, for Marx, will be realized in a classless society, 'the complete manifestation of everyone's individuality'. Compare, finally, Marx's view that history moves on when the 'fetters' on new productive forces are 'burst asunder' with Spencer's belief that 'forms that have ceased to facilitate and have become obstructive . . . are swept away in all cases'.[56] The difference between Spencer and Marx in their perception of their times was that, for the former, the fetters to be burst asunder were those put on an emerging industrial society by landed interests, not those imposed by the capitalist flagbearers of that society.

At the broader philosophical level, Marxism and Social Darwinism were united in their materialism, in the sense of the naturalistic project of explaining human and social development in terms of material conditions of life. Some of the 'zoological materialists' were also materialists in the older eighteenth-century sense. Karl Vogt opined that thought is secreted from the brain like bile from the liver; Ernst Haeckel, who regarded evolution as 'the magic word by which we shall solve all . . . riddles', held that all phenomena, mental included, 'may be ultimately referred to the mechanics of atoms'. 'Darwin's bulldog', Thomas Huxley, on the other hand, was an 'epiphenomenalist', taking consciousness to be a non-physical 'collateral product' of bodily processes, but incapable of returning the compliment and having any effect upon the body.[57] Spencer denied being an (old-style) materialist on the ground that, since our investigations cannot reach 'the ultimate nature of things', there exists 'The Unknowable', about whose constitution – 'spiritualistic', 'materialistic', or otherwise – it is forever idle to speculate (446).[58]

Social Darwinism is badly named. Spencer, for one, developed his views before the publication of *The Origin of Species* in 1859, and therefore well before Charles Darwin's own account of human evolution in *The Descent of Man* of 1871. More important, most of the Social Darwinists are more appropriately labelled 'Social Lamarckians'. It was not to Darwin's picture of evolution as a pretty haphazard story of species being favoured or weeded out through natural selection that their view of human progress owed. It was, rather, to Jean Baptiste Lamarck's hypothesis of purposive adaptation, illustrated by the giraffe stretching its neck ever longer to reach the ever receding leaves, and the inheritance of the characteristics so acquired. Darwin himself was no exponent of 'global progressionism', but the 'catalyst' which enabled it to take such a hold in Victorian England.[59] Ironically, the Social Darwinists had less in common with Darwin than with some of his theological critics. These did not reject evolution, but insisted that it must display a purpose and progression suitable to its being the vehicle of a divine plan.

Replace the final two words by 'necessary process' or 'rational order', and you have Spencer's view.

'Who now reads Spencer?', asked a distinguished sociologist some years ago. Well, a few people have blown the dust off the musty tomes that make up his 'Synthetic Philosophy', and perhaps more should. Enormously admired, though unloved (except by George Eliot), in his day, this eminent Victorian was an acute critic of any facile utilitarianism and a precursor of the 'evolutionary epistemology' much in favour today (see ch. 10, sect. 4). Certainly this self-taught, vainglorious puritan ('No Spencer ever dances!') should not be ignored in a history of systematic philosophies, for he was a systemizer of almost Hegelian proportions.

Philosophy is the 'statement of the ultimate principles discernible throughout all manifestations of the Absolute' (xi). Although this Absolute is the Unknowable, we can discern its manifestations in inorganic matter, organic life, and 'super-organic' social existence. What we discover, at all these levels, is the 'law of evolution and dissolution', which is rooted in the still more fundamental law of the 'persistence of forces'. What evolves or dissolves does so in response to impinging 'forces'. Evolution, on which Spencer focuses, is progress from 'confused simplicity' to 'distinct complexity' (438). Species, for instance, become ever more heterogeneous, more sharply distinguished from one another, and exhibit greater internal organization and integration. Barring accidents, evolution tends towards a state of equilibrium, where the maximum diversity and complexity compatible with the material pressures of 'force' are reached.

In the organic world, this equilibrium coincides with 'the highest state of humanity' (441). Here, Spencer finds the key to achieving his 'ultimate purpose . . . that of finding for the principles of right and wrong . . . a scientific basis'.[60] It was he, not Darwin, who coined the phrase 'survival of the fittest', and the thought it encapsulates is not, primarily, the Darwinian one that the evolutionary struggle weeds out the less fit, but the Lamarckian one that it forces the combatants to become fitter. The 'principles of right and wrong' are those which prescribe the conduct that people must adopt if they are to continue to climb the evolutionary tree towards the maximum diversity and individual complexity which their environment permits. These principles will vary according to environment, but are always likely to include thrift and other 'self-improving' virtues.

For Spencer, however, as for many others who see their own age as the outcome of a slow and gradual evolution, the times now call for a radical break in moral development. The old paternalistic norms of society, necessary in their day, have, in the 'Industrial Society', become 'hindrances' to further human evolution. Conditions are now ripe for the 'complete manifestation of everyone's individuality'. For two reasons, a *laissez-faire* principle of individual liberty is the contemporary imperative. Unless people are left at liberty, they will be unable, unlike Lamarck's giraffes, to stretch themselves and hence make themselves properly 'fit' to respond to the challenges of modern life. Second, people molly-coddled by a paternalistic regime and cushioned by hidebound tradition against the march of progress, will not 'pass through [those] *moral ordeals*' which, like the cold showers at Dr Arnold's Rugby [school], are prerequisites of 'fitness'.[61] Some people will doubtless fail to come through their ordeals and go to the wall. But, despite the judgement of many critics, Spencer's Social Darwinism is not the brutal doctrine that we ought so to arrange affairs that some people – and some peoples – go under, on the grounds that we are then emulating nature, 'red in tooth and claw', in weeding out the failures. Rather it is the doctrine that, in technological societies, the appropriate vehicle for continuing the evolutionary progress, discernible in life at all levels, towards diversity and individuality is liberalism. Whether or not Spencer succeeded in putting liberalism on 'a scientific basis', his attempt was not more obiously a failure than those which founded it on a mythical social contract or on the eternal, unevolving 'rights of man'.

• 5 Positivism, Pragmatism and British Idealism •

Herbert Spencer was classed by his contemporaries as a 'positivist'. Philosophy, for him, was not a rival to the sciences, but their synthesis into a general account of knowable reality. (The 'Unknowable' or 'Absolute' was not a proper topic for any discipline.) In the nineteenth century, however, there was a second reason for classification as a positivist: the conviction that the sciences were the way to the moral and social betterment of mankind. Spencer not only shared that conviction, but helped to create it.

It was 'the father of positivism', Auguste Comte (1798–1857), who gave currency to the term as an expression of the twin confidence in the sciences as the sovereign providers of knowledge and our best hope for moral progress. This confidence, of course, continued the optimism of radical Enlightenment thinkers, now boosted by the success of such sciences as chemistry and electro-dynamics in providing both understanding of nature and the tools for techno-logical advance. Intellectual history, for Comte, passes through three stages, theological, metaphysical and positive. At the first stage, people explain things in terms of hidden powers, from tree-spirits to the Christian God, modelled on the human mind. At the second, explanation appeals to abstract forces and causes, while at the final stage, it is recognized that no appeal is required beyond one to empirical laws of 'succession and resemblance' among phenomena. The crowning achievement of this 'positive' stage will be the infant science of sociology, fathered by Comte himself. While it presupposes the development of other sciences, like biology, it will, once mature, embrace these in the sense of explaining their development and logic.[62]

There is no place in positivism for traditional religion, now seen as obfuscating and obstructive of progress. Such was Comte's positivist zeal, however, that he proselytized on behalf of a new 'religion of humanity', complete with a 'priesthood' of scientists and businessmen, and a 'calendar of saints' including such names as Adam Smith (predictably) and Dante and Shakespeare (less so). Comte, one should add, was ill, depressed, and less than fully sane at the time of these proposals.

The 'religion of humanity' was denounced as 'spiritual despotism' by a younger, British philosopher who, nevertheless, had been fired by the Frenchman's positivist view of knowledge. Nor did he abandon Comte's premise that progress must be based on a naturalistic understanding of human behaviour. I refer to John Stuart Mill, destined to become at least as eminent a figure as Spencer in British public life, and in English-speaking philosophy more so.

Inductivism and Phenomenalism

J. S. Mill (1806–73) was educated by his polymath father, James, a disciple of Bentham and the associationist psychologist David Hartley. So gruelling was the pedagogic programme – Greek at three, logic at twelve – that at twenty John Stuart suffered a breakdown, convinced that he was a thinking-machine incapable of normal emotion. Succour came, ironically, from reading Wordsworth, whose mystical pantheism could hardly have been further from the austere empiricism that Mill came to advocate. For most of his career, Mill combined a job in the East India Company with writing on innumerable topics. Later he combined his writing with being a Member of Parliament, eventually retiring to France in order to be close to the grave of his wife with whom, before the death of her first husband, Mill had conducted a long and platonic – though by Victorian standards, *risqué* – liaison. Before his own death, Mill's championship of rising causes, such as women's emancipation, together with his more theoretical writings, had already guaranteed him an influence unmatched, then or at any other time, by an English philosopher.

The constant target of Mill's polemics is 'intuitions', those allegedly innate ingredients of the mind to which philosophers of various stripes appealed in order to explain our knowledge. These philosophers included the 'Scottish School', which treated belief in the external world as part of our inborn 'common sense'; Kant, whose synthetic *a priori* truths are preconditions of experience; and 'ethical intuitionists', for whom moral truths are delivered by an innate 'moral sense'. Mill's hostility had various grounds. In the moral sphere, for example, intuitions provide reactionaries with an excuse for disallowing moral debate. But his main complaint is that reliance on intuition has the advantage of theft over honest toil. Where we can explain our knowledge as arising from what really is indubitably given to us, then we should do so, and not shirk this work by treating the knowledge as intuitive and underivable.

All that is truly *given* to us, for Mill, are the mind's 'outward feelings or sensations, and its inward feelings' (L 4.1.2).[63] Nothing else, strictly speaking, is observed; rather, it is inferred from what is given. Inference, in turn, rests on 'the laws of the association of ideas': laws which, for example, make us expect one sensation to follow another because of the previously observed 'order of our sensations' (WH 177–8). There was nothing original in these claims, out of step though they may initially have been with the prevailing climate. We have encountered them in Hume and Condillac, for instance. Mill's virtue is his tenacity in protecting the claims against objections which admirers of Kant and others had come to deem fatal. There are at least four problems faced by associationism: how to account for, respectively, knowledge of necessary truths, the methodology of science, belief in external reality, and consciousness of the self. Only in the face of the last problem does Mill soften his robust empiricism.

The existence of necessary truths had often been cited, for example by Leibniz, in refutation of empiricism. Experience can inform us how matters *are*, not how they *have* to be. Mill concedes this, but bluntly denies there is a way matters *have* to be. There are no necessary truths, other than those 'purely verbal' ones, of the 'All bachelors are unmarried' ilk, which 'give no informa- tion' at all (L 1.6.4). A geometrical axiom, like 'Two straight lines cannot enclose a space', only seems to be necessary, unlike an 'ordinary physical truth', because it is confirmed by experience 'almost every instant of our lives' (L 2.5.4). This produces such a conviction of the axiom's truth that we naturally, yet mistakenly, imagine that it *could* not have been false. Even the axioms of logic are inductive generalizations. 'A proposition cannot be both true and false' registers the fact, known 'by the simplest observation of our own minds', that belief and disbelief are 'different mental states, excluding one another' (L 2.7.5).

Mill is equally harsh with the objection that science does not typically employ the one principle of inference he allows, inductive extrapolation from observed to unobserved cases. He concedes to his opponents, like William Whewell, that scientists often proceed by setting up hypotheses, on little or no evidence, which they then test against experience. But to conclude that induction is inessential to scientific truth is to confuse 'Invention and Proof'. Inventing a hypothesis is heuristically useful in directing us towards relevant observations, but these cannot prove the hypothesis, nor even render it probable. This is because any number of rival hypotheses which might be conceived would also be compatible with those observations (L 5.14.6).

The greatest challenge, however, for radical empiricism is to honour our commonsense belief in an external world. An empiricist, it seems, must hold that tables and trees are either observable or, if not, inferable from what is observable. But a radical empiricist, like Mill, seems to block both alternatives. We experience nothing but sensations, and inductive inference can only be from what we have experienced to what we will or might experience.[64] There could, therefore, be no legitimate inference from experience to Kant's things in themselves. Yet Mill accepts that there are external objects in the sense of things which exist even if not 'perceived by man'. His problem is now the one Berkeley faced, having claimed that the only immediate objects of experience are 'ideas'. The Bishop's solution was that tables and trees, even when unperceived by man, are perceived by God. Some commentators discern a different solution in Berkeley, to the effect that when I talk of an unperceived table in my study, I refer to the ideas I *would* have *if* I returned to the study, looked in the right direction, and so on (see p. 263). This is the line that Mill apparently follows.

'I believe that Calcutta . . . would still exist if every . . . inhabitant were . . . struck dead': for 'the permanent possibility of sensation which I call Calcutta would still remain . . . If I were suddenly transported to the banks of the Hoogly, I should . . . have the sensations which . . . would lead me to affirm that Calcutta exists' (WH 184). Calcutta exists, sure enough, but only in virtue of the fact that *if* certain conditions obtain then people *would* have sensations belonging to that great bundle we label 'Calcutta'. Since this 'possibility of sensation' is there irrespective of anyone actually having sensations, then Calcutta is an external object in the sense of something which need not in fact be perceived in order to exist.

Mill is usually referred to as a 'phenomenalist': reasonably enough, if phenomenalism is the claim that, in the final analysis, there exist nothing but sensations (phenomena) and the minds which experience them. It is not obvious, though, that he holds, like later phenomenalists, that the very meaning of statements about external objects is fully rendered by talking about possibilities of perception. Admittedly, he writes that most people 'conceive of' objects as permanent possibilities of sensation. Against that, however, he writes that not only do we 'fancy' an object to be 'something more', but we are 'compelled' to do so. If he really thought 'Calcutta exists' just meant that certain sensations are possible, he should dismiss as nonsense the speculation that Calcutta might be 'something more' and have 'real externality'. Instead, he says, more circumspectly, that this speculation is not 'capable of proof'. Perhaps his point should have been this: whatever it is we *do* mean by 'Calcutta exists', what we *ought* to mean by it is no more than a possibility of sensations. Not only is there is no reason to think that anything exists other than actual and possible sensations, but the proposed meaning gives us 'the only sense [of external existence] we need care about' (WH 187). When we enquire whether Saddam Hussein's nuclear arsenal exists, all that can matter to us is what experiences we may look forward to. Whether the bombs, if they exist, do so in a sense other than that of promising certain experiences should be a matter of indifference to their potential recipients. Hence, the sense in question is one to abandon.

Philosophers favourable to a phenomenalist analysis of material objects have often baulked at extending it to minds. Even Hume, though unable to discover an abiding ego uniting his experiences, found it hard to believe, when outside his study, that a person is simply a 'bundle of perceptions'. Mill would clearly *like* to treat the mind as 'nothing but the series of our sensations . . . with the addition of infinite possibilities of feeling' (WH 189). If my table is a permanent possibility of being sensed, *I* am a permanent possibility of sensing. Such an analysis, he argues, is compatible with belief in minds other than my own, for why should there not be other 'series of sensations' than the one which comprises me? Mill confesses, however, to a 'final inexplicability' in the notion of mind or self. An analysis of myself into a series of experiences is circular, since some of these make reference to myself. That is, the experiences which go to make up me must be antecedently identified as mine. Memory of something, for instance, includes 'the belief . . . that I myself formerly had . . . the sensations remembered' (WH 194).

Utilitarianism Reformulated

We should not conclude from the insolubility of this problem that the mind is an occult substance or falls outside the laws of nature. On the contrary, 'the law of causality applies in the same strict sense to human actions as to other phenomena' (L 6.2.1). With sufficient effort, indeed, it is possible to establish a science, 'ethology', of how individual characters are formed, the results of which will form the basis of sociology. Policy may be an art, but 'science . . . lends to art' the knowledge needed if our moral and social goals are to be practicable (L 6.12.2).

It is this emphasis on empirical enquiry in ethics which, together with his inductivism and phenomenalism, qualifies Mill as a positivist. One enemy, yet again, is 'intuitionism', this time as a refusal to query 'gut feelings' of right and wrong. Another is Kant's view that our duties can be calculated by pure, armchair reasoning. Thus there can be no *proof* of the principle of utility – the only ultimate good is the greatest happiness of the greatest number – which Mill, son of a disciple of Bentham and godson of the man himself, inherited. Facts about human desire can, however, be marshalled in its favour. Indeed, 'the sole evidence it is possible to produce that anything is desirable, is that people do actually desire it' (U 288). What people always desire is their happiness. This does not mean that a good meal, friendship or esteem are desired only as means to the happiness they are predicted to yield. That is just as well, since an obsessive concern for happiness is self-defeating. 'Ask yourself whether you are happy,' wrote Mill in his *Autobiography*, 'and you cease to be so.' Typically, such things are desired 'for their own sake', as ingredients in a life a person finds satisfying.

This point allows Mill to deal with a matter Bentham had left a mystery. Why, if my pleasure is my sole end, should I care about other people's happiness, except when this chances to facilitate my own? For Mill, the question is badly posed. People naturally desire the happiness of others as an ingredient in their own, not as a means to satisfying selfish desires. Hence, we need not ask *why* someone should care about others. This is not to say that Mill, any more than Bentham, faces up to the problem of how, in cases where my happiness clearly conflicts with the general happiness, I can remain obedient to the principle of utility.

Mill amends his godfather's account in a further respect when he distinguishes between quality and quantity of pleasure and allows that the former may outweigh the latter. 'It is better to be a human being dissatisfied than a pig satisfied' (U 258). Some have seen this as a fatal concession, but Mill defends it by appeal, once more, to the facts of human nature. People who have seriously sampled both the higher human pleasures and the lower pig-like ones prefer smaller doses of the former to larger doses of the latter. And it is what people prefer and desire which furnishes the criteria for happiness. It is hard to resist the impression, however, that there are activities Mill admires – science and philosophy, say – for reasons independent of their pleasurable yield. This is an impression confirmed by his influential case for liberty. His official defence of the principle that 'the only purpose for which power can be rightfully exercised over [someone] . . . against his will, is to prevent harm to others' sounds utilitarian in tone (OL 135). Since individuals are usually the best judges of their happiness, then when the public 'interferes with purely personal conduct, . . . the odds are that it interferes wrongly' (OL 214). But when we read that 'he who lets the world . . . choose his plan of life for him, has no need of any other faculty than the ape-like one of imitation' (OL 187), Mill's attachment to a romantic ideal of self-creation is surely apparent. It is nice to think that he owed something more durable to the arch-romantic, Wordsworth, than a panacea for youthful depression.

Neo-Kantianism and Pragmatism

By the end of the nineteenth century, all the ingredients in the positivism represented by Mill – its associationist psychology, inductivism, phenomenalism, utilitarianism, and faith in a science of society – were under attack. Critics ranged from sympathizers, keen to repair the cracks in positivism, to wholesale demolishers. One attack was launched by the logician Gottlob Frege (1848–1925) on Mill's view of mathematical truths as inductive generalizations. How, he asks, could $1,000,000 = 999,999 + 1$ describe what we observe, when no one wittingly perceives such large groups of objects? Mill's mistake is to confuse its applications, 'which often are physical and do presuppose observed facts, with the pure mathematical proposition itself'. These 'pure' propositions are about numbers, abstract entities of just the kind Mill's empiricism excludes, independent as they are of psychology. 'Psychology,' says Frege, 'should not imagine that it can contribute anything whatever to the foundation of arithmetic.'[65] An attack on a different target, positivist pretensions in social science, was led by Wilhelm Dilthey (1833–1911). Explanation of historical events, for example, requires a mode of empathetic understanding quite foreign to anything provided by the natural sciences.

Frege and Dilthey make their main appearances in chapter 10. For the present, I focus on the overhaul of positivism by various thinkers sympathetic to its empiricist thrust. Some of these belonged, like Dilthey himself, to the loosely knit school of Neo-Kantians. This name might lead one to expect outright hostility to positivism, but most of the school had abandoned two aspects of the Master's philosophy badly at odds with empiricism. They rejected, first, the doctrine of things in themselves standing behind phenomena; and second, the idea of synthetic *a priori* principles as innate structures of mind. To be sure, such principles are not generalizations from experience, as they are for the positivists, since the orderly conduct of observation, which scientists strive for, presupposes them. Nor, however, are they eternally necessary conditions of experience, but either the natural products of human evolution or the cultural ones of historical development. This, for some Neo-Kantians, meant that the principles should not be spoken of as true (or false). Rather, they are 'fictions', owing their entrenchment to their value for guiding empirical enquiry. This approach was applied to scientific laws by Ernst Mach (1838–1916), himself a physicist. Some of these laws cannot be generalizations from experience, since they are 'about' unobservable entities, like atoms. Still, for Mach, a convinced phenomenalist, the laws cannot *really* be about such entities since 'the world consists only of our sensations'. They should not be construed, then, as truths about anything, but as 'economic' instruments for predicting what sensations will occur under what conditions, as 'succinct directions . . . for the employment of . . . experiences, ready for use'.[66]

The criticisms by Frege, the Neo-Kantians and Mach all conspire to marginalize the issue, so important to Mill, of how beliefs are arrived at. The effect of the latter two criticisms is to switch attention to the use and value propositions and laws have for us. With this switch, certain questions are bound to arise. Why confine the emphasis upon use to synthetic *a priori* propositions and scientific laws? Why regard them as 'instruments' which are neither true nor false, instead of elevating use-value to a criterion of truth? These were questions already being explored, not only by Nietzsche, but across the Atlantic.

Pragmatism, still a lively force today, is described by one American as 'the chief glory of our country's intellectual tradition'.[67] For all I know, there once flourished pragmatist schools in Turkey or Norway, but I doubt it: pragmatism has a robust American flavour, redolent of both the Wild West and Wall Street. Surely it had to be an American, William James (1842–1910), who could describe truth both as 'any idea upon which we can ride' and as something we should seek as 'part of our general obligation to do what pays' (382, 441).[68] It was the 'genial', 'open air' version of pragmatism launched by this Harvard Professor that was to make a splash: due, not least, to his attractive personality and a buoyancy of style notably absent from the novels of his brother, Henry. Not that James himself had always felt buoyant, having suffered, in 1870, a deep depression and 'horrible fear of my own existence' (6). He was brought out of this, not by reading Wordsworth, but a French philosopher who convinced him of the efficacy of free will. ('My first act of free will shall be to believe in free will' (7).) James inherited the name and general programme of pragmatism from Charles Sanders Peirce (1839–1914), a logician and something of an outsider, whose prickly character made a university career impossible, and whose last twenty-five years were spent reclusively. James was a constant supporter, intellectually and financially, of the older man, though his revision of Peirce's views prompted the latter to prefer the title 'pragmaticism' in the justified hope that it was 'ugly enough to be safe from kidnappers' (186).[69]

Both writers, despite emphasizing their phenomenalism or 'radical empiricism', distance themselves from positivism. Peirce's phenomenalism, he insists, is not Hume's or Mill's, but Kant's, though without the excrescence of things in themselves. External objects cannot be built up out of sensations, since 'objective validity' or applicability to an external world is presupposed by perceptual experience (84). James has a different objection to sensationalism: it is just not true, psychologically, that we experience isolated sensations, subsequently stitched together on the basis of the 'associations' among them. Rather, consciousness is a 'stream', whose elements are so blended that they can be abstracted only artificially. Anyway, it is arbitrary of positivists to restrict experience to what is directly furnished by the senses. 'Experience,' writes

Peirce, 'is what the course of life has *compelled* me to think' (385). It compels me, for instance, to regard the world I inhabit as one with a long past, though this is not a feature of it that I can directly perceive. For James, it is mere prejudice to exclude from the realm of genuine experiences those of the mystic or 'supernaturalist'. Allowing only the meagre diet of experiences the positivist does is like 'offering a printed bill of fare as the equivalent for a solid meal' (769). Finally, the traditional empiricist assumption that a person constructs his view of reality from his individual resources must be rejected. For one thing, Peirce reminds us, thought is 'of the nature of language', and presupposes a person's membership of a linguistic community, so that he or she is 'not absolutely an individual' (191). For another, the very notion of reality implies a contrast between an individual and a public view of things. The real is what is independent of *my* beliefs.

These criticisms conspire to reject the attempt to understand our concepts in terms of their 'phenomenal equivalents', the sensations associated with our words. How, then, should we spell out the essential connection between concepts and experience? When Peirce remarks that the 'purport' of words or concepts is to be found in their 'purposive bearing', the transition to pragmatism is made (196). In Peirce's hands, at least, pragmatism is first and foremost a theory of meaning. The whole meaning of a concept consists in the 'general modes of rational conduct' ensuing from its application, and there is 'no distinction of meaning . . . [without] a possible difference of practice' (204, 123). The belief that a liquid is wine, say, is not, as for Mill, the anticipation of certain sensations, but a 'notification' that we may act towards it in certain ways. This theme was developed by the leading figure in a second wave of American pragmatists, John Dewey (1859–1952), best–known to the wider public for his influence on his country's educational system. For Dewey, 'it is the characteristic use to which a thing is put . . . which supplies [its] meaning', and to understand the meaning of a word is not to grasp some inner idea or sensation associated with it, but to participate, however vicariously, in putting the thing it stands for to use.[70]

This welding of understanding with action has important implications, first, for the mind–body issue. If thought is essentially tied to practice, then the problem, inherited by empiricists from Descartes, of inferring the body's existence from subjective experience cannot arise. Creatures who think are necessarily embodied, for thought, as Peirce insists, 'can have no concrete being without action' (202). The whole tendency to 'sunder existence' into an inner 'receptacle' and an outer world is erroneous: while, for James, experience is 'neutral', neither mental nor material. These latter terms represent different ways of viewing experiences and of relating them to one another. The essential tie between understanding and action implies, second, a short way with the competing claims of rarified metaphysics. It is not that, as for Mill, these are 'not capable of proof': rather, they are senseless and not genuine rivals at all, being without implications for practice. As James put it, 'there can *be* no difference . . . that doesn't *make* a difference' (379).

If beliefs are 'instruments' of action, they are not pictures or mirrors of reality: so we might expect, in the wake of a pragmatist definition of meaning, an analogous one of truth. This was not a step that Peirce, however, took. Truth cannot, indeed, be a correspondence between beliefs and a reality independent of those beliefs, as manifested in our activities in the world. Rather, truth is to be understood in consensual terms. The true opinion is the one 'fated to be ultimately agreed to' by competent investigators and practitioners, above all scientists, and real objects are the ones recognized in this, perhaps infinitely distant, consensus (133). This definition registers Peirce's belief that a process of 'universal love' drives enquirers and guarantees ever greater convergence among them. No such faith informs Dewey's characterization of truth, otherwise in keeping with Peirce's approach, in terms of the 'warranted assertibility' our theories or beliefs possess.

An overtly pragmatist definition of truth was the contribution of William James, a triumph or disaster according to opinion. 'The true is the name of whatever proves itself to be good in the way of belief'; it is 'the expedient in the way of our thinking'; and our beliefs 'agree' with reality when they enable us to 'handle it . . . better' than others would (388, 438, 434). This marks a more radical departure, in two respects, from Peirce's position than might be imagined. For one thing, James relativizes the 'good' and 'expediency' of a belief to individuals. It is when a new belief 'gratifies the individual's desire' effectively to assimilate novel experiences that it 'counts as "true"' (384). Truth is therefore independent of that consensus, 'in the long run', among a qualified public which was Peirce's criterion. (James, with scant respect for consistency, does at times refer to an 'abstract' or 'absolute' truth which transcends the gratification of individuals.) Second, James – for much of the time, at least – places few, if any, constraints on the 'expedient' effects which make a belief true for an individual. Certainly, we should not confine attention to the 'effects' which scientists invoke when adjudicating beliefs. Pragmatism is 'completely genial', allowing *anything* that is 'better for us to believe' for the conduct of our lives as a reason for holding it true (388–9).

This is why James, the self-proclaimed 'radical empiricist', can nevertheless advocate religious faith. 'If theological ideas prove to have a value for concrete life, they will be true' (387). And a value they indeed have, for the 'reactions' of the believer to the world and to people are healthier and happier than those of the non-believer. The world becomes a 'Thou', not an 'It', and we treat it accordingly (733). Like Pascal before him (see p. 242), James urges us to cultivate our 'will to believe', since the agnostic, as much as the atheist, debars himself from the benefits of faith, rather as an indecisive man misses the opportunity to marry an 'angel' of a woman (732).

In Mill, there was a romantic trying to break out of a positivist shell. With James, romantic themes, in intriguing counterpoint to an underlying empiricism, sound loud and clear: the roles of will and emotion in interpreting the world about us, for example, and the identity which the individual, if free from 'over-intellectualism', will experience with the life of the natural and, indeed, 'supernatural' world. If pragmatism can sometimes seem a philosophy designed for the hard-headed scientist or the hard-nosed Wall Street operator, in James' writings it exudes the air of the pioneering West rather than the atmosphere of the laboratory or the boardroom.

British Idealism

Over the last few pages, we have seen positivism undergoing more or less radical surgery, from local operations on its understanding of science to wholesale replacement of its notion of truth. In the writings of the British (or Oxford) Idealists, however, the patient is buried (only to be resurrected, however, a few decades later in Austria (see ch. 10, sect. 3)). British Idealism marks the return of metaphysics with a vengeance. 'Idealism', here, is something of a pun, for the movement's main protagonists – T. H. Green (1836–82) and F. H. Bradley (1846–1924) – were idealists in both a metaphysical and a moral sense. The metaphysics they embraced owed to Kant and Hegel rather than to Berkeley's 'empirical' idealism or to Mill's phenomenalism. They saw themselves, too, as recalling their contemporaries from the pleasure-seeking goals of utilitarianism to loftier moral ideals. 'The contribution to human perfection', wrote Green, 'must be the object in which [one] seeks self-satisfaction' (191).[71] If Spencer was the champion of Victorian 'self-improvement', and Mill of individual liberty, it was Green whose writings were to be found in the trunks of those high-minded Oxford graduates who sailed away to administer the British Empire. Green was as active as Mill in promoting good causes: less so Bradley, a sickly recluse whom T. S. Eliot, in Oxford to write a dissertation on Bradley at the philosopher's own College, never even saw.

Like many systematic philosophers, the two idealists presented their ethical views as deriving from an underlying metaphysics. But here the tail seems to have wagged the dog. The rejection of rival philosophies – positivism, naturalism – is inspired by their failure to provide an acceptable account of moral life. To view human beings as hedonistic creatures of nature is, for Bradley, 'absolutely irreconcilable with ordinary moral beliefs' (E 83);[72] while, for

Green, it makes moral principles senseless, since 'to a being who is simply the result of natural forces an injunction to conform to their laws is unmeaning' (9). 'Ought' implies 'can'.

Here we find a partial replay of the romantic and idealist reaction, at the beginning of the century, to Enlightenment doctrines. In both cases, a key notion is that of *unity*. Mill's utilitarianism, as much as Bentham's or Helvétius', was accused of atomizing society, of setting people apart by treating the individual as the basic unit of social life. Green, admittedly, says that a nation 'has no real existence except as the life of the individuals composing' it (184). But his constant stress is on the vacuity of a life outside of a community – the family, say, or the nation – which gives it substance. Each person aims at 'self-realization', but cannot achieve this 'without contemplating others not as a means to that better state, but as sharing it with him' (199). Elsewhere, indeed, Green denies individual self-consciousness: we are not so much 'parts of', but 'partakers in . . . [a] self-consciousness' of which the world as a whole is the 'expression'.[73]

The attack on the divisive tendency of individualism is more strident in Bradley. 'The only thing that satisfies our desires' is a 'real identity of subject and object' (E 177) which, at the ethical level, means recognizing oneself as a 'pulse-beat' of a whole community. Strip a man of his birth and education as an Englishman and 'what you have left is not . . . a man, but some I know not what residuum' (E 166). The individual of utilitarian theory, with his or her ready-made character and desires, is a 'delusion'. Self-realization is to be sought, therefore, not through satisfaction of pre-formed desires, but in attending to 'my station and its duties', which record the 'objective' moral will of a community on which my identity depends. Important as the duties of my station – as father, citizen, or whatever – are, however, there are also duties of 'ideal morality'. 'The production of truth and beauty', for example, is a duty, but in so trying to realize oneself, a person does not act 'as a member of a visible community' (E 205). One is reminded, here, of Hegel's elevation of 'Absolute Spirit' – the realm of art, religion and philosophy – over the ethical life. The impression is confirmed by Bradley's claim that moral life cannot 'satisfy wholly the spirit's hunger'. Morality needs to be 'consummated in oneness with God', the ineffable Godhead of Jakob Boehme and other 'vehement' mystics. Only then is unity with reality achieved, through 'dying to' a 'private self' now recognized as an obstacle to identity with the one will that permeates the whole (E 328ff).

For Green and Bradley, then, self-realization is only partially achieved through life in an organic community: necessary, too, is a sense of deeper unity with reality. Like Hegel, they are sometimes willing to call this reality 'God', but are aware that this is misleading. Absolute reality is not, at any rate, 'the God of religion', as Bradley puts it, for He is but one 'factor in the Whole'

(AR 395). Whatever its name, there is, for Green, 'one spiritual self-conscious being, of which all that is real is the . . . expression':[74] a 'spirit', Bradley agrees, 'outside of [which] . . . there cannot be any reality' (AR 489). These Hegelian utterances, though, disguise differences between the two men. On two starting points, to be sure, they are agreed. First, it makes no sense to speak of a reality that cannot be experienced, one that 'sits apart . . . and does not descend into phenomena' (AR 488), like Kant's thing in itself. Second, the key to understanding reality is reflection on the *relations* between phenomena. It is their failure to turn this key which condemns the empiricism of Hume and Mill. How, Green asks, can we account for 'consciousness of events as related' on the basis, simply, of the separate sensations which, for those writers, exhaust experience (16)? After all, we do not have sensations of the cat, the mouse, *and* the one's being bigger than the other. Bradley agrees: the 'togetherness' of elements of experience is impossible to explain on the traditional, atomistic view of experience.

At this point, the two philosophers part company. For Green, if sensation cannot supply us with experience of relations, this must be furnished by *thought*. What Kant said about spatial, temporal and causal relations – that they are imposed by mind – is true of all relations. Green draws the appropriately radical, idealist conclusion. Since nature is 'the system of related appearances', and since relations cannot exist apart from mind, then nature is 'impossible apart from the action of intelligence' (36). Without this 'action', indeed, there could be no experience at all, for even the humblest sensation is only identifiable through its relations to others. Kant was therefore wrong to suppose that anything is *given* to experience, independent of the 'action of intelligence'. Since nothing is, finally, cut off from anything else, we are compelled to regard nature as a seamless whole, the activity or expression of mind. This 'mind' cannot, of course, be yours or mine, for it would be absurd to suppose that nature begins to exist only when 'this or that person begins to think' (36). Individual minds, then, must be relatively localized expressions of this single self-consciousness, of the One with which, at the ethical level, we try to identify through discarding our self-centred interests.

Bradley's view of relations is more radical. There aren't any. Or rather, they do not belong to the fabric of reality, only to appearance. 'A relational way of thought . . . must give appearance, and not truth' (AR 28). To readers who recognize this he announces the good news that they need hardly bother with the remaining 500 pages of his book, since its conclusions – such as the merely apparent nature of space, time, and self – follow in short order. His argument is that the concept of relations is incoherent because it involves an infinite regress. For the cat to be related to the mouse, there must be a relation between them. But how are the creatures linked to this relation, which they must be in order to be linked to each other? Only through a further relation linking them to the original one. But then the question arises as to how this second relation is linked to the first one and to the cat and mouse. And so on. Perhaps Bradley's point is this: given an 'immediate experience' of a kind not yet articulated into separate items and relations between them, we can then abstract these from the experience. What we could not intelligibly do is stitch together an experience of 'unity-in-diversity' from these individual items and relations.[75]

Whatever the worth of this argument, Bradley concludes that 'the Absolute is not many . . . the universe is one' (AR 127). If it were 'many', its ingredients would be related to one another: but that is impossible, since relations are abstractions which we, for our convenience, make from reality. What, then, is reality? Nothing we try to say about it can be adequate, since language is compelled to employ relational concepts, applicable only to the articulated realm of appearances. Nor can reality be anything beyond the 'sensuous curtain' of experience, such as a thing in itself or, as perhaps for Green, 'some unearthly ballet of bloodless categories' of thought (PL 591). Reality, then, must be experience itself: but experience no longer dissected into separate ingredients, including those of the subject and the object of experience, and the relations between them. We have an intimation of such experience in those lazy, sleepy perceptions, later so well described by Proust, where everything – the sunlight, the bird-song, the heaviness of our limbs – blends as one. So we can at least 'form the general idea of an absolute experience in which phenomenal distinctions are merged, a whole become immediate at a higher stage without losing any richness' (AR 141). Only the mystic can do better than form this general idea and actually partake in this experience. (Readers of ch. 2, sect. 3 will understand why Indian philosophers have compared Bradley with Śaṅkara, for appearance and reality, in the former's account, are indeed akin to *māyā* and *Brahman* in the latter's.)

It is ironic, perhaps, that Victorian England, home for many decades of hard-headed positivism and sober empiricism, should enter the twentieth century inspired by an idealist philosophy as exotic as that which dominated continental Europe, only to burn itself out, earlier in the previous one. To be sure, the role-reversal was short-lived, as we will see in chapter 10. First, though, we examine developments, themselves stimulated by those in nineteenth-century European thought, which were taking place further east.

• Notes •

1 Quoted in Roger Scruton, *Kant*, p. 8.
2 References to Kant are to *Critique of Practical Reason* (P); *Fundamental Principles of the Metaphysic of Morals* (F); *Lectures on Ethics* (LE); to section numbers of *Critique of Judgement*

(J); and to the standard page numbers of the first (A) and second (B) editions of *Critique of Pure Reason*.

3 A prime example is Jonathan Bennett, *Kant's Analytic*.

4 Quoted in Scruton, *Kant*, p. 7.

5 Gilles Deleuze, *Kant's Critical Philosophy*, p. 14. For illuminating accounts of Kant's 'transcendental idealism', see Charles Parsons, 'The Transcendental Aesthetic', and P. F. Strawson, *The Bounds of Sense*.

6 Quoted in Scruton, *Kant*, p. 9.

7 Here I follow Paul Guyer, 'Introduction: The starry heavens and the moral law', pp. 22ff. For a different, but useful account, see S. Körner, *Kant*, ch. 9.

8 Quoted in Charles Taylor, *Sources of the Self*, p. 574.

9 References are to *Gedichte: Hyperion*. The importance of this work is stressed by Edward Craig, *The Mind of God and the Works of Man*, pp. 162ff.

10 Taylor, *Sources of the Self*, ch. 21. See also Charles Taylor, *Hegel*.

11 Quoted in Friedrich Nietzsche, *Untimely Meditations*, pp. 140–1.

12 Friedrich Schiller, *On the Aesthetic Education of Man*, 14th Letter.

13 Quoted in Michael Rosen, *Hegel's Dialectic and its Criticism*, p. 103.

14 Friedrich Schlegel, quoted in Andrew Bowie, *Aesthetics and Subjectivity*, p. 43.

15 Julian Roberts, *German Philosophy*, p. 144.

16 References to Schelling are to *Ideas for a Philosophy of Nature* (I), and *System of Transcendental Idealism* (S).

17 References to Fichte are to *Science of Knowledge*.

18 J. G. Fichte, *Die Wissenschaftslehre (1810)*, pp. 25–6.

19 Quoted in Frederick Copleston, *A History of Philosophy*, vol. 7, part I, p. 108.

20 References to Hegel are to section numbers of *Phenomenology of Spirit* (PS), *The Encyclopaedia Logic* (EL), *Philosophy of Mind* (PM), and *Philosophy of Right* (PR); and to page numbers of *The Philosophy of History* (PH), and *Introduction to the Lectures on the History of Philosophy* (HP).

21 See J. P. Eckermann, *Gespräche mit Goethe*, p. 690.

22 Quoted in Rosen, *Hegel's Dialectic and its Criticism*, p. 69.

23 Michael Inwood, *A Hegel Dictionary*, pp. 129–30.

24 Hans-Georg Gadamer, quoted in Rosen, *Hegel's Dialectic and its Criticism*, p. 121.

25 Quoted in Copleston, *A History of Philosophy*, vol. 7, part I, p. 146.

26 Ibid., p. 85.

27 Karl Popper's charge of fascism against Hegel, in his *The Open Society and its Enemies*, vol. 2, rests too heavily on such slogans. Fichte, too, has been unfairly treated as a proto-fascist. Despite the rabidly chauvinistic tone of his *Addresses to the German Nation*, composed at the time of Napoleon's invasion, Fichte's State is a broadly liberal one.

28 Quoted in Patrick Gardiner, *Schopenhauer*, p. 12.

29 Arthur Schopenhauer, *Parerga and Paralipomena*, vol. 2, pp. 614ff.

30 References to Schopenhauer are to volume and page numbers of *The World as Will and Representation*.

31 Gardiner, *Schopenhauer*, p. 183.

32 Michael Tanner, 'Schopenhauer', p. 388.

33 See Copleston, *A History of Philosophy*, vol. 7, part 2, pp. 57ff.

34 References to Nietzsche are to section numbers of *The Will to Power* (WP); *Beyond Good and Evil* (BGE); *The Genealogy of Morals* (GM); *Twilight of the Idols* (TI); *Thus Spake Zarathustra* (Z); and *Daybreak* (D). BGE and GM are in *Basic Writings of Nietzsche*; TI and Z are in *The Portable Nietzsche*. The translations of quoted passages are often my own.

35 Bernard Williams, 'Nietzsche's centaur', p. 17.

36 Michel Foucault, *Power/Knowledge*, pp. 53–4. For other Gallic 'readings' of Nietzsche, see David B. Allison (ed.), *The New Nietzsche*. A more sober account is given by Richard Schacht, *Nietzsche*.

37 Nietzsche, *Werke*, vol. 3, p. 314.

38 See Alexander Nehamas, *Nietzsche: Life as Literature* – an excellent study of Nietzsche. See also Julian P. Young, *Nietzsche's Philosophy of Art*.

39 References to Kierkegaard are to *The Journals* (J); *Philosophical Fragments* (PF); *Concluding Unscientific Postscript* (CUP); *Either/Or*; *Fear and Trembling* (FT); and *The Sickness Unto Death* (SUD), which is in *A Kierkegaard Anthology*.

40 Roger Poole, *Kierkegaard*, p. 7. For a more traditional account, see the excellent Patrick Gardiner, *Kierkegaard*.

41 Alistair Hannay, *Kierkegaard*, pp. 52–3.

42 Alasdair MacIntyre, *After Virtue*, p. 38.

43 See David R. Law, *Kierkegaard as Negative Theologian*.

44 Isaiah Berlin, *Karl Marx*, p. 76.

45 Quotes from Feuerbach, some of them from his famous *The Essence of Christianity* (translated by George Eliot, no less), are culled from Leszek Kolakowski, *Main Currents of Marxism*, vol. 1; Copleston, *A History of Philosophy*, vol. 7; and Hayden V. White, 'Feuerbach, Ludwig'.

46 Quoted in Kolakowski, *Main Currents of Marxism*, vol. 1, p. 112.

47 Letter of 1841, in *The Portable Karl Marx*, p. 22. A few years later, Hess complained of Marx's 'vanity' and 'demand [for] personal submission'.

48 *The Portable Karl Marx*, p. 70.

49 References to Marx are to *The Portable Karl Marx*, in which the following cited works are partly or wholly translated: 'Theses on Feuerbach' (TF), 'Contribution to the Critique of Hegel's *Philosophy of Right*' (HPR), *Economico-Philosophical Manuscripts of 1844* (EP), *The German Ideology* (GI), *Capital* (C), *A Contribution to the Critique of Political Economy* (CPE), *Manifesto of the Communist Party* (M). References to Engels are to *Karl Marx and Friedrich Engels: Selected Works* (SW), vol. 2.

50 For the 'Kremlin' line, see Louis Althusser, *For Marx*; for the 'humanist' line, see Herbert Marcuse, *Reason and Revolution*.

51 Quoted in Kolakowski, *Main Currents of Marxism*, vol. 1, pp. 172–3.

52 Quoted in G. A. Cohen, *Karl Marx's Theory of History*, p. 41.

53 For this criticism, see John Plamenatz, *Man and Society*, vol. 2, and for a response to it, Allen Wood, *Karl Marx*.

54 This is the gist of Cohen's account of Marx's historical materialism, *Karl Marx's Theory of History*; for a criticism of it, see Alex Callinicos, *Marxism and Philosophy*.

55 Quoted in Callinicos, *Marxism and Philosophy*, p. 63.

56 Quoted in J. W. Burrow, *Evolution and Society*, pp. 224–5.

57 On Haeckel, Huxley, etc., see John Passmore, *A Hundred Years of Philosophy*, ch. 2.

58 References to Spencer are to *First Principles*, 2 vols.

59 Peter J. Bowler, *Charles Darwin*, p. 150: a book on which I often rely.

60 Quoted in Burrow, *Evolution and Society*, p. 215.

61 Ibid., p. 187.

62 See *The Positive Philosophy of Auguste Comte*.

63 References to Mill are to book, chapter and section of *A System of Logic* (L), and to page numbers of *Utilitarianism* (U), *On Liberty* (OL), and *An Examination of Sir William Hamilton's Philosophy* (WH).

64 On the importance of Mill's inductivism for his account of the external world, see John Skorupski, *John Stuart Mill*.

65 Gottlob Frege, *The Foundations of Arithmetic*, pp. 13, vi.

66 Quoted in John Skorupski, *English-Language Philosophy (1750–1945)*, pp. 121ff.

67 Richard Rorty, *Consequences of Pragmatism*, p. 160.

68 References to James are to *The Writings of William James*.

69 References to Peirce are to his *Selected Writings*.

70 John Dewey, *Democracy and Education*, pp. 29, 16.

71 References to Green are to section numbers of *Prologomena to Ethics*.

72 References to Bradley are to *Ethical Studies* (E); *Appearance and Reality* (AR); and *The Principles of Logic* (PL).

73 Quoted in Skorupski, *English-Language Philosophy (1750–1945)*, p. 88.

74 Ibid.

75 See Peter Hylton, *Russell, Idealism and the Emergence of Analytic Philosophy*, pp. 48ff, on this point and for an excellent discussion of Green and Bradley.

9
· RECENT NON-WESTERN PHILOSOPHIES ·

· 1 India ·

'The need for philosophy arises when faith in tradition is shaken', wrote a modern Indian philosopher.[1] Certainly it is as true of his culture as of others discussed in this chapter – Chinese, Japanese, and Islamic – that a revitalization of philosophy owed to the shock which tradition received from the impact of the West. (The case of Africa is, perhaps, rather different since it is a debated point, as we shall see, whether 'African philosophy' is a suitable label for the traditional thought of that continent.)

By 1820, British dominion over India, achieved with an ease embarrassing to many Indians, was almost complete. For various reasons, this prompted a re-examination of traditional thought that the earlier Mogul conquest had not. The Islamic Moguls generally took a relaxed, unproselytizing attitude towards the old religions and ways. Nor did they import ideas so uncompromising towards the ancient wisdom as those carried in the baggage-train of the British – Enlightenment naturalism and nineteenth-century positivism. More subtly threatening were idealist systems of thought, such as Hegel's, with an apparent similarity, but perhaps no more, to those of the Indian schools.

We might distinguish between three related challenges to Indian intellectual tradition. First, there was the challenge, replete with the rhetoric of 'the rights of man', equality and liberty, to the Indian moral outlook and the practices, like the caste system, which this seemed to condone. Second, there was the challenge to Hindu religion, seen by many Europeans as a barely intelligible chaos of beliefs in contrast to the clearer, crisper doctrines of Christianity. Finally, Indians faced the challenge of philosophical systems which purported to explain reality in naturalistic terms, without recourse to contemplative intuition or other mysterious access to knowledge.

Faced with such impressive challenges, Indian thinkers were in a predicament still experienced today, to judge from one recent author's confession: that of being 'too intimately visited by "modern" secular winds . . . to take . . . for granted . . . inherited modes of thought', yet unable, with the 'bond with tradition . . . not wholly broken', to reject 'those traditional norms which still reach down . . . with magisterial authority'.[2] The response to this predicament went through two broad phases. During the earlier phase, it was one of guarded welcome to Western ideas. The quintessential figure here was Ram Mohan Roy (1772–1833), founder of the influential *Brahmo Samaj* ('Divine Society'), a cosmopolitan admirer of the Enlightenment and of Christian ethics, and an ally of the British in their efforts to rid his country of its more grotesque customs, such as that of *satis* throwing themselves on the funeral pyres of their husbands. Significantly, though, Ram Mohan insisted that his reformism was in keeping with the authoritative texts of Hinduism, the Vedas and the *Upaniṣads*. For some, however, he exhibited insufficient fidelity to tradition, and in the second half of the nineteenth century, a more militant phase in the response to the Western challenge was evident.

There were, to be sure, diehard conservatives for whom any Western idea was anathema – for none more so, ironically, than those Western Indophiles who formed the Theosophical Society, like the former Fabian socialist Annie Besant. But the more common attitude was that while there was much to admire in Western thought and achievements, these could not be integrated into Indian culture without considerable transformation and were anyway nothing to cause Indians embarrassment over their own tradition. Tagore expresses this attitude in a letter of 1893: 'just as the city streets [of Europe] are hard and paved . . . so the [European] mind and character have to be solidly constructed'. Still, 'I don't see this impractical, self-absorbed, free-roving mind of mine, with its love of imagination, as anything to be ashamed of'.[3] Such statements may make 'Neo-Hinduism' sound more defensive than it was, for an emerging theme was that, whatever benefits Western thought might have to confer, even greater ones can flow in the opposite direction. As Vivekananda put it, 'when the Occidental wants to learn about the spirit, about God, about the soul, about the meaning and mystery of this universe, he must sit at the feet of the Orient to learn'. His countrymen must be ready for the spiritual 'conquest of the whole world by India' (75–6).[4]

Vivekananda (1863–1902) was the disciple of the saintly mystic Ramakrishna, and with his striking performance at the World Parliament of Religions in Chicago in 1893, the first of many Indian spiritual emissaries to the West. He was, however, just one of a remarkable group of thinkers – philosophers, poets, politicians, mystics, often a combination of these – born within a few years of one another and responsible for lending new life to the Indian tradition. Best known, of course, is Mohandas Gandhi (1869–1948). But the group also includes the man who dubbed Gandhi '*Mahātma*' (the Great Soul) and was in turn dubbed 'the Indian Goethe' by Albert Schweitzer, Rabindranath Tagore (1861–1941), the Nobel Prize-winning Bengali poet; Aurobindo Ghose (1872–1950), a fiery political orator before retiring to forty years of meditation in an *āśram*; and, a little later, Sarvepalli Radhakrishnan (1888–1972), university philosopher, diplomat and, finally, President of the nation for whose independence he, like the others mentioned, had prepared the way.

I have spoken of tradition defended in the teeth of the Western challenge but, as we saw in chapter 2, there was no single tradition of Indian thought, even if the various *darśanas* or 'schools' shared a common framework. It is usually said that the tradition revivified at the end of the nineteenth century was the Vedāntic one (see ch. 2, sect. 3, and ch. 6, sect. 1). This is basically true: hence the title 'Neo-Vedānta' for the new movement. Buddhism, certainly, since its salad days under the Mauryan emperors during the third century BCE, had declined in influence, despite its successful export further east. Other systems of thought were not to be re-examined in detail until very recently, and then by Indian philosophers working mainly in Western universities, and impressed by the contributions which these systems, especially Nyāya, had to make to issues salient in twentieth-century analytical philosophy.[5] As we shall see, however, the Vedāntic tradition defended was of a more eclectic variety than anything formulated in earlier times by Śaṅkara or Rāmānuja.

'Practical Vedānta' and Ecumenicalism

Nineteenth-century critics of India often construed the practices they abhorred – the caste system, the arbitrary rule of preening Maharajahs, the immolation of widows – not as corruptions of a traditional ideal, but as all too consistent with the moral quietism encouraged by tradition. If people's only genuine goal is *mokṣa*, liberation from the cycle of rebirth in the empirical world (*saṃsāra*), it might seem a mere distraction to be concerned with social ills. The only moral principles, apparently, would be those personal rules of conduct – temperance, chastity, and the like – which are conducive to detachment from the physical and social world (see ch. 2, sects 1 and 5). Many Indians must have felt as ambivalent towards social reformers as one of R. K. Narayan's characters: 'While he thundered against . . . social shortcomings, a voice went on asking: "Life and the world and all this is passing – why bother about anything?"'[6]

What Vivekananda called 'practical Vedānta' was the rebuttal of this attitude. The goals of the Ramakrishna Mission which he founded were 'self-liberation and service to humanity'. Better, perhaps, is 'self-liberation *through* service to humanity', for he argued that *mokṣa* is only attainable through moral commitment to the well-being of others. (Ironists will note the similarity between this and T. H. Green's ideal of 'self-realization through service to humanity' which, as we saw (p. 354), inspired many of India's colonial administrators.) The central premise, here, is that of Advaita (non-dualist) Vedānta: the 'oneness' of everything, including ourselves, with a spiritual reality, *Brahman*. What is dropped, however, is the impression given by some Advaitins that the everyday world of plurality and individuality is one that should not unduly engage our attention. The plural world, as a manifestation of *Brahman*, is at heart a unity, so there cannot be a genuine conflict between concerns for one's own soul and for those of others. 'When one man serves another, really he serves himself, because essentially . . . all are one.'[7]

Nor can there be any conflict between service to human beings and devotion to God, the 'active' aspect of *Brahman* in the world. For God is only visible to us 'in the human face'. People, therefore, only become 'religious from the day [they] begin to see God in men and women', and behave towards them accordingly (73). In particular, religion demands the effort to educate people − to 'put ideas in their heads, [so] they will do the rest' (78) − and the alleviation of poverty, for an ignorant person living in penury is in no position to progress towards liberation. The effect, then, of Vivekananda's interpretation of Vedānta was to place unprecedented emphasis upon the first of the three 'disciplines' (*yogas*) proposed by the *Bhagavad-Gītā* as routes to *mokṣa* − those of 'action' (*karma*), 'devotion' (*bhakti*) and 'knowledge' (*jñāna*) (see ch. 1, sect. 5).

The *Gītā* was the favourite reading of the man of whom Einstein wrote, 'generations to come . . . will scarce believe that such a one . . . walked upon this earth'. Mahātma Gandhi developed his account of the relation between religion, politics and morality as a young lawyer working among the Indian community of South Africa. His theoretical acumen, organizational skills and charismatic personality made him, after his return to India, the moral leader of his country's independence movement. Assassinated by a Hindu fanatic in 1948, this 'seditious fakir', as Winston Churchill revoltingly described him, lived long enough to witness that independence, and too long to avoid experiencing its bloody partition between Moslems and Hindus. His sole object, Gandhi explained, was 'self-realization, to see God face to face, to attain *mokṣa*' (A x).[8] While on earth, however, the only way to achieve this vision is to 'find God . . . in his creation and be one with it'. This means, in particular, to be one with our fellows since, as creatures of God, we are all 'tarred with the same brush'. 'The immediate service of other human beings', then, 'becomes a necessary part of the endeavour' to realize the spiritual goal (S 30ff). Ideally, this service takes the form of personal devotion and love towards people. But, in the real world, it requires political and social action too: for it is violence, exploitation, social prejudice (against the 'untouchables', for instance) and material greed which stand in the way of *mokṣa*, and these can only be combatted by entering the political fray. The connection between religion and politics is thus made: 'those who say that religion has nothing to do with politics do not know what religion means' (A 420).

Gandhi's achievement has been described as 'the spiritualization of politics', for 'there was hardly a Hindu religious category and practice to which he did not give a . . . secular content'.⁹ This is true, certainly, of *ahimsā* (non-violence), with its central role in his famous doctrine of *satyāgraha*. This term was coined from the words for 'truth' and 'firmness' (A 266), and denotes the ideal of gentle but resolute insistence, not only on speaking the truth, but on enabling people to recognize it. This is something to pursue whether persuading one's wife to desist from a harmful diet or one's rulers to relent from injustice. There are two kinds of reason why *satyāgraha* is, for Gandhi, so central. First, alternative means of persuasion contradict the moral principle of non-violence. Since all life partakes in one divine reality, to harm a single living being is 'to slight [the] divine powers, and . . . the whole world' (S 67). *Ahimsā*, Gandhi stresses, is not 'the crude thing' which those who equate it with 'passive resistance' imagine. Refraining from harming a person is but one expression of the principle, which is also flouted by 'every evil thought, . . . by hatred, by wishing ill to anybody'. Since the principle is also 'violated by our holding on to what the world needs', thereby indirectly contributing to suffering, it enjoins active intervention on behalf of the underprivileged.

The deeper case for *ahimsā* and *satyāgraha* is that they are necessary for the emergence of truth. Truth will out only when people engage in rational discourse with one another. But this is not something they do in a vacuum, and political theorists have been guilty of ignoring the conditions which must obtain for human beings to exhibit rationality. They will not do so where violence lurks, believers rather than their beliefs are attacked, prejudice prevails, or one of the parties to the debate enjoys disproportionate power. *Satyāgraha*, then, enjoins that 'transformation or purification of [the] relationship' between people which is essential if they are to engage as rational beings (S 74).¹⁰ But there is a further reason why 'truth-firmness' must be gentle. While there are absolute truths about God and His will, no single person is able to identify these with certainty, so that 'I must hold by the relative truth as I have conceived it' (A xi). Any such conception is bound to be fragmentary and perspectival and, rather as for C. S. Peirce (see p. 353), absolute truth is an horizon which we can only approach *together*, by combining fragments of individual understanding and partial perspectives. Such a combination presupposes a climate of non-violent discourse in which no views are brutally excluded from consideration, and men and women remain patiently open to revising the fallible and relative truths at which they have so far arrived.

A perspectival view of truth was also operative in another dimension of Neo-Vedāntic thought. To a generation used to the sight of saffron robes mingling with dog-collars, turbans with dreadlocks, at 'festivals' of inter-faith worship, the idea that religions share a common essence may not be news. This was not so a century ago when Vivekananda broke it to the World Parliament of Religions, compounding this controversial message with the claim that Hinduism had a privileged role in securing religious unity. Even if it had been more in the Hindu character, outright hostility towards Christianity would not have been a viable option. For one thing, no religion could be all bad which generated such an eminently attractive social morality. For another, India's greatest nineteenth-century saint, Ramakrishna, in whom the sight of a balloon or a lion could induce religious ecstasy, purported to enjoy direct experience of the Christian God and Allah as well as of Kali, 'the divine mother'. This hospitality to other religions was soon extended: Vivekananda proclaimed his readiness to worship in the Mosque or before the crucifix, while Gandhi could announce 'I consider myself a Hindu, Christian, Moslem, Jew, Buddhist and Confucian' (S 10).

But what could justify this hospitality, this 'harmonizing' of the great religious writings which, for Vivekananda, will 'lead mankind to the place where there is neither the Vedas, nor the Bible, nor the Koran'?[11] First, a Gandhian appreciation of the partiality of any one culture's grasp of truth. 'All religions are true', wrote the Mahātma, yet 'all religions have some error in them' (SG 258). Through careful synthesis, the errors will cancel themselves out. Each religion, continues Radhakrishnan, by emphasizing some aspects of divine reality is bound to understate others. Islam's 'spirit of resignation' and Christianity's 'divine love', say, reflect so many 'visions . . . [which] fertilize each other so as to give mankind a many-sided perfection' in its religious understanding (FC 76).[12] The harmonization of different religions was facilitated, second, by distinguishing not only between religions and their outward forms – the 'treasure within' from its 'earthen vessels', as St Paul put it – but between the absolute Godhead and the various Gods (Allah, Vishnu, and so on) which issue from different peoples' attempts to represent the former. A 'spiritual religion of humanity', says Aurobindo, will not be one of creed or rites, but a 'growing realization' of that 'secret Spirit' which historical religions have struggled to make manifest (158–9).[13] It is, argues Radhakrishnan, 'misleading to speak of different religions', for these are but different symbolic approximations to the single religious-cum-philosophical truth of the Godhead as absolute reality (FC 77f).

But some religions are more equal than others, it seems. Recall Vivekananda's insistence that the West must 'sit at the feet of the Orient'. And there is nothing even-handed in Aurobindo's claim that 'the Hindu religion is really the eternal . . . universal religion which embraces all others' (153). Part of the thought, here, was that Hinduism is well-equipped to serve as a religious melting-pot, already capable of embracing within its fold the devotees of Vishnu, Śiva, Kali, and others. In the doctrine of *avatars* – those appearances of a god in human form, like Krishna in the *Gītā* – there is scope, moreover, to accommodate Christian claims about Jesus' divinity. If a charioteer can be a man–god, why not a carpenter? But the deeper thought was that Hinduism was wedded to a distinction between an ineffable reality (*Brahman*) and God (*Īśvara*) as an active principle in the world. This was just the kind of distinction required for distilling a common religious essence from variable dogmas. Though not unknown to other religious traditions, only in Hinduism was the distinction central and orthodox.

With such a privileged status accorded to Hinduism, one may wonder what substance remains to the rhetoric of 'harmonization' – especially when one encounters passages where Vivekananda, for example, refers to Christian doctrines like that of creation *ex nihilo* as ones which 'have disgusted all the educated' (77). And there is another reason for questioning the candour of the ecumenical effort. Hinduism may be a broad church, but there are genuine philosophical tensions within it, and arguably it was only by pasting over these that Vedānta could be presented as a coherent religious philosophy able to embrace other religions. It is Vivekananda, Gandhi and others whom Karl Potter has in mind when he laments that 'success in philosophy has come to be measured in terms of how many positions one can incorporate into one's world-view without their apparent contradictions becoming any more than apparent'.[14] Some thinkers, however, could not be so readily accused of fudging these 'contradictions' and tried, moreover, to accommodate Vedānta to currents of philosophy imported from the West. Let us consider their attempts.

Intuitive Absolute Idealism

The philosophical task facing the Neo-Vedāntins was twofold. First, both 'practical Vedānta' and the doctrine of religious unity drew heavily on the *Upaniṣads'* theme of the identity of everything with *Brahman*. But, as Rāmānuja and Madhva had long ago observed (ch. 6, sect. 1), it was not easy to square this theme with acceptance of a god who could be a proper object of religious worship. For Tagore to reiterate 'this absolute conception of *Brahman* . . . in which there can be no distinction of this and that', but then to place it 'outside the subject' of religious faith, was surely an evasion of the issue.[15] Moreover, the monistic theme had, historically, encouraged a view of the empirical world as illusory, a view more apt to produce a mood of 'Why bother?' than of moral commitment. Second, the Neo-Vedāntins were well-versed in recent Western philosophies which had either to be refuted or assimilated. A. K. Coomaraswamy, for example, was impressed by Nietzsche whom, however, he managed to construe as a mystic preaching the Indian message of 'the interpenetration of the spiritual and the material', and whose Overman was the sage who had attained liberation in this life.[16] But it was three other Western tendencies which loomed largest: evolutionary materialism, which dispensed with explanatory appeals to spirit; Kantian and positivist strictures on the possibility of knowledge which exceeds the realm of empirical phenomena; and non-mystical idealism of Hegel's sort, which rests the case for an absolute spirit on reason.

Let us begin by looking at Radhakrishnan's attempt to discharge the tasks just noted, one which frequently coincides with Aurobindo's. First, there is his interpretation of evolution. With the scientific story told by Darwin and Spencer there is no need to take issue, but far from supporting a materialistic view of the cosmos, the story refutes it. That story at best shows why some events occur given that others have occurred: it cannot, as a philosophy should, show why the whole process has to be as it is. Mechanistic stories fail to answer the question 'what guides the mechanism?' and must be supplemented by a teleological account of the 'reason or purpose behind it' (IV 331). When we consider 'the successive emergence of the material, the organic, the animal, the human and the spiritual orders of existence', it is apparent that 'the aim of cosmic evolution is to reveal the Spirit' (FC 27, 44). Even if we ignore this final aim, it is impossible to explain the emergence of higher stages from lower ones – of animal life from mere matter, say, or mind from the merely animal. Mind and spirit must, as Aurobindo puts it, be things which 'universal nature has hidden in herself' before their manifest emergence (155). Finally, it would be 'presumptuous' to think that evolution ends with the emergence of human self-consciousness. Indeed, we are already familiar with a 'plane' of 'superconsciousness' – or, as Aurobindo prefers, the 'supramental' – where we enjoy a union with a 'higher world' than the one described by evolutionary science.

If evolution is to be taken seriously, so is the world in which it unfolds: hence, the doctrine of *māyā* cannot 'mean that the empirical world . . . is an illusion'. Granted, it is of a 'lower order' than *Brahman*, being 'subject to change, waxing and waning' (ER 27ff.). It has, too, a 'one-sided dependence' on *Brahman*, since the latter could exist without it, but not vice versa. Still, enjoying a lower, dependent status does not amount to non-existence. Elsewhere Radhakrishnan explains that by 'idealism' he does not intend the doctrine that things are only mental 'images', but the view that all existence has 'meaning or purpose' (IV 15). It follows, as Aurobindo observes, that those 'old yogas . . . [which] found the earth a rather impossible place for any spiritual being' were wrong, and we need have no compunction taking this earth and its inhabitants as sufficiently real for moral and political action to be worth the bother (158). If the empirical world is real, so is that 'active or energizing' force which we discern at work in it and call God or Īśvara. Instead of regarding Īśvara, as perhaps Śaṅkara did, as an illusory appearance of *Brahman*, we should view Him as 'the Absolute in action as Lord and Creator' (FC 39). Hindus need not, therefore, fear that they are worshipping a phantasm when praying or sacrificing to Īśvara in His various aspects, such as Vishnu or Śiva.

Some Western philosophers, swayed by Kant or positivism, will complain that there can be no knowledge of *Brahman*, since this would transcend all possible experience. But, as William James saw, it is arbitrary to restrict experience to the senses, and we 'must submit to the fact of spiritual experience, which is primary' (ER 23). Others, followers of Hegel, may complain that knowledge of absolute spirit can only be reached through reason. But they should, insists Radhakrishnan, concede the primacy of intuition, since what else guarantees the basic principles which reasoning presupposes? 'Logical knowledge', moreover, can at best 'give the structure of being, not being itself'. To be 'put in touch' with being, direct intuition is necessary, of a kind which 'unites' us with it, since in this 'integral' insight 'the subject is not opposed to the object' (FC 61). Hegel's ambition of recognizing that we are 'at home' with spiritual reality requires, then, the primacy of intuition over reason. Aurobindo agrees: if few of us attain to 'direct spiritual knowledge', this is because of more earthly distractions, such as 'the sexual impulse' – quaintly described as a 'mistake' – which the time-honoured yogic disciplines can overcome (156f).

Radhakrishnan seeks further, eclectic support for his intuitive idealism. In Jamesian vein, he holds that the truth in 'integral insight' is 'due to the fact that it satisfies our wants . . . and thus gives peace of mind . . . and contributes to . . . social harmony' (ER 24). In Kierkegaardian fashion, he cites the individual's sense of his or her 'nothingness' as the start of a religious quest which can only end with appreciation of one's dependence on a greater Self.

The sense that 'I am nought' is also important for another, more subtle, philosopher of the period, K. C. Bhattacharyya (1875–1940). Significantly, though, what this sense testifies to is not mere dependence on something greater, but 'the possibility of . . . the individual self being unreal' (477).[17] Generally, Bhattacharyya is critical of the departures from Śaṅkara's monistic philosophy evident in his contemporaries' writings, whilst sharing their aims of finding space for religion and morality, and accommodating the wisdom of the West. He is, for example, hostile to their purposive version of evolution. Any big story of 'cosmic evolution', as distinct from Darwin's limited theory of natural selection, is only 'a species of imaginative literature', with no place in either science or philosophy. No such story could be verified, and the categories it employs – matter, life, mind, and so on – are not an objective classification of the ingredients of reality, but abstract distillations from experience (471ff.).

Such remarks suggest a robust empiricism on Bhattacharyya's part, soon confirmed by his admiration for Kant's restriction of conceptual judgement to items of possible perception. Indeed, he heads in a positivist direction, complaining that Kant should not have allowed for even the 'thinkability' of such items as 'pure' selves and God. Only the things encountered through practical activity and sense-perception are 'literally thinkable'. What, then, is the status of philosophical claims about things in themselves, absolute reality and so on? While they are not, as the logical positivists were currently urging, merely symptoms of a 'disease of speech', they must nevertheless be construed non-literally. Philosophy is the 'systematic symbolism' through which we endeavour to express what is not strictly speakable (460). It does not follow, however, that we cannot have knowledge of the unsayable. The self may not be 'thinkable', but it is not therefore 'utterly unknowable'. We have, as Schopenhauer would agree, a direct, if mysterious, acquaintance with ourselves as embodied subjects. Some of us, moreover, experience an 'identity with the over-personal self' (460), a foretaste of which is that sense of 'I am nought' referred to above. It is this experience which, though 'speakable only in the purely symbolist way', Advaita Vedānta attempts to articulate.

But if the central doctrine of that philosophy is 'the illusoriness of the individual self' (113) and of the empirical world, the old problem of making sense of religious worship and moral duty persists. Bhattacharyya's response begins with distinguishing appearance from the merely imaginary for, as Kant saw, the distinction between, say, waking and dream experiences is one made *within* the world of appearances. He continues in Kantian vein when he writes, 'one has to be a realist to outgrow realism' (120). That is: we must accept that the tables and trees we perceive are not figments of the imagination before we can appreciate that, nevertheless, we are not perceiving reality itself but only the forms in which it appears to us. In Kant's terms, we should be 'empirical realists' but 'transcendental idealists'. In a sense, accepting that the world of *māyā* is one of mere appearance leaves everything where it was. Space and time may not be features of reality, yet we have no option but to think in spatial and temporal terms, and it would be silly to react to their 'illusoriness' by giving up the use of rulers and clocks. Nothing loses its importance simply by being shown to belong to reality as it appears, not as it is, and this is as true of moral action as of anything else. Not to help an injured man on the basis that bodies are appearances would be like refusing to wear a watch on the ground that time is only apparent.

Just as Kant's transcendental idealism is a philosophical interpretation of ordinary experience, and not a criticism of it, so the Advaita doctrine of *Brahman* is 'no rejection but only an interpretation of . . . concrete religion' (123). In everyday experience, we can be aware of ourselves as individuals related to a personal god immanent in the world. That, on philosophical reflection, we appreciate that individuals and this god belong only to appearance is no more reason to denigrate such experience than an analogous reflection serves to discredit our ordinary perception of space and time. Indeed, true self-knowledge – the knowledge that there is only the one Self, *Brahman* – 'derives its whole meaning from the concrete religion of worship and ceremonial' (123). Without the intimations which that religion makes possible, there could be no ascent to its philosophical interpretation. To play this role, worship and ceremonial must, moreover, belong in a genuine tradition: which is one good reason not to 'hustle people out' of their old religious ways. Hence we ought to display the tolerance towards a plurality of religions urged by Vivekananda and others.

In short, there is no need to water down the seemingly stark message of Advaita Vedānta in the manner of Radhakrishnan. Properly understood, it secures the seriousness for us of the world of *māyā*, and hence that of moral action and religious worship. Whether or not Bhattacharyya's reconstruction of Vedānta succeeds, it is surely not open to Potter's criticism of a philosophy whose popularity owes to disguising the contradictions among its eclectic elements. The revival of Vedānta in the nineteenth century by, primarily, religious and moral reformers may not have been an episode of great philosophical sophistication. But through the writings of later philosophers, notably Bhattacharyya, Vedānta is rendered a coherent system of thought, able to match the Western systems which, to an extent, it has now accommodated.

• 2 China and Japan •

As in India, resuscitation of philosophical debate in China and Japan after the mid-nineteenth century owed primarily to the impact of the West, economic, military and intellectual. In both countries, the prevailing orthodoxy had, for centuries, been a tired Confucianism. In China, hardly a thinker of note had emerged since Wang Yang-Ming early in the sixteenth century (see pp. 210ff.); and even in Japan, where debate had been somewhat livelier, the 'aridity' of orthodox Confucianism, to cite one commentator, 'rendered it more and more intellectually vacuous and epistemologically confining as the Tokugawa era [1571–1868] wore on'.[18]

Once Western ways of thought established themselves in the two empires, in the wake of the military and trading enclaves imposed upon them, reactions displayed the same rainbow variety as in India. From conservatives there came the call to 'repel the barbarians' and their new-fangled ideas, from radicals a whole-hearted welcome to ideologies presumed responsible for Western superiority in arms and wealth. As a leading Japanese modernizer, Fukuzawa Yukichi, put it in 1898, 'Chinese philosophy as the root of education was responsible for our obvious shortcomings' and we must 'drive its degenerate influences from our country' (SJT 122).[19] Those Chinese whose cry was for the closing of 'the old curiosity shop of Confucius' agreed. In between these reactions was the search for a syncretic blend of oriental wisdom and occidental reason: for, say, 'the ethics of the East, the science of the West'. (The anger of Emperor Meiji at an indecently early arrival, due to the zeal of a Western engineer showing off the speed of his train, illustrated the problems in getting the right blend.) More subtly, and again with Indian parallels, there were attempts to embrace Western ideas whilst arguing that, not only do they have Eastern precedents, but they can only be fully appreciated when viewed in an Eastern framework.

A further parallel with India was the number of writers on philosophy who were at the forefront of political and social developments in their countries. Sun Yat-Sen (1864–1925) and Mao Tse-Tung (1893–1976) are the best-known of these. One might also mention, among the Japanese, the Western-izing official Nishi Amane (1829–97) and the nationalist revolutionary Kita Ikki (1884–1937), executed for his part in the 1936 mutiny; and, among the Chinese, the Confucian K'ang Yu-Wei (1858–1927), responsible for the last-ditch reforms of the Empire in 1898, and the pragmatist Hu Shih (1891–1962), a leader of the New Culture movement of the 1920s and, later, a prime figure of hate by Mao's intellectual thugs.

In one important respect the East Asian experience was different from India's, for China and Japan were never colonized nor significantly populated by a Western power (until 1946 in Japan's case). This meant that the influence of Christian thought was less marked than in India. More important still were differences between China and Japan in their accommodation to economic and technological invasion, and in subsequent political developments. Within fifty years of the arrival in Japan of an American naval squadron in 1853, she had, through remarkably rapid industrialization, defeated China and stood on the brink of a more impressive victory over Russia. In China, meanwhile, pathetic resistance to Western power – in the Opium Wars, or the Boxer rebellion of 1900 – led to the fall of the imperial system in 1912. During the following years, while Japan enjoyed stable government and status as a world power, China suffered under the burden of warlordship and then of civil war between the Nationalists and the Communists.

These differences were responsible for philosophy taking a different pace and shape in the two nations. Professional philosophy in Japan was able to develop and, as it were, settle down more quickly, the luxury of leisured thought being more affordable than in its chaotic, war-torn neighbour. Again, debates which still split Chinese intellectuals during the 1920s over the acceptability of Western logic and scientific method had been largely settled in Japan forty years before. (Though we will note the phenomenon of 'Japanism' in the 1930s.) Finally, the efficiency with which Japan transformed herself into a modern state meant that her intellectuals were not under the same pressure as their Chinese counterparts to turn against the traditional values of their culture. Whereas a reformist Chinese could blame the obsession with filial piety for his country's failure to modernize, Japanese thinkers could credit their country's success to the virtues long proclaimed in 'the way of the warrior' (*bushido*).

Confucianism Adjusted

Only the diehards in the circle of the ghastly Empress Dowager Tz'u Hsi could, by 1900, imagine that the prevailing Confucian orthodoxy in China should remain intact. For others, the only question was whether Confucianism was an 'old curiosity shop' to be closed up or a philosophy capable of adjustment to new ideas and political developments. This possibility of tailoring Confucianism to a new era was encouraged by the fact that it had never been a tight set of clear and agreed doctrines. Certainly, all Confucians agreed that the universe was a harmonious system, whose nature should be reflected in the life of the 'superior person' (*chung tzu*), and that the primary virtue of this person was *jen* ('compassion', 'humanity'), to be exhibited in service to society. But the import of crucial terms, like *jen*, was flexible, and major tensions between Confucian thinkers had always existed: like that between Mencius and Hsun Tzu over the innate goodness of man (ch. 3, sect. 2), or between the Neo-Confucians Chu Hsi and Wang Yang-Ming over the relative priority of reason and heart (ch. 6, sect. 2).

The leading reconstructor of Confucianism in its practical aspects was K'ang Yu-Wei, an influential reformist monarchist whose successes under both these heads were short-lived. The 1898 reforms he inspired were suppressed after 100 days by the Empress Dowager, while the restoration of the Manchu Emperor in 1917, in which K'ang was instrumental, lasted only twelve days. K'ang combined boundless respect for Confucius – 'the most . . . perfect sage [in] the history of mankind' (SCT 731)[20] – with horror at the practices which his followers had condoned, such as the foot-binding of women. Central to K'ang's thought were two perceptions. First, that of the world as a single, harmonious whole, revealed to him by a sudden experience that 'heaven, earth, and the myriad things were all of one substance with myself' (SCT 724). Second, a Schopenhauerian vision of 'the whole world [as] but a world of grief and misery . . . a great slaughter-yard' (CCP 625). This may sound more Indian than Chinese, but in the first place K'ang's explanation of the world's unity is thoroughly Confucian. The 'myriad things', including human beings, are united since all are, ultimately, parts of the 'all-embracing Primal *ch'i* ['material–spiritual force']' which 'created' the Heaven and Earth from which they spring

(CCP 625). As for suffering, this is not an inevitable aspect of our earthly condition, only to be avoided by release from the world, but something we can take practical steps to eliminate. Our aim should not be Buddhistic contemplation but 'daily to bend our thoughts . . . to means of seeking happiness: this is to progress' (CCP 636). Our thoughts should only turn to Buddhahood once suffering has been made a thing of the past.

Progress is anyway inevitable. 'The course of humanity progresses according to a fixed sequence' from the Age of Disorder, through that of Order (which we are currently approaching), to the Age of Great Peace (SCT 732f). Here as elsewhere, one notices the influence on K'ang of Western notions – evolution, progress – in which he was well-versed but with which he insists on crediting Confucius. Since Confucius is usually construed as holding a cyclical view of history, K'ang's tribute may be more imaginative than scholarly.

The doctrine of the three Ages provides K'ang with his tool for criticizing the Confucianism of his contemporaries. Their trouble, like that of many earlier followers of Confucius, is – as K'ang's pupil T'an Ssu-t'ung pointed out – to treat the duties preached by Confucius as 'the essence of Confucianism', thus failing to recognize that they belonged to a 'system applicable only to the Age of Disorder' (CCP 652). If Confucius had lived in the Age of Order, when people need to be united in a single nation, he would not have preached duties to family and clan. Indeed, as we set course for the Age of Great Peace, when even national boundaries will be erased, filial piety will, says K'ang, be replaced by 'the loving care of the entire race' (SCT 732), or rather of life in general, since animals will not be discriminated against. National boundaries are only one of the nine whose abolition is 'the remedy for suffering': others include those of race, class, and sex. With these boundaries erased, the primary virtue of *jen* can at last be manifested as Confucius intended: in universal compassion and love for all creatures as moral equals. (Some readers may well think that this was the intention of Mo Tzu rather than Confucius – see ch. 3, sect. 3.) K'ang, in effect, was an early enthusiast for today's popular image of morality as an 'expanding circle', whereby the constituency of creatures deserving of moral concern gradually expands from members of one's immediate family to all creatures capable of suffering.[21] Loyalty to class, patriotism and 'anthropocentric' morality are only stages in that process.

As this futuristic vision suggests, K'ang's evolutionism was not that of the Social Darwinists. Competition and struggle may have played their part in humanity's progress, but now constitute the 'greatest evil . . . in the world', and those who enthuse about them are helping to turn the earth into a 'jungle [where] all is blood and iron'.[22] In the harmonious society, there will be no private property to inspire competition, not even private homes, so that 'everyone will dine together, like a great convention' (CCP 637). Though the main case for socialism is one of human harmony, K'ang shared the familiar European conviction that it would lead to material progress and the elimination

of suffering. Jules Verne more than Friedrich Engels, though, seems to inspire K'ang's vision of a technological utopia, replete with its flying hotel rooms, daily medicals, and lavatories 'made pleasant with music and fragrant odours'.

If utopian internationalist socialism is an unexpected product of Confucianism, so presumably is the aggressive nationalism – or fascism – which some Japanese writers manufactured partly from Confucian materials. The clearest statement of this latter attempt was the document published by the Japanese Ministry of Education in 1937, and sold to two million people, *Fundamentals of our National Polity* (SJT 278–88). Here was an attempt to blend elements of Western political thought, Buddhism and Confucianism, spiced with the Shintoist tradition of emperor worship, and to 'sublimate' these into a uniquely 'Japanist' ideology. The Western ingredients in the blend were the nineteenth-century nationalism and historicism which German writers had extracted from Herder's accounts of *Kultur* and *Volk* and Hegel's 'organic' theory of the State. Echoing Kita Ikki's pronouncement that 'every nation has its own national spirit', the authors of the *Fundamentals* complain that in 'abstract theories', like K'ang's internationalism, 'concrete and historical national life became lost in the shadow'. Hegel was right to regard the State as the entity to which individuals owe their loyalty and identity as persons. Hegel, though, was an exception, for Western theories generally fail to recognize that the State 'gives birth to individual beings', instead treating it as an 'expedient for the welfare of . . . independent individuals'. Socialism is no exception, since what it preaches is simply 'class individualism'. Here the East has done better, emphasizing a 'spirit of self-effacement' that means 'living to the great, true self by denying one's small self'.

If that is the Indian contribution, Confucianism also provides essential ingredients. Two of these, 'a sense of obligation [which] binds master and servant' and filial piety, can, when combined with belief in the Emperor's divine origin, nurture the sentiment of 'our country [as] a great family nation', with the Imperial Household as the 'head family', and the Emperor as the master to whom obligations are ultimately owed. It is, moreover, the Confucian doctrine that 'the spirit of harmony is built on the concord of all things' in Heaven and Earth that underpins an ethic of national unity. Within an individualistic climate of thought, there can perhaps be 'co-operation' and 'mitigation' of conflict, but 'there exists no true harmony'. Since traditions and cultures are essentially different from one another, only within the 'national polity', the Emperor at its head, can there be achieved that harmony among human beings which replicates 'the fundamental Way' of the Confucian universe. Only, in other words, in Japan is the Way truly manifest.

K'ang and the authors of the *Fundamentals* reiterate, without elaborating, the broad framework of Confucian metaphysics, their interests being practical. The period is not a vintage one for Confucian metaphysics, but a partial exception

is the work of Fung Yu-Lan (1895–1990), best known for that indispensable aid to us non-sinologists, *A History of Chinese Philosophy*, but the author, too, of 'the most original Chinese philosophical work in this century' (SBCP 751), *A New Rational Philosophy*. Insufficiently 'materialist' for Mao's taste, Fung was to disown the work, after 1949, as symptomatic of 'feudalism'. Fung saw himself as representative of a third stage of that 'meeting of the West and the East [which had] constituted the main current of Chinese thought' since the final decades of the nineteenth century (CCP 732). Instead of rejecting Western ideas wholesale, or of welcoming them so uncritically that the Chinese tradition became an object of contempt, it was high time to make objective comparisons so that Eastern and Western thought might illuminate one another. Fung's ambition is to use the insights of Aristotle and others to provide a new, less fragile basis for the 'rationalist' Neo-Confucianism of Chu Hsi, supplemented by Taoist ingredients.

Chu Hsi was right to regard *Li* ('principle') and *ch'i* ('material') as the central categories of metaphysics (see pp. 208ff.). For anything to exist, there must be the 'principle . . . by which actual things necessarily are what they are' (SBCP 755) – for example, squareness in the case of square things. But there must also be 'that on which [the thing] depends for existence . . . the material which actualizes the principle' (SBCP 757). Unfortunately, the Neo-Confucians misconstrued the status of these metaphysical claims, failing to distinguish their purely 'formal' character from the empirical character of scientific claims. Chu compares *Li*'s relation to things with a parent's relation to children, as if principles were therefore productive powers within the world. In fact, statements like 'There is squareness' tell us nothing about the actual world, only about the conditions necessary for there to be a world of things at all. Chu also speaks of *ch'i* in such terms as 'clear' and 'turbid', as if it were the kind of stuff studied by chemists. But, as Aristotle saw in connection with 'prime matter', if this is to serve as the precondition for everything's existence, it cannot itself have any particular characteristics. 'Matter itself has no nature . . . whatsoever, it is indescribable' (SBCP 757). 'There is *ch'i*', then, is a 'formal' proposition, belonging not to science but to an account of the possibility of science.

Fung takes a similar line with Taoist claims. For there to be a world of change and becoming, there must indeed be a 'process' or 'way' whereby material and principle somehow combine so that things are 'transformed'. But it would be wrong to regard the Tao as some force, akin to God, standing behind this process. Terms like '*tao*' and 'the Great Whole' are shorthand labels for material force, the totality of principles and 'the entire process from material force to principle' taken together (SBCP 759). Put differently, 'The Absolute exists' is a 'formal', summary statement about the conditions for there to be a world, not a reference to some grand entity standing inside or outside that world.

It is tempting to think that, had Fung been working in Austria or Britain during the 1920s and 1930s, he would have subscribed to the Logical Positivist view that metaphysical claims are disguised statements about language (see pp. 443ff.). Maybe he would then have been willing to translate the claim that there must be principles by which actual things are what they are into something like, 'For X to exist, some meaningful general terms must be predicable of X.' But it would not then be easy to understand the moral capital which Fung makes out of the notion of *Li*. As for Chu Hsi, so for Fung, these principles serve as *standards* for things and people. 'The physical nature of things is good' when they 'actually follow their principle' (SBCP 760). *Li*, that is, seem to function like Plato's Forms, a point confirmed when Fung reiterates Chu's conviction that it is by 'investigating principles to the utmost' that human beings realize themselves. They do so, it seems, because in the intellectual endeavour to acquaint themselves with *Li* and the practical endeavour to make their behaviour conform with *Li*, they become 'free from the restriction of [sense-] experience' and from 'self-bondage' (SBCP 761). They are then freed for 'forming one body with all things', and hence for the exercise of *jen* towards the universe as a whole. Confucian metaphysical claims may, then, be 'formal' in the sense that they are not about the world of sense-experience. But they are, it seems, about something: about a reality of essential forms towards which, like Plato's philosophers, the sage must steer himself if he is to realize his rational and moral humanity.

Pragmatism and Maoism

The 'investigation of principles to the utmost' advocated by 'rationalist' Confucians was not wholly characteristic of Chinese thought, with its focus upon practical conduct. Given that focus, it is no surprise that the Western philosophies which captured the imagination of radicals were those which proclaimed the priority of practice over theory. Whereas Westernizing Japanese radicals, such as Nishi, imported the positivism of Comte and Mill, it was pragmatism and Marxism that were embraced by the leaders of the 'New Culture' movement in China during the 1920s. One such leader, Hu Shih, was a student of John Dewey at Columbia University, returning to China with unbounded enthusiasm for his teacher's pragmatism and other American products, like 'Mr Science and Mr Democracy', and scorn for his own culture. 'We are inferior to others not only in technology and political institutions but also in moral values, knowledge, literature, music, fine arts and body physique.'[23] Only Mohism (ch. 3, sect. 3) among Chinese philosophies, with its iconoclastic and utilitarian attitude towards tradition, won Hu's approval. Even the Eastern 'spirituality' vaunted by Hu's conservative contemporaries was dismissed. It is

Eastern cultures which are materialist since, through ignorance and laziness, their peoples remain 'restricted . . . by a material environment from which they cannot escape' (SCT 854). There is more 'spirit', intelligence and imagination invested in the motor car than in the rickshaw. Moreover, spiritual achievements require both the affluence and the 'refined methods' of investigation found only in the West. 'What spirituality is there', Hu asks, 'in the old beggar-woman who dies while still mumbling' the name of a Buddha?[24]

Critics of the West, he argues, are wrong to pit science against 'philosophy of life', for what we need is precisely a naturalistic philosophy of life. By investigating the causes of human behaviour, we can improve the human condition, dispensing with dangerous myths of a divine 'benevolent Ruler' and personal immortality. Science teaches that 'the "small self" is subject to death...', but mankind – the "Large Self" – ... is immortal', and that 'to live for the sake of the species and posterity is religion of the highest kind' (SCT 843). Hu's opponents might wonder how this and other moral prescriptions are conjured out of a naturalistic account of human beings as determined by physical laws. Pragmatism furnishes him with an answer. The truth of any theory, including naturalism, can only reside in its success. Only when a belief's 'utility still remains, [do] we . . . still call it truth' (SCT 833). Utility is the benefit conferred on the human species in the prevailing environment. Pragmatism, for Hu, has profound implications for political action. Principles of loyalty, for instance, which were true in a previous century are now false, because inappropriate to new conditions. What we need are 'particular truths for here and now', something that Chinese conservatives fail to recognize (SCT 832). They fail, too, to see the frivolity of 'abstract' philosophical thinking about principles and everything else. 'Thought is an instrument to deal with environment' (SCT 834), and once removed from its concrete, natural setting evaporates into hot air. Philosophical disputes that cannot be settled by the criterion of coping with the environment have no genuine meaning. Hence the proper duty of the philosopher can only be to seek a 'fundamental solution' to the 'basic and crucial problems of human life'.[25]

That remark, reminiscent of Marx's injunction to philosophers to 'change the world', could have been made by any of Hu Shih's communist contemporaries. These were not people whose ranks he could join, however, partly because of a love of American 'individualism', partly because their 'economic determinism' rendered any intervention by intellectuals pointless. If Marxists were right, he argued, they should await the inevitable revolution in their armchairs. Given a Hobson's choice between the Communists and the Nationalists in the 1930s, Hu's preference was for the latter, themselves adherents to an ideology with a strong pragmatist streak. Indeed, the founding-father of the movement, Sun Yat-Sen, put practice so far ahead of theory that it was only in 1924, a year before he died, that he provided a considered and cogent statement of this ideology.

Sun – founder of the Kuomintang (National People's Party) and a main agent in the overthrow of the Manchu dynasty – showed his pragmatist streak by attacking Wang Yang-Ming's maxim that 'it is not difficult to know but difficult to act'. It was his countrymen's acceptance of this maxim, Sun believed, which accounted for the difference between 'lethargic China' and 'enterprising Japan'. Whereas the Japanese learned from the West and 'effected their reforms without [first] knowing the principle involved', China had refused to 'undertake reform measures until she understood them', failing to grasp that 'one who acts does not have to know' (SCT 784–5). A similar mistake was made by those who insisted on first devising a precise theory of revolution before embarking on it. Hu Shih criticized Sun for making an artificial distinction between theory and practice, but Sun's point was that while practice must indeed incorporate understanding in the form of implicit know-how, explicit theoretical articulation of the practice need not, and cannot sensibly, precede the practice.

This seems to be his point when he writes, 'we cannot decide whether an idea is good or not without seeing it in practice', for it is only good if of practical value to us. Consider the internationalism promoted by K'ang. 'Theoretically, we cannot say it is no good', but history and current events show that it is. China would not have become a 'semi-colony' of the Western powers, if imbued with a fiercer nationalist spirit (SCT 770). Hence nationalism is the first of the 'Three People's Principles' – the others being democracy and the 'People's Livelihood' (by 1924, a kind of state socialism, tempered by small capitalist enterprises) – which the Kuomintang took to Taiwan after Mao's victory in 1949.

Mao Tse-Tung, of peasant stock, was a librarian when, in 1921, he helped found the Chinese Communist Party of which he became the leader after the famous 'Long March' of 1935. He was supreme ruler of his country from 1949, but his authority slipped after the economic disaster known as the 'Great Leap Forward'. To reassert this authority, Mao launched the 'Cultural Revolution' when, to the large indifference of Western philosophers more concerned with injustice in Paraguay or South Africa, thousands of their Chinese colleagues were humiliated, forced to work in the rice-fields, imprisoned and otherwise silenced. Mao's political career did not prevent him churning out several works which, 'primitive, clumsy, . . . even childish' though they have been judged,[26] became almost the only philosophical reading available in the libraries where he had once worked.

Maoism may seem the most striking instance of Asia's adoption of a Western philosophy, Marxism. But it is arguable that Maoism is indelibly Chinese in heritage and that its 'dominant values seem completely alien to Marxism',[27] more akin to the communism which Marx and Engels called 'primitive' and 'utopian' than to their own 'scientific' version. To be sure, Mao was fond of the rhetoric of dialectical materialism, outdoing even Engels in detecting 'contradictions'. 'Contradiction exists in the process of development of all things' (19),[28] but when he goes on to illustrate this universal 'movement of opposites' his debt is more to *Yin–Yang* cosmology and Lao Tzu (see p. 80) than to Marxism. For besides the 'contradictions' between the people and feudalism or the proletariat and the bourgeoisie, we hear of those between above and below, fortune and misfortune, life and death (42ff.). To understand the nature of any situation, the relations between such polar opposites must be properly diagnosed. In particular, the Party must distinguish between contradictions which are 'antagonistic' and those which are not, lest it settles by force what it can leave to resolve itself, or vice versa.

Mao also adopts a pragmatist approach to knowledge, of the kind hinted at in Marx's *Theses on Feuerbach*. 'Social practice alone is the criterion of the truth of his . . . knowledge' (283). Since 'practice' is taken in so wide a sense as to include perception, the claim is in danger of becoming trivial; but Mao's point seems to be that perceptual data need to be worked on, 'remodelled and reconstructed', in order to furnish knowledge (290f). For Mao, it is this emphasis on practice as prior to knowledge, yet responding to it and generating further understanding, that constitutes the truth of materialism, for he rejects that 'mechanistic materialism' which treats ideology as a mere function of productive forces (40). Indeed, he grants to ideology a greater power than do orthodox Marxists, and perhaps he had to. The 'objective' conditions of China – its absence of an industrial proletariat, for instance – were hardly those under which Marx deemed a communist revolution possible. Without faith in the autonomous power of zeal and ideals – of the kind instilled into the Red Guards – there could have been no prospect of securing the revolution.

To the doctrine of the priority of practice over theory, Mao gave one peculiar twist, at once unMarxian, rooted in Chinese tradition and, for his country's intelligentsia, disastrous. The Taoists, recall, admired the unspoken wisdom embodied in the skilled practice of craftsmen, favourably contrasting this with voluble, artificial book-learning. Moreover, it was in the countryside that men of wisdom, cleaving close to nature, were to be found. It is easy to recognize this tradition in Mao's polemics against book-learning ('to read too many books is harmful') and in the 'cult of the peasant' he fostered: factors which were combined, during the Cultural Revolution, when professors were ordered into the fields, not only by way of emphasizing the dignity of manual work, but so that they might imbibe the raw, honest understanding implicit in such work. Already in 1927 Mao had praised peasant schooling as 'something quite different from the futile clamour of the intelligentsia and so-called "educators"' (57).

There is nothing Marxist in this elevation of the peasantry or denunciation of intellectual life. Nor is there in Mao's sweeping hostility to individualism, which, he holds, capitalism derives from and nurses. For Marx, communism will mean the release of people's true individuality; but for Mao, its virtue is that of a 'state of universal fraternity' in which all 'join in common effort'.[29] When he speaks of 'a splendid ancient culture' of China, despite its 'feudal dross' (SCT 890), he may have in mind, as did K'ang Yu-Wei and the Confucians, an age when people regarded themselves as integral units of an organic society. Marx, with his vestiges of romantic individualism, would then be one of those Westernizing imports which, Mao warns, the Chinese must 'never swallow raw or absorb . . . uncritically' (SCT 889). In his way, then, Mao reconjures his country's ancient vision of a 'Great Whole' in which people only truly participate by effacing themselves.

The Kyoto School

The distance between Maoism and twentieth-century Japanese metaphysics can seem like that between a bustling collective farm in Canton and a tranquil temple garden in Kyoto – for it is at the university of the old imperial capital that most of the philosophers I shall mention worked. Yet there are themes in common: the ubiquity of 'contradictions', for example, and the denial that individuals are the basic constituents of society. The Japanese absorbed Western philosophy with the same alacrity as Western technology and political institutions. Escape from internal strife and, after 1945, from a totalitarian ideology meant that the debates galvanized by the encounter with the West matured in a calmer, freer atmosphere than the Chinese enjoyed. The first European imports, brought back by Nishi Amane, who also discharged the difficult job of inventing Japanese equivalents to Western philosophical terms (including 'philosophy' itself), were positivism and its ethical bed-fellow utilitarianism. But by the early years of the twentieth century, it was Kant and German Idealism which exerted the main influence, joined later on by Heidegger. For political reasons, it was German professors who staffed the new, European-style universities; and, anyway, German philosophical preoccupations – notably with the nature of the self and its relation to the world and society – engaged more closely with the Japanese Buddhist tradition. Indeed, it was this tradition which prevented Japan from becoming an Eastern outpost of European philosophy, and enabled Kyoto thinkers to speak of a 'Japanese spirit which goes to the truth of things' and provides 'something equal, if not superior to, Occidental conceptions' (Nishida, JPT 365 and 352).[30]

In the kind of comment echoed by sociologists studying the 'group-orientation' of Japanese factory-workers and tourists, one philosopher writes that his people 'attach unduly heavy importance to their human nexus in disregard of the individual'.[31] The remark might have been directed against his colleagues in Kyoto where a central, critical theme was individualism, both as a cultural phenomenon and as a doctrine about the structure of society. Many of them argued, as did novelists like Natsume Soseki and, later, Mishima Yukio, that 'the cult of the individual' merely masked selfishness. Or, as with Nishitani Keiji (1900–90), it was held that individualism, when yoked with technologism, engendered a sense of estrangement from other people and from nature, an 'uncanny homelessness'.[32] As for individualism as a social philosophy, we saw this under attack in the *Fundamentals of our National Polity* (see p. 375) where, in Hegelian vein, the individual was said to owe his very being to the State. What that document expressed for a popular audience, Kyoto philosophers elaborated for one more versed in metaphysics.

Tanabe Hajime (1885–1962), for example, rejected Kant's attempt to base a universal morality upon the will of the autonomous, rational self. Just as a dog belongs to a genus only through belonging to a certain species, whose nature forms the dog's behaviour, so, according to Tanabe's 'logic of species', people are only related to humankind through membership of a particular nation state, whose character shapes them and provides them with moral direction. A more original critique of individualism is found in the writings of Watsuji Tetsurō (1889–1969). He argued, in an intriguing book on *Climates and Cultures*, that climate and geography profoundly shape religious experience. It is no accident, for instance, that the tough gods of monotheism – Jehovah, Allah – arose in a region where people needed strength and resolve to overcome a hostile desert terrain. The more general point was the central role played by the experience of *space* in shaping human lives. While Western philosophers, like Heidegger, are right to make time 'play a part in the structure of subjective existence', Watsuji complains that 'space also was not postulated as part of the basic structure of existence'.[33] 'Space' is to be taken in both a physical and a social sense, and it is a person's occupation of and movement within both spaces that define him or her. Watsuji makes much of the fact that the Japanese term for person (*ningen*) is composed of characters meaning 'man' and 'between'. As embodied creatures, our lives are structured by the spatial, physical relations we stand in to others. But 'betweenness' is also a social matter, the 'space' we occupy being defined by a network of social relationships – marriage, workplace, local community, and so on. Or better, perhaps, the relationships which we *are*. For Watsuji's point is that the rational, autonomous individual of Western tradition is a pale abstraction from the webs of bodily and social interaction apart from which persons, in any full-blooded sense, cannot be identified. As for Tanabe, there can be no individual morality transcending the loyalties and duties that circumscribe the 'space' in which I live, move and have my being.

The Buddhist doctrine of 'No self', we saw in chapters 2 and 6, applied not only to the human self, but to substances in general. King Milinda's chariot was no more a discrete, independent entity in the world than he himself was (see

p. 47). Likewise, the status of the individual or self as discussed in Kyoto was part of the wider problem of 'the one and the many'. I shall focus on the approach, shared in broad outline by many of his colleagues, of the central figure of the school, Nishida Kitarō (1870–1945). My remarks apply to his 'later' thought, from around 1927 on, when he was trying to fuse the insights of various Western thinkers, including Leibniz and Kant, with those of Mahāyāna Buddhism, especially in its Japanese incarnation, Zen. Those familiar with these contributions will not expect Nishida's fusion to make for an easy read.

Nishida's philosophy is an attempt to escape the impasses into which Kant was apparently led. Kant, recall, felt compelled to postulate both an empirical self, subject to mechanistic causal laws, and a 'pure' self which is not within the empirical world, but its spectator and, to boot, the locus of the moral will, rational and free. The relation between the 'two selves', Kant conceded, was incomprehensible. Beyond our understanding, too, is the relation, more generally, between the world as a mechanistic order and as a purposive whole, between the world of causes and the world of ends. Nishida agrees that it is impossible to regard the self as either 'merely instinctive' and empirical or 'merely rational' (LW 99).[34] Equally, the world cannot be one of 'merely . . . mechanical causation' – for then 'life itself could not be accounted for' – nor a purposive whole in which everything has a predetermined end, for 'in such a world there is no freedom' (SJT 360). But we cannot rest with the idea of two selves and two worlds, nor with that of incomprehensible unions between them. The task is to rethink the terms which generate these impasses.

For Nishida, the dilemmas which Kant and his idealist successors failed to resolve are due to deep, and deeply mistaken, commitments of the main Western philosophical tradition since Aristotle. To begin with, this tradition is founded on an 'object logic', which 'substantializes the self' and the items we experience (LW 53): for it treats 'the world . . . as an aggregation of innumerable things', of particular, logically independent substances that combine with one another (SJT 356). This treatment of self and world is due, in large measure, to a second persistent tendency of Western philosophy: to view things 'from the standpoint of the mere intellectual self' (FP 93). For when we disengage from active life, perhaps turning our gaze inwards, we are indeed inclined to view the world as so many persistent, separate objects standing over against us, and to regard our own selves as objects too, only of a more ghostly variety.

One requirement, then, is to abandon – except for special limited purposes – the purely intellectual, spectatorial standpoint, and employ the perspective of the socially and historically placed 'active self': the self which engages with the world in a constant process of forming, and being formed by, it (SJT 360). This perspective will help prise us away from the 'object logic' of the West towards the 'concrete logic' of the East, also referred to, more ominously, as 'the logic of nothingness' and of 'contradictory identity'. What Nishida has in view is a 'logic' which treats reality holistically, as a 'one' within which things are constantly being transformed and losing their momentary identities and hence 'negating' themselves (SJT 356f). The central concept of such a logic is not that of the object or substance, but of the 'place' (*basho*) or 'centre' of a 'transformational matrix' where things interact and merge (LW 56). As for Watsuji, it is relations between things – their 'betweenness' – which is fundamental, with the things themselves being abstractions from the webs or matrices which define them.

Nishida traces this 'concrete logic' back to Nāgārjuna (see pp. 44ff.) and finds it expressed in such Zen *koans* as 'When you call this a bamboo stick, you are wrong; and when you don't you are also wrong.' Be that as it may, once acclimatized to this logic, we can unblock the Kantian impasses of the 'two selves' and 'two worlds'. First: being rid of 'the dogmatism of the reified objective self', we recognize ourselves as fluid processes ever on the move from 'the created to the creating', placed at any given time within a social-historical situation, yet always transcending it through our 'self-determining' activities. If we emphasize 'the past tense' – our created, given situation – we view ourselves empirically as items in a causal mechanism; to emphasize our transcending, self-determining activities, on the other hand, is to view ourselves as free and rational (LW 90ff). For limited, pragmatic purposes both perspectives are valid, and to that extent the self is a 'contradictory identity' of opposed aspects. But provided we recognize the artificiality of these perspectives and the abstraction they involve from the full life of the 'concrete active self' – provided, that is, we do not 'reify' these aspects into two selves, an empirical and a transcendental one – the 'contradiction' creates no impasse.

Second, when we likewise appreciate that the mechanistic and teleological perspectives on the world as a whole are abstractions we make only by stepping 'outside the world of historical actuality' (SJT 361), the 'contradiction' between them is no longer a dilemma. These perspectives may be valid in their place, but they cannot be true, yet conflicting, views of how reality itself is. For 'concrete logic' teaches us that reality is not an 'agglomeration' of distinct substances in causal, mechanical interaction, nor a seamless purposive whole of which individual people and things are the mere accidents.

But how, if not in mechanical or teleological terms, are we to characterize the world and the relation to it of selves and things? Here Nishida shows a debt to Leibniz's monadology (see pp. 272ff.). The world is not a mechanism or a single purposive substance, but a vast 'calculus of self-expression': each person and thing is 'an expressive monad' of this world, a 'formative position' within its matrix (LW 52). So entwined with the world am I, that I mirror and am mirrored by the whole 'calculus'. It is as if the world were a great dance, a self-expression impossible without its individual steps and movements, just as they would be without sense outside of the dance. The dance is nothing without the steps, but cannot be reduced to them. Similarly, the world is both one and many, a 'manyness-of-oneness' and a 'oneness-of-manyness' (SJT 360). For the logic of expression requires that, while a whole can only express through its parts, the parts can only express through belonging to the whole.[35]

Steeped in Zen literature, Nishida likes to formulate his position in paradoxical terms. If the self is not a substance, then it is 'nothingness', so that as Dōgen (see pp. 276ff.) put it 'to study the self is to forget the self'. And our enmeshment in the world is such that 'subject and object are one': we think and act only by 'becoming things' (LW 55). Nishida thinks his philosophy helps articulate Zen religiousness, especially its sense of the ordinary world, and the simplest things and activities within it, as religiously imbued. *Pace* Kant, religious sense has nothing to do with morality and cosmic purpose. Rather, the self is 'essentially religious' because it has, potentially at least, a sense of its 'absolutely contradictory existence', its 'nothingness', and hence of its total dependence on an 'absolute other' (LW 77). But this view of the self is precisely the message of 'concrete logic'. The religious person is one who, receiving this message, seeks to realize it in his life, to 'negate' himself or, as one Zen verse advocates, to 'be thoroughly dead . . . while alive'.

In the West, unfortunately, the 'other' before which we are nothing is understood as a transcendent being, a person. This is to remain in the grip of 'object logic'. Once freed from its grip, we recognize that the religious domain is one with the familiar world, that *nirvāṇa* is *saṃsāra* (see p. 46). It is this world on which the self is utterly dependent, not just contingently but as a matter of logic. Moreover, the world as a whole – the absolute – is, like the individual self, continually 'negating itself', giving rise to, *inter alia*, selves. In that sense, we can say of it that it 'causes mankind to be, and truly saves mankind'. We can even say that it 'loves' us, for what is true love but self-denial for the sake of people (LW 100)? That which gives rise to us, 'saves' and 'loves' us might surely be described as the religious. It is this sense of the familiar world as religious, of an everyday 'face-to-face relation with the absolute', that prompts 'the Zen celebration of ordinary human experience', of hoeing, eating and sleeping (LW 111). Though, as an individual – a particular 'position' in the world – I am not the whole of reality, my enmeshment with it is such that, as one Zen Master wrote, 'Buddha and I [are] not separate for one instant; facing each other the whole day through' (LW 78). There are few more radical attempts than this to cure the 'uncanny homelessness' that afflicts us, to give each of us a place in a world that we can, in quiet and simple ways, love and celebrate.

• 3   The Islamic World •

It would be impossible, here, to chart all the philosophical currents to have passed through the Islamic world during the past two centuries. The *ummā*, or community of Muslims, extends across countries as distant from one another, geographically and culturally, as Algeria and Indonesia, Pakistan and Sudan. Some developments, morever, have taken place outside any of these countries. The Sūfi tradition, for example, largely eclipsed in the Middle East, has been continued primarily by Europeans. In this section, I shall focus on the 'modernist' rethinking of Islam, which first arose in Egypt and pre-partition India, and on the theocratic doctrine of the Islamic State practised in Pakistan and Iran.

Already in the eighteenth century, many Muslim thinkers were oppressed by a sense of decay in the Islamic world. For the Wahhābi movement – named after al-Wahhāb (1703–92), the inspiration for today's Saudi regime – decay was visible in the religion of the Prophet itself. Schisms and sects, heresies like saint-worship and Sūfi pantheism, rituals and superstition had combined with the dead hand of the *ulamā* – learned scholars who based their judgements less on the Koran than on the commentaries of their predecessors – to produce a parody of the pristine faith that flourished during the years following the death of Muhammad in 632 CE.

By the nineteeth century, a one-sided confrontation with Europe compounded and extended this sense of decay. The French, then the British, invaded Egypt, the Dutch Indonesia, the Russians Turkestan. India, with its 50 million Muslims, was now part of the British Empire, and most of what remained of the Islamic world was part of an Ottoman Empire already diagnosed as 'the sick man'. With the occupation of Turkey's territories by European powers after 1918, 'there was scarcely such a thing left as a Muslim state not dominated by the Christian West'.[36] As the French general who rode into Damascus proclaiming 'Saladin, we have returned!' knew, all this was especially galling to a civilization that had once been the match for Europe. As late as 1683, the Turks had laid siege to Vienna. Equally galling to many Muslims was the manifest superiority of Europe in scientific, philosophic and political thought. After all, mediaeval Christendom had largely got its philosophy and science, especially medicine and engineering, from the Arabs. Moreover, in comparison with the brutal, squabbling states of mediaeval Europe, the Arab polity had been one of tolerance and peace.

The perceived decay in religion, intellect, political institutions and military power occasioned, unsurprisingly, much soul-searching. Here are just a few of the questions one 'modernist', Muhammad Abduh (1845–1905), addressed to his fellow Muslims: 'If Islam granted to reason and will the honour of independence, how [has] it bound them with such chains? If it has established the principles of justice, why are . . . its rulers such models of tyranny? . . . Why have Muslims spent centuries enslaving the free?' (152).[37] For some 'secularists', especially in Turkey, the remedy for these ills was, if not abandonment of Islam, then its relegation to the reduced status of Christianity in post-Enlightenment Europe, no longer a dominant influence in intellectual and political affairs. But for the majority of Muslim reformers, an opposite remedy was called for, the 'Islamicization of society', a return to the original essence of Islam and the adaptation of its principles, where necessary, to modern conditions. 'Why are the Muslims in such a sad condition?', asked Jamāl al-Dīn Afghānī (1839–97), and answered 'When they were [truly] Muslims . . . the world bears witness to their excellence. As for the present, I will content myself with this holy text: "Verily, God does not change the state of a people until they change themselves inwardly" (Koran 13.11)' (173).[38] Muslims, that is, are responsible for their 'sad condition', but in that case they also have the capacity to raise themselves out of it by becoming 'truly' Muslim again.

'Modernism'

Those words of Afghānī could have been spoken by 'fundamentalists', such as the Wahhābis, as could his and Abduh's diatribes against the ossified traditionalism of the *ulamā* and their call to 'open the gate' to *ijtihād* (independent interpretation of texts and laws). It is, therefore, 'something of an irony to pit the fundamentalists against the . . . modernists', for both insist that 'Muslims must go back to the original and definitive sources of Islam and perform *ijtihād* on that basis'.[39] Still, there were important differences between the two groups. (One must not, incidentally, confuse the 'fundamentalists' with the bomb-throwing zealots so labelled by today's journalists, nor the 'modernists' with those later figures whom one author describes as believing that 'religion as a force . . . is no longer valid in our age'.[40] The 'modernists' I discuss all believed in Islam as a regenerative force in society.)

The two related platforms on which the 'modernists' stood, in contrast with the 'fundamentalists', were those of receptivity to the West and, relatedly, the rehabilitation of science and philosophy in the Muslim world. Afghānī called on Muslims to 'march resolutely in the path of civilization after the manner of Western society' (183), while Syed Ahmed Khan (1817–98) said it would be 'suicidal' not to acquire Western science and educational practices (189).[41] As for philosophy, Abduh concedes that the mediaeval Arab philosophers, like Avicenna, were 'too precipitate' in accepting the authority of Aristotle, but bemoans the success of Ghazāli and others in branding philosophy as irreligious and in stifling philosophical debate for nearly a thousand years (37ff). In a lecture which had him expelled from Turkey, at the behest of the *ulamā*, Afghānī defined philosophy as 'man's becoming man and living in the light of sacred rationality' (110).

There were, to be sure, differences among the 'modernists' over the warmth of the welcome to be extended to Western thought. One broad approach was to 'start from the basic principles of Islam and to restate them in the light of the contemporary situation'; another to 'start from a selected Western philosophy and . . . to integrate Muslim doctrine with it'.[42] The best example of the latter approach is Muhammad Iqbāl, whom I discuss later. But even among those who professed the former approach, there were significant differences, one of which was political. Afghānī – a colourful figure from Iran who, for some reason, called himself an Afghan – spent much of his life being expelled from one country after another for preaching a pan-Islamic revolt against European imperialism. This inspired a bitter hatred towards Ahmed Khan who, 'to ingratiate himself with the English' (177), advised his fellow Muslim Indians to accept the enlightening influence of imperial rule. Abduh, at first a disciple of the fiery Afghānī, eventually took the compromise position of accepting British rule as an interim, necessary evil, and in fact became Mufti of Egypt during that rule.

Afghānī's animosity towards Ahmed Khan may have caused him to exaggerate a further difference between them: this time over Islam's accommodation to Western 'naturalism' or 'materialism'. Khan is accused of 'hoaxing' his countrymen with Muslim rhetoric whilst striving 'to erase the traces of religious zeal' (178) in favour of a purely naturalistic view of the world. This seems an unfair construal of his insistence that the 'touchstone of a true religion' is its conformity with the laws of nature, human nature included (191). It is doubtful, moreover, that Afghānī – not a patient commentator – properly understood the 'naturalism' he attacked. The calibre of his grasp of the theory of evolution, for example, might be gauged from the following 'refutation' of it: if Darwin were right then Arab and Jewish boys, having been circumcised for millennia, should now be born without foreskins (137). That said, there are recent writers who wonder if Ahmed Khan was more than a 'naturalistic deist'. Come to that, there are those who wonder the same about Afghānī for, as we shall see, his arguments for religious belief are ones available to an atheist.[43]

Whatever their differences, the 'modernists' were emphatic about the *rational* credentials of Islam. It is this, above all else, which explains their rejection of traditionalism in favour of *ijtihād*, their rehabilitation of philosophy and confidence that Islam can absorb European thinking, and their conviction that a 'truly' Muslim society will be a good and well-ordered one. Ahmed Khan speaks for them all in saying, 'Islam is not irrational superstition; it is a rational religion which can march hand in hand with the growth of human knowledge. Any fear to the contrary betrays lack of faith in the truth of Islam' (189–90).

As that remark suggests, there are at least two senses in which Islam is held to be rational: its doctrines are rational, and it encourages rational enquiry in all areas, such as the natural sciences. The doctrines are rational in both positive and negative respects. Positively, the central beliefs in a single transcendent God, creator of the world and protector of mankind, are ones that can be logically defended against alternative conceptions. Negatively, Islam is not saddled with the irrational accretions of other religions: the belief in a person who is at once a man and God, for example, or as Afghānī points out, unwarranted distinctions among human beings according to their membership of a caste or priesthood. The true Muslim, writes Abduh, will moreover avoid spouting the nonsense of the theologians of other religions by heeding the Prophet's injunction 'not [to] take your meditations into the Divine essence, or you will perish'. One reason, that is, why Islam is rational is its recognition, enabling it to remain within the bounds of sense, that 'reason quite lacks the competence to penetrate to the essence of things' (54).

Islam is rational, second, because of its injunction to human beings to pursue knowledge. All our authors like to cite passages from the Koran or the Prophet which sound this theme: for example, 'Oh my Lord, increase my knowledge', 'Whoever wishes to have the benefits of the Herafter, let him acquire knowledge', or 'Bring your evidence if you are speaking the truth'. Those who might think that the knowledge referred to is only religious knowledge are reminded by Ahmed Khan of the Prophet's instruction that 'Muslims should seek knowledge even if they have to go to China to find it' (189). Since the Chinese could hardly enlighten Muslims on Koranic knowledge, what is referred to here must be scientific knowledge of the world and human beings. There is, then, divine sanction for the confidence that no true science or philosophy could contradict the claims of Islam. Those Muslims who fear the findings of such enquiries must, then, 'lack faith in the truth of Islam'.

Those Muslims are equally misguided who pit the claims of reason against those of revelation, to the advantage of the latter. Islam, writes Abduh, is 'built squarely on reason', with revelation its 'surest pillar' (39). Revelation has a triple rational justification. First, there is good reason for it to occur, since the pronouncements of the prophets serve to bind people together in a religious community in a way that dry logic cannot. Second, as both Ahmed Khan and Abduh insist, prophecy is not an 'unnatural' phenomenon, but an innate capacity akin to other remarkable, yet well-attested, ones human beings possess. Finally, there are rational methods for sorting the wheat from the chaff, authentic from fraudulent prophecy. 'The proof of the . . . truth of what [a prophet] delivers from his Lord', says Abduh, 'is evident before the eye-witness who sees' the prophet: hence, later belief in its truth is warranted provided that the eye-witness' testimony has been reliably passed on (99).

There is a further, third sense in which Islam is rational according to the 'modernists', especially Afghānī. Irrespective of the truth of its doctrines, there are good reasons of a broadly utilitarian kind for people to embrace these rather than the beliefs of the atheist or infidel. Various 'social virtues', such as honesty and a capacity for shame, can only be secured by belief in a wise and powerful Creator who punishes evil deeds. Hence even 'the basest of religions' is better for society than irreligion, but Islam is, on several counts, more conducive to the 'social virtues' than any other faith. For example, Afghānī argues – in keeping with today's pedagogical ideal of 'self-esteem' – that Islam, with its emphasis on human nobility and equality, deters a person from 'imagin[ing] in himself deficiencies, decadence, and lack of ability'. People will then be confident competing with others, seeking 'greatness and honour', and so benefitting their society (170).

It is a mark, finally, of the rational person to perform *ijtihād*. Crucial here is a willingness to adapt all but the unambiguous, defining tenets of Islamic theology and ethics to conditions very different from those which prevailed in Muhammad's time. This distinction between, as it were, the fixed constitution of Islam and principles open to new interpretation was important for all the 'modernists', and especially for Abduh, a lawyer suitably enough. It was on the basis of this distinction that he called for changes in the system of polygamy. More important, it provided scope for incorporating Western concepts into the fabric of Muslim social morality. Thus *shurā*, the practice of consulting the leaders of the community, should in modern times convert into parliamentary democracy; while *ijmā*, the seeking of agreement among the learned, should now be understood as respect for public opinion. For Abduh's follower Rashīd Ridā (1865–1935), *jihād* – too often understood by Muslims to mean 'holy war' – should be interpreted as a call, simply, for defending Islam and for 'positive effort' on its behalf.[44] As we shall see later, not all Muslims proclaiming a return to the original essence of Islam were hospitable to such interpretative flexibility.

None of the 'modernists' so far discussed were 'original thinkers' in the sense of supplying a new philosophical basis for Islam. The 'old time religion', freed from the clutter of dogma that had accumulated since 'the golden age', and made adaptable – as surely the Prophet intended – to modern conditions, was in order as it was. Metaphysical speculation was neither necessary nor desirable, being all too liable to exceed the limits of reason. There was one thinker, however, often counted among the 'modernist' ranks, less reluctant to review his religion's conception of reality.

Iqbāl's Reconstruction of Islam

The 'spiritual father of Pakistan', Muhammad Iqbāl (1873–1938), born in the Punjab, is also the 'poet laureate' of the nation whose birth he died too soon to witness. There and elsewhere, his poems are today read in a way his philosophical works are not. My library's copy of the poems is well-thumbed whereas, until I intruded, its copy of his main theoretical work had been unmolested for twenty years. Iqbāl's was the second and currently disapproved of the approaches mentioned above, that of integrating Islam into a 'selected Western philosophy'. (Like Ahmed Khan, he also bears the stigma of a knighthood.) Much of Iqbāl's thought is continuous with that of the 'modernists': the insistence that reason and revelation are mutually supportive; the complaint that 'Europe has been slow to recognize the Islamic origin of her scientific method' (R 181);[45] the criticism of a quietistic, pantheistic tradition in Islam; and, above all, the call for *ijtihād* to rescue the *sharī'a*, the law of Islam, from 'a state of immobility' (R 209).

What distinguishes Iqbāl's position is an underlying metaphysics – the fruit of 'rethink[ing] the whole system of Islam without completely breaking with the past' (R 136) – that might have surprised his fellow 'modernists'. His philosophy might be dubbed 'dynamic idealism', for reality is said to be 'spiritual', an 'absolute ego', and 'rationally directed creative life' (R 80ff). It is misleading, perhaps, to speak of him starting from *a* Western philosophy. The authors he quotes most are Bergson and Whitehead (see ch. 10, sect. 1), but his eclectic position also owes to Berkeley, Leibniz, Hegel, Nietzsche, and Einstein. It would be wrong, morever, to speak of Western philosophers as Iqbāl's *authorities*. These are the Koran, the *hadīth* (the 'traditions' of the Prophet), and the testimonies of Sūfi mystics like the poet Rumi. Still, Iqbāl's strategy is to articulate a synthesis of recent Western philosophies and then to look in these Islamic sources for early intimations of it. If the strategy succeeds, the Western philosophies themselves articulate and elaborate what was previewed implicitly, symbolically, or simply more sparely, in those sources.

'The great point in Christianity,' argues Iqbāl, was its 'revelation of a new world within [man's] soul.' Unfortunately this revelation was at the expense of any spiritual concern with the 'outer' world of nature, the inevitable results being a 'sharp opposition between the subject and the object' and the 'ideal and the real', and the 'unhappy consciousness' of people to whom the 'outer' world is alien. Islam, on the contrary, 'recognizing the contact of the ideal with the real, says "yes" to th[is] world', and holds that 'nature is to the Divine Self [what] character is to the human self', an 'expression' of the 'inner' (R 11–13, 76). Christianity would be justified in pitting the soul against nature if the latter were simply a mechanistic system of material substances. But, as Einstein and Whitehead have established, it isn't this, but a 'continuous creative flow' which thought artificially carves up into discrete objects (R 47). Moreover, as Berkeley had shown, postulating an unobservable material world behind the phenomena of experience is at best gratuitous.

This does not mean, however, that reality is simply a big bundle of phenomena or experiences. To establish what it is, Iqbāl uses Schopenhauer's tactic (see

p. 321): to begin with 'that privileged case of existence' – our own selves – where 'we are in absolute contact with reality', and to use this to 'throw a flood of light' on reality at large (R 63). When I examine myself, I do not discover a mere sequence of distinct experiences bound into a bundle by relations like succession and coherence. Rather, as Bergson saw, I am a 'unity of directive purpose', an 'organic whole', in which 'states of consciousness melt into each other', so that it is only artificially that I can be cut up into discrete, successive states (R 144, 65ff). What introspection reveals, then, is that the self which unites my experiences is to be understood in terms of a striving for preservation, integrity and unity, and expansion. Unlike Schopenhauer's will, however, Iqbāl's 'deeper ego' is not blind or irrational: it is purposive intelligence, as much thought as will.

Since it is only in self-knowledge that we are directly acquainted with reality itself, our understanding of the 'outer' world must be derived from it. 'On the analogy of our conscious experience', we are then entitled to conclude, 'the universe is a free creative movement' (R 69). This nicely accords, therefore, with the view of the world as 'process' reached, from a different direction, by Einstein and other scientists. What they ignore, however, is that there must be an 'all-embracing concrete self', God, who is the 'ultimate source' of the unity and direction of the universe, by analogy with the human self which unites and directs a person's experiences (R 75).

This conception of God as the 'absolute ego' manifested in a dynamic, organic and purposive universe is, Iqbāl holds, Islam's. In an imaginative exercise of *ijtihād*, Iqbāl interprets various Koranic passages in this light. The reference to 'the succession of the night and of the day [as] signs for men of understanding' (3.189), for example, is held to convey that the universe is not only a dynamic process, but one which expresses God's nature. The orthodox may worry that Iqbāl steers far too close to pantheism. 'Existence is an effect of the Self' (SIT 208), he writes, and if 'the absolute Ego is the whole of reality', what room is there for the separate identities of you and me? Certainly he quotes with approval Sūfi utterances, of the 'I am God' variety, usually interpreted pantheistically (see p. 191). But this is an interpretation Iqbāl rejects: Sūfis do not experience 'the finite ego effacing its own identity by . . . absorption into the Infinite Ego', but simply its 'sharing in the life and freedom' of God (R 151ff). In fact, Iqbāl ends up with a metaphysics resembling Leibniz's (see ch. 7, sect. 4). The universe consists of innumerable 'sub-egos' which are somehow combined into those higher egos we call human selves by a 'profounder Ego', God, who is therefore 'other' than the rest of the egos (R 144). Since Iqbāl's argument for God seemed to rest on treating the universe as a single Self analogous to the human self which unites experiences, it is not clear that this switch to regarding reality as a vast 'colony' of plural selves is a cogent one.

This is not a switch that disturbs Iqbāl, however. What does concern him is the seemingly aggressive, almost Nietzschean, individualism which permeates his account of the human self, busy with 'self-assertion', the 'effort to be something', and 'sharpen[ing] its will'. Such an image, threatening to alienate people from one another and place them in opposition, seems incompatible with the Islamic emphasis on the community of believers, and indeed of all life. In several poems, Iqbāl insists that the individualism and 'self-assertion' of which he speaks actually require intimate membership of a community. 'A common aim . . . is unity which . . . forms the Community; the many live only by virtue of the single bond' (SIT 210). But this leads us into Iqbāl's political views and the idea of the Islamic State.

Theocracy

One Western ideological import which appealed to many Muslim reformers, especially in more 'secularist' circles, during the nineteeth and twentieth centuries was nationalism – not least because it provided a weapon to aim against Western imperialism. But already among some of the 'modernists' there was unease with this import. Would the division of the Islamic world into sovereign nation states be compatible with the idea of a united Muslim community, the *ummā*? And while nationalist aspirations might effectively challenge the West's political intrusion, were they not too secular and liberal in spirit to provide a bulwark against 'cultural colonialism'? The nationalist call might have helped secure Iran's independence from Western control but, as that country's leader after 1979, Ayatollah Khomeini, had long argued, something else was needed if it was to be cleared of the 'wine-shops [which] wear off the brain of [our] youth', and the kind of music which 'rouses the spirit of . . . unlawful sexuality'.[46] A Muslim nation must be Muslim first, a nation second, and someone who is an Iranian before he is a Muslim, says Khomeini, is a 'polytheist'.

A tension between the claims of nationalism and Islamicization is discernible in Iqbāl's writings. It was only at the end of his life that this 'father' of Pakistan advocated a Muslim state outside of India, as distinct from a semi-autonomous region within it. No 'Fatherland do we profess', he had written, 'except Islam' (SIT 211). Even if 'for the present every Muslim nation must . . . focus on herself alone', the aim must be to 'form a living family of republics' within which the 'horizons' of people are not artificially restricted by national boundaries (R 223). Rashīd Ridā displayed the same tension. Often regarded as an Arab nationalist, he nevertheless called for the resurrection of the Caliphate, the unity of Muslims under a single head, analogous to a mediaeval Pope and Holy Roman Emperor rolled into one. People whose loyalty is to a nation are bound only in 'natural solidarity', by geography and the need for self-defence, and this cannot be, unlike religion, the ground of a moral system. Even infidels will fare better under the Caliphate, for they are tolerated and respected in a polity based upon Koranic principles of justice in a way that they are not by people who have nothing to worship but national unity.

The Islamic State, then, is not founded on an ideal of nationhood, and its advocates, like Khomeini, recognize it as a *pis aller*, a step towards the distant goal of an integrated Islamic world. Pakistan's most radical advocate of an Islamic State, Abul-Ala Maududi (1903–79), was, like Iqbāl, at first hostile to an independent Muslim nation. Events convinced him, however, of the interim need for a 'separate homeland . . . for translating into practice the ideals envisaged by Islam', but then only with the proviso that what explicitly and 'exclusively' binds its citizens together should be their common faith (SIT 404).

The Islamic State can be described as a theocratic one, though not necess-arily in the narrow sense of rule by clerics. To be sure, the Parisian-trained Iranian sociologist Ali Sharī'atī (1933–77) demanded that those who 'specialize in the theoretical knowledge of Islam', whom he compared to Plato's philoso-pher-kings, should appoint from among themselves the 'most enlightened and purest person', an Imam, as ruler in 'the place of the Prophet'.[47] But other writers are content with a secular Head of State, provided he strictly follows the guidance of the *ulamā* or some new breed of theological experts. Nor, on the other hand, is the Islamic State a theocracy only in Iqbāl's anodyne sense of a State which endeavours to realize religious principles 'in a definite human organization' (R 216f). Crucial, in addition, is the constitutional supremacy of the *Sharī'a*, Islamic law, explained by one critic as follows: 'the law to be found in the Koran and the *sunna* [Islamic custom] is above all man-made laws, and in case of conflict . . . , the latter . . . must yield to the former' (Munir, SIT 395). The same writer goes on to charge that the Islamic State is a contradic-tion in terms, for a State is, by definition, a sovereign entity not subject to any outside law, Koranic included. To this charge, the standard reply is that God alone is sovereign, so that any authority possessed by governments is delegated from Him. 'Man has no right to legislation', declares Khomeini, and is 'subject to no command except that of God', adding that those 'rotten' governments which fancy themselves to enjoy a different source of authority are all founded on 'coercion and force'.[48]

Christians, and indeed many Muslims, tend to respond to a view like Khomeini's by saying that, while God's word in matters on which He has pronounced is sovereign, there are plenty of matters on which He is silent, or – as with adultery, say – on which His word, though sovereign, binds only 'privately' or 'in conscience'. Theocracy, therefore, requires both belief in a God who is explicit on a large range of social and moral matters, and rejection of the distinction between private morality and public law. Hence we find

Khomeini warning his followers, 'Never say that Islam is composed only of a few precepts concerning relations between God and His creation!'[49] Doubtless there are subjects on which even the Koran is vague or inexplicit: but in such cases, a ruler must consult expert theological opinion as to which policies are most consonant with the general principles of holy law.

Of greater philosophical interest is the case against the private/public divide so central to contemporary liberal thought under the influence of Mill's *On Liberty*. A common criticism levelled against Christianity by Muslim thinkers is the divorce it seems to condone, encouraged by New Testament verses of the 'Render unto Caesar' type and by Augustine's doctrine of the 'two cities', between religious morality and secular law. Iqbāl complains that in Europe 'religion is a private affair of the individual and has nothing to do with . . . man's temporal life'. Islam, by contrast, 'does not bifurcate the unity of man into an irreconcilable duality of spirit and matter' (SIT 219). Elsewhere he quotes with approval the Prophet's dictum that 'The whole of this earth is a mosque'. To emerge from the mosque, having heard some practice denounced as irreligious, into a world where that same practice is happily permitted, is to live a schizoid life. Religion is not a matter only for Sunday (or Friday) mornings: Khomeini's point, presumably, when he remarks that the mosque is not a church.

It is one thing, however, to urge that religious morality should suffuse everyday life, another to conclude that it should be enforced by the state *in toto*. To clinch the case for that, it needs to be argued that the *Sharī'a* is an organic whole which would collapse – and with it a recognizably Islamic society – if particular rules were selected from it as matters for private conscience alone. This is precisely what Maududi argued. The *Sharī'a* can only function at all if 'the entire system of life is practised in accordance with it', so that it is impossible to remove this or that injunction from the legal system. Consider adultery. In a 'filthy society [of] sexual excitement, . . . obscene books and vulgar songs', where 'economic and social conditions have made marriage extremely difficult', it is both pointless and wrong to punish adultery. For such a law must be 'part of a complete system of life': one where titillating pornography is absent, where women are well-protected and nothing militates against marriage, and where 'piety and charity are current coins'. In such a society, the law against adultery is an integral part of a whole set of laws 'essential for protecting the Islamic system of life from deterioration' (SIT 408ff). *Pace* Mill, there are no 'self-regarding' actions which, though immoral, do not harm society. For a society is defined by a seamlesss web of principles and mores, the violation of any of which threatens to unravel the whole and hence to destroy the society whose identity they determine.[50]

Except for someone who, in the name of 'cultural relativism', condones almost anything provided it is 'their way', people outside of Islamic States are generally appalled by punishments such as stoning to death for adultery. A good dose of *ijtihād*, one feels, might reasonably revise the traditional insistence on such punishments. But it is harder to see what arguments against the general theocratic idea could cut any ice with its advocates. To hold, for example, that the State should be a 'minimal' and morally neutral one, there only to facilitate individuals' pursuit of their 'life-choices', is merely to contradict the social vision expressed in the Koran. What needs to be challenged, presumably, is the view of society as a seamless fabric, tinkering with whose parts unravels the whole, put forward by thinkers like Maududi. It is not obvious that this challenge can be laid down with any great confidence by Westerners who have witnessed the moral and social deterioration of their own societies as more and more areas of behaviour are left to private discretion, and the sanctions against unacceptable behaviour accordingly reduced. Put differently, it is not clear that a society in which people feel 'at one' with their fellows can permit the degree of 'privacy' which liberal ideology requires.

• 4 Africa •

In the previous sections of this chapter, the developments being traced were developments in ancient philosophical traditions forced to reconsider by the impact of Western thought. In the case of Africa, there was the same impact, following in the wake of the chaotic 'scramble' for and partition of that continent which, by 1900, left only Morocco and Ethiopia as independent states, their turn as colonies yet to come. But it is less clear what the impact was upon. In the vestiges of an earlier, Arab empire, in the monophysite Christian empire of Ethiopia, and in Dutch southern Africa, there were, to be sure, philosophical traditions, but these are not the regions which presently concern us. In those that do – in 'traditional', 'darkest' Africa of the Kikuyu, the Dogon, the Yoruba, to name but a few – there were no literary traditions at all, philosophical included. What there was of writing was put to more utilitarian ends than the recording of metaphysical schemes. So whatever needed defending, revising or scrapping in the face of the Western challenge, it was not the great texts of an intellectual culture.

For some writers, this lack of a literature means that there is no African philosophical tradition. 'The first precondition for a history of philosophy . . . is the existence of science as . . . organized . . . in discourse. . . . [T]he chief requirement of science itself is writing.'[51] Others demur: a literature may be a desirable medium for a philosophy, but is not essential. One thing, at any rate, is certain. Whatever else 'African philosophy' currently covers, it certainly includes the prolonged, often passionate debate of the last three decades on the issue of what African philosophy is. As one contributor to a book of 'essential readings', all of which address this issue, puts it, 'current African professional philosophy is predominantly a meta-philosophy. Its central theme is the question "What is philosophy?" [and its] corollary... "What is African philosophy?" '[52]

African Philosophy?

For those who think it is best to get on with philosophy, without racking one's brains to define what one is getting on with, this preoccupation with 'meta' questions is a distraction. But this ignores the sensitive context in which they are set. 'Philosophy', a distinguished African practitioner reminds us, 'is the highest-status label of Western humanism', and 'the urge to find something in Africa that "lives up to" the label is . . . a question of wanting to find something that *deserves* the dignity' accorded to, say, Greek or Enlightenment thought (148).[53] To secure the label for traditional African beliefs is then one way of responding to the charge made, early in the twentieth century, by the French anthropologist Lévy-Bruhl, in a book sub-titled by his translator *Mental Functions in Inferior Societies*, that Africans are 'pre-logical' and incapable of abstract thinking.

Still, it is surely best to insulate, as far as possible, the issue of whether there is a traditional African philosophy from the ideological debates which the issue has spawned. For one thing, it is less clear than the previous paragraph implied that 'dignity' is best won by securing the label 'philosophy' for the old ways of thought. Certainly there are those, as we shall see, who locate this dignity in styles of thought disjoint from the 'abstract' one characteristic of philosophy. Moreover, as the poet of anti-colonialism, Aimé Césaire, argued, harping upon respect for 'Bantu philosophy' can all too easily divert from the respect which really matters – for native property, freedom and nationhood.[54]

Césaire refers here to a book, *Bantu Philosophy*, published in 1945 by a Belgian missionary, Placide Tempels, a pioneering attempt to discover a philosophical world-view in the oral wisdom of African peoples. This kind of attempt, much emulated in subsequent years, has been dubbed 'ethnophilosophy' by its strongest critic, Paulin J. Hountondji (from Benin). It is the attempt to uncover an 'implicit "philosophy" conceived as an unthinking, spontaneous, collective system of thought, common to all Africans or . . . to such-and-such an African ethnic group' (112).[55] (By extension, 'ethnophilosophy' is sometimes used to refer to such a system of thought, rather than to the study of it.) Before examining criticisms of ethnophilosophy, let us glance at its practitioners' justification of their labour and at its alleged fruits.

The assumption of ethnophilosophy is that no culture can exist whose members do not share conceptions of the world and of themselves sufficiently deep and broad to deserve the title of a world-view or philosophy. Without such a view, there is no stability or order in the society, hence 'we can and should talk of African philosophy, because the African culture has its own way of establishing order'.[56] Tempels, for one, conceded that Bantu people are not 'capable of formulating a philosophical treatise', but that is no objection to the latent existence of such a 'treatise'. With patient questioning, the ethnophilosopher can formulate it so as to be able to tell the Bantu what, for example, 'their inmost concept of being is'.[57] The charge that a philosophy is surely something that *individual* thinkers articulate is either bluntly rejected (perhaps as a Western 'individualist' prejudice), or accommodated by pointing to certain 'sages' found in African cultures, men able to elaborate the world-view implicitly embraced by their fellows. (The classic case is the Dogon sage Ogotommeli, whose words were transcribed by a French anthropologist, Marcel Griaule.) The charge that a philosophy must exist in writing is also rejected (perhaps as another, rather recent Western prejudice). Were that charge valid, after all, Socrates and the Buddha could not count as philosophers.

To illustrate what might emerge from ethnophilosophical retrieval of a native world-view, Tempels' discovery of the Bantus' 'inmost concept of being' must suffice. Western metaphysics, he argues, is static and atomistic: the basic unit of reality is the individual substance, 'the thing insofar as it is', with its attached properties. For the Bantu, conversely, being is dynamic and holistic, 'existence-in-relation'. The basic concept is that of force: reality consists of countless forces, such as spirits, only intelligible in terms of their interplay with one another. Being is, so to speak, alive and not, therefore, something set over against human beings. On the contrary, a person or rational being (*muntu*) is but one force among the rest, distinguished by a capacity to control non-rational forces. 'The human being, apart from the . . . interaction of forces, has no existence.'[58] Tempels also discerns in the Bantu world-view the notion of a Great Force above the welter of spirits and lesser forces. This parallel to a concept of God provides the welcome news, to a missionary, that the Bantu are more amenable than many had imagined to conversion.

It is hard to know where to begin with the myriad criticisms which have been levelled against the ethnophilosophical approach. Some, we saw, are of a broadly moral kind. To Césaire's complaint that currying respect for folk beliefs distracts from more urgent forms of respect, the point can be added that one does not honour, but insults, a people by supposing that they go about with a philosophy inside their heads which they are without the *noûs* to articulate. Others lament the way the approach diverts professional African philosophers from participating in the wider, international philosophical world. Here, attention is drawn to the disanalogy between 'African philosophy', as construed by the ethnophilosophers, and 'British philosophy', say, where what is intended is not the everyday beliefs of people in Manchester or Brighton, but a disciplined tradition of professional work. Yet other critics take issue with the ethnophilosophers' nonchalance towards the absence of a literary tradition, and with their elevation of 'sages' to the status of genuine philosophers. It is of course possible to philosophize without putting one's thoughts in writing, but in the absence of a literature, there is no publicly available body of thought to develop and criticize – no philosophy, therefore. And it is only in relation to such a body that an individual thinker counts as a philosopher. Ogotommeli may lend beautiful expression to the inchoate beliefs of the Dogon but, speaking in a literary and critical vacuum, that is all he does and so he cannot be placed in a class alongside Aristotle or Kant, participants in an authentic discourse.

There are, though, two more fundamental, if somewhat competing, criticisms to be heard. The first is, bluntly, that the folk philosophies allegedly uncovered by ethnophilosophers are too crude, too much myth and superstition, to deserve a place on the world-stage. Anyway, a philosophy wins its spurs, primarily, through the arguments used to defend its conclusions, and these are notoriously absent in the case of traditional world-views, where the monotonous appeal is always to 'what our ancestors said'. Second, Tempels and his followers are not, as they imagine, discovering and transcribing Bantu or whatever philosophy; rather, complains Hountondji, they 'project on to [traditions] their own philosophical beliefs'. Hence, when ethnophilosophers disagree over the Bantu concept of power, there is no genuine issue to resolve, for theirs is a 'science without an object . . . accountable to nothing' (119). Or as Kwame Anthony Appiah adds, having rejected the claim that the Akan of Ghana are mind–body dualists, 'But I don't think that it makes sense to say that they are monists either: like . . . all Westerners without a philosophical training . . . most simply do not have a view about the issue at all' (160). To recall an earlier example, is it any more plausible to credit a Bantu farmer with a theory of force than a French grocer with a Thomist view of substance?

If African philosophy is not ethnophilosophy, and excludes it even, what is it? Hountondji's influential, minimalist definition is 'a literature produced by Africans and dealing with philosophical problems', the context making clear that the Africans primarily intended are professional, Western-trained university teachers (120). This is at once too narrow and too broad: too narrow in its insistence that only Africans can participate in African philosophy (a criterion which would exclude Wittgenstein and Popper from a history of twentieth-century British philosophy), but too broad in not restricting the range of philosophical problems falling under the heading of 'African philosophy'. It may be too narrow in another direction to proclaim that 'African philosophy is first of all the search for a theory of . . . African national liberation' or the 'thinking the problems . . . that arise from the lived actuality of post-colonial "independent" Africa'.[59] Still, one can appreciate the suggestion that if there is to be African philosophy as distinct from, simply, philosophy done in Africa, a tradition must be forged and that the most obvious materials for this will be issues of special, if not unique, interest to Africans.[60]

Without wanting to prejudice the direction of this enterprise, I shall focus on two areas in the remainder of this section, ones which have already received much discussion and must surely belong in the wider field of a distinctively African philosophy. First, there is the task – one for a philosophy of science, natural and social – of 'making sense' of the seemingly bizarre beliefs and practices of traditional African religion. This is not to advocate a return to ethnophilosophy, for it is not necessary to suppose that these beliefs themselves constitute a philosophy. The philosophy goes on only at the 'meta' level of understanding the beliefs. Second, there is the area of broadly moral and ideological issues related to Africa's colonial experience: ones of nationalism, liberty, and 'negritude', for example. These two areas cannot be kept entirely apart. After all, to hold, as some do, that the great crime of colonialism was to suppress a distinctive 'negritude' imbuing African culture is also to hazard a view about the mentality underlying traditional beliefs.

Philosophical Anthropology

Making sense of strange beliefs and practices is not, of course, the preserve of students of Africa or other tribal cultures. Renaissance alchemy and magic are hardly less puzzling than Zande witchcraft or Ndembu divination, and some of *our* current obsessions – from 'Royal-watching' to dead pop-star cults – surely invite ethnographical attention. Still, not all Renaissance men and women were alchemists, any more than all Britons today are 'Royal-watchers'. Both practices, moreover, are relatively hived-off from the rest of people's everyday behaviour. Also, they are liable to atrophy: there are few alchemists around today and enthusiasm for Royal antics waxes and wanes with the particular Royals on display. By contrast, magic, divination, witchcraft and invocation of spirits seem to be universal, pervasive and persistent aspects of African life, at least in the countryside (100 'witches', according to a TV news report, were 'necklaced' in South Africa during 1994). Africans, one reads, are 'notoriously religious', and 'religion permeates into all departments of life so fully that it is not easy to or possible to isolate it'.[61] It is this which makes their traditional cultures such a focus of ethnographic interest.

'Precisely', someone will say, 'it's of *ethnographic* interest. What has *philosophy* to do with empirical explanation of alien beliefs and practices?' Scientific beliefs and practices may provide a useful analogy by way of answer. There is surely a task for philosophers of science somewhere between the 'purely' philosophical one of prescribing proper criteria of evidence and truth and the 'merely' empirical one of describing how actual scientists spend their working-hours. This is the attempt to construct a model which makes rational sense of what seem to be anomalous features of their practice – the tendency, say, to hold on to certain hypotheses despite plenty of counter-evidence. Empirical enquiry is doubtless needed to establish that the model actually applies, but the construction of the model itself, incorporating as it does a conception of rational behaviour, is a philosophical project. So is the construction of like models for making sense of traditional folk beliefs and practices. The whole enquiry of which this construction is a part can be labelled 'philosophical anthropology'.

There have, to be sure, been those, like Lévy-Bruhl, for whom there is nothing for such an enquiry to enquire into. We do not understand worship of water-spirits or the witch-doctor's consultation of chicken-bones, but that is because such phenomena are genuinely unintelligible, the manifestations of a 'pre-logical', barely human mentality. Among those who find this hard to swallow, the most popular approaches for many years were ones which treated the alien beliefs as non-literal and the corresponding practices as merely symbolic. After all, as the sociologist Emile Durkheim had argued, no culture can survive whose view of the world is hopelessly false and whose practices are completely inefficacious. Taken at face value, this is just what traditional African beliefs and practices must be. Hence we cannot take them at face value.

How, then, should they be taken? Consider the invoking of water-spirits to protect the fish on which the natives depend. There is not a whit of evidence that these spirits exist, nor that, even if they do, invoking them has any effect. Moreover, so the argument goes, the natives know all this, 'deep down' at least. Still, the invocation is effective in other ways: it brings the natives together in their resolve to protect their fisheries, say, and enables them to vent their spleen, in a socially harmless way, at the ill-luck which has recently plagued them. The explanatory model, here, is one of ceremony and ritual, understood as socially functional and emotion-releasing forms of behaviour. Britons who toast 'God save the Queen!' may be atheists, and certainly doubt that God intervenes on behalf of the House of Windsor. But we can still understand this practice when we grasp its symbolic, functional and expressive character. Likewise with the 'exotic' behaviour which 'naïve' anthropologists once took at face value.[62]

This approach is implausible. The loyal toast is indeed a ceremonial relic, useful in its way, of a dead system of belief. It is not credible, however, that Africans are constantly engaged in symbolic ceremony, indifferent to the truth of beliefs they ritualistically mouth. All the evidence suggests that the Azande, say, believe in the efficacy of witchcraft oracles, and if they did not, it is hard to see how consulting the oracles could serve to cement social relations and perform other useful functions. Of greater interest, then, is the model proposed by the anthropologist and philosopher of science, long resident in Nigeria, Robin Horton. Beliefs in spirits, oracles and the like are to be taken at face value, and understood as playing analogous roles to the hypotheses of Western scientific theory. In both cases, we see the 'quest for unity underlying apparent diversity; . . . for order underlying apparent disorder' (209).[63] In both cases, unobservable 'theoretical entities' – hydrogen nuclei in one case, say, 'spirit anger' in the other – are cited to 'link events in the visible, tangible world', a dropped bomb and the subsequent mushroom cloud, or a 'breach of kinship morality' and the subsequent illness of the offender (212–13).

This model, argues Horton, allows otherwise puzzling features of African thought to fall into place: for example the 'jump' which is suddenly made from commonsense explanation to one in terms of spirits or spells. This is not, as some have imagined, an inexplicable 'jump . . . to mystical thinking', but akin to, and made in similar circumstances to, the scientist's switch from everyday to theoretical explanation – when, for instance, the everyday account is inadequate or insufficiently broad in scope (219). There is, to be sure, a major difference between the 'impersonal idiom' of Western science and the 'personal' one of African religion. The theoretical entities of the former are modelled on inanimate things, billiard-balls or waves, while those of the latter are modelled upon human agents. That is hardly surprising. In the West, order and predictability are 'lamentably absent' from human relations in comparison with those governing mere things. Not so in traditional Africa, where 'the human scene is the locus *par excellence* of order, predictability, regularity' (224). Theoretical explanation is always of the less in terms of the more ordered and familiar, and given the differences between African and Western cultures, it is this which accounts for the difference in their theoretical 'idioms'.

Still, as Horton himself insists, African religion and witchcraft are not science. Indeed, the traditional cultures have, as one African puts it, 'throttled the impulse towards sustained inquiry' of a scientific kind.[64] Hence, we find no experimental method at work in these cultures, and an extreme resistance to revision of beliefs and practices. Horton explains this in terms of the 'closed' nature of African thought – the inability, for geographical and other reasons, to envisage genuine alternatives to established beliefs. Here, he takes his lead from the anthropologist Evans-Pritchard's observation that a Zande cannot step outside his 'web of belief' since 'it is the only world he knows . . . It is the texture of his thought and he cannot think his thought is wrong' (230). A Western scientist can, with some sanguinity, contemplate the overthrow of his pet theory, since he is confident that alternative theories are standing in the wings. But for the Zande or Kalabari diviner, the only alternative to his present system of beliefs is epistemic chaos and a consequent sense of a world too opaque and irregular to be at home in.

Horton's account, though much admired, has been challenged on a number of grounds. Perhaps he overdoes the 'closed' character of African cultures, which have, after all, long had considerable contact with alien ones. (In later writings, indeed, his emphasis has switched from this 'closed' character to the relative lack, in African thought, of a tradition of 'second order' reflection on notions like knowledge and truth.) More seriously, he is accused of ignoring the importance in African culture – as in many earlier ones – of explaining events in a manner which shows their point or meaning, not just of identifying their causal antecedents.[65] Maybe the 'personal idiom' reflects more than the Africans' familiarity with a stable, ordered social world. Among peoples for whom the natural world is still, in Weber's sense, an 'enchanted' one replete with significance, purpose and value, it would be unsurprising if the theoretical entities appealed to were at least akin to intelligences, beings with something like a moral purpose in mind for the world they control. A man breaches the kinship code of his tribe and falls ill. However adequate, at one level, an explanation of his illness in terms of catching a germ might be, it cannot satisfy people with an urge to ask 'But why did *he* catch it?' or 'Why was the germ around in *that* house?' For what such questions register is the sense, only recently lost in the modern world, of a moral balance in the cosmos. Where such a sense endures, no science, however sophisticated, can substitute for moral accountancy.

'Negritude', History and Humanity

Frantz Fanon described the struggle against colonialism, of which he was a leading theorist, as a 'metaphysical experience'. Whether because it was harsher, more bare-faced, more patronizing, or simply because it lingered on for so long in the changed world after 1945, African colonialism has attracted philosophical attention to a degree that no other has. Did it, despite ending Arab and indigenous slave-trading and revolutionizing hygiene and medicine, constitute a unique crime? What would post-colonial liberation be liberation from and for, exactly? These were among the questions debated by African and Afro-Caribbean intellectuals, some of them at the forefront of the anti-colonial struggle, and their answers are still examined by contemporary African philosophers, including most of those already mentioned in this section.

The questions are not unrelated to those of the status of African philosophy and the nature of traditional African mentality. Someone who holds that colonialism's crime was its debasement of *négritude* or *Africanité* is liable both to admire the 'ethnophilosophical' task of retrieving the thought-systems in which such an 'essence' is embodied, and to reject the view that such systems are at all akin to Western ones. Conversely, those – Marxists, for example – with more 'universalist' conceptions of philosophy and human mentality are liable to regard colonialism as an instance, extreme perhaps, of a familiar kind of oppression.

For several decades after 1945, the most popular conceptual weapon in the anti-colonial armoury was that of *négritude* or *Africanité*. I use the French spellings since it was primarily Francophone writers, like the Martiniquian Aimé Césaire and Senegal's first President and French Academician, Léopold Senghor, who forged and wielded the notion. *Négritude*, wrote Fanon, was 'the emotional if not the logical antithesis of the insult which the white man flung' at the black (212).[66] For while the apostles of *négritude* largely accepted the white *description* of African mentality and culture, they reversed the usual *evaluation* of them. The differences between European and African minds alleged by Lévy-Bruhl and others should occasion, among black people, not shame but pride. 'Reason is hellenic and emotion is negro'; 'white reason is analytic . . . Negro reason is intuitive'; 'the European is empiric, the African is mystic'. In making these contrasts, Senghor argues, Western anthropologists were dead right, even to the extent of regarding the negro world as 'the kingdom of childhood'. Where they went wrong was in concluding that these differences established the inferiority of black peoples. Being 'childlike' is something to nurture, not to revile. For one thing, it is a mark of that special affinity with, and sensitivity to, the world about him which makes 'the Negro . . . the man of Nature'. Again, it is in 'the kingdom of childhood' that a person feels the closest bonds with other people: he 'assimilates himself with the Other . . . in symbiosis', without the 'ruthless analysis' to which Europeans submit personal relations. More generally, there is a host of 'cultural values of the black world', rooted in the essential *négritude* which divides it from the Western one, and making it a kinder, more sympathetic culture from which the world at large should learn.[67]

Even at the height of enthusiasm for *négritude*, in the 1960s, the concept had its severe critics among black writers. For many, it was a distraction from the liberation struggle, turning the spotlight on cultural rather than political affairs. The Ghanaian leader, Kwame Nkrumah, for example, argued that effective 'socialist action' required 'the elimination of fancifulness' about 'racial social-ism'.[68] Worse still, it reinforced the very racism which was surely a main target of the struggle. Reading lines like Césaire's, 'There flows in our veins a blood that requires of us a unique attitude towards life', no one can deny the racist character of the notion, hardly mitigated by Sartre's apology for it as an 'anti-racist racism'.[69] As noted above, Senghor and his colleagues did not challenge European racist thought, but merely changed its evaluative from negative to positive. Anyway, critics continued, Senghor's account of Africans as intuitive rather than rational, mystical rather than analytic, is plainly false. As Amilcar Cabral, leader of the revolt in Guinea-Bissau against the Portuguese until his assassination by them in 1971, observed: anyone who works with African peasants soon realizes their 'capacity for reasoned discussion and clear exposition of ideas, the facility for understanding and assimilating concepts' (54).[70] For Cabral, Fanon and others, the popularity of *négritude* was largely due to its acceptability to Europeans. In France, especially, a veritable cult of *Africanité* allowed people at once to sing the praises of Africans whilst insisting that such childlike innocents still require, in an all too adult world, the protection of colonial government.

The writings of Cabral and Fanon have been described as 'paradigmatic for African philosophy', eschewing the sentimentality of *négritude* and ethnophilosophy yet, by focusing upon the 'concrete historicity' of the African situation and its interpretation, refusing to be side-tracked by the totally general concerns of, say, Marxism.[71] Both writers, certainly, refuse to interpret colonialism and liberation from it in terms of a *négritude* insulted and then retrieved. Neither, for example, has time for romanticism about tribal society. Africans must 'detribalize and unite the nation', insists Fanon (201–2), while Cabral calls for 'the progressive liquidation of the remnants of tribal mentality' (54). Both, too, implicitly reject Senghor's image of the peacable, childlike native in demanding *violent* struggle. For Cabral, this is required not only to get rid of the colonialists, but as 'a determinant of culture' for a new Africa.[72] In Fanon's book, a 'handbook for the black revolution' according to the cover blurb, violence is sanctioned, if not quite for its own sake, then for investing people with 'positive and creative qualities', and because it 'binds them together as a whole', imbued with nationalist consciousness (93).

For Fanon, a Martiniquian psychiatrist later active in the Algerian fight against the French until his death from cancer in 1961, colonialism was a crime, not against *Africanité*, but against humanity itself. It has turned men into 'things', so that, in the liberation struggle, 'the "thing" which has been colonized becomes man during the . . . process by which it frees itself' (37). The 'most horrible' of the crimes of colonialism, through its total disruption of indigenous life, was committed 'in the heart of man' and 'consisted of the pathological tearing apart of his functions and the crumbling away of his unity' (315), leaving him alienated and schizoid, no longer able to co-ordinate feeling and reason, individuality and loyalty to a community. Liberation spells nothing less than the recreation of 'the whole man'.

The indigenous life so disrupted is rooted, not in race, but in history, and colonialism's crime can also be described as that of stealing their history from a people. With liberation, this people 'begin to go forward again . . . to make history' (69), instead of having it made for them. The same thought is expressed by Cabral's famous call for a 'return to the source'. This is not a return to some primaeval stage of African innocence, but the returning to 'uprooted, alienated' men and women of their capacity to 'make history'. For these people, colonialism has meant 'the paralysis or deviation or even the halting of [their] history'.[73] To be fully human is to have one's destiny in one's own hands, and this requires critical appropriation of the past, to be extended, according to one's own will, into the future one thereby shapes. In removing destiny from the hands of Africans, the colonialists have thereby denied them their full humanity.

Critics may wonder, as they watch the latest atrocities in Rwanda and even Algeria on the TV, whether putting down the ills of modern Africa to colonialism alone is not simplistic. Other forces – modern technology imping-ing upon tribal cultures, nationalism, fundamentalist religious revivalism, and so on – also play their role. There is surely a double irony in Cabral's and Fanon's diatribes against the West – 'We have better things to do than . . . follow Europe' (Fanon 312) – and their zeal, in reaction against sentimental *négritude*, for national consciousness, technology, advanced medicine and the like. For one thing, these thoroughly modern goals are also thoroughly Western ones in origin. For another, it is perhaps the pursuit of these goals, with the transformations they entail for traditional African ways, and not the legacy of colonialism *per se*, which best explains why the 'making of history' after liberation has not fulfilled the hopes with which Fanon, Cabral and countless others invested it.

• Notes •

1   S. Radhakrishnan, 'Fragments of a Confession', p. 9.
2   J. L. Mehta, *On Heidegger, Hermeneutics and the Indian Tradition*, p. 219.
3   Rabindranath Tagore, *Selected Short Stories*, p. 283.
4   References to Vivekananda are to Stephen Hay (ed.), *Sources of Indian Tradition*, vol. 2.
5   Outstanding examples are B. K. Matilal, *Perception*; and J. N. Mohanty, *Reason and Tradition in Indian Thought*.
6   R. K. Narayan, *Mr Samprath – The Printer of Malgudi*, p. 30.
7   N. B. Chakraborty, 'Vivekananda and practical Vedanta', p. 51.
8   References to Gandhi are to *An Autobiography* (A); *The Sayings of Mahātma Gandhi* (S); and *Selections from Gandhi* (SG).
9   Bhikhu Parekh, *Gandhi's Political Philosophy*, p. 109, is an excellent study of Gandhi. Also useful is Peter Serracino Inglott, 'The philosophy of Mahātma Gandhi'.
10 I follow Parekh here, *Ghandhi's Political Philosophy*, ch. 6, who points out Gandhi's anticipation of twentieth-century 'Critical Theory'.
11 Quoted in Chakraborty, 'Vivekananda and practical Vedanta', p. 50.
12 References to Radhakrishnan are to 'Fragments of a confession' (FC); *An Idealist View of Life* (IV); and *Eastern Religions and Western Thought* (ER).

13 References to Aurobindo are to *Sources of Indian Tradition*. Robust readers will want to look at his massive *The Life Divine*.

14 Karl H. Potter, *Presuppositions of Indian Philosophies*, p. 254.

15 Rabindranath Tagore, *The Religion of Man*, pp. 127f.

16 Ananda K. Coomaraswamy, *The Dance of Śiva*, pp. 115ff.

17 References to Bhattacharyya are to his *Studies in Philosophy*.

18 Thomas R. H. Havens, *Nishi Amane and Modern Japanese Thought*, p. 11.

19 References beginning 'SJT' are to Ryusaku Tsunoda et al. (eds), *Sources of Japanese Tradition*, vol. 2.

20 References to Chinese authors are to Wm. Theodore de Bary et al. (eds), *Sources of Chinese Tradition* (SCT); Wade Baskin (ed.), *Classics in Chinese Philosophy* (CCP); and Wing-Tsit Chan (ed.), *A Source Book in Chinese Philosophy* (SBP).

21 See Peter Singer, *The Expanding Circle*.

22 Quoted in Donald H. Bishop, 'K'ang Yu-Wei', pp. 329–30.

23 Quoted in Y. C. Wang, *Chinese Intellectuals and the West*, p. 395.

24 Quoted in Hsu Sung-Peng, 'Hu Shih', p. 387.

25 Ibid., p. 367.

26 Leszek Kolakowski, *Main Currents of Marxism*, vol. 3, p. 484.

27 Ibid., p. 485.

28 References to Mao, unless otherwise specified, are to his *Selected Works*, vol. 1.

29 Quoted in Donald H. Bishop, 'Mao Tse-Tung and the Chinese Tradition', pp. 417–18.

30 For useful surveys of recent Japanese philosophy, see John C. Maroldo, 'Contemporary Japanese philosophy', and, less fully, Yuasa Yasuo, 'The encounter of modern Japanese philosophy with Heidegger'.

31 Nakamura Hajime, 'Basic features of the legal, political and economic thought of Japan', p. 148.

32 Keiji Nishitani, 'Reflections on two addresses by Martin Heidegger', p. 150.

33 *Climates and Cultures – a Philosophical Study*, preface.

34 References to Nishida are to *Last Writings* (LW); *Fundamental Problems of Philosophy* (FP); and 'The problem of Japanese Culture', in *Sources of Japanese Tradition* (SJT).

35 For related accounts of 'the one and the many', see Ueda Yoshifumi, 'The status of the individual in Mahāyāna Buddhist philosophy', and Nishitani, 'Reflections on two addresses by Martin Heidegger'.

36 Edward Mortimer, *Faith and Power*, p. 86. This book can be usefully consulted on all the topics discussed in this section.

37 References to Abduh are to *The Theology of Unity*.

38 References to Afghānī are to his writings contained in Nikki R. Keddie, *An Islamic Response to Imperialism*.

39 Fazlur Rahman, *Islam and Modernity*, p. 142.

40 Akbar S. Ahmed, *Postmodernism and Islam*, p. 163.

41 References to Ahmed Khan are to Stephen Hay (ed.), *Sources of Indian Tradition*, vol. 2.

42 H. A. R. Gibb, *Islam*, p. 119.

43 On the religiousness of Ahmed Khan, see Rahman, *Islam and Modernity*, p. 52; on Afghānī's, see Mortimer, *Faith and Power*, p. 116.

44 On Abduh and Ridā, see Albert Hourani, *Arabic Thought in the Liberal Age 1798–1939*, chs 6 and 9.

45 References to Iqbāl are to his *The Reconstruction of Religious Thought in Islam* (R), and to *Sources of Indian Tradition* (SIT).

46 Quoted in Mortimer, *Faith and Power*, p. 324.

47 Ibid., p. 340.
48 Quoted in F. Rajaee, *Islamic Values and World View*, pp. 54, 76.
49 Quoted in Mortimer, *Faith and Power*, p. 326.
50 This line of argument is not a Muslim preserve. Lord Devlin followed it when opposing the legalizing of homosexuality in Britain recommended by the Wolfendon Report.
51 Paulin J. Hountondji, *African Philosophy*, p. 99.
52 Henry Odera Oruka, 'Sagacity in African philosophy', p. 48.
53 Kwame Anthony Appiah, *In My Father's House*. References to Appiah are to this book.
54 Aimé Césaire, *Discourse on Colonialism*, p. 37.
55 Paulin J. Hountondji, 'African philosophy: myth and reality'. References to Hountondji are to this article, a chapter from his book of the same name.
56 Innocent Onyewuenyi, 'Is there an African philosophy?', p. 38.
57 Placide Tempels, *Bantu Philosophy*, p. 36.
58 Ibid., p. 104.
59 E. Wamba-Dia-Wamba, 'Philosophy in Africa: challenges of the African philosopher', pp. 231–2; Tsenay Serequeberhan, *The Hermeneutics of African Philosophy*, p. 7.
60 On African philosophy requiring a tradition, see Kwasi Wiredu, 'On defining African philosophy'.
61 John Mbiti, *African Religions and Philosophy*, p. 1.
62 See John Skorupski, *Symbol and Theory*, for a detailed philosophical discussion of symbolist approaches.
63 References to Horton are to 'African traditional thought and Western science'.
64 Kwame Gyekye, 'Technology and culture in a developing country'.
65 See Appiah, *In My Father's House*, pp. 198ff.
66 References to Fanon are to *The Wretched of the Earth*.
67 Quoted in Serequeberhan, *The Hermeneutics of African Philosophy*, pp. 42ff. A useful source for Léopold Senghor's views is his *Prose and Poetry*.
68 Serequeberhan, *The Hermeneutics of African Philosophy*, p. 41.
69 Quoted in Appiah, *In My Father's House*, pp. 316, 47.
70 References to Cabral are to *Return to the Source*.
71 Serequeberhan, *The Hermeneutics of African Philosophy*, p. 118.
72 Quoted in Basil Davidson et al. (eds), *Southern Africa*, p. 65.
73 Quoted in Serequeberhan, *The Hermeneutics of African Philosophy*, p. 103.

10
• TWENTIETH-CENTURY WESTERN PHILOSOPHIES •

• 1 Philosophies of Life •

The adage goes that the nineteenth century ended in 1914. As a comment on the political and social caesura marked by the Great War, it has its point, but in the cultural and intellectual arenas a new era had arrived more punctually. Debussy and Schoenberg, Picasso and Matisse, Einstein and Freud produced some of their most important work during the opening decade of the new century as, in philosophy, did Frege, Husserl, Russell and Bergson. The tolling of the new century, it seems, inspired a re-examination of the doctrines which had dominated the closing decades of the old. The response to the idealism which held sway in Britain and even the USA will be considered in section 3. In the first two sections, I discuss philosophies consciously designed to counter the positivist and materialist trends which, we saw at the end of chapter 8, provided the main philosophical direction in continental Europe. The phenomenologists and existentialists of section 2 rejected the claim that empirical science is able to furnish an adequate and complete account of the world, let alone of human existence. Their criticisms were preceded and to a degree prefigured, however, by those of a loose group of thinkers whom I shall call 'philosophers of Life'.

Comparisons can be made between the response of these thinkers to nineteenth-century positivism and that of the romantics to eighteenth-century Enlightenment. Enlightenment optimism about the epistemic prospects of observation and reason had been spurred by the success of the physical sciences, notably mechanics. Hume had hoped to do for the mind what Newton had done for matter. One tactic of romantic critics, therefore, was to draw attention to the life-sciences, such as biology, to the inapplicability of mechanical models in such areas, and to a corresponding need for notions like purposiveness and design. By the end of the nineteenth century, however, this seemed a shaky platform on which to resist the prospects for a mechanistic, materialist cosmology. The theory of natural selection promised to provide a mechanical model for biological development, while fledgling advances in neurophysiology and the study of psychiatric disorders lent empirical support to the guess that the mind is an automatic function of, or perhaps identical with, the brain.

Despite these advances, there was a growing sense in some circles that Life, a process or force which underlies the phenomena studied by the life-sciences, cannot itself be an object of scientific knowledge. Within those circles, 'Life', 'Das Leben', 'La Vie' became, during the first few decades of the century, talismans to invoke in the way that 'Reason', 'Sentiment' and 'Progress' had in earlier times. Those who invoked them were, to be sure, a mixed bunch – academics, artists, men of letters, propagandists – ranging from professional philosophers like Bergson and Whitehead to the Fauvist painters, from the Italian Futurists such as Marinetti to the 'reactionary modernists' in Germany, like Spengler, who supplied the more romantic ingredients of Nazi ideology. Whatever the differences between these groups, their common theme was one of the need for human beings to tap in, both in thought and action, to the dynamic, vital process of Life which orthodox science, 'static' and 'analytical', ignored. Science, as they saw it, offers a picture of the world that is not only partial but, when taken as complete, desiccating: for it distances us from that 'great river of life' which, for Bergson, flows through everything and, above all, through 'the body of humanity' (CE 284).[1] Clearly, we are hearing yet again our recurrent *Leitmotiv* of a quest for a unitary account of a reality into which human existence is integrated.

'Elan Vital'

Henri Bergson (1859–1941) was Life's most eloquent advocate. Doubtless it was this eloquence which helped him become the most celebrated philosopher in Europe before the First World War and, later, to win the Nobel Prize for literature. The stirring, sometimes erotic, terms in which he described the Life which constantly explodes within and around us attracted to his lectures, at the Collège de France, the same racier elements of Parisian society who, of an evening, swooned at Diaghilev's ballets. Although Bergson's interests moved more and more towards the mystical, his work over the course of forty years was a consistent elaboration of an initial insight into the incapacity of 'analytical' science to capture the seamless flux of which we are aware in ordinary experience. Bergson's star has since fallen. Much of the science on which he based some of his arguments for its inherent limitations has been superseded, but he was also branded, notably by Bertrand Russell, as 'anti-scientific'. Perhaps his star will rise again for, as we will see in section 5, his thinking should evoke sympathy among more recent critics – deconstructivists included – of the pretensions of the intellect.

The vision Bergson invites us to share is that of a spiritual, potentially conscious force – Life or 'the vital impetus' (*élan vital*) – galloping through time in 'an overwhelming charge able to beat down every resistance' offered by 'inert' matter. Life, from its humblest beginnings to its climax in man, is 'consciousness launched into matter' (CE 286, 196). Science and intellect are equipped to articulate only the products of this vast process, not the inner 'true nature of Life, the full meaning of the evolutionary movement' (CE x). For that we require mystical intuition, itself a retrieval on a higher plane of the animal instinct, long suppressed by intellect, which unites living creatures with Life itself. The 'creative energy' and 'love' which the mystic intuits coursing through the universe may be described as 'the essence of God' (MR 218). Provided, then, that we do not conceive of God as 'a *thing* . . . already made', but as 'unceasing Life, action, freedom' (CE 262), Bergson's vision is a religious one. (Bergson, it seems, only refused to join the Catholic church out of solidarity for the suffering of his fellow Jews during the 1930s.)

God, in this vision, is not an intellect ruling the world according to a preordained plan. Nevertheless, human life is the apex of evolution: for it is into man alone that the impetus of Life which threatened 'to come to a stand' has 'passed freely' (CE 280). But this impetus will grind to a halt even among human beings unless they ascend to a vision of Life which enables them to break out of a circle of self-enclosed interests and of intellectual preoccupations which are geared to the pursuit of these interests. Otherwise people will remain entrapped in the 'closed' moralities and 'static', myth-ridden religions which, though binding them together into distinct social bodies, segregate them from humanity and nature as a whole. Only with the vision vicariously granted the rest of us by mystical 'heroes', shall 'we feel ourselves no longer isolated in humanity [and] in the nature that it dominates' (CE 285).

Although it is in mystical intuition, and through the works of visionary artists, that direct acquaintance with Life is vouchsafed, it was through critical reflection on evolutionary theory that Bergson first arrived at the hypothesis of an *élan vital*. None of the doctrines of evolution on the market were, in his view, adequate. Evolution does not display the smoothness and tendency to increasing harmony which we should expect on the 'finalist' doctrine of a goal to which it advances. The Lamarckian doctrine of 'effort' requires the false hypothesis of the inheritance of acquired characteristics. Darwinism may explain the details and 'sinuousities of the movement of evolution, but not . . . the movement itself'. Simple organisms, Bergson holds, were perfectly adapted to their environments: hence, to explain the development of more complex species, we must posit 'an original impetus . . . an internal push that has carried Life . . . to higher and higher destinies' (CE 107). The emergence of species and of sophisticated organs like the eye are not fully explicable in terms of chance mutations and adaptation. It would be better to think of nature, the *élan vital, using* matter to 'express' itself. It is not, for example, the hardware of the eye which explains vision: rather, this 'visual organ . . . only expresses . . . the exercise of the function', seeing, towards which there is a natural 'push' (CE 101).

This leads to Bergson's deeper criticism of orthodox evolutionary science – indeed, of science at large – when it exceeds its brief. Bergson had a robustly pragmatist view of science, one which influenced William James (see pp. 351ff.). The object of science is 'not to show us the essence of things, but . . . the best means of acting on them' (CE 98). The categories employed by the sciences and the intellect are those which best enable us to deal with things and, especially, to construct devices and machines for our use. There is not the least reason to suppose that these categories correspond to the real structure of the world. Science and intellect have 'carved up' the world for our convenience, and then promptly forget that they have done so. For Bergson, Russell explains, the intellect may be compared to a carver with the 'peculiarity of imagining that the chicken always was the separate pieces into which the carving-knife divides it'.[2]

Closely related to science's urge to foist upon reality categories devised merely for practical expediency is its tendency to view the world as a collection of discrete things, composed in their turn of physical parts whose operations govern their behaviour. In a way, science is 'right to do so', for acting upon the world and manufacturing things requires that we break them down into constituents, that we decompose and recompose them at will. It is wrong, nevertheless, to imagine that reality in itself is divided into these atomic constituents. In particular, to treat the living world in the manner of orthodox biology, as a mechanism decomposable into immobile, discontinuous parts is to view the seamless flux of Life in the fashion that chemists regard inert matter (CE 206).

If science and intellect do not 'show us the essence of things', however, it seems that scepticism looms, that the only 'knowledge of things is a practical knowledge aimed at the profit to be drawn from them'. But there is an alternative: 'placing oneself within the object by an effort of intuition' (IM 39). That there is a faculty of knowledge which 'transcends the point of view of the understanding' or intellect (CE xv) is something Bergson had argued long before occupying himself with evolutionary theory, in his studies of memory, time and motion. There is 'nothing mysterious in this faculty' of intuition (IM

59), but something patently at work in ordinary experience, if we would but pay attention to this experience in the manner of a 'true empiricism', uncontaminated by theoretical prejudices. For example, to know that I am raising my arm, I do not have to observe it passing through a series of spatial points in temporal succession. I know it as a simple, indivisible act.

More importantly, there is certainly 'one reality . . . which we all seize from within, by intuition . . . not by . . . analysis'. This is 'our own personality in its flowing through time – our self which endures'. The intellect, and professional psychology, may pretend that the self is analysable into discrete, successive mental states, but there is 'beneath these sharply cut crystals . . . a continuous flux'. Our inner life is one of 'pure duration' (*durée*), a continuity in which memories, moods, perceptions flow into and give shape to one another (IM 24ff). Conveniently for Bergson and his readers, the invention of cinema provided him with a useful model. The 'mechanism of our ordinary [intellectual] knowledge is of a cinematographical kind' (CE 323), for it treats our mental life as composed of separate 'images' rapidly succeeding each other. The treatment is misguided, for in the case of our mental life, nothing corresponds to the frozen frames at which the film can be stopped.

Bergson draws several important conclusions from this account of 'our personality flowing through time'. First, the usual determinist argument against free will must be mistaken: for it requires that whenever a person is in a certain state, he or she will then, by law-like necessity, act in a certain way. But, for Bergson, each state a person is in is unique. 'Consciousness cannot go through the same state twice' (CE 6), for a state's identity depends on its place within a whole flow of experience. Or better, to speak of a state of a person is to make an artificial abstraction from a single ongoing flux. Second, and for a similar reason, there can be no 'parallelism' between mind and brain: for that would require that mental life be divisible into constituents to be paired off with brain-states. The brain, Bergson ingeniously suggests, does not produce conscious experience but acts as an 'obstacle' or 'filter' whereby consciousness, for good practical reasons, restricts the amount of data that would otherwise overwhelm it.[3] Finally, somewhat in the style of Schopenhauer, Bergson assumes that since it is knowledge of our own personality which is the most vivid instance of intuitive knowledge, it must also provide us with the model for our knowledge of reality as a whole. At any rate, once we recognize ourselves as personality flowing through time, we are compelled to regard reality 'as if a broad current of consciousness had penetrated matter' (CE 191). In other words, we must interpret reality as Life.

Bergson was under no illusion as to the difficulty of 'invert[ing] the habitual direction of . . . thought' and intellect, so as to rehabilitate intuition (IM 51). While people continue to live in conditions of scarcity and material need, their primary focus is bound to be upon practical matters, such as manufacturing, which, we have seen, are the province of the intellect. Language, too, presents an obstacle to the desired inversion. The existence and entrenchment of this eminently successful system of symbols encourages not only the belief that the concepts they express correspond to a pre-given structure of reality itself, but the conviction that what cannot be expressed in such symbols cannot be known. This latter militates against any receptivity towards intuition, since its deliverances are ineffable. The personality I know from within, for example, cannot be 'expressed by symbols, being incommensurable with everything else' (IM 22).

Equally inexpressible, of course, are the mystic's intuitions of Life. Nevertheless, the mystic's attempts to communicate his or her experiences produce 'the whisper of an echo' in the 'innermost being of most men' (MR 182). And the time will come, Bergson believes, when human beings are freed from their pressing material concerns and when, therefore, intuition – though 'a lamp almost extinguished' – will 'pierce the darkness of the night in which the intellect leaves us' (CE 282). Many more of us than of old will then be afforded the vision that their inner life 'also is Life in general' (CE 272). The 'madly inflated' and 'frenzied' pursuit of material goods which encouraged the development of intellect, and was in turn reinforced by it, will 'deflate just as suddenly'. Men and women will then return to a 'simpler life', enjoying the 'security and serenity' that only a sense of 'at homeness' with Life itself can guarantee (MR 258ff, 181).

Process

Life was, in the main, a continental European speciality. Yet it was the unlikely figure of an English mathematical physicist, Russell's collaborator on *Principia Mathematica*, who elaborated, during his advanced years at Harvard, the most systematic metaphysics of Life. I refer to the 'process philosophy' or 'philosophy of the organism' of Alfred North Whitehead (1861–1947). The impact on Whitehead, then a Professor of applied mathematics in London, of reading Bergson during the First World War 'can hardly be exaggerated'.[4] They were, though, philosophers of very different characters, Whitehead sharing little of Bergson's confidence in mystical intuition as the route to truth. Mysticism may provide 'insight into depths as yet unspoken', but the job of philosophy is to 'rationalize' such insight (MT 924).[5] Whitehead's was the traditional rationalist ambition to 'frame a coherent, logical necessary system of general ideas in terms of which every element of our experience can be interpreted' (PR 567). And he means *every* element. This single system must give a coherent and adequate account of aesthetic and moral experience as much as of sense-perception and mathematical intuition. It is this universality of the scheme which distinguishes it from the particular sciences, but the methodology is similar: generalization from limited experiences to hypotheses then tested against further ones.

Like Bergson's, Whitehead's philosophy was partly inspired by reflection on the science of his day, but this time the new physics of relativity and quantum mechanics rather than biology. It disturbed him that people's conception of the world had not yet responded to the new physics with its talk of vectors, vibrations of energy, and the like, and was fixated instead on the mechanics of inert matter formulated in an earlier century.[6] The new physics confirmed for Whitehead, as biology had for Bergson, the centrality of *process*. Instead of making things and facts ultimate, his philosophy 'makes process ultimate' (PR 572). What must be discarded are the assumption of 'static spatio-temporal and physical forms of order' (MT 862) and its related fallacies – those of 'misplaced concreteness' and 'simple location'. These involve, respectively, taking what are in fact abstractions from processes as real ingredients of the world (points in time, for example), and conceiving of the world as composed of independent substances with qualities. It is not easy to overcome these fallacies since our language reinforces them. In particular, its subject–predicate form fosters the 'evil' impression that its terms refer to independent things and their properties (PR 599).

The 'static' picture must be discarded for at least two reasons. First, it is not true to experience, especially bodily experience, which, typically, does not record anything neatly divided into discrete data or objects. Second, it makes change and causation unintelligible. If a process were a succession of discrete states, we should have incoherently to suppose that features 'transfer' from one state, the cause, to another, the effect. Hence it must be the process itself which is basic, a single 'active' thrust from which discrete states are only artificially, as it were posthumously, abstracted (MT 918).

Reality has, in a sense, its atomic units – 'actual occasions', which are 'pulsations' or momentary events that issue in a universe different, however slightly, from the one antecedent to these events. Here we have 'the final real things of which the world is made up' (PR 585), with the more familiar items of experience, like tables and chairs, being relatively stable constructs from, or 'societies' of, these basic units. But they are not atoms in the sense of units independent of one another. There are 'no self-contained matters of fact capable of being understood [except] as an element in a system'. Each 'leads . . . beyond itself' to, finally, 'a systematic universe [which] supplies its . . . status' (PR 581, 577). An 'occasion', moreover, requires something else to be what it is: a 'form', such as a colour, which, because it is the same form on different 'occasions', and neither lives nor perishes, must be eternal (SMW 422). These forms or 'eternal objects' might be thought of as potentialities for 'occasions' to embody, provided they are somehow fitted for, or 'relevant' to, each other.

For 'actual occasions' to manifest the 'togetherness' or coherence required for stable processes, like tables and chairs, to occur, there must be some principle of agency at work in the world. As indeed there must for that 'basic adjustment' whereby the forms or 'eternal objects' find, as it were, relevant 'occasions' in which to be realized. This principle is what Whitehead calls 'God', a primordial 'urge' towards both the realization of forms in nature and a relatively stable continuation of past processes into the future (MT 599ff).[7]

This talk of an 'urge', or 'appetition', at work in the world begins to explain why Whitehead's is a philosophy of Life. It is part of a wider, Bergsonian vocabulary of nature as 'throbbing', 'pulsating' and 'vibrant', reflecting Whitehead's conviction that the concept of Life – 'the central meeting point of all . . . strains of systematic thought' – must be 'fused' with that of physical nature if we are to grasp reality (MT 904ff). The centrality of Life is at its clearest in his account of 'prehensions', the relations of 'togetherness' between 'actual occasions' which produce the processes we experience as physical objects. No such processes could emerge unless the 'occasions' somehow 'involved' one another. Since this involvement or togetherness cannot be one of interaction between independent entities, we must seek a different model from that of mechanics. This is provided by the emotions, for we speak of people enjoying one another, being together in feeling, and being emotionally involved. 'Prehensions', in general, then may be described as 'feelings' (PR 591), and Life or process at large is 'enjoyment of emotion' (MT 919).

No more than Leibniz in connection with his monads is Whitehead suggesting that events such as puffs of smoke or a sunset consciously enjoy or experience anything: their Life 'lies below this grade of mentality' (MT 919). But nor is this psychological talk mere metaphor, for we have no handle on the 'involvements' among the basic entities of reality other than that provided by our own affective experiences. There is another reason, as well, why we must attribute feeling to 'merely' physical processes. It is impossible to believe that colours, smells and other so-called 'secondary properties' are not part of the furniture of the real world, but are only features of our 'ideas', as Locke held, thereby falsely 'bifurcating' nature into its real ingredients and its effects upon us. 'Sensa', such as colours, must therefore be 'participating in nature as much as anything else'. Whitehead accepts, though, that there cannot be sensa without experience. Since this experience need not be ours, nor that of any other conscious creature, it follows that in unconscious nature itself there must be 'emotional enjoyment' of, say, 'sheer redness'.[8]

Such remarks will only sound absurd to people wedded to a mind–body dualism, with its crippling corollary that 'mental functionings are not properly part of nature', but only reflections of it within the soul (MT 911). When we descend the scale from human beings through higher and lower animals down to vegetables, the arbitrariness of saying 'Mental functioning ends just here' is apparent. So it is when we consider the smooth gradation from vivid visual perception through dim bodily sensations down to automatic yet adaptive behaviour. Life or experience, then, should be conceived as the whole world-process manifested, however modestly, by the simplest events in nature as well as by the fugues of Bach or the sonnets of Shakespeare.

For Whitehead, as for Bergson, this conception cannot but transform our view of ourselves and our place in the order of things. It represents the fusion of 'religion and science into one rational scheme of thought', for it both explains our experience and invests it with 'emotion and purpose' (PR 582). It affords human beings the sense of being within, not outside of, the natural world-process, and articulates the 'intuition of [this] universe as everlasting process, unfading in its deistic unity of ideals' (MT 874).

Human Life, Reason and Technology

Philosophies of Life were, I noted at the outset, critical responses to the positivist climate of the late nineteenth century. With Bergson and Whitehead, the response was to develop metaphysical systems of a kind no positivist could entertain, but not all of those who deployed the notion of Life in their critique of positivism had such large ambitions. I shall conclude by discussing some more limited, though radical, ventures in the philosophy of Life.

Wilhelm Dilthey's strictures against importing the methods of the natural sciences into the social and human ones were mentioned in chapter 8 (p. 350), and his prominence as a pioneer of 'hermeneutic' philosophy will emerge later (p. 428). Here I focus on the role that Life played in his thinking. Dilthey announces that he will 'confine the term "life" to the human world' (232).[9] Far from Life being what humans share with organic nature, or with the whole cosmos, it is what distinguishes their existence from any other kind. It is manifested or 'objectified', not in 'animal' activities, like sex, but in art, political institutions, and culture in general. In Dilthey, then, there is no Bergsonian talk of Life, as a universal force, coursing through all our being.

Although a mechanistic, positivistic account of the natural world might be adequate, no such account is appropriate to human history and culture, where there is a 'conflict between the tendencies of Life and the goal of science'. This is for two reasons. First, students of history, religion and the like are 'involved in Life' and 'want to influence it': hence they are incapable of attaining the neutrality and objectivity required by the positivist ideal of science (183). Second, as Vico and Herder appreciated (see ch. 7, sect. 5), the student only properly understands the religious beliefs, say, of an epoch when he or she grasps or enters into the form of Life which shaped them. This Life of the epoch is no mere aggregate of separate cultural, economic, religious and political phenomena. Rather, it is 'the basis for all its individual forms and systems, for our experience [and] understanding . . . of them' (232). The positivist social scientist, like J. S. Mill, then, in his attempt to explain a culture as a whole in terms of its atomic parts, commits the same fallacy that, for Bergson and Whitehead, scientists generally commit. He ignores that 'general property of Life' which gives shape and identity to the very parts in terms of which he hoped to arrive at an overall picture. It must, then, be through something akin to empathy or intuition that this 'basis' for the parts, Life itself, is discerned. Objective observation of the data, even if it were possible, could not suffice, for without a grasp of the whole, the data cannot come alive nor show themselves for what they are.

Dilthey was confident that, purged of its zeal to emulate the natural sciences, a genuine science of history and culture was possible, one which would, moreover, help us to overcome 'our attitude to the world as something other, alien and terrible' which the failure to understand Life has allowed to persist (136). No more than Whitehead, then, does he belong among those thinkers of the period who intoned the word 'Life' in a litany of abuse against reason, science, and rational morality. And there were many such thinkers, D. H. Lawrence (1885–1930), for example, who wrote that 'the intellect is only a . . . bridle . . . All I want is to answer to my blood, direct, without the fribbling intervention of mind, or morals, or what not.'[10]

Hardly less extreme, if philosophically more sophisticated, was the leading Spanish man of letters of his day, Miguel de Unamuno (1864–1931), with his call upon 'the man of flesh and bone' to live with 'the tragic sense of life' that recognizes the irreconcilable 'struggle between reason and life' (115).[11] For Unamuno, our own lives or vitality are the one thing we can be sure of, and unless we have become jaded or depressed by grey science, our attachment to life must produce a craving 'hunger for personal immortality . . . [an] effort to persist indefinitely' (36). So intense is our vitality that we are impelled to 'personalize everything and discover that the total All, . . . the universe, is also a Person possessing a Consciousness' (139). Unfortunately, this faith in immortality and the urge to personalize are contradicted by reason and science. It is reason's 'forcing [us] to submit to the inevitable, to mortality' which is above all responsible for the 'tragic sense' (115). More generally, however, 'reason is the enemy of life', for all that is vital escapes it, so that it must seek to 'congeal the living stream in blocks of ice' (90).

It might seem that if reason contradicts faith in immortality, God, and so on, then we should try to dispel such faith. But not so, says Unamuno. For one thing, it is perfectly in order to use the 'goodness or utility' of a belief as a mark of its truth. For another, as Hume and other sceptics saw, reason corrodes itself, for its very own principles fail to withstand rational examination. We should anyway remember that the language of rational philosophy is not sacrosanct, but an historical product, a 'humanly elaborated' inheritance that might have developed very differently (310). Finally, filled with vitality, we cannot but hope for immortality and view the universe as a conscious organism, so that reason's objections are doomed to be ineffective. This does not mean that we should, instead, abdicate from rational thought, for that too is impossible. Rather we must travel to 'the bottom of the abyss . . . at the irreconcilable conflict between reason and vital feeling', and there find a 'despair' which is also a source of strength, the 'basis for a vigorous life' (124). For it is from this conflict that man's greatest achievements, in morality, art and religion, have been sparked.

This defiant despair, a sort of 'up yours' attitude to a recalcitrant universe, was also meat and drink to various German philosophers of Life, the so-called 'reactionary modernists', such as Oswald Spengler (1880–1936), author of the best-selling Domesday scenario, *The Decline of the West*. But it is in a different work, *Man and Technics*, 'a contribution to a philosophy of life', that Spengler most closely addresses our current theme. Impressed by Nietzsche's doctrine of the will to power and by the 'red in tooth and claw' school of Social Darwinists, Spengler understands Life – 'active, fighting, and charged' – as identical with 'conflict' (10f).[12] Belonging to Life, man remains a 'beast of prey', even if most contemporary human beings have, on the surface, been tamed by civilization and 'herbivore' ethics. Needless to say, this 'charged' Life cannot be grasped by science with its 'chemical' methods and preoccupation with 'static . . . details'. Life is 'revealed only through unsophisticated living with it' (20). More generally, Spengler leaves us in no doubt as to whom he sides with, the 'Vikings of the blood' or the 'Vikings of the mind'.

Unlike Lawrence and many other reactionaries of the period who made similar utterances about Life and blood, Spengler was no primitivist enjoining a return to the jungle (hence the label 'reactionary *modernist*'). On the contrary, it is in modern technology that 'the proud blood of the beast of prey revolts for the last time against the tyranny of pure thought' and 'herbivore' constraints (79f). Other creatures continue their conflicts within nature, but man's 'destiny [is to] pit himself against her', to 'enslave and harness her very forces' (78, 84). Technology is his means. Spengler is keen, of course, to distinguish his enthusiasm for technology from that of Comte and other positivist advocates of technical progress. These 'progress-philistines' base their case on utilitarian considerations: technology will benefit us. But the true technologist's 'passion . . . has *nothing whatever* to do with its consequences': rather, it is the Faustian urge to 'triumph over difficult problems' and to 'build a world *oneself*, to be *oneself* God' (85f).

There is another reason why technology is not to be justified on utilitarian grounds, for while it represents the apex of man's struggle against nature, it is also the beginning of the end. 'The creature is rising up against its creator', like

Frankenstein's monster, and 'the Lord of the World is becoming the slave of the Machine'. Endless traffic jams, global warming, and much else in the future will guarantee that our technological 'Faustian civilization will lie in fragments, *forgotten*' (90, 103). Man, that beast of prey, will lose the battle – but no matter. 'Better a short life, full of deeds and glory, than a long life without content', and the 'great' and the 'thoroughbred' among human beings will at least attain honour as they enter, bravely facing their doom, into a crumbling Valhalla (103f).

A Spenglerian vision of Life, conflict, technological passion, and even of ultimate doom, is clearly discernible in Nazi ideology. Here is Joseph Goebbels, Hitler's Minister for Propaganda, writing in 1939: 'We live in an age that is both romantic and steellike, that has not lost its depth of feeling . . . National Socialism understood how to take the soulless framework of technology and fill it with the rhythm and hot impulses of our time.'[13] In 1941, Bergson died of pneumonia, probably contracted through lining-up with other Jews on an icy day in front of Nazi officials in Paris. It was an irony that this man should fall victim to the henchmen of an ideology which his own ideas about Life, however unintentionally and modestly, had played a role in forging.

• 2 Phenomenology, Hermeneutics and Existentialism •

The philosophical movements discussed in this section share the mood of those considered in the previous one. We encounter again hostility to the hubristic claims of scientism or positivism on behalf of the sciences, and a similar perception of human beings enervated and estranged in a modern world where these claims are received wisdom. There are important differences, however. The thinkers who now concern us do not counter positivism by substituting a metaphysics of Life for orthodox science, intuitions of nature for empirical enquiry, or 'blood' for reason. They emphasize, rather, the secondary, derivative character of science, and its unavoidable presuppositions and prejudices – features which disqualify it as a fundamental and objective account of reality. Second, the antidote to the modern condition is not the pretence that human beings are continuous with the Life which courses through the rest of nature. On the contrary, they must recognize their uniqueness, yet in doing so also appreciate that the world they inhabit is a human one, to be 'at home' in.

The above mood, with the modulations mentioned, was fully expressed during the first third of the century by Edmund Husserl, 'the father of phenomenology'. Empirical science, he argued, can at best apprise us of 'facts', not of 'essential being' (I 40),[14] and anyway must take too much for granted to exhibit the 'rigour' of a truly fundamental and objective account of the world. Such rigour belongs only to a style of philosophical examination of experience which Husserl calls 'phenomenology' or – borrowing his teacher, Franz Brentano's, misleading term – 'descriptive psychology'. In old age, Husserl's attention turned to 'the crisis of European existence' evident in a new 'barbarian hatred of spirit' and reason, of the kind displayed by fascists and some of the writers discussed in the previous section. Dreadful as this hatred was, it was an inevitable 'revulsion' against the 'mistaken rationalism' of the positivists (C 179). For the effect of their elevation of the sciences had been, first, to void the world of all meaning and value, by 'mathematicizing' it, and thereby promoting a dualist image of 'nature . . . alien to spirit' (C 154): and, second, to reduce the human mind to a mere object, a brain perhaps, in the grip of the same mechanical processes as a train or a stone. If such are the products of reason, it is no wonder that reason itself should be feared.

In this section, I begin with Husserl's position, often called 'pure' phenomenology to distinguish it from the 'existential' phenomenology to which some of his followers, most famously Martin Heidegger, moved. In their view, Husserl's version was itself all too infected by the 'mistaken rationalism' of which he rightly accused the positivists. Existential phenomenology, we will see, incorporates themes which, blended with the ideas of earlier thinkers – Dilthey, in one case, Kierkegaard and Nietzsche, in the other – yields the movements known as hermeneutics and existentialism respectively.

Pure Phenomenology

The life of Edmund Husserl (1859–1938) – a Moravian Jew, whose career was mainly spent at the German universities of Göttingen and Freiburg – was almost entirely uneventful, at least until towards its end, which came just soon enough to save him from persecution, though not humiliation and harrassment, by the Nazis. It was one, too, of dedication to his calling: a prolonged effort to rethink an abiding set of problems. His amazing output testifies to a power of concentration confirmed by a tendency to forget about other obligations, such as dining with his own guests, when summoned to his study by a philosophical problem. Dry and turgid his writings may have been, but they, like his life, bear witness to his conviction that only through honest philosophical toil is it possible to 'shape oneself into the . . . free, autonomous "I" ', to 'find oneself' (C 338). This conviction remained firm from his early preoccupation with the foundations of mathematics to his late concerns with the constitution of reality and the crisis of modern Europe. It is one Husserl imparted to the many students, themselves important figures, who critically continued the tradition he founded.[15]

The longer tradition to which he himself belonged was that of rationalism, whose goal, as he saw it, was 'fundamental description', the presentation of truths at once necessary, indubitable and self-evident. It is because the claims of empirical science are none of these that, despite positivist pretensions, it cannot be fundamental. Science aims to *explain*, but a prior aim is to *describe* what there is to explain. Hence we must go 'back to the things themselves' (I 74f), to a stage prior to science's interpretation of things. That is the task of a truly 'rigorous science', a philosophy which 'aims exclusively at establishing "knowledge of essences"' (I 40). These essences, the materials for fundamental description of 'the things themselves', are objects for 'intuition', a non-perceptual 'seeing', not for empirical investigation. In Husserl's senses of the terms, it is these essences which are 'phenomena' and the investigation of them is 'phenomenology'. (Earlier philosophers had used 'phenomena' quite differently, to refer to sensory appearances or sense-data.)

Focusing on essences is not easy, since our everyday thinking is powerfully influenced by information about contingent matters of fact, by scientific interpretations of things, and so on. To obtain this focus, it is necessary to perform various *epoches* or 'abstentions'. The term is borrowed from the Greek sceptics who spoke of 'abstaining' from, 'disconnecting' or 'bracketing' our everyday beliefs. To begin with, we need to bracket the scientific picture of the world and recall the 'life-world', the world as it is 'for all of us' (C 209). Colours, for example, must be thought of as what we see, not as invisible light-waves impinging on the retina. Then, more radically, we must bracket the whole physical world, debar ourselves 'from using any judgement that concerns spatio-temporal reality' (I 100). This manoeuvre is reminiscent of Descartes', but its point is different: not seriously to call physical reality into doubt, but to put 'out of action' facts irrelevant to essences. Whether, say, a man exists in reality or only in a novel is a contingent matter which has no bearing on his essence, on what makes him who he is.

A third, even more radical suspension of our 'natural standpoint' is needed for a truly Augean cleansing of our usual assumptions. For we must also abstain from belief in the existence of the 'empirical' or 'natural' self, the abiding, embodied human character or persona studied by psychology. Whether there are selves in that sense is a contingent, dubitable matter. Still, there must be an 'I' which survives abstention from belief, namely the 'transcendental' or 'pure' ego which does the abstaining. (Here, of course, there are echoes of Descartes' *cogito* argument – see p. 244). This 'I' cannot itself be part of the world – which, recall, has been put in abeyance – but is the pure subject or 'spectator' which remains when all else has been bracketed. This final *epoche* completes what Husserl calls his 'phenomenological reduction', by which nearly all the items we normally take to exist have been put out of play so that the philosopher may now focus, unimpeded, on what is directly given in our experiences and upon the essences embodied in these experiences. Everything, to be sure, 'goes on appearing as it appeared before' this reduction, but in the armchair of the phenomenologist 'all natural believing' is suspended (CM 20).

How are we to understand these essences and the enquiry into them? Early in his career, Husserl defended a view of mathematical truths which he later saw as unacceptably close to J. S. Mill's 'psychologistic' account of them as empirical generalizations. What he retained, however, and extended to necessary, essential truths in general, was the thought that these are founded upon 'mental acts' we perform. To enquire into essences, then, is to examine mental acts. Such acts have two sides to them. A description of my hoping for a long life might focus on what I hope for or on my hoping for it: on the content or 'noema' of the act (shared with such acts as expecting and dreading a long life), or on its psychological character (not shared with those very different acts). Now it is on the 'noematic' content of mental acts that the study of essences must focus. Any such act is 'intentional' in the sense of being 'directed' towards some object (I 241ff) – a long life, in the above example. It is the act's content that dictates which object it is directed towards, the one which would, if it really exists, 'fulfil' or 'satisfy' the act of, say, hoping. So, to know an object's essence *is* to know the content of the acts directed towards it. The object's essence is what makes it, of necessity, the object it is – namely the one with the features required for it, and no other object, to 'fulfil' the mental acts which 'intend' it.

Husserl writes that the 'noema is . . . a generalization of the idea of meaning [*Sinn*] to the field of all acts', not just linguistic ones.[16] There is a helpful analogy, certainly, between a word's sense and reference, on the one hand, and a mental act's content and object, on the other. Just as, for Frege, the sense or meaning of a word determines what it refers to, so, for Husserl, mental acts are 'related to things through their posited meaning' (I 346). Just as an expression, like 'Santa Claus', can have a sense but fail to refer, so the 'intentional object' of a mental act may fail to exist, like the woman combining the attributes of Marilyn Monroe and Mother Theresa whom I hope to marry. But just as to understand what an expression means I must, in principle, be able to tell of objects whether the expression refers to them or not, so to grasp the content of a mental act I must be able to tell whether an object 'fulfils' it or not.

Many philosophers this century have construed their job to be the establishing of 'conceptual' truths through examination of the meanings of the words we employ for talking about the world. That is not Husserl's view, but only because he sees no reason to restrict 'meaning-conferring acts' to the utterances of words. If hoping, believing and perceiving are also to be viewed as such acts, whereby objects are 'intended', the kinship between 'conceptual analysis' and pure phenomenology is close. The champions of these approaches are at any rate agreed that philosophical enquiry must be immunized from irrelevant and contingent matters of mere fact and existence.

In one direction of Husserl's later thought, however, few practitioners of 'conceptual analysis' would follow him. Although in bracketing the physical world, Husserl does not mean to deny its existence, he does speak of the world as in some sense 'constituted' by the mental acts of a 'pure' ego, describing himself as being, like Kant (see p. 299f.), a 'transcendental idealist'. Few commentators agree on the exact nature of this idealism, but two features, at least, are clear. First, the world as we experience it is 'animated' by the meanings which we project, in our perceptions and desires as much as our linguistic acts, so that we have no conception of what objects outside such a field of meanings might be like. Second, to say of objects that they exist can only mean that the mental acts – perceptions, say – 'directed' towards them are 'fulfilled' by further, confirming experiences. Roughly, that is, 'The dagger really exists' means that the further experiences which I predict to occur, as part of the sense of my current perception, actually will occur. In that case, it is nonsense to speak of the existence of objects or the world as such, independent of mental acts.

'Being-in-the-World'

'Existential' phenomenologists – pre-eminently Martin Heidegger (1889–1976) and the two French contemporaries, Jean-Paul Sartre (1905–80) and Maurice Merleau-Ponty (1907–61) – owed a considerable debt to Husserl. He was right, as the last of the trio put it, to 'foreswear science' in order to return to primordial descriptions of experience on which scientific explanation is parasitic (viii).[17] Right, too, to see that human beings cannot be natural objects, however sophisticated, alongside others: a conviction registered by Sartre's description of human existence as 'Being for-itself', in contrast to the 'Being in-itself' of everything else. Husserl was right, finally, to locate human uniqueness in 'intentionality', in our being, as Merleau-Ponty puts it, 'condemned to meaning' (xix). The final verdict of these authors on Husserl, however, was one of 'so near and yet so far'. Husserl, says Sartre, was not 'faithful to his first intuition[s]' (BN lvii),[18] and didn't know when to stop. It is one thing to 'foreswear' science, quite another to 'bracket' the whole physical world; one thing to deny that the self is an empirical object, like the brain, quite another to 'reduce' it to a 'pure', unembodied 'I'. As Heidegger will insist, there is only 'the concrete person', whose 'knowledge presupposes existence' in a world which cannot be 'bracketed' or 'put out of play' (BP 276).[19]

Responsible for his excesses was Husserl's overly intellectual conception of intentionality, one which elevated cognition over action, mental processes over practice. As Sartre puts it, since 'meaning came into the world only by the activity of man, practice superseded contemplation'.[20] If it is primarily through purposive practice that meaning is projected onto things, Husserl should not have 'abstained' from belief in the physical world nor, Merleau-Ponty holds, underestimated the crucial role of the body in the 'imposition of meaning' (147). (One should note that in his last writings, partly in response to Heidegger's criticisms, Husserl did come to emphasize the roles of our 'life-world' activities and the 'lived body' in the generation of meanings.)

Husserl's mistake was a fatal one, since it rendered nugatory the whole point of the doctrine of intentionality. He had himself criticized earlier philosophers, like Descartes and Hume, for treating objects of experience as *internal* to experience, as ideas or impressions. They had thereby ignored the centrifugal character of experience, its 'directedness' towards what is outside of mental activity. When Sartre learned of Husserl's doctrine of intentionality, he 'turned pale with emotion', scenting a way of escape from the 'alimentary' view of perception which restricts direct awareness to the inner contents of experience. But he soon came to see that Husserl's own version did not offer this escape. By 'bracketing' the world, Husserl was in effect guaranteeing that perceptual and other acts are so many 'flies bumping their noses on the window without being able to clear the glass' (BN 100). Or, in Heidegger's words, Husserl's 'idea of a subject which has intentional experiences merely inside its own sphere' is a 'perverted subjectivization of intentionality', betraying the whole charm of the notion, its promise of showing how experience can engage with the world (BP 64).

The 'existential' phenomenologists give a workmanlike, 'Stakhanovite reading' of notions like intentionality and meaning, tying them to embodied, purposive practice in the world, and not, like Husserl, to the conscious performance of mental acts.[21] To appreciate the kind of account of human beings and their world to emerge from such a reading, I turn to Heidegger's *Being and Time* (1927), that 'most profound turning point in German philosophy since Hegel'.[22]

Martin Heidegger rarely strayed from his native Black Forest region of southern Germany, whose costume and customs he frequently assumed. Most of his university career was spent at Freiburg, where he inherited Husserl's Chair. After 1945, banned for several years from teaching for his association with the Nazis, Heidegger devoted himself to writing at his mountain retreat on Todtnauberg. With Wittgenstein, he is increasingly perceived as one of the two seminal philosophers of the century, but no other has been so controversial – 'possibly Lucifer in person', for Iris Murdoch; the model of an obscurantist metaphysician, for Rudolf Carnap; the fount of gnostic wisdom, for the poet Paul Celan. Recently, controversy has centred on the extent of his involvement with and sympathies for National Socialism. The former he later played down, the latter he refused entirely to recant.[23] As with Wittgenstein, it is usual to distinguish between an 'early' and 'late' Heidegger, before and after his 'turn' during the 1930s: a turn away from the position discussed in this section to a more gnomic one which prompted Sartre, on visiting Heidegger after the war, to declare that his erstwhile hero had 'gone mystical'. (I discuss his later views in section 5.)

The declared topic of *Being and Time* is 'the question of Being', one ignored, according to Heidegger, since the Pre-Socratics in favour of enquiry into particular beings or entities. Fortunately, some will think, little of this uncompleted work discusses Being in general, most of it consisting in often earthy descriptions of the kind of Being, *Dasein* ('being-there'), enjoyed by human beings. Since 'we always conduct our activities in an understanding of Being', however inchoate, 'the question of Being' is best tackled by exploring our understanding of it – we for whom 'Being is . . . an issue', a matter of concern in a way it is not for any other creature (BT 25, 42). Human existence, *Dasein*, is essentially 'Being-in-the-world'.

This is not the banal claim that people, as it happens, live in a world, but a challenge to the whole tradition, from Descartes to Husserl, which construes human beings as intellectual 'spectators' of a world, their own bodies included, to which they are at most contingently related and in the absence of which they could, at least in logic, still exist. Cartesian doubt, Humean scepticism, Husserl's *epoche* are only possible if the human being can, in thought, be detached or abstracted from the world. Heidegger's aim is to show that this is absurd. *Dasein* is not 'mere cognition in the . . . spectator sense' (BP 276): it is engaged with the world in such a way that neither can be conceived without the other. *Dasein* is necessarily 'always already with other beings' (BP 157), and 'Reality is . . . grounded in the Being of *Dasein*' (BT 255). Heidegger might here have quoted Martin Buber's remark, in his influential *I and Thou*, that it is absurd to 'split' experience into two separate factors, a 'ghostly I' and a 'ready-made world'.[24]

The world as we 'proximally' experience it is not composed of ready-made objects 'present-at-hand' (*vorhanden*) for cognition and perception. Rather, things are 'proximally' encountered as 'ready-to-hand' (*zuhanden*), as 'equipment', as items – like hammers and inkwells – which are what they are in virtue of having an 'in-order-to', a 'for-the-sake-of', within purposive human activities. This is true even of items in nature, such as the south wind, for these, too, are initially 'discovered . . . only by the circumspection with which one takes account of things in farming' and other practices (BT 112). 'Proximally', moreover, nothing is encountered in isolation, as an independent 'substance'. Rather, each thing is 'sign-like', pointing to the other things and the people that provide the contexts which give it an identity. The ink points to the pen, the pen to the study, the study to the academic institution. The world, indeed, is a great 'referential totality', the complete context in which everything 'ready-to-hand' has its place. (To look for the essences of things one by one, in isolation from one another, in the manner of Husserl, is therefore impossible.)

Why does Heidegger think that our 'proximal' encounter must be with the 'ready-to-hand'? 'To the extent that any entity is discovered in its Being . . . it is already something ready-to-hand . . . not a "world-stuff" that is merely present-at-hand' (BT 118). That is, there is no 'access' to a thing – it wouldn't be 'lit up' for us – without its place in activities that matter to us. In the absence of these, the world would be shapeless, with nothing standing out in relief for us. Once things have been 'lit up', it is then possible to abstain from our usual practical interests and 'just stare' at them, examine them for their 'intrinsic' properties, like shape, and merely 'cognize' them. We are then viewing them as 'present-at-hand'. This way of viewing them, as physical substances, is assumed in the Cartesian tradition to be the basic way of experiencing objects. But it cannot, insists Heidegger, be basic: not only because things must first have been 'discovered' in their pragmatic roles, but because even this 'spectatorial' view has, originally, a practical motive. Only when breakdowns occur in our practical dealings – when, say, a tool ceases to function – do things become 'conspicuous' or 'obtrusive', so that we inspect them, measure them, examine what they are made of – in short, treat them as 'present-at-hand' (BT 102ff). What tradition views as our primary way of experiencing things, then, is in fact derivative, parasitic.

This account of the world has important, equally non-traditional implications for the nature of the we who have our being 'in' it. *Dasein* is not 'in the world' in the dull, geometric sense that the ink is in the pen; rather, it 'dwells in' the world and is 'absorbed in' it. The fundamental relation between ourselves and the world is not causal or spatial, but 'intentional': a relation holding within a field of significance. *Dasein* is not essentially perceptual or cognitive: rather, its 'Being reveals itself as *care* (*Sorge*)' (BT 227). For something to be perceived, it must first show up for us within the field of our concernful dealings. 'Care' is not, for Heidegger, an exercise of consciousness, of 'mental acts', though of course one can come consciously to care about or disregard something. It is, rather, implicit in the 'absorbed coping' with 'equipment' which is our normal mode of being-in-the-world. Those intellectual 'spectators' – Descartes' *cogito* and Husserl's 'pure' ego – are, therefore, no more to be identified with human beings than are the physical substances of tradition with things as 'proximally' encountered. *Dasein's* relation to the world is not that of a subject to an object, a spectator to the passing show. Only by an extreme and distorting abstraction can our being be detached from that of the world we are 'in'.

Hermeneutics

The world as 'proximally' encountered is one of 'possible significance' (BT 184), a 'referential totality' of 'sign-like' items. But signs need interpreting, and a defining capacity of *Dasein* is interpretative understanding of its world. This is easy to overlook if we think of interpretation as a theoretical procedure applied by individuals to raw data of experience. 'Primordial' interpretation, for Heidegger, has none of these features, however. It is 'carried out not in a theoretical statement but in an action' (BT 200), as when one 'interprets' something as a hammer by using it as such. Nor is it carried out by an individual, who is, on the contrary, 'always already' in a world interpreted for him by 'the "they"' (*Das Man*), anonymous people at large. Finally, in basic interpretation, we do not 'throw a "signification" over some naked thing' (BT 190), for nothing is encountered in the raw, but always *as* a door, house, or whatever. Heidegger, accordingly, describes *Dasein*'s relation to its world as 'hermeneutic', a term designating the 'business of interpreting'. Since phenomenology, whose aim is 'the disclosedness of Being', can only proceed by uncovering *Dasein*'s own implicit understanding, it follows that phenomenology itself is hermeneutics (BT 61f). The phenomenologist is, therefore, doubly involved in the 'business of interpretation', for what he tries to interpret are themselves interpretations.

'Hermeneutics' was the romantic theologian Schleiermacher's label for the methodology of biblical interpretation. It was Wilhelm Dilthey, however, already met with as a critic of positivism in the social sciences and a 'philosopher of Life' (see p. 350 and p. 417), who first extended the scope of the discipline. By 'hermeneutics', Dilthey meant the 'methodology of the understanding of recorded expressions' (261), not just written texts like the Bible, but all the items, from paintings to gardens, in which the 'spirit of an age' has been 'objectified'. All cultural products are at least analogous to written texts, and the historian's aim, as much as the literary critic's, is 'understanding [of] the relationship . . . of expression to what is expressed' (229).

This relationship cannot be grasped through the analytical techniques of the natural sciences because of its holistic character. 'Meaning means nothing except belonging to a whole' (233), so that to interpret an old painting, say, the historian must empathetically enter into the whole Life or spirit of its century. This gives rise to the first of two dilemmas that taxed Dilthey. If something can only be understood in terms of the whole to which it belongs, how can understanding ever begin, for surely the whole must also be understood in terms of its parts? This is one version of the famous 'hermeneutic circle'. The second dilemma was how, if all expression is 'determined by a horizon' of thought peculiar to an age, the historian himself could achieve any objective interpretation of ages alien to his own.

These problems seem to become more general with Heidegger's radical extension of the scope of hermeneutics. As his valetudinarian student, Hans-Georg Gadamer (b. 1900), explains, hermeneutics is now 'universal in scope', since all 'being that can be understood is language' (xii).[25] It is not, that is, just cultural products, but *everything*, which is 'sign-like' and so analogous to verbal expressions. Since 'sign-like' things can only be understood relative to the 'relational totality' to which they belong, it follows that the 'circle' mentioned above infects all interpretation, not just the cultural historian's. Heidegger insists, moreover, that any interpretation – whether *Dasein*'s own or the phenomenologist's – can only occur against a background of 'fore-conceptions', so that it is 'never a presuppositionless apprehending of something presented to us' (BT 191–2). Later it is made clear that these presuppositions belong to *Dasein*'s historical situatedness. Hence Dilthey's other worry, about the possibility of objectivity in the humane sciences, becomes universal in scope.

Gadamer, the leading champion of hermeneutic phenomenology, does not try to solve these problems so much as reduce our perception of them as problems. That we oscillate between a grasp of the whole and understanding its parts is not a disaster befalling interpreters, but definitive of the very activity of interpretation, and not something that usually causes trouble. If it did, translating a foreign text would be a rare event, since in translation we are constantly adjusting our sense of the whole text and our understanding of individual expressions in terms of one another. Again, while we should indeed try to uncover and critically examine 'fore-conceptions' or 'pre-judices', we must also recognize the absolute necessity for these if understanding or interpretation is ever to begin. 'Pre-judices' are 'biases of our openness to the world . . . conditions whereby we experience something' and upon which there depends the selection of 'some possibilities of questioning' to the exclusion of others (9). Unless things were, initially, taken in some way rather than another, nothing would be 'lit up' as worth questioning.

Finally, Dilthey's worry that the historical situatedness of the enquirer may cut him off from the past which he is trying to interpret is misplaced. Our consciousness, says Gadamer, is an 'effective-historical' one, formed by the historical traditions into which we are born. Since 'the horizon of the present cannot be formed without the past', a constant 'fusion of horizons', past and present, is always occurring (273f). In other words, what places the enquirer firmly in his own age is precisely what gives him access to earlier ones, enabling him to 'conquer a remoteness', as another hermeneuticist puts it:[26] namely, a lived acquaintance with developing tradition. This same acquaintance means, moreover, that the phenomenologist – the enquirer into our current understanding – is not hermetically sealed inside a scheme of interpretation which he can in no way transcend. At any rate, his access to earlier, alternative schemes provides some basis for distancing himself from current 'fore-conceptions' and to eliminate those which Heidegger called 'fancies and popular conceptions' (BT 195).

Existentialism

The concern of hermeneutics is with the public, anonymous structures of meaning which imbue the life of a culture, and in which an individual is 'always already' immersed or 'thrown', as Heidegger puts it. Alongside this concern, however, Heidegger had another, inherited from Kierkegaard's diatribes against 'the Public's' suppression of the individual. The individual *Dasein* is not merely 'thrown' into a public world, but is abjectly 'fallen' and 'absorbed' into 'average' attitudes and interpretations, taking pleasure 'as *they* take pleasure' and finding shocking 'what *they* find shocking'. A person has thereby 'lost itself', its 'ownmost possibilities of Being' delegated to 'the "they"'' (BT 163f, 220ff). For however 'communal' it is in practice, human being is, in essence, individualized. As Heidegger's fellow *Existenzphilosoph*, Karl Jaspers (1883–1969), put it, 'Although I am in my social I, I no longer coincide with it . . . I am not a result of social configurations . . . [for] I retain my own original potential'.[27] For both thinkers, I am called to a sense of my 'authentic' individual potential through both the uncanny mood they describe as 'anxiety' (*Angst*) and anticipation of death. The latter 'utterly individualizes *Dasein*', for dying is the most striking example of something which each *Dasein* 'must take upon itself' (BT 310, 284).

With the introduction of these themes, existential phenomenology has become existentialism, for the classic statement of which we turn to Jean-Paul Sartre. Indeed, the label was invented around 1944, by the Catholic philosopher Gabriel Marcel, for the recently emerging ideas of Sartre and his friend Simone de Beauvoir (1908–86), only later being applied retrospectively to those of Heidegger, Jaspers and, with less warrant perhaps, Kierkegaard and Nietzsche. Of all twentieth-century thinkers, Sartre's name is the most widely known: the only one, surely, that could have appeared, rhyming with 'Montmartre', in a Fred Astaire musical. Philosopher, novelist, playwright, essayist, song-writer, editor, political activist, prodigious lover and drinker, Sartre filled life to the brim. Dictating to his secretary from the lavatory, even the most intimate moments of his day were not to be wasted. At first a teacher of philosophy, Sartre was enabled by the success of his novels and his great tome *Being and Nothingness* (1943) to devote himself to writing and politics. He gradually abandoned existentialist tenets in favour of an idiosyncratic Marxism, so that by the 1960s this erstwhile fixture of Left Bank cafés was more often to be seen, with De Beauvoir, handing out Maoist pamphlets and at student demonstrations. His complex relationship with De Beauvoir, recorded with only partial frankness in her autobiography, seems destined to intrigue connoisseurs of the world's great loves well into the future.

That Sartre could figure in Hollywood musicals is one small testament to the vogue or cult that existentialism became in the post-war years, with its 'clique of . . . young people who prowled' between nightclubs, feigning *Angst* and *ennui*, and wearing 'the new "existentialist" uniform' of all black.[28] Few of these youths, one guesses, had ploughed through the 600 pages of Sartre's tome, and it is important to distinguish the vogue from Sartre's own philosophy. Popular characterizations of existentialism as 'the expression of the spiritual dishevelment of a post-war age' and 'an anti-intellectual philosophy of life' only apply to the former.[29]

The centrepiece of existentialism is a doctrine of radical freedom and responsibility. We are, says Sartre, 'condemned to be free' (EH 34) and 'nothing foreign has decided what we are' (BN 554). Hence, our responsibility is 'overwhelming' and we are 'without excuses'. For Sartre, this doctrine flows from the existential phenomenologist's insight that a human being's relationship to the world is 'intentional' and 'hermeneutical', not the causal one of an object interacting with others. Circumstances or situations only impinge upon our actions in virtue of the interpretations we give to them in the light of our 'projects'. The steepness of the mountain only 'causes' me to walk round it if construed in a certain way: as an obstacle, say, rather than a challenge. The Spanish existentialist Ortega y Gasset (1883–1955) puts it well: 'the world is . . . a conjunction of favourable and adverse conditions . . . [with] no being independent of us; it consists . . . in facilities and difficulties . . . in respect of our aspirations'.[30] A human being, Heidegger had said, is always 'ahead of itself' (BT 236), always on the way towards achieving purposes in the light of which alone circumstances figure as motives or reasons. Sartre is making the same point when he denies that 'the motive causes the act', for it is an 'integral part of the act', idle apart from the 'project' which brings it into play (BN 437–8).

But what of a person's character or emotional make-up? Does this not determine or constrain action? In a famous passage, Sartre writes that 'there is at least one being whose existence comes before its essence, . . . which exists before it can be defined by any conception of it. That being is man' (EH 34). The point is not simply that a person, in a godless world, has no essence in the sense of a preordained function. It is, as well, that a person has no fixed constitution or nature, his or her character being constantly shaped through action. Since a person is 'nothing else but the sum of his actions' (EH 41), there is no such thing as, say, a cowardly temperament, only people who frequently take the coward's way-out. Even our emotions and passions are 'chosen' rather than 'given', for they are at once strategies for coping with situations and functions of 'projects' freely engaged in. Ortega sums it up nicely: 'the stone is given its existence: it need not fight for what it is . . . Man has to make his own existence at every moment.'[31]

Not all of Sartre's fellow existentialists were sympathetic to his talk of our continually 'choosing' ourselves, our situations and our characters. 'Not to refuse is not the same thing as to choose', explains Merleau-Ponty. We are too obviously 'thrown' into situations to speak of our choosing them. Still, while 'I can no longer pretend to choose myself continually from nothing at all', I possess the powers of 'general refusal' and 'begin[ning] something else' (452) – of standing back from my situation or motives, appraising and so altering them. My responsibility remains 'overwhelming', therefore. Indeed, for Sartre, it extends well beyond my own person and actions. By not actively opposing what is evil, I comply with it: my hands are dirty and I bear responsibility for the evil. Again, whenever I act deliberately I give a green light to others to emulate my action: I am 'a legislator deciding for the whole of mankind' (EH 30) and so bear responsibility for the consequences of their acting as I do.

Appreciation of this responsibility, of what hangs on my own personal commitments, is one of several sources of *Angst* or 'anguish'. Indeed, a degree of *Angst* – akin to the vertigo of someone who knows that nothing prevents his throwing himself over the precipice – is inseparable from awareness of freedom. The aware person cannot take comfort that his 'character', his good record, or his past resolutions will dictate the appropriate decision when the moment comes: for none of these – nothing at all, in fact – constrains his choice at that moment. There is an even more disturbing dimension of *Angst*, first highlighted by Heidegger. As the individual 'resolutely' and 'authentically' stands back from the everyday interpretations and valuations of things into which he is 'thrown', everything becomes 'uncanny' and shows itself 'in an empty mercilessness' (BT 393). Nothing any longer has its usual significance, and the individual experiences an 'absurd' world without secure 'foundations': he is therefore thrown back upon himself as the source of values and meanings.

Angst, then, is no fun, and 'fleeing' from it into a more 'tranquillized' condition explains that form of self-deception Sartre calls 'bad faith' (*mauvaise foi*). In bad faith, a person 'gives to himself the type of being of the object' (CM 484), thereby refusing to own to his unique freedom. Thus Sartre's cast of café characters includes the waiter who – too eager and polite, his step a little too quick – is 'playing at *being* a waiter', identifying too closely with a fixed role so as to exonerate him from facing up to decisions; and the woman who tries to avoid responsibility for the direction a flirtation will take by pretending that the events are merely 'happening' to her, leaving her hand in the man's clasp as if it were a lump of meat instead of the instrument of action and decision that it is (BN 56ff). The primary form taken by bad faith is to 'think of [oneself] from the position of the Other' (CM 485), to surrender to other people's pigeon-holing of oneself as, irretrievably, this or that kind of person.

This surrender, and the motive behind it, are apparent in the words of a character from a Sartre novel: 'I am myself for all eternity paederast, villain, coward . . . I need no longer bear the responsibility of my turbid and disintegrating self: he who sees me causes me to be. I am as he sees me' (R 116, 345). A main complaint in Simone de Beauvoir's best-seller, *The Second Sex*, is that her fellow women too readily identify themselves with the 'objects' that men are said to view them as.

The antithesis of bad faith is what existentialists call 'authenticity'. Critics often accuse them of adopting the spirit of the song-title, ''T'ain't what you do, it's the way that you do it': of, that is, holding that it doesn't matter what actions people perform provided that they do so authentically. When Sartre writes that it is impossible to judge someone who 'chooses his purpose . . . in all clearness and . . . sincerity, whatever that purpose' (EH 50), he seems to confirm the accusation. So, it seems, does his famous example of the wartime student who must decide between joining the Free French and looking after his aged mother, and to whom Sartre says 'You are free, therefore choose – that is to say invent. No rule of general morality can show you what you ought to do' (EH 38).

Appearances, however, are misleading here, for Sartre is emphatic that there is a criterion for moral choice, namely freedom, which is 'the foundation of all values' (EH 51). To begin with, the authentic person must will to be free, frankly to acknowledge responsibility for his or her life. But, as Jaspers remarked, 'man only becomes free in so far as the other becomes free'.[32] The point here is not a political one. It is, rather, that I can only view myself as free if I regard and treat other people as free too. This is because my view of myself is indelibly coloured by how others regard me, and I cannot suppose they regard me as free unless I so regard them. Someone who knows what it is to be free in his or her own case, then, must respect the freedom of another. (The influence of Hegel's Master–Slave parable is apparent here – see p. 315.) This is why 'my freedom impl[ies] mutual recognition of others' freedom' (CM 487), and why 'I cannot make liberty my aim unless I make that of others equally my aim' (EH 52).

How a person best promotes authenticity or mutual recognition of freedom is another, and difficult, issue – the one, in effect, faced by the student. For what he must choose between is a 'morality of sympathy, of personal devotion' (to his mother), and a 'morality of wider scope' (enjoining a just war against the Nazis) (EH 36). Familiar rules of 'general morality' are indeed unhelpful here, since any such rule is culled from within one or other of the competing moral perspectives and cannot, therefore, be used to adjudicate between them. Sartre's own vision of the authentic life devoted to mutual recognition of freedom seems to be of one committed to principles and moral causes of 'wider scope' – anti-racism, anti-colonialism, and the like. But other, more quietistic visions are compatible with the idea of authenticity. For Gabriel Marcel (1889–1973) and other 'religious existentialists', it is through intimate personal relations – love and friendship – that I best 'apprehend' the freedom of another, 'help him to be freed [and] collaborate with his freedom'.[33] If there is no party line among existentialists on the practical implications of the quest for authenticity, this is not because they are indifferent to the 'what' of moral action, and concerned only with its 'how'. It is because of an honest, and indeed perennial, dilemma. If I am to 'collaborate' with my fellow human beings, to live in community with them, as I must if I am myself to realize my humanity, shall I best do so by playing a strident role on the world-stage or by cultivating human intimacy within my own backyard?

• 3 Logical Atomism and Logical Positivism •

Sections 1 and 2 examined philosophies hostile towards the positivist trends which held sway in mainland Europe at the end of the nineteenth century. We now examine views which develop those same trends, but in a new key furnished by investigations into logic and language. Logical Positivism, as the name implies, was a continuation of the Comtean brand by other means, but its champions also owed a debt to the Logical Atomism formulated during the First World War. I consider these movements in chronological order, postponing until the end their implications for ethics, religion, and the nature of philosophy.

In Britain, we saw, it was not positivism which held sway, but a home-brewed Absolute Idealism, according to which reality is a monistic whole of spirit or experience. Two young Cambridge philosophers who had momentarily succumbed to this heady brew were to be its main critics. For Bertrand Russell (1872–1970) and G. E. Moore (1873–1958), Bradley's idealism did intolerable violence to common sense. That judgements about parts of reality can only be relatively true; that there are no non-mental objects; that no objects can be identified except in relation to the whole – these are doctrines of last resort. For Russell, at least, mathematics proved no such resort was necessary, for there we discover absolute, non-mental truths, and sharply discriminable items of reality.

Both men, however, veered in the short term towards a metaphysics which, on reflection, was no less offensive to common sense. According to this 'Platonic atomism',[34] reality contains *everything* we can significantly talk about. '*Being*', wrote Russell, 'belongs to . . . every possible object of thought', including 'numbers, the Homeric gods, relations [and] chimeras' (PM 427).[35] If such an entity did not have being, there would be nothing for propositions in which it is mentioned to be *about*: they would then be nonsense, which clearly they are not. Moore, his common sense twice offended by his own theories, largely abandoned metaphysical speculation. Russell, also twice bitten but less shy, embarked instead on developing a metaphysics which would steer between the excesses of monism and 'Platonism'. There are indeed many real entities, but these no longer include the gods and chimeras, for 'logic must no more admit a unicorn than zoology can' (IM 169). Since the only real entities turn out, however, to be 'logical atoms', with nearly everything in which we normally believe relegated to 'fictions', the results hardly square with common sense. Indeed, we 'end with something so paradoxical that no one will believe it': but that, Russell consoles us, is after all 'the point of philosophy' (LA 193).

Russell's Logical Atomism

Russell's Logical Atomism marked but one stage in a long philosophical career frequently suspended for work in mathematics and for moral causes – pacifism during the First World War, progressive education in the 1930s, nuclear disarmament in the 1960s. The much-married Russell's *risqué* views on sexual freedom caused him the same run-ins with the US authorities that his political activism did with the British. The most influential British philosopher of the century, a logician of genius (the main author of the monumental *Principia Mathematica*) and, for his admirers, the moral conscience of his nation, Russell was second to none of his contemporaries in intellectual stature. Despite George VI's verdict, 'a queer-looking fellow', he certainly looked the part: white-maned, dome-headed, eagle-eyed. He died aged 98, robust but depressed both by the direction of a world which had produced the nuclear bomb and the Vietnamese war, and by the increasingly trivial preoccupations of philosophers that left his own work, outside of logic, largely ignored.

Despite the novel, logician's apparatus of Russell's metaphysics, he had the 'old-fashioned' empiricist aim of establishing on the basis of sense-experience what we really can know.[36] If the world we can know turns out to have a certain 'dryness or dulness', that does not detract from the grandeur of philosophy. Human beings are diminished when they live in a 'prison' of prejudices that put an 'impenetrable veil' between themselves and the world beyond. Through philosophy we 'so enlarge our interests as to include the whole outer world', and hence enlarge our selves, so securing 'a form of union of Self and not-Self'. It is not mysticism's goal, therefore, but its deprecation of rational knowledge, that is to be condemned. Moreover, 'dry' as the world may be, it is also infinitely great, so that through philosophical understanding 'the mind also is rendered great, and becomes capable of that union with the universe which constitutes its highest good' (PP 91ff).

Russell describes his position as *Logical* Atomism to distinguish it from that of the physicists. Logical atoms are those which analysis must reach in order to dissolve various logical paradoxes, to show how we manage to mean anything by our words, and to exhibit how we can really know some of the things we claim to. Unlike the physicist, moreover, the philosopher analyses, not the world, but our talk about it. Though since there is 'a certain fundamental identity of structure between a fact and the symbol for it' (LA 197), the results of this analysis are transferable to the world of facts.

In his mathematical work, Russell had encountered paradoxes which he attributed to treating subject expressions, like 'The class of all classes', in subject–predicate sentences, as naming or referring to actual entities. (This, we saw, was how Russell himself treated them in his 'Platonist' days.) To dissolve a paradox arising from such a sentence, the trick was to translate it 'into a form in which it does not mention the class at all', thereby dispelling the conviction that such a class must exist (LA 262). Russell soon generalized this strategy, known as 'the theory of descriptions'. Take a so-called 'definite description', like 'The present king of France', which on the surface seems to name a particular person. On Russell's theory, any sentence containing this expression can be translated into one which does not even *seem* to refer to, and so demand the existence of, this person. 'The present king of France does not exist', for instance, becomes 'It's not the case that there exists one and only one thing with the property of being a present king of France.' The translation illustrates how paradox is avoided. If the subject expression really were a name, there would have to be a French king it named, in which case it would be absurd to deny his existence. But on Russell's translation, the sentence comes out as unproblematically true.

Some expressions, however, must name entities, otherwise language would have no direct contact with reality. We could not describe something unless '*it* itself' could be 'mention[ed] by means of a name' (LA 200). We wouldn't know *what* we were talking about unless our propositions turned out, on analysis, to be 'composed wholly of constituents with which we are acquainted' (p. 32). To be acquainted with something is to be 'directly aware' of it, without the help of inferential or descriptive knowledge. So the questions 'Which expressions genuinely name?' and 'Which entities are we acquainted with?' are two sides of the same coin. By looking at one side, we see that ordinary names or name-like expressions, such as 'Piccadilly', 'Romulus' or 'My pen', are not genuine or 'logically proper' names. By looking at the other, we see, equivalently, that places, people and physical objects are not genuine objects of acquaintance.

Take 'Piccadilly'. If this were a genuine name, its meaning would require the existence of the famous street. But clearly it does not: the expression would still have a sense even if, like El Dorado, the street were a figment of the imagination. But isn't Piccadilly something that some of us are directly acquainted with? In denying this, Russell reveals his debt to empiricists like Hume. It is not the place with which I am acquainted, but 'sense-data' (patches of colour, noises, and the like) and their simple properties (red, loudness, and so on). At one time, he thought of physical objects and other 'external' things as entities whose existence we infer in order to explain our sense-data. His considered view, though, was that 'logical constructions are to be substituted for inferred entities' (ML 115). Piccadilly is a 'construction' or 'fiction' (LA 191): to speak of it is a shorthand way of referring to a mass of related sense-data and their properties. (Rather as talk of the average family is an abbreviation for talking about people and the relations among them.) It may be, Russell concedes, that Piccadilly and my pen have an existence over and above sense-data: but we have no reason to suppose so, and their doing so could do nothing to explain our experiences nor our understanding of the terms in which we speak of them.

Combining linguistics and epistemology, it emerges that the only genuine atomic sentences, into which all others are ultimately analysable, are ones like 'This (is) red', where 'this' means, not a physical object, but 'an actual object of sense' (LA 201). The only genuine names, pairing off with atomic objects, are, then, demonstratives like 'this' and 'that', when employed in the above manner. The only other candidate Russell considers is 'I'. Am I not acquainted with myself, the direct referent of 'I' as uttered by me? But the candidate is turned down on Humean grounds. I am indeed acquainted with various experiences called 'mine', but not with a 'persistent' or 'metaphysical ego' which has these experiences. 'A person is [simply] a certain series of experiences' (LA 277). The self, then, is as much a 'fiction' as Piccadilly and my pen. None of them are denizens of Russell's parsimonious world of 'ultimate simples' that enjoy 'a kind of reality not belonging to anything else' (LA 270).

The *Tractatus*

The self and 'ultimate simples' were issues on which the other great version of Logical Atomism, composed by a young Austrian soldier during 1914–18, differed from Russell's. Ludwig Wittgenstein (1889–1951) had been a student of Russell's on the eve of the war though, as the older man readily conceded, his teacher as well. Relations were eventually to cool, Russell seeing little in Wittgenstein's later philosophy, while the latter despised Russell's high-profile moral postures. Wittgenstein is one of the most intriguing characters in the history of the subject, indeed a cult-figure, as the battery of memoirs, novels and films about his life attest. These days one does not have to be a philosophy student to be familiar with this son of a plutocratic and suicide-prone Viennese family who turned to philosophy from engineering, lived in a remote Norwegian hut, carried his first masterpiece about in a soldier's knapsack, and who, sure that he had solved all the problems of philosophy, left the subject to teach at a village school and design a bizarre house for his sister. No less familiar are the tortured remorse over his homosexuality, the return to philosophy in the 1930s and the dismantling of his earlier position, the abandonment of a Cambridge Chair to work in hospitals during the Second World War, and the final years of wandering and cancer.[37]

The young Wittgenstein shared Russell's view that ordinary language, like clothing which fails to reveal the form of the body, 'disguises thought' (T 4.002),[38] and so calls for analysis into 'elementary propositions' which 'picture' elementary facts in the world. But it was out of different motives from Russell's that he wrote *Tractatus Logico-Philosophicus*, a haunting work whose terse, enigmatic utterances might have been (as indeed they have become) the libretto for a modernist cantata. The inspiration is not Hume's empiricism, but Kant's attempt to place limits on reason, not with the aim of discrediting what lies beyond – God and moral freedom, for example – but of securing them against illegitimate speculation. Wittgenstein's is the related attempt to 'draw a limit . . . to the expression of thoughts', to what can significantly be said (T Preface). Talk of matters outside this limit – religion, ethics, the meaning of life – can only be 'nonsense'. But this is not to dismiss such matters, for 'there are, indeed, things that cannot be put into words . . . They are what is mystical' (T 6.522). The point, rather, is to prevent people 'just *gassing*' about these, the truly 'important', things.[39]

A second motive was at work. Despite his admiration for Frege's and Russell's work on logic, Wittgenstein believed they had failed to identify the unique character of the propositions of logic, like the law of the excluded middle ('p or not-p'). His 'fundamental idea' is that the 'logical constants', like 'or' and 'not', are not 'representatives' (T 4.0312). They do not stand for items or relations in the world: if they did, the truths of logic would, as Mill wrongly thought, be like those of science. Logic, urges Wittgenstein, is '*prior* to every experience. To 'look at the world' for an answer to a question of logic is to be on a 'completely wrong track' (T 5.551–2). Analysis, then, must show us both how to set limits to language and how the propositions of logic are possible. The strategy will be to identify the elementary units of meaning and the operations which can be performed upon them. The output of these operations exhausts what can significantly be said, and logic and the 'mystical', in their different ways, are seen to lie outside this realm.

Wittgenstein accepts Russell's view that ordinary propositions must be analysable into ones containing genuine names, such a name being one whose 'object is its meaning' (T 3.203). These 'simple signs' combine into elementary propositions, said to 'picture' facts since an object corresponds to each sign and the proposition and the fact share a common 'form', somewhat as with photography. But why must analysis come to an end in these simple elements? Logic, the answer goes, requires that each proposition has a determinate sense (T 3.251). The sense of a proposition is given by the conditions under which it would be true or false, so that an *in*determinate proposition would allow for conditions under which it was neither of these: but that would contradict the law of the excluded middle, which demands that every proposition is either true or false. Indeterminacy is only avoided if the analysis of a proposition ends with a complete specification of conditions, divided into those which would make the proposition true and false respectively.

Notoriously, the *Tractatus* offers no examples of atomic signs and objects. There must be such for language to be meaningful, but we are unable to identify what they are. Russell's sense-data cannot fit the bill because propositions concerning them do not have the required logical independence to count as elementary. 'A is red' and 'A is green', for example, contradict each other, and where the 'product of two propositions is a contradiction', any appearance that they are elementary must be 'deceptive' (NB 91). One or both must conceal a complexity which, unpacked, reveals an explicit contradiction of the form 'p and not-p'. (Compare 'A is a bachelor' and 'A is married': the former, unpacked into 'A is an unmarried man', explicitly contradicts the latter.)

That elementary propositions or facts must be independent of one another, so that none can entail or contradict another, is crucial to Wittgenstein's understanding of the propositions of logic. These arise only through our combining propositions into more complex ones with the help of 'truth-functional' operators like 'and' and 'not'. Some, like 'p or not-p', are 'tautologies': that is, they 'admit *all* possible situations', so that we know *a priori* that they cannot be false, whatever the truth-value of their component proposition(s) ('p' in this example). Others, like 'neither p nor not-p', admit of no situations, and are *a priori* false (T 4.462). Strictly speaking, tautologies and contradictions 'say nothing' and therefore 'lack sense', for they can never provide information. 'I know nothing about the weather when I know that it is either raining or not raining' (T 4.461). It is now clear why elementary propositions must be independent of one another. If p and q were elementary *and* incompatible, then logical relations would not be the result, solely, of our combining propositions into complex ones: and that would spoil Wittgenstein's whole attempt to capture the unique status of logic.

If tautologies and contradictions 'lack sense', they are not the 'non-sense' of talk about ethics and religion. Ethical propositions, if such there were, would be neither contingent elementary ones nor the result of combining these with the help of 'not', 'or', and the like. Hence they stand beyond the limits of language. I shall return to Wittgenstein's remarks on these 'mystical' matters, contenting myself here with a glance at his opaque comments on the self.[40] When he writes that 'there is no such thing as the subject that thinks' (T 5.632), he is agreeing with Russell that 'I' is not the name of some simple object in the world, and that the self which psychology studies is a complex set of thoughts and experiences. Nevertheless, there is a 'non-psychological' self, a 'metaphysical subject' (T 5.641). In the *Notebooks*, such a subject is required, rather as for Kant, in order to explain the possibility of ethics. Since good and evil are 'not properties in the world', they must be ones of a subject somehow outside of it.

A further argument for this 'metaphysical self' is hinted at when Wittgenstein writes that the subject is 'a presupposition' (NB 79) or 'limit of the world – not a part of it' (T 5.641). There is nothing we can say about this metaphysical self, whose nature is 'completely veiled': 'The world as I found it', which is all I can talk about, does not contain the I who finds it (T 5.631). Still, this self is needed, for the world I find is '*my* world'. To imagine another world, I must be able to speak about it: but to do that I must employ 'the language which alone I understand' (T 5.62). How, though, is this language understood by me? The expressions of that language can only have meaning through the correlations which *I* make between them and objects in the world I know. Hence, the world I imagine is not after all another one, but at most a different arrangement of the objects belonging to my world. The world, then, is mine in that it presupposes – and so does not contain – the 'I' that is a precondition for meaningfully talking about it and so for 'finding' it.

That I am not 'part of the world' may seem a depressing, alienating conclusion. This is not how Wittgenstein sees it. I am not some peculiar entity, an 'outsider', within the world but at odds with it, like Descartes' *cogito*. The metaphysical subject has no nature or content to set it apart from worldly things: it is, as it were, 'a point without extension' (T 5.64), whose whole being is exhausted in finding the world as it is. '*Nothing* is left over' when that world is removed, and in that sense, 'I see that I too belong with the rest of the world' (NB 85).

Logical Positivism

According to the *Tractatus*, one should tell someone who 'wanted to say something metaphysical' that he had 'failed to give a meaning' to his words (T 6.53). This was music to the ears of a group of Austrian scientists and philosophers of science who gathered round Moritz Schlick (1882–1936) in the 1920s, its older members already versed by the positivist Ernst Mach (see p. 350) in hostility towards metaphysics. This 'Vienna Circle' included Rudolf

Carnap (1891–1970) and Otto Neurath (1882–1945), and attracted such visitors as A. J. Ayer (1910–89), author of that vivid report on the Circle's ruminations, *Language, Truth and Logic*, and Wittgenstein himself, when on furlough from his village school or sister's house. The proselytizing zeal of the members only partially abated with Schlick's murder by a crazed student and the emigration of many of them after Hitler's invasion of Austria.

The *Tractatus* provided the Circle not only with a declaration against metaphysics, but with the materials for conducting the campaign against it. These were, in particular, the theses that the limits of significant language are exceeded by statements irreducible to elementary empirical ones, and that all necessary truths are tautologies, and so uninformative or 'trivial'. These theses were enough to persuade the Circle that 'metaphysics was not merely outdated as the old positivism had it, but was a logically impossible enterprise, being excluded by the essential nature of language'. Here, then, was a new 'positivism on logical grounds': *Logical* Positivism (or Logical Empiricism), as it was soon to be called.[41]

With one central doctrine of the *Tractatus*, however, the Vienna Circle were unable to agree: its claim to be delineating the structure of the reality 'pictured' by language. Must not such a claim, by Wittgenstein's own criteria, be outlawed? For it is neither a tautology nor an empirical statement that reality structurally corresponds to language. The *Tractatus*, it seemed, was as metaphysical a work as any other, confirming Bradley's tart remark that he who tries to prove metaphysics impossible simply has a rival metaphysics to peddle. To be sure, Wittgenstein was aware of the problem, pointing out the impossibility of a picture's picturing its relation to what it depicts, and cheerily confessing that his own propositions are 'nonsensical', ladders to be thrown away once climbed (T 6.54). But as Carnap said, it is intolerably paradoxical to write a whole book, instead of keeping silent, about matters whereof, allegedly, one cannot speak (PL 37–8).[42]

The pressure was on, then, to defend the elimination of metaphysics, and to justify the kind of analysis of language pursued by the Atomists, but without recourse to atomistic metaphysics. The clue to how this might be done was provided by Wittgenstein himself. Suitably construed, his dictum that 'to understand a proposition means to know what is the case if it is true' (T 4.024) would yield the notorious 'verificationist theory of meaning', and its associated 'principle of verifiability'. Schlick sloganized the theory as follows: 'The meaning of a proposition is the method of its verification.' The associated principle is that, unless we know 'how the truth of our assertion can be tested . . . our words . . . are mere noises without meaning' (MV 34–5).[43]

Three comments can be made on this right away. First, Schlick's slogan is ambiguous. Does understanding a proposition's meaning consist in grasping some technique for ascertaining whether it is true, or in knowing what observations *would* confirm it? Schlick himself oscillates between these, but the favoured view was to construe 'the method of verification' as referring to the observations which would verify a proposition. Analysis of propositions is then justified as elucidating their meaning in terms of statements which describe how they are confirmed: no mention of a world of atomic facts is required. Second, a large exception to the slogan and the principle was made for mathematical and other 'analytic' statements. These do not *need* verifying, since the validity of any such statement – '2 + 2 = 4', 'Vixens are female foxes', or whatever – depends, as Ayer put it, 'solely on the definitions of the symbols it contains' (78).[44] Third, it is possible to accept the principle of verifiability but hold back from the verificationist theory of meaning: to accept, that is, that no statement is meaningful which is unverifiable, but to doubt that understanding its meaning just *is* to grasp how it is verified. Some Positivists, certainly, baulked at such implausible implications as that the meaning of a statement about the past must be spelled out in terms of present and future observations (of old bones or historical documents, say). The principle by itself, after all, seemed enough to perform the main task, the elimination of metaphysics.

How, quite, *did* it perform that task? Carnap defines as 'metaphysical' those propositions which purport to be about 'something . . . over or beyond all experience', citing claims like 'Everything is material' and 'Everything is a shadow of eternal ideas' (PL 15–16). *Ex hypothesi*, these claims are compatible with all our experiences, and no observations we make could serve to support them. They are 'pseudo-theses', therefore, 'disguised nonsense'. 'Nonsense', here, is nothing as complimentary as 'rubbish' or 'codswallop' but, quite literally, 'lack of meaning'. Thus Schlick says to the metaphysician, *not* ' "Your words assert something false", but "Your words assert nothing at all!" . . . "I do not understand you" ' (PR 110). Quite a thing is made of even-handedness towards rival metaphysical claims. Materialism is not defended against idealism, nor pluralism against monism. In all such debates, there is a plague on both houses. But one wonders, for example, whether the philosopher who holds that there are immortal souls doesn't suffer more than his rival from the news that both their positions are senseless. The rival, after all, might welcome the switch from denying immortality to regarding the notion as meaningless.

A major problem was to formulate the principle of verifiability in a way that would not cast some respectable statements of natural science into the same pit as metaphysics. Consider an open generalization, like 'All ravens are black'. This cannot be conclusively verified by observation, since maybe in the infinite future there will be a green raven. Another Austrian, Karl Popper (1902–94), suggested that its scientific credentials resided in its being conclusively *falsifiable* by observation of a non-black raven.[45] But then the problem shifts to the status of a statement like 'There exists a green raven', which cannot be falsified by a finite number of observations. One rather desperate suggestion, Schlick's, was that since 'All ravens are black' is meaningful, yet unverifiable, it cannot be a statement or proposition, but a rule or piece of advice: 'When you come across a raven, expect it to be black!' Those who found this strategy implausible preferred to weaken the requirement that verification must be conclusive. Thus, Ayer suggested that a proposition is meaningful provided that some 'observations [are] relevant to the determination of its truth or falsehood?' (38). The trouble with this is that metaphysicians worth their salt would surely argue that *some* observations are at least *relevant* to their claims. (Hegel, after all, cites almost the whole of history in support of his.) Ayer and others tried hard to tighten up this notion of 'weak' verifiability, but not to anyone's final satisfaction.[46]

Discussions of the above problem took for granted the existence of basic, directly and conclusively verifiable statements in terms of which, ultimately, all other meaningful statements could be understood. What were these, and how were *they* verified? The popular answer was that they refer to the 'given', to 'the content of a single experience, and what . . . verif[ies] them conclusively is the occurrence of the experience' (Ayer 10). So we find Schlick, for example, claiming that statements about bodies can be 'transformed into propositions . . . about the regularity of occurrence of sensations', descriptions of which are directly verified by these sensations (PR 109).

Some Positivists, notably Carnap, rejected this answer. For one thing, if basic or 'protocol' statements referred to sensations, their meanings would be 'private' to the person having the sensations. Then 'there would be no intersubjective protocol language' (PF 158) of the kind surely required for the very public discourse of science. Worse still, talk of correspondence between basic statements and sensations violated Wittgenstein's strictures against speaking of the relation between language and reality. What would be the status of such talk, which doesn't sound either tautologous or empirical – the only meaningful kinds allowed by Positivist lights? For Carnap, talk of protocol statements referring to 'directly given experience' is not exactly *wrong*, but it needs translating into a different, 'formal' idiom which avoids any appearance of making claims about language's relation to reality. Instead of speaking of statements referring to the given, we should speak, simply, of statements which 'need . . . no justification and serv[e] as a foundation for all the remaining statements of science' (PF 153). Asked *why* certain statements need no justification – and Carnap's preference is for ones couched in the vocabulary of physical objects, not of sensations – his reply is the 'conventionalist' one that these are the statements which the scientific community has opted to treat as basic and unproblematical. Few other Logical Positivists were willing to follow Carnap here in what was, after all, an anticipation of the 'postmodernist' refusal to allow that there is anything 'outside of the text'. Nor, unfortunately, did they adequately answer his charge that their position violated their own strictures on meaningfulness.

Philosophy, Ethics and Religion

A striking feature of twentieth-century philosophy has been a concern with its own status. This owes less to an onanistic fetish than to the perception that this status is problematic. The effect of the philosophies just discussed was, after all, to call into question their own possibility. The author of the *Tractatus* was forced to denounce the book's own propositions as nonsense, while the Logical Positivists were soon to realize that their lynch-pin threatened to self-destruct. The principle of verifiability insists that a proposition must be either verifiable or tautologous. Yet the principle itself seems to be neither of these and so entails its own meaninglessness.

The above concern was accompanied by attempts to construe the activities of other, earlier philosophers. These were divided into two groups. Wearing the white hats were those, primarily the British empiricists, who could be seen as precursors of logical analysis, writing in a different and misleading idiom. Take Hume's famous command to 'commit to the flames' works that indulge in anything but mathematical or experimental reasoning. What is this, asks Ayer, but a 'rhetorical version of our own thesis' that only analytic and empirical statements have 'literal significance' (54)? Similarly, Hume's claim that 'ideas' must come from 'impressions' was read as a crude expression of the truth that meaningful statements must be reducible to ones describing sense-data. Wearing the black hats were the metaphysicians, whose claims could not be thus rechauffé. It was insufficient, however, to brand these as nonsense: they are not nonsense in the manner of Edward Lear's verses, and those who make them were not just exercising their voices or pens to no purpose whatever. For Carnap, metaphysics is indeed akin to poetry but, for that reason, it is, like 'laughing, lyrics and music, *expressive*' (PL 29). Metaphysical systems express different 'emotions' towards the world. His suggestion that realism and idealism reflect, in turn, an 'extrovert' and 'introvert' personality may raise a smile. But the thought that idealism marks a 'tendency to withdraw from the unfriendly world' is not absurd if taken to mean that it is a way of solving the problem of alienation by, so to speak, 'humanizing' the world which seems to stand over against human beings.

Attention focused, however, on the status of the Positivists' own work. This was to be seen, not as a body of 'doctrine', but as an 'activity' of analysis and elucidation of language. As to the exact character of the activity, there was less agreement. To regard it, with Wittgenstein, as elucidatory nonsense was too paradoxical, and attempts were made to show that the analysts' claims were, despite appearances, either empirical or tautologous, and hence respectable. Schlick, for example, said that 'we have done nothing but formulate the rules which everybody always follows' when explaining the meanings of their words (MV 34). But it is hard to believe that 'everybody' explains the meaning of, say, statements about the past in terms of current sensations: and even if they do, the question arises as to the status of *their* explanations. Carnap, who wanted philosophy to be the study of 'logical syntax', held that analysis merely makes explicit the 'formation' and 'transformation' rules implicit in scientific language. But it is implausible, surely, to suppose that the 'transformation' of statements about electricity into ones about pointers and copper wires is a linguistic 'rule' followed by scientists. Conceding this, Carnap later veers towards the view that analysis and the principle of verifiability itself are 'recommending' to scientists that they adopt certain rules and avoid utterances not reducible, by those rules, to basic, empirical statements. As recommendations, the philosopher's words sidestep the charge that they are meaningless statements, because neither verifiable nor tautologous: they are not *statements* at all.

Carnap was here taking a leaf from his and other Positivists' accounts of ethical language. I called the verificationist theory of meaning 'notorious', and it was its damning implications for moral and religious belief, rather than for abstract metaphysics, which outraged the wider public. A sentence like 'Pleasure is a good thing' creates no problem if taken as an empirical report of what people in unpuritanical societies admire or desire. But as G. E. Moore had allegedly shown, no normative moral judgement can be equivalent to an empirical statement of this sort. If 'Pleasure is good' always meant 'Pleasure is generally desired', it would be impossible significantly to raise the question 'Is what people generally desire good?' – which clearly it is not. Moore's diagnosis, seconded for a time by Russell, of the mistake involved in treating the two sentences as equivalent was that a 'naturalistic fallacy' is thereby committed. This is the fallacy of equating a simple, 'non-natural' quality, *good*, known by moral intuition, with a 'natural' property, *being generally desired*, discoverable only empirically.[47]

The Logical Positivists, predictably, gave a different diagnosis of the mistake, for Moore's 'non-natural' moral properties were clearly anathema, being unavailable to observation by the senses. The real mistake, of which Moore himself was also guilty, is to treat moral judgements as *any* kind of statement of fact. If 'Killing is evil' were such a statement, we could deduce from it further statements about future sense-experience: but we cannot. Since it is not, either, a trivial tautology, not something true by definition, the guillotine must fall: 'Killing is evil' fails to state anything at all. It is without 'factual', 'cognitive' or 'literal' meaning. These qualifiers were needed, since one could hardly dismiss all moral judgements as nonsense *tout court*. Clearly they have some role, though not that of telling how things are. But what role? Carnap says of 'Killing is evil' that it is 'merely an expression of a certain wish', with only 'the grammatical form' of a statement (PL 24). According to Ayer, the function of an 'ethical word' in a moral judgement is 'purely "emotive". It is used to express feeling about certain objects' (108).

This 'emotivist', or 'hurrah/boo', account of moral judgements was subjected to various refinements. Some writers, noting the 'dynamic' role played by these judgements, emphasized their role in affecting other people's emotions, as distinct from expressing the speaker's own. Others, picking up on Carnap's description of a moral judgement as 'nothing else than a command', would downplay the importance of emotion, concentrating instead on the behavioural and interpersonal roles of moral language.[48] None of these refinements, of course, could mollify those for whom moral judgements state truths which, through reason or intuition, human beings are capable of ascertaining. For them, the 'disenchanted world' appears naked in the writings of the new positivists: a world containing nothing of value or meaning, a world bereft of anything that the natural scientist cannot find there.

For, of course, religion fell under the same verificationist guillotine as ethics. The religious believer is not even credited with making an honest mistake: rather, his statements are senseless, since his God is nothing whose existence could make any observational difference. Even 'agnosticism is ruled out', says Ayer: the agnostic hovers between 'God exists' and 'God does not exist', unsure which sentence is true. But, of course, neither is: neither expresses a proposition at all (116). This makes it sound as if atheism is as disreputable as theism: but as Ayer's readiness to describe himself as an atheist before a wider, less subtle audience suggests, it is surely the believer, not his opponent, who loses most from the news that God is neither alive nor dead, but a senseless notion. As with moral and metaphysical judgements, the Vienna Circle allowed religious utterances, by way of consolation, to possess 'emotive' meaning. 'God exists' expresses a sense of awe before the universe, or supreme admiration for the life of Christ, or whatever. It is one of the twentieth century's ironies, surely, that this treatment of religious language, at first the hallmark of positivist atheism, is now almost *de rigueur* among the professedly Christian 'new' theologians of the 'Honest to God' school.

Wittgenstein wrote of the ethical and the mystical that 'what we cannot speak about we must pass over in silence' (T 74). Certainly the Vienna Circle passed over his own remarks on these matters. That ethics and the mystical 'cannot be put into words' indeed implies that moral and religious utterances are not statements of fact and so are 'non-sense'. But in Wittgenstein's case, this is not a prelude to treating them as outbursts of emotion or devices for affecting the feelings of other people. What he intends – what is *shown* by our inability to speak of morality and religion – is famously hard to discern, but here is an attempt to do so, based mainly on the *Notebooks* (pp. 73–87).

Kant was right to see that ethical value must belong unconditionally, 'non-accidentally', and this has two implications. First value 'cannot lie *within* the world', for everything within it is accidental, contingent (T 6.41). Second, only 'the willing subject' can be good or evil, since it is the will alone which is immune from accident, unlike the success or failure of the actions willed. It is quite wrong to think of the will as operating within the world. My desires are, of course, sometimes satisfied, but this is due solely to the 'grace of fate', not to a connection between will and worldly events, which are entirely independent of will. Willing affects the 'boundaries of the world', not what happens in it: and it does so through being 'an attitude of the subject to the world', for with the adoption of an attitude, the world 'becomes an altogether different world' (T 6.43). The good will is the happy one, whose world waxes rather than wanes, which 'renounc[es] any influence on happenings', and which resolves to be in harmony or 'agreement with the world'.

There is an Eastern flavour to this idea of the good will happily acquiescing in the world, abstaining from fruitless attempts to change its course and from 'the amenities of life'. This is no accident, since Wittgenstein's inspiration here was Schopenhauer who derived *his* inspiration from the *Upaniṣads* and Buddhism. This Eastern flavour grows stronger with Wittgenstein's remarks on God and the mystical. To take an attitude towards the world, I must be able to *view* or *feel* it as a whole, not as a mere collection of atomic facts. It is this 'feeling the world as a limited whole . . . that is mystical' (T 6.45), for no amount of empirical observation can reveal it to me in that light. Since I can only talk about particular facts, I must be silent – well, almost – about this world-as-a-whole. The world so viewed may also be called 'God'. For, first, when we view it thus, we 'see that the facts of the world are not the end of the matter', but have meaning as ingredients in a whole: and to believe in God is to attribute meaning to life. Second, in the quiescent vision of the world-as-a-whole, we recognize our utter dependence upon it, as if upon an 'alien will': and 'what we are dependent on we can call God'.

My dependence on the world is a double one. As an empirical ego – an embodied person – I am an ingredient in the world as a whole, and no sense can be made of me except as enmeshed with it. As a metaphysical subject – a will that takes up a stance towards the world – I am, so to speak, a nothing, a 'point without extension', whose whole being consists in an attitude which, in the absence of the world, would have no object. Coherent or not, beyond the bounds of sense or not, we have here a position at the opposite pole from the 'disenchanted' perspective of the Logical Positivists, an attempt in a long tradition to integrate the self with a meaningful world which is, after all, '*my* world'.

• 4 Naturalisms •

Few of the Vienna Circle who emigrated to Britain and the United States were to adhere, on this new soil, to the strict tenets of Logical Positivism. By the 1950s, a writer could fear, only half in jest, that calling his position by that name would bring it into 'unjustifiable disrepute'.[49] What, then, has been happening on this soil from, say, 1945 to the present? What philosophies, if any, have dominated? This question is hard to answer. For one thing, there is the sheer scale of philosophical activity. My 1993 *Directory of American Philosophers* lists some 11,000 teachers, 150 societies and 140 journals with, in each case, interests ranging from Augustine to animal rights, set theory to sex. Second, there has been, in some circles, hostility towards the idea of *a* philosophy. Philosophy, one is told, is an 'activity', and it is common to classify movements in Anglo-American philosophy in terms not of doctrinal '-isms', but of methods or objectives. Philosophy, according to taste, has been 'the analysis of ordinary language' or 'formal semantics'. Its aim was to 'dissolve' problems caused by misunderstanding of language, or to make explicit the '*conceptual structure* of which our daily practice shows us to have a tacit . . . mastery'.[50]

Such classifications capture divisions found in recent philosophy, but are not ideal in a book whose focus *is* upon doctrines and '-isms'. I want to suggest that, despite the motley, there has been a dominant *urge*, at least, in favour of doctrines within a circumscribed range. To be sure, positions outside that range have been much discussed, but then that is *because* they buck the trend. It was news when one philosopher insisted that bats have an 'inner' life, that there is something it is *like* to be a bat;[51] but only because the prevailing fashion had been to define intelligence in terms of overt behaviour or functional states of an organism. The 'dominant urge' is not one which recent philosophers all obey: but it sets the context in which they are at work.

Two Kinds of Naturalism

The most influential postwar American thinker, the Harvard philosopher W. V. Quine (b. 1908), writes that 'knowledge, meaning and mind are part of the same world they have to do with, and . . . are to be studied in the same empirical spirit that animates natural science. There is no place for prior philosophy' (OR 26).[52] This expresses the 'naturalism' which has been the 'dominant urge' referred to above. Naturalisms of various sorts – from the Pre-Socratics to Hume – have been encountered earlier. What I now have in mind might crudely be characterized as the view that 'nature is all there is [and] the natural man is the whole man'.[53] The naturalistic urge is at any rate the *endeavour* to understand everything essential about human life, for all the changes wrought through 'culture', on the basis of its development as part of the natural order, the only one we can have any reason to suppose there is.

Naturalism takes shape by way of contrast with what it excludes. The *super*natural, of course, is excluded, and we find precious few English-language philosophers of recent note with an 'orthodox' conception of a transcendent God. The transcendent more generally is in disrepute. That we can occupy, as Plato and Kant imagined, a standpoint outside nature, or be equipped with 'intuitions' of an order which is neither constructed by human activity nor amenable to empirical investigation, is increasingly found incredible. Cartesianism in almost all its aspects is also excluded: we are not souls that happen to be connected to bodies, nor can we identify genuine *knowledge* by 'internal' tests like the 'clarity and distinctness' of ideas. Embodiment is essential to any understanding of mind, and criteria of knowledge must invoke our 'external' interaction with the world about us.

A more precise characterization of naturalism is impeded by the fact that two kinds have flourished during our period. Both fit the broad rubric and share the enemies just mentioned, but it is also the tensions between them which have given much of its life to recent philosophy. First, there is 'scientific naturalism', according to which the natural sciences promise to provide a complete account of the world and ourselves, so that a philosophical view which contradicts scientific wisdom must for that reason be rejected. This entails that our understanding of, *inter alia*, meaning, mind and value must be compatible, and preferably consonant, with the scientific world-view. For example, belief in free will, to survive at all, must at least square with an explanation of behaviour in purely physical terms, and ideally be seen to require it.

Second, we have 'anthropological naturalism'. This holds no particular brief for natural science, and registers no urge to ensure that our understanding dovetails with physics. What it emphasizes is that human beings are embodied practitioners within the world, and that no understanding of them is possible without that emphasis. This barely distinguishes the approach from that of existential phenomenology (see pp. 424ff.), and indeed it would be quite wrong, on the assumption of some schism between 'continental' and 'analytical' philosophy, to deny the similarities. But what we do find in anthropological naturalism is a focus, less on culturally variable practices, than on their natural bases. It is not that the practices could not vary, but they are typically grounded in a shared 'form of life' – the tendency to count in certain ways, for example, or to respond sympathetically to the suffering of others.

Those examples, and the phrase 'form of life', are Wittgenstein's, during his later period from around 1930. He will serve as our leading anthropological naturalist, constantly rooting our psychological concepts, say, in physical practices, and these in a shared 'form of life'. Commanding, questioning and the like are 'as much part of our natural history as walking [and] eating', so that analyses of these and other intelligent practices are 'really remarks on the natural history of human beings' (PI §25, §415).[54] These remarks, though, make 'observations which no one has doubted', but which get overlooked because they are 'always before our eyes'. The sophisticated observations of science, by contrast, have little or nothing to offer by way of elucidating our familiar concepts, and the philosopher has no obligation to tailor his analyses to them. This contrasts with the attitude of Quine, for whom 'philosophy . . . is continuous with science' – fortunately in his view, since 'whatever can be known can be known by means of science' alone (PP 1). We should, for example, be willing to stop referring to beliefs if these play no explanatory role within a science of mind.

Wittgenstein and Quine, then, are respective champions of the two naturalisms. But the labels are mine, and many writers could be neatly fitted under neither, perhaps because they adopt different approaches to different issues. The two naturalisms are tendencies which coalesce in their hostility towards Cartesianism, Platonism and other brands of anti-naturalism. In what follows, it will sometimes be the alliance, sometimes the conflict, between them which is the more apparent. It is worth noting that my distinction cuts across an important one, between 'realism' and 'anti-realism', which some commentators see as central in recent philosophy.[55] One might expect scientific naturalists to take a 'realist' view of scientific theory as something validated by correspondence with objective reality. Conversely, one might expect their rivals, with their stress on human activity, to think of science in an 'anti-realist' way, as just one more practice whose claims are 'validated' by criteria, internal to the practice, which the practitioners happen to have agreed upon. Their sympathies, perhaps, would be with Thomas Kuhn's view of 'competing paradigms' in science, whose emergence and demise can owe more to fashion than to firm evidence. Indeed, these paradigms so shape scientists' outlooks that they do not see the same evidence: they are 'practicing in different worlds', and no data can neutrally decide between competing paradigms.[56]

Matters are not so simple, however. Quine berates Kuhn for 'belittl[ing] the role of evidence and accentuat[ing] cultural relativism' (OR 87), yet his own case for science's privileged status is not one of correspondence with objective reality. It is the explanatory richness and pragmatic success of science that set it above religion or magic, and oblige us to tailor the rest of our understanding to its findings. Indeed, so-called 'metaphysical realism' – the idea of *the* world to which *any* correct theory must correspond[57] – is the exception rather than the rule among scientific naturalists. The grounds on which they accord science an elevated status vary – correspondence with reality, explanatory sweep, pragmatic success: *that* they do so is what ties them together.

Let me now turn to the problems which have exercised naturalists in the areas of language, knowledge, mind and value: areas occupied by that creature who has proved so resistant to naturalistic treatment, man.

'Scientific Semantics'

Philosophers this century have liked to recast questions about beliefs and ideas into ones about linguistic notions, such as propositions and meanings. This has been credited to Frege's appreciation that the 'only proper method for analysing thought consists in the analysis of *language*'.[58] Language is the more concrete, tractable target of analysis, *via* which one then proceeds to the more shadowy realm of the mind. Some go further: no sense, even, can be made of a notion like belief except in terms of the use of language. Donald Davidson (b. 1917) – second only to his teacher, Quine, in influence on the American scene – argues that no creature can have beliefs unless it has the concept of belief. This it can only have if it understands the possibility of being mistaken and hence the contrast between truth and error. And this contrast can be grasped only through participation in a shared language.[59] A thinking creature like man is therefore essentially linguistic.

Little is gained, however, from the naturalist point of view, by the switch from a psychological to a linguistic idiom, if language itself proves resistant to naturalistic explanation. To judge from the theories of meaning on offer early in the century, the omens were not good. Some theories, in the tradition of Locke, treated meanings as mental items – ideas or images – associated with words whose job it is to transmit these items from one head to another. This approach was rejected by Frege, but he left the notion of a meaning or sense (*Sinn*) obscure. The sense of a name cannot be the object in the world it refers to since two names (such as 'the Morning Star' and 'the Evening Star') may have the same reference, but clearly differ in sense. Nor can it be a private 'inner picture', since it is in a 'common store': different speakers can share or apprehend one and the same sense. The meaning of the name must be an abstract entity, neither in the head nor in the world.[60]

For the naturalist, there is little to choose between Locke and Frege. Both treat meanings as entities nowhere to be found in the publicly observable world, and describe the relation of words to their meanings and to the world in terms that would hardly figure in a scientifically respectable account of language. For example, words are said to 'express' their senses, which in turn 'correspond' to objects. Both, finally, permit the Cartesian possibility of a person understanding a language in total isolation from other people and the rest of the world. Provided a person associates words with the appropriate ideas or senses, they understand them, even if there is *no* world beyond the veil of these meanings.

Approaches like these prompted a Polish logician and émigré to the USA, Alfred Tarski (1902–83), to complain of the failure to bring semantics into 'harmony with the postulates of the unity of science and of physicalism'.[61] It was his work on the notion of truth, in fact, which provided the clue to a new approach. Unhappy with the usual notion of truth as 'correspondence with the facts', he showed how such troublesome notions can be defined in a vocabulary to which no physicalist could take exception. (Actually, he thought this could only be done for certain formal languages: 'true' as applied to sentences of a natural language is an incoherent term.) The procedure is, first, to reduce the notion of truth to that of 'satisfaction'. Bonzo is said to 'satisfy' the description 'is a dog' just in case he is a dog. Talk of 'satisfaction' can in turn be eliminated, as in this example, through replacing a statement about an expression's being satisfied by an equivalent one about the conditions under which it is satisfied. If this procedure works, we need not, in principle, employ troublesome semantic terms like 'true', 'correspond', 'refer' and so on.

How does this help with the notion of meaning? Well, suppose we extend Tarski's eliminative account of truth to natural languages, and then link this with the familiar idea (see p. 441) that to know a language is basically a matter of grasping the conditions under which its sentences would be true. The result will be a view of linguistic understanding as, essentially, the capacity to pair sentences of one's language with the conditions of their truth: to pair, say, 'Snow is white' or '*Schnee ist weiss*' with snow's being white. Although we at first learn to pair whole sentences with conditions in the world, the ability we soon display to understand new sentences on the basis of their parts shows that crucial in knowledge of a language is the pairing of words and other sub-sentential expressions with what 'satisfy' them: 'is white', say, with snowflakes and bridal gowns. Just such an approach has been championed by Davidson. 'To know what it is for a sentence – any sentence – to be true . . . amounts . . . to understanding the language.' No appeal need be made to ideas or Fregean senses which intervene between words and the world. The link-up is direct, and these ideas or senses simply have 'no demonstrated use' in explaining our understanding of a language.[62] Sentences, to be sure, have meanings in the sense that they are used to utter truths or falsehoods: but that just shows that talk of meaning can be reduced to talk of truth, which, in turn, can be eliminated *à la* Tarski. The result is not a physicalist theory of meaning: but since the account uses no terms – 'sense', 'express', and so on – offensive to physicalist ears, it is at least compatible with such a theory. Some writers have tried to provide a physicalist theory, arguing that Tarski's definition of 'true' is unacceptably silent on the physical, causal connections between words and the objects which 'satisfy' them.[63] The jury, among scientific naturalists, is still out on this point. For some, it is enough that those notions can be rendered innocuous. We needn't, in addition, bring physical connections into their very analysis.

Among the attempts to tear away the veil of meanings is the account of 'natural kind' terms (like 'water' and 'aluminium') urged by the American philosophers Saul Kripke (b. 1940) and Hilary Putnam (b. 1926). The traditional view was that these terms must express ideas or senses, their meanings, in order to refer to anything. This, it is held, must be wrong. If the reference of 'water' were dictated by an idea we have of the stuff, such as 'clear, potable liquid', we should have to regard as water any stuff on another planet which fits this idea. But this we would not do if the stuff were other than H_2O. If the term has *a* meaning at all, it is this very stuff, water or H_2O, not some idea or sense expressed by it. 'Cut the pie any way you like,' says Putnam in vernacular mood, ' "meanings" just ain't in the *head*.'[64] If they were, two speakers, one on earth, the second on this other planet, who associated the same idea with 'water', would mean the same by it, despite talking about totally different stuffs. That result, holds Putnam, is surely counter-intuitive.

It is worth noting that this account challenges the traditional link between the *necessary* and the *a priori*: the assumption – from Leibniz to Ayer – that experience cannot reveal necessities in the world. For Kripke and Putnam, 'Water is H_2O' is necessary, true in all possible worlds, since nothing could be water except H_2O: still, *that* water is H_2O was an empirical discovery, not something worked out *a priori*. The most important feature of the account, however, in the present context, is the bringing of the world into our understanding of words. Putnam accuses Locke, Frege and others of a 'solipsistic' view of understanding, as something available to a speaker independent of contact with actual objects. They have thereby left out 'the contribution of the real world' to our grasp of words.[65] That the real world *must* make a decisive contribution is clear from how natural kind terms are given their use, for this involves something like ostension, pointing to what the words refer to. 'Water', say, is defined as the term for *this* stuff, which I am pouring into my whiskey, and for any stuff which is relevantly the same (H_2O, as it has turned out).

Other naturalists reject ideas and meanings as insufficiently disciplined by behavioural criteria, the only ones with which scientific methodology should have truck. 'I ask no more,' pleads Quine, 'than for a rough characterization [of these notions] in terms of dispositions to verbal behaviour' (WO 207). Since, in his view, that plea has remained unanswered by those who employ such notions, we should be rid of the 'myth of a museum' ('the mind') in which ideas and meanings are stored. Consider the 'propositions' said to be expressed by sentences. There must, people have argued, be such entities for translation to occur: for what is a correct translation but a sentence which expresses the same proposition as the foreign one? But the idea of a 'uniquely correct translation' is a 'pernicious illusion', both fostering and fostered by the myth of propositions (WO 208). The fact is that any number of translations of a sentence, all compatible with any possible behavioural evidence, are feasible. True, we prefer some to others, but on aesthetic grounds and ones of convenience. There is no sense to the idea that just one of them is correct, and hence we should reject any theory, like that of propositions, which pretends that there is. Such theories have no place in a 'scientific semantics'.

'Language-games'

Writers towards the anthropological end of the naturalist spectrum have criticized views of the kind so far sketched for paying inadequate attention to the social practices with which language is entwined.[66] As with other naturalists, the later Wittgenstein's target is any 'veil of meanings' doctrine. The main culprit is the Lockean view of meanings as images or other mental items, but Wittgenstein's attack would also strike more recondite candidates, such as Frege's senses. Whereas for Quine, meanings turn out to be empirically ungrounded entities, for Wittgenstein, any tendency to think of them as entities in the first place is confused. Acquaintance with an image or a sense cannot, to begin with, be *required* for understanding a word. 'The same thing can come before our minds' when we hear a word on two occasions, yet our applications of it be entirely different. 'Has it the *same* meaning both times? I think we shall say not' (PI §140). More crucially, such an acquaintance cannot be *sufficient* for understanding. Consider a mental image. This cannot confer understanding of the word, the ability to apply it, since it is 'just another sign' whose application to anything would in turn need to be explained. 'The interpolation of a shadow between [a] sentence and reality loses all point' (BB 37) once we see that the shadow needs interpreting as much as the sentence. If we could explain how it is applied, we could then by-pass it and offer a like explanation of the sentence itself.

For 'a *large* class of cases', at least, we can say that 'the meaning of a word is its use in the language' (PI §43). The negative point, here, is that understanding is not a matter of acquaintance with some entity, nor of being in some cognitive state. The positive one is that understanding is a matter of 'know-how', the 'master[y] of a technique', akin to a craftsman's understanding of his tools. That analogy can be extended, for words, like tools, only have a use and meaning within shared practices. To change the analogy, words are moves within games – 'language-games' – whose rules give them their point. It is in this idea that understanding words is a practical capacity to 'obey rules' that both the anthropology and the naturalism in Wittgenstein's account emerge.

'"Obeying a rule" is a practice . . . Hence it is not possible to obey a rule "privately": otherwise thinking one was obeying a rule would be the same thing as obeying it' (PI §202). To 'obey the rules' of games, including 'language-games', is to participate in 'customs' and 'traditions' alongside other people. No account, therefore, can be given of linguistic understanding which ignores shared human practices.[67] Talk of 'rules', however, might encourage the view that understanding is simply a matter of grasping *conventions*, and that would be to overlook the massive contribution of 'natural life'. Generally, 'when I obey a rule, I do not choose. I obey the rule *blindly*', since 'I have been trained to react to this sign in a particular way' (PI §219, §198). If this makes me seem like a trained dog raising its paw, the answer is that using words *is* much more like this than often imagined. In particular, it is not, typically, either required or possible to give reasons – including appeal to some convention – which justify applying a word in this, rather than that, way. Justifications must run out at some point, one at which we can only say 'I have reached bedrock, and my spade is turned . . . "This is simply what I do"' (PI §217). That they run out, however, is no impediment to shared language, for there is, fortunately, 'agreement in . . . form of life' (PI §241). We just do find it natural to 'go on' in certain ways having been 'trained' to 'react' on various occasions. If we did not, no amount of training – nor of rules and conventions – would avail to ensure that we will continue to understand one another. (The importance of this for issues of knowledge and rationality will emerge later.)

For Wittgenstein, then, we are bound to the natural world through language: not because our words must be directly paired with objects and states of affairs, but because obeying the same rules as our fellows is ultimately rooted in the natural dispositions we all share.

Knowledge

We again find alliance and conflict between the two naturalisms over the age-old questions about knowledge – the analytic question of what is meant by 'knowledge', and the sceptic's question whether our claims to knowledge are ever justified: alliance against the traditional answers, and conflict over their replacements. The old answers are rejected for ignoring the role of nature, but the new ones differ over this role. A striking feature of traditional analyses of knowledge is that the world plays no part in them, beyond the obvious one of having to match our beliefs in order for them to be true and hence count as knowledge. When Descartes and Spinoza are asked what distinguishes a mere true belief, a lucky guess perhaps, from an item of genuine knowledge, their answer appeals to 'internal' marks of the latter, its 'clarity and distinctness'. Later writers focused on the justifications we can offer for our beliefs: we only *know* that cats don't grow on trees if, say, we can produce good evidence that they don't. There is no more mention, here, than in Descartes, of any *interaction* between ourselves and cats which would make our belief a case of knowledge. But this, according to several recent writers, is just what is needed, here picking up on the not-so-recent remarks of that prodigy of a logician, Frank Ramsey (1903–30). 'A belief was knowledge', he wrote, 'if it was (i) true, (ii) certain), (iii) obtained by a reliable process'. That process can only be a 'causal process connecting what happens' with my knowledge of it.[68]

Without this connection, there is no way, it is argued, to explain how there can be justified true belief that nevertheless falls short of knowledge – as when I truly believe that it is 3.00 p.m. on looking at my normally reliable clock which, however, has stopped 24 hours earlier.[69] Here, clearly, I don't know that it is 3.00 p.m., and the suggested reason is that there isn't the appropriate causal connection between me, my clock and the time of day. The crude, general idea, then, is that I only know that p if my belief is suitably caused by p's being the case. This idea would be appealing to the scientific naturalist quite apart from offering a solution to problems like the clock one. For the only notion it invokes to convert true belief into knowledge is the eminently naturalistic one of causality.

This 'causal theory of knowledge' is not intended to show that we *do* know anything. Indeed, it offers a hostage to fortune, for the sceptic will quickly ask 'Why assume that our beliefs ever are in suitable causal relations with the world?' To that question, however, some naturalists offer a partial answer by invoking Darwin. 'Creatures inveterately wrong in their [beliefs] have a pathetic but praiseworthy tendency to die before reproducing their kind' (OR 126), writes Quine. That we humans have not died out suggests that the bulk of our beliefs about the world must be correct, and correct because of biological mechanisms which allow the world itself to shape the beliefs we have about it. Without those mechanisms, creatures would be unable to satisfy their desires, including those at work in reproducing their kind. For to satisfy desires, creatures must be able correctly to represent the conditions which would satisfy them. As successful creatures, then, ones pretty good at getting what they want, humans must have been favoured by natural selection to arrive at their beliefs because those beliefs are true. None of this will persuade the diehard sceptic, who will challenge the credentials of the theory of evolution. But then it is characteristic of scientific naturalism not to indulge in 'prior philosophy' – in this instance, an attempted knockdown of scepticism – but to regard 'all scientific findings' as 'welcome for use in philosophy as elsewhere' (OR 127). There can be no objection to thus using Darwin's findings, and their implications for how our beliefs come about, in support of the assumption that many of these beliefs constitute knowledge.

Wittgenstein – our champion of anthropological naturalism – has no more sympathy for this analysis and vindication of knowledge than for traditional ones. When we reflect on the 'normal' use of 'I know', the things philosophers have said about knowledge turn out to be mistaken or too sweeping. It is only in context, as 'a move in one of our language-games' (OC §622), that 'I know' makes sense. Unless a special context is specified, 'I know you', said to a friend during a walk, is unintelligible. Often, though not always, 'I know' announces that I have 'proper grounds' for making a statement whose certainty has been called into question (OC §18). Because its use is so dependent on context, it is wrong, for a start, to think of it as describing a mental state, such as the self-luminous one with which Descartes identified knowledge. It is wrong, too, to look for a general test for converting true belief into knowledge. This is as true of the 'causal' criterion discussed above as of any other. Sometimes we check that a person's belief was appropriately caused before crediting him with knowledge: sometimes not. It depends on the rules of the language-game in which 'know' is being used.

Wittgenstein's main target, however, is the assumption, common to sceptics and their orthodox critics alike, that it is sensible to ask for justification of our basic beliefs. They thereby 'fail to realize the groundlessness of our believing' (OC §166). Remarks like that, or 'I cannot say that I have good grounds for the opinion that cats do not grow on trees or that I had a father and a mother' (OC §282), might give the impression that Wittgenstein himself is a sceptic: one reinforced by his denial that, special context apart, we can speak of *knowing* that cats don't grow on trees, and the like. But that impression is wrong. Such beliefs are 'groundless' only because any ground we produce could be no surer than the beliefs themselves are. And if they are not knowledge, this is not because they are something less – mere conjectures, say – but, as it were, something more. We can speak of knowing something only where doubts would at least be in order: which they are not in the case of beliefs like 'Cats don't grow on trees.' Such beliefs 'stand fast' for us, and form the 'substratum' of all our 'enquiring and asserting' (OC §162). If *they* could be doubted, *everything* could: but 'a doubt that doubted everything would not be doubt' (OC §329). Questions would have no point if every possible resolution of them is excluded from the start.

Wittgenstein does not discuss the Darwinian attempt to justify our beliefs sketched earlier, but for him this would be as superfluous as any other. His own account of our 'substratum' beliefs, however, is itself naturalistic. It is not a matter of convention that they 'stand fast': where there is 'human agreement' is not over decisions as to what is true, but in forms of life. It is these which have 'to be accepted' and are 'the given' (PI §241 and p. 226). Nor, therefore, does it just so happen that we share these beliefs: they belong to an 'inherited background', the product of our 'natural history'. This inheritance, finally, is not one of self-evident intuitions, of 'certain propositions striking us immediately as true': for it is 'not a kind of *seeing* on our part; it is our *acting* which lies at the bottom' of our language-games (OC §204). Our basic beliefs, then, express those shared, natural forms of behaviour without which no other beliefs, no enquiries, and no language would be imaginable.

Mind

We have been cheerfully talking about *beliefs*. But what are these? What, more generally, are 'mental phenomena' and 'the mind'? Nowhere has the naturalistic urge been more rampant during the last 50 years than over these questions – unsurprisingly, since it is traditional theories of the mind, notably Descartes', which have done most to detach human beings from the natural order, cuccooning them inside an immaterial medium. In a 'clear instance of intellectual progress', writes Richard Rorty, there is a 'developing consensus' that Cartesianism is entirely wrong,[70] and that any adequate account of mind must fully acknowledge behavioural criteria for psychological descriptions. Still, within this consensus there are different tendencies. For some writers, Descartes' dualism is, by scientific canons, just a bad theory, and an emphasis on behaviour is required by the principle that to be 'respected scientifically . . . mental ascriptions would have to be pegged to publicly, physically testable verification-conditions'.[71] For others, Cartesianism is *incoherent*, and no *sense* can be made of 'mental ascriptions' except in behavioural terms. This division roughly corresponds to that between scientific and anthropological naturalists. Certainly, writers in the first group show an eagerness missing in the second to calibrate their position with the latest wisdom of cognitive science and neurophysiology.

The story begins in 1949, with Gilbert Ryle's (1900–76) *The Concept of Mind*, a stylish diatribe of 'deliberate abusiveness' against Descartes' 'dogma of the Ghost in the Machine', the immaterial soul or *cogito* 'inside' the body (17).[72] For Ryle, Descartes' error is a whopping 'category-mistake', which treats the mind as something of the same logical type as the body, only made of a different stuff. Rightly seeing that minds cannot be physical mechanisms, Descartes wrongly concluded that they are non-physical ones, 'bits of not-clockwork' rather than of clockwork (21). In reality, once we describe people's dispositions to behaviour, we already describe their minds. A belief, for example, is not an inner state over and above dispositions to act and speak in certain ways. To talk of a person's body *and* mind is like talking of some colleges, administrative offices, laboratories etc. *and* the university, as if the latter were something in addition to the former.

Failure to perceive this results in absurdities. If, for instance, it is held that intelligent behaviour must be the result of an inner and 'prior theoretical operation', we get caught in an infinite regress: for that inner operation, to be intelligent, must then be preceded by another such operation (31). Worse, I could never know that other people acted intelligently, not being privy to their inner operations. Worst of all, I could not even tell if *I* acted intelligently, since to do so I need to be able to 'compar[e] [my] own performances with those of others' (22). This last point is reminiscent of Wittgenstein's famous argument against 'private languages'. Suppose that, as for Descartes, Locke and others, my psychological vocabulary referred to 'immediate private sensations' or 'ideas'. In that case, another person, confined to his or her own sensations or ideas, cannot understand my language (PI §243). But, then, not even *I* could understand it. I would have no criterion of using its words correctly, of applying them consistently from occasion to occasion. Hence 'whatever is going to seem right to me is right. And that only means that here we can't talk about "right"' (PI §258). A meaningful word must be used in accordance with a rule: but there can be no rule without a criterion for whether it is being followed or not. The conclusion in the present context is that 'an "inner process" stands in need of outward criteria' (PI 580), behavioural ones, rooted in 'forms of life' which determine the very sense of terms like 'belief', 'pain' or 'hope'.

Ryle and Wittgenstein are often called 'logical' behaviourists, to distinguish them from the school of behavioural psychology. As Ryle saw it, this school either ignored inner processes as a methodological policy, thereby implicitly conceding their occurrence; or it embraced a crude, mechanistic materialism like Hobbes' (see p. 257), which commits the same 'category-mistake' as Descartes' 'para-mechanical' doctrine. 'Crude' is an apt epithet, certainly, for the views of the pioneer behaviourist, J. B. Watson, who once described thinking as 'subvocal talking', the latter being defined in terms of 'muscular combinations' developed through 'laryngeal movements . . . in overt speech'.[73] Nor did Ryle see much mileage in the thin 'stimulus and response' model of behaviour, barely applicable even to their rats, with which psychological behaviourists usually operated.

Crude though Hobbes' and Watson's versions may have been, it is a materialist view which has held centre-stage since the 1960s. Common to the new materialists, despite their agreement with Ryle's rejection of dualism and his emphasis upon behaviour, is a refusal to accept that there are no inner states or processes. Not only does it offend common sense to deny that pain, say, is such a state, but we typically invoke pains or beliefs to *explain* behaviour, something we could hardly do if they are only dispositions to behave in certain ways. We must by all means do justice to behavioural criteria, but this can be done, as one materialist puts it, by defining a mental state as one 'apt to be the cause of certain effects or . . . to be the effect of certain causes'. We then leave it to empirical investigation to identify the real nature of such states. Nothing as crude as 'muscular combinations' will do; but it would surely be 'quite unpuzzling . . . if mental states should turn out to be physical states of the brain'.[74] Pain, on this view, just *is* a brain-state in the way that water just *is*

H$_2$O. If someone objects that by examining a brain-state one does not experience pain, the reply is that nor, by chemically analysing the glass of Perrier, does one taste it. There is no reason, that is, why 'two' things discovered to be identical through empirical investigation should not be encountered or experienced in totally different ways.

This 'mind–brain identity thesis', however, faces a difficulty which critics were quick to detect. If a certain kind of pain just is a kind of brain-state, then whenever that pain occurs, so must the corresponding brain-state. But maybe Martians experience the pain, yet have wires inside their heads, not brains. As Putnam put it, it is *possible* that 'evolution, all over the universe, might *always* lead to *one and the same* physical "correlate" of pain', but it is 'ambitious' to assume it does.[75] His solution is to understand mental states 'functionally', especially in terms of their bringing about behaviour, but to leave open how these 'functions' are physically 'realized'. Any particular 'token' of pain will be identical with some physical state: but we cannot assume that all 'tokens' of this type of pain correlate with physical states of the same kind.

Neither the 'identity thesis' nor its 'functionalist' successor questions the propriety of our everyday mental vocabulary. Provided that 'belief' refers to well-defined functional states, the term is in order. Other writers are less friendly towards our familiar 'folk psychology'. They make two general points. First, recent neuroscience suggests that there can be no smooth 'match-ups' between beliefs, say, and neural processes. The favoured model for these processes is one of a 'society' of myriad mechanisms occurring, none of which can be neatly correlated with the elements in a belief. The grossness of a belief contrasts, as it were, with the fineness of the neural process. Second, there is 'the widespread explanatory [and] predictive . . . failure of folk psychology'.[76] Centuries of it have not enabled us to explain memory and madness, dreaming and distinguishing faces. The 'soft' conclusion is that, while folk concepts are useful and permissible in their place, they should not be taken too seriously. 'Belief' should not be construed as referring to anything 'real': it is a 'fictional' term, like 'the average man'.[77] This is too pussy-footing a reaction for those, the 'eliminative materialists', who reach the 'hard' conclusion that folk psychology is so 'hopelessly primitive and deeply confused' that it deserves the same fate as other failures, such as alchemy.[78] No one thinks that 'ensouled by Mercury' is 'useful and permissible in [its] place', since the total failure of the conceptual scheme such a notion belongs to means it has no place anywhere. Why should softer treatment be meted out to the concepts of folk psychology?

'The idea that man stands outside the order of nature', wrote Ayer, 'is one that many people find attractive on emotional grounds.'[79] Those at work in San Diego, capital of 'eliminative materialism', and elsewhere over the preceding decades are clearly not among these people. Indeed, they seem to have found the ultimate strategy for ensuring that man does not stand outside the order of nature: that of denying that there is any such creature as ordinarily conceived – a creature of beliefs, emotions, and ideas. Time, I suppose, will tell whether the strategy marks the triumph of naturalism or suffers the fate that, as its creators remind us, befell alchemy and witchcraft.

Moral Naturalism

If human beings have constituted a general obstacle to naturalism, their moral existence has presented a particular one. Where in the world, conceived as a purely natural, causal order, is there room for that freedom of the will which moral judgements on people's actions seems to presuppose? Where, indeed, is there room for the *values* which these judgements assign to actions? One broad approach, traditionally, was to remove the obstacles. Hume, for example, argued that freedom of the will is simply 'liberty of spontaneity', the capacity to act according to one's desires: something, therefore, which is compatible with causal, naturalistic explanations of behaviour. As for value, this belongs to actions according to how they please or offend a natural sentiment like sympathy towards suffering (see p. 277). The alternative broad approach was to treat morality as proof of the limits of naturalism. For Kant, we cannot, as natural creatures, be free: hence we must, in one aspect, be 'pure' selves outside the empirical order. As such selves – moral wills immune to natural desires and obedient to a 'categorical imperative' of reason – we are also the source of moral value (see p. 302).

It is fair to say that in the 'broad, useful' sense of an 'ethical view that stems from the general attitude that man is part of nature', most Anglo-American moral philosophy in the twentieth century has been naturalistic.[80] Thus a head-count would favour the 'compatibilist' view that an action's being freely performed is consistent with its being, at some level, causally explicable. I do not act freely, of course, if I act under compulsion: but, as many writers insist, not all causes should be described as compelling. As for values, there have been few defenders of such views as that right is what God commands; or that 'good' names a 'non-natural' property intuited by a non-empirical 'sense'. Nor has there been much sympathy with Kant's idea that moral principles are ones we light upon and obey in defiance of natural inclination.

How, then, in 1967 could a commentator write, albeit with exaggeration, that 'there do not appear . . . to be any self-confessed naturalists among moral philosophers'?[81] The answer is that something of a misnomer caught on after G. E. Moore labelled as 'naturalists' those guilty of the alleged 'naturalistic fallacy' of identifying *good* with a 'natural' property, such as pleasure (see p. 445). Later writers, including the Logical Positivists, largely agreed that this was a fallacy and indeed interpreted it more widely. 'Naturalism' came to be the name of the view that 'certain kinds of facts or features are necessarily relevant criteria of moral evaluation'.[82] In this new sense, naturalism has indeed been rejected by many writers. Consider such once-popular interpretations of 'Killing is wrong': it expresses a hostile feeling towards killing; it registers a personal commitment not to kill; it is a means of persuading others not to kill; or, it is a prescription, 'Do not kill!' On such construals, an evaluation is not a statement at all, and so neither true nor false: hence nothing, no fact or feature, can be a 'necessarily relevant criterion' for it. The 'new' naturalism rejected here is, of course, a different fish from naturalism in the 'broad, useful' sense. Indeed, emotivists, existentialists, prescriptivists and others who reject the former often boast of robust adherence to 'the general attitude' that man – his moral life included – is 'part of nature'. That is why 'most modern ethical works' can be 'broadly' naturalistic, despite there being so few 'self-confessed naturalists'.

During the last third of the century, however, more of this self-confessing breed have emerged, in something of a revolt against the sharp fact *versus* value divide insisted upon by the emotivists and their successors. The central charge made by these writers is that the image of human nature from which emotivist etc. views of morality stem is an impoverished one. A richer, more adequate one will demonstrate that moral evaluations are not, as emotivists *et al.* contend, individual choices or adoptions of attitudes which float free from people's perception of the 'facts or features' of their situations. For the Irish-born novelist and philosopher Iris Murdoch (b. 1919), at the heart of emotivism and its relatives is the notion of the will – the self which chooses and takes up attitudes – as 'the creator of value': and this reflects the view, variously heralded by Kant, Nietzsche and Kierkegaard, that a human being is, in essence, a will – that 'what I am "subjectively" is a footloose, solitary, substanceless will' (80 and 16).[83] That is why it is found so intolerable that my moral evaluations can be dictated, or even constrained, by facts.

These connected views of human being and morality do not withstand examination, according to Murdoch. Once we turn from the bland evaluative terms, 'good' and 'bad', to the richer vocabulary of 'brave', 'vulgar', 'snobbish' and the like, the idea that we *first* neutrally establish the facts and *then* 'choose' an attitude towards them, looks silly. Given proper attention to a person's behaviour, we feel 'compelled' to describe him as, say, vulgar, snobbish and insensitive, and we are thereby under a compulsion to evaluate him negatively. This is why to ordinary people, untainted by philosophy, 'it is perfectly obvious that goodness *is* connected with knowledge', values with facts (38). What the image of the human being as, essentially, will ignores is our rich inner 'life of the emotions'. Our charged perceptions of one another, our natural (though educable) responses to people's words and behaviour, our attentive sensitivity to the features of a situation – all these prepare us in our making of moral judgements, not by serving as mere data for a subsequent attitude or choice, but as rendering what is good or bad, right or wrong, '*compulsively* present' to us (39).

In his influential *After Virtue*, the Scottish philosopher Alasdair MacIntyre (b. 1929) also berates emotivists and existentialists for turning moral conviction into a matter of will. They can do so only by ignoring human nature, albeit in a sense of 'nature' different from Murdoch's. Emotivists and their allies are quite right to deny that moral conclusions can be derived from an account of 'untutored human nature', of 'man-as-he-happens-to-be'. For example, nothing of moral substance follows from the brute fact that people naturally seek pleasure. But what the emotivists ignore is the possibility of grounding morality in an account of 'man-as-he-could-be-if-he-realized-his-essential-nature'. What modern philosophers – indeed we moderns generally – have lost, and wrongly so, is the Aristotelian conception of a human nature in the sense of 'an essential purpose . . . function' or *telos* (50, 56).[84] Without such a conception, moral debate becomes interminable and unsettlable, thereby giving grist to the idea that morality is just a matter of personal choice or commitment.

Although there can be disagreement over the good life which accords with our essential nature or *telos*, three things can be said with confidence. First, it involves '*seeking* for the good life for man'. Second, this search requires the exercise of certain virtues, and third, a person cannot 'exercise the virtues only *qua* individual' (204). This is partly because the virtues must be understood as internal to various social practices, and partly because the notion of a person or 'self . . . detachable from its social and historical roles and statuses' (205) is a myth of modern secular liberalism. Moral persons – if conditions ever revive in which they can flourish – are, then, ones who participate in a communal tradition comprising practices which at once confer an identity on individuals and provide scope for the virtues whereby they seek for the good life and realize their *telos*.

This revival of a communal notion of personal identity – encountered several times in this book – forms a crucial part of the case made by MacIntyre and like-minded thinkers against that recent liberal classic, the Harvard philosopher John Rawls' (b. 1921) *A Theory of Justice*. Here, if anywhere in the postwar literature, is 'anti-naturalist' ethics in the tradition of Kant: for it is Rawls' ambition to ground the basic principles of justice – those which should govern the distribution of goods, powers, and liberties in a society – on disengaged rationality. The proper principles are those which 'free and rational persons concerned to further their own interests would accept in an initial position of equality' (11).[85] To guarantee this equality, crucial for the choice of principles in this 'social contract' to be fair, people must be put behind a 'veil of ignorance'. That is, they must be ignorant of, *inter alia*, their strengths and weaknesses, their religious affiliations, their social positions, and their particular conceptions of what is good. For knowledge of such factors would, given their natural egoism, enable and motivate people to opt for the kind of society which favours themselves, doubtless at the expense of others. The parallel with Kant's dissociation of the moral will from empirical factors, though by no means complete, is striking.

What principles does Rawls expect would be accepted in the initial and supposedly fair contract position he has stipulated? There are three: first, 'each person is to have an equal right to the most extensive liberty compatible with a similar liberty for others'; second, social and economic inequalities are only justified if the 'least advantaged' maximally gain from them; and third, there must be 'fair equality of opportunity' to benefit from any of these justified inequalities (60, 302). Rawls' amnesiac contractors, it seems, reason as follows in support of the crucial second principle: 'I don't have any idea how I'll land up in society, but maybe at the bottom of the heap. Still, in a society governed by this principle, that bottom is further from the pits than in any other society. So, if I'm sensible, I shall assent to that principle.'

The main point of Rawls' critics is not so much that his contractors, behind their 'veil of ignorance', would be too remote from flesh-and-blood men and women for us to have any idea what principles they would opt for. It is, rather, that whatever principles they opted for could not and should not be compelling for real people who do, *inter alia*, have religious affiliations and particular conceptions of the good. Granted, if I did not belong to a certain moral tradition or had no loyalties to a particular community, I should not vote for a society which favoured that tradition or community. But I do belong and do have my loyalties. What is it to me what some bloodless creature, whom I can in no way identify with, might opt for? Very probably, he or she would opt for a society in which the worship of no one God is favoured. Yet if that God is my God, why should I let this creature's deliberations deter me from driving out the false gods? How, the naturalist will urge, *could* I, being the man I am, defined in large part by the convictions and loyalties I have?

The signs are that the liveliest debate in English-speaking moral philosophy – a partial reprise of the one between Kant and Hegel – will continue to be between those who ground our obligations and values in the deliverances of detached reason and those for whom any abstraction from our historical and communal lives can result in a morality fit only for bloodless aliens, not real men and women.[86]

• 5 Postmodernism •

The disengaged rational self under attack from MacIntyre and other 'naturalists' in section 4 is also a main target of more iconoclastic writers of the last third of the twentieth century. For various postmodernist thinkers, indeed, the deserved 'fall of the self' is part of the welcome demise or 'end of philosophy' itself. After all, if there is no rational subject – no locus, therefore, for what the German philosopher and sociologist Jürgen Habermas (b. 1929) calls 'subject-centred reason' (34)[87] – then philosophy as traditionally pursued is left without its favourite topic and anyone to pursue it.

The phrase 'the end of philosophy' is taken from one of the two thinkers – Nietzsche being the other – to whom these iconoclasts owe most. This is Martin Heidegger, but after his so-called 'turn' away from the existentialist position described in section 2 towards one which, we saw, prompted Sartre to remark that he had 'gone mystical'. Philosophy, he states, 'in the present age has entered its final stage' (BW 373).[88] There had, to be sure, been earlier obituaries. For Hegel and Marx, the purpose of philosophy – the overcoming of alienation – was completed with, respectively, Hegel's own writings and the victory of the proletariat (see p. 320 and p. 337). For positivists like Comte, philosophy comes to an end with its replacement by more professional disciplines, the sciences. The death-sentence passed by Heidegger and his followers is very different. Far from completing its grand purpose, philosophy from Plato on has been a misconceived enterprise. What should replace it, however, cannot be science, since it too assumes the integrity of 'subject-centred reason'. Our postmodernists share, too, Heidegger's conviction that traditional philosophy has been morally, as well as intellectually, flawed. Its assumptions have at least conspired to produce our 'destitute', 'homeless' age.

Postmodernism and its Heroes

The 'postmodernist' label has been attached, not always with their consent, to a number of predominantly French philosophers. They include the Parisian trio, Michel Foucault (1926–84), whose title 'Professor of History and Systems of Ideas' gave a fair indication of his interests; Jacques Derrida (b. 1930), the Algerian-born founder of 'deconstruction'; Jean-François Lyotard (b. 1925), author of the manifesto *The Postmodern Condition*; and the American 'neo-pragmatist', Richard Rorty (b. 1931). But the label has also been a 'buzz-word' for a whole late twentieth-century cultural tendency manifested not only in the arts, but in fashions in clothing and food and, indeed, in a distinctive life-style. Characteristic of this movement has been its enthusiasm for irony and play, parody and pastiche, pluralism and eclecticism. Such features have their echoes, certainly, in postmodernist philosophizing: in Derrida's orthographical tricks (words which are crossed out, neologistic puns, and so on), in Lyotard's plea that the scientific 'game' should seek for dissent not consensus (66),[89] or in

Rorty's hope that 'in the ideal liberal society, intellectuals would...be ironists'.[90]

The connection between the philosophers and the wider cultural movement becomes clearer, however, when we identify two deeper *motifs* of the latter. The first, to sound paradoxical, is a marked hostility to 'depth'. One commentator speaks of the 'contrived depthlessness' of postmodernist architecture, its concern with facades for their own sake, for instance.[91] Another refers to the postmodernist painter's rejection of the modernist belief that the use of multiple perspectives would reveal 'the true nature of a unified...underlying reality'.[92] A Guide to an exhibition of postmodernist works boasts that they have 'no implication of a higher level of experience, no promise of a deeper intellectual experience'. The same Guide stresses that the works 'reveal...little about the artist': their 'subject is the viewer'. This illustrates the second deeper *motif*: the recessiveness of the artist, which Roland Barthes dramatized as 'the death of the author'. The idea is at least this: romantic and modernist images of the solitary author/artist struggling to communicate exaggerate the individual's power to control the message that will be received, not least through underplaying the role of the reader or viewer in determining what the work 'means'. The two *motifs* are connected. If a work had depth, it would convey some 'inner' message of the artist. So, if no such messages can be conveyed, works lose their depth, and the artist who recognizes this will cease to agonize over his or her calling, revelling instead in eclectic parody of those yet to hear the news of the death of the author/artist.

The *motifs* of depthlessness and the demise of the controlling artist find their parallels, in postmodernist philosophy, in two related themes. First, the rejection of 'metaphysics', understood in Heidegger's sense as the attempt to provide grounds or foundations for our basic practices, discourses, and beliefs (BW 374). According to Lyotard's widely-quoted definition of 'postmodern', it refers to 'incredulity towards metanarratives', these being grand attempts to 'legitimate' science or discourse, such as Hegel's dialectic of Spirit or the Enlightenment appeal to reason (xxiii–xxiv). The second theme, already alluded to, is 'the fall of the self', in the sense of the rational subject, the figure – familiar since Descartes – deemed capable of first subjecting all beliefs to critical examination and then justifying them from the ground up. So put, the two themes are connected: for foundationalism has required confidence in the rational individual's capacity to get down to the foundations. Derrida combines the themes in pleading that we 'pass beyond man . . . that being who, throughout the history of metaphysics, . . . has dreamed of . . . the reassuring foundation' (WD 292).[93]

The best way to examine the postmodernists' treatment of these themes is by tracing their debt to the two heroes they all acknowledge – Nietzsche and Heidegger. (Rorty cites other 'edifying' precursors including, astutely enough, the later Wittgenstein.) According to Habermas, it is Nietzsche who marks 'the entry into postmodernity' (83), for he was the first to refuse to take metaphysics at face value, as disinterested enquiry into the structure of reality and the foundations of knowledge. Like Christianity, metaphysics for Nietzsche manifests a 'tremendous historical need' felt by 'our unsatisfied . . . culture' since the demise of the ancient myths which had furnished a comforting picture of our place in the world.[94] Metaphysics is a function of 'the will to power', the invention of a 'true world', the imposition of stable structures of 'Being' upon the flux of experience by people unable to bear the thought that all is ephemeral 'Becoming' (see pp. 326f.). Philosophical systems are metaphors or perspectives, and should be investigated not for their truth or falsity, since there are 'no facts, only perspectives', but 'genealogically', for the factors – historical, psychological, physiological – which give rise to them. As for the rational self, this is a 'fiction' for Nietzsche: the invention of 'moralists' who need to postulate something which can be held responsible and duly punished for the actions that offend them.

With much of Nietzsche's diagnosis, Heidegger agrees. Metaphysics is an historically locatable and misguided substitute for something human beings have lost since pre-Socratic Greece; and the rational subject supposed to conduct metaphysical enquiry is the invention of a particular era of metaphysics. Yet, for Heidegger, Nietzsche failed to 'overcome' metaphysics, being instead 'the last metaphysician', the perpetrator of an 'inverted Platonism'. With Nietzsche, 'the essential possibilities of metaphysics are exhausted' (N4 148), since he carried to an extreme the two main tendencies which, ever more insistently, metaphysics has always displayed. Metaphysics is understood by Heidegger as the examination of 'the Being of beings' – people, physical objects, or whatever – in the conviction that Being is the ultimate cause or 'ground . . . from which beings as such are what they are . . . [and] can be known, handled and worked upon' (BW 374). Being is thereby construed as 'a "being" after the fashion of the familiar sort of beings which act as causes' (BW 214), as a 'presence' responsible for whatever else is 'present' in reality. Whether it is Plato's Form of the Good, the Christian God, Spinoza's Substance, or Hegel's Absolute Spirit, Being is always construed by analogy with some more familiar being – a person, say, or a physical stuff. Common to all metaphysics, though not always explicit, is a 'productive' or 'technical interpretation' of the world as a product or artifact of something, Being.

This tendency towards a 'productive' view of reality is accompanied by one towards a 'subjectivist' account of the 'ground' of beings. The two are connected, for the paradigm example of a producer is surely the human subject. This latter tendency was already there in Protagoras' doctrine that 'man is the measure of all things': one which, says Heidegger, Descartes virtually repeats in defining reality as that which can be 'represented . . . *through* and *for* the representing subject' and in 'grounding' truth 'on the self-certainty of the human subject'. But it is with Nietzsche that 'the metaphysics of subjectivity' and 'productivity' reaches its climax. In Nietzsche's 'metaphysics of the absolute subjectivity of will to power', the world is almost literally the product of the human subject, of man considered as a bodily complex of 'drives and affects', no longer the *animal rationale* of Descartes, but a *brutum bestiale* (N4 86, 147f). The doctrine of 'will to power' may overturn more orthodox metaphysical systems, yet it too strives to explain reality and knowledge in terms of a special, underlying ground – one which, moreover, starkly displays the tendencies implicit in the earlier systems.

Heidegger accuses metaphysics of an 'oblivion of Being', of failing to heed the vital 'ontological difference' between Being and (particular) beings. The metaphysician tries to explain or 'ground' beings-as-a-whole in terms of just one kind of being (substance, self, will to power, or whatever). But this is incoherent, since 'Being [is] essentially broader than all beings', including those regarded as the ground of everything. To be anything at all, *every* being owes its existence to Being, and none, therefore, can qualify as Being itself. In one of his favourite metaphors, Heidegger compares beings to objects which are lit up and Being to 'the lighting itself' (BW 216–17). Just as no lit up object can account for how objects are lit (cannot, that is, itself be the lighting), so no being can explain how it or anything else *is* (cannot itself be Being). Being is not a kind of being but the *way* – or, rather, the series of ways – in which, historically, beings get 'revealed' or 'lit up' for us. It is Being itself, not man, which is responsible for these ways of revealing. Thus the history of metaphysics is also 'the history of Being': metaphysicians merely articulate these revelations, in the deluded belief that they are plumbing the eternal foundations of reality. Nietzsche, for instance, is merely giving voice to Being's latest 'lighting up' of things as objects to be used and dominated. The human subject is a cipher or messenger of Being, and so not the autonomous rational being of traditional philosophy.

With metaphysics 'overcome', is there another kind of discourse innocent of the 'oblivion of Being'? Not if by this is meant a language for representing and conceptualizing Being, for just as I can see the objects lit up in my room, but not the lighting of them, so I can represent to myself the beings revealed in the world, but not the revealing of them. Still, 'there is a thinking more rigorous than the conceptual', a non-representational thinking which can 'bring to language' the 'advent of Being' (BW 235, 241). This 'thinking' [*Denken*], it seems, is less likely to occur in the philosophy seminar than when smoking a pipe over a *Stein* of beer among sturdy peasants, albeit fortified by reading Sophocles and Hölderlin. 'Thinking' requires hearing 'the right word[s] within . . . traditional language' (BW 213), especially poetry, through which we are somehow 'attuned' to 'the call of Being', somehow experience the 'nearness of the unobtrusive power' whose 'gift' of 'light' is responsible for anything being what it is. The nature of this 'attunement' may become clearer later, when I discuss Heidegger's critique of technology, the main engine of the 'homelessness' which is the legacy of metaphysics.

Genealogy and 'Bio-Power'

Let us now trace the development of the anti-foundationalist theme by the postmodernists, focusing first on Foucault and then on Derrida. Little love, it seems, was lost between the two men, with Foucault branding his former pupil an unserious 'little pedagogue' after his book on madness had been 'deconstructed' by Derrida. Their differences were due, in part, to their different inspirational sources – Nietzsche in Foucault's case, Heidegger in Derrida's. Foucault owes to Nietzsche, first, the 'nominalist' conviction that language does not mirror an objective order, but imposes order and structure on the world. Nietzsche grasps 'the secret that [things] have no essence or that their essence is fabricated' (FR 78).[95] The second debt is to Nietzsche's 'genealogical' method, 'a form of history' which accounts for 'the constitution of knowledges [and] discourses' in terms of *power*. Nietzsche's own approach, however, is insufficiently historical for Foucault, appealing as it does to a metaphysically suspect 'will to power' and a handful of drives supposed to stem from an abiding human nature. Foucault's genealogy is, by contrast, a 'gray, meticulous, and patiently documentary' examination of 'the systems of subjection' and 'play of dominations' – at work in medicine, the penal system, sexual practices and elsewhere – of which claims to knowledge and permissible ways of speaking are 'effects' (FR 76, 83). (For a time, no sociology department in Britain was complete without its Foucault look-alike, sporting rectangular dark glasses beneath a shaven pate – an indication that his influence on sociology has been at least as great as on philosophy.)

To understand Foucault's genealogy, we must first glance at the 'archaeological' approach which, under the influence of postwar 'structuralism', he had earlier adopted. Here his concern was with what he took to be the more-or-less autonomous 'codes of knowledge' or 'discourses' of the human sciences which, since the Renaissance, had succeeded one another in abrupt, discontinuous fashion. These, he held, dictated which claims to knowledge, ideas, and arguments could, at a given time, be entertained. The 'codes', in turn, were shaped by the prevailing *'epistëme'* of the time – 'the total set of relations that unite . . . the discursive practices that give rise to . . . sciences' (AK 191). Thus, Renaissance science was governed by the *epistëme* of 'resemblance', the image of the universe as a system of 'correspondences' to be uncovered by the scientist: while, in 'the Classical Age', the controlling *epistëme* became that of 'representation' and 'taxonomy', the idea being that something is understood when it is allocated its place in a complicated hierarchical ordering of the world.

What was 'lacking' in this 'archaeological' approach, Foucault came to see, was appreciation of 'the problem of the "discursive regime", of the effects of power peculiar to the play of statements' (FR 55). Discourses, that is, need to be understood in relation to non-discursive practices, to 'systems of subjection'. Foucault's main concern was now with 'the era of "bio-power"', which gathered steam at the end of the eighteenth century with 'an explosion of . . . techniques for . . . the subjugation of bodies and the control of populations', of a whole 'political technology of the body'. Thus, it is as a 'means of access to the life of the body and the life of the species' that we should view the medical and psychiatric discourses surrounding sexuality which have proliferated over the last two hundred years (HS 146). This is not the banal claim that the development of knowledge requires suitable social and political conditions, nor a rehash of the Marxist view that prevailing forms of knowledge are 'ideological' tools of a power elite: for the kind of power that interests Foucault is 'anonymous', diffused through the 'capillaries' of society but without a controlling organ. Power and knowledge are not contingently related: they are not mere means to one another, rather they 'directly imply' and 'constitute' one another (DP 27).

It is in dense, detailed descriptions of 'power/knowledge' – of surveillance, internment, censuses and so on – that Foucault excels. But what concerns us is the relativist and anti-foundationalist conclusions he draws from them. Where truth, in his 'archaeological' writings, was relative to the 'codes' which enabled the production of statements and theories, now it is a 'system of ordered procedures' for their production 'linked in a circular relation with systems of power'. 'Truth is not outside power', but 'the product of multiple constraints', and 'each society has its own regime of truth' (FR 72ff). Since it is only relative to such a 'regime' that statements can be held as true or arguments regarded as valid, it makes no sense to ask for the rational credentials of the 'regime' itself. The psychological theories, for example, which prosper in the 'era of "bio-power"' are incommensurable with those which hold sway in different eras. To suppose there could be some objective foundation on the basis of which such different theories could be adjudicated is to forget that there are no 'essences' which are not 'fabricated'.

Writing and *Différance*

A starker way than Foucault's of demolishing foundationalism would be to argue that thought is reducible to language and that outside of language there is nothing at all – *ergo*, nothing to 'legitimate' our talk and thought. Taken at face value, this is the position of Derrida, Director of Studies at the *Ecole des Hautes Etudes* in Paris. 'We *think only in signs*' and 'there are nothing but signs' (G 50). It is such remarks that have made 'Jacques de Ripper' a darling of radical literary critics, but a clown or fraud for many professional philosophers, including the Cambridge ones who refused to support his Honorary Doctorate. With allowance made for Gallic hyperbole, however, his position may be less novel than friend and foe imagine.

Derrida's target, like Heidegger's, is 'the metaphysics of presence': the idea that there are entities which 'ground' our thought and language. In his view, however, the German's own account of Being, especially his 'quest' for special words which would directly 'address' Being, still 'belong[s] to metaphysics' (P 10). Derrida's strategy is to attack a familiar view of language – 'logocentrism' – which, among its sins, 'support[s] the determination of . . . being . . . as presence'. Both logocentrism and the 'metaphysics of presence' reflect the misguided yet 'irrepressible desire' for a 'transcendental signified' – for something independent of language to serve as its anchor (G 14, 49). When, as a prime example of logocentrism, Derrida cites the view that a sign 'signifies "mental experiences" which themselves . . . mirror things by natural resemblance' (G 11), it is clear that his target is the same as that of Quine, Davidson and other 'naturalists' discussed in section 4 – the idea that words mean by standing for entities (images, senses, or whatever) directly present to consciousness. He may pick on Husserl rather than Locke or Frege, but it is the same kind of enemy, attacked with similar weapons, moreover.[96]

To appreciate Derrida's attack, we need to consider his bizarre-sounding claim that *all* language is a 'species of writing' (G 8). This is not the mad claim that pen and ink preceded and determine the nature of spoken language. Rather, it registers a 'new concept of writing' (P 26) motivated by the consideration that all language possesses crucial features which writing *obviously* has – ones to which, however, a 'phonocentric' obsession with the spoken word, especially in 'inner monologue', blinds us. When I 'hear-myself-speak', I imagine an 'absolute proximity . . . of voice . . . and meaning' (G 12). The silent word seems too gossamer-like to intervene between consciousness and an item, not itself belonging to language, directly present to it as the word's meaning – an image, say. The word seems imbued with its meaning, and to be naturally rather than arbitrarily connected with it. Nor, in 'hearing-myself-speak', do I have any sense that the word's meaning depends on its use in other contexts and its relations to other words.

We are not, however, prone to such illusions in the case of written signs. The connection between the letters 'c-a-t' and feline animals is obviously arbitrary, not natural. Moreover, we recognize that the sequence 'stands for' another sign, the word 'cat'. Written signs also patently belong to a whole system of such signs and depend for their meaning on doing so. Equally obviously, their intelligibility is not tied to a particular context, since the context in which they are read is very likely to be quite different from that in which they were written. They are, therefore, 'iterable' – repeatable and decipherable in different contexts. Derrida's point is that all this is true, though less obviously, of spoken words, of signs in general indeed. Thus, the written word is a 'sign of a sign', but it would be 'more profoundly true' to say this of all signs (G 43). Again, 'the possibility of repeating, and therefore identifying, marks, is implied in *every* code, making of it a communicable, transmittable, decipherable grid that is iterable . . . for *any* possible user' (MP 315, my emphases).

Before seeing how Derrida deploys this point to discredit logocentrism and the 'metaphysics of presence', a note on the notorious notion of 'deconstruction'. In Derrida himself, there is no single pattern of argument, no one set of deconstructive 'axioms', of the kind forged by literary critics who pay him homage. There is, though, a typical form to his arguments. The target, usually, is a claim to the effect that a concept A (e.g. speech) is more fundamental and 'privileged' than a concept B (e.g. writing). The aim is then to show, primarily by *ad hominem* argument, that A is in fact derivative, not quite from B itself, but from a 'wider' concept B★. Both A and B turn out to be instances of B★. Thus both speech and writing are instances of a 'wider concept of writing', generated by reflecting that all signs have features which belong more obviously to writing than to speech. Another example: literal talk is typically privileged over metaphorical talk, but deconstructive reflection shows that both kinds are instances of a widened notion of rhetorical language. Even 'literal' talk displays crucial features usually associated with metaphorical talk. When Derrida calls philosophical discourse a 'particular literary genre' (MP 293), he does not deny the obvious differences between Kant and Wordsworth, Plato and Sophocles, but insists that even in the first members of these pairs one finds 'rhetorical organization', 'a set of tropic resources', and so on. This illustrates the *ad hominem* character of Derrida's arguments. 'The movements of deconstruction do not destroy structures from the outside' (G 24), but from 'within', by showing that an author who privileges A over B himself displays the falsity of his claim. Kant wants metaphor excluded from philosophical writing, but himself employs metaphor to state his point. Plato minimizes the importance of writing in relation to speech, but betrays an essential reliance on written signs.

The conclusions Derrida draws from his claim that all language is a 'species of writing' are best teased out from his neologism *'différance'*, defined as 'the movement according to which language . . . is constituted "historically" as a weave of differences' and 'deferrals' (MP 12). (The term is coined from the French words for 'differ' and 'defer' and is intended to combine their senses.) Our language is a 'weave of differences' in that the meaning of a word is a function of its contrasts with other words. Each word bears the 'trace . . . of other elements of the . . . system' (P 26). 'Red' could not mean what it does in the absence of 'blue', 'orange' and so on. Language is a weave of 'deferrals' in two senses. First, any item said to be signified by a word – a concept, say – is 'also in the position of a signifier' (P 20), for it too needs to be interpreted and applied. The word's meaning is therefore 'deferred' to this item, and so cannot be explained in terms of it. Second, the meaning of an expression on some occasion is 'related no less to . . . the future than to . . . the past' (MP 13). As 'iterable', an expression's meaning is 'deferred' in that a grasp of it always refers us to further contexts and occasions of the expression's use.

The grand conclusion is that a meaning cannot be some item present to consciousness – an image, concept or whatever of direct acquaintance. To grasp a meaning inevitably refers us to a whole system of meanings and to past and future uses of a term – to matters, that is, which could not be regarded as present to the speaker. The 'play of differences', then, forbids that there should be 'a simple element . . . *present* in and of itself' that could be identified as a word's meaning (P 26). It is no good replying that an *intention* to pair a word with an image or whatever fixes the term's meaning. For not only does the problem remain that this image is itself a signifier requiring interpretation, but no intention could determine the term's place in the language as a whole, nor its use in indefinitely many different contexts.

Nor can we seek a foundation for our language in the structure of the real world, for this world is itself the 'product' of *différance* in that 'we have access to . . . "real" existence only in the text' of language (G 158). 'There is nothing outside of the text' is not the crazed claim that only words exist, but the assertion that there is no sense to the idea of what the world is like independent of the linguistic system in which things are classified and differentiated. That might not worry the foundationalist overmuch if our linguistic ordering of the world were severely constrained by permanent inbuilt structures of the mind or brain, as the structuralist anthropologist Claude Lévi-Strauss (b. 1908) imagined. *Différance*, however, is 'historical': our current system of distinctions is 'neither inscribed in the heavens, nor in the brain' (P 9), but constantly 'drifting'. There would, in fact, be far more drift and instability in communication were it not for 'socio-institutional conditions . . . [and] nonnatural relations of power' which keep the members of a linguistic community more or less in line.[97] Whether it is something 'nonnatural' or, as Wittgenstein held, 'something animal', which keeps speakers in line, it is nothing of a kind to *justify* or *ground* our language and thought.

Despite a tendency to personify *différance* as a 'power' which 'produces' our systems of meanings, Derrida's insistence elsewhere that 'it reigns over nothing . . . and nowhere exercises any authority' (MP 22) is surely intended to proclaim the sheer anchorless contingency of language and thought. Language is 'something unpredictable . . . it is not based on grounds. It is not reasonable (or unreasonable). It is there – like our life.'[98] These just might have been Derrida's words, though they are those of Wittgenstein, who really did over-come any urge to postulate a 'deep' power behind our linguistic practices. If, for Derrida, *différance* is to be 'wondered' at, this is surely not, as Habermas suggests, because he 'remains close to Jewish mysticism', with its belief in the ever deferred 'event of revelation' (183). It is because, as for Wittgenstein, life as it is, with 'nothing hidden', is wondrous.

'The Fall of the Self'

I noted earlier a broad connection between postmodernist anti-foundationalism and the slogan of 'the fall of the self'.[99] The rational subject of Enlightenment optimism is a chimera if it is deemed to be one which can suspend all preconceptions and then represent an objective reality which would 'legitimate' beliefs and values. However, the slogan does not announce the demise of a single creature. Rather different notions, not always distinguished by the obituarists, are being buried. We should distinguish at least three: the Cartesian *cogito*, 'individualism' and 'humanism'. The *cogito*, and such relatives as Husserl's 'pure ego', were of course under attack by Merleau-Ponty, Heidegger and other existential phenomenologists (see ch. 10, sect. 2). Consciousness cannot belong to a self-enclosed, disembodied self, but is an aspect, rather, of our 'Being-in-the-world', of our embodied engagement with the world. This attack, predictably, has been continued. Thus for Derrida, the *cogito* is a prime instance of 'the metaphysics of presence' since, on Descartes' view, self-consciousness is 'the perception of self in presence' or 'self-presence' (MP 16). In that case, it is a myth: a person, like all else, belongs in a 'weave' of differences and deferrals, and cannot therefore be present to an act of con-sciousness, not even his or her own.

For most postmodernists, including Derrida, the *cogito* is not worth wasting critical energy on. A worthier target is 'individualism', the idea that individuals are the basic engines of social change, and hence an important ingredient in the 'distinctively modern picture of the self as finally independent of . . . history'.[100] If selves make history, they are not made by it. Inspiration for criticisms of this idea comes from both Marx and Nietzsche. The Marxist philosopher Louis Althusser (1918–90), for example, argued that a central thesis of Marx's, once he had got over his youthful 'humanism', was that 'the human subject . . . is not the "centre" of history . . . except in the imaginary misrecognition of the "ego"'. Indeed, the very notion of autonomous human subjects was an 'inven-tion' of capitalism. If people could be persuaded that this is what they were, they would be more ready, in the belief that they were exercising autonomy, to 'accept [their] subjection' to 'ideological State apparatuses'.[101] In a more Nietzschean vein, Foucault also argues that history is not made by individuals, since it is largely 'a history of the different modes by which . . . human beings are made subjects' (SP 208). In particular, the exercise of 'bio-power' requires a zeal for 'dividing practices' which sort people into the mad and the sane, the deviant and the normal, and so on. These, together with an obsession for digging 'inside' people – by eliciting 'confessions', for example – encourage us to see ourselves as unique, 'interesting' selves, autonomous and 'private' little domains divided off from one another.

It is a third, related target which has provoked the most splenetic postmodernist outbursts, including Foucault's famous remark that 'man is a recent invention' who will be 'erased, like a face drawn in the sand at the edge of the sea' (OT 386–7). Following Heidegger, I shall call it 'humanism': the idea that individuals are, or can be, relatively autonomous sources of meaning, understanding and intelligibility. This idea had already been savaged by the French structuralists: 'Not man, but structures are decisive! Man is nothing!', had been their slogan in the 1950s.[102] Thus, for Lévi-Strauss, we are not rid of the Cartesian spirit merely by rejecting the *cogito*. It remains alive if the self, even when considered as social and embodied, is deemed potentially independent of the 'codes' which structure thought.[103] Hence, his animosity towards existentialism, 'a shop-girl's philosophy' catering to the romantic illusion that the individual, if sufficiently 'authentic', can disengage from, and rise above, the public structures of meaning and value that he or she inherits.

Such criticism was levelled against Heidegger as much as Sartre, but Heidegger, we earlier saw, himself turned against the humanist aspects of his original position. Man in his later writings is no longer the Promethean *Dasein* of *Being and Time*, but more a passive recipient of the world as Being chooses to reveal it. In particular, a person 'belongs' to the language he or she speaks. Indeed, it is less true to say that man speaks language than that 'language speaks man'. The latter would better convey that language is 'not merely of the making or at the command of our speech activity' (WL 125). Rather, it is the language we are 'sent' in a given era which dictates the activities of speech and thought in which we can engage. It is this theme, common to Lévi-Strauss and Heidegger, that the autonomy of the self is vitiated by our being creatures of language which the postmodernists continue. When the literary critic Roland Barthes announced 'the death of the author', he did so on the grounds that a 'play of codes' intervenes between author and reader, so that the former cannot control the latter's interpretation of the text.[104] Worse, the author is not privileged to decide what the text *does* mean: for this is a function of the 'codes' on which it draws. Derrida goes further. The self or subject is 'inscribed in [and] a "function" of language', for I can only be a self at all through speaking, and this means 'making [my] speech conform . . . to the system of . . . language as a system of differences', to the prevailing 'movement of *différance*' (MP 15). This entails that there is *no* subject, in the sense of a creature who is 'agent, author, and master' of language (P 28). It will then follow that the rational subject of Enlightenment dreams is an illusion. For that subject, to wipe the slate of prejudice and mere opinion clean, would have to stand back from and then fully master the language which will be the instrument of his pristine enquiries. But that is precisely what no one can do if everyone is 'inscribed in' or 'spoken by' language.

Liberation and Alienation

Despite their parallel criticisms of traditional views, the 'polemics' of English-language philosophers like Quine 'lack the apocalyptic tone' of those who, as Rorty puts it, share with Heidegger and Derrida 'the sense of "Western metaphysics" as . . . all-encompassing'.[105] This 'tone' voices the feeling that metaphysics is as much a moral as an intellectual aberration. 'Moral' is not a word of which Heidegger and postmodernists are fond, and one might indeed wonder with what right such iconoclasts could indulge in moralizing. Still, there is no disguising the antipathy towards modernity in which, they hold, metaphysics is deeply implicated: nor the preference for attitudes which, they hope, might emerge in a 'postmetaphysical' age.

To begin with, there is the idea that metaphysics has helped to impose constraints from which, with its demise, we might hope to be liberated. Consider, first, the 'authority' which the sciences have enjoyed in modernity. For Lyotard, once it is appreciated that these are so many 'games', the 'rules' of which are 'specific to each particular kind of knowledge', the sciences lose all claim to 'legitimate' other discourses – a point reinforced by the realization that scientific 'knowledge' is merely what happens to get 'accepted in the social circle of the "knower's" interlocutors' (52). Even the sciences have to gain, Rorty says, from confessing that 'the only sense in which science is exemplary is that it is a model of human solidarity', of open and free debate, rather than of objective reality.[106] Second, there are those like Jean Baudrillard – 'the hottest property on the New York intellectual circuit' of the 1980s, according to *The Guardian* – for whom, with the demise of metaphysics and the 'liqui-dation of all referentials', our culture will feel free to luxuriate in the 'hyperreal' or 'simulacra'. These are creations which do not even pretend to correspond to anything, but 'the generation by models . . . without origin'. Once 'truth, reference and objective causes have ceased to exist', we are at last freed from the obligation to 'feign' and 'simulate'.[107]

Slightly less frenetic, finally, are Foucault's and Derrida's hopes for the liberation of various 'voices' – those of the mad, delinquents, and so on – which have been 'excluded' since the Enlightenment. For Foucault, these groups suffer in two stages at the hands of Enlightenment reason. With its obsession for 'division', they are set up *as* groups, ripe for special treatment and possible exclusion. Then they are invested with characteristics deemed hostile to the cool exercise of reason – emotion, wildness, and the like – so that possibility becomes actuality, and their voices are suppressed. Derrida has been especially concerned with the marginalization of women. 'Phallocentrism and logocentrism are indissociable' – so much so that he mints the term 'phallogocentrism' to mark their union (AL 57ff.). The reasons for this union have appealed to several feminist writers, who argue that the sharp divisions of metaphysics – reason *versus* feeling, mental *versus* physical, etc. – which Derrida wants to deconstruct are a prerogative of the male mind. They sympathize, too, with the suggestion that the rational self or subject, so crucial to metaphysical thought, has a 'phallic character', the 'cutting virility' of an intelligence that penetrates into things (AL 366).

Of greater interest, perhaps, than these liberationist aspirations is Heidegger's exposure of metaphysics' involvement in the 'estrangement' or 'homelessness [which] is coming to be the destiny of the world' (BW 218). The engine of this homelessness is technology, which, in its 'essence', is not practical activity but a 'way of revealing' the world. 'The earth now reveals itself as a mining district, the soil as a mineral deposit' (BW 296). Indeed, everything is treated as 'standing reserve' (*Bestand*), to be utilized, put on tap, 'challenged'. This way of revealing is the culmination of metaphysics, which, we saw, has always construed Being as a 'productive' cause. Once a 'subjectivist' twist is given to this idea, so that *man* becomes the 'ground' of everything, the world gets viewed as a human commodity.

What makes this way of revealing 'monstrous' is not that it is false: things really can 'show up' as equipment to be utilized. It is monstrous, first, because it 'drives out every other possibility of revealing' (BW 309) to an extent that, say, an aesthetic way could not. Even the extreme aesthete must sometimes regard things in a more mundane light, whereas a pragmatic attitude towards the environment all too easily emerges as the only reasonable one for 'practical', 'sensible' people. Second, it is the most hubristic way of revealing, at the farthest remove from a willingness to 'let beings be', to allow them to display their own natures instead of mobilizing them for our purposes. By regarding 'man [as] the lord of beings', technology uproots his more intimate relation to the world as 'the shepherd of Being' (BW 221). Paradoxically, by viewing the world as there 'for us', we are set over against it, as exploiters not communers. 'The Rhine itself appears to be something at our command . . . a water-power supplier' (BW 297), no longer the river running through the soil of a native land to which people once owed their identity. (Unsurprisingly, Heidegger's writings have inspired many later environmental thinkers and 'eco-philosophers'.)[108]

Technology, as the culmination of metaphysics, is monstrous, finally, because it infects our stance to *everything* – most crucially, to our language. 'Language is at once the house of Being and the home of human beings' (BW 239): the 'place' where Being is intimated to us and where we, 'hearkening' its intimations, realize our humanity. Just as a house is not a home when viewed instrumentally – as a building in which to invest capital or hang one's hat – so a collection of signs ceases to be a true language when treated simply as a set of tools. So to treat it is to become homeless, to distance our language from us – as something to survey, control and utilize – instead of seeing it as defining and giving us our being. This was Derrida's point, too, when denying that we are 'masters' over the language we 'inhabit'. It was the point, too, of romantic critics of Enlightenment like Herder (see p. 283), for whom a vicious aspect of 'subject-centred reason' was the pretence that the language in which we dwell is something we can step back from and assess. We should indeed be masters of our language in a sense: but this is not akin to the domination of nature and tools by technologists. It is, rather, the kind which, as one writer sees it, Wittgenstein invokes: 'a mastery analogous to that achieved by athletes and craftsmen . . . a grace and seamless self-mastery which constitutes the fulfillment of a distinctively human possibility'.[109]

There has, in closing, perhaps emerged a double irony. A *Leitmotiv* of the book has been the endeavours of philosophy to 'cope with' estrangement or homelessness: to provide accounts of the world which, as it were, give us a place within it, but not at the expense of denying our uniqueness. Is it not ironic, then, that some of the most influential thinkers of the twentieth century should charge philosophy itself – metaphysics, at least – with producing our sense of estrangement? Ironic or not, the charge is one we have often encountered, in various guises, over the preceding chapters – in Ghazāli's exposure of 'the incoherence of the philosophers', for example (see p. 163). It would be boring, I think, to battle over the word 'philosophy'. It matters little whether, with Heidegger, we proclaim 'the end of philosophy' or speak, with Wittgenstein, of philosophy as a remedy for the disease of which it is the cause. What does matter is to appreciate the perennial sense that a certain kind of rational enquiry, however elevated its motives, must ultimately distort our relation to the world, and in doing so set us over against it.

I say a 'perennial' sense: and here, perhaps, is a second irony. It is sometimes remarked that philosophy has not 'progressed' over 2,500 years. That is clearly wrong if it means that bad arguments have never been weeded out. But it is sobering to reflect on the closeness between Heidegger's view of our place in the universe, his hostility towards theory, his call for 'rigour of meditation, carefulness in saying, frugality with words' (BW 241) and the utterances of the ancient sages – of the Buddha and Lao Tzu, for example – with which our history virtually began. But, then, if Heidegger is right and the 'old words' are the ones we must try to hear, the irony of circling back to where we began is a trivial price to pay.

• Notes •

1 References to Bergson are to *Creative Evolution* (CE), *The Two Sources of Morality and Religion* (MR), and *An Introduction to Metaphysics* (IM).
2 Bertrand Russell, *History of Western Philosophy*, p. 759.
3 For a sympathetic account of Bergson's accounts of time, mobility, and free will, see Leszek Kolakowski, *Bergson*.
4 F. S. C. Northrop, 'Whitehead's philosophy of science', p. 169.
5 References in the text to Whitehead are to *Modes of Thought* (MT), *Process and Reality* (PR), and *Science and the Modern World* (SMW), as partially reprinted in *Alfred North Whitehead: An Anthology*.
6 Victor Lowe, 'The development of Whitehead's philosophy', p. 90.
7 On Whitehead's difficult conception of God and much else, see Wolfe Mays, *The Philosophy of Whitehead*, and Dorothy Emmett, 'Whitehead, Alfred North'.
8 Quoted by Mays, *The Philosophy of Whitehead*, p. 169.
9 References are to Wilhelm Dilthey's *Selected Writings*.
10 Quoted in George Lichtheim, *Europe in the Twentieth Century*, p. 184, a useful book on the currents of thought under discussion.
11 References to Unamuno are to *Tragic Sense of Life*.
12 References are to Oswald Spengler's *Man and Technics*.
13 Quoted in Jeffrey Herf, *Reactionary Modernism*, p. 196, an excellent book on Spengler and other German thinkers of the period.
14 References to Husserl are to *Ideas* (I); *The Crisis of European Sciences* (C); and *Cartesian Meditations* (CM).
15 By placing Husserl in a section alongside existentialist and hermeneutical thinkers, I follow the convention of treating him as a 'continental' philosopher. But much recent interest in his work relates it to that of Frege and other founding fathers of 'analytical' philosophy. See, especially, Michael Dummett, *Origins of Analytical Philosophy*. On Husserl and later phenomenologists, see M. Hammond et al., *Understanding Phenomenology*.
16 Quoted by Dagfinn Føllesdal, 'Husserl's notion of noema', p. 74, an article to which my discussion owes much.
17 References to Merleau-Ponty are to his *Phenomenology of Perception*.
18 References to Sartre are to *Being and Nothingness* (BN); *Existentialism and Humanism* (EH); *Cahiers pour une morale* (CM); and *The Reprieve* (R).
19 References to Heidegger are to *The Basic Problems of Phenomenology* (BP), and *Being and Time* (BT).
20 Quoted by Simone de Beauvoir, *Force of Circumstance*, p. 13.
21 Arthur C. Danto, *Sartre*, p. 104.
22 Jürgen Habermas, quoted in Hubert L. Dreyfus, *Being-in-the-World*, p. 9; an excellent book on Heidegger.

23 On Heidegger's life and Nazi connections, see Hugo Ott, *Martin Heidegger*.
24 Martin Buber, *I and Thou*, p. 26.
25 References to Gadamer are to *Truth and Method*.
26 Paul Ricoeur, 'Existence and hermeneutics', p. 249.
27 Karl Jaspers, *Philosophy*, vol. 2, p. 30.
28 De Beauvoir, *Force of Circumstance*, p. 152.
29 The definitions of, respectively, *The Oxford Companion to French Literature*, 1st edition, and *The Concise Oxford English Dictionary*, 5th edition.
30 José Ortega y Gasset, *History as a System*, p. 114.
31 Ibid., p. 111.
32 Karl Jaspers, 'Philosophical Autobiography', p. 85.
33 Gabriel Marcel, *Being and Having*, p. 107.
34 On 'Platonic atomism', see Peter Hylton, *Russell, Idealism and the Emergence of Analytic Philosophy*, part II.
35 References to Russell are to section numbers of *The Principles of Mathematics* (PM), and to page numbers of 'The Philosophy of Logical Atomism' (LA); *The Problems of Philosophy* (PP); *Mysticism and Logic* (ML); and *Introduction to Mathematical Philosophy* (IM).
36 A. J. Ayer, *Russell*, p. 35.
37 On Wittgenstein's life, see Ray Monk, *Ludwig Wittgenstein*.
38 References in this section to Wittgenstein are to proposition numbers of *Tractatus Logico-Philosophicus* (T), and page numbers of *Notebooks 1914–1916* (NB).
39 Paul Engelmann, *Letters from Ludwig Wittgenstein*, p. 143.
40 On the 'mystical' and the self, see Michael P. Hodges, *Transcendence and Wittgenstein's Tractatus*.
41 J. O. Urmson, *Philosophical Analysis*, p. 107 – an excellent account of the transition from Atomism to Positivism.
42 References to Carnap are to *Philosophy and Logical Syntax* (PL), and 'Protocol statements and the formal mode of speech' (PF).
43 References to Schlick are to 'Meaning and verification' (MV), and 'Positivism and realism' (PR).
44 References to Ayer are to *Language, Truth and Logic*.
45 Karl Popper, *The Logic of Scientific Discovery*.
46 See the Editor's Introduction to Barry Gower (ed.), *Logical Positivism in Perspective*, a useful collection of obituary articles on this philosophy.
47 See G. E. Moore's *Principia Ethica*.
48 See Charles Stevenson, *Ethics and Language*; and R. M. Hare, *The Language of Morals*, for the more refined 'emotivist' and 'prescriptivist' accounts.
49 David Rynin, 'Vindication of L★g★c★l P★s★t★ v★sm', pp. 60–1.
50 P. F. Strawson, *Analysis and Metaphysics*, p. 7.
51 Thomas Nagel, 'What is it like to be a bat?', in his *Mortal Questions*.
52 References to Quine are to *Ontological Relativity* (OR); *Word and Object* (WO); 'Philosophical progress in language theory' (PP); and *From a Logical Point of View* (LP).
53 John Skorupski, *English-Language Philosophy 1750–1945*, p. 15.
54 References to Wittgenstein in this section are to section numbers of part I and page numbers of part II of his *Philosophical Investigations* (PI); *The Blue and Brown Books* (BB); and *On Certainty* (OC).
55 See, for example, John Passmore, *Recent Philosophers*.
56 Thomas Kuhn, *The Structure of Scientific Revolutions*, p. 149. For good discussions of realism and anti-realism concerning science, see Passmore, *Recent Philosophers*, and Anthony O'Hear, *What Philosophy Is*.

57 On 'metaphysical realism' as 'incoherent', see Quine's Harvard colleague and, at times in his mercurial career, fellow scientific naturalist, Hilary Putnam, *Meaning and the Moral Sciences*, part 4.

58 Michael Dummett, *Truth and Other Enigmas*, p. 458.

59 Donald Davidson, *Inquiries into Truth and Interpretation*, p. 170.

60 Gottlob Frege, *Philosophical Writings*, pp. 60ff.

61 Alfred Tarski, *Logic, Semantics, Metamathematics*, p. 406.

62 Davidson, *Inquiries into Truth and Interpretation*, pp. 21, 24.

63 See Hartry Field, 'Tarski's theory of truth'.

64 Hilary Putnam, *Mind, Language and Reality*, p. 227. For Kripke's similar view, see his *Naming and Necessity*. Both writers, incidentally, also attack Frege's view that proper names must have senses *via* which they refer.

65 Putnam, *Mind, Language and Reality*, pp. 220, 245.

66 See, for example, P. F. Strawson, *Meaning and Truth*.

67 Though see Colin McGinn, *Wittgenstein on Meaning*, who criticizes this 'social' interpretation. Chapter 1, pp. 77ff, incidentally, provides a limpid account of Wittgenstein's general position.

68 Frank Ramsey, *The Foundations of Mathematics*, p. 258.

69 Similar cases are raised in the much-discussed Edmund L. Gettier, 'Is justified true belief knowledge?'

70 Richard Rorty, review of Daniel Dennett, *Consciousness Explained*, 1991, p. 3.

71 William Lycan, in his editorial introduction to *Mind and Cognition*, p. 3 – a vast source of recent writings in the philosophy of mind.

72 References are to Gilbert Ryle's *The Concept of Mind*.

73 'Talking and thinking', in Lycan (ed.), *Mind and Cognition*, pp. 14ff.

74 David Armstrong, 'The causal theory of mind', in ibid., pp. 40–1.

75 'The nature of mental states', in ibid., p. 53.

76 Paul M. Churchland, *Matter and Consciousness*, p. 45.

77 See Daniel Dennett, *Brainstorms*.

78 Churchland, *Matter and Consciousness*, p. 45.

79 A. J. Ayer, *Man as a Subject for Science*, p. 5.

80 Bernard Williams, *Ethics and the Limits of Philosophy*, p. 121.

81 G. J. Warnock, *Contemporary Moral Philosophy*, p. 62.

82 Ibid., p. 68.

83 References to Murdoch are to *The Sovereignty of Good*.

84 References to MacIntyre are to *After Virtue*.

85 References to Rawls are to *A Theory of Justice*.

86 Naturalists like MacIntyre, with their stress on practice and tradition, would count as 'anthropological' ones, to recall the distinction made earlier in this section. One should note the recent revival, in the shape of sociobiology, of a form of evolutionary and 'scientific' moral naturalism. 'It simply has to matter that we are modified monkeys', writes one enthusiast for this updated version of the kind of evolutionary ethics discussed in ch. 8, sect. 4. Michael Ruse, 'The significance of evolution', p. 43.

87 References to Habermas are to *The Philosophical Discourse of Modernity*.

88 References to Heidegger in this section are to his *Basic Writings* (BW); *Nietzsche*, vol. 4 (N4); and *On the Way to Language* (WL).

89 References to Lyotard are to *The Postmodern Condition*.

90 Richard Rorty, *Contingency, Irony, and Solidarity*, p. 87.

91 Fredric Jameson, 'Postmodernism, or the cultural logic of capitalism'.

92 David Harvey, *The Condition of Postmodernity*, p. 30.

93   References to Derrida are to *Writing and Difference* (WD); *Of Grammatology* (G); *Positions* (P); *Margins of Philosophy* (MP); and *Acts of Literature* (AL).

94   From *The Birth of Tragedy*, quoted by Habermas, *The Philosophical Discourse of Modernity*, p. 87.

95   References to Foucault are to *The Foucault Reader* (FR); *The Archaeology of Knowledge* (AK); *Discipline and Punish* (DP); *The History of Sexuality, Vol. I* (HS); *The Order of Things* (OT); and 'The subject and power' (SP).

96   On these similarities, see Samuel C. Wheeler III, 'Indeterminacy of French interpretation: Derrida and Davidson', and Richard Rorty, *Essays on Heidegger and Others*.

97   Quoted in Charles Spinosa, 'Derrida and Heidegger: iterability and *Ereignis*', p. 284.

98   Wittgenstein, *On Certainty*, §559. On the relation between the two thinkers, see Henry Staten, *Wittgenstein and Derrida*.

99   I borrow the phrase from the subtitle of Robert C. Solomon, *Continental Philosophy Since 1750*.

100 James C. Edwards, *The Authority of Language*, p. 57.

101 Quoted in Richard Kearney, *Modern Movements in European Philosophy*, p. 305.

102 Vincent Descombes, *Modern French Philosophy*, p. 105.

103 See Claude Lévi-Strauss, *Structural Anthropology*, vol. I.

104 See Roland Barthes, *S/Z*.

105 Rorty, *Essays on Heidegger and Others*, p. 110. See also, Cooper, 'Analytical and continental philosophy'.

106 Richard Rorty, *Objectivity, Relativism, and Truth*, p. 39.

107 Jean Baudrillard, *Selected Writings*, pp. 166ff.

108 See Michael E. Zimmerman, *Heidegger's Confrontation with Modernity*.

109 Stephen Mulhall, *On Being in the World*, p. 201.

• BIBLIOGRAPHY •

Abduh, Muhammad. *The Theology of Unity*, trans. I. Musaad and K. Cragg (London: Allen & Unwin, 1966).

Abe, Masao. *Zen and Western Thought* (Honolulu: University of Hawaii Press, 1985).

Ackrill, J. L. 'Aristotle on *eudaimonia*', in A. Rorty (ed.), *Essays on Aristotle's Ethics*, 1980.

—— (ed.). *A New Aristotle Reader* (Oxford: Clarendon Press, 1987).

Adorno, Theodor and Horkheimer, Max. *Dialectic of Enlightenment*, trans. J. Cumming (London: Verso, 1973).

Aeschylus. *The Oresteian Trilogy*, trans. P. Vellacott (Harmondsworth: Penguin, 1959).

Afghānī, *See under* Keddie, Nikki R.

Ahmed, Akbar S. *Postmodernism and Islam: Predicament and Promise* (London: Routledge, 1992).

Allinson, Robert E. 'An overview of the Chinese mind', in R. E. Allinson (ed.), *Understanding the Chinese Mind*, 1989.

—— (ed.). *Understanding the Chinese Mind: The Philosophical Roots* (Hong Kong: Oxford University Press, 1989).

Allison, David B. (ed.). *The New Nietzsche* (Cambridge, Mass.: MIT Press, 1986).

Alston, A. J. (trans. and ed.). *A Samkara Source-Book*, vol. 5 (London: Shanti Sadan, 1989).

Althusser, Louis. *For Marx*, trans. B. Brewster (Harmondsworth: Penguin, 1969).

Anacker, S. (trans.). *Seven Works of Vasubandhu: The Buddhist Psychological Doctor* (Delhi: Motilal Banarsidass, 1986).

Anscombe, G. E. M. and Geach, P. T. *Three Philosophers: Aristotle, Aquinas, Frege* (Oxford: Blackwell, 1961).

Appiah, Kwame Anthony. *In My Father's House: Africa in the Philosophy of Culture* (London: Methuen, 1992).

Aquinas, St Thomas. *Philosophical Texts*, trans. T. Gilby (Oxford: Oxford University Press, 1956).

——. *Summa Theologiae*, 60 vols, various translators (London: Eyre & Spottiswood, 1963–75).

——. *On Politics and Ethics*, ed. P. E. Sigmund (New York: Norton, 1988).

Arberry, A. J. *Sufism: An Account of the Mystics of Islam* (London: Allen & Unwin, 1950).

Aristotle. *Works of Aristotle* (complete translation), ed. J. Barnes (Princeton: Princeton University Press, 1984). *See also under* Ackrill, J. L., 1987.

Armstrong, A. H. *Plotinus* (London: Allen & Unwin, 1953).

Arnold, Matthew. *Essays in Literary Criticism* (New York: Home Library, 1902).

Augustine, St. *Confessions*, trans. R. S. Pine-Coffin (Harmondsworth: Penguin, 1981).

——. *The City of God*, trans. H. Bettenson (Harmondsworth: Penguin, 1984).

Aurobindo. *See under* Ghose.

Averroes. 'The decisive treatise determining the nature of the connection between religion and philosophy', and 'Long Commentary on *De Anima*', in A. Hyman and J. Walsh (eds), *Philosophy in the Middle Ages*, 1974.

——. *Tahafut Al-Tahafut* (Incoherence of the Incoherence), trans. S. Van Den Bergh (London: Luzac, 1978).

——. *See also under* Genequand, C.

Ayer, A. J. *Man as a Subject for Science* (London: Athlone, 1964).

——. *Language, Truth and Logic* (London: Gollancz, 1967).

——. *Russell* (London: Fontana, 1972).

——. *Hume*, in *The British Empiricists* (Oxford: Oxford University Press, 1992).

Baba, Bangali (trans.). *The Yogasūtra of Patañjali* (Delhi: Motilal Banarsidass, 1976).

Bacon, Francis. *The New Organon and Related Writings* (Indianapolis: Bobbs-Merrill, 1960).

Barnes, Jonathan. *The Presocratic Philosophers* (London: Routledge & Kegan Paul, 1982).

——. *Aristotle* (Oxford: Oxford University Press, 1986).

Barthes, Roland. *S/Z*, trans. R. Miller (London: Cape, 1975).

Bary, Wm. Theodore de. *The Liberal Tradition in China* (Hong Kong: Chinese University Press, 1983).

——. Chan, Wing-Tsit and Watson, Burton (eds). *Sources of Chinese Tradition* (New York: Columbia University Press, 1960).

Baskin, Wade (ed.). *Classics in Chinese Philosophy* (New Jersey: Helix, 1984).

Baudrillard, Jean. *Selected Writings* (Cambridge: Polity, 1988).

Beauvoir, Simone de. *The Second Sex*, trans. H. Parshley (London: New English Library, 1962).

——. *Force of Circumstance*, trans. R. Howard (Harmondsworth: Penguin, 1987).

Bennett, Jonathan. *Kant's Analytic* (Cambridge: Cambridge University Press, 1966).

——. *A Study in Spinoza's* Ethics (Cambridge: Cambridge University Press, 1984).

Bergson, Henri. *Creative Evolution*, trans. A. Mitchell (London: Macmillan, 1911).

——. *The Two Sources of Morality and Religion*, trans. R. Audra and C. Brereton (London: Macmillan, 1935).

——. *An Introduction to Metaphysics*, trans. T. Hulme (New York: Liberal Arts, 1949).

Berkeley, George. *The Works of George Berkeley*, 9 vols (London: Nelson, 1948).

——. *Philosophical Writings* (London: Nelson, 1952).

Berlin, Isaiah. *Karl Marx: The Man and His Environment* (Oxford: Oxford University Press, 1939).

——. *Vico and Herder* (London: Hogarth, 1980).

Bhagavad Gita, The. trans. J. Mascaro (Harmondsworth: Penguin, 1976).

Bhattacharyya, Krishnachandra. *Studies in Philosophy* (Delhi: Motilal Banarsidass, 1983).

Bishop, Donald H. 'K'ang Yu-Wei' and 'Mao Tse-Tung and the Chinese Tradition', in D. H. Bishop (ed.), *Chinese Thought*.

——. (ed.) *Chinese Thought: An Introduction* (Delhi: Motilal Banarsidass, 1985).

Bowes, Pratima. 'Mysticism in the *Upaniṣads* and in Śaṅkara's Vedānta', in K. Werner (ed.), *The Yogi and The Mystic*.

Bowie, Andrew. *Aesthetics and Subjectivity: From Kant to Nietzsche* (Manchester: Manchester University Press, 1990).

Bowler, Peter J. *Charles Darwin: The Man and His Influence* (Oxford: Blackwell, 1990).

Bradley, F. H. *The Principles of Logic* (Oxford: Oxford University Press, 1928).

——. *Ethical Studies* (Oxford: Oxford University Press, 1962).

——. *Appearance and Reality: A Metaphysical Essay* (Oxford: Oxford University Press, 1969).

Brooke, John Hedley. *Science and Religion: Some Historical Perspectives* (Cambridge: Cambridge University Press, 1991).

Buber, Martin. *I and Thou*, trans. R. Gregor Smith (Edinburgh: Clark, 1937).

Burckhardt, Jacob. *The Civilization of the Renaissance*, trans. S. Middlemore (Oxford: Phaidon, 1945).

——. *History of Greek Culture*, trans. P. Hilty (London: Constable, 1963).

Burnyeat, Myles. 'Can the sceptic live his scepticism?', in M. Schofield, M. Burnyeat and J. Barnes (eds), *Doubt and Dogmatism*.

——. (ed.). *The Skeptical Tradition* (Berkeley: University of California Press, 1983).

Burrell, Roy. *The Greeks* (Oxford: Oxford University Press, 1989).

Burrow, J. W. *Evolution and Society: A Study in Victorian Social Theory* (Cambridge: Cambridge University Press, 1966).

Burton, Richard (trans.). *The Illustrated Kama-Sūtra, Ananga-Ranga, Perfumed Garden* (London: Hamlyn, 1991).

Cabral, Amilcar. *Return to the Source: Selected Speeches* (New York: Monthly Review, 1973).

Callinicos, Alex. *Marxism and Philosophy* (Oxford: Oxford University Press, 1985).

Candrakīrti. *See under* Stcherbatsky, T.

Canfield, John V. 'Wittgenstein and Zen', *Philosophy*, vol. 50, 1975.

Canfora, Luciano. *The Vanished Library* (London: Vintage, 1991).

Carnap, Rudolf. *Philosophy and Logical Syntax* (London: Kegan Paul, 1935).

——. 'Protocol statements and the formal mode of speech', in O. Hanfling (ed.), *Essential Readings in Logical Positivism*.

Carr, Brian and Mahalingam, Indira (eds), *Encyclopedia of Asian Philosophy* (London: Routledge, 1995).

Césaire, Aimé. *Discourse on Colonialism* (New York: Monthly Review Press, 1972).

Chadwick, Henry. *Augustine* (Oxford: Oxford University Press, 1986).

Chakraborty, N. B. 'Vivekananda and practical Vedānta', in S. N. Chattopadhyay (ed.), *Culture and Quest: Vivekananda Volume* (Calcutta: ISISAR, 1993).

Chan, Wing-Tsit (ed.). *A Source Book in Chinese Philosophy* (Princeton: Princeton University Press, 1963).

——. (ed.). *Chu Hsi and Neo-Confucianism* (Honolulu: University of Hawaii Press, 1986).

Chuang Tzu. *See under* Wieger, L.

Chung-Ying Cheng. 'Chinese metaphysics as non-metaphysics: Confucian and Daoist insights into the nature of reality', in R. E. Allinson (ed.), *Understanding the Chinese Mind*.

Churchland, Paul M. *Matter and Consciousness: A Contemporary Introduction to the Philosophy of Mind* (Cambridge, Mass.: MIT Press, 1988).

Clark, Stephen R. L. *God's World and the Great Awakening: Limits and Renewals*, vol. 3 (Oxford: Clarendon Press, 1991).

Cohen, G. A. *Karl Marx's Theory of History: A Defense* (Oxford: Clarendon Press, 1978).

Collins, Steven. *Selfless Persons: Imagery and Thought in Theravāda Buddhism* (Cambridge: Cambridge University Press, 1982).

Comte, Auguste. *The Positive Philosophy of Auguste Comte*, trans. H. Martineau (London: Bell, 1896).

Condorcet, Antoine-Nicolas de. *Sketch for a Historical Picture of the Progress of the Human Mind*, trans. J. Barraclough (London: Wiedenfeld & Nicolson, 1955).

Confucius. *The Analects*, trans. D. C. Lau (Harmondsworth: Penguin, 1979).

Coomaraswamy, Ananda K. *The Dance of Śiva: Essays on Indian Art and Culture* (New York: Dover, 1985).

Cooper, David E. 'Analytical and continental philosophy', *Proceedings of the Aristotelian Society*, vol. 94, 1993.

——. 'Is Daoism green?', *Asian Philosophy*, vol. 5, 1994.

——. (ed.). *A Companion to Aesthetics* (Oxford: Blackwell, 1992).

Copenhaver, Brian P. and Schmitt, Charles B. *Renaissance Philosophy* (Oxford: Oxford University Press, 1992).

Copleston, Frederick. *A History of Philosophy*, 7 vols (New York: Image, 1985).

Cornford, F. M. *Principium Sapientiae* (Cambridge: Cambridge University Press, 1952).

——. *From Religion to Philosophy* (New York: Harper & Row, 1957).

Cottingham, John. *The Rationalists* (Oxford: Oxford University Press, 1990).

Craig, Edward. *The Mind of God and the Works of Man* (Oxford: Clarendon Press, 1987).

Crombie, I. M. *An Examination of Plato's Doctrines*, 2 vols (London: Routledge & Kegan Paul, 1962).

Curley, E. M. *Spinoza's Metaphysics: An Essay in Interpretation* (Cambridge, Mass.: Harvard University Press, 1969).

Cusanus, Nicolas. *Of Learned Ignorance*, trans. G. Heron (London: Routledge & Kegan Paul, 1954).

Danto, Arthur C. *Sartre* (London: Fontana, 1975).

——. *Mysticism and Morality: Oriental Thought and Moral Philosophy* (Harmondsworth: Penguin, 1976).

Dasgupta, Surendranath. *A History of Indian Philosophy*, 5 vols (Delhi: Motilal Banarsidass, 1988).

Davidson, Basil et al. (eds). *Southern Africa: The New Politics of Revolution* (Harmondsworth: Penguin, 1976).

Davidson, Donald. *Inquiries into Truth and Interpretation* (Oxford: Clarendon Press, 1984).

Dawson, Raymond. *Confucius* (Oxford: Oxford University Press, 1981).

Deleuze, Gilles. *Kant's Critical Philosophy: The Doctrine of the Faculties*, trans. H. Tomlinson and B. Habberjam (London: Athlone, 1984).

Dennett, Daniel. *Brainstorms* (Montgomery, Vermont: Bradford, 1978).

Derrida, Jacques. *Of Grammatology*, trans. G. Spivak (Baltimore: Johns Hopkins University Press, 1976).

——. *Writing and Difference*, trans. A. Bass (London: Routledge & Kegan Paul, 1978).

——. *Positions*, trans. A. Bass (Chicago: University of Chicago Press, 1981).

——. *Margins of Philosophy*, trans. A. Bass (Chicago: University of Chicago Press, 1982).

——. *Acts of Literature* (London: Routledge, 1992).

Descartes, René. *Descartes: Philosophical Letters*, trans. A. Kenny (Oxford: Oxford University Press, 1970).

——. *Selected Philosophical Writings*, trans. J. Cottingham, R. Stoothoff, and D. Murdoch (Cambridge: Cambridge University Press, 1988).

Descombes, Vincent. *Modern French Philosophy*, trans. L. Scott-Fox and J. Harding (Cambridge: Cambridge University Press, 1980).

Deussen, Paul. *Outlines of Indian Philosophy* (Delhi: ESS Publications, 1976).

Dewey, John. *Democracy and Education* (New York: Free Press, 1966).

DeWoskin, Kenneth. 'Chinese and Japanese aesthetics', in D. E. Cooper (ed.), *A Companion to Aesthetics*.

Dhammapada, The. trans. J. Mascaro (Harmondsworth: Penguin, 1986).

Diamond Sūtra, The – With Supplemental Texts from the Final Teachings of the Buddha (New York: Concord Grove Press, 1983).

Dilthey, Wilhelm. *Selected Writings*, trans. H. Rickman (Cambridge: Cambridge University Press, 1976).

Dōgen Zenji. *Shobogenzo: The Eye and Treasury of the True Law*, vol. I, trans. K. Nishiyama and J. Stevens (Tokyo: Nakayama Shobo, 1975).

Dover, Kenneth J. *Greek Popular Morality in the Time of Plato and Aristotle* (Oxford: Oxford University Press, 1974).

Dreyfus, Hubert L. *Being-in-the-World: A Commentary on Heidegger's Being and Time, Division I* (Cambridge, Mass.: MIT Press, 1991).

Dummett, Michael. *Truth and Other Enigmas* (London: Duckworth, 1978).

——. *Origins of Analytical Philosophy* (London: Duckworth, 1993).

Dunn, J. G. D. *Christology in the Making* (London: SCM Press, 1980).

Eckermann, J. P. *Gespräche mit Goethe* (Wiesbaden: Tempel, n.d.).

Eckhart, Meister. *Meister Eckhart*, 2 vols, trans. C. de B. Evans (London: Watkins, 1924 and 1931). *See also under* Fleming, U.

Eco, Umberto. *Foucault's Pendulum* (London: Picador, 1990).

Edwards, James C. *The Authority of Language: Heidegger, Wittgenstein and the Threat of Philosophical Nihilism* (Tampa: University of South Florida Press, 1990).

Edwards, Paul (ed.). *The Encyclopedia of Philosophy*, 8 vols (New York: Macmillan and Free Press, 1967).

Eliade, Mircea. *Yoga: Immortality and Freedom* (London: Arkana, 1989).

Emmett, Dorothy. 'Whitehead, Alfred North', in P. Edwards (ed.), *The Encyclopedia of Philosophy*.

Engelmann, Paul (ed.). *Letters from Ludwig Wittgenstein with a Memoir*, trans. L. Furtmuller (Oxford: Blackwell, 1967).

Engels, Friedrich. *See under* Marx, Karl.

Epicurus. *See under* B. Inwood and L. Gerson (eds).

Epstein, Isidore. *Judaism* (Harmondsworth: Penguin, 1959).

Erasmus, Desiderius. *Praise of Folly*, in E. Rummel (ed.), *The Erasmus Reader* (Toronto: Toronto University Press, 1990).

Euripides. *The Bacchae and Other Plays*, trans. P. Vellacott (Harmondsworth: Penguin, 1973).

Fakhry, Majid. *A History of Islamic Philosophy* (New York: Columbia University Press, 1970).

Fanon, Frantz. *The Wretched of the Earth*, trans. C. Farrington (New York: Grove, 1968).

Feuerbach, Ludwig. *The Essence of Christianity*, trans. G. Eliot (New York: Harper & Row, 1957).

Fichte, J. G. *Science of Knowledge (Wissenschaftslehre): with First and Second Introductions*, trans. P. Heath and J. Lachs (New York: Appleton-Century-Crofts, 1970).

——. *Die Wissenschaftslehre in ihrem allgemeinen Umriss (1810)* (Frankfurt: Klostermann, 1976).

Field, Hartry. 'Tarski's theory of truth', *Journal of Philosophy*, vol. 69, 1972.

Finkielkraut, Alain. *The Undoing of Thought*, trans. D. O'Keeffe (London: Claridge, 1988).

Finley, M. I. (ed.). *The Legacy of Greece: A New Appraisal* (Oxford: Clarendon Press, 1981).

Fleming, Ursula (ed.). *Meister Eckhart: The Man from whom God Hid Nothing* (London: Collins, 1988).

Føllesdal, Dagfinn. 'Husserl's notion of noema', in H. L. Dreyfus (ed.), *Husserl, Intentionality and Cognitive Science* (Cambridge, Mass.: MIT Press, 1982).

Foucault, Michel. *The Archaeology of Knowledge*, trans. A. Sheridan (New York: Harper, 1972).

——. *Discipline and Punish: The Birth of the Prison*, trans. A. Sheridan (New York: Random House, 1979).

——. *The Order of Things: An Archaeology of the Human Sciences*, trans. not given (London: Tavistock, 1980).

——. *Power/Knowledge: Selected Interviews and Other Writings 1972–7*, trans. C. Gordon (London: Harvester, 1980).

——. *The History of Sexuality*, vol. I, trans. R. Hurley (Harmondsworth: Penguin, 1981).

——. 'The subject and power', in H. Dreyfus and P. Rabinow, *Michel Foucault: Beyond Structuralism and Hermeneutics* (Brighton: Harvester, 1982).

Frede, Michael. *Essays in Ancient Philosophy* (Oxford: Clarendon Press, 1987).

Frege, Gottlob. *The Philosophical Writings of Gottlob Frege*, trans. P. Geach and M. Black (Oxford: Blackwell, 1966).

——. *The Foundations of Arithmetic*, trans. J. Austin (Oxford: Blackwell, 1974).

Fung Yu-Lan. *A History of Chinese Philosophy*, 2 vols, trans. D. Bodde (Princeton: Princeton University Press, 1952).

Furley, D. J. and Allen, R. E. (eds). *Studies in Presocratic Philosophy*, vol. I (London: Routledge & Kegan Paul, 1970).

Gadamer, Hans-Georg. *Truth and Method*, trans. W. Glen-Doepel (London: Sheed & Ward, 1979).

Galileo Galilei. *Dialogue Concerning the Two Chief World Systems*, trans. S. Drake (Berkeley: University of California Press, 1953).

Gandhi, M. K. *An Autobiography: or, The Story of My Experiments with Truth*, trans. M. Desai (Ahmedabad: Navajivan, 1927).

——. *Selections from Gandhi* (Ahmedabad: Navajivan, 1957).

——. *The Sayings of Mahātma Gandhi* (Singapore: Brash, 1984).

Gardiner, Patrick. *Schopenhauer* (Harmondsworth: Penguin, 1963).

——. *Kierkegaard* (Oxford: Oxford University Press, 1988).

Geach, Peter. 'Aquinas', in G. E. M. Anscombe and P. T. Geach, *Three Philosophers* 1961.

——. 'Nominalism', in A. Kenny (ed.), *Aquinas*, 1969.

Genequand, Charles (trans.). *Ibn Rushd's Metaphysics: A Translation with Introduction of Ibn Rushd's Commentary on Aristotle's Metaphysics, Book Lam* (Leiden: Brill, 1984).

German, Terence J. *Hamann on Language and Religion* (Oxford: Oxford University Press, 1981).

Gettier, Edmund L. 'Is justified true belief knowledge?', *Analysis*, vol. 23, 1963.

Ghazāli, Abu Hamid Al-. *Tahafut Al-Falasifah* (Incoherence of the Philosophers), trans. S. A. Kamali (Lahore: Pakistan Philosophical Congress, 1963).

——. *Mishkat Al-Anwar* (The Niche for Lights), trans. W. Gairdner, in *Four Sufi Classics* (London: Octagon, 1980).

Ghose, Aurobindo. *The Life Divine* (Pondicherry: Sri Aurobindo Ashram, 1955).

Gibb, H. A. R. *Islam: A Historical Survey* (Oxford: Oxford University Press, 1987).

Gilson, Etienne. *The Mystical Theology of Saint Bernard*, trans. A. Downes (London: Sheed & Ward, 1940).

——. *History of Christian Philosophy in the Middle Ages* (London: Sheed & Ward, 1955).

Goodman, L. E. 'Did al-Ghazāli deny causality?', *Studia Islamica*, vol. 47, pp. 83–120, 1978.

Gosling, J. C. B. *Plato* (London: Routledge & Kegan Paul, 1973).

Gower, Barry (ed.). *Logical Positivism in Perspective: Essays on Language, Truth and Logic* (London: Croom Helm, 1987).

Graham, A. C. 'The place of reason in the Chinese philosophical tradition', in R. Dawson (ed.), *The Legacy of China* (Oxford: Clarendon Press, 1964).

——. *Chuang-tzu: The Inner Chapters* (London: Allen & Unwin, 1981).

——. 'What was new in the Ch'eng-Chu theory of human nature?', in Wing-Tsit Chan (ed.), *Chu-Hsi and Neo-Confucianism*.

Green, Deidre. 'Living between the worlds: *bhakti* poetry and the Carmelite mystics', in K. Werner (ed.), *The Yogi and the Mystic*.

Green, T. H. *Prologomena to Ethics* (Oxford: Clarendon Press, 1890).

Guyer, Paul (ed.). *The Cambridge Companion to Kant* (Cambridge: Cambridge University Press, 1992).

Gyekye, Kwame. 'Technology and culture in a developing country', in R. Fellows (ed.), *Philosophy and Technology* (Cambridge: Cambridge University Press, 1995).

Habermas, Jürgen. *The Philosophical Discourse of Modernity*, trans. F. Lawrence (Cambridge: Polity, 1987).

Hakuin. *See under* Yampolsky, P. B.

Haldane, John. 'Aquinas on sense-perception', *Philosophical Review*, vol. XCII, no. 2, 1983.

——. 'Medieval and renaissance ethics', in P. Singer (ed.), *A Companion to Ethics*.

Hamann, J. G. *See under* German, Terence J.

Hamlyn, D. W. *A History of Western Philosophy* (Harmondsworth: Penguin, 1987).

Hammond, M., Howarth, J. and Keat, R. *Understanding Phenomenology* (Oxford: Blackwell, 1991).

Hanfling, Oswald (ed.). *Essential Readings in Logical Positivism* (Oxford: Blackwell, 1981).

Hannay, Alistair. *Kierkegaard* (London: Routledge, 1982).

Hansen, Chad. 'Language in heart-mind', in R. E. Allinson (ed.), *Understanding the Chinese Mind*.

——. *A Daoist Theory of Chinese Thought: A Philosophical Interpretation* (Oxford: Oxford University Press, 1992).

Happold, F. C. (ed.). *Mysticism: A Study and an Anthology* (Harmondsworth: Penguin, 1970).

Hare, R. M. *The Language of Morals* (Oxford: Oxford University Press, 1952).

——. *Plato* (Oxford: Oxford University Press, 1982).

Harvey, David. *The Condition of Postmodernity: An Enquiry into the Origins of Cultural Change* (Oxford: Blackwell, 1989).

Harvey, Peter. *An Introduction to Buddhism* (Cambridge: Cambridge University Press, 1990).

Havens, Thomas R. H. *Nishi Amane and Modern Japanese Thought* (Princeton: Princeton University Press, 1970).

Hay, Stephen (ed.). *Sources of Indian Tradition*, vol. 2 (New York: Columbia University Press, 1988).

Hegel, G. W. F. *The Philosophy of History*, trans. J. Sibree (New York: Dover, 1956).

——. *Philosophy of Right*, trans. T. Knox (Oxford: Clarendon Press, 1962).

——. *Philosophy of Mind*, trans. W. Wallace (Oxford: Clarendon Press, 1971).

——. *Phenomenology of Spirit*, trans. A. V. Miller (Oxford: Oxford University Press, 1977).

——. *Introduction to the Lectures on the History of Philosophy*, trans. T. M. Knox and A. V. Miller (Oxford: Clarendon Press, 1987).

——. *The Encyclopaedia Logic*, trans. T. Geraets, W. Suchting and H. Harris (Indianapolis: Hackett, 1991).

Heidegger, Martin. *On The Way To Language*, trans. P. Hertz (New York: Harper & Row, 1971).

——. *Basic Writings*, trans. D. F. Krell (London: Routledge & Kegan Paul, 1978).

——. *Being and Time*, trans. J. Macquarrie and E. Robinson (Oxford: Blackwell, 1980).

——. *The Basic Problems of Phenomenology*, trans. A. Hofstadter (Bloomington: Indiana University Press, 1982).

——. *Nietzsche: vol. 4, Nihilism*, trans. D. F. Krell (San Francisco: Harper & Row, 1982).

Herder, J. G. *On Social and Political Culture*, trans. and ed. F. M. Barnard (Cambridge: Cambridge University Press, 1969).

Herf, Jeffrey. *Reactionary Modernism: Technology, Culture and Politics in Weimar and the Third Reich* (Cambridge: Cambridge University Press, 1984).

Herrigel, Eugen. *Zen in the Art of Archery* (Harmondsworth: Arkana, 1985).

Hiriyanna, M. *Essentials of Indian Philosophy* (London: Allen & Unwin, 1985).

Hobbes, Thomas. *The English Works of Thomas Hobbes*, 9 vols, ed. W. Molesworth (London: 1839–45).

——. *Leviathan* (Oxford: Blackwell, 1960).

Hodges, Michael P. *Transcendence and Wittgenstein's Tractatus* (Philadelphia: Temple, 1990).

Holbach, Paul Henri d'. *Système de la nature* (Hildesheim: Olms, 1966).

Hölderlin, Friedrich. *Gedichte: Hyperion* (Augsburg: Goldmann, 1981).

Homer. *The Iliad*, trans. E. V. Rieu (Harmondsworth: Penguin, 1961).

——. *The Odyssey*, trans. E. V. Rieu (Harmondsworth: Penguin, 1966).

Horton, Robin. 'African traditional thought and Western science', in M. F. D. Young (ed.), *Knowledge and Control: New Directions for the Sociology of Education* (London: Collier-Macmillan, 1971).

Hountondji, Paulin J. *African Philosophy: Myth and Reality*, trans. H. Evans (Bloomington: Indiana University Press, 1983).

——. 'African philosophy: myth and reality', in T. Serequeberhan (ed.), *African Philosophy*.

Hourani, Albert. *Arab Thought in the Liberal Age 1798–1939* (Cambridge: Cambridge University Press, 1983).

Hsu Sung-Peng. 'Hu Shih', in D. H. Bishop (ed.), *Chinese Thought*.

Hsun Tzu. *See under* Watson, B.

Hughes, E. R. (ed.). *Chinese Philosophy in Classical Times* (London: Dent, 1960).

Hui-Neng. *See under* Yampolsky, P. B.

Hume, David. *A Treatise of Human Nature* (Oxford: Clarendon Press, 1960).

——. *Essays: Moral, Literary and Political* (Oxford: Oxford University Press, 1965).

——. *An Enquiry Concerning Human Understanding* (Indianapolis: Hackett, 1977).

——. *Dialogues Concerning Natural Religion* (Indianapolis: Bobbs-Merrill, 1977).

Hume, R. E. (trans.). *The Thirteen Principal Upanishads* (Delhi: Oxford University Press, 1990).

Husserl, Edmund. *Cartesian Meditations*, trans. D. Cairns (The Hague: Nijhoff, 1960).

——. *Ideas: General Introduction to Pure Phenomenology*, trans. W. Boyce-Gibson (New York: Collier, 1962).

——. *The Crisis of European Sciences and Transcendental Phenomenology*, trans. D. Carr (Evanston: Northwestern University Press, 1970).

Hylton, Peter. *Russell, Idealism and the Emergence of Analytic Philosophy* (Oxford: Clarendon Press, 1990).

Hyman, A. and Walsh, J. (eds). *Philosophy in the Middle Ages: The Christian, Islamic and Jewish Traditions* (Indianapolis: Hackett, 1974).

Inwood, B. and Gerson, L. (eds). *Hellenistic Philosophy: Introductory Readings* (Indianapolis: Hackett, 1988).

Inwood, Michael. *A Hegel Dictionary* (Oxford: Blackwell, 1992).

Iqbāl, Muhammad. *The Reconstruction of Religious Thought in Islam* (Lahore: Kapur, 1930).

Irwin, Terence. *Classical Thought* (Oxford: Oxford University Press, 1989).

Īśvarakṛṣṇa. *See under* Sastri, S. S.

Jaeger, Werner. *Aristotle: Fundamentals of the History of his Development* (Oxford: Oxford University Press, 1934).

James, William. *The Writings of William James* (Chicago: University of Chicago Press, 1977).

Jameson, Fredric. 'Postmodernism, or the cultural logic of late capitalism', *New Left Review*, vol. 146, 1984.

Jami. *Salaman and Absal*, trans. E. Fitzgerald, in *Four Sufi Classics* (London: Octagon, 1980).

Jaspers, Karl. 'Philosophical autobiography', in P. Schilpp (ed.), *The Philosophy of Karl Jaspers* (Illinois: Open Court, 1957).

——. *Philosophy*, 3 vols, trans. E. Ashton (Chicago: Chicago University Press, 1969–71).

Kama-Sūtra, The. See under Burton, R.

Kant, Immanuel. *Lectures on Ethics*, trans. L. Infield (New York: Harper & Row, 1963).

——. *Critique of Pure Reason*, trans. N. Kemp Smith (London: Macmillan, 1964).

——. *Critique of Judgement*, trans. J. Bernard (New York: Hafner, 1966).

——. *Critique of Practical Reason*, trans. L. White Beck (Indianapolis: Bobbs-Merrill, 1976).

——. *Fundamental Principles of the Metaphysic of Morals*, trans. T. Abbott (New York: Prometheus, 1987).

——. *Political Writings*, trans. H. B. Nisbet (Cambridge: Cambridge University Press, 1991).

Katz, Steven T. 'Language, epistemology, and mysticism', in S. T. Katz (ed.), *Mysticism and Philosophical Analysis* (London: Sheldon, 1978).

Kearney, Richard. *Modern Movements in European Philosophy* (Manchester: Manchester University Press, 1986).

Keddie, Nikki R. *An Islamic Response to Imperialism: Political and Religious Writings of Sayyid Jamal al-Din al-Afghānī* (Berkeley: University of California Press, 1968).

Kenny, Anthony. *Descartes: A Study of his Philosophy* (New York: Random House, 1968).

—— (ed.). *Aquinas: A Collection of Critical Essays* (London: Macmillan, 1969).

——. *Aquinas* (Oxford: Oxford University Press, 1980).

Kierkegaard, Søren. *The Journals 1834–54*, trans. A. Dru (London: Fontana, 1958).

——. *Concluding Unscientific Postscript*, trans. D. Swenson and W. Lowrie (Princeton: Princeton University Press, 1968).

——. *Either/Or*, 2 vols, trans. W. Lowrie (Princeton: Princeton University Press, 1971).

——. *A Kierkegaard Anthology*, ed. R. Bretall (Princeton: Princeton University Press, 1973).

——. *Fear and Trembling*, trans. A. Hannay (Harmondsworth: Penguin, 1985).

——. *Philosophical Fragments: Johannes Climacus*, trans. H. and E. Hong (Princeton: Princeton University Press, 1985).

King, Sallie B. 'Two epistemological models for the interpretation of mysticism', *Journal of the American Academy of Religion*, vol. 56, 1988.

Kirk, G. S., Raven, J. E. and Schofield, M. *The Presocratic Philosophers* (Cambridge: Cambridge University Press, 1983).

Kirwan, Christopher. *Augustine* (London: Routledge, 1989).

Knowles, David. 'The historical context of the philosophical work of St. Thomas Aquinas', in A. Kenny (ed.), *Aquinas* 1969.

Kolakowski, Leszek. *Main Currents of Marxism*, 3 vols, trans. P. Falla (Oxford: Oxford University Press, 1981).

——. *Bergson* (Oxford: Oxford University Press, 1985).

Körner, S. *Kant* (Harmondsworth: Penguin, 1967).

Kripke, Saul. *Naming and Necessity* (Cambridge, Mass.: Harvard University Press, 1980).

Krishna, Daya. *Indian Philosophy: A Counter Perspective* (Delhi: Oxford University Press, 1991).

Kristeller, Paul Oskar. 'Humanism', in C. B. Schmitt and Q. Skinner (eds), *The Cambridge History of Renaissance Philosophy*.

Kuhn, Thomas. *The Structure of Scientific Revolutions* (Chicago: University of Chicago Press, 1962).

Lao Tzu. *Tao Te Ching*, trans. D. C. Lau (Harmondsworth: Penguin, 1985).

Law, David R. *Kierkegaard as Negative Theologian* (Oxford: Clarendon Press, 1993).

Leaman, Oliver. *An Introduction to Medieval Islamic Philosophy* (Cambridge: Cambridge University Press, 1985).

Lear, Jonathan. *Aristotle: The Desire to Understand* (Cambridge: Cambridge University Press, 1988).

Leibniz, Gottfried Wilhelm. *Basic Writings*, trans. G. Montgomery (Illinois: Open Court, 1962).

——. *Philosophical Writings*, ed. G. Parkinson (London: Dent, 1990).

Lévi-Strauss, Claude. *Structural Anthropology*, vol. I, trans. C. Jacobsen and C. Grundfest (London: Allen Lane, 1968).

Lichtheim, George. *Europe in the Twentieth Century* (London: Cardinal, 1974).

Lin Yutang. *My Country and Its People* (London: Heinemann, 1936).

Lipner, Julius. *The Face of Truth: A Study of Meaning and Metaphysics in the Vedantic Theology of Rāmānuja* (Albany: State University of New York Press, 1986).

Locke, John. *An Essay Concerning Human Understanding* (London: Dent, 1961).

———. *Two Treatises of Government* (Cambridge: Cambridge University Press, 1967).

Long, A. A. *Hellenistic Philosophy: Stoics, Epicureans, Sceptics* (London: Duckworth, 1986).

——— and Sedley, D. N. (eds). *The Hellenistic Philosophers*, vol. I (Cambridge: Cambridge University Press, 1987).

Lovejoy, Arthur O. *The Great Chain of Being* (Cambridge, Mass.: Harvard University Press, 1964).

Lowe, Victor. 'The development of Whitehead's philosophy', in P. Schilpp (ed.), *The Philosophy of Alfred North Whitehead*, 1941.

Lucretius. *On the Nature of the Universe*, trans. R. Latham (Harmondsworth: Penguin, 1986).

Lycan, William (ed.). *Mind and Cognition: A Reader* (Oxford: Blackwell, 1990).

Lyotard, Jean-François. *The Postmodern Condition: A Report on Knowledge*, trans. G. Bennington and B. Massumi (Manchester: Manchester University Press, 1986).

McGinn, Colin. *Wittgenstein on Meaning: An Interpretation and Evaluation* (Oxford: Blackwell, 1984).

Machiavelli, Niccolo. *The Prince*, trans. W. Marriott (London: Dent, 1960).

MacIntyre, Alasdair. *A Short History of Ethics* (New York: Macmillan, 1966).

———. *After Virtue: A Study in Moral Theory* (London: Duckworth, 1982).

Maimonides, Moses. *Guide of the Perplexed*, trans. S. Pines (Chicago: University of Chicago Press, 1963).

Malebranche, Nicolas. *The Search After Truth*, trans. T. Lennon and P. Olscamp (Columbus: Ohio State University Press, 1980).

Mao Tse-Tung. *Selected Works*, 4 vols (New York: International Publishers, 1954–6).

Marcel, Gabriel. *Being and Having*, trans. K. Farrer (London: Dacre, 1949).

Marcus Aurelius. *The Meditations*, trans. J. Collier (London: Walter Scott, n.d.).

Marcuse, Herbert. *Reason and Revolution* (New York: Humanities, 1955).

Maroldo, John C. 'Contemporary Japanese philosophy', in B. Carr and I. Mahalingam (eds), *Encyclopedia of Asian Philosophy*, 1995.

Martin, C. B. and Armstrong, D. M. (eds). *Locke and Berkeley: A Collection of Critical Essays* (London: Macmillan, n.d.).

Marx, Karl. *The Portable Karl Marx*, trans. and ed. E. Kamenka (Harmondsworth: Penguin, 1983).

——— and Engels, Friedrich. *Selected Works*, 2 vols (Moscow: Foreign Languages Publishing House, 1962).

Matilal, B. K. *Logic, Language and Reality: Indian Philosophy and Contemporary Issues* (Delhi: Motilal Banarsidass, 1985).

———. *Perception: An Essay on Classical Indian Theories of Knowledge* (Oxford: Clarendon Press, 1986).

Matthiessen, Peter. *The Snow Leopard* (Harmondsworth: Penguin, 1978).

———. *The Tree Where Man Was Born* (London: Picador, 1984).

Mays, Wolfe. *The Philosophy of Whitehead* (London: Allen & Unwin, 1959).

Mbiti, John. *African Religions and Philosophy* (New York: Doubleday, 1970).

Mencius. *Mencius*, trans. D. C. Lau (Harmondsworth: Penguin, 1970).

Merleau-Ponty, Maurice. *Phenomenology of Perception*, trans. C. Smith (London: Routledge & Kegan Paul, 1981).

Michael, Franz. *China Through the Ages: History of a Civilization* (Colorado: Westview Press, 1986).

Mill, J. S. *A System of Logic* (London: Longmans & Green, 1886).

——. *Utilitarianism and On Liberty* (London: Fontana, 1962).

——. *An Examination of Sir William Hamilton's Philosophy* (Toronto: University of Toronto Press, 1979).

Mo Tzu. *See under* Watson, B.

Mohanty, Jitendra Nath. *Reason and Tradition in Indian Thought: An Essay on the Nature of Indian Philosophical Thinking* (Oxford: Clarendon Press, 1992).

Monk, Ray. *Ludwig Wittgenstein: The Duty to Genius* (London: Cape, 1990).

Montaigne, Michel de. *An Apology for Raymond Sebond*, trans. M. Screech (Harmondsworth: Penguin, 1987).

Moore, Charles A. (ed.). *The Japanese Mind: Essentials of Japanese Philosophy and Culture* (Honolulu: University of Hawaii Press, 1967).

Moore, G. E. *Principia Ethica* (Cambridge: Cambridge University Press, 1989).

Mortimer, Edward. *Faith and Power: The Politics of Islam* (London: Faber & Faber, 1982).

Mulhall, Stephen. *On Being in the World: Wittgenstein and Heidegger on Seeing Aspects* (London: Routledge, 1990).

Murdoch, Iris. *The Sovereignty of Good* (London: Routledge & Kegan Paul, 1985).

Nāgārjuna. *See Under* Stcherbatsky, T.

Nagel, Thomas. *Mortal Questions* (Cambridge: Cambridge University Press, 1979).

Nakamura Hajime. 'Basic features of the legal, political and economic thought of Japan', in C. Moore (ed.), *The Japanese Mind*.

Narayan, R. K. *Mr. Samprath – The Printer of Malgudi* (London: Mandarin, 1990).

Nasr, Seyyed Hossein. *Sūfi Essays* (London: Allen & Unwin, 1972).

Nauman, St. Elmo. *Dictionary of Asian Philosophies* (London: Routledge, 1979).

Needham, Joseph. *Science and Civilization in China, vol. 2: History of Scientific Thought* (Cambridge: Cambridge University Press, 1956).

Nehamas, Alexander. *Nietzsche: Life as Literature* (Cambridge, Mass.: Harvard University Press, 1985).

Nietzsche, Friedrich. *The Portable Nietzsche*, trans. W. Kaufmann (New York: Viking, 1954).

——. *Basic Writings of Nietzsche*, trans. W. Kaufmann (New York: Modern Library, 1968).

——. *The Will to Power*, trans. W. Kaufmann and R. Hollingdale (New York: Vintage, 1968).

——. *Werke*, 3 vols (Munich: Hanser, 1969).

——. *Daybreak*, trans. R. Hollingdale (Cambridge: Cambridge University Press, 1982).

——. *Untimely Meditations*, trans. R. Hollingdale (Cambridge: Cambridge University Press, 1985).

Nishida Kitarō. 'The problem of Japanese culture', in Ryusaku Tsunoda et al. (eds), *Sources of Japanese Tradition*, 1967.

——. *Fundamental Problems of Philosophy: The World of Action and The Dialectical World*, trans. D. Dilworth (Tokyo: Sophia University Press, 1970).

——. *Last Writings: Nothingness and the Religious Worldview*, trans. D. Dilworth (Honolulu: University of Hawaii Press, 1987).

Nishitani Keiji. 'Reflections on two addresses by Martin Heidegger', in G. Parkes (ed.), *Heidegger and Asian Thought*.

Northrop, F. S. C. 'Whitehead's philosophy of science', in P. Schilpp (ed.), *The Philosophy of Alfred North Whitehead*, 1941.

Nussbaum, Martha C. *The Fragility of Goodness: Luck and Ethics in Greek Tragedy and Philosophy* (Cambridge: Cambridge University Press, 1986).

O'Hear, Anthony. *What Philosophy Is* (Harmondsworth: Penguin, 1985).

Onyewuenyi, Innocent. 'Is there an African philosophy?', in T. Serequeberhan (ed.), *African Philosophy*.

Ortega y Gasset, José. *History as a System and Other Essays towards a Philosophy of History*, trans. H. Weyl et al. (New York: Norton, 1962).

Oruka, Henry Odera. 'Sagacity in African philosophy', in T. Serequeberhan (ed.), *African Philosophy*.

Ott, Hugo. *Martin Heidegger: A Political Life*, trans. A. Blunden (London: Harper Collins, 1993).

Otto, Rudolf. *Mysticism East and West*, trans. B. Bracey and R. Payne (New York: Macmillan, 1932).

Panofsky, Erwin. *Meaning in the Visual Arts* (Harmondsworth: Penguin, 1983).

Parekh, Bikhu. *Gandhi's Political Philosophy: A Critical Examination* (London: Macmillan, 1989).

Parel, A. J. 'The question of Machiavelli's modernity', in T. Sorell (ed.), *The Rise of Modern Philosophy*.

Parfit, Derek. *Reasons and Persons* (Oxford: Clarendon Press, 1984).

Parkes, Graham (ed.). *Heidegger and Asian Thought* (Honolulu: University of Hawaii Press, 1987).

Parrinder, G. (ed.). *The Sayings of the Buddha* (London: Duckworth, 1991).

Parsons, Charles. 'The Transcendental Aesthetic', in P. Guyer (ed.), *The Cambridge Companion to Kant*.

Pascal, Blaise. *Pensées*, trans. A. Krailsheimer (Harmondsworth: Penguin, 1980).

Passmore, John. *A Hundred Years of Philosophy* (Harmondsworth: Penguin, 1968).

——. *Recent Philosophers: A Supplement to A Hundred Years of Philosophy* (London: Duckworth, 1985).

Patañjali. *See under* Baba, B.

Pater, Walter. *The Renaissance* (Oxford: Oxford University Press, 1986).

Peirce, Charles S. *Selected Writings* (New York: Dover, 1958).

Penelhum, Terence. 'Skepticism and fideism', in M. Burnyeat (ed.), *The Skeptical Tradition*.

Pico Della Mirandola, Giovanni. *Oration on the Dignity of Man*, trans. A. R. Caponigri (Chicago: Gateway, 1956).

Plamenatz, John. *Man and Society: A Critical Examination of Some Important Social and Political Theories from Machiavelli to Marx*, 2 vols (London: Routledge & Kegan Paul, 1963).

Plato. *Collected Dialogues*, ed. E. Hamilton and H. Cairns (Princeton: Princeton University Press, 1961).

Plotinus. *The Enneads*, trans. S. MacKenna (Harmondsworth: Penguin, 1991).

Plutarch. *The Rise and Fall of Athens: Nine Greek Lives*, trans. I. Scott-Kilvert (Harmondsworth: Penguin, 1960).

Poole, Roger. *Kierkegaard: The Indirect Communication* (Charlottesville: University of Virginia Press, 1993).

Popkin, Richard H. *The History of Scepticism from Erasmus to Spinoza* (Berkeley: University of California Press, 1979).

——. 'Scepticism and modernity', in T. Sorell (ed.), *The Rise of Modern Philosophy*.

Popper, Karl. *The Open Society and its Enemies*, 2 vols (London: Routledge & Kegan Paul, 1945).

——. *The Logic of Scientific Discovery* (London: Hutchinson, 1959).

Potter, Karl H. (ed.). *Encyclopedia of Indian Philosophies: Vol. III, Advaita Vedānta Up To Śaṁkara and His Pupils* (Delhi: Motilal Banarsidass, 1981). Contains reductions of all Śaṅkara's authenticated works.

——. *Presuppositions of Indian Philosophies* (Delhi: Motilal Banarsidass, 1991).

Putnam, Hilary. *Meaning and the Moral Sciences* (London: Routledge & Kegan Paul, 1978).

——. *Mind, Language and Reality: Philosophical Papers*, vol. 2 (Cambridge: Cambridge University Press, 1979).

Qadir, C. A. *Philosophy and Science in the Islamic World* (London: Routledge, 1988).

Questions of King Milinda, The, trans. T. W. Rhys Davids (Delhi: Motilal Banarsidass, 1988).

Quine, W. V. O. *From a Logical Point of View* (New York: Harper & Row, 1963).

——. *Word and Object* (Cambridge, Mass.: MIT Press, 1964).

——. *Ontological Relativity and Other Essays* (New York: Columbia University Press, 1969).

——. 'Philosophical progress in language theory', *Metaphilosophy*, vol. 1, 1970.

Quinton, Anthony. *Francis Bacon* (Oxford: Oxford University Press, 1980).

Radhakrishnan, Sarvepalli. *Eastern Religions and Western Thought* (Oxford: Clarendon Press, 1939).

——. *An Idealist View of Life* (London: Allen & Unwin, 1947).

——. 'Fragment of a confession', in P. Schilpp (ed.), *The Philosophy of Sarvepalli Radhakrishnan* (New York: Tudor, 1952).

——. *The Hindu View of Life* (London: Unwin, 1980).

—— and Moore, Charles (eds). *A Source Book in Indian Philosophy* (Bombay: Oxford University Press, 1957).

Rahman, Fazlur. *Islam and Modernity: Transformation of an Intellectual Tradition* (Chicago: University of Chicago Press, 1984).

Rajaee, F. *Islamic Values and World View* (Lanham: University Press of America, 1983).

Rāmānuja. *See under* Thibaut, G.

Ramsey, Frank. *The Foundations of Mathematics and other Logical Essays* (London: Routledge & Kegan Paul, 1950).

Rawls, John. *A Theory of Justice* (Oxford: Oxford University Press, 1973).

Ricoeur, Paul. 'Existence and hermeneutics', in J. Bleicher (ed.), *Contemporary Hermeneutics* (London: Routledge & Kegan Paul, 1980).

Roberts, Julian. *German Philosophy: An Introduction* (Oxford: Polity, 1988).

Rorty, Amelie O. (ed.). *Essays on Aristotle's Ethics* (Berkeley: University of California Press, 1980).

Rorty, Richard. *Consequences of Pragmatism* (Brighton: Harvester, 1982).

——. *Contingency, Irony, and Solidarity* (Cambridge: Cambridge University Press, 1989).

——. Review of Daniel Dennett, *Consciousness Explained, London Review of Books*, 21 Nov. 1991.

——. *Essays on Heidegger and Others* (Cambridge: Cambridge University Press, 1991).

——. *Objectivity, Relativism, and Truth* (Cambridge: Cambridge University Press, 1991).

Rosen, Michael. *Hegel's Dialectic and Its Criticism* (Cambridge: Cambridge University Press, 1982).

——. 'The first Romantic?', *Times Literary Supplement*, 8 Oct. 1993.

Ross, G. MacDonald. *Leibniz* (Oxford: Oxford University Press, 1992).

Ross, W. D. *Aristotle* (London: Methuen, 1949).

Rousseau, Jean-Jacques. *The Social Contract and Discourses*, trans. G. D. H. Cole (London: Dent, 1963).

——. *Emile*, trans. B. Foxley (London: Dent, 1977).

Ruse, Michael. 'The significance of evolution', in P. Singer (ed.), *A Companion to Ethics*.

Russell, Bertrand. *Introduction to Mathematical Philosophy* (London: Allen & Unwin, 1919).

——. *The Principles of Mathematics* (Cambridge: Cambridge University Press, 1937).

——. *Mysticism and Logic: and Other Essays* (London: Unwin, 1963).

——. 'The philosophy of Logical Atomism', in *Logic and Knowledge: Essays 1901–50* (London: Allen & Unwin, 1968).

———. *The Problems of Philosophy* (Oxford: Oxford University Press, 1980).

———. *History of Western Philosophy* (London: Routledge, 1993).

Ryle, Gilbert. *The Concept of Mind* (Harmondsworth: Penguin, 1963).

Rynin, David. 'Vindication of L★g★c★l P★s★t★v★sm', in O. Hanfling (ed.), *Essential Readings in Logical Positivism*.

Ryusaku Tsunoda, Bary, Wm. Theodore de, and Keene, Donald (eds), *Sources of Japanese Tradition*, vol. 2 (New York: Columbia University Press, 1964).

Śaṅkara. *The Thousand Teachings*, trans. A. J. Alston (London: Shanti Sadan, 1990). *See also under* Alston, A. J. and Potter, Karl H.

Sartre, Jean-Paul. *Being and Nothingness: An Essay on Phenomenological Ontology*, trans. H. Barnes (London: Methuen, 1957).

———. *Existentialism and Humanism*, trans. P. Mairet (London: Methuen, 1966).

———. *Cahiers pour une morale* (Paris: Gallimard, 1983).

———. *The Reprieve*, trans. E. Sutton (Harmondsworth: Penguin, 1986).

Sastri, S. S. (trans.). *The Sāṃkhya-Kārikā of Īśvarakṛṣṇa* (Madras: University of Madras, 1948).

Schacht, Richard. *Nietzsche* (London: Routledge, 1983).

Schelling, F. W. J. *System of Transcendental Idealism*, trans. P. Heath (Charlottesville: University of Virginia Press, 1978).

———. *Ideas for a Philosophy of Nature*, trans. E. Harris and P. Heath (Cambridge: Cambridge University Press, 1988).

Schiller, Friedrich. *On the Aesthetic Education of Man*, trans. E. Wilkinson and L. Willoughby (Oxford: Clarendon Press, 1967).

Schilpp, P. A. (ed.). *The Philosophy of Alfred North Whitehead* (Illinois: Open Court, 1941).

Schlick, Moritz. 'Meaning and verification' and 'Positivism and realism', in O. Hanfling (ed.), *Essential Readings in Logical Positivism*.

Schmitt, Charles B. and Skinner, Quentin (eds). *The Cambridge History of Renaissance Philosophy* (Cambridge: Cambridge University Press, 1988).

Schneewind, J. B. (ed.). *Moral Philosophy from Montaigne to Kant: An Anthology*, vol. 2 (Cambridge: Cambridge University Press, 1990).

Schofield, M., Burnyeat, M. F. and Barnes, J. (eds). *Doubt and Dogmatism: Studies in Hellenistic Epistemology* (Oxford: Clarendon Press, 1980).

Scholem, Gershom G. 'General characteristics of Jewish mysticism', in R. Woods (ed.), *Understanding Mysticism* (New York: Image, 1980).

Schopenhauer, Arthur. *The World as Will and Representation*, trans. E. Payne (New York: Dover, 1969).

———. *Parerga and Paralipomena*, 2 vols, trans E. Payne (Oxford: Clarendon Press, 1974).

Screech, M. A. *Montaigne and Melancholy: The Wisdom of the Essays* (Harmondsworth: Penguin, 1991).

Scruton, Roger. *Kant* (Oxford: Oxford University Press, 1990).

———. *Spinoza* (Oxford: Oxford University Press, 1991).

Seneca. *Letters From A Stoic* (Harmondsworth: Penguin, 1987).

Senghor, Léopold. *Prose and Poetry*, trans. J. Reed and C. Wake (London: Heinemann, 1976).

Serequeberhan, Tsenay. *The Hermeneutics of African Philosophy: Horizon and Discourse* (London: Routledge, 1994).

——— (ed.). *African Philosophy: The Essential Readings* (New York: Paragon, 1991).

Serracino Inglott, Peter. 'The philosophy of Mahātma Gandhi', *Scientia*, vol. 32, 1969.

Seth, Vikram. *A Suitable Boy* (London: Phoenix, 1993).

Singer, Peter. *The Expanding Circle: Ethics and Sociology* (New York: Farrar, Strauss & Giroux, 1981).

—— (ed.). *A Companion to Ethics* (Oxford: Blackwell, 1991).

Skorupski, John. *Symbol and Theory* (Cambridge: Cambridge University Press, 1976).

——. *John Stuart Mill* (London: Routledge, 1989).

——. *English-Language Philosophy 1750–1945* (Oxford: Oxford University Press, 1993).

Smart, Ninian (ed.). *Historical Selections in the Philosophy of Religion* (London: SCM Press, 1962).

Solomon, Robert C. *Continental Philosophy Since 1750: The Rise and Fall of the Self* (Oxford: Oxford University Press, 1988).

Sophocles. *The Theban Plays*, trans. E. Watling (Harmondsworth: Penguin, 1949).

Sorell, Tom (ed.). *The Rise of Modern Philosophy* (Oxford: Clarendon Press, 1993).

Spencer, Herbert. *First Principles*, 2 vols (London: Williams & Norgate, 1911).

Spengler, Oswald. *Man and Technics: A Contribution to a Philosophy of Life*, trans. C. Atkinson (London: Allen & Unwin, 1932).

Spinosa, Charles. 'Derrida and Heidegger: iterability and *Ereignis*', in H. Dreyfus and H. Hall (eds), *Heidegger: A Critical Reader* (Oxford: Blackwell, 1992).

Spinoza, Benedict de. *Spinoza: The Political Writings*, ed. A. Wernham (Oxford: Oxford University Press, 1958).

——. *The Collected Works of Spinoza*, vol. I, trans. E. Curley (Princeton: Princeton University Press, 1985).

Staten, Henry. *Wittgenstein and Derrida* (Lincoln: University of Nebraska Press, 1984).

Stcherbatsky, Theodore. *The Conception of Buddhist Nirvana* (Delhi: Motilal Banarsidass, 1977). Contains translations of works by Nāgārjuna and Candrakīrti.

Stevenson, Charles L. *Ethics and Language* (Yale: Yale University Press, 1944).

Strawson, P. F. *The Bounds of Sense: An Essay on Kant's* Critique of Pure Reason (London: Methuen, 1966).

——. *Meaning and Truth* (Oxford: Oxford University Press, 1970).

——. *Skepticism and Naturalism: Some Varieties* (London: Methuen, 1985).

——. *Analysis and Metaphysics: An Introduction to Philosophy* (Oxford: Oxford University Press, 1992).

Suzuki, D. T. *Zen Buddhism: Selected Writings of D. T. Suzuki* (New York: Doubleday, 1956).

——. *Zen and Japanese Culture* (Princeton: Princeton University Press, 1959).

Tagore, Rabindranath. *Gitanjali* (London: Unwin, 1986).

——. *The Religion of Man* (London: Unwin, 1988).

——. *Selected Short Stories* (Harmondsworth: Penguin, 1991).

Tanner, Michael. 'Schopenhauer, Arthur', in D. E. Cooper (ed.), *A Companion to Aesthetics*.

Tarski, Alfred. *Logic, Semantics, Metamathematics*, trans. J. H. Woodger (Oxford: Clarendon Press, 1956).

Taylor, Charles. *Hegel* (Cambridge: Cambridge University Press, 1975).

——. *Sources of the Self* (Cambridge: Cambridge University Press, 1989).

Tempels, Placide. *Bantu Philosophy* (Paris: Présence Africaine, 1969).

Thibaut, G. (trans.). *The Vedānta-Sūtras: With the Commentary by Rāmānuja* (Delhi: Motilal Banarsidass, 1989).

Thomas à Kempis. *Of the Imitation of Christ* (London: Kegan Paul & Trench, n.d.).

Tsongkapa. *The Principal Teachings of Buddhism: With a Commentary by Pabongka Rinpoche*, trans. Geshe Lobsang Tharchin (New Jersey: Mahayana Sutra and Tantra Press, 1988).

Tung Chung-Shu. *See under* Baskin, W. and Hughes, E. R.

Ueda Yoshifumi. 'The status of the individual in Mahayana Buddhist philosophy', in C. Moore (ed.), *The Japanese Mind*.

Unamuno, Miguel de. *Tragic Sense of Life*, trans. J. Crawford Flitch (New York: Dover, 1954).

Upaniṣads, The. See under Hume, R. E.

Urmson, J. O. *Philosophical Analysis: Its Development Between the Two World Wars* (Oxford: Clarendon Press, 1956).

——. 'Aristotle's doctrine of the mean', in A. Rorty (ed.), *Essays on Aristotle's Ethics*, 1980.

——. *Berkeley*, in *The British Empiricists* (Oxford: Oxford University Press, 1992).

Urvoy, Dominique. *Ibn Rushd* (Averroes), trans. O. Stewart (London: Routledge, 1991).

Vasari, Giorgio. *Artists of the Renaissance*, trans. G. Bull (Harmondsworth: Penguin, 1982).

Vasubandhu, *See under* Anacker, S.

Vico, Giambattista. *Selected Writings*, trans. L. Pompa (Cambridge: Cambridge University Press, 1982).

Vlastos, Gregory. 'Review of F. M. Cornford: *Principium Sapientiae*', in D. Furley and R. Allen (eds), *Studies in Presocratic Philosophy*, vol. I.

——. 'Equality and justice in early Greek cosmologies', in D. Furley and R. Allen (eds), *Studies in Presocratic Philosophy*, vol. I.

Wamba-Dia-Wamba, E. 'Philosophy in Africa: challenges of the African philosopher', in T. Serequeberhan (ed.), *African Philosophy*.

Wang, Y. C. *Chinese Intellectuals and the West: 1872–1949* (Chapel Hill: University of North Carolina Press, 1966).

Warnock, G. J. *Contemporary Moral Philosophy* (London: Macmillan, 1967).

Watson, Burton (ed.). *Basic Writings of Mo Tzu, Hsun Tzu, and Han Fei Tzu* (New York: Columbia University Press, 1967).

Watsuji Tetsurō. *Climates and Culture: A Philosophical Study*, trans. G. Bownas (Tokyo: Kokuseido, 1971).

Watts, Alan. *The Way of Zen* (London: Arkana, 1990).

Werner, Karel (ed.). *The Yogi and the Mystic: Studies in Indian and Comparative Mysticism* (London: Curzon, 1989).

Wheeler III, Samuel C. 'Indeterminacy of French interpretation: Derrida and Davidson', in E. LePore (ed.), *Truth and Interpretation: Perspectives on the Philosophy of Donald Davidson* (Oxford: Blackwell, 1986).

White, Hayden. 'Feuerbach, Ludwig', in P. Edwards (ed.), *An Encyclopedia of Philosophy*.

Whitehead, Alfred North. *An Anthology*, ed. F. Northrop and M. Gross (Cambridge: Cambridge University Press, 1953).

Wieger, Leon (trans.). *Wisdom of the Daoist Masters: The Works of Lao Zi (Lao Tzu), Lie Zi (Lieh Tzu), Zhuang Zi (Chuang Tzu)* (Lampeter: Llanerch, 1984).

Williams, Bernard. 'Philosophy', in M. I. Finley (ed.), *The Legacy of Greece: A New Appraisal*.

——. *Moral Luck: Philosophical Papers 1973–1980* (Cambridge: Cambridge University Press, 1981).

——. 'Nietzsche's centaur', *London Review of Books*, 3 October 1981.

——. 'Descartes's use of skepticism', in M. Burnyeat (ed.), *The Skeptical Tradition*.

——. *Ethics and the Limits of Philosophy* (London: Fontana, 1985).

Wiredu, Kwasi. 'On defining African philosophy', in T. Serequeberhan (ed.), *African Philosophy*.

Wittgenstein, Ludwig. *Notebooks 1914–16*, trans. G. Anscombe (Oxford: Blackwell, 1961).

——. *Philosophical Investigations*, trans. G. Anscombe (London: Macmillan, 1969).

——. *The Blue and Brown Books: Preliminary Studies for the* Philosophical Investigations (Oxford: Blackwell, 1969).

——. *On Certainty*, trans. D. Paul and G. Anscombe (Oxford: Blackwell, 1969).

——. *Tractatus Logico-Philosophicus*, trans. D. Pears and B. McGuinness (London: Routledge, 1988).

Wood, Allen. *Karl Marx* (London: Routledge, 1981).

Woolhouse, R. S. *The Empiricists* (Oxford: Oxford University Press, 1992).

Wu, Laurence C. *Fundamentals of Chinese Philosophy* (Lanham: University Press of America, 1986).

Yampolsky, P. B. (trans.). *The Platform Scripture Of The Sixth Patriarch: The Text of the Tun-Huang Manuscript* (New York: Columbia University Press, 1967).

——. *The Zen Master Hakuin: Selected Writings* (New York: Columbia University Press, 1971).

Yates, Frances A. 'Bruno, Giordano', in P. Edwards (ed.), *The Encyclopedia of Philosophy*.

Young, Julian P. *Nietzsche's Philosophy of Art* (Cambridge: Cambridge University Press, 1992).

Yuasa Yasuo. 'The encounter of modern Japanese philosophy with Heidegger', in G. Parkes (ed.), *Heidegger and Asian Thought*.

Zimmerman, Michael E. *Heidegger's Confrontation with Modernity: Technology, Politics and Art* (Bloomington: Indiana University Press, 1990).

• INDEX •